T0338313

The Samuel Gompers Papers

THE
Samuel Gompers
PAPERS

VOLUME
10
The American Federation of Labor
and the Great War, 1917–18

Editors
Peter J. Albert
Grace Palladino

Assistant Editors
Marla J. Hughes
Mary C. Jeske

UNIVERSITY OF ILLINOIS PRESS
Urbana and Chicago

A portion of the publication costs of this book was provided by
the National Historical Publications and Records Commission.
© 2007 by the Board of Trustees
of the University of Illinois
All rights reserved
Manufactured in the United States of America
C 5 4 3 2 1

University of Illinois Press
1325 South Oak Street   Champaign, IL 61820-6903
www.press.uillinois.edu

*The paper in this book meets the guidelines for permanence and
durability of the Committee on Production Guidelines for
Book Longevity of the Council on Library Resources.* ∞

Library of Congress Cataloging-in-Publication Data

The Samuel Gompers Papers

Includes bibliographies and indexes.
Contents: v. 1. The making of a union leader, 1850–86
— v. 2. The early years of the American Federation of Labor,
1887–90 — v. 3. Unrest and depression, 1891–94 — v. 4. A
national labor movement takes shape, 1895–98 — v. 5. An
expanding movement at the turn of the century, 1898–1902
— v. 6. The American Federation of Labor and the rise of
progressivism, 1902–6 — v. 7. The American Federation of
Labor under siege, 1906–9 — v. 8. Progress and reaction in
the age of reform, 1909–13 — v. 9. The American Federation
of Labor at the height of progressivism, 1913–17 — v. 10. The
American Federation of Labor and the Great War, 1917–18.
    1. Gompers, Samuel, 1850–1924—Archives. 2. Trade-
unions— United States—History—Sources. 3. Labor
movement—United States—History—Sources. I. Gompers,
Samuel, 1850–1924.
HD6508.S218   2007   331.88'32'902   84-2469
ISBN-10 0-252-01138-4 (alk. paper : set)
ISBN-13 978-0-252-01138-2 (alk. paper : set)
ISBN-10 0-252-03041-9 (alk. paper : v. 10)
ISBN-13 978-0-252-03041-3 (alk. paper : v. 10)

CONTENTS

INTRODUCTION

Samuel Gompers never favored war, but when it came he knew which side he was on. As an American, he was on his country's side—there was no other choice, he believed, once war was imminent. As a trade unionist, he was on the American Federation of Labor's side—wartime demands put a premium on all-out production, opening new opportunities for the labor movement. "This war is a people's war," Gompers proclaimed. "The final outcome will be determined in the factories, the mills, the shops, the mines, the farms, the industries, and the transportation agencies of the various countries." Victory abroad would require industrial peace at home, he knew, but it would also require some fundamental changes in industrial relations. As the AFL Executive Council put it in the spring of 1917, economic justice was the cornerstone of national defense. "War has never put a stop to the necessity for struggle to establish and maintain industrial rights," the Council noted. "Wage-earners in war times must . . . keep one eye on the exploiters at home and the other upon the enemy threatening the national government."[1]

This volume of the *Samuel Gompers Papers* focuses on the AFL's struggle to serve the nation and the labor movement during a critical period in American history, when this country's official policy of neutrality gave way to the forces of war. Beginning with Gompers' last-minute effort to persuade German workers to help prevent war with the United States, it follows the labor movement's internal debate over the meaning of American participation and the Executive Council's pragmatic—and in some cases reluctant—pledge of support, offered just weeks before war was declared. Consensus did not come easily, since opposition to entering the war was widespread at the time. Leaders of the needle trades unions, the Chicago Federation of Labor, and the Pennsylvania State Federation of Labor, for instance, all opposed American involvement. Once the United States joined the Allied forces in April, however, debate grew less fierce, particularly after the Socialist Party of America denounced participation in the war. As the Socialist party lost credibility with most of the labor movement, Gompers was able to solidify AFL support for the war effort, a crucial step in his campaign to "render constructive service that will not only have its influence in war situations," as he told the Executive Council, "but will also affect the standing of wage-earners in time of peace."[2]

This volume also charts the evolution of a new relation between organized labor and the federal government that began with Gompers' controversial promise to forgo labor's fight for the "closed" union shop and gave rise to a series of labor-adjustment boards that supported the eight-hour day, equal pay for equal work, and labor's right to organize and bargain collectively with employers. Thus for the first time in American history, organized labor was recognized as a vital partner in the war effort, a radical change in national policy that President Woodrow Wilson acknowledged when he addressed the AFL's convention in the fall of 1917. Praising Gompers for "his patriotic courage, his large vision, and his statesmanlike sense of what has to be done," Wilson frankly admitted that, "While we are fighting for freedom, we must see . . . that labor is free . . . that the conditions of labor are not rendered more onerous by the war . . . [and] that the instrumentalities by which the conditions of labor are improved are not blocked or checked."[3]

This potent combination of wartime demand and government support revitalized the labor movement nationwide. Jobs were plentiful, expectations were high, and labor turnover was widespread, conditions that nurtured the rising popular demand for industrial democracy. As war-related production increased between 1916 and 1917, workers called a record number of strikes—in fact more than 2,000 strikes erupted during the first six months of the war, usually over issues of work rules and union recognition. By 1918 more than 2.7 million workers claimed membership in the AFL—an increase of 31.5 percent since 1916, and 86 percent since the rise of the open shop movement in 1903.[4] With new affiliates as varied as the National Federation of Federal Employes and the International Union of Timber Workers, the AFL also launched wartime organizing campaigns among steel, packinghouse, electrical manufacturing, and railroad shop workers, and met with representatives of the black community to spur organization among shipyard workers and others. At the same time, the Federation kept up its campaign to organize women workers who were rapidly entering iron and steel, glass, leather, and chemical factories. During the war women were producing bombs, operating drills, reading blueprints, and driving cranes, as well as sewing tents and uniforms, thereby changing the face of industry—although not necessarily the minds of male coworkers—almost overnight.[5]

For Gompers, these years were the high point of his career. Long recognized as a talented administrator, negotiator, organizer, and public speaker within the labor movement, he now joined the ranks of national policy makers, serving as a member of the Advisory Commission of the Council of National Defense (CND) and chairman of its Committee on Labor. As the official liaison between the federal government and organized workers, Gompers was directly involved in matters of economic mobilization, particularly manpower mobilization, and he played a central role in the development of wartime labor policies, with an eye to increasing production, reducing industrial conflict, and advancing labor's wage and hour standards. Trading ideas, and in some cases vehement criticisms, with CND colleagues, including financier Bernard Baruch, railroad president Daniel Willard, and head of the American College of Surgeons Franklin Martin (who initially considered Gompers to be an "'agitator,' anarchist . . . and all-round bad man"), Gompers zealously argued labor's case for the eight-hour day, safe working conditions, union wage standards, and collective agreements. He also championed federal legislation to protect the families of servicemen and improve living conditions in wartime "boomtowns," and lobbied for labor representation on district draft boards, the Railroad Wage Commission, the War Industries Board, and the Committee on Taxation of War Profits, among many others. "We are not going to give up our liberty. We are not going to give up our rights," he told the CND. "What matters it to the men of labor, if, in the struggle for the freedom and the democracy of the United States . . . chains in the guise of slavery are fastened upon them?"[6]

Gompers relished the public attention and access to governmental power that came with his committee chairmanship. But he was fully aware that his appointment to the Advisory Commission was a means, not an end, for organized labor. From the very beginning the AFL leader was on the defensive, fighting state efforts to conscript skilled labor, waive hard-won protective legislation, and resurrect child labor, all under the guise of wartime necessity. At the same time, Gompers used his position with the CND to educate his new colleagues, for as Dr. Martin acknowledged, "he had to convince those of us associated with him that the conditions among the working people of the country were as desperate as they afterwards proved to be."[7] By most accounts, he acquitted himself well. "From every side the word comes to me of a new appreciation, not only of Mr. Gompers, himself," Secretary of Commerce William Redfield noted in the summer of 1917, "but of the great cause of which he is the able leader." His fellow commissioners agreed. "He always talked to the point, he always interested, he always finally convinced," Dr. Martin noted. "His influence grew from the first day of our meeting until the war was over." Even his erstwhile nemesis, Daniel Willard, had to concede that Gompers was doing a good job. "If anyone had told me that my personal antagonism toward Samuel Gompers would change within 1 week to ardent admiration and real affection," he confessed, "I would have pronounced that individual a fit candidate for an insane asylum."[8]

In the process of proving his competence and reliability, though, Gompers never abandoned his trade union goals. On the contrary, he stood his ground—whether he stood alone or not—on a number of controversial issues, from protecting prevailing union standards to opposing wartime Prohibition for soldiers.[9] And according to Ralph Easley, his longtime associate on the National Civic Federation—and an early proponent and organizer of the CND—Gompers sought no outside advice when it came to matters like "mediation, restrictions, output, [and] standards." In fact, he was making "better headway from the standpoint of labor than if we had all been in it," Easley reported, "because we certainly would not have agreed with all the propositions that the A.F. of L. people have put up to the Government."[10] During this period Gompers also worked behind the scenes to win a new trial for Tom Mooney, a labor radical and alleged bomb-thrower, and publicly endorsed the idea of taxing corporate war profits out of existence. In fact, his blunt assessment of capital's failure to match labor's wartime contributions drew increasing support—and requests for help—from a broad range of wage earners. Enraged citizens called on him to fight sky-high food and housing costs. German-American workers, unjustly maligned as enemy agents, looked to Gompers to help them regain their jobs. Unorganized workers of all kinds—black, female, and immigrant—called on him for advice and assistance.

Consequently, Gompers was working harder than ever before—no mean feat for a man who was already known to schedule meetings on the train, so as not to waste travel time. Although he could rely on an extremely competent staff, led by Frank Morrison and R. Lee Guard in the AFL office, and James Sullivan and Gertrude Beeks Easley at the Committee on Labor of the CND, the AFL president was always in demand. Mothers begged him to save their sons from the battlefield, and friends and acquaintances pestered him for jobs, draft deferments, or help getting placed in the military. The United Garment Workers kept him busy with their fight against the Amalgamated Clothing Workers over the right to sew military uniforms. The Carpenters regularly challenged his authority to make agreements with the government or interfere with their right to strike. And the rise of the People's Council of America for Democracy and Peace—which called for immediate peace negotiations and drew support from foreign-born workers and socialist union leaders—led Gompers to participate in founding the American Alliance for Labor and Democracy (AALD), a government-funded organization of trade unionists and prowar socialists determined to "Americanize" the immigrant workforce and insure their wartime support.[11]

At the same time, Gompers was trying to resolve serious fights that threatened fragile ties between government and labor. In Bisbee, Arizona, striking copper miners were loaded on cattle cars and "deported" to New Mexico; in Northwest timber camps recurring IWW strikes induced an army officer to launch his own union—the Loyal Legion of Loggers and Lumbermen; and in shipyards along the Pacific Coast, government mediation boards repeatedly failed to satisfy striking workers. The AFL leader was also expected to take a leading role in wartime organizing campaigns. As Edward Nockels put it—when he wanted Gompers' help to "clinch" the packinghouse workers' campaign in Chicago—"All we need is Sam."[12]

By any measure, these were momentous years. In Russia the Bolsheviks were rising to power, and all over Europe new socialist labor alliances were beginning to take shape. In the United States, black Americans were starting the great migration from farms to cities that would eventually remake American society, and young women—especially young working women—were claiming a measure of personal freedom that would make them "new women" in public. At the same time, though, a reaction against too much change on the labor front was also beginning to take hold. The arrest and conviction of militant IWW and antiwar leaders, including Bill Haywood and Eugene Debs, heralded the first—and at the time, almost unnoticed—steps of a Red Scare that would take an enormous toll on the labor movement in the years to come. These and other critical issues were on Gompers' mind during the war, and he was kept up to date by a wide range of correspondents, including William Appleton and Arthur Henderson in England, organizers John Fitzpatrick and Emmet Flood in Chicago, C. O. Young in Seattle, and Ernest Bohm in New York, former members of the Socialist party John Spargo and Chester Wright, who worked with him on the AALD, and a host of government officials and reformers of every stripe.

For Gompers, these years were profoundly significant on a personal level too. In 1917, the AFL president celebrated fifty years of service to the labor movement and fifty years of marriage to Sophia Julian Gompers—the former sixteen-year-old cigar stripper from Brooklyn who had eloped with him the day after his seventeenth birthday. The following year, Gompers proudly traveled to Europe, at the urging of the Wilson administration, attending the British Trade Union Congress in Derby and the Inter-Allied Labour and Socialist Conference in London. He then traveled to Belgium, France, and Italy, where he saw the destructive power of war at first hand. Doing his best to promote President Wilson's Fourteen Points wherever he was asked to speak, Gompers publicly debated pacifists and European "Bolsheviki," as he put it, and tried "like the mischief . . . [to put] some stiffening into the backbone of the people . . . [to make them] stand behind their countries at least until after the war was won."[13]

In the midst of carrying out this duty for his country, however, Gompers received shattering news from home. Sadie, his youngest child and cherished "pet," had died unexpectedly, a victim of the Spanish influenza epidemic of 1918. This was not the first time he had lost a close family member while he was away from home, and it was not the first time he had buried a child—both his mother and his daughter Rose had died while he was traveling on behalf of the AFL, and his son Abraham had died in 1903 from tuberculosis. But Sadie still lived at home, where she had made family life "happy, mirthful, and musical" for her parents, and her death was a blow from which they never truly recovered. Without her, "there was no music," Gompers wrote a few years later, adding that his wife, Sophia, "never came back to herself after our Sadie's death."[14]

A "welcome home" meeting had been scheduled for Chicago to honor Gompers' service, but acting AFL president John Alpine took it for granted that it would be canceled or at least postponed so that Gompers might have time to grieve. It would be "inhuman," he thought, to expect from Gompers "what everyone else seems to expect, that it will be a relief to his feelings" to go on with things as planned. But perhaps because it was the only way he knew how to survive, Gompers did exactly that. Following the same advice he had given to so many others during the war, he "stiffened his backbone" and made his way to Chicago and then Laredo, Texas, giving speeches, conducting meetings, and demonstrating the strength of character and self-discipline that, for better or worse, had shaped his longtime leadership of the AFL.[15]

Firm in his belief that the war had been a crusade for "justice, freedom and democracy," Gompers reminded the cheering crowd in Chicago that labor's fight was not over yet. "The principles of democracy do not flash in the air, they are not fanciful, they are not theoretical. . . . Democracy must be practiced and acted every day of our lives to be true," he explained. "As a result of this war there must come new relations not only between nation and nation but between man and man. . . . We want . . . the right to life, liberty and the pursuit of happiness not to be mere generalities but the rules of every-day life." This was the vision that had propelled him during these years, the idea that the destruction of war would give way to "new ideals and conditions based upon broader and truer concepts of human rights." And now that the war had triumphantly ended, as he wrote to President Wilson on the day the armistice was signed, Gompers was confident that a "new era in the life of the peoples and nations of the world" was about to begin, one in which he and the AFL were determined to play a role.[16]

ACKNOWLEDGMENTS

The Samuel Gompers Papers is indebted to many institutions and individuals, both for ongoing, long-term support of the Project and for specific contributions to this volume. Two federal agencies, the National Endowment for the Humanities (NEH) and the National Historical Publications and Records Commission (NHPRC), have provided the core of our funding, and we are very grateful for their support. In addition, NEH matching grants enable us to raise additional funding for the Project and the NHPRC subventions to the University of Illinois Press offset a portion of the publication costs of the volumes.

We also deeply appreciate the labor movement's long-standing support of the Gompers Project, in partnership with the University of Maryland, the NHPRC, and the NEH. The AFL-CIO Executive Council, the George Meany Memorial Archives, and many national and international unions have given us access to their Gompers-era records, granted us permission to photocopy and publish pertinent material, and followed the progress of our work with interest and encouragement.

We are also most grateful to the AFL-CIO Executive Council for its support of the Gompers Project with major financial contributions on an ongoing basis in response to NEH matching grants. And we want to acknowledge as well the financial support in the Project's crucial early years from the George Meany Memorial Archives; the Joseph Anthony Beirne Memorial Foundation of the Communications Workers of America; the Associated Actors and Artistes of America; the United Automobile, Aerospace, and Agricultural Implement Workers of America International Union; the Bakery, Confectionery, Tobacco Workers', and Grain Millers' International Union; the International Brotherhood of Boilermakers, Iron Ship Builders, Blacksmiths, Forgers, and Helpers; the International Union of Bricklayers and Allied Craftworkers; the United Brotherhood of Carpenters and Joiners of America; the International Brotherhood of Electrical Workers; the International Union of Electronic, Electrical, Salaried, Machine, and Furniture Workers; the International Union of Operating Engineers;

the Association of Flight Attendants; the United Food and Commercial Workers' International Union; the Glass, Molders', Pottery, Plastics', and Allied Workers' International Union; the American Flint Glass Workers' Union; the American Federation of Government Employees; the Graphic Communications International Union; the Laborers' International Union of North America; the National Association of Letter Carriers; the International Longshoremen's Association; the International Association of Machinists and Aerospace Workers; the Mechanics' Educational Society of America; the United Mine Workers of America; the Union of Needletrades, Industrial and Textile Employees; the Newspaper Guild; the Office and Professional Employees' International Union; the International Brotherhood of Painters and Allied Trades of the United States and Canada; the Paper, Allied-Industrial, Chemical, and Energy Workers' International Union; the United Association of Journeymen and Apprentices of the Plumbing and Pipe Fitting Industry of the United States and Canada; the American Postal Workers' Union; the International Federation of Professional and Technical Engineers; the Brotherhood of Railway Carmen of the United States and Canada; the Retail, Wholesale, and Department Store Union; the United Rubber, Cork, Linoleum, and Plastic Workers of America; the Seafarers' International Union of North America; the Service Employees' International Union; the International Alliance of Theatrical Stage Employees, Moving Picture Machine Technicians, Artists, and Allied Craftsmen of the United States, Its Territories, and Canada; the American Federation of State, County, and Municipal Employees; the United Steelworkers of America; the American Federation of Teachers; the International Brotherhood of Teamsters; and the Amalgamated Transit Union.

We deeply appreciate as well the continuing support we receive from the University of Maryland at College Park. We want to express our gratitude to Gary Gerstle, chair of the Department of History, James F. Harris, dean of the College of Arts and Humanities, and Charles B. Lowry, director of the University of Maryland Libraries, as well as to our colleagues in the History Department, the members of the staff of the University's McKeldin Library, where our principal offices are located, and to Kathleen R. Cavanaugh and Jon K. Boone of the Academic Computing Services Office of the College of Arts and Humanities. The department, the library, and the university assist and encourage our work in countless ways, including giving us substantial financial support, office space, and computer and other technical assistance.

We have been helped by the staffs and used the collections of many area libraries and research institutions in preparing this volume, particularly those of the George Meany Memorial Archives, the Library of Congress, the Library of the U.S. Department of Labor, and the National Archives.

Many individuals gave us invaluable assistance in our work on this book, including, among others, Fiona Aitken and Alan R. Bell, National Library of Scotland, Edinburgh; Andrew Bethune, Edinburgh City Libraries and Information Services; Maria Barbara Bertini, Archivio di Stato di Milano; John Dallison and Patricia Kenny, Local Studies Library, Derby City Libraries; Lynda A. DeLoach, the George Meany Memorial Archives, Silver Spring, Md.; Ian Glen, University of Wales, Swansea; George H. Goebel, Dictionary of American Regional English, University of Wisconsin, Madison; Michael Hussey, Shawn Russell, and Mitch Yockelson, National Archives and Records Administration, Washington, D.C.; Leslie Martin, Chicago Historical Society; Byron Perrine of Olivia, Minn.; Donald A. Ritchie, U.S. Senate Historical Office, Washington, D.C.; Patrizia Sione, Kheel Center for Labor-Management Documentation and Archives, Cornell University; and Charlotte Tucker, Local Studies Library, Birmingham Central Library. Megan Simms transcribed the documents in this volume with her usual skill and care, and Thomas A. Castillo, Jeffrey T. Coster, Claire Goldstene, and Amy J. Rutenberg helped with proofreading the galley pages.

Finally, we wish to acknowledge our great debt to David Brody, Melvyn Dubofsky, David Montgomery, and Irwin Yellowitz, members of our board of editorial advisors, for so very generously taking the time to give this volume a critical reading while still in manuscript and for making invaluable suggestions for improving the book.

Notes

1. Samuel Gompers, "Labor's Service to Freedom," American Memory Historical Collections, DLC; "American Labor's Position in Peace or in War," Mar. 12, 1917, below.

2. See, for example, "Excerpts from the Minutes of a Meeting of the AFL Executive Council," Mar. 9, 1917, below. For a more general discussion see David Montgomery, *The Fall of the House of Labor: The Workplace, the State, and American Labor Activism, 1865–1925* (New York, 1987), Joseph A. McCartin, *Labor's Great War: The Struggle for Industrial Democracy and the Origins of Modern American Labor Relations, 1912–1921* (Chapel Hill, N.C., 1997), and Elizabeth McKillen, *Chicago Labor and the Quest for a Democratic Diplomacy, 1914–1924* (Ithaca, N.Y., 1995). Gompers quotation from "To the Executive Council of the AFL," Feb. 28, 1917, below.

3. AFL, *Proceedings*, 1917, p. 3.

4. Bruce I. Bustard, "The Human Factor: Labor Administration and Industrial Manpower Mobilization during the First World War," Ph.D. diss., University of Iowa, 1984, pp. 69–70; Melvyn Dubofsky, *The State and Labor in Modern America* (Chapel Hill, N.C., 1994), p. 62. According to the U.S. Department of Labor there were nearly 3,800 strikes in 1916, more than 4,400 in 1917, and

over 3,300 in 1918, with 1.6 million strikers in 1916, 1.2 million in 1917, and
about the same number in 1918 (Florence Peterson, "Strikes in the United
States, 1880–1936," U.S. Department of Labor *Bulletin* 651 [1937]: 21, 35).
AFL membership was 1,465,800 in 1903, 2,072,702 in 1916, and 2,726,478 in
1918 (AFL, *Proceedings,* 1919, p. 62).

5. According to Gompers, the AFL had seven women organizers on staff
during the war (to D. S. Leighty, May 21, 1918, reel 235, vol. 247, p. 300,
SG Letterbooks, DLC). For women war workers and their jobs, see Maurine
Weiner Greenwald, *Women, War, and Work: The Impact of World War I on Women
Workers in the United States* (Westport, Conn., 1980). According to a U.S. Department of Labor Women's Bureau survey, women constituted at least 20
percent of all workers manufacturing electrical machinery, airplanes, optical
goods, leather and rubber products, as well as food, paper, and printed material, among others (Greenwald, *Women, War, and Work,* p. 21).

6. Franklin H. Martin, *Digest of the Proceedings of the Council of National Defense
during the World War,* 73d Cong., 2d sess., 1934, S.Doc. 193, p. 40; Valerie Jean
Conner, *The National War Labor Board: Stability, Social Justice, and the Voluntary
State in World War I* (Chapel Hill, N.C., 1983), p. 23; AFL, *Proceedings,* 1917,
pp. 81–88; AFL, *Proceedings,* 1918, pp.73–74; Bustard, "The Human Factor,"
p. 46; Speech of Samuel Gompers, May 15, 1917, Records of the Committee
on Labor, RG 62, Records of the Council of National Defense, DNA.

7. "Personal Reminiscences of Samuel Gompers," Extract from Franklin
Martin's diary, John Frey Papers, DLC. For Gompers' work on war-risk insur-
ance and soldiers' and sailors' compensation, see Newton Baker to John Frey,
Dec. 6, 1926, Frey Papers.

8. William Redfield to Robert Maisel, Aug. 14, 1917, Files of the Office of
the President, General Correspondence, reel 87, frame 218, *AFL Records;* Martin, "Personal Reminiscences of Samuel Gompers"; Daniel Willard is quoted
in Martin, *Digest of Proceedings,* pp. 55–56.

9. Martin, *Digest of Proceedings,* pp. 150–53, 240.

10. [Ralph Easley] to Louis B. Schram, Oct. 9, 1917, Records of the Committee on Labor, RG 62, Records of the Council of National Defense, DNA.

11. Philip S. Foner, *History of the Labor Movement in the United States,* vol. 7,
Labor and World War I, 1914–1918 (New York, 1987), pp. 112–14; Montgomery,
Fall of the House of Labor, pp. 372–73; McKillen, *Chicago Labor and Democratic
Democracy,* pp. 10–11.

12. Edward Nockels to William B. Rubin, Feb. 12, 1918, Files of the Office
of the President, General Correspondence, reel 92, frame 477, *AFL Records.*

13. "An Address at a Reception in Chicago Honoring the Members of the
American Labor Mission to Europe," Nov. 8, 1918, below.

14. Samuel Gompers, *Seventy Years of Life and Labor: An Autobiography,* 2 vols.
(New York, 1925), 1: 478, 508.

15. John Alpine to James Duncan, Oct. 18, 1918, below.

16. "To Woodrow Wilson," Nov. 11, 1918, below; "An Address at a Reception
in Chicago," below; "Labor and the War" in "Report of A.F. of L. Executive
Council," AFL, *Proceedings,* 1917, p. 72; Gompers, *Seventy Years,* 2: 513.

SYMBOLS AND ABBREVIATIONS

AFL	American Federation of Labor
ALS	Autograph letter, signed or stamped with signature
CIO	Congress of Industrial Organizations
DLC	Library of Congress, Washington, D.C.
DNA	National Archives and Records Administration, Washington, D.C.
ICHi	Chicago Historical Society
IWW	Industrial Workers of the World
KOL	Knights of Labor
NN	New York Public Library, Astor, Lenox, and Tilden Foundations
PD	Printed document
PLS	Printed letter, signed or stamped with signature
PLSr	Printed letter, signature representation other than stamp
RG	Record Group
SG	Samuel Gompers
T and ALS	Typed and autograph letter, signed or stamped with signature
T and AWSr	Typed and autograph wire (cable or telegram), signature representation other than stamp
TD	Typed document
TDc	Typed document, copy
TDpS	Typed document, letterpress copy, signed or stamped with signature
TDtcSr	Typed document, transcribed, copy, signature representation other than stamp
TL	Typed letter
TLc	Typed letter, copy
TLcS	Typed letter, copy, signed or stamped with signature
TLcSr	Typed letter, copy, signature representation other than stamp
TLp	Typed letter, letterpress copy
TLpS	Typed letter, letterpress copy, signed or stamped with signature
TLpSr	Typed letter, letterpress copy, signature representation other than stamp
TLS	Typed letter, signed or stamped with signature
TLSr	Typed letter, signature representation other than stamp

xxiii

TLtcSr   Typed letter, transcribed, copy, signature representation other than stamp

TLtpSr   Typed letter, transcribed, letterpress copy, signature representation other than stamp

TUC   Trades Union Congress of Great Britain

TW   Typed wire (cable or telegram)

TWcSr   Typed wire (cable or telegram), copy, signature representation other than stamp

TWpS   Typed wire (cable or telegram), letterpress copy, signed or stamped with signature

TWpSr   Typed wire (cable or telegram), letterpress copy, signature representation other than stamp

TWSr   Typed wire (cable or telegram), signature representation other than stamp

TWtcSr   Typed wire (cable or telegram), transcribed, copy, signature representation other than stamp

TWtpSr   Typed wire (cable or telegram), transcribed, letterpress copy, signature representation other than stamp

SHORT TITLES

The Samuel Gompers Papers, vol. 4   Stuart B. Kaufman et al., eds., *The Samuel Gompers Papers*, vol. 4, *A National Labor Movement Takes Shape, 1895–98* (Urbana, Ill., 1991)

The Samuel Gompers Papers, vol. 7   Stuart B. Kaufman et al., eds., *The Samuel Gompers Papers*, vol. 7, *The American Federation of Labor under Siege, 1906–9* (Urbana, Ill., 1999)

The Samuel Gompers Papers, vol. 8   Peter J. Albert and Grace Palladino, eds., *The Samuel Gompers Papers*, vol. 8, *Progress and Reaction in the Age of Reform, 1909–13* (Urbana, Ill., 2001)

The Samuel Gompers Papers, vol. 9   Peter J. Albert and Grace Palladino, eds., *The Samuel Gompers Papers*, vol. 9, *The American Federation of Labor at the Height of Progressivism, 1913–17* (Urbana, Ill., 2003)

1917 Jan. 16   German foreign minister Arthur Zimmermann cables German minister in Mexico proposing Mexican alliance with Germany and Mexican reconquest of southwestern United States

Jan. 28   Celebration of SG's sixty-seventh birthday and fiftieth wedding anniversary

Jan. 31   Germany notifies United States it will resume unrestricted submarine warfare on Feb. 1. United States cuts diplomatic relations with Germany on Feb. 3

Mar. 4   Naval Appropriation Act signed into law, authorizing president to suspend federal eight-hour laws but stipulating overtime pay for extra work

Mar. 12   Conference at AFL headquarters adopts statement "American Labor's Position in Peace or in War"

Mar. 15
(Mar. 2, Old Style)   Abdication of Tsar Nicholas II

Apr. 2   Committee on Labor of Advisory Commission of Council of National Defense organized. On Apr. 5 the executive committee recommends neither employers nor employees take advantage of war to change existing standards

Apr. 6   Congress passes joint resolution declaring war on Germany

Apr. 7–14   Socialist Party of America convention in St. Louis condemns war and urges workers to refuse to support war effort

May 18   Selective Service Act of 1917 authorizes creation of local draft boards, requires men between ages of twenty-one and thirty to register for military service, and empowers president to conscript one million men. On Aug. 31, 1918, registration is extended to those between eighteen and forty-five

June 15	Espionage Act prohibits giving foreign agents information harmful to national defense, promoting insubordination or disloyalty in armed forces, or obstructing recruiting or enlistment, and authorizes postmaster general to deny use of mails to materials advocating treason or insurrection
June 19	SG and Secretary of War Newton Baker sign Cantonment Construction Agreement, later extended to other War Department construction work (July 27), aviation fields (Aug. 8), navy construction work (Aug. 10), warehouses and other storage facilities (Sept. 4), and all other War Department construction work (Dec. 28)
June 27– Nov. 6	Bisbee, Ariz., copper miners' strike
July 2	East St. Louis, Ill., race riot
July 15	Chicago Federation of Labor authorizes organizing campaign in Chicago stockyards. Stockyards Labor Council organized to carry on the work
July 29	In response to activities of People's Council of America for Democracy and Peace, American Alliance for Labor and Democracy is formally launched in New York City with SG as chairman and Robert Maisel as director. Alliance convention meets in Minneapolis, Sept. 5–7
July	War Industries Board established by Council of National Defense. It becomes an independent agency in May 1918
Aug. 1	Frank Little abducted and lynched in Butte, Mont.
Aug. 10	Lever Food and Fuel Control Act authorizes president to regulate production, distribution, and price of food, fuel, and other essential commodities, prohibits hoarding, and bans manufacture or importation of distilled liquors
Aug. 20	Shipbuilding Labor Adjustment Board created to resolve disputes involving wages, hours, or conditions of labor on work undertaken for U.S. Shipping Board or Emergency Fleet Corporation

Sept. 5	Department of Justice agents raid IWW offices in Chicago and other cities and the homes of IWW officials. 166 IWW members are indicted; 100 of them are tried in Chicago in 1918 on charges of conspiracy to interfere with the war effort; all are found guilty
Sept. 19	President Wilson appoints commission to investigate and mediate labor unrest in the West and Northwest
Nov. 7 (Oct. 25, Old Style)	Bolsheviks overthrow Provisional Government in Russia (the October Revolution)
Nov. 12–24	AFL convention meets in Buffalo
Nov. 22	Coronado Coal Co. wins district court judgment under Sherman Act against United Mine Workers of America
Dec. 10	U.S. Supreme Court affirms injunction against organizing the Hitchman Coal and Coke Co. by United Mine Workers of America
Dec. 26	President Woodrow Wilson issues proclamation authorizing federal takeover of railroads and appointing William McAdoo Director General of Railroads
1918 Jan. 8	President Woodrow Wilson outlines Fourteen Points in address before Congress
Feb. 20–23	Inter-Allied Labour and Socialist Conference, London
Mar. 3	Treaty of Brest Litovsk ends hostilities between Russia and Germany
Apr. 8	National War Labor Board established
Apr. 20	Sabotage Act passed to punish damage to or destruction of war-related materials, premises, or transportation facilities
April–May	American labor mission visits England, France, and Ireland
May 13	Secretary of Labor William B. Wilson creates War Labor Policies Board to standardize policies of government agencies on wages, hours, working conditions, and distribution of labor
May 23	Provost Marshal General Enoch Crowder issues "Work or Fight" order requiring all draft-age men either to engage in some useful or essential occupation or serve in the military

May–June	American labor mission visits Mexico
June 3	U.S. Supreme Court strikes down Keating-Owen Act prohibiting interstate commerce in goods produced with child labor
June 10–20	AFL convention meets in St. Paul
June 30	Eugene Debs is arrested for violating Espionage Act in a speech before Ohio Socialist party convention in Canton. In September he is tried, convicted, and sentenced to ten years in prison
July 23	President Wilson issues proclamation placing U.S. telegraph and telephone systems under control of government as of midnight July 31, under supervision of Postmaster General Albert Burleson
July	Gov. William Stephens of California grants temporary reprieve to Thomas Mooney. In November he commutes Mooney's sentence to life imprisonment
Aug. 1–2	Trade union conference held in Chicago on organizing iron and steel industry
Aug. 15/16– Nov. 3	SG and American labor mission visit England, Scotland, France, and Italy, attend TUC meeting at Derby (Sept. 2–7) and Inter-Allied Labour and Socialist conference in London (Sept. 17–20), and inspect sectors of the front in Belgium, France, and Italy
Oct. 14	Sadie Julian Gompers dies in influenza epidemic
Nov. 11	Cease-fire takes effect on Western Front
Nov. 13–16	Pan-American Federation of Labor organized at Laredo, Tex.

Documents

To the Executive Council of the AFL

Washington, D.C., Feb. 4, 1917.

Personal and Confidential.
Extra.
Executive Council, American Federation of Labor.
Colleagues:

Since the rapidly developing critical situation[1] between this country and Germany, I have given constant thought to the matter. I came to my office this morning for several conferences, and also to attend to some pressing matters that could not be deferred. After thinking further over the foreign situation, I concluded that with the President's approval, I would send a cablegram to Mr. Carl Legien,[2] urging the German labor movement to try to prevail upon the German government to avoid a break with this government, and thereby prevent universal conflict. I called up the White House by telephone, talked with Secretary Tumulty,[3] and told him what I had in mind. I then read to him the cablegram I had prepared, which he wrote down as I read it over the phone. It is as follows:

"February 4, 1917.

["]Legien,
["]Berlin
["]Can't you prevail upon German government to avoid break with United States and thereby prevent universal conflict?

["]Gompers."

I then asked him to bring the matter to the attention of the President and to say to the President that I desired to send the cablegram, but I would refrain from doing so unless it met with his approval. Mr. Tumulty said that he would immediately take the matter up with the President, and he, Mr. Tumulty, expressed his appreciation of what I contemplated doing.

Some time this afternoon Mr. Foster,[4] assistant secretary to the President, called me up over the telephone and said:

"The President desires me to say that he has read the cablegram which you, Mr. Gompers, propose to send to Mr. Legien at Berlin. He

3

says that he not only approves it but thinks it is a splendid service and the President is very grateful."

I have sent the cablegram.[5] It seemed to me that in this crucial hour every honorable effort should be made to try and prevent the United States being dragged into the war and without time for consultation with the members of the Executive Council, I concluded to pursue the course I have and trust it may meet with your approval.

Please return your *vote, marked "personal and confidential"* as to your approval of the course I have pursued in this matter.[6]

This document is indicated by the word "extra" and not by any number, and it will be kept in my confidential records.

Fraternally yours,   Saml Gompers.
President,   American Federation of Labor.

TLS, Files of the Office of the President, General Correspondence, reel 82, frames 229–30, *AFL Records.*

1. On Jan. 31, 1917, Germany notified the United States that it would resume unrestricted submarine warfare on Feb. 1. President Woodrow Wilson cut diplomatic relations with Germany on Feb. 3.

2. Carl LEGIEN was secretary of the Generalkommission der Gewerkschaften Deutschlands (General Commission of German Trade Unions; from 1919, the Allgemeiner Deutscher Gewerkschaftsbund [General German Federation of Trade Unions]) from 1890 to 1920 and was secretary of the International Federation of Trade Unions (to 1913, the International Secretariat of the National Centers of Trade Unions) from 1903 to 1919.

3. Joseph Patrick Tumulty (1879–1954) served as private secretary to Wilson from 1911 to 1921.

4. Actually Rudolph Forster.

5. SG to Legien, Feb. 4, 1917, reel 217, vol. 229, p. 927, SG Letterbooks, DLC. On Feb. 10 SG quoted the cable in a letter to Johann von Bernstorff, the German ambassador to the United States (Files of the Office of the President, General Correspondence, reel 82, frames 286–88, *AFL Records*). Legien replied on Feb. 11 that "no intervention with government on my part has any chance of success unless America prevails upon England to discontinue starvation war as being contrary to law of nations" (Files of the Office of the President, General Correspondence, reel 82, frames 299–300, *AFL Records;* quotation at frame 299).

6. The AFL Executive Council voted to approve SG's actions.

From John Fitzpatrick[1] and Edward Nockels

Chicago Ill Feb 4 1917

The Chicago Federation of Labor in regular meeting assembled pro-test against this country taking part in the war of Europe We demand that American citizens be prevented from entering the war zone

Chicago Fedn of Labor
John Fitzpatrick   President
E N Nockels   Secy

TWSr, Files of the Office of the President, General Correspondence, reel 82, frame 226, *AFL Records.*

1. John J. FITZPATRICK served as president of the Chicago Federation of Labor (1900–1901, 1906–46) and as an AFL salaried organizer (1903–23).

To William McAdoo

Washington, D.C., February 5, 1917.

Hon. William G. McAdoo,
Secretary of the Treasury,
Washington, D.C.
Sir:

The following is contained in the Diplomatic and Consular Appro-priations Bill:[1]

"The President is authorized to extend to the Governments of Cen-tral and South America an invitation to be represented by their min-isters of finance and leading bankers, not exceeding three in number in each case, to attend the Second Pan American Financial Confer-ence[2] in the city of Washington, at such date as shall be determined by the President, with a view to carrying on the work initiated at the First Pan American Financial Conference and establishing closer and more satisfactory financial relations between their countries and the United States of America, and authority is given to the Secretary of the Treasury to invite, *in his discretion, representative citizens* of the Unit-ed States to participate in the said conference, and for the purpose of meeting such actual and necessary expenses as may be incidental to the meeting of said conference and for the entertainment of the foreign delegates during the conference, to be expended under the direction of the Secretary of the Treasury, to be immediately available and to remain available until expended, $50,000."

Two years ago a similar item was contained in the appropriations bill for the same purpose, and I wrote[3] you stating that if a Pan American conference was to take place upon the subject of banking, finances or any other matter, that the whole populations of all Pan American countries were vitally interested as well as the very limited group in each country which controls banking and financial agencies.

You will remember that when I wrote you about this same matter two years ago you called my attention[4] to the fact that the wording of the law gave you no choice in selecting the group from which the American representatives on the High Commission were to be chosen—bankers alone were specified. The proposed law, however, does not contain such limitation but authorizes the Secretary of the Treasury to invite, in his discretion, representative citizens of the United States. This broad grant of authority, if enacted into law, will leave you free to choose from all groups of citizens affected by trade with Pan America.

It is unnecessary to tell you that the banking interests of all countries which have control over credit agencies have a determining control over all industrial, commercial, agricultural and mining operations within the various countries. It has to do with problems that are part of the lives of all of the people.

In your letter to me of two years ago you expressed such broad appreciation of the importance of closer relationships with Pan American countries that I again urge the matter upon your attention in order that you may have it in mind in making arrangements for the Commission.

It is of great regret to all American citizens that there does not exist between the United States and Spanish-American countries that confidence and mutual respect which are the indispensable basis for cooperation and for the attainment of those high ideals which the majority of the citizens of all the countries desire to see the directing forces of international relations.

Nor is this attitude of suspicion on the part of Latin Americans altogether without justification. The great masses of the citizens of the United States have never had an opportunity to make known to the masses of Latin American countries their real purposes and desires. There has been no personal contact that would disclose the warm sympathy and the mutual interests that really exist between the great majority of citizens of the United States and of those countries that are trying to work out the problems of democracy.

Control over official relations between the two countries has been monopolized by a very narrow group of citizens of this country. Until recent months there has been no way by which communications could be established between the masses of the people of Pan American countries. The only relations existing were those established by American business and enterprise.

It is a matter of common information that unfortunately the morality and the ideals of good business are not always representative of the best thought of the people of the United States. The practices and the principles which big business has followed in this country have characterized its activities in Pan American countries. In truth, its methods have been even more unscrupulous and more flagrant there than in this country. Big business as expressed in Pan American relations has been interested only in the dollar. The people of Pan American countries and their natural resources have meant to big business only opportunities for exploitation.

Since business relationships were the only point of contact between our country and Latin American countries, and citizens engaged in these enterprises demanded the protection of the American government, there has been developed a policy under which the American flag followed and protected American business, even in its worst aspects. Unfortunately, the United States has been associated in the minds of many Latin Americans with the [im]morality—yes the immorality and ruthlessness of big business. Such a concept so far as it applies to the masses of the great citizenship of this republic is a grave injustice.

I am sure that I am voicing the firm conviction of the masses of the citizens of the United States when I declare that the time has come when the ideals, the interests and the welfare of human beings must be the chief concern of the government of the United States.

I urge for your most serious consideration the proposition that no international conference ought to be held in which the masses of the people have not duly accredited representatives voicing and advocating their interests.

If the United States government can afford to again appropriate $50,000 to develop banking interests of Pan American countries there can be no justification for confining that amount to financial interests alone, unless an equal amount is appropriated to promote the best human relationships between the various countries.

The United States is now facing an extremely critical period in its history. It may be that the very existence of the nation will depend upon mutual confidence and cooperation of the republics of the Western Hemisphere. It is necessary that we give our best thought to preparedness or democracy to meet the dangers that confront it. There can be no true preparedness without mutual confidence between those who desire the same purposes. Confidence cannot exist between the

United States and these South American countries under the present policies. It can only exist when there has been some way opened up for free democratic exchange of ideas between the masses of the peoples of these various countries. There can be no better way to accomplish that purpose than to provide for a Pan-American conference of the representatives of these masses.

Again I urge upon you, as I did two years ago, the fundamental importance of a democratic conference representing the human interests and the human problems of the peoples of the Western Hemisphere.

You may know that for several years it has been the purpose of the American Federation of Labor to establish the best possible relations between the governments and the peoples of the United States and Mexico, and it may be interesting for you to have the information that for the past year a movement has been on foot, which is now about to be consummated, in the establishment of a Pan American Federation of Labor,[5] not only concerned with the immediate protection and promotion of the rights and interests of the workers of Pan American countries, but also for the crystalization of the spirit of unity and solidarity of the peoples and the governments of Pan American countries. As the result of a conference of the committee[6] having the Pan American Federation of Labor in charge, in the name of the American Federation of Labor I have the honor to address this letter to you for your consideration and action, and it is the earnest hope that both will be in sympathetic accord with the matters and suggestions with which this communication deals.[7]

Very truly yours,   Saml Gompers.
President   American Federation of Labor.

TLS, William McAdoo Papers, DLC.

1. H.R. 19,300 (64th Cong., 1st sess.), making appropriations for the diplomatic and consular service for the fiscal year ending June 30, 1918, was introduced on Dec. 21, 1916, by Henry Flood, a Democratic congressman from Virginia and chairman of the House Committee on Foreign Affairs. The bill became law on Mar. 3, 1917 (U.S. *Statutes at Large*, 39: 1047–58).

2. The Second Pan-American Financial Conference eventually met in Washington, D.C., Jan. 19–24, 1920, with Secretary of the Treasury Carter Glass serving as presiding officer and representatives of twenty Latin American and Caribbean nations in attendance.

3. Probably SG to William McAdoo, June 23, 1915, reel 195, vol. 207, pp. 296–98, SG Letterbooks, DLC. See also SG to McAdoo, July 2, 1915, *The Samuel Gompers Papers*, vol. 9, pp. 296–99.

4. McAdoo to SG, June 29, 1915, RG 174, General Records of the Department of Labor, DNA.

5. The founding meeting of the Pan-American Federation of Labor was held Nov. 13–16, 1918, at Laredo, Tex.

6. The Pan-American Federation of Labor Conference Committee.

7. McAdoo replied on Feb. 9, 1917, that he himself had suggested the phrase "representative citizens" to insure he would have a wider range of candidates to choose from as delegates to the next Pan-American financial conference (McAdoo Papers, DLC).

A Circular[1]

Pan-American Federation of Labor
Conference Committee
Washington, D.C., February 9, 1917.

MANIFESTO

To the Workers of Latin America.

Fraternal Greetings:

The convention of the American Federation of Labor, held in November, 1916,[2] in the city of Baltimore, United States of North America, passed resolutions and gave authority to its Executive Council whereby this, the Pan-American Federation of Labor Conference Committee, is called into being.[3]

In accordance with this action there has been established in the building of the American Federation of Labor in Washington, D.C., an office in charge of the Pan-American Federation of Labor Conference Committee whose mission it is to give form to the projected conference of bona fide labor representatives from all Pan-American countries.

The Conference Committee is composed of Samuel Gompers, Chairman, representing the American Federation of Labor; John Murray, Secretary, and the following committeemen: Santiago Iglesias,[4] representing the organized workers of Porto Rico, and Carlos Loveira, representing the organized workers of Yucatan, Mexico. The committee welcomes representatives from the organized labor movements of Latin-American countries to join with us. All are urged to select their representatives as soon as possible. If an official selection can not be made early, the name and address of some one should be given the committee, who will correspond with the Committee and with whom it and others can correspond.

By means of correspondence with all the labor centers of the American continent, and through the daily, weekly and monthly press friendly to Labor, the Conference Committee proposes to carry on an active propaganda for the attainment of practical, immediate benefits as well as the ideals of organized labor.

As is well known, the capitalists of North America and some European countries are scattering millions and millions of dollars through Latin-America acquiring concessions and business properties which are disposed of to them by Latin-American politicians and speculators without taking into consideration the rights of the masses of the people, the masses of the people who by these transactions have their future endangered for decades and perhaps centuries.

If the employers, the capitalists, of Pan-America thus unite for the protection of their common advantage, it becomes all the more evident that the wage-earners of these countries must also unite for their common protection and betterment.

It will be the duty of the Pan-American Federation of Labor to show to the world that its purpose is to permeate the Western Hemisphere with a humane influence. This influence will more truly represent the sentiments of the American people than the influence of all the corporations of the United States, and is in strong contrast with those capitalists who are eternally crying "Business, business," and "Dollars, dollars."

Above all things, the Pan-American Federation of Labor should stand as a guard on watch to protect the Western Hemisphere from being overrun by military domination from any quarter.

The Conference Committee desires to impress upon its brother workers throughout Pan-America that in its opinion each national organization should be autonomous within the jurisdiction of its own country. The Conference Committee stands for the right of the workers of every American country to work out their own problems in accord with their ideals and highest conceptions.

Authorized by the American Federation of Labor, the Executive Council held a most important conference in Washington, during the month of July, 1916, with representatives of the organized labor movement of Mexico.[5] It is generally conceded that this conference was one of the main factors in averting war between the two countries which at that very moment was made imminent by the Carrizal affair.

Two of the Mexican delegates participating in this conference, Baltasar Pages and Carlos Loveira, left Washington on a tour of propaganda and study through South American countries. They carried with them credentials from organized labor of the State of Yucatan, Mexico, and from President Gompers of the American Federation of Labor.[6] This propaganda tour lasted for over five months, the delegates going as far south as Chile and Argentina, besides visiting other Latin-American countries. Everywhere Loveira and Pages, speaking for the ideal of a Pan-American Federation of Labor, were received with a warm welcome, and a full report was made by Mr. Loveira to the Thirty-sixth Annual Convention of the American Federation of Labor held in Baltimore.[7] The report cited the significant situation now existing between Chile and Peru. These countries had been at war with one another and, officially, still regard each other with suspicion. In spite of this, however, the labor movements of these countries have established the most friendly relations, each country maintaining a fraternal delegate in the land of the other and holding labor congresses from time to time. The report went on to show that between Costa Rica, Nicaragua and Guatemala the same fraternal labor conditions exist.

The Conference Committee hopes that every bona fide labor organization in Latin-America will immediately establish correspondence, one with another, and for this purpose and to facilitate this correspondence, the Conference Committee encloses a list of names and addresses so that there may be a free interchange of opinions and suggestions to bring about the purposes expressed in this document.

It is earnestly requested that labor organizations which desire any further information in regard to matters of trade union tactics, rules, regulations and customs may freely ask this Conference Committee for them, in order that all may acquire fraternal solidarity.

The working people of all our countries should give their first attention to securing better standards of life and work:

Higher wages.

Shorter workdays.

More safe and sanitary conditions in all places of employment.

Better homes.

Better surroundings.

Prohibition of child labor.

Protection of children.

Legislative enactments to achieve and maintain equal rights:

The right of association.

The right of free assemblage.

The right of free speech.

The right of free press.

The right, singly or collectively, to withhold our labor power—the right to strike.

Latin-American labor organizations are asked to spread the suggested ideals of this conference by means of correspondence, by means of the press at their disposal, and through pamphlets. In order to facilitate this great work it is desired that all possible information in relation to unions, syndicates, federations and confederacions be sent to the Pan-American Federation of Labor Conference Committee, American Federation of Labor Building, Washington, D.C., U.S.A., giving in detail names and addresses of leaders, number of members and other matters of moment.

It is not the purpose of the Conference Committee in this circular letter to undertake to discuss all that this Pan-American Federation of Labor may encompass or portend. Suffice it to know that this Conference Committee has in mind the establishment of the most cordial and fraternal relations, cooperation for the protection and the promotion of the rights and interests of the working people—this to maintain the integrity of our several countries in order that the largest field of helpfulness may be utilized, and that the people and all the governments of Pan-America may stand as one great unit for our common protection and advancement.

It is with these thoughts and hopes uppermost in our minds and our hearts, the spirit of which we have but barely expressed, that we appeal to our fellow-workers of Pan-America to give this, our solemn purpose, their immediate, hearty and constant support.

. . .

Note—The thought and hope for a Pan-American Federation of Labor have been, as is well known, long in contemplation and for nearly a year in the course of preparation. This manifesto has been in course of preparation for several weeks, and is not based upon the present critical international situation between the United States and Germany. Indeed, it was written before the break came, but between the time of its production in the English language and its translation into Spanish, the crisis was reached and its printing held up to incorporate this paragraph. That which precedes this is all the more significant by reason of the crisis in which the United States and necessarily the Latin-American countries find themselves, and emphasizes more clearly than ever the necessity for a Pan-American Federation of Labor and a spirit of Pan-Americanism. It is hoped that the best fraternal relations shall be established between the workers and all the peoples of Pan-America with the peoples of all other countries, but come what may, at least the workers and the peoples of Pan-America must stand true, not only to their geographical situation but for the common protection and the opportunity for the development and maintenance of their ideas and ideals of democracy, justice and freedom.

Fraternally,   Conference Committee.

Saml Gompers.
John Murray
C. Loveira.
Santiago Iglesias

PLS, Files of the Office of the President, General Correspondence, reel 82, frames 276–80, *AFL Records*.

1. This document was published in a two-column format, with one column in English and the other in Spanish.

2. The 1916 AFL convention met in Baltimore, Nov. 13–25.

3. The recommendations were included in the report of the Committee on International Relations to the 1916 AFL convention, which adopted them on Nov. 25.

4. Santiago IGLESIAS Pantín served as president of the Federación Libre de los Trabajadores de Puerto Rico (Free Federation of the Workers of Puerto Rico) from 1900 to 1933 and as AFL salaried organizer for Puerto Rico and Cuba from 1901 to 1933.

5. See *The Samuel Gompers Papers*, vol. 9, pp. 436–42.

6. SG to the Workers of All American Countries, July 6, 1916, reel 209, vol. 221, pp. 911–14, SG Letterbooks, DLC.

7. The report of Carlos Loveira y Chirinos to the 1916 AFL convention is printed in AFL, *Proceedings*, 1916, pp. 387–89.

To the Executive Council of the AFL

Washington, D.C., Feb. 10, 1917

No. 14
Executive Council American Federation of Labor.
Colleagues:

The members of the Executive Council have approved the course pursued by me in the document to the E.C. marked "extra,"[1] and some have declared[2] that I should make some declaration regarding the attitude which they and I have felt ought to be made regarding the present critical international situation.

In a way I have already done this.

On Sunday February 4, I with a number of my assistants spent the entire day at the office and then saw in the Congressional Record a discussion in the House of Representatives in which it was clearly manifest that there was a disposition to repeal the Eight Hour law.[3] I immediately prepared a letter[4] and saw that it was delivered to Hon. Champ Clark, Speaker of the House of Representatives that evening and asked him to kindly present the letter to the House of Representatives, read it there to the members and have it printed in the Record.[5] It was an argument showing there was no necessity for the repeal of the Eight Hour law, that the emergency provided in the Eight Hour law of August 1, 1892 contemplated the waiving of the Eight Hour day in government establishments in case of emergency, and surely either war or the imminence of war is such an emergency as contemplated by the law. For convenience and for your information I sent you a copy of that letter and Speaker Clark's reply.[6]

I had important engagements in New York[7] and Secretary Morrison[8] has forwarded[9] you copy of the Congressional Record containing the letter. In connection with the first subject mentioned in this letter, I quote from the expression of my opinion upon the subject of the willingness of the workers of America to do duty to the United States in any emergency in which our country may be confronted. It is as follows:

"There need be no apprehension entertained by any one that the working people of the United States will fail in the performance of duty and to give service for the safety, the integrity and the ideals of our country.

["]I think I am in a position to know as well as any other man in America the feeling and the spirit of America's workers. While I am sure they earnestly hope that war may be averted, yet when the emergency arises they will give a good accounting of themselves."

I have seen various newspaper comments, editorial and otherwise upon this declaration and all of them have been favorable toward the attitude of our movement.

With best wishes, I am,

Fraternally yours,　Saml Gompers.
President　American Federation of Labor

TLcS, Executive Council Records, Vote Books, reel 15, frames 287–88, *AFL Records*.

1. See "To the Executive Council of the AFL," Feb. 4, 1917, above.

2. Replies to SG's letter to the AFL Executive Council of Feb. 4, 1917, from John Alpine, Henry Perham, John Lennon, William Green, James Duncan, and W. D. Mahon can be found in Files of the Office of the President, General Correspondence, reel 82, frames 243, 252, 263, 281, 283–85, and 291, *AFL Records*.

3. The possibility of temporarily suspending federal eight-hour laws was discussed during a debate in the House of Representatives on Feb. 3, 1917, on H.R. 20,632 (64th Cong., 2d sess.), the naval appropriation bill for the fiscal year ending June 30, 1918. The appropriation act, which became law on Mar. 4, included a provision authorizing the president to suspend federal eight-hour legislation in case of national emergency, but it stipulated overtime pay rates of at least time-and-a-half for time worked beyond eight hours in a day (U.S. *Statutes at Large*, 39: 1168–95).

4. SG to Champ Clark, Feb. 4, 1917, reel 218, vol. 230, SG Letterbooks, DLC.

5. Clark read SG's letter on Feb. 6, 1917, in the House of Representatives, and it was subsequently printed in the *Congressional Record* (64th Cong., 2d sess., 1917, vol. 54, pt. 3, p. 2701).

6. For Clark's reply, dated Feb. 6, 1917, see AFL Microfilm Convention File, reel 28, frame 1474, *AFL Records*. On Feb. 5 SG sent the AFL Executive Council a copy of his letter to Clark, and on Feb. 9 he forwarded a copy of Clark's reply (Executive Council Records, Vote Books, reel 15, frames 267, 286, *AFL Records*).

7. SG left Washington, D.C., on Feb. 5, 1917, for New York City, where he held a number of conferences, attended a meeting of the National Civic Federation executive council, and testified before the New York Public Service Commission. He returned to AFL headquarters on Feb. 10.

8. Frank MORRISON served as secretary (1897–1935) and secretary-treasurer (1936–39) of the AFL.

9. Morrison to the AFL Executive Council, Feb. 7, 1917, vol. 491, pp. 781–82, Frank Morrison Letterbooks, George Meany Memorial Archives, Silver Spring, Md.

To Mahlon Garland[1]

Feb. 20, 1917.

Hon. Mahlon M. Garland,
U.S. House Office Building, Washington, D.C.
Dear Sir:

Replying to your letter of February 8, in which you enclosed to me copy of the Adamson bill H.R. 20752[2] with report No. 1434[3] of same, let me call to your attention the statements I made before the House Committee on Interstate Commerce on a similar measure[4] previously introduced by Mr. Adamson.[5] You will have to obtain these hearings from the Committee on Interstate and Foreign Commerce, as it has been impossible for us to get more than sufficient number to furnish copies to the members of our Executive Council. My statements on those occasions were clear, emphatic and complete and I trust that you and your associates in Congress will see to it that I am properly quoted when this matter comes before the House for discussion.

In your letter of the 8th, you say: "I believe in the last session of Congress you urged the passage of the Adamson bill—so-called Eight Hour Law." I did no such thing, neither did my associates nor any of the representatives of the Railroad Brotherhoods. I interviewed no legislator, no Representative, no Senator, nor did I request their support in behalf of the Adamson bill. Some Senators and Representatives complained because we did not solicit their support—some of these gentlemen occupied the most influential relations in the councils of the Republican party. They voluntarily offered to speak for Labor. I positively declined to ask their assistance, or the assistance of any others. The matter was in the hands of the President and the Congress of the United States and we confined our efforts to a protest against incorporating in such a bill compulsory investigation or any language in the law that could be eventually interpreted to mean compulsory service. We accepted the law, as passed, in good faith and expected that it would be put into operation. The railroad officials gave their assent to its enactment and then as soon as Congress had adjourned, they attacked the President and those who voted for the Adamson Law and they inspired thousands of columns of abuse, in the public prints of the nation, of the men who advocated and voted for the law. They started their legal machinery to work in the courts.[6]

You know the present situation. The blame can not be laid at the doors of the American Federation of Labor and the Railroad Brotherhoods. The railroad officials have played a double-acting game, and while they have, so far, succeeded in deferring the establishment of a basic eight-hour day for railroad men, they have not yet succeeded in defeating that principle nor will they succeed. The basic eight-hour day for railroad men is going to be established and the American Federation of Labor will do everything within its power to assist the Railroad Brotherhoods towards that much desired end.

I hope that neither you nor your friends will allow this issue to again become confused. Neither the Adamson bill as now written nor the Newlands bill[7] is satisfactory to Labor.

I send you marked copies of the *American Federationist* for February 1917 and the Weekly News Letter of the American Federation of Labor which make reference to both these bills. I shall have something further to say concerning them at a later date in the *American Federationist.*[8] Note the articles under the captions "The Yoke will not be Worn" page 126 of the *Federationist,*[9] "'Can't Strike' Law Offered in New Form" and "'Round-About Method to Prohibit Strikes," in the News Letter.[10] I think with these statements before you and a perusal of my argument before the Committee, you will be thoroughly and completely advised as to my attitude on the whole proposition, and in which I express the declarations of the organized labor movement of America.

Very truly yours,   Saml Gompers.
President   American Federation of Labor.

TLpS, reel 218, vol. 230, pp. 593–95, SG Letterbooks, DLC.

1. Mahlon Morris GARLAND, president of the Amalgamated Association of Iron and Steel Workers of the United States from 1892 to 1898 and an AFL vice-president from 1895 to 1898, served as a Republican congressman from Pennsylvania from 1915 until his death in 1920.

2. H.R. 20,752 (64th Cong., 2d sess.), was introduced by Democratic congressman William Adamson of Georgia on Feb. 5, 1917, to amend the Newlands Mediation, Conciliation, and Arbitration Act of 1913. It proposed fines or imprisonment for obstructing the mail or interstate or foreign commerce, and it authorized the president to take control of the railroads in case of war or national emergency and draft railroad employees into military service. The bill did not become law.

3. U.S. Congress, House, Committee on Interstate and Foreign Commerce, *Operation of Railroads in Times of Peace and War,* 64th Cong., 2d sess., 1917, H. Rept. 1434.

4. H.R. 19,730 (64th Cong., 2d sess.), introduced by Adamson on Jan. 6, 1917, would have amended the Newlands Act to prohibit strikes by railroad workers while labor disputes were under investigation. SG testified against the bill on Jan. 17 and 19 before the House Committee on Interstate and Foreign Commerce (U.S. Congress, House, Committee on Interstate and Foreign Commerce, *Interstate Commerce on Railroads. Hearings before the Committee on Interstate and Foreign Commerce of the House of Representatives,* 64th Cong., 2d sess., 1917). The bill did not become law.

5. William Charles Adamson (1854–1929) served as a Democratic congressman from Georgia from 1897 to 1917.

6. A test case challenging the constitutionality of the Adamson Act was initiated in November 1916 and was argued before the U.S. Supreme Court in January 1917. On Mar. 19 the court handed down its decision—on a five-four vote—upholding the law (*Wilson* v. *New et al.,* 243 U.S. 332 [1917]).

7. S. 8201 (64th Cong., 2d sess.), introduced by Democratic senator Francis Newlands of Nevada on Feb. 9, 1917, included many of the same provisions as H.R. 20,752. It did not become law.

8. "Freedom Gives National Virility," *American Federationist* 24 (Mar. 1917): 201–3.

9. *American Federationist* 24 (Feb. 1917): 126–27.

10. *AFL Weekly News Letter,* Feb. 10 and 17, 1917.

To the Executive Council of the AFL

Washington, D.C., Feb. 28, 1917.

No. 22.
Executive Council, American Federation of Labor.
Colleagues:

Our country cannot remain unaffected by events that are rocking the very foundations of world civilization. Even though we should be able to maintain our rights without being drawn into the present and pending world conflict, yet we shall be compelled to meet the problems and the changed conditions growing out of the war and adjust our affairs to meet the changed conditions that will prevail in these European countries after the war.

There is an immediate critical problem that the labor movement must meet. The whole world is afire and there is imminent danger that at any time the United States may be involved in the conflagration. The organized labor movement cannot stand idly waiting until some dire catastrophe shall happen before formulating a definite constructive policy of defense of ideals, rights, freedom and justice, and deciding upon the part labor must take to maintain them.

Wage-earners constitute such a large portion of the whole nation that no plan for preparedness or defense can be evolved that does not vitally concern them; in fact, creative labor power will necessarily be a fundamental factor in any plan whether concerned with military or naval defense or the mobilization of industrial forces to supply munitions of war. It is inevitable that some plan of defense will be adopted, whether we will it or not, with our advice or against our protest.

There are two ways in which the matter can be approached, either with the aid and cooperation of Labor, with Labor's representatives maintaining certain ideals of human welfare that are just as essential to national defense as any military purpose or if Labor should hold aloof from the entire situation, plans will be adopted by those out of touch with the labor movement and out of sympathy with the needs and ideals of the workers. In other words, duties and service in connection with national defense will be imposed upon the workers without asking their advice in formulating these plans or Labor can make this an opportunity for emphasizing the tremendous service that it renders to society both in peace and in war, and insisting upon a helpful guiding voice in the determination of affairs that so vitally affect the masses.

Labor has an opportunity to render constructive service that will not only have its influence in war situations but will also affect the standing of wage-earners in time of peace, or else it will find itself confronted with the necessity of obeying directions which will involve fundamental injury to workers physically as well as place them in the position of inferiors with no part in helping to guide governmental policies.

As you know, President Wilson appointed me a member of the Advisory Commission of the Council of National Defense.[1] The Executive Council approved my acceptance of the position. I have been working with the Council and with the Advisory Commission. General policies are now in the making and can be directed either for or against the interests of humanity. Organized labor cannot delay in expressing itself upon the present and impending critical situation. Now is the time for Labor to speak, but inasmuch as the justification for Labor's participation in determining national policies is based upon democratic principles, it is necessary that the same spirit should determine the principles and plans which the wage-earners among themselves shall agree upon. It is imperative, therefore, that the representatives of the labor movement shall consider this entire subject and shall agree upon the fundamental principles which Labor will accept in national defense and in which it will cooperate.

Representatives of the Railway Employes Department of the A.F. of L., in which a number of the metal trades are represented, were and are holding a meeting in Washington, and conferring with railroad companies regarding wages, standards and schedules,[2] and as the situation which I am discussing in this letter became increasingly critical, I asked these representatives to meet me in conference last evening. The following were present:

Mr. Frank Morrison, Secretary of the A.F. of L.

Mr. A. J. Berres,[3] Secretary of the Metal Trades Dept.

Mr. A. O. Wharton,[4] President of the Railroad Employes Dept.

Mr. J. A. Franklin,[5] President of Boiler Makers and Iron Ship Builders Union.

Mr. Wm. J. Spencer,[6] Secretary Building Trades Dept.

Mr. Wm. H. Johnston,[7] President International Association of Machinists.

Mr. P. J. Savage,[8] member Executive Board, International Association of Machinists.

Mr. J. F. Anderson,[9] Vice-President, International Association of Machinists.

Mr. N. P. Alifas,[10] Business Agent, District #44, International Association of Machinists.

Mr. O. E. Hoard,[11] Vice-President, Amalgamated Sheet Metal Workers' International Alliance.[12]

Mr. G. C. Van Dornes,[13] representing the International Brotherhood of Blacksmiths.

Mr. Arthur E. Holder,[14] Legislative representative of the A.F. of L.

Mr. C. A. Chism,[15] member of Washington local of Blacksmiths.

The importance of the conference is manifest by the fact that those present in the conference represented the metal trades—the trades which will be most vitally affected by war.

After the entire situation had been thoroughly presented and discussed, it was the unanimous opinion of all present that the labor movement would lose a great opportunity if it did not make a definite statement as to how far it was willing to go in the movement for preparedness. The labor movement represents the democratic ideals of the masses. It is a constructive, idealistic force, and if it fails to suggest plans then it cannot with justice rebel against plans devised by others.

It was the sentiment of this conference that the labor movement must cooperate in the formulation of plans, and that the President of the A.F. of L. ought to call a special meeting of the Executive Council; and also to call a conference consisting of the officers of all national and international unions and departments.

Whatever action the American labor movement shall take must be taken quickly in order that we may exercise a beneficent guidance rather than be forced to submit to emergency measures. In view of this entire situation and under authority of the constitution of the A.F. of L., Article 6, Section 4, which provides that the President shall call meetings of the Executive Council when necessary, etc., I therefore exercise that authority and call a meeting of the Executive Council to meet at the A.F. of L. Building, Washington, D.C., at ten o'clock the morning of Friday, March 9, 1917,[16] and urge that every member of the Executive Council be present.

In addition I submit the following proposition and ask you to transmit your votes[17] thereon by telegraph as promptly as possible:

Resolved, That the President of the A.F. of L., in the name of the Executive Council, invite the officers of all international and national unions and of departments affiliated to the A.F. of L., to participate in a conference with the Executive Council in Washington, D.C., Monday, March 12, 1917.[18]

Anticipating that the Executive Council realizes the importance of the situation, the call for the Executive Council meeting, and the call for the conference, I feel warranted in assuming that the call will receive your approval. I have therefore sent out a circular letter[19] to the officers of all international unions and departments, placing the situation before them and stating that the matter of calling the conference has been submitted to you, and asking them to hold themselves in readiness upon a telegraphic request from me to attend the general labor conference at Washington on Monday, March 12, 1917.

At the special meeting of the Executive Council we shall have the opportunity of considering the subject for more than two days and formulating at least a tentative program which can be submitted to the conference on Monday.

Again I urge every member of the Executive Council to be in attendance at the meeting herein called for ten o'clock, Friday morning, March 9, 1917, and to promptly telegraph your votes upon the proposition authorizing the call for the conference.

With best wishes, and hopes for the best results in the interests of labor and our country, I am,

Fraternally yours,   Saml Gompers.
President,   American Federation of Labor.

TLcS, Executive Council Records, Vote Books, reel 15, frames 332–34, *AFL Records.*

1. The Council of National Defense was created by the Army Appropriation Act of Aug. 29, 1916. Essentially a research and planning agency—although it later took on some administrative responsibilities—its purpose was to coordinate the country's industries and resources. Its members included the secretaries of agriculture, commerce, interior, labor, navy, and war. In October 1916 an Advisory Commission of seven was appointed to work with the Council, and in February 1917 the Advisory Commission

was divided into seven committees, with each member chairing the committee in his own field of expertise: Bernard Baruch, raw materials, minerals, and metals, Howard Coffin, munitions and manufacturing, including standardization, Hollis Godfrey, engineering and education, SG, labor, including conservation of the health and welfare of workers, Franklin Martin, medicine and surgery, including sanitation, Julius Rosenwald, supplies, including clothing, and Daniel Willard, transportation and communication. Numerous additional subsidiary committees and boards were set up as well—for example, under SG's Committee on Labor there were subcommittees on wages and hours, mediation and conciliation, welfare work, women in industry, information and statistics, press, publicity, and cost of living and domestic economy. The War Industries Board, originally created as a subordinate body of the Council in July 1917, became an independent agency in May 1918 and absorbed many of the functions of the Council and the Advisory Commission. The Committee on Labor and its subcommittees ceased functioning in 1919. The activities of the Council were suspended in 1921.

2. A joint conference opened in Washington, D.C., on Feb. 26, 1917, between general managers of fourteen southeastern railroads, known as Division 3, and representatives of some thirty-five thousand workers in railroad-related unions. Arthur Wharton, president of the AFL Railway Employes' Department, served as chairman of the union delegation. The negotiations extended over a period of six months and concluded on Aug. 24 with an agreement providing for higher wages, a reduction of hours, and overtime pay.

3. Albert Julius BERRES served as secretary-treasurer of the AFL Metal Trades Department from 1908 to 1927.

4. Arthur Orlando WHARTON was president of the AFL Railway (to 1915, Railroad) Employes' Department from 1912 to 1922.

5. Joseph Anthony FRANKLIN was president of the International Brotherhood of BOILER MAKERS, Iron Ship Builders, and Helpers of America from 1908 to 1944.

6. William J. SPENCER was secretary-treasurer of the AFL Building Trades Department from 1908 to 1924 and from 1927 to 1933.

7. William Hugh JOHNSTON was president of the International Association of MACHINISTS from 1912 to 1926 and served on the National War Labor Board from 1918 to 1919.

8. Thomas J. Savage, a member of Machinists' local 634 of Charlestown, Mass., was a member of the Machinists' general executive board (1915–18) and served as an alternate for Johnston on the National War Labor Board (1918).

9. John F. Anderson, a member of Machinists' local 308 of St. Louis, served as an organizer (1912–13) and as a vice-president (1913–25) of the Machinists.

10. Nels P. Alifas, a member of Machinists' local 174 of Washington, D.C., was president of Machinists' District 44 (Navy Yards and Arsenals) from 1912 until at least 1951.

11. Otto E. Hoard was a member of Amalgamated Sheet Metal Workers' International Alliance 319 of Kansas City, Mo. (Railroad Shopmen) and served as the local's recording secretary (1908–9) and financial secretary (1909–11). He also served as a vice-president of the international union (1909–20) and as a member of Railway Board of Adjustment No. 2 of the U.S. Railroad Administration (1918–20).

12. The Amalgamated SHEET Metal Workers' International Alliance.

13. Gus C. Van Dornes of Letona, Ark., served as a member of the board of trustees (1909–13) and as a vice-president (1914–24) of the International Brotherhood of BLACKSMITHS and Helpers (from 1919, the International Brotherhood of Blacksmiths, Drop Forgers, and Helpers). He was also a member of Railway Board of Adjustment No. 2 (1918–21).

14. Arthur E. Holder served on the AFL Legislative Committee from 1906 to 1917.

15. Clarence A. Chism, a drop forger, was recording secretary of Blacksmiths' local 217 of Washington, D.C. (1916–17).

16. The AFL Executive Council met in Washington, D.C., Mar. 9–12, 1917.

17. The AFL Executive Council voted in favor of the proposal.

18. The conference on Mar. 12, 1917, was attended by the members of the AFL Executive Council and more than 140 representatives from eighty affiliated national and international unions, five unaffiliated organizations (the railroad brotherhoods and the National Window Glass Workers), and the five AFL departments. It adopted the statement "American Labor's Position in Peace or in War" (printed below).

19. Actually the circular was not sent out until Mar. 2, 1917 (SG to Dear Sir and Brother, Mar. 2, Files of the Office of the President, reel 82, frames 439–43, *AFL Records*). After receiving the AFL Executive Council's approval, SG sent a second letter on Mar. 3 confirming the Mar. 12 meeting (ibid., frame 452).

From John White[1]

United Mine Workers of America[2]
Indianapolis, Indiana March 3, 1917.

Dear Sir and Brother:

Referring to your favor of February 27th,[3] I desire to say that I note your request but I am personally against the whole scheme of war and preparedness that is now so prevalent and I have taken a very advanced position against the scheme of preparedness and military training that I find myself out of harmony with the entire program. My deep and honest convictions against this whole plan, including the desire for war, is, I assure you, the result of mature thought. I see no humanitarian issues in the present war. I believe that it is distinctly a commercial war. In my broad travels I find little sentiment among the working people in favor of this terrible war. The United Mine Workers of America has gone on record in a very pronounced manner against compulsory military training and we believe that the great masses of the people should determine whether or not they should engage in this unjust and uncalled for war. Therefore, recognizing the sentiments of the people that I represent and expressing my own views personally, I would most respectfully beg to be excused from participating in the matter referred to in your letter.

With kind regards, I remain,

Yours very truly,　John P. White
President.

TLS, Files of the Office of the President, General Correspondence, reel 82, frame 458, *AFL Records.*

1. John Phillip WHITE served as president of the United Mine Workers of America (1911–17).

2. The United MINE Workers of America.

3. In his letter of Feb. 27, 1917, SG asked White to become a member of the Committee on Labor of the Advisory Commission of the Council of National Defense and to suggest others who might serve with him (reel 218, vol. 230, p. 871, SG Letterbooks, DLC).

Excerpts from the Minutes of a Meeting of the Executive Council of the AFL

Washington, D.C. March 9, 1917.

[MORNING SESSION]

Mr. Gompers: Gentlemen of the Executive Council: In accordance with your vote I have asked Mr. Howard Coffin[1] to meet with us and to give us such information as he thinks he may impart to us in connection with the present national and international situation, both industrial and from a military and naval standpoint. I would not undertake to say that Mr. Coffin will even refer to all the information that he has, for it is so vast that it would take him more time and take more of our time than he or we can give, but I may say this. In my judgment I think there is no doubt of it that Mr. Coffin is possessed of a wider range of information, general and detailed, than is possessed by any other man in America. Mr. Coffin has for the last year and a half given his undivided time to the investigation in the effort at mobilization of the industries of the country. . . .

. . .

Mr. Coffin: . . . I judge that in the brief time that you want to give to anything I may say that you would like to have me deal with the phases of the work as I see them which involve what we may term industrial relations in this country. By industrial relations I mean the whole fabric of our machinery involving the relations of workers and manufacturers, and manufacturers and the government, and perhaps also the question of the methods of purchase or procurement whereby the government will have to produce under war conditions the various materials which go to make up not only the sphere of the fighting forces, but the sphere of the civilian population as well.

The situation in England of course has been very unsatisfactory and that situation has been entirely due to certain fundamental weaknesses in England's organization, but largely due to the fact that England was caught utterly unprepared in every department of her national institutions. To evidence that I brought down to you, just to show you, the war legislation—only the emergency legislation which was developed between the dates of the beginning of the war, 1914, and the 31st of August, 1915. These five volumes cover the emergency legislation which England found it necessary to enact for the control of her wartime conditions dealing with industrial relations to a certain extent, and other matters as well. We unquestionably would be very much in the same boat. I am not sure that we would not be worse off. We are going to find immediately upon declaration of war, whether in two or three weeks or the next five years, that there is going to be a stampede for the enactment of half baked legislation to meet the momentary needs of the moment, or meet those needs as they seem to exist at the moment without any well considered plan or well considered theory behind it. Now I do not think that we as intelligent American citizens ought to let this thing happen. We certainly have had lesson enough without going beyond England's experience to realize about what we would have to go through. None of us here in this room want of course to see a war come upon this country, but as someone put it the other day, when someone comes along with a bigger navy and a tougher conscience, what are you going to do about it? It may be forced upon us, as the present situation is being forced upon us, and while we are all very much in the dark as to what this immediate situation may develop, there is not very much doubt in our minds as to some ultimate situation which may develop five or ten years hence, provided we are forced at that time into a war with some one or two of the first class powers. There is little doubt in our minds as to what that situation would be like because we have seen and know what modern warfare means.

· · ·

. . . I think you can very readily see what would happen if the Ordnance Department, and the Commissary, and the Quartermaster, and the Engineers' Departments would begin to place orders suddenly among four or five, or among thousands of American manufacturers for supplies, the essential elements of which all went back to about the same sources of material supplied. Every manufacturer who had bid on a contract for the War Department would of course immediately try to cover for material before he made his bid. The result is that all of these thousands of manufacturers would be trying to cover for copper and steel and cloth, and all of the fundamentals that go into the forty thousand items, and the Commissary Department would be trying to cover for flour, etc., and the result would be inevitable that not only the cost of all these commodities would go up two or three hundred percent, but the cost of living would go up at the same time, because you would not go into the market with a wholesale request for bids on materials in the quantities that we now know would be necessary, and expect to have any other result. . . .

England has found out to her cost that you can no longer deal in finished commodities under war conditions. You must go straight to the source of the raw materials, whether food stuffs or steel, or copper, or whatever it is, and the government must control the sources of that material, and the prices, etc. The transportation of the country will unquestionably be under government also. It is clear that the private manufacturer has no chance to even have materials delivered to him except by direction of the government. Now those things are, I think, about the facts as they lie. We may theorise, if we like, that it can be done in some other way, but the actual experience in these foreign countries has seemed to indicate that that is the way it would really be done, provided the necessary direction is employed at the head of the government to avoid the confusion and the expense, and the inconvenience that accompanied Great Britain's entry into the war.

Now that means that in the industrial relation all along the line, you must have first a control of the raw commodities of the country, and a control of the price of those raw commodities. You must have a control of the price of the finished article, that the government has turned out by the manufacturer. You must have some control or understanding or agreement as to the price of the labor which goes into those commodities, and that whole thing must be based upon a sliding scale of raw products. If the price of raw products is to be increased for any reason, then the whole scale, all up the line, must also be increased, and in looking at the methods of handling these matters in the various countries it seems that the French system is perhaps to be preferred over the English system.

England has taken over under governmental direction a very large number of manufacturing plants. France has not done this to any extent at all. France has permitted the manufacturing institutions to remain in the control of the private manufacturer, but has controlled her raw materials, and is fixing the price at which the government obtains its supplies.

Now these things are very radical, I admit, but there is not anything about war that follows precedent, and there is not anything about war that has to do with law, because if it were governed by laws, we would not have war. Therefore, our best guide as to what we must do over here must be found from what has actually had to be done in these foreign countries.

. . .

. . . Both in England and in France they are trying to make all of these transactions profitable, because they realize that it is only through such a procedure that they can keep the whole economic machine oiled up. That is, labor must have a fair return; the producers of the raw materials must have a fair return, and the finisher of the product must have a fair profit, in order that economically the nation may go along as a successful institution. If labor was working for half what it ought, and the manufacturer selling at 25% less than it was costing him to produce, of course there would be a catastrophe, and there would be bankruptcies, etc.

Mr. Morrison: Have you any information in regard to the percentage they allow the manufacturer?

Mr. Coffin: It varies somewhat. I have some books here which are accessible to your office—I got them from the War College a few days ago—giving statistics. However, in England, in the controlled plants, they were permitted to go ahead and make their normal profit, whatever it might be, as a manufacturing institution. It might be 5%, or more; but when the period of accounting came, everything above a 10 or 15% basis, as the case might be, went into the government's hands. . . .

. . .

They are tying to operate the French nation as a big industrial machine, on the basis of reasonable and fair returns to all concerns, but on the basis of not permitting abnormal profit to anyone along the line.

Now our conditions in this country are such that I think we ought to make a start on this thing right away in a very serious minded way, and of course Mr. Gompers knows we have statistics on many of these subjects.

This question of an industrial reserve is one of the things that is most vital, following the control of raw materials and the control of profits arising from war. I do not think that I need say anything as to the necessity for keeping the skilled men, or the craftsmen of this country in the places where they will do the most good in an emergency. It would be utterly frivolous for a man who has spent forty years of his life in becoming an expert tool maker, merely because he happens to feel a surge of patriotism, to shoulder a musket and go marching to the front, because his value many, many times over would be at his job of tool making. All of the skilled workers of this country, whether they be textile workers, or workers in metals, certainly during the first period of any war that we might get into, would be of the most value in their usual line of work. As it became necessary possibly, if we were involved in a situation as serious as that which now confronts Europe, it might be necessary to begin to call out even skilled labor for military purposes.

We can see in England they are having now to substitute women very largely for men, and I must pay the ladies the compliment of saying that in a very great many lines of work where highly developed skill, particularly with the hands and the fingers, and accuracy in the using of measuring instruments and that sort of thing is required, the women have done even better work than the men ever did on those same jobs. They have a faculty for that sort of thing which the men apparently do not possess.

This industrial reserve is something that I think the American Federation of Labor must give its immediate attention to. If there were a declaration of war next week, the probabilities are that the next move within twenty-four or forty-eight hours thereafter, would be a call for half a million volunteers. I say half a million because I think that would be about the number that we could expect to put into shape in a reasonable time; and immediately after that a call for half a million more to go into training just as soon as the first half million were under way. There we are confronted immediately with this whole subject of the industrial reserve, and how to keep skilled men out of the ranks. The better men among the skilled workers of the country are very patriotic, and in Europe they did volunteer and they did go to the front, and I have no doubt at all but that we would be surprised at the percentage of our skilled workers who would do that thing in this country. . . . And I might say in this connection that the law as it now stands, apparently gives to the President no power of exclusion of any man of a military age and of physical fitness. Whether a law can be passed in time to meet that need is of course a question, in view of the present situation. Just what that method of exclusion should be is somewhat of a question. Mr. Gompers and myself have discussed the age limitation. History has shown, and the foreign war has shown, that the young men are the ones who fight the battles of the country and they are the men who are capable of withstanding the hardships they must encounter. They can go without upsetting the machinery of the country nearly so much. They have not usually large families, and they can be spared better than the older men, and if we could establish an age limit and say that in the event of a call that no man over 25 years of age, unless he has seen military or naval service, would be accepted on the first call, we would go far to keep the skilled worker out of the army. I imagine that very few men under 25 years might be rated as the real skilled portion of the country's workers, who have spent years in learning a certain art that cannot be built up in a short time. That is merely a thought. Nothing has been done on it, and it is before you gentlemen for discussion and suggestion. As a matter of fact, this whole industrial reserve idea is before you gentlemen for discussion and suggestion. . . .

. . .

Mr. Morrison: In your mobilization of industries have you considered the proposition of women in industry?

Mr. Coffin: Well, of course, as a general proposition we would hope that we would not have to use them, but if we should, we could. . . .

. . .

Mr. Morrison: Well, the women are active themselves, and their activity takes this form: that the women who go into the industry must receive the same wages as paid to the men.

. . .

Mr. Gompers: A question that might interest the Executive Council is the peculiar geographical position in which is located the plants engaged in the manufacture of powder and munitions from the strategic standpoint.

Mr. Coffin: There probably is not a war department in any foreign country which has not within its war data plans relating to this country, the plan to establish a line from the Chesapeake Bay to Lake Erie. It would be comparatively easy for any one of the foreign powers as they are at present fitted to do that, and if they should do it, they cut off, of course, the whole eastern munition making territory, in a space of about 200 miles, and if a landing were made over here, the probabilities are that that would be the attempted stroke, because they would have the country pretty nearly at their mercy if they established that line. They would have the whole great area of the country cut off from the limited area upon which it would be utterly dependent for the supply of many things that must go into the making of war materials. The whole gauge making craft, almost, is located in the New England States. The present great arms manufacturing institutions are all there, and there is no doubt, I believe, but that is the weak point. I believe that was what you wanted me to bring out.

Mr. Morrison: Well, do you think that there are any countries combining [that] could land on and overrun that part of this country?

Mr. Coffin: I do not think there is the least doubt of it. Here are the estimates made at about the beginning of the war, which would have to be revised somewhat, as to the ability of foreign countries to make landings in this country, and we find here that Germany, using only three-quarters of her tonnage for troop ships, it is estimated she could land 440,000 men in this country within thirty days. Great Britain, which had no army before the war, but had a tremendous tonnage in shipping, three times as much as any other country in the war, it is estimated she could have used only 50% of her tonnage and landed 170,000 men within fourteen days. Great Britain, of course, since that time has created an army of five or six millions, whereas she only had not to exceed 750,000 men in her service.

Mr. Duncan:[2] All of that is predicated upon no opposition.

Mr. Coffin: It is predicated upon first defeating the American Navy, which England, of course, could very easily do, and Germany could probably easily do, and furthermore, upon a state of affairs which I think is a pretty true state of affairs, that is, without armed resistance, trained armed resistance, that there could be very little serious resistance.

. . .

Mr. Duncan: We would have to be asleep for all those things to happen.

Mr. Coffin: As we are now, or as we have been? Had we suddenly been embroiled in war, there is not any question but that Germany would have simply walked away with us.

. . .

There is one thing I would like to mention, Mr. Gompers. I do not know, of course, anything as to the ideas of the gentlemen present on the question of universal service, but to thousands of us who have studied this situation, there does not seem any other answer of a comprehensive nature. Some form of universal service, I believe, is before us, and I think is coming whether or no. I know some of the gentlemen of the Committee on Military Affairs told me they considered it unavoidable. Now the thing which we should all do is to face that issue with the others and do in so far as we can, or work as far as we can to get the sensible and logical thing in that line, something which will accomplish the maximum good with the minimum amount of evil connected with it.

Mr. Duncan: A few minutes ago you referred to another phase of this same subject, and reference was made to the advantage we hope to have that as the result of this great conflict in Europe, great international wars, at least, might be ended. What would be the use of universal service when we are endeavoring to build affairs and shape our thoughts upon no more war? The military man in my opinion is the poorest authority on the subject. To a military man nothing is right except a uniform and a gun, and anyone who does not appreciate it is a witless critter whose education has been sadly neglected. General Scott[3] is a great general, I mean in his work apart from what he is doing at the present time, apart from the economics he has entered into such as doing work under government contracts, etc. These are great things. But he is a militarist, everything to him comes through a military mind, and universal training and service is one of them. In the view General Scott and some of those leaders have, if we were to become true we would all of us become soldiers more or less. Now to the extent they would be educated to be soldiers, they would be dedicated to the same kind of work as those militarists and therefore what is the use of pursuing our economic thought and endeavoring to make our country great as an industrial country?

Mr. Coffin: I think those things are all true in a degree. If we do as Germany did, make every man serve three years and drill into him the fact that the military phase of the national life is the only one worth while, I think you are right. I do not, on the other hand, believe we are ever going to do that, and I do not think that our whole makeup will ever permit us to do that sort of thing. I think that the maximum training would be not to exceed a period of months when a man is possibly 19 or 20 and endeavor to give him enough of a nucleus of military training so that we would not have to go through so much of a military training if necessary to call him.

Mr. Duncan: I question if there is in all history a group of better fighters than the Confederate soldiers when their numbers and general conditions are considered. They gave the United forces of the north, with all their money and foreign assistance the fight of their lives, yet it was not the military stuff that gave it to them. It was the spirit that was in them. And we would rise to the occasion as they did then. The same spirit was aroused among our people when we got into a quarrel with Spain about Cuba. Some of the greatest generals we had were volunteers.

. . .

Mr. Coffin: . . . I feel that this situation that may confront us, or this whole planning to meet the emergency of war in this country, is one in which we are all so vitally interested and one in which we must take a fair view of the situation so that we stand or fall together, is so essential that we ought to all take that view of it, and I want to impress again the thought that it is vital that the government control the sources of all materials. I think we are all agreed that in most instances, take our big corporations such as telegraph and telephones, I think figures prove that the service is more efficient under ownership such as now exists. . . .

Mr. Duncan: In regard to your parting words about the government taking hold of things, we are hoping that you will second several of Mr. Gompers' motions on the commission[4] to differentiate between the workers and the materials, because the labor power of the workers is not a commodity, and we want to carry this into our line of thought, because if we do not we might thereby be supplying evidence that we considered the labor power of the worker as being on a par with or equal to materials.

. . .

You will find as far as the organized workers are concerned, that the claim that is made by many of the manufacturers and their attorneys that we are unfriendly to the government, is a lot of the rankest humbug. If we unfortunately have to get into war, we will prove it. Those people who claim that those are qualities of organized labor, will be among the carpet baggers, who will be leaving to look after their interests in the Orient or elsewhere, while our people will go to the front trying to defend the interests of the United States. Our unions in the Civil War enlisted to such an extent that frequently there were not enough left at home to form a quorum to conduct the meetings. And in many instances not enough came back from the war to hold a meeting.

. . .

[AFTERNOON SESSION]

Mr. Gompers: Gentlemen of the Executive Council: In compliance with the motion made this morning that Honorable William B. Wilson,[5] Secretary of the Department of Labor, be invited to give us the benefit of his advice this afternoon regarding the situation and conditions for the consideration of which this special meeting of the Executive Council was called, I got in touch with Mr. Wilson, and it was agreeable to him and he accepted the invitation and stated that the hour set, about three o'clock this afternoon, would be entirely agreeable to him, and Secretary Wilson is with us now. I may say, Mr. Secretary, that the call to the national and international trade unions you have had, and you know the purport of it. I have had the opportunity of meeting with you, sir, and as a member of the Council of National Defense, as a member of its Advisory Commission, and the attitude which the workers should take in the present situation and any emergency or eventuality is, of course, the prime purpose for which this special meeting and the conference for Monday have been called. We should be very glad to have you give us the benefit of your advice and your understanding.

Mr. Wilson: Mr. Chairman and Gentlemen of the Council: The world is passing through one of its greatest crises at the present time. We are almost face to face with the problem of whether or not a democracy can withstand the onslaughts of a benevolent despotism. It has been said by many writers that the final determination of all questions is force, and that is practically true. There are two factors in determining questions. The first and the best factor is reason. But when reason fails, then the final determination undoubtedly rests with force. If I understand the trade union movement properly, it is built upon that concept, that reason should be the determining factor, but when reason has failed, then it is absolutely necessary that there should be force on the side of right, because if there is not force on the side of right, then force on the side of wrong will prevail.

. . .

. . . If the worst comes, if we are embroiled in the difficulties that now obtain in Europe, and I hope we will not be, then the preservation of our institutions requires that the wage workers of our country and that portion of the wage workers that gives the most concrete expression to them, the trade union movement, must take its place in a determined effort to maintain our institutions. If it does not, then it will meet with the same fate that other organizations have met with under similar circumstances when the tendency is towards the defense of human liberty—other organizations that failed to do their share. It would be crushed; it would be run over as with a juggernaut.

I do not believe the trade union movement can afford to be placed in that kind of a position. I believe that it should take its place when the occasion arises as a cooperator, a willing cooperator, for the maintenance of human liberty, and by taking its place as a willing cooperator for the maintenance of human liberty, not only retain its strength, but have greater strength when the crisis is over to promote the welfare of the wage earners, who constitute the mass of our society. To take any other course is likely to lead to the destruction or the weakening at least of the trade union movement, so that when the crisis is over it should be in a position to protect the welfare of the wage earners. Mr. Chairman, briefly stated, that is my concept of the situation. I believe that the trade union movement of the country should tender its services in an effort to cooperate with the government in any eventuality. Out of it will grow greater strength and greater assurance of the continuation of democratic institutions and the maintenance of human rights.

. . .

Mr. Morrison: I want to ask this question. You made the statement that the labor movement should tender its services. Now have you in looking at it from the standpoint of the position you occupy, with the knowledge that you have, have you any definite statement or suggestion as to just what the movement should offer to the government?

Secretary Wilson: Mr. Chairman, there are some things that occur to me, at least, I do not know that they cover all the field, but there are some things that occur to me as being of great importance which the labor movement could offer. It has been very thoroughly demonstrated in the present conflict in Europe that the services of the workmen at home are of as much importance in the preparation and transportation of the supplies, the equipment, the munitions necessary for the support of the army, as the armies themselves. The tremendous amount of material used by modern armies makes that a fact. Whenever such a condition arises in any country, there must of necessity be a tremendous readjustment of the working forces. There must be a movement from the class of work least needed to the class of work most needed. If the trade union movement offers its services, if it presents to the government the opportunity of using its machinery for developing the mobility of labor, then those transfers, those changes, are more likely to be made under conditions favorable to labor than if the government is to develop other agencies for developing the mobility of labor. . . .

Mr. Mahon:[6] . . . I have not yet been convinced by anyone that there is a necessity of war, and I do not think that it is a question of preparing for war until there is a reason for war. It strikes me that the position as trades unionists we should take is to continue that that we have always taken, that we are decidedly opposed to any war; that we stand unalterably opposed to war. That is the position the trade union has always assumed, and I as a trade unionist am not ready to change my position at all, and that is the declaration that should be made, and that is the position of the American people. The main issue of the last campaign was, "Wilson kept us out of war." He was elected because he kept us out of war, and I can't agree that we have reached the time yet where we should go into the preparation for war, involve our unions and our forces into that, lend encouragement to that military spirit, that is going on throughout this whole country to create and establish military conditions that we are all opposed to. I have not as I said, been convinced that there is a necessity for war.

Secretary Wilson: Mr. Chairman, I think that last statement is exactly the position that has been taken by President Wilson and by his advisers and by the Congress of the United States; that there is not as yet a necessity for war; that war may be brought to us whether we want it or not, however, has been more clearly impressed upon our people during the past two months than ever before since the struggle in Europe began. As to the first proposition, I could take exactly the same attitude if I had never had any trade union training, but having had a trade union training and that training having taught me that it was absolutely necessary to prepare when there was no struggle, or when there was no struggle in sight, in order that I might engage successfully in the struggle when it did come, having been taught that in the trade union movement, I can't follow the first part of your suggestion. The trade union movement is only valuable because it is a militant movement. The moment the trade union movement takes the ground that under no circumstances will it fight, under no circumstances is there any reason for industrial war, just that moment the trade union movement becomes valueless to the wage workers of the country. Applying the same principle to international affairs that we apply to our trade union affairs, then it is our duty as American citizens to avoid war as far as we can avoid war. To keep out of it if it is possible for us to keep out of it, but to be prepared to meet it if we must meet it in order to maintain that which is right and just and due to us and to maintain our freedom.

. . .

Mr. Mahon: I can't see the powers that are going to oppose our government at the present time. I have thought it over carefully and studied it from every phase, and I can't conceive of any danger. From Europe now, or from Germany in the condition it is in, I can't conceive of it coming from them or from any other quarter. I think it is just simply an excitement that is unnecessary.

. . .

Secretary Wilson: Let me make one more suggestion on this point. The recently published instructions of the German government to its Mexican Ambassador required the Mexican Ambassador under certain circumstances to make an effort to secure the cooperation of certain other countries in making war upon the United States, and to hold out to those other countries as an inducement for them to make that war, the dismemberment of the United States.[7] If by pursuit of any such arrangement, if it were successful, our country was dismembered, if the southwest was given to Mexico, and the Pacific Coast was given to some other country, if other parts of the United States were handed over to foreign countries, what would become of the institutions that we have struggled so hard to establish?

Mr. Mahon: If there was that condition and that danger, of course, we would fight to preserve our country, but there is not anything to show that that is more than a myth. The German government is struggling wherever it is possible, but there has nothing developed to my mind, and to my mind there will nothing develop on the Mexican and Japanese situation. It is simply a myth, that is all.

. . .

Mr. Duncan: The point that I want to mention is another phase that has been touched upon by Vice-President Mahon. In the first place, on this subject in its broader sense we are confronted with the situation which, when something similar arises in other countries, we strongly condemn namely the labor organizations falling in with the military line of thought in their respective countries. It applied to almost each of the countries, although in other countries than Germany and Austria they claimed they were on the defensive. We have been in hopes, and it was developing that the influence of the economic organizations in the civilized countries would be sufficient to offset war because of the underlying concepts among organized workmen that war meant murder of the producers. As far as our own country is concerned at the present time, the great danger lies in governmental activities, principally through Congress in enacting legislation which would of necessity be, I do not say entirely permanent, but for a considerable time practised, when so far as the cooperation of the laboring people with the government is concerned if left to voluntary action, the assistance of the working people would be freely and fully given and when the need for the special activity was over the whole of that line of activity and procedure would revert to normal conditions. The greatest danger at the present time in connection with our government affairs, is the evident desire on the part of those inclining towards militarism to introduce a system of military service. Such would not be in accordance with anything which the labor movement had stood for or desired.

. . .

Any overt act by a German submarine such as the sinking of one of our ships, would look to me like an informal perhaps a formal declaration of war. In connection with such an event the working people should voluntarily offer their assistance for the defense and preservation of our government, our institutions and our country and not as bolstering up an offensive movement against a foreign power. They should do it voluntarily, but should use all economic as well as their voting power against any compulsory act which might be attempted to be forced upon them either by executive or by legislative action. As citizens they should do what would be fitting for them to do and when the need for the unusual activities is ended everybody would return to their pacific and industrial pursuits without having thereafter to contend with laws which has been enacted and which would fasten upon us a military system which could only be detrimental to a great democratic system of government. The desire of those opposed to us was apparent when they recently wanted to try to repeal our eight-hour bill. Representatives of the army insist that we must have compulsory universal service. Such would mean that our pacific intentions, our democratic purposes, our civilized developments would have as their guiding tendencies, instead of general peace, a species of militarism as promulgated by the war office, the Navy department, our enlisted officers and the war college. This to me seems to be the worst phase of the whole situation and I hope that the President and his advisors including the influence [of] Secretary Wilson as a militant trade unionist, will do everything they can do to prevent it. . . .

Mr. Gompers: I would like to address myself to this subject. From my earliest boyhood or my earliest young manhood, up to within the past two years I have been an ultra pacifist, insofar as military training, military service is concerned. I belonged to nearly every peace association or peace league in existence in the United States, as well as in the international peace movement. I have relied upon the increased intelligence of the peoples of all countries and upon the fraternity established by the organized workers to bring about its realization. My fondest dream and hope were Tennyson's couplet of the brotherhood of man and the federation of the world.[8]

. . .

I cannot convey to any mind the shock which I received when I learned that the workmen of Germany had responded to the call to the colors and were invading Belgium. The workingmen of the other countries responded to the call of their governments to the colors. It showed me that my hopes and life-long aspirations for international peace and international brotherhood had been shattered—that the old command to "love thy neighbor as thyself" in practice had been shot to pieces; that men loved themselves, their families and their localities and their countries better than they loved their neighbors, both in the same street, city, state or country,—than they loved the people of any other district, city, state or nation, and it showed too the fact that men would fight for the cause they believe to be right or they are made to believe is right.

. . .

Now in the United States we have a situation as can only in part be discussed. Certainly, not discussed publicly. We may imagine that we know the situation, but we do not know it.

I am a sworn officer now of the Government of the United States and my oath of office as a member of the Advisory Commission of the Council of National Defense prevents my disclosing some of the information which has come to me. The dangers confronting our country—the dangers by which we are threatened vitally affect our Republic—dangers not alone from Germany, not alone from Austria, but from the country to which the labor movement has given the cause, by reason of which that country feels a grievance against the United States—China. The grievance against the United States which she alleges she has is because the labor movement of the United States has produced that alleged cause. We have excluded the Chinese from the United States and by law.[9] That demand went forth as the demand of the workers of the United States. China is an awakening country.

At the instance of the labor movement of America we found that the President of the United States entered into what is known as a "gentlemen's agreement" with the government of Japan to exclude Japanese workmen from the United States, and Japan is an awakening country and one of the great powers of the world. There is a grievance or she alleges she has a grievance against the United States, because at our demand her people have been excluded from the United States by agreement first and now by law,—the provisions of the Immigration Law enacted within these past few weeks. There are no other frictions between the United States and these two countries than the questions that we as a labor movement are primarily responsible for, because of the enactment into law of the demands which we have made. If you gentlemen think that this friction between these two countries and the government of the United States is superficial, you are making a mistake. It may have been an unpropitious time for Japan to take the step which Germany in her intrigue sought to bring about.

In addition to the newspapers, I have had opportunities for information that I doubt is obtainable by any five men in the United States. There are in the United States not less than 250,000 reservists of the German army. Within these past six weeks more than 50,000 of the German reservists have gone into Mexico. There is on the Canadian border a situation of a similar character, the nature of which I cannot even by indirection reveal. The revolt in Cuba[10] is the result of the machinations and the money of the Teutonic allies. The revolutionary movements stirred up in the Latin-American countries are due to the same cause. The German reservists in the United States and those who have gone into Mexico and are on the border between the United States and Canada are trained men, are armed men with as much ammunition in their possession or at convenient points as the United States itself possesses now. My opposition to militarism today is as great as at any time, but I hold that what we are now facing is not militarism nor a militaristic spirit, but a militant spirit, the willingness to do, the willingness to fight for the right. General Wood expressed this significant remark at a conference a few months ago, and this morning I jotted it down from memory,—"An armed people trained in the use of arms cannot have their liberties taken away from them."

At this point, Mr. Duncan objected to Mr. Wood being quoted on account of his militaristic training and sympathies.

Mr. Gompers replied: "You do not know General Wood or you do not know his utterances if you say that. As a matter of fact, his whole scheme of camp training, his whole proposition for training in the training camps was for the democratization of any militant action on the part of the people of the United States. In every word that he has uttered that I have seen or heard and in the correspondence that I have had with him, he is against militarism and is in favor of universality of service in order to accomplish its democracy."

Mr. Gompers then read again the statement of General Wood which he had jotted down from memory—"An armed people cannot have their liberties taken away from them."[11]

. . .

TDc, Executive Council Records, Minutes, reel 5, frames 1327–35, 1339–60, *AFL Records.*

1. Howard Earle Coffin (1873–1937), vice-president and construction engineer at the Hudson Motor Car Co. (1910–30), was chairman of the Committee on Production, Organization, Manufacture, and Standardization of the Naval Consulting Board, known as the Committee on Industrial Preparedness (November 1915–December 1916), a member of the Advisory Commission of the Council of National Defense (December 1916–18), and head of the Aircraft Production Board (from October 1917, the Aircraft Board; 1917–18).

2. James DUNCAN was president of the Granite Cutters' International Association of America (1912–23) and an AFL vice-president (1895–1928).

3. Maj.-Gen. Hugh Lenox Scott (1853–1934) served as army chief of staff from November 1914 to September 1917 and was a member of the Root commission to Russia in 1917.

4. That is, the Advisory Commission of the Council of National Defense.

5. William Bauchop WILSON was the first U.S. secretary of labor, serving from 1913 to 1921.

6. William D. MAHON was president of the Amalgamated Association of Street and Electric Railway Employes of America (to 1903, the Amalgamated Association of Street Railway Employes of America) from 1893 to 1946 and an AFL vice-president from 1917 to 1923 and from 1936 to 1949.

7. A reference to a telegram sent by Arthur Zimmermann, the German foreign minister, to Heinrich von Eckhardt, the German minister in Mexico, on Jan. 16, 1917, informing him of the resumption of unrestricted submarine warfare and directing him to propose a German alliance with Mexico in the event of war between the United States and Germany. Eckhardt was to offer German financial support to Mexico and approval of the Mexican reconquest of Texas, New Mexico, and Arizona and was also to suggest that the president of Mexico invite Japan to join the alliance. On Feb. 25 President Woodrow Wilson was shown a copy of the telegram, which had been intercepted and decoded by the British government. It was published in the press on Mar. 1.

8. The passage in Alfred, Lord Tennyson's "Locksley Hall" reads: "Till the war-drum throbbed no longer, and the battle-flags were furled / In the Parliament of man, the Federation of the world."

9. The Chinese Exclusion Act.

10. In the wake of a disputed presidential election held the previous November, an armed uprising began in Cuba in February 1917 under the leadership of former president José Miguel Gomez. Characterized in the American press as part of a German plot, the revolt was quickly suppressed in western Cuba, Gomez and other insurrectionary leaders were captured on Mar. 7, and fighting in eastern Cuba ended later in the spring.

11. For a further statement by Duncan, see his letter to SG of Mar. 17, 1917, AFL Microfilm National and International Union File, Granite Cutters Records, reel 38, frame 1559, *AFL Records.*

American Labor's Position in Peace or in War

Washington, D.C., March 12, 1917.

AMERICAN LABOR'S POSITION IN PEACE OR IN WAR

A conference of the representatives of the national and international trade unions of America, called by the Executive Council of the American Federation of Labor, was held in the American Federation of Labor Building, March 12, 1917, in which conference the representatives of affiliated national and international trade unions and the railroad brotherhoods participated.

The Executive Council of the American Federation of Labor had the subject-matter for three days under advisement prior to the conference and submitted a declaration to the conference.[1] The entire day was given over to a discussion of the recommendation and such suggestions as were submitted. After a thorough discussion the following document was adopted by a unanimous vote:[2]

We speak for millions of Americans. We are not a sect. We are not a party. We represent the organizations held together by the pressure of our common needs. We represent the part of the nation closest to the fundamentals of life. Those we represent wield the nation's tools and grapple with the forces that are brought under control in our material civilization. The power and use of industrial tools is greater than the tools of war and will in time supersede agencies of destruction.

A world war is on. The time has not yet come when war has been abolished.

Whether we approve it or not, we must recognize that war is a situation with which we must reckon. The present European war, involving as it does the majority of civilized nations and affecting the industry and commerce of the whole world, threatens at any moment to draw all countries, including our own, into the conflict. Our immediate problem, then, is to bring to bear upon war conditions instructive forethought, vision, principles of human welfare and conservation that should direct our course in every eventuality of life. The way to avert war is to establish constructive agencies for justice in times of peace and thus control for peace situations and forces that might otherwise result in war. The methods of modern warfare, its new tactics, its vast organization, both military and industrial, present problems vastly different from those of previous wars. But the nation's problems afford an opportunity for the establishment of new freedom and wider opportunities for all the people. Modern warfare includes contests between workshops, factories, the land, financial and transportation resources of the countries involved; and necessarily applies to the relations between employers and employes, and as our own country now faces an impending peril, it is fitting that the masses of the people of the United States should take counsel and determine what course they shall pursue should a crisis arise necessitating the protection of our Republic and defense of the ideals for which it stands.

In the struggle between the forces of democracy and special privilege, for just and historic reasons the masses of the people necessarily represent the ideals and the institutions of democracy. There is in organized society one potential organization whose purpose is to further these ideals and institutions—the organized labor movement.

In no previous war has the organized labor movement taken a directing part.

Labor has now reached an understanding of its rights, of its power and resources, of its value and contributions to society, and must make definite constructive proposals.

It is timely that we frankly present experiences and conditions which in former times have prevented nations from benefiting by the voluntary, whole-hearted cooperation of wage-earners in war time, and then make suggestions how these hindrances to our national strength and vigor can be removed.

War has never put a stop to the necessity for struggle to establish and maintain industrial rights. Wage-earners in war times must, as has been said, keep one eye on the exploiters at home and the other upon the enemy threatening the national government. Such exploitation made it impossible for a warring nation to mobilize effectively its full strength for outward defense.

We maintain that it is the fundamental step in preparedness for the nation to set its own house in order and to establish at home justice in relations between men. Previous wars, for whatever purpose waged, developed new opportunities for exploiting wage-earners. Not only was there failure to recognize the necessity for protecting rights of workers that they might give that whole-hearted service to the country that can come only when every citizen enjoys rights, freedom and opportunity, but under guise of national necessity, Labor was stripped of its means of defense against enemies at home and was robbed of the advantages, the protections, the guarantees of justice that had been achieved after ages of struggle. For these reasons workers have felt that no matter what the result of war, as wage-earners they generally lost.

In previous times Labor had no representatives in the councils authorized to deal with the conduct of war. The rights, interests and welfare of workers were autocratically sacrificed for the slogan of "national safety."

The European war has demonstrated the dependence of the governments upon the cooperation of the masses of the people. Since the masses perform indispensable service, it follows that they should have a voice in determining the conditions upon which they give service.

The workers of America make known their beliefs, their demands and their purposes through a voluntary agency which they have established—the organized labor movement. This agency is not only the representative of those who directly constitute it, but it is the representative of all those persons who have common problems and purposes but who have not yet organized for their achievement.

Whether in peace or in war the organized labor movement seeks to make all else subordinate to human welfare and human opportunity. The labor movement stands as the defender of this principle and undertakes to protect the wealth-producers against the exorbitant greed of special interests, against profiteering, against exploitation, against the detestable methods of irresponsible greed, against the inhumanity and crime of heartless corporations and employers.

Labor demands the right in war times to be the recognized defender of wage-earners against the same forces which in former wars have made national necessity an excuse for more ruthless methods.

As the representatives of the wage-earners we assert that conditions of work and pay in government employment and in all occupations should conform to principles of human welfare and justice.

A nation can not make an effective defense against an outside danger if groups of citizens are asked to take part in a war though smarting with a sense of keen injustice inflicted by the government they are expected to and will defend.

The cornerstone of national defense is justice in fundamental relations of life—economic justice.

The one agency which accomplishes this for the workers is the organized labor movement. The greatest step that can be made for national defense is not to bind and throttle the organized labor movement but to afford its greatest scope and opportunity for voluntary effective cooperation in spirit and in action.

During the long period in which it has been establishing itself, the labor movement has become a dynamic force in organizing the human side of industry and commerce. It is a great social factor, which must be recognized in all plans which affect wage-earners.

Whether planning for peace or war the government must recognize the organized labor movement as the agency through which it must cooperate with wage-earners.

Industrial justice is the right of those living within our country. With this right there is associated obligation. In war time obligation takes the form of service in defense of the Republic against enemies.

We recognize that this service may be either military or industrial, both equally essential for national defense. We hold this to be incontrovertible that the government which demands that men and women give their labor power, their bodies or their lives to its service should also demand the service, in the interest of these human beings, of all wealth and the products of human toil—property.

We hold that if workers may be asked in time of national peril or emergency to give more exhausting service than the principles of human welfare warrant, that service should be asked only when accompanied by increased guarantees and safeguards, and when the profits which the employer shall secure from the industry in which they are engaged have been limited to fixed percentages.

We declare that such determination of profits should be based on cost of processes actually needed for product.

Workers have no delusions regarding the policy which property owners and exploiting employers pursue in peace or in war, and they also recognize that wrapped up with the safety of this Republic are ideals of democracy, a heritage which the masses of the people received from our forefathers, who fought that liberty might live in this country—a heritage that is to be maintained and handed down to each generation with undiminished power and usefulness.

The labor movement recognizes the value of freedom and it knows that freedom and rights can be maintained only by those willing to assert their claims and to defend their rights. The American labor movement has always opposed unnecessary conflicts and all wars for aggrandizement, exploitation and enslavement, and yet it has done its part in the world's revolutions, in the struggles to establish greater freedom, democratic institutions and ideals of human justice.

Our labor movement distrusts and protests against militarism, because it knows that militarism represents privilege and is the tool of special interests, exploiters and despots. But while it opposes militarism, it holds that it is the duty of a nation to defend itself against injustice and invasion.

The menace of militarism arises through isolating the defensive functions of the state from civic activities and from creating military agencies out of touch with masses of the people. Isolation is subversive to democracy—it harbors and nurtures the germs of arbitrary power.

The labor movement demands that a clear differentiation be made against military service for the nation and police duty, and that military service should be carefully distinguished from service in industrial disputes.

We hold that industrial service shall be deemed equally meritorious as military service. Organization for industrial and commercial service is upon a different basis from military service—the civic ideals still dominate. This should be recognized in mobilizing for this purpose. The same voluntary institutions that organized industrial, commercial and transportation workers in times of peace will best take care of the same problems in time of war.

It is fundamental, therefore, that the government cooperate with the American organized labor movement for this purpose. Service in government factories and private establishments, in transportation agencies, all should conform to trade union standards.

The guarantees of human conservation should be recognized in war as well as in peace. Wherever changes in the organization of industry are necessary upon a war basis, they should be made in accord with plans agreed upon by representatives of the government and those engaged and employed in the industry. We recognize that in war, in certain employments requiring high skill, it is necessary to retain in industrial service the workers specially fitted therefor. In any eventuality when women may be employed, we insist that equal pay for equal work shall prevail without regard to sex.

Finally, in order to safeguard all the interests of the wage-earners organized labor should have representation on all agencies determining and administering policies for national defense. It is particularly important that organized labor should have representatives on all boards authorized to control publicity during war times. The workers have suffered much injustice in war times by limitations upon their right to speak freely and to secure publicity for their just grievances.

Organized labor has earned the right to make these demands. It is the agency that, in all countries, stands for human rights and is the defender of the welfare and interests of the masses of the people. It is an agency that has international recognition which is not seeking to rob, exploit or corrupt foreign governments but instead seeks to maintain human rights and interests the world over, nor does it have to dispel suspicion nor prove its motives either at home or abroad.

The present war discloses the struggle between the institutions of democracy and those of autocracy. As a nation we should profit from the experiences of other nations. Democracy can not be established by patches upon an autocratic system. The foundations of civilized intercourse between individuals must be organized upon principles of democracy and scientific principles of human welfare. Then a national structure can be perfected in harmony with humanitarian idealism—a structure that will stand the tests of the necessities of peace or war.

We, the officers of the National and International Trade Unions of America in national conference assembled in the capital of our nation, hereby pledge ourselves in peace or in war, in stress or in storm, to stand unreservedly by the standards of liberty and the safety and preservation of the institutions and ideals of our Republic.

In this solemn hour of our nation's life, it is our earnest hope that our Republic may be safeguarded in its unswerving desire for peace; that our people may be spared the horrors and the burdens of war; that they may have the opportunity to cultivate and develop the arts of peace, human brotherhood and a higher civilization.

But, despite all our endeavors and hopes, should our country be drawn into the maelstrom of the European conflict, we, with these ideals of liberty and justice herein declared, as the indispensable basis for national policies, offer our services to our country in every field of activity to defend, safeguard and preserve the Republic of the United States of America against its enemies whomsoever they may be, and we call upon our fellow workers and fellow citizens in the holy name of Labor, Justice, Freedom and Humanity to devotedly and patriotically give like service.

American Labor's Position in Peace or in War ([Washington, D.C., 1917]). Printed note: "Issued by American Federation of Labor, A.F. of L. Building, Washington, D.C., Samuel Gompers, President, Frank Morrison, Secretary."

1. A draft of this statement was submitted to the AFL Executive Council on Mar. 9, 1917. It was discussed section by section, amended, and approved on Mar. 10, and the two introductory paragraphs were adopted by the Council on Mar. 12.

2. Writing SG on Mar. 17, 1917, James Duncan noted criticisms of the statement at the conference by Andrew Furuseth, John Frey, Daniel Tobin, and Joseph Skemp. Nonetheless, he observed, "What amazed me the most was that such well known,

well meaning, and constructive minded men as offered amendments found no one to second same. It was evident that after the document was—shall I say carefully and deliberately read?—that it seemed to convey the general and constructive thought of the delegates, and that because there was evident care displayed in its makeup the delegates felt that dismemberment or alteration would not better it" (Files of the Office of the President, General Correspondence, reel 82, frame 572, *AFL Records*).

To Nikolai Chkheidze[1]

Washington DC March 21 1917

N S Chekheiji
Russian Duma Petrograd
We rejoice with Russia's workers in their newly achieved liberty.[2] The splendid proclamation of your provisional government, declaring for free speech and press and the right of workers to organize and if necessary to strike, for their rights guarantees to Russia's workers opportunity for freedom and progress and assures the New Russia her future greater glory. International labor welcomes the triumph of freedom and the downfall of despotism throughout the world.

Gompers[3]

TWpSr, reel 219, vol. 231, p. 761, SG Letterbooks, DLC.

1. Nikolai Semenovich Chkheidze (1864–1926), a leader of the Menshevik faction of the Russian Social Democratic party, was chairman of the Provisional Executive Committee of the Petrograd Council of Workers' Deputies (subsequently the All-Russian Council of Workers' and Soldiers' Deputies) and a member of the Provisional Committee of the Duma.

2. Severe shortages of food and fuel triggered widespread civil unrest in the Russian capital of Petrograd in early 1917. Strikes and other protests began on Mar. 8 (Feb. 23, Old Style), and by Mar. 10 (Feb. 25) over two hundred thousand demonstrators were in the streets. On Mar. 12 (Feb. 27) the city's military garrison mutinied and joined the insurgents, and two committees were created that assumed de facto governmental authority—the Provisional Committee of Duma Members for the Restoration of Order and the Provisional Executive Committee of the Petrograd Council of Workers' Deputies. Tsar Nicholas II abdicated three days later, on Mar. 15 (Mar. 2).

3. On Mar. 23, 1917, David Francis, the American ambassador to Russia, suggested to the State Department that messages from SG and other labor leaders would strengthen the position of the new Provisional Government. Frank Polk, counselor to the State Department, conveyed the request to SG on Apr. 1. In response, SG cabled Francis on Apr. 2, enclosing both his note to Chkheidze of Mar. 21—to which he had received no acknowledgment—and a second, longer message, which he asked Francis to deliver to Chkheidze and make public. The second message again congratulated the Russians on their "newly established liberty" but warned that "it is impossible to achieve the ideal state immediately." Only after "the right foundation has been established," SG continued, could "the masses . . . utilize opportunities for progress, more complete

justice, and greater liberty. Freedom is achieved in meeting the problems of life and work. It cannot be established by revolution only—it is the product of evolution" (Files of the Office of the President, General Correspondence, reel 83, frame 6, *AFL Records*). Francis confirmed receipt and delivery of the second cable on Apr. 7. SG, together with the other members of the AFL Executive Council, cabled Chkheidze again on Apr. 23, urging the Russians "to build practically and constructively" as they formed a new government (reel 220, vol. 232, p. 873, SG Letterbooks, DLC).

From Matthew Woll[1]

Office of the President
International Photo-Engravers' Union of North America[2]
Chicago, Ill. March 21, 1917.

Personal

Dear Mr. Gompers:—

Last Tuesday morning I waited as long as I possibly could to take up one or two matters with you; not being able to wait until you arrived at your office, I take this opportunity of submitting the several matters to you for your consideration, and I am doing so in strict confidence, and in my personal capacity.

Some time ago, while in conference with Mr. Olander[3] of the Illinois State Federation of Labor, he informed me that the officers of the Amalgamated Clothing Workers[4] had come to see him regarding their status in the labor movement. He of course advised them that they had no standing whatever in the American Federation of Labor and that they ought to take steps to become a part of the labor movement. Mr. Olander suggested to me that he thought the Amalgamated Clothing Workers would possibly consider a proposition which calls for a convention of the two organizations in the clothing trade; this convention to settle all of the difficulties which has parted the clothing workers.

Mr. Olander did not encourage them, however, in this matter, but he believed that inasmuch as the outside clothing workers are so great in number that some steps ought to be taken to bring about an adjustment of the differences, and he thought that if the Amalgamated Clothing Workers would apply to you for a Charter that this would then afford you the opportunity of trying to have both factions in the clothing trade get together and to agree upon holding a joint convention as herein indicated.

Olander does not, however, want to urge the Amalgamated Clothing Workers to file an application for a charter, unless he felt certain that this course, or one similar to it, could be followed. In other words, he does not want to start something that he believes for the best of the movement and then find in the end that he has only aroused criticism and condemnation against him.

I have asked Olander to submit a statement to me on this matter and assured him that I would take it up with you in a confidential way.

I am enclosing copy[5] of this statement for your consideration.

I am very sorry I did not have the opportunity of talking this matter over with you, because I fully appreciate your position in this matter, and the danger of giving any assurance of any kind. However, if you can trust me in this matter, and if you believe the proposal of Mr. Olander of sufficient merit to encourage it, your advice to me on this subject will be greatly appreciated.

I want to assure you that whatever suggestion you may make to me on this question will be treated with strict confidence and that I will be guided entirely by your wishes in this matter.

Another matter I believe I ought to advise you of is one relating to the Legal Department of the American Federation of Labor. In going to Milwaukee yesterday I met Mr. Rubin on the train. He was somewhat peeved that I opposed his scheme of lawyerizing the labor movement. He was also grieved because he had not been consulted further by the Executive Council or yourself regarding the establishment of the Legal Department A.F. of L., and from his talk I judged that he was hopeful of securing the appointment to this department. Unquestionably you know about his ambitions in this matter and what he would like to accomplish in that capacity. If he were successful the dangers I have indicated in my statement to you some time ago upon the Legal Department would be realized without question. The point, however, I want to emphasize is that Mr. Rubin is determined to induce as many Central Labor Unions and State Federations that he possibly can, to institute Legal Departments under his own guidance, and by thus working up an organization of lawyers within the several State and Central bodies, he will force the American Federation of Labor, through these influences, to establish himself at the Legal Department in Washington. That seems to be his ambition.

I do not know whether this information will be of value to you; nevertheless I feel it my duty to inform you of this development. I understand he has just been successful in Detroit in establishing a Legal Department there.

One other matter I wanted to have you consider and that has to do with the Smith-Hughes Bill[6] as recently enacted by Congress, having to do with vocational education.

If I am correctly advised, under this law the President will appoint a

Commission which is to enforce the provisions of this law, and on which Commission labor will be represented. I am not informed whether the members of this Commission shall devote all of their time to this work or whether they will meet only occasionally to generally supervise the operation of this law.

If this Commission is one to meet only occasionally, to administer and supervise the law in question, may I not have your opinion as to the advisability of my seeking an appointment on this Commission. I have been urged by several leaders in Illinois to seek this appointment, and I know some of the School people would be highly pleased to see me in this position. For the last two or three years I have given considerable of my time to all questions pertaining to the public schools and particularly to the subject of vocational education. The last two reports to the Illinois State Federation of Labor on this subject have been prepared by myself, copies of which I enclose herewith.

During the past year I have been constantly in conference with the different civic organizations, employers' associations and organizations of the school teachers and school men on this subject and largely through my efforts I have been able to bring all of these conflicting interests to a point where we are about to agree upon a bill for the unit system of control to be submitted to the Illinois Legislature at an early date.

I mention these matters only to indicate to you that I am not without experience on this subject.

I would like your opinion upon this suggestion and wish to assure you beforehand that I will be guided entirely by your opinion and wishes in this matter.

Again assuring you that whatever response you may make to the several matters touched herein will be treated in strict confidence, and that your wishes in all these matters will be followed out in toto, extending my very best wishes and kindest personal regards, I am

Fraternally yours,   Matthew Woll

TLS, AFL Microfilm National and International Union File, Photo Engravers Records, reel 43, frames 2497–98, *AFL Records.*

1. Matthew WOLL served as president of the International Photo-Engravers' Union of North America from 1906 to 1929.

2. The International PHOTO-ENGRAVERS' Union of North America.

3. Victor A. OLANDER served as secretary (1909–20) of the Lake Seamen's Union (from 1919, the Sailors' Union of the Great Lakes), vice-president (1902–25) of the International Seamen's Union of America, and secretary-treasurer of the Illinois State Federation of Labor (1914–49). During World War I he was a member of the National War Labor Board and the Illinois State Council of Defense.

4. The Amalgamated CLOTHING Workers of America.

5. Olander to Woll, Feb. 12, 1917, AFL Microfilm National and International Union File, Photo Engravers Records, reel 43, frame 2498, *AFL Records*.

6. The Smith-Hughes Act (U.S. *Statutes at Large*, 39: 929–36), which became law on Feb. 23, 1917, created a federal vocational education board, consisting of the secretaries of agriculture, commerce, and labor, the U.S. commissioner of education, and three citizens appointed by the president to represent agriculture, industry, and labor. President Woodrow Wilson appointed Charles Greathouse of Indianapolis, James Munroe of Boston, and Arthur Holder to the board. The act also authorized federal grants, to be matched by state contributions, to promote education in agriculture, home economics, and the trades.

To Carl Legien

Washington DC April 2 1917

Carl Legien
Berlin SO 16 Engelufer 15 Berlin
This may be the last word the labor movements of our respective countries will have an opportunity to express before war conditions lasting perhaps for years may put an end to peaceful fraternal intercourse and communication. You know that the United States cannot influence another country with which it is at peace to prevent a siege or blockade of a city or a country with which that country is at war.[1] The United States must however protect its citizens from unlawful and unwarranted destruction of their lives. We are all doing our level best to avert actual war and we have the right to insist that the men of labor of Germany exert their last ounce of effort to get your government to make an immediate and satisfactory avowal that shall save all from America's entrance into the universal conflict.[2]

Samuel Gompers

TWpSr, Files of the Office of the President, Letterbooks, Advisory Commission, Council of National Defense, reel 20, p. 91, *AFL Records*.

1. See "To the Executive Council of the AFL," Feb. 4, 1917, n. 5, above.

2. In response to the repeated sinkings of American ships following Germany's resumption of unrestricted submarine warfare, President Woodrow Wilson, speaking before a joint session of Congress on Apr. 2, 1917, asked for a declaration that a state of war existed with Germany. The Senate passed the measure (S.J. Res. 1, 65th Cong., 1st sess.) by a vote of 82 to 6 on Apr. 4; the House of Representatives approved it 373 to 50 on Apr. 6.

An Address at the Organizational Meeting[1]
of the Committee on Labor of the
Advisory Commission of the Council
of National Defense

Washington, D.C. Monday, April 2, 1917.

. . .

Mr. Gompers. Just a word in addition to what Mr. Morrison has so well said. What matters it if we gain the heavens if we lose our own souls. I am free to tell you that I am not a lover of the United States of America simply because it has that name. To me the Republic of the United States has a meaning. If the autocracy of Russia as it obtained of old existed in the United States I would not be willing to fight for it. It is the ideals of the Republic, the standards of the Republic, the guarantee the Republic gives for human freedom or liberty, the opportunity and the right to life, liberty and the pursuit of happiness. It is because of these ideals that this Republic is so dear to us. I had not the happiness to be born in the United States but very soon, as soon as I was permitted, I took upon myself the obligation of loyalty to the United States and I have tried to keep the faith. The men of labor form the great masses of the people, and if freedom has any meaning it applies to them, for as a rule those men who are blessed with wealth are free and have been free the world over no matter what the form of government, and that the masses of the people, if there be tyranny or injustice or burdens, it is they who have to bear them. Now we have made wonderful progress in this great country of ours and raised these standards and concepts of human liberty and human freedom. We have sacrificed much during the fray but there must be the star of hope for the men of labor, the masses of the people, after the sacrifices which have been made that those of us who will remain and our children and children's children will look to that star of hope as their encouragement to fight on for freedom and the Republic.

Heinrich Heine said—I know it is hardly appropriate at this time a German may be quoted but inasmuch as we are not yet at war, I may be privileged to use a quotation from one of his lines—"Bread is freedom; freedom is bread." Without the opportunities of rightful living the term of freedom is a mockery. You can understand that in the event of strife and storm, beleaguered and besieged, that men will go hungry and see their wives and children cry and wail because they are hungry and yet would rather die than surrender. But so long as conditions of this character do not prevail men must be sustained in their ability to fight and you can't make good fighting men if you lower the standards of men at home.

The Council of National Defense created by authority of law of the country and the Advisory Commission confronted with the experience of the European countries in this war, and particularly England, selected a representative of labor, and how can you get a representative of labor, I mean in his representative capacity, unless it comes from a concerted expression, and how can that expression be obtained unless through organization? I was selected as the representative of labor as a member of that Council and Commission and when the Commission was divided up into committees, I was selected as Chairman of the Committee on Labor for the conservation and welfare of workers, and that is what this conference was called upon to consider and determine and act. How can we conserve the health and welfare of workers and their families, that is our mission. Do you think for a moment that if I desired simply to cultivate the acquaintance of those most congenial to me that I would have taken upon myself the appointments of the representatives of the United States Steel Corporation? Has the National Manufacturers Association been so kindly disposed toward me that I would ask their representatives to meet and become members of this committee? I should certainly not enter into details as to that, but to me all these things were of lesser consequence. I realize that no matter what attempts are made by the National Association of Manufacturers or the United States Steel Corporation or the Cotton Manufacturers Association or other associations of employers, that was not the question. Either they made an earnest, effective effort or by the stars above us, the acceptance of membership in this committee will mean that they do active work. I have no feeling in the matter at all. Men are men. We judge men by their acts. If I can't altogether forget, I can forgive, and what I want, as a member of this committee, is that men shall give service to accomplish the purpose for which this committee has been created for the conservation and welfare of the workers. While this struggle is on, cooperate. Men and women, we are in the making of a new world. The events which will transpire within the next five years will be more potential in the reconstruction of the character of the peoples of this and other countries than have taken place in one hundred years in any previous time in the history of the human race, and it is a question of are you and I going to give our contribution toward the attainment of it and the realization of our highest hopes; to maintain the best we have; to sacrifice the least that need be sacrificed; to give up all but not one jot or tittle more than is necessary for the defense of the ideals of this Republic; that is my conception of it. I have said it all along and I am justified in my thought by what has transpired in former controversies in which our country was involved.

During the Civil War unions of workingmen, both north and south, adjourned until the war was over and volunteered into their respective armies of the North and South and fought under their respective flags, and it was the organized labor movement which first recognized the fraternity of the men of the north and the south. Perhaps influenced by necessity, but be that as it may, the first fraternal relations reestablished after the Civil War were between the unions still in existence in the North and in the South. So the men of labor are going to give a good accounting of themselves in this fight and it seems inevitable. God grant that it may not be as gigantic a struggle as it now seems to those who know, that peace may come sooner than we anticipate, and that out of the crisis will come the real relations which should exist between man and man, no matter in which country he may live or to which country he may owe his first allegiance, when the war drum will beat no longer and the battle flags be furled in a universal brotherhood of man and a federation of workingmen. (Applause).

. . .

TDc, Records of the Committee on Labor, RG 62, Records of the Council of National Defense, DNA.

1. The organizational meeting of the Committee on Labor of the Advisory Commission of the Council of National Defense, held at AFL headquarters on Apr. 2, 1917, was attended by some 150 labor and business representatives and others involved with the health and welfare of workers. The meeting discussed a variety of proposals and endorsed SG's appointment of an executive committee consisting of SG (chair), Lee Frankel, vice-president of the Metropolitan Life Insurance Co., Elisha Lee, general manager of the Pennsylvania Railroad, James Lord and James O'Connell, presidents of the AFL Mining and Metal Trades departments, V. Everit Macy and Louis Schram of the National Civic Federation, Frank Morrison, A. Parker Nevin of the National Association of Manufacturers, Warren Stone, grand chief of the International Brotherhood of Locomotive Engineers, and William B. Wilson, secretary of labor. Ralph Easley was appointed assistant to the chairman and Gertrude Beeks temporary secretary.

From James Wilson[1]

Pattern Makers League of North America[2]
Cincinnati, April 2, 1917.

Dear Sir & Bro.:

Ever since the first of the year, we have had a contention with the Navy Department relative to the wage rate paid to pattern makers in the employ of the Government at the Brooklyn Navy Yard.

I have taken this matter up personally with the Secretary[3] and with the Assistant Secretary of the Navy.[4] Brother Berres of the Metal Trades Department has taken it up, and we have likewise taken the matter up with the Secretary of Labor, Mr. Wilson, and he has presented the matter to the Secretary of the Navy.

Under date of March 22d, I wrote the President calling his attention to our inability to secure a wage rate for our members in the Brooklyn Navy Yard in accordance with the laws. Under date of March 31st, I received a letter from the Assistant Secretary of the Navy, in which he states, that they will not re-open the question of wages at the Brooklyn Navy Yard.[5]

I am enclosing a copy of this letter, also a copy[6] of a letter I am this day sending to the Secretary of the President.

The maximum wages paid to the pattern makers in the Brooklyn Navy Yard is $4.48, our minimum in that district is $4.50.

The General Executive Board of our Organization have sanctioned a movement of our men employed in the Navy Yard to strike for a higher wage rate. We have put forth our best efforts to continue the men at work in view of the serious situation that is confronting our Government.

The Navy Department will need more of our men in all navy yards, and the Government cannot expect men to work for the government under wages much less than that paid by private establishments. The continued refusal of the Navy Department to recognize that we are right in our contention, we are gradually being forced into a position, where we will have to grant our members the right to strike or leave the employment of the Government in this yard, and we hesitate to permit this step to be taken, and if you could use your influence with the President, so that we would be relieved of the necessity of taking such a course, we will greatly appreciate any thing you can do.

We are willing to submit our case to arbitration, let the President select the entire Arbitration Board and all we want is a right to present to any one whom he may select so long as they are not Naval Officers, our contention, and we are satisfied to abide by such decision. We do not even desire to have a voice in the selection of one to represent our side on such an Arbitration Board, for we know that any fair minded men who look into the case would readily see that a great injustice is being done the pattern makers in the employ of the Brooklyn Navy Yard.

With best wishes, I remain,

Fraternally yours,   James Wilson
Gen'l Pres.[7]

TLS, Files of the Office of the President, General Correspondence, reel 83, frames 11–12, *AFL Records.*

1. James Adair WILSON served as president of the Pattern Makers' League of North America from 1902 to 1934.

2. The PATTERN Makers' League of North America.

3. Josephus Daniels (1862–1948) served as secretary of the navy from 1913 to 1921.

4. Franklin Delano Roosevelt (1882–1945) was assistant secretary of the navy from 1913 to 1920. A Democratic member of the New York state senate from 1911 to 1913 and the Democratic candidate for vice-president of the United States in 1920, he later served as governor of New York (1929–33) and as president of the United States (1933–45).

5. Roosevelt wrote Wilson on Mar. 31, 1917, refusing to reconsider the question of a wage increase for the pattern makers because, he said, civilians employed by the Department of the Navy had already been given a 5– to 10–percent increase under the provisions of the Naval Appropriation Act of Mar. 4, 1917 (Files of the Office of the President, General Correspondence, reel 83, frame 14, *AFL Records*).

6. [Wilson] to Joseph Tumulty, Apr. 2, 1917, Files of the Office of the President, reel 83, frames 18–19, *AFL Records.*

7. SG replied on Apr. 9, 1917, that he would take the matter up with the secretary of the navy in his official role as a member of the Advisory Commission of the Council of National Defense (reel 220, vol. 232, pp. 501–2, SG Letterbooks, DLC). He later reported to the 1917 AFL convention that, in addition to the 5– to 10–percent wage increase mandated by law, metal trades workers in government navy yards had negotiated wage increases averaging 16 percent.

Excerpts from the Minutes of the First Meeting of the Executive Committee of the Committee on Labor of the Advisory Commission of the Council of National Defense

E.C. Room, American Federation of Labor Building,
Washington, D.C. Ten o'clock, April 5, 1917

. . .

Mr. Gompers then presented the following resolution from the meeting of April 2[1] with reference to maintaining existing standards:

"We recommend that the Council of National Defense urge upon the legislatures of the states, as well as all the administrative agencies charged with the enforcement of labor and health laws, the great duty of rigorously maintaining the existing safeguards as to the health and the welfare of workers, and that no departure from such present standards, in state laws or state rulings affecting labor, should be taken without request of the Council of National Defense that such a departure is essential for the effective pursuit of the national defense."[2]

After consideration and discussion[3] in which there was raised the legal power of the federal government and the possible necessity for Congress to pass an enabling act in the event that it should become necessary for the states to be requested to modify their labor laws, it was decided to refer the matter of advocating that standards be not relaxed until essential for the defense of the country to a sub-committee. Mr. Lee[4] also outlined the importance of advocating that the present status of employers and employes' contracts be maintained until emergency necessitates change.

Upon motion duly seconded the following committee was appointed to prepare a statement covering the entire subject with relation to existing standards: Honorable William B. Wilson, Elisha Lee, and Louis B. Schram.[5] This committee was authorized to report to the afternoon session.

. . .

REPORT OF THE AFTERNOON SESSION.
CONVENED AT 2:30 O'CLOCK.

. . .

The report of the sub-committee was presented by Secretary Wilson and read by the secretary at his request. After discussion and amendment, upon motion by Secretary Wilson, the following resolution was adopted:

RESOLUTION ADOPTED AT MEETING OF EXECUTIVE COMMITTEE
LABOR COMMITTEE—CONSERVATION OF HEALTH AND WELFARE OF
WORKERS. SAMUEL GOMPERS, CHAIRMAN

April 5, 1917.

"The defense and safety of the nation must be the first consideration of all patriotic citizens. To avoid confusion and facilitate the preparation for national defense and give a stable basis upon which the representatives of the Government may operate during the war, we recommend:

["]First: That the Council of National Defense should issue a statement to employers and employes in our industrial plants and transportation systems advising that neither employers nor employes shall endeavor to take advantage of the country's necessities to change existing standards. When economic or other emergencies arise requiring changes of standards, the same should be made only after such proposed changes have been investigated and approved by the Council of National Defense.

["]Second: That the Council of National Defense urge upon the legislatures of the states, as well as all administrative agencies charged with the enforcement of labor and health laws, the great duty of rigorously maintaining the existing safeguards as to the health and the welfare of workers, and that no departure from such present standards, in state laws or state rulings affecting labor, should be taken without request of the Council of National Defense that such a departure is essential for the effective pursuit of the national defense.

["]Third: That the Council of National Defense urge upon the legislatures of the several states that before final adjournment they delegate to the Governors of their respective states the power to suspend or modify restrictions contained in their labor laws when such suspension or modification shall be requested by the Federal Government; and such suspension or modification, when made, shall continue for a specified period and not longer than the duration of the war.

["]Fourth: That the Council of National Defense should recommend to Congress that adequate and proper provisions be made by the Government for the care of families of individuals who are accepted for service in the military or naval forces of the United States."[6]

. . .

TDc, Records of the Committee on Labor, RG 62, Records of the Council of National Defense, DNA.

1. That is, the organizational meeting of the Committee on Labor of the Advisory Commission of the Council of National Defense.

2. This resolution was presented by Felix Frankfurter at the meeting on Apr. 2, 1917.

3. A verbatim transcript of this discussion can be found in the Records of the Committee on Labor, RG 62, Records of the Council of National Defense, DNA.

4. Elisha Lee (1870–1933), a member of the executive committee of the Committee on Labor, was general manager and later vice-president of the Pennsylvania Railroad.

5. Louis B. Schram (1856–1921) was a member of the executive committee of the Committee on Labor, president of the Indian Wharf Brewing Co. of Brooklyn, N.Y., and chairman of the labor committee of the United States Brewers' Association.

6. The Council of National Defense adopted these resolutions with slight changes at a joint meeting with the Advisory Commission on Apr. 7, 1917. The approved text, with the exception of resolution four, which was not made public, is printed in "To Daniel Tobin," Apr. 17, 1917, below.

William B. Wilson, Lee, and Schram subsequently prepared an "Amplification" of the resolutions, which was adopted by the executive committee of the Committee on Labor on Apr. 16 and by the Council of National Defense on Apr. 23. It reads:

"There seems to be some misunderstanding of the scope of the statement made by the Council of National Defense when it advised 'that neither employers nor employees shall endeavor to take advantage of the country's necessities to change existing standards.' In order that that misunderstanding may be removed, the following amplification is made:

"There have been established by legislation, by mutual agreement between employers and employees, or by custom certain standards constituting a day's work. These vary from seven hours per day in some kinds of work to twelve hours per day in continuous operation plants. The various states and municipalities have established specific standards of safety and sanitation and have provided inspection service to enforce the regulations. They have also established maximum hours of work for women and minimum age limits for children employed in gainful occupations. It is the judgment of the Council of National Defense that the Federal, State and Municipal Governments should continue to enforce the standards they have established unless and until the Council of National Defense has determined that some modification or change of these standards is essential to the national safety; that employers and employees in private industries should not attempt to take advantage of the existing abnormal conditions to change the standards which they were unable to change under normal conditions.

"The one other standard that the Council had in mind was the standard of living. It recognizes that the standard of living is indefinite and difficult to determine, because it is in a measure dependent upon the purchasing power of wages. It believes, however, that no arbitrary change in wages should be sought at this time by either employers or employees through the process of strikes or lockouts without at least giving the established agencies, including those of the several states and of the federal Government, the Mediation Board in the transportation service and the Division of Conciliation of the Department of Labor in the other industries, an opportunity to adjust the difficulties without a stoppage of work occurring. While the Council of National Defense does not mean to intimate that under ordinary circumstances the efficiency of workers is the only element that should be taken into consideration in fixing the hours of labor, safety, sanitation, women's work and child labor standards, such efficiency is the object that must be attained during the period when the nation's safety is involved. It may therefore be necessary for the Council as a result of its investigation and experience to suggest modifications and changes in these standards during that time. It is not the purpose of the Council, however, to undertake to determine the wage rate that will be sufficient to maintain the existing standards of living. Such questions as cannot be adjusted by private negotiations should be referred to the mediation agencies above referred to or to such other constituted agencies as may exist to the end that such questions may be adjusted in an orderly and equitable manner to avoid the stoppage of industries which are so vital to the interests of the nation at this critical time" (Records of the Committee on Labor, RG 62, Records of the Council of National Defense, DNA).

From Edward Anderson[1]

Denver Colo Apl 9 1917

Press reports today[2] quote you as recommending to organized labor that no demands be made by them for improved working conditions of labor at this time without the approval of the National Defense Committee and that said committee recommends that the governors of various states be given the power to suspend or modify restrictions of labor laws are you in accord with this statement and recommendation[3]

Ed Anderson
Sec Tres

TWSr, Files of the Office of the President, General Correspondence, reel 83, frame 59, *AFL Records.*

1. Edward E. ANDERSON was secretary-treasurer (1916–22) of the Colorado State Federation of Labor.

2. On Apr. 9, 1917, in an article entitled "Labor Promises Nation Loyal Support in War," the *Rocky Mountain News* (Denver) printed the preamble and the three resolutions on labor standards adopted by the Council on National Defense on Apr. 7.

3. See "To Edward Anderson," Apr. 10, 1917, below.

To Edward Anderson

Washington, D.C., April 10, 1917.

Mr. Ed Anderson,
301 German American Trust Bldg., Denver, Colo.
Telegram received.[1] The declaration is in effect that fundamental standards shall not be disturbed but in no wise precludes the effort to obtain necessary improved conditions. The declaration further holds that legislatures should rigorously uphold and officers enforce labor and health laws and that no relaxation of them should be attempted. It further provides that the legislatures be asked to pass a law placing in the hands of the governors of the states the power to modify for a specified period and not longer than the duration of the war the labor laws and those only when the Council of National Defense shall decide that an extraordinary emergency exists requiring such action even though temporary. The declaration is designed to maintain the laws in all their force and to stop the hysteria manifest in so many quarters for the repeal or modification of these laws.

Samuel Gompers.

TWSr, Files of the Office of the President, General Correspondence, reel 83, frame 93, *AFL Records.*

1. See "From Edward Anderson," Apr. 9, 1917, above.

From Daniel Tobin[1]

Office of Daniel J. Tobin, Gen'l Pres.
International Brotherhood of Teamsters, Chauffeurs,
Stablemen & Helpers of America[2]
Indianapolis, Ind. April 12, 1917

Dear Sir and Brother:

The following is a copy of a telegram I have received today, which is only one of the many which I received within the last week or ten days, pertaining to the statement appearing in the press[3] that Mr. Gompers, President of the American Federation of Labor had practically pledged labor organizations of the country to have no trouble during the war, such as occurred in Europe—or some such statement:

"Sioux City, Iowa. April 11, 1917

["]Daniel J. Tobin,
["]222 E. Michigan St., Indianapolis, Ind.

["]We have endeavored to get a meeting with the bosses and they ignore us on every occasion. Will not grant an audience of any kind. The boys are very restless. President Gompers' article in press stating there will be no strikes has made bosses stand pat. What would you advise. Answer by wire, local 315.

["]C. W. Easley,[4]
["]Secretary."

In view of the fact that I have not seen this statement denied by you, I want to know what there is to it. I am not saying until I hear from you whether or not you made such a declaration. Still the fact remains that the statement has not been denied by you, and it leads me to believe that there must be something to it, and I want to be plain with you, and say my personal opinion is, if you made any such pledge or promise to the Council of National Defense, the President, or any other body in Washington, you had no right to do so. Before any such action should be taken or a pledge of this kind made, my opinion is, a special convention of the American Federation of Labor should have been held, and before it was held International officers should have been asked to consult with their several unions and get instructions so that when they did attend the special convention of the American Federation of Labor they would be in a position to know the feeling of their membership.

I want to say to you that the International I represent will continue to fight and struggle, even to the extent of striking for better conditions, war or no war; that we are dealing, in many instances, with employers who are absolutely unfair and who take every advantage they can possibly take in order to overcome the strength of the union, and while we endeavor to negotiate with our employers and settle with them without a strike, we are forced, in many instances, to call men out on strike. This particular time is the worst period in the history of our International Union, due principally to the fact that our membership are starving resulting from high prices and low wages. We are building up and organizing continually, but doing so conservatively, gradually, slowly and surely. Our per capita tax for the month of March was the highest in the history of the International, we receiving per capita tax on over seventy-five thousand members, and this necessitates, as you understand, more energy, more plotting and planning on the part of the officers, to better the conditions of the membership.

All I can say in answer to a telegram, such as above, is that our International Union is going along just as we did before—settling with our employers who are willing to be fair, but determined to fight unfair employers, many of whom we still have with us.

Kindly answer[5] this letter and let me know what there is to the statement that appeared in the papers as coming from you—if you have been properly quoted, as I have had several communications of this kind, and want to know what there is to this statement, before I make any open declaration to our General Executive Board or to the public in behalf of this International Union.

Fraternally yours,   Daniel J. Tobin
General President.

TLS, Files of the Office of the President, General Correspondence, reel 83, frames 134–37, *AFL Records.*

1. Daniel Joseph TOBIN, of the International Brotherhood of Teamsters, Chauffeurs, Stablemen, and Helpers of America, served as president of the union from 1907 to 1952.

2. The International Brotherhood of TEAMSTERS, Chauffeurs, Stablemen, and Helpers of America.

3. For example, "No Strikes Part of War Program," published in the *Indianapolis Star* of Apr. 9, 1917, reported that "no strikes or labor disputes of any kind during the war is the program of the labor committee of the council of national defense's advisory commission, headed by Samuel Gompers." An article published in the *Indianapolis News* the same day, "Prevention of Labor Trouble Being Sought," carried a similar report, announcing that "strikes such as hampered England early in the war would be avoided in the United States under the committee's recommendation 'that neither employers nor employes shall endeavor to take advantage of the country's necessities to change existing standards' without special approval of the defense council."

4. Crouch W. Easley of Sioux City, Iowa.

5. See "To Daniel Tobin," Apr. 17, 1917, below.

From Abraham Baroff[1]

International Ladies' Garment Workers' Union,[2]
New York, N.Y. April 16th, 1917.

My dear President:

This is an urgent matter to which I want to call your attention and ask your advice and cooperation.

Big orders for military raincoat garments have been placed in a number of shops which are controlled by our Waterproof Garment Workers' Union, Local #20, in this city. When prices were about to be fixed in some of these factories the employers declared to their workers that owing to the fact that these were military garments they would have to accept the prices which they would be given without choice or election. When our people remonstrated they were curtly informed that they have no more union shops; that they have no right to strike, and that they will simply have to take what they are given. When the officers of this local union came to us and told us that they were ready to go down on strike, we stopped them from doing so in order to give ourselves a chance to investigate this matter. We found that the prices offered to them were far below the standards which were usually paid by these firms for regular civilian garments. It became clear to us that these shops were ready to take advantage of the fact that they were making military garments in war time. Feeling, however, that we should not call our workers down in strike unless as a method of last resort, and knowing the desire of the Federation to avoid strikes on war materials by all means possible, we got in touch with Brother Frayne[3] and asked him to try to adjust this matter in the name of the Federation. This morning we learned that Brother Frayne had left New York for the entire week.

I am bringing this matter to your attention because I believe that in the very near future we may have complications of this nature on a large scale. Military garments will very likely be made in New York in many cloak shops, and if such will be the attitude of the employers, some permanent committee of arbitration in shops where military work is being made must be established at once. I am very anxious, Brother Gompers, to prevent this strike in the raincoat shops and am doing my best to keep the workers in.[4]

I would therefore request you to inform me by wire, if possible, as to whether the creation of such a committee within the next few days is a feasible thing, as I am afraid that we will have to stop work on these orders unless a reasonable arrangement will be arrived at within this week.[5]

Thanking you in advance for your kind attention, I am,

Fraternally yours,   (signed) Abraham Baroff,

General Secretary-Treasurer.

TLtcSr, RG 174, General Records of the Department of Labor, DNA. Enclosed in SG to William B. Wilson, Apr. 18, 1917, ibid.

1. Abraham BAROFF served as secretary-treasurer of the International Ladies' Garment Workers' Union from 1915 to 1929.

2. The International LADIES' Garment Workers' Union.

3. Hugh FRAYNE, an AFL salaried organizer, was in charge of the AFL's New York City office and chaired the labor division of the War Industries Board.

4. During the summer and fall of 1917, members of Ladies' Garment Workers' local 20 (Waterproof Garment Workers) struck several New York City clothing firms with government contracts to make rainwear for the army because of wage disputes. The first strike, against H. E. Lazarus and Co. and involving from three to five hundred workers, began in late June and lasted about five weeks. Rowland Mahany, a U.S. Department of Labor commissioner of conciliation, brought about a settlement that included a pay increase. In September a similar controversy led to strikes by about two thousand workers against thirteen firms. Mahany was again brought in, and between Sept. 24 and Oct. 15 arranged settlements in which the firms agreed to meet the union's demands for higher wages.

5. SG sent a copy of Baroff's letter to Secretary of Labor William B. Wilson on Apr. 18, 1917, noting that "this case is typical of many which are being received at this office, and indicates that as the war progresses these complaints will grow in volume." SG went on to suggest that an agency should be created "whereby the occurrences detailed in the letter can be met and overcome" (RG 174, General Records of the Department of Labor, DNA). Wilson referred the matter to Walter Gifford, the director of the Council of National Defense.

To Marguerite Browder[1]

April 17, 1917.

Miss Marguerite Browder,
Secretary, Stenographers, Typewriters, Bookkeepers & Assistants'
     Union #14268,[2]
1112 North Ninth St., Kansas City, Kansas.
Dear Madam:

The following telegram[3] was received by me on Saturday:

"Passage of censorship,[4] draft,[5] espionage,[6] war college[7] and Chamberlain compulsory service[8] bills by Congress means autocracy for America and menace to organized labor. We call upon you to start vigorous opposition at once to forestall establishment of Prussianism in America under guise of Democracy. Act at once before too late.

["]Stenographers, Typists, Bookkeepers & Assistants
["]Union No. 14268."

Last Saturday I presented the following statement to the Military Affairs Committee:[9]

"The organized labor movement has always been fundamentally opposed to compulsion. It has maintained that institutions and relations of a free people can and should be based upon the voluntary principle. It now maintains that what has been the directing basic principle in industrial organization and service must be the initial basic principle in the military. The declaration unanimously adopted by the representatives of the entire organized Labor movement of the United States is based upon this adherence to the voluntary principle.

["]It has been the hope of the men and women of labor that if this Republic should inevitably be drawn into active participation in the present world conflict that the Republic of the United States might demonstrate to the world that free institutions and ideals are effective and sufficient in war as well as in peace.

["]It is the hope of organized labor to demonstrate that under voluntary conditions and institutions the Republic of the United States can mobilize its greatest strength, resources and efficiency.

["]We know that only under voluntary institutions can the nation mobilize good will. Good will is essential to enthusiastic and effective united action.

["]The labor movement stands firmly by the voluntary principle. We declare that at no time have voluntary institutions been given a real effective and conclusive test. Until such a test shall have been given there is no good reason for abandoning the principle which was born of the spirit of 1776 and which has enabled us to establish the ideals and the traditions that have given this Republic meaning as a country, free, efficient and capable of meeting any condition or emergency."

The Judiciary Committee of the House, before which the Espionage bill has been under consideration, has also been presented the objections of the American Federation of Labor to the Espionage bill in its present form.[10] The American Federation of Labor had already taken vigorous action upon the subjects contained in your telegram, prior to its receipt.[11]

With kind regards and best wishes, I am

Fraternally yours,   Saml Gompers.
President,   American Federation of Labor.

TLpS, reel 220, vol. 232, pp. 747–48, SG Letterbooks, DLC.

1. Marguerite Browder, a resident of Kansas City, Kans., was employed as a stenographer in Kansas City, Mo., where she served in 1917 and 1918 as secretary of Stenographers', Typewriters', Bookkeepers', and Assistants' Union 14,268. She was the sister of Earl Browder, who had previously served as president and secretary of the union and was later the secretary of the American Communist party.

2. AFL 14,268 was chartered in 1912.

3. Stenographers', Typists', Bookkeepers', and Assistants' Union 14,268 to SG, Apr. 13, 1917, Files of the Office of the President, General Correspondence, reel 83, frame 198, *AFL Records*.

4. See n. 6, below.

5. On Apr. 5, 1917, the War Department submitted legislation to the chairmen of the House and Senate Military Affairs committees authorizing use of the draft. The Selective Service Act of 1917, signed into law on May 18, authorized creation of local draft boards, required males between the ages of twenty-one and thirty to register for military service, and empowered the president to raise one million men through conscription (U.S. *Statutes at Large*, 40: 76–83).

6. H.R. 291 (65th Cong., 1st sess.) was introduced by Democratic congressman Edwin Webb of North Carolina on Apr. 2, 1917, and became law on June 15 (U.S. *Statutes at Large*, 40: 217–31). Known as the Espionage Act, it authorized the death penalty, imprisonment, or fines to punish espionage, damage to ships or cargo for export, or the promotion of insubordination or disloyalty in the armed forces or the obstruction of recruiting or enlistment. The act also empowered the postmaster general to deny use of the mails to those advocating treason, insurrection, or forcible resistance to the law.

7. Probably a reference to H.R. 92 (65th Cong., 1st sess.), a universal military training bill drafted by the Army War College and introduced by Republican congressman Julius Kahn of California on Apr. 2, 1917. The bill did not become law.

8. S. 1 (65th Cong., 1st sess.), a bill providing for universal military training, was introduced by Democratic senator George Chamberlain of Oregon on Apr. 3, 1917. It did not become law.

9. On Apr. 14, 1917, M. Grant Hamilton presented SG's statement to the House Committee on Military Affairs at its hearings on voluntary enlistment and conscription. The statement was published in the *AFL Weekly News Letter* of Apr. 21 and in the May issue of the *American Federationist* (24: 376). The AFL Executive Council at its April meeting also adopted a declaration opposed to conscription, which it sent to the president of the Senate and the Speaker of the House of Representatives on Apr. 27 (reel 221, vol. 233, pp. 96–103, SG Letterbooks, DLC).

10. The House Committee on the Judiciary held hearings on the espionage bill on Apr. 9 and 12, 1917. Arthur Holder testified before the committee on Apr. 12.

11. In June 1917 Earl, Ralph, and William Browder were arrested in Kansas City, Mo., on charges of conspiracy to obstruct the operation of the draft law. Subsequently convicted, they were each fined $1,000 and sentenced to terms of two years' imprisonment.

To Daniel Tobin

April 17, 1917

Mr. Daniel J. Tobin,
President, Int'l. Brotherhood of Teamsters, Chauffeurs, Stablemen
  and Helpers of America,
222 E. Michigan Street, Indianapolis, Ind.
Dear Sir and Brother:

Your letter of April 12th[1] received and contents noted. In reply thereto, I can find no better way to set the matter clear than by giving you substantially the same reply which I have made to various inquirers as to the misleading statement which appeared in the press and to which you refer.

Neither myself nor any other representative of the American Federation of Labor has announced to the public or made any promise to any one in any form that "there shall be no strikes of any kind during the war."

The sole apparent basis for the rumor that I joined in such a promise is the fact that at a meeting of the Executive Committee of the Labor Committee recommendations were made to and finally approved by the Advisory Commission of the Council of National Defense. The resolutions relate to the preservation of existing labor standards and are as follows:

First: That the Council of National Defense should issue a statement to employers and employes in our industrial plants and transportation systems advising that neither employers nor employes shall endeavor to take advantage of the country's necessities to change existing standards. When economic or other emergencies arise requiring changes of standards, the same should be made only after such proposed changes have been investigated and approved by the Council of National Defense.

Second: That the Council of National Defense urge upon the legislatures of the states, as well as all administrative agencies charged with the enforcement of labor and health laws, the great duty of rigorously maintaining the existing safeguards as to the health and the welfare of workers, and that no departure from such present standards in state laws or state rulings affecting labor should be taken without a declaration of the Council of National Defense that such a departure is essential for the effective pursuit of the national defense.

Third: That the Council of National Defense urge upon the legislatures of the several states that before final adjournment they delegate to the Governors of their respective states the power to suspend or modify restrictions contained in their labor laws when such suspension or modification shall be requested by the Council of National Defense; and such suspensions or modification when made, shall continue for a specified period and not longer than the duration of the war.

In the course of the meeting at which these resolutions were passed, it was clearly stated and understood that the intent of the proposition, that is, the first resolution regarding possible emergencies requiring modifications in existing standards, was to maintain existing standards. The attention of the Committee was directed to the fact, and it was generally understood for the basis of our action, that workmen employed in the transportation systems and industrial plants may find their wages of the present time out of proportion to the increased cost of living, and in that case a maintenance of the present status of labor conditions obviously implied an advance in wage scales.

In the discussion on this point which followed in the Committee consideration was given to the circumstances in which, during the war, organized English miners were obliged to demonstrate the necessity of a wage increase, the award being in their favor when they had proved the considerable changes that had taken place in the cost of living. Plainly, in similar cases in this country, higher wage scales must be adopted. Therefore there are incorporated in the resolutions the recommendation that proposed changes should be made only after investigation and approval by the Council of National Defense, whose duty in this respect should also be a vigorous maintenance of safeguards to the health and welfare of workers.

The resolutions in question clearly apply only to the large industries and the transportation systems whose operation are essential to the prosecution of the war. They are not intended to cover every petty labor difference in the country, though it is hoped that patriotic regard will be had by all citizens to the need of a possible maximum of industrial peace everywhere. It is, of course, not expected by the committee that negotiations, or even strikes, now on in various occupations shall be wholly suspended irrespective of the merits of the questions under discussion. On such points each trade union is the judge of the principles which should prevail in its action.

The special attention of trade unions is called to the fact that the committee's resolutions declare that legislatures should uphold and public officers enforce existing labor and health laws, and that the modifications or standards authorized in extraordinary emergencies by the Council of National Defense should be only for specified periods and in any event not longer than the duration of the war.

With this statement, I feel that each case of differences arising between employers and employes, as well as the trade agreements or other matters now under discussion, may be left to the common sense of men who are willing and anxious to perform their duty to their country in the present grave situation.

I trust that the above will clarify the misunderstanding which really occurred, not so much from what was published in the newspapers, but the scare head-lines which had really no relation to the substance of the body of the resolutions.

I take it that in this crisis in our nation's history everyone will do his level best, not only for service, but for a united spirit and action.

With kind regards, I remain,

Yours fraternally, Saml Gompers
President American Federation of Labor.

P.S. Enclosed you will please find statement as published in this week's A.F. of L. News Letter which you will kindly accept as part of this letter.[2]

TLpS, reel 220, vol. 232, pp. 755–58, SG Letterbooks, DLC.

1. See "From Daniel Tobin," Apr. 12, 1917, above.
2. The statement, written by SG, was published under the heading "To Study, Not to Hinder" in the *AFL Weekly News Letter* of Apr. 21, 1917. It made essentially the same points as SG's letter to Tobin.

George Diefenbach[1] and L. N. Abrams[2] to Walter Larkin,[3] with an Appended Note from Larkin to SG

[East] St. Louis, Ill., April 17, 1917.

Mr. Walter Larkin,
Vice Pres. Sheet and Tin Div.
Martin's Ferry, Ohio.
Dear Sir and Bro.

I know you wonder what is wrong but say we have had one awful experience. We went to Gary and were on the job at once and succeeded in getting 26 men together in a short time and took them to the hotel. There we explained our mission to them and then they wanted to get more men which they all set out to do, and on Monday we had some cards printed as to our whereabouts, and passed them out to the men as we met them, and they also came to our room in droves or flocks and gangs, but they wanted a Saturday meeting which we arranged for and we have all reason to believe that at least 300 men would have been there. We had arranged to use the Labor Hall for Saturday and Sunday afternoon. Friday night we met all the men who go out on the train at 11:25 P.M. and the ones coming back at 12:20 A.M., and they surely were enthused. About 1 o'clock A.M. we retired and at 2:30 A.M. a rap came to our door and we very naturally answered, and they were Secret Service men who told us to get up and dress and pack our grips, we were wanted by the Federal authorities in Chicago. We had our money in the safe in the hotel. They would not even wait for us to get that. I had a suit of clothes in a tailor shop getting pressed (and I guess it's still there). They took us to the Gary Police Station and searched us and took everything away from us and then put us into an auto and took us to Chicago. There we were again searched (but of course had nothing on us) and put in jail and kept there in the most rotten place I ever saw until late Saturday afternoon, then we were taken to the Federal Building to the United States Marshall's Office, and Walter you will never know or realize what we were put through with the finish being if we agreed to stay out of Gary at this present war time we would be released, and of course that was the only course for us to take and they very emphatically told us that if any of our people came there they would get the same as we did or worse, and for us to inform all our people, (the police force framed this all up in our opinion), and that during this war time we must not interfere with any plant filling government orders, and Walter they showed us where we had our choice of returning to Gary and face 30 years in prison or possibly the sun rise squad, which you no doubt are aware of the meaning.

But Walter the feeling in Gary is remarkable, and I would not be surprised at all to see those men proceed of their own accord. Walter they had all manner of charges drummed up against us; false and nothing true, but we had no way of proving an alibi.

Now Walter you write the U.S. Marshall, Chicago, Ill., Federal Building, and get the dope that was handed to us and you will then realize what we went against. We surely were disappointed at our finish for we had a beautiful start and we surely wish to congratulate you and Bro. Robinson on your splendid work in the valley, and I feel sure that Gary, Ind. and others will follow suit.

Well Walter we must close for this time as we do not know any more that we could put on paper, and no doubt we will see you soon in Granite City and we want the privilege of appearing before the convention[4] and making a verbal report, or, at least, to you, and we want all the national officials and members of the convention to feel and know that our homes are always open at all times to all. And if there is any further information we can give you, wire us or write, and we will sure be more than pleased to give you any information we can.

Wishing yourself and family everything in life and best regards to Bro. Robinson and family, and further success in your great undertaking, we beg to remain,

Yours fraternally,   (Signed) Geo. Diefenbach,
L. N. Abrams.

[Appended Note]

Mr Samuel Gompers
President A.F. of L.
Washington D.C.
Dear Sir and Brother:—
Please give me your opinion on the above and advise what course to persue and oblige,

Yours Fraternally,   Walter Larkin
Vice Pres AA
Martins Ferry Ohio[5]

TLtcSr and ALS, Files of the Office of the President, General Correspondence, reel 83, frames 229–31, *AFL Records.* Typed notation: "*Copy.*"

1. George Diefenbach was a member of Amalgamated Association of Iron, Steel, and Tin Workers' lodge 11 of Granite City, Ill., and an organizer for the international union.

2. L. N. Abrams of Granite City was an organizer for the Iron, Steel, and Tin Workers.

3. Walter Larkin (1865–1925), a member of Iron, Steel, and Tin Workers' lodge 46 of Martin's Ferry, Ohio, was vice-president of the international union's tin division (1905–10) and then of its sheet and tin division (1910–25).

4. The 1917 Iron, Steel, and Tin Workers' convention met May 2–25 in Granite City.

5. SG received a second letter on the same subject, dated May 22, 1917, from president John Williams and secretary-treasurer M. F. Tighe of the Iron, Steel, and Tin Workers. He sent it on to Secretary of Labor William B. Wilson, who referred it in turn to the Department of Justice. Hinton Clabaugh, a division superintendent for the department's bureau of investigation in Chicago, reported on the matter to the department on June 26. His statement reads in part:

["]Chief of Police Forbis of Gary, Indiana, called on the telephone and stated that two agitators in Gary were causing considerable trouble which might result in violence and he was of the opinion that their activities were financed or inspired by German interests. He stated that if the Government did not act in the matter, he personally would on behalf of the local authorities; that the present was no time for improper agitation, strikes, etc. and that he would not permit it. I replied that I could not concern myself in ordinary labor disputes, unless specifically instructed by my superiors to make an investigation, and that we even followed this policy with reference to agitation in factories which were making munitions for the Army and Navy.

["]Chief of Police Forbis replied that he was under the impression that the American

Sheet and Tin Plate Co. of Gary were making supplies for either the Army or Navy, and possibly both. At any rate he reiterated that there was strong reason for believing that the two agitators in question were supplied with more money than ordinary organizers or business agents; and in addition the wages paid at the plant where the business agents were agitating were in excess of that paid by similar institutions and as I now recall it, possibly in excess of the Union scale.

["]I told Chief Forbis that I would send an agent to Gary to make an investigation for the purpose of determining whether the agitators in question were directly or indirectly in the employ of interests unfriendly to this Government. Chief Forbis stated that the men would voluntarily accompany him and that he would be glad to bring them to Chicago for a conference.

["]He and Mayor Johnson accompanied them to Chicago in an automobile and in so far as I have been advised, I did not know that they were under arrest. If they were under arrest it was upon a State cha[rge of] disorderly conduct, or inciting riot, or whatever statute Chief [Forbis] had in mind.

["]The men came to the office, and both of them, I think had an American flag pasted on their linen collars. They gave evidence of being loyal, patriotic American citizens, and there was no evidence to indicate that they were in any way involved in any German plot, except circumstantial evidence not susceptible of proof. In other words, it looked like a plain case of two labor agents endeavoring to organize a non-union factory["] (AFL Microfilm National and International Union File, Iron, Steel and Tin Workers Records, reel 38, frame 2446, *AFL Records*).

Wilson forwarded Clabaugh's report to SG on July 17, and SG sent it on to Williams and Tighe on July 25.

To Robert Lansing

Washington, D.C. April 19, 1917

Hon. Robert Lansing
Secretary of State
Washington, D.C.
Sir:

Newspapers of today report that it has been officially stated by the State Department that this government will send a commission to the new Republic of Russia.[1]

Inasmuch as the revolution in that country had its origin primarily in those most oppressed, and the workers of Russia have been one of the directing influences in establishing the new freedom of that country, I think you will appreciate the value and the importance of including in the American commission at least one representative of the organized labor movement of this country as the official spokesman for the American labor movement.[2] I have already been in communication[3] with the leaders of the revolution of Russia, and I am sure that no step could do more toward cementing the bonds between our two nations than that which I now urge upon your consideration and favorable action.

In connection with this matter it is not inappropriate to call to your attention my recent cablegrams to Lloyd George[4] and Premier Ribot[5] asking them to send representatives of the organized labor movement of Great Britain and France to the United States[6] in connection with the Government Commission[7] appointed to come here. Premier George cabled[8] me in reply that he would be delighted to comply with my request and cable information reaches me that Mr. Charles W. Bowerman[9] and James R. Thomas[10] of the British Trade Union movement have been appointed to come to the United States to perform that mission.[11] I have reason to believe that the French Government will also send two representatives.[12]

President Menocal[13] of Cuba, to whom I also cabled,[14] cabled an affirmative compliance[15] with my request.

There are already representatives of the Mexican Labor movement in Washington and an international conference of the representative labor movements of France, England, Cuba and Mexico and of the United States would do much to be helpful to our people here and also have a beneficial influence upon the minds of Russia's people, as well as the rank and file of the workers of Germany.

It is one of the most striking developments of the whole war situation that all countries are coming to appreciate the importance and the significance of the organized labor movements and the indispensable service these organizations render to society.

I sincerely hope that you will give favorable consideration to my suggestion of sending a representative of the American labor movement to Russia to join with the American Commission and convey fraternal good will of the working masses of the United States to the workers of Russia.

> Very truly yours,   Saml Gompers.
> President   American Federation of Labor

TLS, RG 59, General Records of the Department of State, DNA.

1. A nine-member commission under the leadership of Elihu Root was sent to Russia in the summer of 1917 to demonstrate American support for the Provisional Government and encourage Russia to remain in the war.

2. On Apr. 10 and 11, 1917, respectively, Edward House and Robert Lansing had recommended SG as a member of the commission. President Woodrow Wilson turned down the idea because he felt SG's "pronounced" opposition to socialism would diminish his influence in Russia but suggested he be consulted on who the labor member of the commission should be (Wilson to Lansing, n.d., RG 59, General Records of the Department of State, DNA). Subsequently discussing the matter with Lansing, when the two were among the guests who attended a dinner given on Apr. 23 at the White

House for the members of the Balfour mission, and then with William B. Wilson, SG recommended James Duncan. President Wilson asked Duncan to serve on May 5.

3. See "To Nikolai Chkheidze," Mar. 21, 1917, above.

4. David Lloyd George (1863–1945) served as a Liberal member of Parliament (1890–1945), chancellor of the Exchequer (1908–15), minister of munitions (1915–16), secretary of state for war (1916), and prime minister of Great Britain (1916–22).

5. Alexandre Ribot (1842–1923) served as premier of France (1892–93, 1895, 1914, 1917).

6. The cables were sent on Apr. 12, 1917 (Files of the Office of the President, Letterbooks, Advisory Commission, Council of National Defense, reel 20, p. 174, *AFL Records*).

7. The British and French governments sent commissions to the United States in April 1917 to discuss the joint war effort with their new ally. Foreign Minister Arthur Balfour led the British mission; the French mission was headed by former premier René Viviani and included former commander-in-chief Joseph Joffre. These delegations were followed later in the year by commissions from Italy, Russia, Belgium, Romania, Japan, and Serbia.

8. Lloyd George to SG, Apr. 13, 1917, Files of the Office of the President, General Correspondence, reel 83, frame 140, *AFL Records*.

9. Charles William BOWERMAN served as secretary (1911–23) of the Parliamentary Committee of the TUC (from 1921, the General Council of the TUC) and was a Labour member of Parliament (1906–31).

10. Actually James Henry THOMAS, secretary of the National Union of Railwaymen (1917–31) and a Labour member of Parliament (1910–36).

11. In addition to Bowerman and Thomas, the British labor mission included Joseph Davies (1866–1954), a member of the prime minister's secretariat, and Heathcote William Garrod (1878–1960), a member of the faculty at Merton College, Oxford, who served in the Ministry of Munitions during the war. The mission arrived at New York on May 4, 1917, and visited Washington, D.C., Pittsburgh, Chicago, Cleveland, Boston, and Albany and Schenectady, N.Y., before returning to England at the end of the month.

12. SG had asked Ribot to send Léon Jouhaux and Auguste Keufer to the United States as the French labor representatives. Jouhaux informed SG on May 16, 1917, that the two were unable to come (Files of the Office of the President, General Correspondence, reel 83, frame 941, *AFL Records*).

13. Mario García Menocal y Deop (1866–1941), a member of the Conservative party, served as president of Cuba from 1913 to 1921.

14. SG to Menocal, Apr. 16, 1917, Files of the Office of the President, Letterbooks, Advisory Commission, Council of National Defense, reel 20, p. 237, *AFL Records*.

15. Menocal to SG, Apr. 18, 1917, Files of the Office of the President, General Correspondence, reel 83, frame 279, *AFL Records*.

A Memorandum by Samuel Gompers

Washington, D.C. April 19, 1917

MEMORANDUM

In order to facilitate the organization and the conduct of the offices of the Committee on Labor, to conserve the time of those who are so generously assisting me in the work, to relieve myself as far as possible of the necessity for consultation as to the working of the office, I respectfully ask that the following be observed:

All correspondence, documents, etc., addressed to or intended for me, will go to Mr. Sullivan[1] in conformity with my request[2] of Mr. Gifford.[3]

Mr. Sullivan will have a fac simile of my signature, with authority to use it; he will be personally responsible to me for any and all matter that goes out in my name. In correspondence of which he is not absolutely sure of his position, he will hold the letters for my personal signature. In the A.F. of L. office, Miss Guard[4] is the only person authorized to sign my name. With her, I have always followed the course that if there is any doubt whatever, the letters must be held for my scrutiny and signature.

Upon all matters purely labor, Mr. Sullivan will act as per above.

On matters other than labor, Mr. Sullivan will consult with Mr. Easley.[5]

Letters and matters regarding the committees to be turned over to Miss Beeks,[6] to be attended by her subject to approval by me.

The filing of correspondence, the keeping of records, etc. will be done under Miss Beeks' direction.

Miss Beeks will keep the minutes of the Executive Committee meetings and before reporting them to the following meeting of the Executive Committee, will submit them to me.

TD, Files of the Office of the President, General Correspondence, reel 83, frames 318–19, *AFL Records.*

1. During World War I James William SULLIVAN served as an assistant to SG on the Committee on Labor of the Advisory Commission of the Council of National Defense and then headed the labor and consumer division of the U.S. Food Administration.

2. SG to Walter Gifford, Apr. 17, 1917, Files of the Office of the President, Letterbooks, Advisory Commission, Council of National Defense, reel 20, p. 251, *AFL Records.*

3. Walter Sherman Gifford (1885–1966) was acting director (December 1916 to March 1917) and then director (March 1917 to October 1918) of the Council of National Defense, with charge of the administrative work of both the Council and the Advisory Commission. Chief statistician of the American Telephone and Telegraph

Co. and later the company's president and chairman of the board, he had previously served as supervising director of the Committee on Industrial Preparedness (January to December 1916).

4. Rosa Lee GUARD was SG's private secretary.

5. Ralph Montgomery EASLEY was chairman of the National Civic Federation executive council (1904–39).

6. Gertrude Brackenridge Beeks (1867–1950) was secretary of the executive committee of the Committee on Labor and secretary of the National Civic Federation executive council. In September 1917 she married Ralph Easley.

From Felix Frankfurter[1]

Law School of Harvard University,
Cambridge, Mass. April 20, 1917.

My dear Mr. Gompers:

Mr. Lloyd George's advice to this country "America should begin where England now is" applies with special force to the handling of labor questions raised by the war. Every candid student of England's conditions knows that failure to deal wisely with labor problems at the outset of the war was the most hampering factor of England's conduct of it during the first year. The task for us, as it was for England, is to secure an uninterrupted output of labor at its most efficient maximum, while at the same time to assure rigorous maintenance of just conditions for labor. Patriotic spirit will go far but of itself will not secure these ends. We must anticipate inevitable friction as time wears on, and, particularly, as the cost of living will rise. Just relations between management and labor do not enforce themselves; we must provide authoritative machinery, representative of the interests of the whole country, for working out sound conditions, and constant supervision in enforcing such conditions.

Specifically, it is necessary, first, to provide in all contracts made by the Government against letting down existing safeguards, adapting general principles to the requirements appropriate to different industries and different localities. Secondly, it is necessary to establish machinery for the adjustment of controversies that are bound to arise.

To that end an organ for action in the field of labor questions[2] should be created similar to the Munitions Board[3] and the Food Board[4] in their respective field. Such a board cannot be established too soon. Its activities are now called for. In various parts of the country difficulties in regard to Government contracts are already manifesting themselves. These danger signals should be heeded. Such a labor board, impartial and expert, acting under the authority of the Council of National Defense, would be the instrument for assuring the just interests of labor as well as the reasonable conditions under which industry can discharge its duties. Only thus will the industrial energies called for by the national crisis be efficiently and peacefully secured.

Cordially yours,   Felix Frankfurter.

TLS, Files of the Office of the President, General Correspondence, reel 83, frames 340–41, *AFL Records.*

1. Felix Frankfurter (1882–1965), a professor at the Harvard Law School (1914–39) and later a justice of the U.S. Supreme Court (1939–62), served as a special assistant to Secretary of War Newton Baker (1917–18), secretary and legal counsel to President Woodrow Wilson's mediation commission (1917–18), and chairman of the War Labor Policies Board (1918–19).

2. Frankfurter drew up a proposal for a nine-member board of labor adjustment that SG presented to the Advisory Commission of the Council of National Defense on Apr. 23, 1917, and to the AFL Executive Council on Apr. 25. It was to consist of two trade unionists, two manufacturers, a woman, a member of the U.S. Civil Service Commission, and three representatives of the public. SG presented a revised draft of the plan—with a seven-member board—to the Executive Council on Apr. 26 (see "Excerpts from the Minutes of a Meeting of the Executive Council of the AFL," Apr. 26, 1917, below). On Aug. 1, after much debate and many revisions, the Council of National Defense and the Advisory Commission approved a version of the plan which again envisioned nine members—three for "labor," three for employers, and three representing the government (Franklin Martin, *Digest of the Proceedings of the Council of National Defense during the World War,* 73d Cong., 2d sess., 1934, S.Doc. 193, p. 240). SG had strong objections, however, and instead called for a seven-member board with three trade unionists, three employers, and an arbitrator. The proposal for a nine-member board was reconsidered at later meetings of the Advisory Commission but never implemented. (For other versions of Frankfurter's proposal see SG to Robert Bass, Apr. 21, 1917, and SG to Daniel Willard, Apr. 28, 1917, Files of the Office of the President, Letterbooks, Advisory Commission, Council of National Defense, reel 20, pp. 313–16, 427–30, *AFL Records.* See also Frankfurter to SG, [May 7, 1917], Files of the Office of the President, General Correspondence, reel 83, frames 678–79, *AFL Records,* and Frankfurter memoranda for the secretary of war, May 22 and June 9, 1917, RG 407, Records of the Adjutant General's Office, DNA.)

3. The Council of National Defense established the General Munitions Board on Apr. 4, 1917, to coordinate and facilitate the work of purchasing and supply agencies in the war and navy departments. The War Industries Board took over its functions in July.

4. On Apr. 7, 1917, the Council of National Defense and the Advisory Commission, meeting in joint session, voted to set up an advisory committee on food supply and prices and asked Herbert Hoover to serve as its chair. He agreed on Apr. 11.

To Edward McGrady[1]

April 25, 1917.

Mr. Edward F. McGrady,
President, Boston Central Labor Union,
987 Washington St., Boston, Mass.
Dear Sir and Brother:

Your letter of April 20th,[2] stating that there was probability of the Massachusetts legislature considering similar proposals[3] to those made in the New York[4] and Connecticut[5] legislatures, that is, to suspend all labor laws for the duration of the war, was received.

It was just because of such proposals and the danger of a movement to destroy existing standards under the misguided impression that the action would further national defense that the Executive Committee of my Committee on Labor recommended to the Advisory Commission that a declaration be issued to the effect that present standards ought to be maintained. The declaration was intended to act as a steadying force and to prevent a threatened stampede and disruption of existing conditions.

In view of the fact that a serious emergency might arise and that several of the state legislatures would shortly adjourn for a period of two years, we advised that the state legislature place in the hands of the governor of the state the authority to suspend laws, if that course should be recommended by the Council of National Defense as indispensable to national safety.

The declaration of the Council of National Defense was misinterpreted with strange unanimity by the metropolitan press of the country. The purpose of the declaration was to steady, not to hinder.

Several members of my Committee on Labor were authorized by the Council of National Defense to go to Albany to protest against the enactment of the proposed legislation giving the Industrial Commission authority to suspend labor laws, without definite specification of the duration of suspension. The general movement to suspend all labor laws seems to be an effort not wisely to promote national defense but to take advantage of the situation to exploit workers.

I wish you would do everything within your power to prevent any other action being taken by the Massachusetts legislature except that recommended by the Council of National Defense. I am glad you wrote me about the matter so that I can assure you that this course will not only not embarrass me, but will further the purposes of the Advisory

Commission of the Council of National Defense as well as safeguard the welfare of the workers.

With best wishes, I am,

Fraternally yours, Saml Gompers.
President American Federation of Labor.

TLpS, reel 221, vol. 233, pp. 40–41, SG Letterbooks, DLC.

1. Edward Francis McGrady (1872–1960), a member of International Printing Pressmen's and Assistants' Union of North America 3 (Web Pressmen) of Boston and president of the Boston Central Labor Union, later served as vice-president of the Massachusetts State Federation of Labor (1919–20), a member of the AFL Legislative Committee (1920–33), assistant secretary of labor (1933–37), and director (later vice-president) of labor relations for the Radio Corporation of America (1937–51).

2. McGrady to SG, Apr. 20, 1917, Files of the Office of the President, General Correspondence, reel 83, frame 354, *AFL Records.*

3. The Commonwealth Defence Act (Massachusetts, Laws of 1917, chap. 342), enacted May 26, 1917, authorized employers to apply for a waiver of any state labor laws that interfered with war work and established a five-member committee to investigate and rule on such requests.

4. On Apr. 20, 1917, New York state senator Elon Brown introduced Senate bill 2149, which authorized the suspension of any of the state's labor laws that interfered with the war effort. The bill passed both houses of the legislature but was vetoed on June 2 by Gov. Charles Whitman.

5. Connecticut, Laws of 1917, chap. 326, enacted May 16, 1917, authorized the governor to modify or suspend any of the state's labor laws during the war if necessary for the national defense and if asked to do so by the Council of National Defense.

To Daniel Willard[1]

Advisory Commission of the Council of National Defense
Washington April 25, 1917.

Mr. Daniel Willard,
Chairman, Advisory Commission, Council of National Defense,
Munsey Building, Washington, D.C.
My dear Mr. Willard:

Under date of April 18 you referred to me a telegram from F. N. Hoffstot,[2] President of the Pressed Steel Car Company of New York. The telegram referred to the custom of the working men of the Pittsburg District of celebrating numerous holidays, a custom which seriously interferes with the desire of the Pressed Steel Company to hasten production at the present time.

I at once wired[3] to Mr. John Williams, President of the Amalgamated

Association of Iron, Steel and Tin Workers,[4] to come to Washington for a conference,[5] as Mr. Williams knows more of the conditions among the steel workers in Pittsburg than any other person.

A conference[6] was arranged with Secretary Redfield,[7] Secretary Wilson, a representative[8] of the American Federation of Labor, and Mr. Williams. The latter was accompanied by another official[9] of his organization.

As you know the Steel Companies have pursued policies hostile to the organized labor movement and have done everything possible to prevent organization among their workers. One policy which was adopted for this purpose was to secure immigrant workers. It is a matter of common knowledge and Congressional record that in the steel industries of Pennsylvania and around Pittsburg, the groups of foreign workers were kept isolated so that there could be the least possible communication and intercourse. No effort was made to Americanize them; on the contrary, the companies did everything within their power to prevent the greatest agency which has proved its effectiveness in Americanizing foreign workers from operating in that field. Consequently these steel operators now find themselves with workers out of harmony with American customs and institutions. In the preparation for a national defense they are dependent upon these foreigners and have found their efforts frustrated by foreign customs such as that mentioned in the telegram to you.

Among another class of workers in the state—the miners—there are also a great number of foreigners, but the United Mine Workers' Organization has succeeded in establishing some of the American ideals among the miners, and the organization has been able to control the celebration of holidays. This illustrates one of the effects of the organized labor movement.

Mr. Williams briefly presented this matter to the conference I mentioned. Another point was brought out by Secretary Wilson, who stated that he knew of union organizations in the steel industry that were unable to keep up their usual productivity because they were unable to secure the raw materials. Secretary Redfield asked for the names of these union concerns and stated that he would see to it that they received raw products and were able to secure the cars in which to transport the same.

Altogether, those participating in this conference felt that an understanding resulted which might be the basis for preventing similar occurrences if no obstacles were interposed to the efforts of those competent to deal with the situation.

I am very glad you referred the matter to me, as I think a better understanding has resulted.

Very truly yours,   Saml Gompers.
Chairman,   Committee on Labor.

P.S.: It may also be interesting to say that as the result of my committee's work and through the agency of Mr. Williams and Secretary Wilson, a strike[10] in the tin plate industry was brought to a speedy and mutually advantageous close.

S. G.

TLS, RG 62, Records of the Council of National Defense, DNA.

1. Daniel Willard (1861–1942), president of the Baltimore and Ohio Railroad (1910–41), was a member of the Advisory Commission of the Council of National Defense (1916–18) and served as its chairman from March 1917 until October 1918, when he was commissioned for a short time as a colonel of engineers in the army. He also served briefly (November 1917–January 1918) as chairman of the War Industries Board.

2. Frank Hoffstot to Willard, n.d., Files of the Office of the President, General Correspondence, reel 91, frame 109, *AFL Records*. Hoffstot was president of the Pressed Steel Car Co. from 1908 until 1933.

3. SG to John Williams, Apr. 20, 1917, Files of the Office of the President, General Correspondence, reel 83, frame 351, *AFL Records*.

4. John WILLIAMS was president (1911–19) of the Amalgamated Association of IRON, Steel, and Tin Workers.

5. In reference to the calling of this conference, see also Bernard Baruch to SG, Apr. 19, B. E. V. Luty to Baruch, Apr. 16, and SG to Baruch, Apr. 20 (Files of the Office of the President, General Correspondence, reel 83, frames 281, 283–87, 291, *AFL Records*).

6. The meeting was held in Washington, D.C., Apr. 23, 1917.

7. William Cox Redfield (1858–1932) was the secretary of commerce (1913–19). He had previously served one term as a Democratic congressman from New York (1911–13).

8. M. Grant HAMILTON, the AFL representative, was a member of the AFL Legislative Committee (1908, 1912–13, 1915–18).

9. Iron, Steel, and Tin Workers' vice-president Walter Larkin. Also attending the conference was James Sullivan, representing the Committee on Labor of the Advisory Commission of the Council of National Defense.

10. Some seven hundred workers at the Yorkville, Ohio, mill of the Wheeling Steel and Iron Co. struck on Apr. 11, 1917, demanding reinstatement of a discharged worker and recognition of Iron, Steel, and Tin Workers' local 81 of Yorkville, which had been organized the week before. Federal mediators Hywel Davies and William Fairley assisted the two sides in reaching a settlement on Apr. 21, under which the company agreed to pay the union wage scale—a pay increase of about 10 percent.

Excerpts from the Minutes of a Meeting[1] of the Executive Council of the AFL

Thursday, April 26, 1917.

AFTERNOON SESSION

. . .

President Gompers submitted the following[2] to the Executive Council, which was read:

If the issues of the present war are to be brought to a successful termination, the best possible relations must be maintained in industry. Vast quantities of materials will be manufactured by the government in its own establishments, much of it purchased in the open market, and contracts entered into with many manufacturing concerns. The continuous flowing of output from all these agencies is a vital necessity.

If our government will profit by the experience of the war-stricken countries, many of the serious industrial difficulties encountered by them can be avoided. The establishment of just relations between employes and employers engaged in the production of materials for government use can be maintained providing the proper agency is created where differences can be dealt with speedily and with a due regard to the rights and interests of both employes and employers. The rightful handling of disagreements occurring in industry and the adoption by this government of proper and recognized minimum standards and maintaining them through a competent agency will prevent unnecessary waste of time and promote a feeling of good will which will act as a stimulus to our citizenship generally.

In order that such an agency may be created for the duration of the war, it is hereby suggested:

First: That there be created by the Council of National Defense a National Board of Labor Adjustment of seven members, to be selected because of their peculiar fitness to deal with the problems which will be assigned to the board, and two of whom shall be trade unionists and two manufacturers, and three persons representing the public.

Second: It shall be the duty of this Board to enforce the maintenance of existing standards and conditions of labor employed in executing Government contracts or orders. No changes in such standards and conditions shall be made without the approval of this Board and all changes shall be determined only after conferences which the Board shall hold with representatives of employers and employes of the industry affected.

Third: That the Board shall have authority when it deems such action necessary, to cause to be established in each manufacturing concern employed on Government contracts a conference committee of four; two to be selected by the employes in any manner they choose, and two representatives of the owners of the plant. Such committee shall take up any grievances arising in that particular plant. In the event that such committee be unable to agree, the grievance shall be appealed to the Board whose decision shall be final and binding upon both parties.

Fourth: All Government contracts shall contain such provisions as are necessary to enforce the findings and the orders of this Board in relation to the standards and conditions of labor employed on Government contracts or orders.

Fifth: This plan shall become inoperative when the Peace treaty is signed.

. . .

TDc, Executive Council Records, Minutes, reel 5, frames 1386–87, *AFL Records.*

1. The AFL Executive Council met in Washington, D.C., Apr. 20–27, 1917.

2. SG was submitting a revised version of a plan for a board of labor adjustment that he had first presented to the AFL Executive Council the day before. See Executive Council Records, Minutes, reel 5, frame 1383, *AFL Records,* and "From Felix Frankfurter," Apr. 20, 1917, n. 2, above.

From Elizabeth Maloney[1] et al.

Chicago Ills April 26 1917

Press reports the appointment of a new committee by you for cooperation with the government in the handling of industrial disputes during war time During these critical times when women are a greater factor than ever before in industry we deplore the ommission of trade union women on these various committees We feel this is a serious oversight and earnestly urge the appointment of representative trade union women on all such committees[2] England has seen the wisdom of representation of working women who have been ably represented in war councils by trade union women We look to America to do even better

Elizabeth Maloney,   Vice President Hotel and
Restaurant Employes Alliance,[3]
Mary Anderson[4]   Int Executive Board Member
Boot and Shoe Workers Union,[5]

Agnes Noster [*sic*][6]   Vice President Int Glove
Workers Union of America,[7]
Olive Sullivan[8]   Office Employee Union,[9]
Emma Steghagen   Boot and Shoe Workers Union,
Elizabeth Christman,[10]   Secty Treas
Int Glove Workers Union,
Margaret Haley[11]   Chicago Teachers Federation,
Mrs Lydia Trowbridge[12]   High School Teachers
Federation,
Mary McEnerney[13]   Bindery Womens Union,
Agnes Johnson[14]   Boot and Shoe Workers Union,
Mary Haney[15]   United Garment Workers Union

TWSr, Files of the Committee on Labor, RG 62, Records of the Council of National Defense, DNA.

1. Elizabeth Maloney (d. 1921), a Chicago waitress, served as secretary of Hotel and Restaurant Employees' International Alliance and Bartenders' International League of America 484 of Chicago (1909–21) and as a vice-president of the Hotel and Restaurant Employees (1911–21). She was also an officer of the Chicago Federation of Labor and a member of the executive board of the Chicago Women's Trade Union League.

2. On Apr. 27, 1917, SG replied that he was "in full accord" with the suggestion and that "women will be represented on committees appointed" (SG to Christman, Files of the Committee on Labor, RG 62, Records of the Council of National Defense, DNA). With few exceptions, however, he did not appoint women to Committee on Labor subcommittees other than the subcommittee on Women in Industry. For a discussion of those appointments, see "A Circular," May 16, 1917, below.

3. The HOTEL and Restaurant Employees' International Alliance and Bartenders' International League of America.

4. Mary Anderson (1872–1964) was a member of the general executive board of the Boot and Shoe Workers' Union from 1906 to 1919 and an organizer for the National Women's Trade Union League from 1911 to 1918. During World War I she served on the subcommittee on Women in Industry, as assistant director of the Women's Division of the Army Ordnance Department (1918), and as assistant director (1918–19) and then director (1919–20) of the Women-in-Industry Service of the Department of Labor (DOL). She later served as director of the Women's Bureau of the DOL (1920–44).

5. The BOOT and Shoe Workers' Union.

6. Agnes NESTOR was vice-president of the International Glove Workers' Union of America (1903–6, 1915–38) and president of the Chicago branch of the Women's Trade Union League (1913–48). During World War I she served on the subcommittee on Women in Industry and on the Council's Committee on Women's Defense Work.

7. The International GLOVE Workers' Union of America.

8. Olive M. Sullivan, a Chicago stenographer, became secretary of the Chicago Women's Trade Union League later in 1917 and served in that office until mid-1919.

9. The AFL chartered Stenographers' and Typists' Association 12,755 of Chicago in 1909. The union changed its name to the Office Employes' Association in 1913.

10. Elisabeth CHRISTMAN of Chicago served as secretary-treasurer of the Glove Workers (1913–31) and was a member of the subcommittee on Women in Industry.

11. Margaret Angela Haley (1861–1939) was a founder of the Chicago Teachers' Federation in 1897 (from 1916 to 1917, American Federation of Teachers 1) and served as its full-time business agent from 1901 until her death. She served as an organizer for the American Federation of Teachers from 1916 to 1917 and was a member of the subcommittee on Women in Industry.

12. Lydia J. Trowbridge of Winnetka, Ill., was vice-president and later president (1918–20) of American Federation of Teachers 3 (the Chicago Federation of Women High School Teachers), a member of the board of trustees of the American Federation of Teachers (1917–18), and a member of the subcommittee on Women in Industry.

13. Mary McEnerney (d. 1946), a member of the subcommittee on Women in Industry, was secretary of International Brotherhood of Bookbinders 30 of Chicago (1905–46) and later a vice-president of the Illinois State Federation of Labor (1922–46).

14. Agnes Johnson, who served on the subcommittee on Women in Industry, was a member of Boot and Shoe Workers' local 94 of Chicago and a salaried organizer for the Boot and Shoe Workers from 1917 until 1926.

15. Mary E. Haney, a seamstress and president of United Garment Workers of America 33 of Chicago, served on the subcommittee on Women in Industry and was later an organizer and secretary of the Chicago Women's Trade Union League.

To William Spencer

Washington, D.C. April 27, 1917

Mr. Wm. J. Spencer,
Secretary-Treasurer Building Trades Department, A.F. of L.,
A.F. of L. Building, Washington, D.C.
Dear Sir and Brother:

At the meeting of the Executive Council this morning you presented a matter for our consideration. You stated that there was a proposal to workmen that they work longer than the regulated hours of labor, that is, longer than the eight hour day and that when such over work is performed the workmen should receive compensation as for "straight time."[1]

This matter received the serious consideration of the Executive Council and I am directed to advise you that the proposal to pay overtime as for straight time would be most injurious, if accepted.

First: The eight hour work day should be maintained as far as possible and only in case of an immediate emergency and for an exceedingly limited period of time should there be overtime. It has been demonstrated that a longer work day than eight hours is unprofitable, unhealthful, uneconomic.

Second: If for any limited period to meet an immediate emergency more than eight hours work shall be required in any day, the compensation should be as for time and one-half.

If straight time is paid for overtime, the hours of labor will be lengthened to that overtime which will become the accepted rule of the hours of daily labor; for the payment of time and one-half for overtime is not to be regarded as a benefit to the workers, but as a penalty to the employers so that the day's work shall not be lengthened without its absolute necessity.

If workmen would voluntarily accept straight pay for overtime in one trade and in one city then employers elsewhere and the government would take advantage and insist upon a like "privilege" there can be no doubt, and thus a period of re-action would set in and the longer work day generally practiced throughout America.

The workers of our country are doing and will continue to do their level best in industrial or any other service. They cannot be accused of slacking, shirking, or lack of patriotism but it is necessary to check the unwarranted greed or hysteria upon those who would unnecessarily sacrifice, by undermining the health, the strength, as well as the spirit of the workers of the United States upon which our government will depend for its safety and defense.

Fraternally yours,   (signed) Samuel Gompers
President   American Federation of Labor

By Direction of the Executive Council of the American Federation of Labor.

TLtcSr, Files of the Office of the President, General Correspondence, reel 83, frames 479–80, *AFL Records*. Typed notation: "Copy."

1. William Spencer had reported that the Washington, D.C., district council of the United Brotherhood of Carpenters and Joiners of America had directed its members to work ten hours a day straight time on the construction of buildings at Ft. Myer, Va., pending advice on the matter from the AFL Executive Council (Executive Council Records, Minutes, reel 5, frame 1393, *AFL Records*).

To William Hamrick[1]

Advisory Commission [of the Council
of National Defense]
May 4, 1917.

Mr. W. P. Hamrick,
General Superintendent, Pacific Mills,
Columbia, South Carolina.
Dear Sir:

Your letter of recent date to the Honorable A. F. Lever,[2] Chairman
of the Committee on Agriculture, House of Representatives, was transmitted to me.

As you say in your letter, there is on foot a movement to render child
labor and compulsory education inoperative, or to secure the suspension of provisions restricting hours of work. This movement seems to
be part of a larger movement to nullify or to destroy all humanitarian safeguards that protect the health and welfare of those who work.
Those directing this movement have taken advantage of the first period of transition during which the people are appalled by their new
problems and are fearful of what the immediate future may contain
for them; there is an effort being made to confuse change and activity
that will direct intelligent plans for self-defense.

The declaration of war means that the activities and resources of this
country shall be diverted to an entirely different purpose from what
obtains under conditions of peace. Transition to a war basis means a
re-direction of activity, not a change of fundamental principles and
policies. Under all conditions the purpose of our government is to
conserve and further the interests of humanity. Those standards which
safeguard the health and well-being of the people cannot justifiably
be suspended or removed unless the nation is reduced to the direst
extremity. We are not facing such emergencies, nor have we exhausted our resources to such a degree that we would be justified in setting aside safeguards that insure the physical and mental well-being
of future citizens. In protecting the childhood of the nation we are
protecting the nation itself. This protection is just as necessary as the
military defense of the nation. There can be no justification for ren-
dering child labor laws inoperative during this war except when it
shall have been demonstrated that all other methods have failed and
an extreme emergency shall have been proved to that body charged
with the defense of the nation—the Council of National Defense.

You say in your letter that to suspend the child labor law[3] would
be of advantage to manufacturers in helping them to overcome the

shortage of labor. Until the manufacturers shall have first tried to re-adjust their industries to a war basis, shall have made all mechanical substitutes for human labor wherever that is possible, and shall have done everything within their power to meet the needs of the nation, and then demonstrate the inadequacy of the number of workers to be secured and the indispensable character of the product under consideration, they will have no good reason for demanding that the children shall be deprived of their right to opportunity for physical and mental growth in order that the industrial needs of the country may be served. The men and women of the country must first try to defend the nation and do its work before they call upon the children to give like service.

Yours very truly,
Chairman,   Committee on Labor.

TLp, Files of the Office of the President, General Correspondence, reel 83, frames 624–26, *AFL Records*.

1. William Pinckney Hamrick was general superintendent of the Pacific Mills in Columbia, S.C., from 1917 until 1941.

2. Asbury Francis Lever (1875–1940) was a Democratic congressman from South Carolina (1901–19). Hamrick wrote Lever on Apr. 19, 1917, urging the suspension of the federal child labor law during the war (Files of the Office of the President, General Correspondence, reel 83, frame 321, *AFL Records*).

3. Federal child labor legislation (the Keating-Owen Act) was signed into law on Sept. 1, 1916, and went into effect on Sept. 1, 1917 (U.S. *Statutes at Large*, 39: 675–76). It barred from interstate and foreign commerce the products of mines or quarries that employed children under sixteen, and articles produced in factories, mills, or other manufacturing establishments that employed children under fourteen or that allowed children between the ages of fourteen and sixteen to work more than eight hours a day or more than six days a week. The Supreme Court declared the law unconstitutional in 1918.

From Albert Berres

Metal Trades Department
American Federation of Labor
Washington, D.C., May 5, 1917

Dear Sir & Brother:

I have had handed to me Secretary Daniels' reply[1] to your letter of April 28th[2] in which you endorsed the brief submitted by the Electrical Workers employed in the Brooklyn Navy Yard which set forth the reasons why they should receive an increase in their wage rate.[3]

The fact that the Naval Appropriation bill contains a provision granting an increase of five and ten per cent to employees of the navy yards beginning July 1st, is no reason why the Electrical Workers should not receive an increase based upon the data submitted. In other words, after they receive the percentage increase granted by Congress they will still be working for twenty cents less than the data shows they are receiving in the locality in which the Brooklyn Yard is located.

I desire to ask what step you propose taking next in order to convince the Secretary of the Navy that it is necessary that these matters should receive the consideration due them and that the mere fact that the provision in the Naval bill calls for an increase, is not sufficient to bring the rates of wages in some cases up to the prevailing rate in stated zones.

I wish also to say that there is not sufficient attention and time being given us to present matters of vital import to these employees before the proper officials at this time. There seems to be time for everyone having something to sell or to recommend but there is not time to give to the representatives of labor. The time is here when Government officials must be made to understand that we are no small factor in this crisis and that we demand proper recognition. Unless this is given they can not expect the hearty and loyal support of the mechanics in the Government service or elsewhere.

I hope you will find the time to have a conference with Secretary Daniels and that you will bring to the attention of the Council of National Defense that it is just as essential, in fact more so, to hear what the representatives of labor have to say, than it is that they meet with the representatives of other interests. With best wishes, I am

Fraternally yours,   A. J. Berres
Secretary-Treasurer.

TLS, Files of the Office of the President, General Correspondence, reel 83, frame 646, *AFL Records.*

1. Josephus Daniels wrote SG on May 2, 1917, that the Department of the Navy would not consider the request of electrical workers at the New York navy yard for a wage increase because of the 5– to 10–percent increase mandated by the Naval Appropriation Act passed earlier in the year (Files of the Office of the President, General Correspondence, reel 83, frame 578, *AFL Records*).

2. SG to Daniels, Apr. 28, 1917, reel 221, vol. 233, p. 162, SG Letterbooks, DLC.

3. SG had met with a committee of electrical workers from the Brooklyn Navy Yard on the afternoon of Apr. 28, 1917.

To the Executive Committee of the Petrograd Council of Workers' and Soldiers' Deputies[1]

Washington, D.C., May 6, 1917.

Executive Committee of the Council of Workmen's and Soldiers'
Deputies.
Petrograd, Russia.

The gravest crisis in the world's history is now hanging in the balance and the course which Russia will pursue may have a determining influence whether democracy or autocracy shall prevail. That democracy and freedom will finally prevail there can be no doubt in the minds of men who know, but the cost, the time lost and the sacrifices which would ensue from lack of united action may be appalling. It is to avoid this that I address you. In view of the grave crisis through which the Russian people are passing we assure you that you can rely absolutely upon the whole-hearted support and co-operation of the American people in the great war against our common enemy *Kaiserism.* In the fulfillment of that cause the present American government has the support of ninety-nine percent of the American people, including the working class of both the cities and of the agricultural sections.

In free America as in free Russia the agitators for a peace favorable to Prussian militarism have been allowed to express their opinions so that the conscious and unconscious tools of the Kaiser appear more influential than they really are. You should realize the truth of the situation. There are but few in America willing to allow Kaiserism and its allies to continue their rule over those non-German peoples who wish to be free from their domination. Should we not protest against the pro-Kaiser Socialist interpretation of the demand for "No annexation," namely, that all oppressed non-German peoples shall be compelled to remain under the domination of Prussia and her lackeys Austria and Turkey. Should we not rather accept the better interpretation—that there must be no forcible annexations, but that every people must be free to choose any allegiance it desires, as demanded by the Council of Workmen's and Soldiers' Deputies.

Like yourselves, we are opposed to all punitive and improper indemnities. We denounce the onerous punitive indemnities already imposed by the Kaiser upon the people of Serbia, Belgium and Poland.

America's workers share the view of the Council of Workmen's and Soldiers' Deputies that the only way in which the German people can bring the war to an early end is by imitating the glorious example of the Russian people compelling the abdication of the Hohenzollerns and the Hapsburgs and driving the tyrannous nobility, bureaucracy and the military caste from power.

Let the German Socialists attend to this and cease their false pretenses and underground plotting to bring about an abortive peace in the interest of Kaiserism and the ruling class. Let them cease calling pretended "international" conferences[2] at the instigation or connivance of the Kaiser. Let them cease their intrigues to cajole the Russian and American working people to interpret your demand, "No annexation, no indemnities" in a way to leave undiminished the prestige and the power of the German military caste.

Now that Russian autocracy is overthrown neither the American government nor the American people apprehend that the wisdom and experience of Russia in the coming constitutional assembly will adopt any form of government other than the one best suited to your needs. We feel confident that no message, no individual emissary, and no commission has been sent or will be sent with authority to offer any advice whatever to Russia as to the conduct of her internal affairs. Any commission that may be sent will help Russia in any way that she desires to combat Kaiserism wherever it exists or may manifest itself.

Word has reached us that false reports of an American purpose and of American opinions contrary to the above statement have gained some circulation in Russia. We denounce these reports as the criminal work of desperate pro-Kaiser propagandists circulated with the intent to deceive and to arouse hostile feelings between the two great democracies of the world. The Russian people should know that these activities are only additional manifestations of the "Dark Forces" with which Russia has been only too familiar in the unhappy past.

The American government, the American people, the American labor movement, are wholeheartedly with the Russian workers, the Russian masses in the great effort to maintain the freedom you have already achieved and to solve the grave problems yet before you. We earnestly appeal to you to make common cause with us to abolish all forms of autocracy and despotism and to establish and maintain for generations yet unborn the priceless treasures of justice, freedom, democracy, and humanity.

American Federation of Labor.
Samuel Gompers, President.

T and AWSr, RG 59, General Records of the Department of State, DNA.

1. This cable was initially drafted by Charles Flint, Elihu Root, and Melville Stone and then brought to SG for his approval. Flint, an industrial capitalist and trust organizer, had founded the American Committee for the Encouragement of Democratic Government in Russia in March 1917; at his invitation, SG had joined the group in early April. Root had recently been named by President Woodrow Wilson to lead an

American commission to Russia (see "To Robert Lansing," Apr. 19, 1917, n. 1, above). Stone was general manager of the Associated Press.

SG met with Flint and William English Walling on May 5 and substantially revised the document, and he met with Flint, Walling, and Frank Polk, counselor to the State Department, on May 6 for further discussion and revision of the cable ([R. Lee Guard], Memorandum, May 5, Files of the Office of the President, General Correspondence, reel 83, frames 662–63, *AFL Records;* Flint to SG, May 19, ibid., reel 84, frames 3–4). The State Department cabled the message to the American ambassador in Petrograd on May 7, and the AFL released the text to the press the same day. Another, slightly different version of the cable, typed on the letterhead of Flint's committee, is in private hands.

2. On Mar. 28, 1917, Karl Durr, secretary of the Schweizerischen Gewerkschaftsbund (Swiss Federation of Labor), proposed that an international conference of trade union delegates meet at Berne to draw up labor demands that could be submitted to the peace conference following the war. On May 14 Jan Oudegeest, head of the auxiliary office of the International Federation of Trade Unions (IFTU), called for an IFTU conference with the same agenda, to meet in Stockholm on June 8. Trade union delegates from the Central Powers and several neutral countries met in Stockholm in response to Oudegeest's invitation, but the labor movements of the United States, Great Britain, France, Switzerland, and Belgium did not send delegates. Nor did delegates from the United States, Great Britain, France, or Belgium attend an international trade union conference that eventually met in Berne that October. The AFL Executive Council rejected the meetings, involving as they did representatives from enemy nations, as "premature and untimely" and likely to "place obstacles in the way to democratize the institutions of the world and hazard the liberties and opportunities for freedom of all peoples" (SG to [Herman] Lindqvist, June 27, 1917, Files of the Office of the President, General Correspondence, reel 85, frame 424, *AFL Records*).

Meanwhile, during the spring and summer of 1917, various socialist groups—the International Socialist Bureau, the All-Russian Council of Workers' and Soldiers' Deputies in Petrograd, and a Dutch-Scandinavian committee organized by Swedish socialist Karl Branting—called for an international socialist meeting in Stockholm in August 1917, in an attempt to bring about an early end to the war. This conference was cancelled after the American, British, French, and Italian governments refused to issue passports to delegates from their countries—the American delegation included Morris Hillquit, Victor Berger, and Algernon Lee—and only representatives from Russia, the Central Powers, and neutral countries were able to attend. In SG's opinion, this conference "was called by the German socialists and certain other notoriously pro-German agitators in other countries either to bring about a Kaiser-dictated peace under the deceptive catch-phrase 'no annexations, no indemnities,' or in the hope of deceiving the Russian socialists into betraying the great western democracies into consenting to a separate peace." It was to thwart Russian participation in the conference, he said, that he sent this cable to the Council of Workers' and Soldier's Deputies at Petrograd (SG to Léon Jouhaux, Louis Dubreuilh, and G. J. Wardle, May 7, 1917, ibid., reel 83, frame 691).

To Godfrey Ott[1]

May 7, 1917.

Mr. G. A. Ott,
Business Representative, United Garment Workers of America,[2]
702 Bromo Seltzer Tower Bldg., Baltimore, Maryland.
Dear Sir and Brother:

Your communication[3] of a few days ago with reference to the information which you say was secured through the press, that the Henry Sonneborn & Company of Baltimore had secured a contract amounting to a million and a half, is hereby acknowledged.

I am aware of course that this firm has been consistent in its opposition to your organization as well as the general labor movement. You suggest that some plan be evolved whereby this and other unfair firms can be prevented from securing government contracts.

For your information I desire to say that practically all government contracts are let upon the competitive basis, the law requiring the various departments to call for bids for the manufacture of supplies for the government, where not manufactured in its own establishments. The letting of government contracts being regulated by law, the lowest bidder usually secures the contract.

In order to change this system it would be necessary to change the existing law, which probably could not be done at this time. It is quite likely that the contracts to be let by the government in the future will be of such enormous size that the fair or union clothing manufacturing establishments will be awarded contracts, so that the non-union houses will not be able to secure a monopoly of this work.

The American Federation of Labor is doing everything possible to maintain the present standards of work and the Council of National Defense has gone on record in favor of that policy. The Federation will exercise every influence it has to secure government contracts for union houses wherever that is possible. You may rest assured that we shall do our very best to guard the best interests of the organized working people of the country.

For your further information let me say that the Naval Appropriation Law passed by the first session of the Sixty-fourth Congress, and approved March 4, 1917, Public No. 391, contains the following clause:

"That in case of national emergency the President is authorized to suspend provisions of law prohibiting more than eight hours labor in any one day of persons engaged upon work covered by contracts with the United States; Provided further, That the wages of persons employed upon such contracts shall be computed on a basic day rate of eight hours work, with overtime rates to be paid for at not less than time and one-half for all hours work in excess of eight hours."

Notwithstanding the fact that this section is incorporated in the Naval Appropriation Law, it is worded so broadly that it applies to all contracts made by the United States with private employers or contractors. The American Federation of Labor will exert itself in behalf of the full enforcement of this broadly written law, and I think it would be of distinct advantage in the case that you have reported to me concerning the contract secured by the Sonneborn Company.

With kind regards and best wishes, I am,

Yours fraternally,   Saml Gompers.
President,   American Federation of Labor.

TLpS, reel 221, vol. 233, pp. 428–30, SG Letterbooks, DLC.

1. Godfrey (variously Gottfried) A. Ott, a Baltimore clothing cutter, was business agent and financial secretary (1917–24?) of United Garment Workers of America 15 (Clothing Cutters and Trimmers) of Baltimore.

2. The United GARMENT Workers of America.

3. Ott to SG, Apr. 25, 1917, Files of the Office of the President, General Correspondence, reel 83, frame 451, *AFL Records.*

To John O'Connell[1]

May 9, 1917

James [*sic*] O'Connell,
Labor Temple, San Francisco, Cal.

Have had most interesting conference with Attorney-general[2] regarding the newly discovered evidence in Mooney case.[3] While the Department of Justice can not take up the matter I am to have conference with other representatives of the government and hope that a new and fair trial may be accorded Mooney.

Samuel Gompers

TWSr, AFL Microfilm Convention File, reel 28, frame 1616, *AFL Records.*

1. John A. O'Connell was a member of International Brotherhood of Teamsters, Chauffeurs, Stablemen, and Helpers of America 85 of San Francisco. He served as secretary and business agent of the San Francisco Labor Council from 1913 to 1928 and as the council's secretary-treasurer from 1928 until his death in 1948.

2. Thomas Watt Gregory (1861–1933) served as attorney general of the United States from 1914 to 1919.

3. Evidence was uncovered in March 1917 that Frank Oxman, a key prosecution

witness in the case against Thomas MOONEY, had committed perjury in his testimony and had suborned perjury from Edward Rigall to support his statements. These revelations, made public in April, set off protests and demonstrations at home and abroad in support of Mooney, who was to be executed on May 17. After meeting with Gregory on May 9, SG asked Mooney's lawyer for photographic copies of Oxman's letters to Rigall, and he turned these over to Secretary of State Robert Lansing on May 10. Lansing gave the copies to President Woodrow Wilson, urging him to ask California governor William Stephens to commute Mooney's sentence or delay his execution until the perjury charges against Oxman could be investigated. Wilson agreed and on May 11 wired Stephens, who replied that Mooney's sentence had been automatically stayed when he appealed his conviction to the California supreme court on the grounds of perjured evidence.

From Louis Lochner[1] et al.

New York NY [May 10, 1917]

Strong group representing labor socialism peace religion politics plans first American conference for democracy and terms of peace New York May thirtieth[2] Basis of invitation to be acceptance in principle of following speedy and universal peace no indemnities no forcible annexations no foreign alliances international organization after the war statement of terms by our government opposition to conscription democratization of diplomacy defense of free speech and press opposition to lowering industrial standards heavy taxation of war industries and incomes May we use your name on call for conference Please reply[3] Wire collect Room Sixty Holland House New York

Emily Balch[4]
Joseph Cannon
Morris Hillquit[5]
Judah Magnes[6]
Louis Lochner Sec.

TWSr, Files of the Office of the President, General Correspondence, reel 83, frames 764–65, *AFL Records.*

1. Louis P. Lochner (1887–1975) served as secretary of the Chicago Peace Society (1914–15), recording secretary of the League to Enforce Peace (1915), manager of the Ford Peace Ship expedition (1915–16), and executive secretary of the People's Council of America for Democracy and Peace (1917–18).

2. The First American Conference for Democracy and Terms of Peace met in New York City, May 30–31, 1917. Attended by some four hundred pacifists and socialists, it called for peace without territorial annexations or punitive indemnities, advocated the repeal of conscription, and demanded that the United States make a separate peace with Germany in exchange for an end to unrestricted submarine warfare. The conference adopted resolutions leading to the establishment of the People's Council.

3. See "To Louis Lochner," May 10, 1917, below.

4. Emily Greene Balch (1867–1961), chair of the Department of Economics and Sociology at Wellesley College, later served as secretary-treasurer (1919–22) and secretary (1934–35) of the Women's International League for Peace and Freedom.

5. Morris HILLQUIT was a leading figure in the Socialist Party of America and served as a member of its national executive committee (1907–12, 1916–19, 1922–33).

6. Rabbi Judah Leon Magnes (1877–1948) was chairman of the Jewish Community (Kehillah) of New York City (1909–22).

To Louis Lochner

Washington, D.C., May 10, 1917.

Mr. Louis Lochner,
Room 60, Holland House, New York, N.Y.
Telegram[1] received. I prefer not to ally myself with the conscious or unconscious agents of the Kaiser in America.

Samuel Gompers.

TWSr, Files of the Office of the President, General Correspondence, reel 83, frame 774, *AFL Records.*

1. See "From Louis Lochner et al.," May 10, 1917, above.

To Allen Thurman

Washington, D.C., May 11, 1917.

Mr. A. G. Thurman,
Secretary, Local Union No. 64, United Brotherhood of
    Carpenters and Joiners of America,[1]
300 Commercial Bldg., Louisville, Ky.
Dear Sir and Brother:

Your letter of May 2 received, in which you protest against the appointment of Mr. Thruston Ballard[2] as Chairman of the Committee on High Cost of Living, which is a sub-committee of the Committee of Labor and assists me in my work as a member of the Advisory Commission.

The Advisory Commission of the Council of National Defense is part of the government machinery for dealing with the defense of the nation in the war in which we are engaged. As a member of that

Commission and as Chairman of my Advisory Committee on Labor, I act in the capacity of a government agent.

The problem which confronts my committee is a national one concerning all of the elements that constitute the nation. The purpose of the committee is to reach an adjustment of industrial relations so as to protect wage-earners who render war service.

The committee must deal with employers of all types, and must protect workers, both organized and unorganized. As employers who are friendly to organized labor and employers who are antagonistic to the aims and purposes of the labor movement both have a part in determining industrial relations, it is necessary that they be represented on this committee in order to reach a general understanding and agreement. It is for this reason that I have asked to serve on this committee employers of both union and non-union labor.

The name of my committee is Committee on Labor, Including Conservation and Welfare of Workers. The standards which are the basis for the work of the committee are the standards established by the organized labor movement. Everything that the committee has done has been to maintain these standards. The committee has been the agency by which the aims and views of the organized labor movement could be directly presented to the Council of National Defense.

Enclosed are copies of a resolution and amplification adopted by the Advisory Commission of the Council of National Defense. Both of these statements originated in my Committee on Labor. From them is evident the kind of work the committee is doing. Association with members of organized labor and employers of union labor in the work of the Committee on Labor cannot be without effect upon employers who have been hostile to organized labor. When these employers of non-union labor have placed upon them the responsibility for maintaining conditions that will enable the government to secure continuous output of necessary supplies and mobilize the good will of workers, they will have a new sense of the function and the work of the organized labor movement.

These, in brief, were reasons that constituted [. . .] of my thought in asking employers to accept membership on the committee.

The other members of the Advisory Commission have made up their committees wholly of employers and experts. Naturally the workers have criticized the makeup of these committees. For instance, the railroad men very justly claim that they ought to be represented on the committee that has to do with transportation, and the coal miners have stated that the men who do the work in the mines ought to be represented on the committee that has to do with the production of coal. You can see, therefore, that had I not appointed employers upon my Committee on Labor I would have been open to the same criticism—that I had not sought the advice and counsel of all elements concerned in production.

With best wishes, I am

Fraternally yours,
President,　American Federation of Labor.

TLc, Files of the Office of the President, General Correspondence, reel 83, frames 825–27, *AFL Records.*

1. The United Brotherhood of CARPENTERS and Joiners of America.
2. Samuel Thruston Ballard (1855–1926), a former member of the U.S. Commission on Industrial Relations, was chairman of the subcommittee on Cost of Living and Domestic Economy of the Committee on Labor of the Advisory Commission of the Council of National Defense. He was vice-president of the Louisville, Ky., flour manufacturing firm of Ballard and Ballard and of the Louisville National Bank, and he later served as lieutenant-governor of Kentucky (1920–23).

A Circular

Advisory Commission of the Council of National Defense
Washington, D.C., May 16, 1917.

To Trade Union Women, Greeting:

Inquiries received at this office[1] show that there is a misunderstanding of that part of the work of my Committee on Labor which has to do with women in industry. An erroneous idea, which is strikingly general, is that wage-earning women are not represented by women with trade union cards in the sub-committee on Women in Industry. From the inquiries it is evident that many have only a vague or an incorrect conception of the organization of the Council of National Defense and its various advisory agencies. The following will clarify the situation.

The Naval Appropriations Law of 1916 provided for a Council of National Defense to be composed of the following members of the President's Cabinet: Secretary of War, Secretary of the Interior, Postmaster General, Secretary of Commerce, Secretary of Agriculture and Secretary of Labor. The law further provided for an Advisory Commission to consist of seven civilians. The President of the American Federation of Labor was appointed by President Wilson as a member of the Advisory Commission. In order to facilitate its work, the Council of National Defense and the Advisory Commission made each member of the latter, chairman of a committee, to assist him in the work of national defense apportioned to him. The undersigned was made chairman of the Committee on Labor, including Conservation and Welfare of Workers. This Committee on Labor acts in a capacity advisory to and co-operative with the chairman of the committee in his work as a member of the Advisory Commission.

I invited to assist me in the work of this Committee on Labor representative trade unionists, employers of labor, financiers, publicists, experts in various scientific fields and students. The large Committee on Labor consists of approximately three hundred members.

An Executive Committee was appointed to plan the work of the committee. On this Executive Committee there are, in addition to myself and my assistant in my work as a member of the Advisory Commission, Mr. James W. Sullivan, (member of I.T.U.), five trade unionists.

Among the committees provided for by the Executive Committee is the sub-committee on Women in Industry. When preparing for this committee an additional number of trade union women were added to the General Committee on Labor.

Since there is no provision for salaries or expenses for any member on any sub-committee, and as the work of the Committee on Women in Industry in order to be effective must be continuous, it was necessary to appoint some woman as chairman who could afford to give all of her time and perform the work gratuitously.

The names of several trade union women were considered while the chairmanship was under consideration, but all were performing indispensable service to their organizations and were financially dependent upon salaries received for their work. They could not continue their work for their organizations and take up the additional work as chairman of this committee. For these reasons, together with her general sympathy and proven ability, Mrs. Borden Harriman[2] was selected as chairman of the committee. The committee consists of 43 members, of whom 24 are members of trade unions.

Recently the Council of National Defense appointed a Woman's Board.[3] One of the members of this board is Agnes Nestor, who is also a member of my sub-committee on Women in Industry. It is evident that this committee will be able to co-operate with the Woman's Board through Miss Nestor, who will be in touch with the work done by the committee.

It seems to me that in view of these facts ample provision has been made for protecting the interests of women in industry so far as the machinery of the Council of National Defense is concerned and, as all readers can see for themselves, trade union women have a representation that will enable them to protect the standards of women in industry and to assist these women in asserting and maintaining their rights. The declarations and the positions taken by women who are members of the Woman's Board are of such a character as to warrant the opinion that this board also is fully aware that industrial justice is fundamental in protecting the interests of women. Much serious consideration has been given to this matter in order that the rights of women may be protected as well as the interests of the entire labor movement. The tendency is apparent that in the months to come the number of women going into industry will be vastly increased. It will take the united effort of all to secure the protection of these women who shall go into industry and new occupations.

I hope, therefore, that the hearty support and cooperation of every woman and man in the labor movement can be counted upon for this work, which is of fundamental importance.

The following are the names of the members of this committee as thus far appointed.[4] The work of the committee is yet in a formative stage.

Sincerely yours,   Saml Gompers.
Chairman   Committee on Labor

TLS, Files of the Office of the President, General Correspondence, reel 83, frames 932–33, *AFL Records.*

1. Letters of inquiry from trade union women can be found in the Files of the Committee on Labor, RG 62, Records of the Council of National Defense, DNA.

2. Florence Jaffray Harriman (1870–1967) served on the board of managers of the New York State Reformatory for Women (1906–18) and on the U.S. Commission on Industrial Relations (1913–16).

3. The Committee on Women's Defense Work (later the Woman's Committee) of the Council of National Defense.

4. The list of the women already appointed to the subcommittee on Women in Industry can be found in Files of the Office of the President, General Correspondence, reel 83, frames 935–36, *AFL Records.*

To Thomas Cranwell[1]

Washington, May 19, 1917.

Mr. T. G. Cranwell,
President, Continental Can Company,
Syracuse, New York.
Dear Sir:

In reply to your letter of May 11:[2]

Permit me to present to you a general statement bearing on the case which you submit to me. That case is that you, as President of the Continental Can Company, desire "a modification of our working hours for female help."

You asked some weeks ago the Industrial Board of the Department of Labor and Industry in Pennsylvania to authorize this modification. In support of your request, the manager[3] of a can manufactory of your company at Canonsburg, Pa., stated that male help is a scarcity in the Pittsburgh district, in which Canonsburg is situated. You plead that there is an extreme need of cans in the canning districts, as set forth in a letter written by Secretary Redfield, of the Department of Commerce. You also say that your women employes are anxious to work overtime.

As an argument in support of your request to the Pennsylvania Industrial Board you cite as a precedent the fact that in the state of New York "the Governor has been given authority to suspend the operation of the labor law in so far as it applied to women working overtime during the continuance of the war." That which prevents you from going ahead with your proposed overtime is a letter from Mrs. Samuel Semple[4] of the Pennsylvania Industrial Board, giving the opinion of that Board that, "at least for the present, the established standards of hours and working conditions in Pennsylvania should remain undisturbed." Mrs. Semple says, "This decision has been reached after consultation with the Council of National Defense, and is in line with the policy which the governor[5] of this state has presented for adoption in this state."

Mrs. Semple refers to the experience of Great Britain illustrating the loss of ultimate efficiency coming from the abandonment of established labor standards, and also to the policy adopted by the State of New Jersey in following the recommendations of the Council of National Defense.

Really Mr. Cranwell, after reading your letter and the copies of the enclosed letters written by you to Dr. E. E. Pratt,[6] Chief of the Bureau of Foreign and Domestic Commerce, and the one written by your Canonsburg manager,[7] and of the letter by Mrs. Semple giving the opinion of the Pennsylvania Industrial Board, I gather the impression that you have been exercising extraordinary energy in this phase of the prosecution of your business. How you have come to entertain the idea that you could successfully apply to me in the matter for "some assistance," as you phrase it, I am at a loss to understand.

My efforts have persistently been in the direction of maintaining the highest standards established in industry up to the present time, and especially those relating to the employment of women and children.

As to the reasons you advance in support of your request, they do not seem to me to be well-founded. While the Governor of New York, it is true, is given authority in a bill not yet a law to suspend the operation of the labor law in its application to women working overtime during the continuance of the war, that authority has not been called into exercise. On the contrary, any proposed suspension of the law by the Governor will be watchfully supervised by a large number of public-spirited persons prepared to urge the claims of society in general against the interests of those employers in particular who have not yet heard the call of patriotism and humanity. Your reference to this authority given the Governor of New York is made in such phraseology as to be interpreted as a statement that women are now working overtime in New York by reason of a suspension of the labor law on that subject. I take it that the wording of your letter on this point has not been intentionally equivocal.

As to the anxiety of your women employes to work overtime, it is unfortunately true that some women in the employ of certain manufacturers do at times manifest a willingness to work to an extent that is daily exhausting, injurious to themselves permanently, and detrimental to their families eventually. To what extent this alleged anxiety to work is true no one may know, for a fact which obscures certainty in the matter is that many persons struggling for a living give such answers to questions put by their employers as they know will please those employers.

With respect to your assertions relative to the scarcity of men and women, it is to be regretted that there is no public method by which such assertions may be proved or disproved.

There may be a scarcity of some kinds of labor in your district at lower wages than are acceptable to unemployed persons who might fill a demand at what they regard as living wages at steady work. Labor of all kinds may be scarce in one town or district of the country while not many miles distant there may be a surplus; or there may be a scarcity of labor for the time being while all concerned may know that the work on which hundreds or thousands are employed is to come to an end in the immediate future. At the present time, throughout the country, general contracts in various branches of industry are expiring without a probability of employment being soon given to the labor which has been engaged upon them.

In all these cases, the absence of public employment agencies which might indicate the movement of supply and demand of workers leaves the interested observers without other help than their own or other men's guess-work.

I would be interested, Mr. Cranwell, in any statement which you might make with regard to efforts made by you, or other employers in your district, to substantiate your assertions with respect to a scarcity of such labor as might with co-operative management and public spirit be brought to the doors of your manufactory.

A reference is made by you to the "extreme need of cans, particularly as set forth in a letter of Mr. Redfield," Secretary of the Department of Commerce. I am in position to say that in the course of a conference, in which Mr. Redfield, officials of the Amalgamated Association of Iron, Steel and Tin Workers, the Secretary of Labor, and others were present, the representations of the union men were such as to raise in the mind of Mr. Redfield the question whether any of the deficit in the output of cans was to be laid at the door of labor, especially as the union representatives stated that they were able to show that in certain places their members were not working full time.

Mr. Redfield himself has just urged upon the National Association of Manufacturers (May 16) at their annual convention[8] in New York, the necessity for preserving the standards of labor.[9]

Finally, Mr. Cranwell, I beg leave to direct your attention to the address[10] of the President of the United States, made to the Committee on Labor of the Advisory Commission of the Council of National Defense, at the White House, May 15. Too long to reproduce here, that address contains these two sentences concerning the possibility of lowering the standards in the employment of labor:

"I have been very much alarmed at one or two things that have happened; at the apparent inclination of the legislatures of one or two of our states to set aside even temporarily the laws which have safeguarded the standards of labor and of life. I think nothing would be more deplorable than that."

Reviewing the foregoing facts bearing upon your request, I am persuaded, sir, that it is your duty to bestow further reflection upon its consequences if granted, as well as upon what you owe to your country and upon the evil example of regarding a thriving business as justification of all the means employed in its prosecution. Further, since we are now in a crisis demanding sacrifice, the first obligation for sacrifice rests on those best able to bear it.

What efforts have you made outside of your immediate district to attract labor to your employ at wages which would pay the workers to enter upon the term of employment you can offer them? Could you not by somewhat raising wages considerably increase the class in the community upon which you and your fellow can-makers might draw for the labor necessary to fill your shops?

Suppose you and your fellow manufacturers were willing to suspend entirely, in this hour of the country's emergency, the pursuit of profits; would there be any possibility of a shortage in tin cans?

Permit me to assure you that my letter is not intended to be merely discursive or critical, but to be reflective and suggestive, and I earnestly hope it may be helpful to the great cause in which our country finds itself contesting.

Very truly yours,   Saml Gompers.

Chairman,   Committee on Labor.

TLpS, Files of the Office of the President, Letterbooks, Advisory Commission, Council of National Defense, reel 20, pp. 688–91, *AFL Records.*

1. Thomas George Cranwell was president of the Continental Can Co. from 1904 to 1927.

2. Cranwell to SG, May 11, 1917, Files of the Office of the President, General Correspondence, reel 83, frame 787, *AFL Records.*

3. Jessie E. Abrams.

4. H. M. Semple to Abrams, Apr. 30, 1917, Files of the Office of the President, General Correspondence, reel 83, frame 529, *AFL Records.* Helen M. Semple, a resident of Titusville, Pa., was a member of the Pennsylvania Industrial Board from 1913 to 1927.

5. Martin Grove Brumbaugh (1862–1930) served as Republican governor of Pennsylvania from 1915 to 1919.

6. [Cranwell] to E. E. Pratt, May 11, 1917, Files of the Office of the President, General Correspondence, reel 83, frame 789, *AFL Records.* Edward E. Pratt was chief of the Bureau of Foreign and Domestic Commerce of the U.S. Department of Commerce.

7. Abrams to Cranwell, May 2, 1917, Files of the Office of the President, General Correspondence, reel 83, frames 574–75, *AFL Records.*

8. The 1917 convention of the National Association of Manufacturers met May 14–16 in New York City.

9. In his address, Secretary of Commerce William Redfield emphasized the importance of cooperation between employers and employees.

10. Woodrow Wilson's address is printed in the July 1917 issue of the *American Federationist* (24: 454).

R. Lee Guard to Ralph Easley

Washington, D.C., May 22, 1917

Mr. R. M. Easley,
New York City.
Dear Mr. Easley:

It is 9 P.M. and I am still here trying to wind up a lot of things that could not be finished during office hours. The chief wanted me to say to you that he will be in New York on Saturday for the luncheon to the British Labor delegates. He will have to leave that night for Pittsburg as he has a mass meeting there at 2 P.M. on Sunday.[1] He did not say whether he could attend the meeting Saturday night,[2] but I don't suppose he can do so. Anyway, a meeting Saturday night, trying to sleep on the train, then a mass meeting on Sunday afternoon would be very strenuous for him at this particular time.[3] The Dr.[4] continues to urge him to get away if only for a few days, so lessen up on things as much as you can while he is in New York, but for pity's sake, don't let him have an idea I suggested it. We tucked him up in the steamer chair on the roof to day where he had a nice little rest, and then had his lunch up there and got through quite a lot of work while out in the air in that way.

He further said to tell you that your suggestion for the meeting on the 30th would be out of the question—he could not undertake it. So don't announce his name for that.

Things have been going at such a rapid pace that I'm in doubt as to whether I am a fish or a bird, or just a plain Pollywog. I think it is the latter. I want to go off into a nice green pool under the willows and hide—but even there I could not forget the German subs.

Sincerely yours,

TLc, Files of the Office of the President, General Correspondence, reel 84, frame 162, *AFL Records.*

1. SG left Washington, D.C., on May 25, 1917, for New York City, where he attended a luncheon reception in honor of the British labor delegates on May 26, hosted by the National Civic Federation. From New York he traveled to Pittsburgh, where he was principal speaker at a patriotic rally on the afternoon of May 27. He returned to Washington later that day.

2. A mass meeting chaired by Hugh Frayne.

3. SG was deeply affected at this time by the death of his long-time friend, physician, and confidante, Jacob Allen. For Franklin Martin's account of SG's reaction to Allen's death and the process of finding him a new doctor, see his *Digest of the Proceedings of the Council of National Defense during the World War,* 73d Cong., 2d sess., 1934, S.Doc. 193, pp. 250–53.

4. Henry Pickering Parker, a Washington D.C., physician, was SG's new doctor.

To Truman Zilliox

May 23, 1917.

Mr. T. M. Zilliop [*sic*],
Secretary Lodge #241, International Association of Machinists,
Hamilton, Ohio.
Dear Sir and Brother:

Your communication of May 21st has been received. While it may be true that the migration of negroes from the South to the North may have some bearing upon the industrial situation in your locality, yet I am quite sure that you would object to any laws which would prohibit locomotion of workmen from one section of our country to another. However, I am sending a copy of your letter to Hon. William B. Wilson, Secretary Department of Labor, for his information.[1]

I trust that you will keep me advised as to the situation in your locality with reference to this particular subject.

With kind regards and best wishes, I am

Fraternally yours,　Saml Gompers.
President　American Federation of Labor.

TLpS, reel 222, vol. 234, p. 95, SG Letterbooks, DLC.

1. SG to William B. Wilson, May 23, 1917, reel 222, vol. 234, pp. 93–94, SG Letterbooks, DLC.

To the Executive Council of the AFL

Washington, D.C. May 24, 1917

No. 54

Executive Council American Federation of Labor
Colleagues:

The following cablegram[1] was received from Oudegeest[2] at Amsterdam, Holland, today:

"I am charged by the International Federation of Trade Unions to invite you to assist at an International Congress of Trade Union Centres which is to be held in Stockholm Folkshus on June eight[3] Agenda discussion and establishment of claims of Trade Unionists at peace negotiations I beg information by wire of the names of your delegates The Dutch Federation of Trade Unions in charge."

Vice-President Alpine[4] and Secretary Morrison were at headquarters at the time and I asked them to consult with me relative to an answer which should be made. As a result I sent the following cable answer:[5]

"Washington May 24 1917

["]Oudegeest
["]Amsterdam
["]Long before United States entered the war American Federation of Labor proposed an International Conference after the war and at the time and place where the representatives of each government were to meet to determine the treaties and international relations. That proposition was rejected. Now after United States is in the war

you propose a conference be held at Stockholm at same time and place when the so-called International Socialist Conference[6] is to be held at Stockholm and this proposition too without consultation with trade un[ion] centers of United States and other countries. There is no time by which American organized labor could select delegates to attend the Stockholm Conference, June eight and cannot see how any good could co[me] from our participation in such a Congress at this time.

["]Gompers."

The members of the Executive Council will please send in their vote[7] to the undersigned as to whether the course pursued meets with your approval.

Fraternally yours, Saml Gompers.
President American Federation of Labor.

TLcS, Executive Council Records, Vote Books, reel 15, frame 413, *AFL Records.*

1. Jan Oudegeest to SG, May 24, 1917, Files of the Office of the President, General Correspondence, reel 84, frame 267, *AFL Records.*

2. Jan OUDEGEEST was president of the Nederlandsch verbond van vakvereenigingen (Netherlands League of Trade Unions; 1908–18) and head of the auxiliary office of the International Federation of Trade Unions (IFTU) in Amsterdam.

3. See "To the Executive Committee of the Petrograd Council of Workers' and Soldiers' Deputies," May 6, 1917, n. 2, above.

4. John R. ALPINE was president of the United Association of Plumbers and Steam Fitters of the United States and Canada and an AFL vice-president.

5. SG to Oudegeest, May 24, 1917, Files of the Office of the President, General Correspondence, reel 84, frame 255, *AFL Records.*

6. See "To the Executive Committee of the Petrograd Council of Workers' and Soldiers' Deputies," May 6, 1917, n. 2, above.

7. The AFL Executive Council voted to approve SG's action.

To Theodore Johnson

May 24, 1917.

Mr. Theodore Johnson,
Secretary, Law and Legislative Committee, San Francisco Labor
  Council,
Labor Temple, San Francisco, Cal.
Dear Sir and Brother:

It has been impossible for me to reply to your letter of May 5 at an earlier date. You can well appreciate the additional demands made upon my time by the serious emergency in which our nation finds itself. The situation affects the labor movement directly and it is necessary under all circumstances to maintain the rights of the workers.

The matter of which you write me deserves most serious consideration. Some months ago I saw something of a national labor defense organization,[1] of which I think Mr. Frank Walsh was leader. The group interested included several who had also been active in the work of the federal commission on industrial relations. As all members of the labor movement know, much could be done by that commission through publicity given to the wrongs against which labor complains, and you also know that not all of the recommendations of the commission were in accord with the adopted principles of the labor movement.[2]

While organized labor is glad to have the cooperation of any agency that will be helpful, yet we cannot have our course, our policies, and our methods decided by those who do not belong to the ranks of the workers. There is an understanding of the labor movement that only comes through actual experience with its problems and responsibility for the maintenance of the movement.

There was an effort to perpetuate the Federal Commission on Industrial Relations through the organization of a Committee on Industrial Relations. Much confusion arose over the similarity of the name and the personnel of the new committee, which included many who had belonged to the Commission. The publicity sent out by the committee secured considerable prestige through this misunderstanding.

As you know the Committee on Industrial Relations appealed to the workers for funds. Many wrote to this office asking for advice as to contributions.[3] Invariably the advice was given that the work of the labor movement is so important and so large that all available money could well be spent in direct furtherance of the purposes of the movement. The effectiveness of the labor movement has been commensurate with the funds at its disposal, and we have failed to do many things only because the necessary money was lacking. It is impossible for the labor movement to maintain its effectiveness as an organization if the labor movement does not determine its own agencies and keep them under its direct control.

An organization for the defense of workers, if it is to receive the support of the organized labor movement ought to first receive the approval of the movement itself. Of course there is a broad, wide field for legal defense of workers. There are as yet many unorganized workers and some that belong to organizations not yet affiliated to the American Federation of Labor, and it is not my intention to minimize the injustices from which many wage earners have suffered.

Such an organization as described in the clipping you sent me could be very helpful to the organized labor movement and to the workers, but it seems to me that if the organization announces that it is to give free legal defense there ought to be no qualification to that statement, and that the organizations of labor ought not to be asked to contribute to an organization to which the national labor movement has never given approval or assumed responsibility for its policies or methods.

Several of those specifically mentioned by me are men who have at heart the welfare of wage earners and regard injustice to workers as a stigma on our nation. But they can be helpful by cooperating with the labor movement and assisting those in need of legal advice without entering into such a quasi official relationship as that planned; a relationship of that kind can be a source of which to hamper both the proposed organization and the labor movement.

With best wishes, I am

Fraternally yours,   Saml Gompers.
President,   American Federation of Labor.

TLpS, reel 222, vol. 234, pp. 115–17, SG Letterbooks, DLC.

1. The National Labor Defense Council, chaired by Frank Walsh, was organized to consult with workers on legal matters and to investigate and publicize the legal aspects of strikes and lockouts. Its efforts were handicapped by a lack of funds and support.

2. For the U.S. Commission on Industrial Relations, see *The Samuel Gompers Papers,* vol. 8, pp. 331–32, n. 2. For SG's reaction to the report of the commission, see ibid., vol. 9, pp. 321–23.

3. See *The Samuel Gompers Papers,* vol. 9, p. 464.

To Charles Lewis[1]

May 25, 1917.

Mr. Chas. H. Lewis,
Secretary, Detroit Federation of Labor,[2]
205 Equity Building, Detroit, Mich.
Dear Sir and Brother:

Your letter and enclosed resolution[3] were received.

One of the results of war conditions in all European countries has been the extension of employment of women. When men in large numbers are taken out of industry and transportation, and yet there remains the necessity of maintaining material output and transporting this output for the support of the nation as well as for those fighting for the nation, it becomes necessary to draw upon many able bodied persons who had previously not been gainfully employed in order to secure enough workers to carry on the necessary economic work of the nation.

The principle upon which the American Federation of Labor proposes to act is to prevent *unnecessary substitution* of women for men, and to conserve standards of work so that *women doing equal work with men shall receive equal wages.* The European war had affected American industry even before our country declared war with Germany. As a result of war time developments women have been employed in industry in increasing numbers in the past years.

It would be impossible to prevent the extension of employment of women. Our task is to direct such employment so that women shall not be employed in industries for which they are physically unfit, and that they shall not be exploited through lower wages or by conscious or unconscious competition with men for employment. The fundamental provision necessary to prevent their being used in competition with men is to assure to women equal pay for equal work.

It has been my purpose that the Committee on Labor which assists me as a member of the Advisory Commission to the Council of National Defense, shall assist in the work of protecting the women and conserving standards in industry. I have appointed a committee on Women in Industry which has already had one meeting and adopted resolutions[4] looking particularly to the purposes of which you write me, namely, to prevent women from being unnecessarily drawn into industry, and to protect them when they must be so employed. A number of trade union women have been appointed to that committee, which is ample assurance that the industrial welfare of women will be the guiding thought.

Realizing as I do that one of the important developments of war conditions is this matter of women's work, you may be assured that I am endeavoring to give it the attention which it deserves.

Fraternally yours,   Saml Gompers.
President,   American Federation of Labor.

TLpS, reel 222, vol. 234, pp. 121–22, SG Letterbooks, DLC.

1. Charles H. Lewis served as recording secretary of the Detroit Federation of Labor (FOL) from at least 1915 until 1918.

2. The Detroit Council of Trades and Labor Unions, founded in 1880 and chartered by the AFL in 1894, changed its name to the Detroit FOL in February 1906 and was rechartered under that name the following month.

3. Lewis to SG, May 11, 1917, Files of the Office of the President, General Correspondence, reel 83, frame 833, *AFL Records*. Lewis enclosed a resolution adopted May 9 by the Detroit FOL calling on the AFL to prevent an increase in the employment of women during the war and insure that women already working received the same wages as men for the same work (ibid., frames 835–36).

4. At its first meeting, held on May 24, 1917, the subcommittee on Women in Indus-

try of the Committee on Labor of the Advisory Commission of the Council of National Defense adopted resolutions calling for the maintenance of existing labor standards, opposing any increase in the employment of married women with young children, and calling the attention of working women to the dangers of undercutting existing wage standards or displacing other workers.

To Frank Sudduth[1]

June 8, 1917.

Mr. F. R. Sudduth,
Secretary, Federal Labor Union No. 7087,[2]
404 Weber Avenue, Belleville, Illinois.
Dear Sir and Brother:

Your communication of June 2nd has been received.

You state that a large number of negroes are now in your district and that they have been shipped in as strike breakers and that many of them are trying to work their way into the different unions. You ask whether you can refuse negroes membership that are not residents of your district.

The fundamental principles of the American Federation of Labor ignore questions of race, creed and color. It is true that in certain sections of the country where race feeling has been accentuated, especially referring to the South, colored men are permitted to have organizations exclusively confined to their race.

Your letter states that at least some of these negroes are applying to your organization for membership.

When men evince a desire to become members of unions and make common cause with those who are organized, the opportunity certainly should be afforded these men to become union men. The organizations of labor have no moral or economic right to deny to any man, even though he be of a different color, the right to join with his fellow workmen for the purpose of bettering his condition.

While it may be true that those who are responsible for the migration of these negroes from the south to the north have ulterior purposes, yet if these negroes realize that they are being exploited by these employers, make an effort to join with organized labor to maintain the present standards, and increase them, an opportunity ought to be afforded them.

It is a serious mistake for any organizations of labor to place any obstacle in the way of those who desire to organize, even though they may be black men.

The negroes are an economic factor in industry and that fact must be recognized and if organized labor refuses to extend to them the same rights and privileges as it does to all other workers, then we must expect the antagonism of the black man instead of his cooperation. The negro has desires and ambitions as well as the white man and if organized labor refuses to assist the negro in securing economic justices, then he must remain a retarding factor to the organized labor movement of the Country.

I trust that the members of your organization will take a broad view of this question and that the best interests of the men who toil may be conserved.

With kind regards and best wishes, I am,

Fraternally yours, Saml Gompers.
President American Federation of Labor.

TLpS, reel 222, vol. 234, pp. 776–77, SG Letterbooks, DLC.

1. Frank R. Sudduth, a coal miner, served as secretary of AFL Federal Labor Union (FLU) 7087 of Belleville, Ill., from late 1916 or early 1917 through 1919.
2. The AFL chartered FLU 7087 in 1898.

A Circular

Washington, D.C. June 13, 1917.

To All Workers:

Legislation to administer the distribution of the necessities of life must be enacted before July 1 if the prices of food necessities are to be reduced to something near normal.

After July 1 the new crops will be moving to the markets, food speculators will have cornered crops, prices will be forced up and the people will feel actual want.

Since the war wages have not kept pace with the increasing costs of living. They have remained practically stationary, while prices have more than doubled. The only practical way to increase the spending incomes of all is to decrease the costs of living.

A grave danger confronts the American people; the danger of hunger which, unless our government takes effective and immediate action to prevent, will portend greater injury than the threats of the foreign foe.

Abnormal conditions exist—the ordinary checks of competition have disappeared. Food speculators are gambling on the people's necessities. We must devise new machinery to meet tremendous, vital needs. We will have to establish economic agencies to control food so that the people may be insured subsistence. This problem strikes at the very roots of life.

This is a problem that has a strong appeal to the whole nation. Legislation can not be accomplished without the persistent, intelligently directed efforts of all.

There is an intense and general desire and need for the benefits of food regulation. Legislation accomplishing that can be secured if this general desire is expressed to those in position to take action.

The House Committee on Agriculture has just reported to the House of Representatives the Lever Food Administration Bill.[1] This bill creates government control of necessities, prohibits hoarding and cornering products and illegitimate speculation by introducing a stabilizing control at the most effective point in the distributive chain, and seeks to stimulate production.

The proposed bill does not set up a food dictatorship or methods that infringe upon the liberties of the citizens. It does not purpose to ration the people but attempts to protect the people against speculation by rational practical means.

In order to secure the fullest benefits from the Lever Bill it must be made law before July 1. Every worker who wishes lower prices of the necessities of life can be helpful in securing the immediate enactment of the Lever Bill. The following suggestions are made to those who wish to help.

Let every trade union, every central body, every state federation of labor, every international organization take official action upon this matter and communicate that to your respective congressmen in the House of Representatives, your Senators, and to the President of the United States.

In addition to this formal official action let every individual member of the organized labor movement write a personal letter or send some communication to his or her Representative and Senator. Ask your friends to take similar action, ask all organized bodies within your locality to express to their representatives at the national capital their desire for the immediate passage of legislation that will reduce the cost of the necessities of life. Present the matter to your local government—city council, town administrators or whatever the agency may be called.

The need of immediate, effective action is demonstrated by the fact that the world's grain crop is seriously below normal. The wheat crop in this country is even smaller than that of last year, and we are confronted with the gigantic task of feeding our allies and maintaining our own army and civilian population.

The war can not be fought by hungry men. The work necessary to maintain the continuity of this nation can not be done by starving people. Food administration is effective, as is demonstrated by the fact that bread is cheaper in Belgium, France and Italy than it is in this country, and this even when we ship the grain to Belgium from which their lower priced bread is made.

You are urged to act immediately to make known your need and your desires to those who are charged with the responsibility of creating agencies by which sufficient food will be assured to this nation and to those fighting the world's war for human freedom.

Press home upon all the necessity that the Lever Bill should be on the statute books before July 1.

Fraternally yours,   Saml Gompers.
President.   A.F. of L.

PLS, Files of the Office of the President, General Correspondence, reel 84, frames 823–24, *AFL Records*.

1. H.R. 4961 (65th Cong., 1st sess.) was introduced by Democratic congressman Asbury Lever of South Carolina on June 11, 1917, and became law on Aug. 10 (U.S. *Statutes at Large*, 40: 276–87). Known as the Lever Food and Fuel Control Act, it empowered the president to regulate the production, distribution, and pricing of food, fuel, and other commodities necessary for the war effort, prohibited the hoarding or monopolization of necessities, and banned the manufacture or importation of distilled liquors.

From Daniel Willard

Advisory Commission of the Council of National Defense
Washington—June 16, 1917.

My dear Mr. Gompers:

I have just read copy of the minutes of the joint meeting of the Council and Advisory Commission, held on June 13th, at which time you spoke at some length concerning matters having particularly to do with the labor situation, and in that connection I regret to say that I find myself unable to accept fully what I understand to be your views concerning the labor question generally as it confronts us at the present time.

I have recently read a very interesting article on the same subject by Sidney Webb, which appeared in the last number of the North American Review[1] and about which I spoke to you the other evening. I have also read an article concerning the matter by Mr. Robert W. Bruere[2] in a recent issue of the New Republic.[3]

I regret very much that owing to my absence from Washington, I was not able to hear the statements made by the English labor representatives when they were in this country and I have so far been unable to obtain a report of what they said. As I understand the matter, labor has gained from the English Government many concessions since the beginning of the war, but labor has also made many concessions itself—that is, if the first paragraph of the article referred to in the New Republic is true,[4] and I can well understand that with such an attitude on the part of both parties, that there should be, and I hope there is, a better understanding in England between the Government and the people than has ever existed before, and I trust that an adjustment which will be measurably satisfactory to both parties may be brought about in this country also. It appears to me, however, that so far labor in this country has seemed reluctant to make such concessions as were freely and quickly granted in England, although asking similar concessions from this Government.

I do not believe the best results will be accomplished unless both parties are willing to give up something. It is possible, of course, that I am mistaken in my understanding of the situation as it exists in our country. If labor, in an effort to contribute to the greatest extent possible toward the winning of the war, has removed restrictions, discountenanced strikes, etc., all in the interest of a greater and more sustained output, I have not been aware of that fact, and it is possible that others may be equally uninformed. I believe that this is one of the most important problems growing out of the war, with which our country will have to deal, and while it so happens that at the present time I am classed, I suppose, as one of the employers, I am first of all a citizen of the United States and have all my life been a worker in some capacity or other, and I am anxious to see this problem of labor settled in the way that will bring the greatest good to the greatest number.

I think the matter is of such importance as to justify its discussion by the Advisory Commission at a special meeting called for that purpose, and at which time I think all would be glad to have as complete a statement from you as you are in position to make concerning the attitude and aspirations of labor at the present time. If my suggestion is agreeable, I shall be glad to arrange for a meeting as soon as possible.[5]

Very truly yours,   D. Willard
Chairman,   Advisory Commission.

TLS, Files of the Office of the President, General Correspondence, reel 85, frames 88–89, *AFL Records*.

1. Sidney Webb, "British Labor under War Pressure," *North American Review* 205 (June 1917): 874–85.

2. Robert Walter Bruère (1876–1964) was a member of the board of arbitration for the New York City garment industry under the Protocol agreement and a writer on labor and industrial issues whose articles appeared in the *New Republic,* the *Nation,* and the *Survey.* He served as director of the Bureau of Industrial Research and Publicity (later the Bureau of Industrial Research), which he and Herbert Croly organized in late 1917 or early 1918, and he was later an instructor at the New School for Social Research in New York City.

3. Bruère, "English Labor and the War," *New Republic,* May 26, 1917, pp. 106–8.

4. Bruère's article summarized the provisions of the Munitions of War Act of 1915 and the Munitions of War (Amendment) Act of 1916, which required workers to give up the right to strike, subjected disagreements over wages and working conditions to binding arbitration, and provided for hiring less-skilled male workers and women during the war. The statutes also mandated limitations on industry profits for the duration of the war. See *The Samuel Gompers Papers,* vol. 9, p. 385, n. 1, and "To William Hutcheson," Aug. 10 [9], 1917, n. 3, below.

5. For SG's reply, see "To Daniel Willard," June 19, 1917, below.

A Memorandum of Agreement[1] between Samuel Gompers and Newton Baker

Washington, D.C., June 19, 1917.

For the adjustment and control of wages, hours and conditions of labor in the construction of cantonments,[2] there shall be created an adjustment commission of three persons, appointed by the Secretary of War; one to represent the Army, one the public, and one labor; the last to be nominated by Samuel Gompers, Member of the Advisory Commission of the Council of National Defense, and President of the American Federation of Labor.

As basic standards with reference to each cantonment, such commission shall use the union scale of wages, hours and conditions in force June 1, 1917, in the locality where such cantonment is situated. Consideration shall be given to special circumstances, if any, arising after said date which may require particular advances in wages or changes in other standards. Adjustment of wages, hours or conditions made by such boards are to be treated as binding by all parties.[3]

Newton D. Baker
Samuel Gompers

I designate General E. A. Garlington.[4]
Mr. Gompers designates Mr. John R. Alpine.
The third man will be designated in a day or two.[5]

TDtcSr, Files of the Office of the President, General Correspondence, reel 85, frame 145, *AFL Records.* Typed notation: "*Copy.*"

1. On July 27, 1917, SG and Newton Baker signed a memorandum authorizing the secretary of war to extend this agreement, at his discretion, to other War Department construction work. Baker subsequently extended it to aviation fields (Aug. 8), warehouses and other storage facilities (Sept. 4), and, finally, all other construction work undertaken by the War Department (Dec. 28). On Aug. 10 Secretary of the Navy Josephus Daniels agreed to apply the arrangement to navy construction work.

2. That is, the encampments where soldiers could be trained for military service, especially the quarters for the troops.

3. For a memorandum outlining the procedures to be followed by the Cantonment Adjustment Commission, see Files of the Office of the President, Reference Material, reel 128, frames 342–43, *AFL Records.*

4. Brig. Gen. Ernest Albert Garlington (1853–1934) served as inspector general of the U.S. Army from 1906 to February 1917.

5. Newton Baker designated Walter Lippmann as the third member of the commission.

To Daniel Willard

Washington, D.C., June 19, 1917.

Mr. Daniel Willard,
Chairman Advisory Commission,
Munsey Building, Washington, D.C.
My dear Mr. Willard:

Yesterday I received your most interesting letter of the 16th instant.[1] Inasmuch as you were present at the joint meeting of the Council and Advisory Commission held on June 13, at which time I presented several matters to the attention of the Council and the Commission, I cannot quite see why you should revert to the minutes of that joint meeting, for as can readily be understood, the minutes of such a meeting cannot be all-comprehensive, although there can be no question as to the accuracy of the minutes as recorded in so far as the subjects with which they deal.

I submitted to the Council and the Commission, generally and in several instances specifically, cases of complaint, of unfair discrimination, injustice, invasion of lawful rights of workers. You recall that I had with me a large package of documents and a brief digest of each separate cause of complaint but that because of the time which would be involved I refrained from presenting them, merely referring to them in a general way.

You will recall, as well as the minutes of the meeting will show, the remarks made by the chairman of the Council, Honorable Secretary of War Mr. Baker, and I am justified in suggesting that the Secretary's remarks should be considered in connection with the subject under consideration. If there was any mental dissent or reservation on the part of any member of the Council to Secretary Baker's statements, they were not expressed.

You say that you find yourself unable to accept fully what you understand to be my views concerning the labor question generally as it confronts us at the present time. I have every reason to believe that this is true. Indeed, there has been no proposition which I have made or suggestion which I have submitted in which the welfare of workers was to be safeguarded on which I have been able to find you in accord with me.

I have not yet had the opportunity to read the article of Mr. Bruere in the New Republic, but I have read the article of Sidney Webb in the North American Review, to both of which you have directed my attention. For the life of me I cannot see how you could approve the views expressed by Mr. Webb in that article and still find yourself unable to accept the views I expressed in the meetings of the Commission and at the meeting of the Council of June 13, for there is nothing contained therein but which clearly shows that the government and the people of England have put into practice what I have tried to impress upon the Commission, the Council, employers and workers generally.

Mr. Webb declares that the trade union movement has given wholehearted support to the country in the struggle to win the war. Has not the trade union movement made declarations of a like character in America? I could place before you complete evidence that this is so. In England, as Mr. Webb's article shows, the trade unions have full representation on every board, agency of the government and in the government itself. Is there any such like representation of organized labor in the United States? Even on the committees appointed by the other six members of the Advisory Commission there has not been appointed one representative labor man or labor woman. On the committee on transportation of which you are chairman, not one representative of the Railroad Brotherhoods has been appointed by you.

It is true that in the past some trade unions in the United States had certain rules which restricted output, but from that course the unions of our country have long departed. In England the trades unions until shortly after the war began continued their rules and restrictions of output and this was due to the imposition by employers generally, of what was known as "stunts" (tasks) and to which the workmen interposed "stints" (limitations). Thus, by reason of the American labor movement throwing off all restraints, stints and restrictions, welcoming the introduction of new and improved tools and machinery, there was and is no necessity for the American trade union movement to make any further declaration upon that subject.

What the American trade union movement declares to employers, is: "Bring on all the new tools and machinery you will. We will operate them to the fullest capacity of production, but we insist that for the greatest continued output, the largest productive capacity, the day's work of the toilers shall be limited to eight hours in any one day, and thus in addition safeguard the health, strength and the lives of the workers from being undermined and destroyed."

In so far as strikes are concerned, there have been and are now fewer than at any time within the past ten years and what few were inaugurated are of comparative unimportance. It may be interesting to note that several of these strikes were provoked by [hostile action on the part of employers interfering with men endeavoring to unite for their own and mutual protection and][2] wholesale discharges made, discharges of men victimized by employers for no other reason than that they have become members of a trade union. When it is borne in mind that the cost of the necessaries of life of the American workers has soared so high that the increases in the cost of living have in many instances advanced from fifty to two hundred percent, within the past two years, it is a cause of astonishment that there have been so few strikes to advance wages. I need not remind so intelligent a man as you of the fact that when the cost of living increases greatly and wages remain practically stationary, the purchasing power of those wages has decreased to that same extent, and that to all intents and purposes it amounts to a reduction in wages.

You will recall the fact that at the joint meeting of the 13th I made a suggestion for conference with the representatives of the government and the representatives of the International trade unions, with a view of reaching an agreement by which there could be secured greater harmony and co-operation and without interruption of industry of any sort. I am quite confident that if that suggestion is carried out we shall obtain by mutual, voluntary action the result so much to be desired, and without the necessity of invoking compulsion by law either for the one side or for the other.

During the first months of the war England practically forced her workers to toil long hours, seven days in the week. Time demonstrated the utter futility of that course, that it had not increased production but impaired the health of the workers so that a return was quickly made for the re-establishment and the maintenance of a normal workday and a day of rest in the week.

We must realize the necessity of maintaining fully equipped with every need our fighting men at the front, for they cannot be expected to do their very best unless their requirements be fully provided; and it is equally true that the civilian workers at home must be not only properly nourished, but their strength and health must not be undermined if they are expected to give their best efforts in the maximum of production.

Inasmuch as you have added the human interest of your own activities in life, I think I too may say that all my life I have been a worker in some capacity or other, and I hope my work has not all been in vain. I believe with you in the greatest good to the greatest number and I know of no way by which that thought can be translated into effect than by the acceptance of several suggestions which I have made to protect and promote the interest of the masses of our people, and which the government of England has put into practice as Mr. Webb in his article so clearly demonstrates.

The subject matter in its entirety is too large with which to deal comprehensively in a letter. Like yourself, my duties are too exacting to permit me to go [into this subject further herein, but I should be very glad to concur in your suggestion for a meeting of the Advisory Commission for a full and free discussion][3] of this entire subject matter, but when such a meeting is held for that purpose, I think that all the members of the Commission should be present and ample time devoted to it so that there can be no mistaking the position of either the one or other members of the Commission.

I shall be glad to go over with you, and as I take it you would desire to consult with the other members of the Advisory Commission, as to the proper date to be set for that purpose.[4]

Very truly yours, Saml Gompers.
Chairman Committee on Labor.

TLpS, Files of the Office of the President, Letterbooks, Advisory Commission, Council of National Defense, reel 21, pp. 127–30, *AFL Records.*

1. "From Daniel Willard," June 16, 1917, above.

2. The text in brackets is supplied from a transcribed copy of this letter in the Files of the Office of the President, General Correspondence, reel 85, frame 171, *AFL Records.*

3. The text in brackets is supplied from a transcribed copy of this letter in the Files of the Office of the President, General Correspondence, reel 85, frame 172, *AFL Records.*

4. Willard's reply, dated June 22, 1917, may be found in the Files of the Office of the President, General Correspondence, reel 85, frames 305–7, *AFL Records.*

Louis Wehle[1] to Frank Morrison

June 20, 1917.

Mr. Frank Morrison,
Secty. American Federation of Labor,
Washington, D.C.
Re Cantonment Construction Labor Conditions.
My dear Mr. Morrison:

Confirming our talk over the telephone this afternoon, it must be clearly understood, as a basis for any labor adjustment machinery, that the Government cannot commit itself in any way to the closed shop, and that the conditions in force on June 1, 1917, which are to serve as part of the basic standards do not include any provisions which have reference to the employment of non-union labor. In our telephone talk just now, I understand that you accede to this view. The word "conditions" is of course clearly understood to refer only to the union arrangements in the event of overtime, holiday work, and matters of that kind. This was clearly understood between Mr. Gompers and myself this morning when we agreed that it would not be legally possible at this time to insert in an understanding—even so much as a provision that preference be given to members of organized labor.[2]

Very truly yours,   Louis B. Wehle

TLS, Files of the Office of the President, General Correspondence, reel 85, frame 227, *AFL Records.* Typed notation: "Copy to Mr. Gompers."

1. Louis Brandeis Wehle (1880–1959), a Louisville, Ky., attorney, served on the legal committees of the General Munitions Board, the Council of National Defense, and the War Industries Board, and was counsel to the Cantonment Labor Adjustment Commission, the Shipbuilding Labor Adjustment Board, the U.S. Shipping Board Emergency Fleet Corporation, and the War Finance Corporation. As special assistant to Secretary of War Newton Baker, he negotiated the cantonment construction agreement with SG in June 1917 (see "A Memorandum of Agreement between Samuel Gompers and Newton Baker," June 19, 1917, above).

2. On June 22, 1917, SG sent a confirming telegram to Wehle, which read: "Your understanding of the memorandum signed by secretary Baker and me is right it had reference to union hours and wages the question of union shop was not included" (Files of the Office of the President, General Correspondence, reel 85, frame 299, *AFL Records*).

From James Duncan

Petrograd. Undated. [c. June 25, 1917]
Recd. July 10th, 1917, 8:15 A.M.

Secretary of State,
Washington, D.C.
Attention Long.[1]
For Samuel Gompers

"Have just returned from Moscow and received your message.[2] Yes Mr. Root's statement[3] to Russian Cabinet was expression of entire mission. Have had many interesting meetings and conferences in Petrograd and in Moscow. Participated in meeting of Moscow Duma, several labor meetings and headquarters cooperative association, including its Central Bank. At three meetings of Workmen's and Soldiers' representatives I made addresses and was most enthusiastically received. Workmen's replies were constructive and inspiring. Have attended many meetings in Petrograd and arrangements are made for my address to the general meeting of Workmen's and Soldiers' delegates. Will report on same later.[4] Great ovations were given us at Vladivostok and all principal stations through Siberia. Workmen and others came to stations to greet us and we addressed them on station platforms and from train steps. We also made impressive visit at Harbin, Manchuria, *but* Siberians were most enthusiastic. Petrograd pessimistic, Moscow less so but cossacks and other militant soldiers are eager for activity. Nowhere is there sentiment for individual peace excepting among certain extremists and the German propagandists. Everywhere and by everyone it is declared that autocracy in Russia is gone forever so while military activities seem dilatory it is encouraging and inspiring to know that Russian Democracy is safe and that therefore economic organizations will proceed in accordance with opportunity and the natural development of the new freedom. Liberty came upon New Russia similar to a bolt from the Heavens and it took the new citizenship some time to realize they were free but the healthy general mind will now develop into a concentrated constructive and representative government which will give the Russian intellect and resources the needed chance to be a most valuable annexation to the roster of real democracies. They may make mistakes for they are human and are feeling their way towards practical and expressive democratic authority but in each move something better will evolve and which with due care will point the way to a new and necessarily better time and to the organization of a great republic. I am well and have stood the strain of travel and official duty very well. The possibilities of the future are so many, so important and so inspiring one is thereby and for the good one can do, much encouraged to perform one's part in the worldwide transformation from the evils of autocracy to the benign influences of representative government and so the work I am performing strongly appeals to me. Duncan."

Root.

TWtcSr, Files of the Office of the President, General Correspondence, reel 85, frames 773–74, *AFL Records*.

1. Breckinridge Long (1881–1958), a St. Louis attorney, served as an assistant secretary of state (1917–20).

2. SG to James Duncan, June 18, 1917, Files of the Office of the President, General Correspondence, reel 85, frame 107, *AFL Records*.

3. Elihu Root addressed the Council of Ministers of the Russian Provisional Government in Petrograd on June 15, 1917.

4. Duncan's report on his trip to Russia, printed in AFL, *Proceedings*, 1917, pp. 322–46, includes the text of his address before the Petrograd Council of Workers' and Soldiers' Deputies, which was probably delivered on June 29 (ibid., pp. 335–38).

The Executive Council of the AFL to the Council of National Defense

June 27, 1917.

The Council of National Defense,
Washington, D.C.
Gentlemen:

As agencies are now organized for national defense work, economic power is largely concentrated in Washington and controlled by the committees established by the Council of National Defense and the Advisory Commission. As the transition from a peace to a war basis progresses, war finance, war contracts, war business will replace the economic basis of peace.

The working people have long ago learned that freedom and democracy have real meaning in other relations only when established in the economic world—they have declared and struggled for democratically organized and controlled relations between employers and employes. Now the workers declare for democracy in all things concerned in a world war for democracy. They demand direct representation by workers, coequal with all other interests, upon all agencies, boards, committees and commissions entrusted with war work.[1]

These boards and committees are now composed almost entirely of business men—able, prominent, men of large affairs who control the placing of contracts and the expenditure of millions of the nation's money. As a matter of precaution to prevent any charge of discrimination or suspicion of scandal, representatives of all citizens contributing to the national funds expended ought to be on the boards or committees. War contracts must not be allowed to be an opportunity for private gain and the accumulation of war profits. As a matter of justice and democratic principle representatives of employes as well as employers ought to determine national economic policies.

Many workers understand the industry in which they work and have a fund of information supplementary to that of their employers. Representation for workers means valuable service to the nation as well as recognition of the fundamentals of democracy. Therefore we, the Executive Council of the American Federation of Labor, urge the Council of National Defense that you endorse the principle of according representation for Labor on all agencies, committees, boards or commissions organized under the Council of National Defense—and recommend that chairmen of all such bodies follow that principle.

Equal participation to all groups in the responsibilities, the duties and the determination of policies concerning the war is necessary to create and maintain a spirit of willing cooperation in the work and sacrifices which all the people of our nation must meet.

The working people of this country have declared their willingness to assist. The men and the women in the labor movement of our country are in wholehearted accord with the declarations of President Wilson as to the causes for which the republic of the United States has entered the war for the dethronement of autocracy and the enthronement of democracy.

We respectfully urge that the matters dealt with herein may receive your favorable consideration and early action.[2]

Very truly yours,
Executive Council American Federation of Labor.
Samuel Gompers.　President.
Frank Morrison　Secretary.

TLpS, reel 223, vol. 235, pp. 346–48, SG Letterbooks, DLC.

1. See AFL, *Proceedings,* 1916, pp. 108–9, 349; AFL, *Proceedings,* 1917, p. 81.

2. For Daniel Willard's acknowledgment of this letter, dated July 2, 1917, see Files of the Office of the President, General Correspondence, reel 85, frame 575, *AFL Records.*

To Woodrow Wilson

Washington, D.C. June 27, 1917.

Honorable Woodrow Wilson,
President of the United States,
Washington, D.C.
Sir:

There was introduced in the United States Senate and passed by that body a bill known as S. 2356.[1] This bill deals with Interstate and Foreign Commerce, and clothes the President of the United States with large powers in the conduct or movement of Interstate and Foreign Commerce in any part of the United States, or of any train, locomotive, car or other vehicle upon any railroad in the United States engaged in Interstate or Foreign Commerce.

This bill was so phrased that in the event it became a law and the provisions thereof strictly enforced, it would be a repeal of the labor provisions of the Clayton Law.

In view of the announced policy of yourself and the Council of National Defense, to maintain existing law until such time as a great emergency made necessary the suspension of any law relating to workers in industry, the representatives of the four great Railroad Brotherhoods requested those in charge of the bill in the United States Senate to incorporate an amendment. Agreeable to the request, the following amendment was adopted by the Senate, unanimously, as part of S. 2356:

"Provided that nothing in this section shall be construed to repeal, modify or affect either Section 6 or Section 20 of an act entitled An Act to Supplement Existing laws against Unlawful Restraints and Monopolies and for other purposes. Approved October 15, 1914."[2]

Upon the unanimous passage by the Senate of the bill referred to with the amendment attached, it went to the House of Representatives where it was referred to the Interstate and Foreign Commerce Committee. This committee, on Monday, June 25, met to consider S. 2356. A majority of the members of the committee present eliminated from the Senate bill the provision that nothing in section one of the bill should be construed to repeal, modify or affect section 6 or section 20 of the Clayton Law. The striking out of this provision from the bill is clearly an effort to repeal the salient sections of the Clayton Law.

Your attention is respectfully called to the fact that during the period when the Sherman Antitrust Law was in the making by Congress, assurances of the most positive character were given that under no strained construction of the provisions of the proposed legislation could the normal activities of the wage-workers of our country regulating hours, wages and conditions of employment be construed by the courts as applicable to such activities. And yet, despite that assurance, the Sherman Antitrust Law, as you well know, has been so construed, much to the injury of a large number of workers, and relief was only secured after twenty-four years of hard work, sacrifice and suffering, by the enactment of the Clayton Law, to which you gave your approval.

Having in mind your clear and concise declaration with reference to the repeal of labor laws, especially a sentence included in your letter[3] to Governor Brumbaugh of Pennsylvania relative to the repeal of the Full Crew Law[4] of that state, I quote one of your forceful statements.

"I take pleasure in replying to your letter of June 1. I think it would be most unfortunate for any of the states to relax laws by which safeguards have been thrown about labor. I feel that there is no necessity for such action and that it would lead to a slackening of the energy of the nation rather than to an increase of it, besides being very unfair to the laboring people themselves."

And, Sir, while addressing you upon this subject your attention is also respectfully called to the fact that the Lever Bill as introduced in the House contained provisions which in effect would repeal the protective features of the Clayton Law by declaring that the ordinary organized activities of the workers engaged in an effort to maintain standards of work and life could be construed and stigmatized as conspiracies, thus laying the workers liable to the charge of treason. To overcome this feature of the bill, Representative Keating[5] of Colorado prepared the following amendment:

"Provided that nothing in this section shall be construed to repeal, modify or affect either Section 6 or Section 20 of an act entitled An Act to Supplement Existing Laws Against Unlawful Restraints and Monopolies and for other purposes, approved October 15, 1914."

Under the spur of zeal or mistaken patriotism, the amendment was defeated.

Now that the House of Representatives has rejected an amendment that would guarantee to all of the workers the right to carry on their necessary organized activities, and the House Committee on Interstate and Foreign Commerce has rejected an amendment that would guarantee the same right to railroad employes, despite the fact that attention was called to the danger that this course would impose upon the workers of the country, there is no assurance that every right which the millions of workers of our country now possess will not be taken from them by Congressional action and by judicial interpretation. The courts of our country will have the right to take cognizance in any case before them that the House of Representatives put their seal of disapproval of the proposed amendments and to place the workers of our country in a position of hazard so far as their rights and their freedom are concerned.

The people of our country are giving and will give wholehearted support to the great enterprise upon which our republic has entered to make the world safe for democracy. Surely in the prosecution of the contest for the establishment of that great principle the toilers of America should not be permitted to lose their rights and their freedom.

It may be additionally interesting to say that there has been no element or group of people in all our country who have done more to clarify the minds of all of the immediate necessity for the enactment of the fundamental principles of the Lever Bill than the organized wage-earners.

We are exceedingly concerned with the present status of these bills, and while we shall make an earnest endeavor to prevent the repeal of the labor provisions of the Clayton Law by indirection, we feel justified in seeking whatever assistance you may be able to render to keep intact and in full force the Clayton Law which you approved on October 15, 1914.

Respectfully,   Samuel Gompers.
President,   American Federation of Labor.

TLS, Woodrow Wilson Papers, DLC.

1. S. 2356 (65th Cong., 1st sess.), introduced by Democratic senator Francis Newlands of Nevada on May 25, 1917, became law on Aug. 10 (U.S. *Statutes at Large*, 40: 272–73).

2. This provision was included in the version of the bill that became law.

3. President Woodrow Wilson's letter to Pennsylvania governor Martin Brumbaugh is printed in Arthur S. Link et al., eds., *The Papers of Woodrow Wilson*, 69 vols. (Princeton, N.J., 1966–94), 42: 446.

4. Pennsylvania, Laws of 1911, pp. 1053–55, enacted June 19, 1911, stipulated the number of railroad crewmen required to operate passenger and freight trains in the state.

5. Edward Keating (1875–1965) served as a Democratic congressman from Colorado from 1913 to 1919.

From Charles Moyer[1]

Denver Colo June 27 [19]17

Our international assumes no responsibility in connection with Bisbee strike[2] It is called by Metal Mine Workers Union of the IWW with western headquarters at Phoenix Ariz The Butte Metal Mine Workers

Union responsible for the strike there[3] is also a branch of the Phoenix local The base of these operations are located in Chicago and it occurs to me that it is time for the Department of Justice or those who have charge of such matters to institute an investigation at that point Kindly hand copy of this telegram to Secretary Wilson

Chas H Moyer

TWSr, Files of the Office of the President, General Correspondence, reel 85, frame 431, *AFL Records.*

1. Charles H. MOYER, of the International Union of MINE, Mill, and Smelter Workers, was president of the union from 1902 until 1926.

2. On June 27, 1917, IWW Metal Mine Workers' Industrial Union No. 800 of Bisbee, Ariz. (formerly Mine, Mill, and Smelter Workers' local 106) went on strike after the three major copper mining companies operating in Bisbee rejected demands that they assign two men to operate machines and lifts, replace the sliding pay scale with a flat rate, and stop all bonus and contract work, blasting during shifts, and discrimination against union members. Within days some thirty thousand copper miners from both the IWW and the Mine, Mill, and Smelter Workers were on strike at Globe, Miami, and Jerome in south-central Arizona and at Clifton, Morenci, and Metcalf near the New Mexico border, virtually shutting down the state's copper mines, which produced almost 30 percent of the nation's output. In Bisbee the strike was effectively ended on July 12 after county sheriff Harry Wheeler and a posse of some two thousand residents rounded up nearly twelve hundred strikers and sympathizers, put them in cattle cars, and dropped them off in the New Mexico desert. The deportees were able to make their way to the army encampment at Columbus, N.Mex., where they took shelter, but they were prevented from returning to Bisbee. Efforts to punish those responsible for the "Bisbee deportations" were unsuccessful (see "To Thomas Gregory," Jan. 19, 1918, n. 6, below).

In September President Woodrow Wilson appointed a commission to investigate labor unrest in the West and Northwest (see "To William B. Wilson," Aug. 27, 1917, n. 3, below). It arranged strike settlements in the Globe-Miami district on Oct. 19, in the Clifton-Morenci-Metcalf district on Oct. 31, and in Bisbee on Nov. 6. The settlements prohibited strikes or lockouts during the war, banned discrimination against union members, called for rehiring some strikers, recognized workers' grievance committees, and provided for the appointment of a federal administrator to settle any grievances not resolved by negotiation. Men accused of making disloyal remarks or those who were members of an organization that refused to recognize contracts—that is, IWW members—were not eligible for reemployment.

3. On June 8, 1917, 164 miners perished in a fire at the Speculator Mine in Butte, Mont. The disaster triggered a spontaneous walkout by the largely unorganized miners in Butte, and within days several thousand had left their jobs and the IWW had sent organizers into the area. At a mass meeting on June 12, the striking miners formed the Metal Mine Workers' Union, which demanded safety improvements and regular mine inspections, a wage increase, union recognition, an end to blacklisting, and reinstatement of blacklisted miners. When the mining companies rejected these demands, AFL-affiliated craft workers also left their jobs, raising the total number of strikers to 15,000. Although technically independent, the Metal Mine Workers' Union was accused of being under the control of the IWW, charges that gained credence with the arrival of IWW organizer Frank Little in July. At the suggestion of U.S. Department of Labor commissioner of conciliation W. H. Rodgers, the companies offered separate

settlements with pay raises to the craft unions, which then voted to return to work. When the miners were offered nominal wage increases as individuals, without union recognition, they rejected these terms and attempted to continue their strike. By the end of September, however, the Butte mines were back in full operation, and on Dec. 20 the Metal Mine Workers' Union called off the strike.

From Ernest Bohm[1]

N.Y. July 3d/[19]17

Confidential.

My dear Sir & Bro.

Just to inform you that the pot is boiling.

At the meeting of our General Executive Committee Monday July 2nd/17, I introduced the following and it was unanimously adopted.

"The General Executive Committee after careful and precise consideration of the documents presented and statement made by President Gompers at the meeting of the C.F.U. on Friday June 29th/17,[2] fully agrees with and endorses his position and recommends, that the C.F.U. co-operate with him and immediately begin activities to Americanize the labor movement in Greater New York.

["]That we condemn the action of the 'Peoples Peace Conference' because it does not represent the American labor movement.

["]For the purpose of effectively carrying out this recommendation, Delegates J. P. Holland,[3] W. Kelly, John Sullivan,[4] V. T. Rybicki[5] and E. Bohm are appointed with power to act."

The following were appointed to co-operate with the National Labor Publicity Organization.[6] J. P. Holland. John Sullivan. E. Bohm.

When the C.F.U. meets on Friday July 13th/17, the boys have been pledged to go to it and after it is over, the disorganizers will remember that they have been in a battle.

Fraternally, Ernest Bohm.

TLS, Files of the Office of the President, General Correspondence, reel 85, frame 576, *AFL Records*.

1. Ernest BOHM was secretary of the Central Federated Union of Greater New York and Vicinity.

2. SG left Washington, D.C., on June 29, 1917, for New York City to address an evening meeting of the Central Federated Union regarding the People's Council of America for Democracy and Peace and its impact on the labor movement in New York. He met the next day with officers of the International Ladies' Garment Workers' Union and the United Cloth Hat and Cap Makers of North America to discuss the

same subject. While in New York SG also attended meetings and functions in connection with a diplomatic mission sent by the Russian Provisional Government, headed by ambassador-designate Boris Bakhmeteff, and on July 6 he addressed a meeting held at Carnegie Hall in honor of that delegation (see "Excerpts from an Article in the *New York Times*," July 7, 1917, below). SG returned to AFL headquarters on July 9.

SG was concerned by efforts of the People's Council to cultivate antiwar sentiment among foreign-born workers in New York City. The council, which claimed the support of "every radical and forward looking force in the nation," had announced it would hold a conference in New York City on June 30 and July 1, 1917, "to bring about the affiliation of hundreds of thousands of workers with the new movement" (People's Council press release, June 28, 1917, Records of the Committee on Labor, RG 62, Records of the Council of National Defense, DNA). It predicted that the meeting, which it referred to as the First Conference for the Maintenance of Workers' Rights and Standards, would attract delegates from four to five hundred trade unions. SG denounced the organizers of the conference as "new-fangled faddists" and dismissed the meeting as an attempt to create "confusion" and "discontent" in the labor movement through "misrepresentation and vilification" ("Gompers Denounces People's Council," *New York Call,* June 30, 1917).

3. James P. HOLLAND served as president of the New York State Federation of Labor from 1915 to 1926.

4. John Sullivan was a member of International Union of United Brewery Workmen of America 59 of New York City and served as a member of the Brewery Workmen's general executive board from 1909 to 1935.

5. Valentine T. Rybicki was a New York City machinist.

6. The Labor Publicity Organization, an independent local organization endorsed by central bodies in the New York City area, was founded in 1915 to publicize information about trade union activities in the region and encourage the growth of the labor press there. It was reconstituted as the National Labor Publicity Organization in January 1917 in an effort to expand its influence in New York, New Jersey, Pennsylvania, and Connecticut. SG spoke at the founding convention of the new organization in New York City, and Bohm and Robert Maisel were selected, respectively, as its president and secretary.

To William Pross[1]

Washington, D.C., July 5, 1917.

Mr. W. L. Pross,
President C.L.U.[2]
Chillicothe, Ohio.
Telegrams[3] received.
The memorandum[4] of the Secretary of War was to the effect that on all cantonment work the union scale of wages, hours and conditions in the district should prevail as of June one, nineteen seventeen. It did not include any provision for union shop. Of course it is not only your right but your duty to persuade workers to join the unions of

their trades and callings but under present circumstances it is urged that a strike should not take place particularly for the establishment of a union shop.

Samuel Gompers.

TWSr, Files of the Office of the President, General Correspondence, reel 85, frame 654, *AFL Records.*

1. William L. Pross was a Chillicothe, Ohio, machinist.

2. The AFL chartered the Chillicothe Trades and Labor Council in 1900 and rechartered it in 1908. The Chillicothe Central Labor Union was chartered in 1916.

3. For Pross's two telegrams to SG of July 3, 1917, see Files of the Office of the President, General Correspondence, reel 85, frames 608–9, *AFL Records.*

4. "A Memorandum of Agreement between Samuel Gompers and Newton Baker," June 19, 1917, above.

Excerpts from an Article in the *New York Times*

[July 7, 1917]

ROOSEVELT AND GOMPERS ROW AT RUSSIAN MEETING

Bitter denunciation of the race riots in East St. Louis[1] by Theodore Roosevelt, an attempt to explain them through the economic opposition of labor to imported negro workers, by Samuel Gompers, and a more impassioned reply by Colonel Roosevelt led almost to a fist fight on the stage of Carnegie Hall last night and provoked wild and prolonged disorder in the audience.

The hall was packed with people who had come to a meeting arranged by the American Friends of Russian Freedom,[2] the American Ambulance in Russia,[3] and the Mayor's Committee for the reception of the Russian Commission, to greet Boris A. Bakhmetieff,[4] the new Russian Ambassador, and his fellow-Commissioners, but Russia absorbed only a minor part of the interest of the evening.

The central feature was the Colonel. He was cheered deafeningly for long minutes when he entered, introduced by Mayor Mitchel as "the foremost private citizen of our country," cheered again in his appeal to America to cast the beam of racial violence out of her own eye and in his attacks on German militarism; and then, when he bent over Mr. Gompers afterward and shook his fist in his face so closely that to people in the auditorium it must have appeared that he was striking him, he was hooted and hissed by a crowd which at times silenced him with boos and made the galleries ring with shouts of protest.

It was the final ceremony of a day of reception to the Russian Embassy, and Mayor Mitchel brought the crowd to quiet with a stern reminder that the meeting had gathered to greet the nation's guests and for no other purpose. Then Ambassador Bakhmeteff took up his speech, already prepared, and read it as if nothing had happened.

. . .

Colonel Roosevelt was the hero of the Carnegie Hall meeting the moment he came on the stage with the Mayor, the Russian Commissioners, and the local committee of reception.

There were cheers for the Mayor and the Ambassador, but they were drowned by the sudden outburst of applause for "Teddy." Carnegie Hall was full; thousands of people had been unable to gain admission; and of the thousands inside there did not seem to be one who was not shouting for him. The Russian Symphony Orchestra, conducted by Modest Altschuler,[5] which had furnished a preliminary musical program, swung into the Russian revolutionary hymn as the commission entered, but people six rows away from them could not tell what they were playing. They went through to the end, and only then, when the Mayor and others on the stage heard the opening of "The Star-Spangled Banner" through the din was the crowd persuaded to stop shouting and join in the anthem.

When it had finished there were more shouts for the Colonel, a group of half a dozen sailors in a box and an old man jumping up and down in the second row being particularly prominent. After perhaps five minutes more the Mayor managed to still the crowd long enough to introduce the Colonel as the first speaker.

. . .

Colonel Roosevelt had his prepared speech in his hand, but did not come to it at the outset.

"Stain on American Name."

"Before we speak of justice for others," he said, "it behooves us to do justice within our own household. Within the week there has been an appalling outbreak of savagery in a race riot at East St. Louis, a race riot for which, as far as we can see, there was no real provocation, and which, whether there was provocation or not, was waged with such an excess of appalling brutality as to leave a stain on the American name. (Applause.)

"Now, friends, the longer I live the more I grow to abhor rhetoric that isn't based on facts, words that aren't translated into deeds. And when we applaud the birth of democracy in another people, the spirit which insists on treating each man on the basis of his rights as a man, refusing to deny to the humblest the rights that are his, when we present such a greeting to the representatives of a foreign nation it behooves us to express our deep condemnation of acts that give the lie to our words within our own country.

"It behooves us to say that it is impossible that there should be a justification for mob violence, for brutality and murder in this democracy. To ask—that isn't strong enough—to demand that the Government agencies shall use with ruthless severity every instrumentality to place the responsibility for this is our first duty.

"We must insist first of all upon the restoration of order, upon the reign of law, and then on the foundation of law and order we can build up the superstructure of justice.

"So much for this brief eulogy of my fellow-citizens," the Colonel finished with a grin, and then turned to his prepared speech. It was praise of free Russia, warning against "doctrinaire idealists and sinister extremists," and then a warning to America, a reminder that Russia had been fighting for three years before we got started, and that it was now our duty to fight as hard as we could. . . .

. . .

Gompers Takes Up Riot.

Mr. Gompers, the next speaker, started by declaring his approval of "the general sentiments" of Colonel Roosevelt's speech.

"But," he said, "I want to explain a feature of the East St. Louis riots with which the general public is unacquainted. I join with you and with him and with all in expressing the detestation of any brutal conduct.

"But I can tell you—and I wish I had brought with me a copy of a telegram received today from Victor Hollander,[6] Secretary of the Illinois Federation of Labor—I can tell you that not only labor men but a member of the Chamber of Commerce of East St. Louis warned the men engaged in luring negroes from the South that they were to be used in undermining the conditions of the laborer in East St. Louis.

"The luring of these colored men to East St. Louis is on a par with the behavior of the brutal, reactionary, and tyrannous forces that existed in Old Russia."

There was vigorous applause at this, not only from the galleries but from the floor, as far as any one could see, from the same people who had applauded Colonel Roosevelt.

"This is not a war against a political fault in one country alone," said Mr. Gompers, "it is a war for real democracy of the world. The poor devil working under debasing conditions in old Russia was no worse off than the man on whom there are imposed the same conditions in free America." (Applause.)

"The authors of the Declaration of Independence based that document on the right of the people to change the Government if it failed to respond to the needs of the people." (At this there was wild cheering from the galleries.)

"Not all the ideals in the heart and mind of the American people have been achieved; there is altogether too much injustice in free America." (Applause, mingled with hisses.) "But even with the faults that we know and the criticism that we believe to be justified we are yet conscious of the fact that there is a larger degree of freedom and justice in America than in any other country in the world."

Then he went on with declarations for firm support of the Government and our allies, denunciation of peace moves as coming from pro-German sources or neutrals too terrorized for free expression, and closed with an expression of the need for war against German militarism. Colonel Roosevelt, who had been fidgeting in his chair, where he sat with only Martin W. Littleton[7] between him and Mr. Gompers, whispered to the Mayor, who announced: "Colonel Roosevelt wants to say another word." And there was another burst of cheers.

FIST IN GOMPERS'S FACE.

"I am not willing," said the Colonel, "that a meeting called to commemorate the birth of democracy and justice in Russia shall seem to have given any approval of or apology for the infamous brutalities that have been committed on negroes at East St. Louis. Justice with me is not a mere phrase or form of words. It is to be translated into living action. How can we praise the people of Russia for doing justice to the men within their boundaries if we in any way apologize for murder committed on the helpless?

"In the past I have listened to the same form of excuse advanced in behalf of the Russian autocracy for pogroms of Jews. Not for a moment shall I acquiesce in any apology for the murder of women and children in our own country. I am a democrat of democrats. I will do anything for the laboring man except what is wrong."

He strode over to Mr. Gompers and shook his fist under the labor leader's nose.

"I don't care a snap of my finger," the Colonel shouted, "for any telegram from the head of the strongest labor union in Illinois. This took place in a Northern state, where the whites outrank the negroes twenty to one. And if in that State the white men can't protect their rights by their votes against an insignificant minority, and have to protect them by the murder of women and children, then the people of the State which sent Abraham Lincoln to the Presidency must bow their heads. We must have investigations—"

Mr. Gompers rose from his chair and broke in: "Investigations afterward, not before—"

"I'd put down the murderers first and investigate afterward," shouted the Colonel, amid a chorus of groans from the gallery. He shook his fist so close to Mr. Gompers's face that he seemed almost to graze it again and again, standing over him as he sat quiet, but burning red and waving his arms up and down. The crowd was howling wildly by this time, in the galleries and on the floor, and there was a burst of boos that completely drowned the Colonel for a time.

"I will go to any extreme necessary to bring justice to the laboring man," he said, "to insure him his economic place, (a burst of groans and howls,) but when there is murder I'll put it down and I'll never surrender." This time the calls of disapproval were drowned by applause. "Oh, friends, we have gathered to greet the men and women of new Russia, a republic founded on the principles of justice to all, equity to all.

"On such an evening never will I sit motionless while directly or indirectly apology is made for the murder of the helpless!"

And then he took his seat, while the crowd raged at him or at Mr. Gompers, with groups downstairs howling at groups upstairs, women shrieking and waving their arms, sailors shouting at men in the boxes opposite or in the dress circle above. All over the house people were standing up, yelling outbursts which were quite indistinguishable in the general din; but as Mayor Mitchel rose and tried to quiet them the volume of sound rolled higher. Finally it paused for a moment and the Mayor said:

"Ladies and gentlemen, we have gathered here to greet the envoys of the Russian people." He was interrupted by more boos and shouts against Roosevelt, but finally obtained quiet and continued sharply: "And for no other purpose than to tender to them this reception and the congratulations of the people of New York." Then he introduced Ambassador Bakhmetieff, and the crowd which a moment before had been howling denunciations back and forth now rose unanimously and cheered the Russian envoy as if there had been no untoward incident at all.

. . .

New York Times, July 7, 1917.

1. Inflamed by rumors that blacks were moving into East St. Louis, Ill., to work as strikebreakers or to bolster the vote count of Republican political operatives, white workers held a protest meeting on May 28, 1917, which was followed by a night of violence targeting blacks. Over the next few weeks racial tensions flared as white gangs attacked black residents and stories circulated that the black community was planning a massacre on July 4 in revenge for the May 28 riots. After black residents defending

their neighborhoods from white drive-by shootings mistakenly shot and killed two white policemen, whites were determined to avenge their deaths and at the same time rid the city of its growing black population. On July 2 armed gangs of white residents roamed the streets, brutally attacking black men, women, and children, looting black homes, setting fire to over two hundred houses, and killing at least thirty-nine blacks. Nine white residents also died in the rioting.

2. Founded in the 1890s, the Friends of Russian Freedom raised funds to support Russian political exiles in the United States and enable them to return to their homeland.

3. The American Ambulance in Russia raised funds to support an ambulance corps and a field hospital on the Eastern Front.

4. Boris Aleksandrovich Bakhmeteff (1880–1951) served as Russian ambassador to the United States from May 1917 to June 1922.

5. Modest Altschuler (1873–1963), a Russian-born cellist and conductor, immigrated to the United States in 1896 and subsequently organized the Russian Symphony Orchestra.

6. Actually Victor Olander, the secretary-treasurer of the Illinois State Federation of Labor.

7. Martin Wiley Littleton (1872–1934), a New York City attorney, served as a Democratic congressman from New York from 1911 to 1913.

From Henry Pope[1]

Porters' & Bootblacks' Union No. 15298[2]
Granite City, Ill., July 12, 1917

Dear Sir:

The above named union in regular meeting convened directs me to call to your attention the existence of certain conditions in Granite City pertaining to organized labor that are a rank injustice to our local, as well as constituting a handicap in the face of which the life of our union is threatened. We are of a firm belief that the American Federation of Labor knows no race or creed, and that the state of affairs as exist here at the present time will not longer be countenanced once the facts are known.

Sponsored by the Central Trades Council[3] the legal number of fellow-workmen applied for and received a charter from the A.F. of L. under date of August 11, 1916, and since that time have abided by and lived up to the law as written in the constitution. We applied for and received admittance to the local Central Trades Council in January, since which time we have been a member thereof and paying our capita tax regularly.

We have persistently endeavored since the beginning to have all porters of what-ever nationality or color to become members and so far every black man working as porter or bootblack here is a member, but with two exceptions no white porters have seen fit to join us, nor can we get the support of the Central Body to assist us beyond mere promises by individual delegates, here in the strongest union town in America. The greatest number of porters here are those employed by saloons, etc., and every saloon or barbershop here is a union place employing union bartenders or union barbers and it would seem that we could get their help, (none doubts that we merit it) but we can't. Now we ask if there be any connections of the above named crafts with the A.F. of L. directly or indirectly, and if they can be urged to give us their support. We feel that we are entitled to assistance from all organized labor, because we are just [as] thorough union men as any regardless of our color, and we are o[nly] asking for moral assistance.

We went to the Central Trades Council and explained that we cared not, that the white porters came into our union if they objected, but should come in or [set up one of their own.] Could there be any more reasonableness asked? [The] Council agreed [that the city was not] so large that it should [require] two locals of the same kind here and that the Teamsters, Hodcarriers, Steel Workers, and all other crafts having workmen of both color employed in Granite City and vicinity have mixed locals, the Porters should have likewise.

But that is all the support we can get, although we have been standing steadily by and seeing our members, one after another lose their jobs, and white men put in their places for no other reason whatever except that he was a union man and that by employing a white porter they could take the help question out of our jurisdiction. The recent trouble in East St. Louis, although too horrible to mention, brings to our minds more forcibly than ever, that after all there is some substance of truth in the oft repeated assertion that organized labor is hostile to the negro. We differ from that belief and think that there was never a more opportune time than the present for organized labor in general, and the A.F. of L. in particular, to disapprove such erroneous impression by taking the position of definite impartiality as regards race or nationality in Labor.

Hoping you will find it convenient to render us whatever assistance you deem best under the circumstances,[4] we respectfully remain,

As ever yours in A.F. of L.   (signed) Henry M. Pope,
Secretary.

TLtpSr, reel 224, vol. 236, pp. 334–35, SG Letterbooks, DLC. Typed notation: "Copy." Enclosed in SG to Thomas Cavanagh, July 21, 1917, ibid., p. 333.

1. Henry M. Pope served as secretary of AFL Porters' and Bootblacks' Union 15,298 of Granite City, Madison, and Venice, Ill., in 1917 and 1918.

2. AFL 15,298 was chartered in 1916.

3. The AFL chartered the Tri-City Central Trades Council (CTC) of Granite City, Madison, and Venice in 1900 and issued a second charter to the organization in 1904.

4. SG wrote Pope on July 21, 1917, that he had sent a copy of his letter to the Tri-City CTC, asking that they look into the matter and assist Pope's organization (reel 224, vol. 236, p. 328, SG Letterbooks, DLC). SG sent a copy of Pope's letter to Thomas Cavanagh, secretary of the council, the same day (ibid., p. 333).

From William Spencer

Building Trades Department
American Federation of Labor
Washington, D.C. July 12, 1917.

Dear Sir and Brother:

Permit me to draw your attention to the unusually large number of building operations that the Government is and will be interested in incident to the war.

Of the contracts that have already been awarded, by far a great majority has been given to those contractors who have in the past utterly failed to maintain a system of collective bargaining with their employes, and in some instances have shown marked discrimination against the employment of Organized Labor.

Still worse, current reports indicate that certain contractors, due to lack of equipment and capacity, are through the medium of advertisements endeavoring to flood the local market with mechanics apparently for the purpose of reducing the labor cost, while taking advantage of the prevailing conditions established by Organized Labor.

We realize that the Government is not in a position to specify that Union Labor shall be employed either in cantonment structures, aviation camps or the permanent buildings that are to be erected, but we do feel there should be no discrimination against union workmen.

The reputable builders of the country, that is the large general contractors who have in the past maintained a system of collective bargaining with their employes, should be more generally recognized by the agency of the Government charged with the letting of building contracts, and we suggest that some representative building tradesman be consulted before contracts are awarded so as to eliminate much of the complaint that now arises.

Thanking you in advance for your earnest consideration of this very important matter, as well as your early reply,[1] I am

Fraternally yours, Wm J Spencer
Secretary-Treasurer, Building Trades Dept.

TLS, Files of the Office of the President, General Correspondence, reel 85, frames 880–83, *AFL Records.*

1. SG informed William Spencer on July 24, 1917, that he had transmitted a copy of his letter to Secretary of War Newton Baker, and he asked Spencer for a list of building trades contractors who conformed to union hours and conditions or who had collective agreements with workmen (reel 224, vol. 236, p. 342, SG Letterbooks, DLC). Spencer sent SG the requested list on July 25.

From Marshall Wright[1] and John Madsen[2]

Seattle, WA Jul 14 1917

Sam Gompers, "Or Frank Morrison"
Waterfront employers association forcing strike by discriminating against union men and compelling all men to hire through their strike-breaking employment office This includes government contractor loading vessels for alaska engineering commission and united states transports We have prevented strike against this outrageous unamerican system by informing the men that the national defense council will surely act on our complaint covering matter dated june 27'th, Men are losing patience We fear they will take drastic action soon We respectfully request you to inform us if anything can be done by your council.[3]

M E Wright. Secy Treasr.
Pacific Coast Dist. ILA[4]
J A Madsen President
Pac Coast dist ILA.

TWSr, Files of the Office of the President, General Correspondence, reel 86, frame 64, *AFL Records.* Handwritten notation: "Submitted to Com. Baruch[5] Take it up with Sec'y Wilson—S.G."

1. Marshall E. Wright, a member of International Longshoremen's Association 38–3 of Tacoma, Wash., served as secretary-treasurer of the Longshoremen's Pacific Coast District from 1917 until 1922.

2. John A. Madsen, a Portland, Oreg., dockworker, served as secretary-treasurer (1916–17) and president (1917–18?) of the Longshoremen's Pacific Coast District. In 1919 he was president of Longshoremen's local 38–6 of Portland.

3. In addition to taking up the matter with Bernard Baruch and Secretary of Labor William B. Wilson, SG wrote J. S. Gibson, president of the Seattle Waterfront Employ-

ers' Association, urging him to use his influence to reconcile differences between waterfront employers and employees (July 17, 1917, Files of the Office of the President,
General Correspondence, reel 86, frame 115, *AFL Records*).

4. The International LONGSHOREMEN'S Association.

5. Bernard Mannes Baruch (1870–1965), a financier, speculator, and, in his later
years, adviser to Democratic political leaders, served from 1916 as a member of the
Advisory Commission of the Council of National Defense, in charge of its division of
raw materials, minerals, and metals. He also served on the War Industries Board, first,
from July 1917, as its commissioner for raw materials, and then, from March 1918, as
its chairman.

From William Thompson[1]

New York, N.Y. July 16th, 1917.

Personal

Dear Mr. Gompers:

On the morning of July 11th I received the following telegram from
Walter Lippman:[2]

"Could you be in Washington tomorrow morning to undertake negotiations, we have already discussed regard to the Garment Unions."

On the afternoon of the 11th of July I telegraphed[3] you as follows:

"Am anxious on account Government to have the Garment amal-
gamation proceed. What suggestions have you about it."

I have not heard from you so far in regard to the matter but presume
that you have been so busy with other matters that you were not able
to give this your attention.

Last week the "Advance," the English organ of the Amalgamated,
printed a very bitter editorial against you in regard to the Roosevelt
episode,[4] which editorial has made both Hillman[5] and myself almost
sick. Schlossberg,[6] General Secretary, Treasurer of the organization
and editor of the paper is a bitter anti-war "Hillquit" type Socialist
and is very much opposed to you. I feel that he can be defeated and a
disavowal of that editorial published, but I feel that we should be able
to give Mr. Hillman and those who stand with him some assurance if
he makes that kind of a life and death struggle. I feel the time is opportune for a successful fight against that element and I should like
as soon as can be to go into it fully with you.[7]

With the highest personal regards and very best wishes,

Sincerely yours,   William O. Thompson

TLS, Files of the Office of the President, General Correspondence, reel 86,
frame 88, *AFL Records*.

1. At this time William Ormonde Thompson was secretary-treasurer of the American Cotton Oil Co. and was serving as a labor mediator for the Cantonment Adjustment Commission.

2. Walter Lippmann (1889–1974), later a Pulitzer Prize–winning columnist, served during World War I as a member of the Cantonment Adjustment Commission and as an assistant to Secretary of War Newton Baker.

3. Thompson to SG, July 11, 1917, Files of the Office of the President, General Correspondence, reel 85, frame 831, *AFL Records.*

4. The editorial, "Gompers Missed a Great Opportunity," was published on July 13, 1917, in the *Advance,* the official journal of the Amalgamated Clothing Workers of America. The editorial criticized SG's comments about the East St. Louis riot at his public meeting with Theodore Roosevelt on July 6 (see "Excerpts from an Article in the *New York Times,*" July 7, 1917, above). The *Advance* termed SG's remarks a "violent speech" and a "moral massacre" that came "perilously near a justification of the bloodshed."

5. Sidney HILLMAN served as president of the Amalgamated Clothing Workers from 1914 to 1946.

6. Joseph SCHLOSSBERG served as secretary (1914–15, 1915–20) and later secretary-treasurer (1920–40) of the Amalgamated Clothing Workers and was editor of the *Advance* (1917–25).

7. SG replied on July 18, 1917, that he was too busy to give the matter any attention, and he suggested Thompson write him again at a later time (reel 224, vol. 236, p. 134, SG Letterbooks, DLC). No further correspondence on the matter has been found. For the creation of the Board of Control of Labor Standards in Army Clothing see "From Thomas Rickert," July 20, 1917, n. 3, below.

To James Sullivan

Committee on Labor
The Advisory Commission of the Council of National Defense
Washington, D.C. July 17, 1917.

Mr. J. W. Sullivan,
Washington, D.C.
Dear Mr. Sullivan:

As my assistant on the Advisory Commission of the Council of National Defense you some time ago tendered your resignation. I have since that time had the matter under consideration. I have a great appreciation of your ability, of your knowledge of the trade union movement, its philosophy, its purposes, its aims, its achievements; of your loyalty to the movement, that you cannot be swerved, cannot be deluded, cannot be swayed from that for which the labor movement stands. Surely, at this critical period as at no other time in the history of our movement, are the services of every loyal man needed. I cannot accept your resignation. I should feel greatly embarrassed to have to say that having put your hand to the plough, you yet had turned back.

While I am not unmindful of the convenience both to you and to me of your being located in the A.F. of L. Building where you can be readily consulted, yet now that the offices of the Committee on Labor have been permanently assigned by the Director of the Advisory Commission, clerks installed, room and desk provided for you as well as for me, and particularly now that Mr. Robbins[1] is no longer in charge of the offices, it seems to me that it is essential that either you or I should personally supervise and direct the offices of the Committee on Labor. In fact, unless some such arrangement is made I fear we may be called upon to surrender rooms for which the Commission is paying rent and which are not being occupied. As it is wholly impractical for me to remove my permanent office from the A.F. of L. Building, I feel that I must ask you to transfer your office to the Munsey Building.

I will go to the offices of the Committee on Labor as frequently as my duties here will permit. When necessary for consultation, you can come to the A.F. of L. Building, or confer by phone, or some one of my assistants here could go down for a brief time and go over with you matters that have transpired here with which you should be made acquainted.

I wish to establish the custom that callers who desire information from or about the Committee on Labor should seek such information in the offices of that Committee. I shall direct that the course be continued of referring to you those persons who desire information on the work of the Committee on Labor unless for some special reason it may be more desirable for me to see them first or last or at all. Without giving offence to those earnest persons who want to help, who may have come long distances for the purpose of conferring with me, it is my hope, as far as possible, to be relieved from the necessity of seeing the greater number of these people who have suggestions or plans to offer, who may seek guidance to the most effective road to service to the committee. I want no one turned away unsatisfied, but I am sure it may be generally so arranged that their time may be given to you and, if necessary to see me, that a few minutes will be sufficient.

Under my instructions Miss Guard has established the custom of sending to the Munsey Building for filing the greater part of the correspondence connected with the Committee on Labor work. There is some of the correspondence which it is necessary to retain here which she understands is subject at any time for reference in this office. She will not deviate from that custom. I wish as far as practicable and possible (with my being compelled to spend the greater part of my time at the A.F. of L. Building) to have all the correspondence of the Committee on Labor on file in the offices of that committee.

For reasons which you understand the report which by order of the Council of National Defense the chairman of the Committee on Labor is required to submit weekly to the Director, I desire to be addressed to the Director and signed by me.

The mail that comes to the Munsey Building offices directed to me you will please open, give to Miss Beeks that which properly goes to her for reply and answer such of it as you may judge should be better answered in your name; that answered in my name will come to the office here for my signature. All letters, even mere acknowledgments, shall be letter-pressed copied.

All correspondence relating to the adjustment of conditions on the various cantonments, to adjustment of troubles between organizations of labor and contractors and companies having government contracts, correspondence relating to the exemption boards, to the food regulation legislation, etc., etc., I have conducted in my name as President of the American Federation of Labor. Letters of this character which may be addressed to me at the Munsey Building you will please send to my office here for reply.

I have not gone over the system for conducting the details of the work in the offices of the Committee on Labor; I am entirely satisfied to leave that to you, Miss Beeks and Mr. Easley.

Such correspondence as is directly connected with the work of the Committee on Labor and its various sub-committees as may come to me at the A.F. of L. offices will be turned over to you, and you in turn will give to Miss Beeks such matters as should properly go to her as secretary of the Executive Committee. I realize that this transfer of mail to and from one office to the other for attention, reply, and signature will cause delay, but under existing circumstances it is the best way that I can now designate.

I have considered the regulations which you submitted. It is not an easy matter to determine where my duties as President of the American Federation of Labor end and my obligations as chairman of the committee on labor of the Advisory Commission of the Council of National Defense begin, no matter how much I or any one else may try to do so. My judgment is that the suggestions as above will be demonstrated to be the better and more effective way in which to meet the situation.

Very truly yours,   Saml Gompers.
Chairman,   Committee on Labor,

The Advisory Commission of the Council of National Defense.

TLcS, Files of the Office of the President, General Correspondence, reel 86, frames 126–30, *AFL Records*.

1. Hayes Robbins (1873–1941) served as secretary of the Civic Federation of New England (1905–8) and later as an assistant to SG on the Committee on Labor of the Advisory Commission of the Council of National Defense (1917). He wrote additional material for a new edition of James W. Sullivan's *Socialism as an Incubus on the American Labor Movement*, which was published in 1918, and he compiled and edited two volumes of SG's writings and addresses, *Labor and the Common Welfare* (1919) and *Labor and the Employer* (1920).

To Chester Wright[1]

July 19, 1917.

Mr. Chester M. Wright,
The Newspaper and Enterprise Association,
Cleveland, Ohio.
My dear Mr. Wright:

Your letter and enclosed articles describing the situation as you found it at East St. Louis was read with the keenest interest and appreciation.

You, of course, saw newspaper accounts of the meeting in New York in which Col. Roosevelt undertook to charge the labor movement with the responsibility for the rioting. However, the attack on me only serves to make more prominent the acute situation which has developed in this country because of rivalry between the standards of living and work of nationalities collected in our industrial centers.

I am glad you covered the situation so fully in your newspaper stories because you are peculiarly adapted to interpret the labor side of the situation. From all indications the organized labor movement will have a stiff fight to maintain standards and protection for the workers against the insidious attempts that are made by any exploiting interests.

I shall be very glad to hear from you often. With best wishes, I am

Very truly yours,   Saml Gompers.
President,   American Federation of Labor.

TLpS, reel 224, vol. 236, p. 154, SG Letterbooks, DLC.

1. Chester Maynard WRIGHT, later the director of the news department of the American Alliance for Labor and Democracy.

To John Mitchell[1]

July 20, 1917.

Mr. John Mitchell,
Chairman, State Industrial Commission,
230 Fifth Avenue, New York City.
My [de]ar Mr. Mitchell:

Your esteemed favor of July 16 to hand, the contents of which have been most carefully noted.

The recent decisions of the United States Supreme Court on the Compensation laws of New York,[2] Washington[3] and Iowa,[4] have caused me much concern, and I have given them as much consideration as my many duties will permit me.

On March 6, the Court maintained the validity of the insurance feature of the Washington Act, in the case Mountain Timber Company, vs. The State of Washington.[5] On the same day, the Court sustained the validity of the general principles contained in the Iowa Act, in the case of J. C. Hawkins, vs. John L. [Bl]eakly, Auditor of the State of Iowa, and Warren Garst, Iowa Industrial Commissioner.[6] On the same day the Court affirmed the award by your Commission in the case of New York Central Railroad vs. [S]arah White,[7] making it perfectly clear in that decision that the Workmen's Compensation law of New York was indisputably applicable in the case of Jacob White, who received fatal injuries while on [du]ty at a new station which was "designed for use, when finished, in interstate commerce," but which the Court decided did not bring his case within the Federal Employers' Liability Act of 1908.[8] A complete and careful reading of that decision leads me to conclude that the Court was consistent with its former decisions rendered in the cases of Bruce Shanks, vs. Delaware, Lackawanna and Western,[9] January 10, 1916; Walsh, vs. New York, New Haven and Hartford R.R. Co., 223 U.S. 1;[10] Norfolk and Western Ry. Co. vs. Earnest, 229 U.S. 114;[11] Pederson vs. Delaware, Lackawanna and Western R.R. Co., 229 U.S. 146;[12] and other cases not necessary to cite herein.

I am disposed to the opinion that the Court, in the decisions herein referred to, have made their lines of demarkation fairly distinct in railroad cases, and that they intend to hold the Federal Employers' Liability Act of 1908, definitely applicable to *all railroad employes* who are injured on or in the course of their employment when it can be clearly and positively shown that at the [ti]me of such injury they are actually engaged either in the movement of interstate commerce or upon some instrumentality which can be clearly shown is used in interstate commerce.

On the other hand, I am of the opinion that the Court has [ma]de it clear and definite that the Compensation Act of New York State and the Compensation Acts of other states which have similar provisions will be applicable to railroad employes who meet [wi]th injuries while on or in the course of their employment and engaged on work that can be clearly proven to be either intra-state commerce or on an instrumentality of the railroad which [i]s not a definite and positive instrumentality in interstate commerce.

The cases decided by the Court on May 21, 1917, seem to me to substantiate the former attitude of the Court, and make it more clear to my mind that what I have herein observed is going to be their practice. I refer herein specifically to the cases of New York Central Railroad, vs. James Winfield,[13] and Erie Railroad vs. Amy L. Winfield, 244 U.S., page—.[14]

I now come to the other portion of your letter in which you refer to the decisions of the Court in Southern Pacific Company, v[s]. Marie Jensen,[15] and the second case of Clyde Steamship Company, vs. Wm. Alfred Walker,[16] both of which will be found in 244 U.S., page—.

Notwithstanding the vigorous dissenting opinions by Associate Justices Brandeis, Clarke,[17] Holmes,[18] and Pitney,[19] the Court decided, by a vote of 5 to 4, that the state legislators had no authority to extend jurisdiction under the state compensation laws for the benefit of workmen injured on wharves and docks, or otherwise employed in distinctly maritime occupations, whether engaged in intra-state or interstate commerce. The Court was very emphatic in the first case cited, wherein it stated:

"The Workmen's Compensation Act conflicts with the general maritime law, which constitutes an integral part of the Federal law under art. 3, paragraph 2, of the Constitution, and to that extent is invalid."

The Court also very distinctly announced that the case was not covered by the Federal Employers' Liability Act, wherein it said:

"Plaintiff in error *being an interstate common carrier by railroad,* is responsible for injuries received by employees while engaged therein under the Federal Employers' Liability Act of April 22, 1908."

"The Southern Pacific Company, a Kentucky corporation, owns and operates a railroad as a common carrier; also the steam ship El Oriente, plying between New York and Galveston, Texas. The claim is that therefore rights and liabilities of the parties here must be determined in accordance with the Federal Employers' Liability Act. But we think that act is not applicable in the circumstances."

Note the emphatic language of the Court in the last sentence—"But we think that act is not applicable in the circumstances."

Then the Court goes on to explain why it declared the first Federal Employers' Liability Act of June 11, 1906,[20] as being invalid,[21] because that act extended to all common carriers engaged in interstate and foreign commerce. That first act was declared invalid because the Court decided, "it embraced subjects not within the constitutional authority of Congress."

In another part of the decision, the Court announced:

"Exclusive jurisdiction of all civil cases of admiralty and maritime jurisdiction is vested in the Federal district courts, 'saving to suitors in all cases the right of a common-law remedy where the common law is competent to give it.' The remedy which the Compensation Statute attempts to give is of a character wholly unknown to the common law, incapable of enforcement by the ordinary processes of any court, and is not saved to suitors from the grant of exclusive jurisdiction."

Upon reviewing the decision more closely, I observe a far-reaching suggestion by the Court, and will quote it herein almost completely:

"Article 3, paragraph 2 of the Constitution, extends judicial power of the United States 'to all cases of admiralty and maritime jurisdiction'; and article 1, paragraph 8, confers upon the Congress power 'to make all laws which shall be necessary and proper for carrying into execution the foregoing powers and all other powers vested by this Constitution in the government of the United States or in any department or officer thereof.'"

Now, please note the following important and suggestive language:

"Considering our former opinions, it must now be accepted as settled doctrine that, in consequence of these provisions, Congress has paramount power to fix and determine the maritime law which shall prevail throughout the country."

Here follows several citations.

["] . . . [22] And further, that, in the absence of some controlling statute, the general maritime law, as accepted by the Federal courts, constitutes part of our national law, applicable to matters within the admiralty and maritime jurisdiction."

It seems to me, therefore, that the Court practically admitted that it was ready to review its former decision on the first Federal Employers' Liability Act, and made it emphatic in this latter decision that there was no question whatsoever concerning the paramount authority of Congress to legislate relative to maritime interstate commerce, provided such maritime law should prevail throughout the whole country uniformly.

I therefore agree with you, that immediate efforts should be made to secure adequate legislation which shall protect the interes[ts] of the workers engaged in the maritime occupations. The difficulty will be, however, to determine just where we should [st]op and how far we should go with such proposed legislation. [I]f we draft a bill covering maritime occupations on docks and on vessels in safe harbor, a contest might be made that it was class legislation because it did not apply to seamen also, and if on the other hand, we urge legislation embracing seamen, we will run afoul of the danger of having such a law declared invalid because it [i]s too sweeping and trespasses upon treaty rights.

At this time I cannot see the advisability of pressing such legislation, but I do think we should make an early preparation for [i]t so that we may bring it before the Congress during the next session (the regular legislative session). Pending that time I think we should give the subject all the consideration we c[an] devote to it, particularly in behalf of the maritime workers.[23]

As I said before, I think the Court has now made a clear and definite demarkation with regards to employes of common carriers engaged in interstate commerce. I foresee no difficulty whatsoever with regards to the power of your Commission. The Court has informed you in the cases I have cited, that the State Compensation law is applicable to all injured workmen who meet with injuries on or in the course of their employment which is not distinctly and clearly interstate commerce, and in all other cases where injuries are received when the injured employe is distinctly and clearly injured while engaged either in interstate commerce or on a definite instrumentality used in interstate commerce, then the Federal Employers' Liability Act of April 22, 1908 applies. With this ruling we can go to the other states which have enacted compensation laws and ask them to change their state laws so that the many thousands of railroad employes engaged in the mechanical departments, the offices, on the tracks, in the warehouses and elsewhere, may be protected equally with other workers. I mention this although apart from the general tenor of your letter because of the fact that in many of the states, these thousands of railroad employes I now refer to have been denied protection under the state compensation laws, and being in doubt about the jurisdiction of the Federal Employers' Liability law, they have been compelled to carry their burdens as formerly, or run the chance of expense and disappointment under the old common law with its abomination of defenses.

I have written this letter at some length because I feel with you, that the subject is an important one, and one that we should meet. If you still think we should have a conference of representatives of unions whose members are employed on vessels and as longshoremen, and a like conference of representatives of unions employed in the transportation industry, I shall be glad to hear from you. It may be that this matter could be deferred until the Buffalo Convention,[24] but if you still feel that a conference should be called, among those interested, previous to that date, kindly let me know. I shall be glad to cooperate and help to the full extent of my ability.

Very truly yours,   Saml Gompers.
President,   American Federation of Labor.

TLpS, reel 224, vol. 236, pp. 437–41, SG Letterbooks, DLC.

1. John MITCHELL was chairman of the New York State Industrial Commission (1915–19) and had previously served as an AFL vice-president (1899–1913).

2. New York, *Laws of 1913*, chap. 816. See *The Samuel Gompers Papers*, vol. 9, p. 76, n. 10.

3. Washington, *Laws of 1911*, chap. 74, and *Laws of 1913*, chap. 148. See *The Samuel Gompers Papers*, vol. 9, p. 75, n. 3.

4. Iowa, *Laws of the Thirty-Fifth General Assembly*, chap. 147, enacted Apr. 18, 1913, provided a scale of compensation for workers injured or killed on the job. Employers who participated in an insurance plan approved by the state were relieved of any additional liability for damages or compensation; those who did not were to be presumed negligent in the case of an injury to one of their employees. The act also created the office of industrial commissioner to carry out the provisions of the law.

5. *Mountain Timber Co. v. State of Washington*, 243 U.S. 219 (1917).

6. *Hawkins v. Bleakly*, 243 U.S. 210 (1917).

7. *New York Central Railroad Co. v. White*, 243 U.S. 188 (1917).

8. U.S. *Statutes at Large*, 35: 65–66. See *The Samuel Gompers Papers*, vol. 8, p. 459, n. 5.

9. *Shanks v. Delaware, Lackawanna, and Western Railroad Co.*, 239 U.S. 556 (1916).

10. *Walsh v. New York, New Haven, and Hartford Railroad Co.* was included among the *Second Employers' Liability Cases* (223 U.S. 1 [1912]).

11. *Norfolk and Western Railway Co. v. Earnest*, 229 U.S. 114 (1913).

12. *Pedersen v. Delaware, Lackawanna, and Western Railroad Co.*, 229 U.S. 146 (1913).

13. *New York Central Railroad Co. v. Winfield*, 244 U.S. 147 (1917).

14. *Erie Railroad Co. v. Winfield*, 244 U.S. 170 (1917).

15. *Southern Pacific Co. v. Jensen*, 244 U.S. 205 (1917).

16. *Clyde Steamship Co. v. Walker*, 244 U.S. 255 (1917).

17. John Hessin Clarke (1857–1945), previously a judge of the U.S. District Court for the Northern District of Ohio (1914–16), served as a justice of the U.S. Supreme Court from 1916 to 1922.

18. Oliver Wendell Holmes (1841–1935), who was earlier a justice of the Supreme Judicial Court of Massachusetts (1882–1902), served as a justice of the U.S. Supreme Court from 1902 to 1932.

19. Mahlon Pitney (1858–1924), previously a Republican congressman from New Jersey (1895–99), served as a justice of the U.S. Supreme Court from 1912 to 1922.

20. U.S. *Statutes at Large*, 34: 232–33.

21. *Employers' Liability Cases*, 207 U.S. 463 (1908).

22. Ellipses in original.

23. SG later reported, "After much deliberation to find a way out, it was finally decided that an amendment to the Judicial Code relating to the jurisidiction of the district courts was the only available remedy" (AFL, *Proceedings*, 1917, p. 116). As a result, he said, Republican senator Hiram Johnson of California introduced S. 2916

(65th Cong., 1st sess.), on Sept. 25, 1917, to amend the code to extend the right to sue under the provisions of state workers' compensation laws to dock workers and other civil claimants who came under admiralty and maritime jurisdiction. The bill became law on Oct. 6 (U.S. *Statutes at Large*, 40: 395).

24. The 1917 AFL convention met in Buffalo, N.Y., Nov. 12–24.

To Woodrow Wilson

Washington, D.C. July 20, 1917.

Honorable Woodrow Wilson,
President of the United States,
Washington, D.C.
Sir:

A number of telegrams have been received by me from several parts of Arizona, calling attention to the treatment accorded to the work-men of that state. I quote herein three telegrams as follows:

["]Phoenix, Arizona,
["]July 18, 1917.

"Samuel Gompers, President,
["]American Federation of Labor,
["]A.F. of L. Building, Washington, D.C.
["]Use your best efforts with President to have all men who were de-ported from Bisbee returned to their homes under military protec-tion. Many American Federation of Labor members with families were deported. Their wives and children are in want. Act at once.

["]W. E. Holm
["]F. J. Perry
["]Former Secretaries Warren District Trade Assembly."[1]

["]Phoenix, Arizona
["]July 19, 1917.

"Samuel Gompers, President,
["]American Federation of Labor,
["]A.F. of L. Bldg., Washington, D.C.
["]Appeal to the President to order men deported from Bisbee returned to their homes with military protection. Many members of American Federation of Labor deported and treated like brutes. Families of deported men suffering with hunger in Bisbee. Quick action is necessary.

["]Thos. A. French,[2]
["]Secretary Arizona State Federation of Labor.["]

["]Phoenix, Arizona.
["]July 19, 1917.

"Samuel Gompers, President,
["]American Federation of Labor,
["]A.F. of L. Bldg., Washington, D.C.
["]Fred W. Brown, Organizer American Federation of Labor, number 7352, a bitter opponent of I.W.W. is among the men deported from Bisbee. Deportation was a general fight on organized labor. We are advised of no action by Federal Government as yet.

["]Thomas A. French,   Secretary.
["]Arizona State Federation of Labor."

The reason I have given these three telegrams is because they are official and from representatives in the labor movement in Phoenix who I know to be trustworthy and truthful.

I assume it is not necessary for me to give any assurance of how utterly out of accord I am with the I.W.W. and any such propaganda; but some of the men deported are said to be law-abiding men engaged in an earnest effort at improvement of their condition. If the men treated as stated have been guilty of any crime, they should be tried in the courts and given the opportunity for defense. There is no law of which I am aware that gives authority to private citizens to undertake to deport from the state any man. If there be lawlessness, it is surely such conduct.

I am fully impressed with your desire not only to see that justice is done but to do justice to all our people alike, regardless of their walk in life, and I respectfully submit this matter to your consideration, confident that you will take such action as the circumstances warrant.[3]

Respectfully,   Saml Gompers.
President,   American Federation of Labor.

TLS, Woodrow Wilson Papers, DLC.

1. The AFL chartered the Warren District Trades Assembly of Bisbee, Ariz., in 1913. Walter E. Holm and F. J. Perry served as its secretaries in 1914 and 1915, respectively.

2. Thomas A. FRENCH was secretary-treasurer of the Arizona State Federation of Labor from 1916 to 1917 and again from 1920 to 1921.

3. President Woodrow Wilson acknowledged SG's letter on July 21, 1917 (Files of the Office of the President, General Correspondence, reel 86, frame 268, *AFL Records*). For Wilson's telegram of July 12 to Arizona governor Thomas Campbell expressing concern about the deportations, see Arthur S. Link et al., eds., *The Papers of Woodrow Wilson*, 69 vols. (Princeton, N.J., 1966–94), 43: 158. See also "To William B. Wilson," Aug. 27, 1917, n. 3, below.

From Thomas Rickert[1]

Chicago, Ill. July 20, 1917.

Dear Sir and Brother:—

I am in receipt of a letter from Secretary Larger,[2] advising me that you wish to meet us in conference in New York on July the 28th, with reference to the danger of Hillman being appointed to look after the interests of the tailors in making government clothes.[3] I find, unfortunately, that it will be absolutely impossible for me to be in New York before July 30th or 31st. Could you change the appointment to either date?[4] If so, advise[5] me here.

Should this be impossible, Secretary Larger with a committee from our Board will meet you on the date that you have set and go over the matter. No doubt you fully realize what it would mean to our organization were the government to select the head of the seceding organization for such important work. For one, I would of course have to immediately resign from the committees connected with the Council of Defense, of which I am now a member. Many other labor leaders would probably do likewise.

Your influence is great, and I know you appreciate the importance of this matter, hence I would urge you to protest most vigorously against his selection. I feel sure that if you will do this the government will not give him consideration.

Assuring you of my kindest personal regards, I remain,

Very truly yours,   T A Rickert.
General President,   United Garment Workers of America.

TLS, Files of the Office of the President, General Correspondence, reel 86, frame 252, *AFL Records*.

1. Thomas Alfred RICKERT was president of the United Garment Workers of America (1904–41) and an AFL vice-president (1918–41). He served on the National War Labor Board (1918–19) and on the subcommittees on mediation and conciliation and on wages and hours of the Committee on Labor of the Advisory Commission of the Council of National Defense.

2. Bernard A. LARGER was secretary of the Garment Workers (1904–28).

3. On Aug. 24, 1917, Secretary of War Newton Baker announced the formation of a Board of Control of Labor Standards in Army Clothing to enforce the maintenance of sanitary labor standards, oversee wages, and resolve disputes in the manufacture of army clothing. The board included no union representatives. Its three members were Louis Kirstein, vice-president and manager of William Filene's Sons Co. of Boston, Florence Kelley, secretary of the National Consumers' League, and Capt. Walter Kreusi of the Army Quartermaster Corps. The board was dissolved on Jan. 23, 1918.

4. SG and Frank Morrison met with Rickert and Larger at AFL headquarters in Washington, D.C., on July 24, 1917.

5. SG et al. to Rickert, July 21, 1917, Files of the Office of the President, General Correspondence, reel 86, frame 263, *AFL Records*.

To Philip Juranovich[1]

July 23, 1917.

Mr. P. S. Jouranovich,
President, Sweetwater County Federated Trades & Labor Council,[2]
Rock Springs, Wyoming.
Dear Sir and Brother:

The resolution of the Federated Trades and Labor Council of Sweetwater County, Wyoming, received. Immediately after the first inadequate reports of the riots in East St. Louis were published, competent reporters and official investigators were sent into East St. Louis to find out the causes of the riots. Their reports were later published in many of the metropolitan papers and an official report made by the Committee of the Illinois State Council of Defense was published in pamphlet form.[3] All of these reports reached practically the same findings as to social and financial causes which brought about a condition that culminated in the dreadful riots.

In an article published in the August American Federationist, which will soon come from the press, the under-lying causes are presented and the official report of the Illinois Committee is incorporated. In order that your organization may be in possession of correct information, I urge that that article be read at an early meeting of your Central Body. Inasmuch as your organization adopted resolutions without knowing all of the facts connected with the situation and has called upon me either to confirm or deny a statement accredited to me in the press, I feel that I have a right to expect that this course will be followed. As to the expression attributed to me in the press, "The war in East St. Louis is real democracy," the statement is false and made without the slightest justification or foundation in fact.

In this critical time in which our nation finds itself confronted by so many outside dangers, it is most important that there should be a spirit of unity and mutual helpfulness within. It is evident that if we do not follow wisest courses and methods, we may have to meet additional dangers of racial antagonism within our border. No true patriot and citizen can consider such a possibility without feeling impelled to do everything within his power to prevent the development of such elements of disruption.

I trust that the organized labor movement will be a forceful element for unity and in support of principles of democracy and freedom.

With best wishes to all members of your organization joined together for the betterment and freedom of American workers, I am

Fraternally,   Saml Gompers.

President,   American Federation of Labor.

TLpS, reel 224, vol. 236, pp. 550–51, SG Letterbooks, DLC.

1. Philip S. Juranovich was a member of United Mine Workers of America 2282 of Rock Springs, Wyo.

2. The AFL chartered the Sweetwater County, Wyo., Trades and Labor Council in 1908.

3. The report by the Labor Committee of the Illinois State Council of Defense, dated June 30, 1917, and signed by John Walker as chair, was printed in SG's article "East St. Louis Riots—Their Causes" in the August 1917 number of the *American Federationist* (24: 621–26). In his article SG himself wrote:

"Even though occurring in a series of unprecedented happenings, the recent race riots in East St. Louis startled and horrified the nation.

"Mobs and riots do not occur in a community that conducts its affairs equitably and with regard to the welfare and best interests of its people, but they indicate diseased, abnormal conditions like festering sores—inflamed by poisons and unwholesome conditions. Such outbreaks are disgraceful and humiliating to all citizens because they demonstrate intellectual or moral incompetence in dealing with community affairs.

"The American nation was horrified and mortified by the brutal race riots recently occurring at East St. Louis, and we want to avoid the possibility of a similar disaster and, therefore, we want to know the causes. An investigation has disclosed the following conditions:

"Negroes imported to lower industrial standards.

"Political corruption and incompetence.

"Absentee corporation control.

"Housing conditions.

"East St. Louis is a commercial and an industrial center—there are the packing plants and stockyards of Armour, Swift and Morris, the Aluminum Ore Company, the American Steel Foundry, the Commercial Acid Company and twenty-seven railroad lines. These corporations have their offices in LaSalle Street, Chicago, or Wall Street,

New York. They employed many foreigners until workers were called home to their colors. They began the policy of negro importation from the south. Negro importation became a regular business—agents were sent throughout the south who collected groups of negroes and paid the railroad fare to East St. Louis. Unsigned advertisements for negro workers to go north appeared in the papers of many localities. As a result, East St. Louis became a sort of convention center for excited, undisciplined negroes who were intoxicated by higher wages than they had ever known. Some of these, as in the case of the Aluminum Ore Company, were used as strike-breakers, and the element of racial industrial competition was added to other trouble-breeding influences.

"Low wage-workers found unfamiliar opportunities involving responsibilities in living and a social obligation for which they were totally unfitted by experience. The city government failed to supplement this deficiency by adequate police for either preventive or repressive purposes. The situation was due to governmental poverty. It is a matter of common information that conditions in East St. Louis made it the gathering place for white and black outlaws and crooks. The situation gave grave concern to the citizens of the town. All the elements necessary for a race war had been gathered.

"Violence became frequent. Minor riots occurred between the whites and the blacks. Six hundred union men marched to the City Hall and asked that further importation of negroes be stopped. They wanted to avert a calamity that they knew was inevitable unless the necessary action was taken. But the profit-mad employers were not checked. Industrial friction and lawlessness continued.

"A racial problem rarely becomes acute except through economic or social friction. There are few who can not dispassionately and philosophically consider racial difference when no personal contact or competition exists. Inevitable conflict comes through a clash of standards—standards of work which mean also standards of life.

"Some unestablished cause precipitated the terrible attack which one race made on the other—the responsibility for which rests fundamentally upon those who profited from the industrial, social and corrupt political conditions in East St. Louis. . . .

"Let no community assume an attitude of self-righteousness toward the terrible violence that has brought shame and horror to East St. Louis and to our whole nation. If the same conditions are permitted to exist in any other locality, the same rioting may be expected. Race problems are serious even when approached with intelligence and always harbor germs of danger. This is why the organized labor movement tries to protect workers from industrial competition with another race, particularly one with lower standards.

"It is particularly timely that this warning be considered now that an effort is being made to destroy the legislation that protects workers against competition with coolie standards of work and life. Our nation is in the fight for democracy and is ready to pour out lives and treasure freely and ungrudgingly for human freedom. Victory means wonderful opportunity but it must be a victory for [the] American people as a whole.

"All students know that the American Federation of Labor, its officers and advocates have valiantly stood in defense and advocacy of the rights of all workers—all our people—white and black, but no one can blind the people to the fact that the negroes became the conscious or unconscious victims to the profit mongers, aided and abetted by a corrupt gang of East St. Louis politicians and grafters. . . .

"The way to prevent riots is to establish justice. Negroes were brought to this country through injustice—that their labor might be exploited. Those innocent, helpless slaves have had a terrible vengeance in the race problem the American people must meet. Similar exploitation of the workers of any other race would inevitably lead to similar results" (ibid., pp. 621–22, 625–26).

From William B. Wilson

Office of the Secretary
Department of Labor
Washington July 24, 1917.

My dear Mr. Gompers:

I am inclosing you herewith copy of telegram addressed to Ashmun Brown[1] by Mr. Dillon,[2] relative to organizing the logging and lumbering industry in the A.F. of L.[3] I have wired the telegram to President Marsh,[4] of the Washington State Federation of Labor, and to Commissioner White,[5] who is acting as a Commissioner of Conciliation for the Department of Labor, copies[6] of which I am inclosing.

The situation in the State of Washington at the present moment is very tense. There is not only the strike in the lumbering camps[7] but street car strikes in Seattle[8] and Tacoma.[9] The street car system is owned by Stone and Webster of Boston, Massachusetts, who control the power plants in the vicinity of Seattle. I have directed former Assistant Secretary of the Treasury Andrew J. Peters[10] to bring what influence he can to bear on Stone and Webster to secure an adjustment.

The strikes, with the unsettled condition among the longshoremen on the waterfront, create a situation likely to materially interfere with the shipment of supplies to Russia and the furnishing of material for the wooden shipbuilding program. I am bringing every influence I can to bear in an effort to get these troubles adjusted. If there is any way in which you can assist us in putting over the suggestion contained in the telegram, so that an adjustment can be reached, it will very materially assist in the solution of the problem.[11]

Sincerely yours,   W B Wilson
Secretary.

TLS, Files of the Office of the President, General Correspondence, reel 86, frames 351–52, *AFL Records*.

1. Ashmun Norris Brown was the Washington, D.C., correspondent for the *Seattle Post-Intelligencer.*

2. Thomas Joseph Dillon was managing editor of the *Seattle Post-Intelligencer.*

3. The telegram, dated July 22, 1917, asked Brown to see SG about organizing logging and timber workers in the AFL since, Dillon asserted, the mill and camp operators had indicated their willingness to grant the eight-hour day to a union affiliated with the AFL (Files of the Office of the President, General Correspondence, reel 86, frame 270, *AFL Records*). The International Union of TIMBER Workers, which had been organized in Washington state the preceding January, applied for an AFL charter on July 23, claiming two thousand members. The charter was issued on Aug. 7. The operators, however, refused to grant the eight-hour day.

4. Ernest P. MARSH was president of the Washington State Federation of Labor

from 1913 to 1918 and a vice-president of the International Shingle Weavers' Union of America from 1916 to 1918.

5. Henry Middleton White, a Bellingham, Wash., attorney, was the commissioner of the U.S. Immigration Service at Seattle from 1913 until 1921 and also served for a time as a commissioner of conciliation for the U.S. Department of Labor.

6. Wilson to Marsh and Wilson to White, both July 24, 1917, Files of the Office of the President, General Correspondence, reel 86, frames 353 and 446, *AFL Records*.

7. Members of IWW Lumber Workers' Industrial Union No. 500 struck on July 14, 1917, when employers, organized in the Lumbermen's Protective Association, rejected demands for an eight-hour day, higher wages, better housing and sanitary conditions, union recognition, and the closed shop. On July 16 the International Shingle Weavers' Union of America and the International Union of Timber Workers joined the strike, which eventually involved between forty and fifty thousand workers and shut down virtually the entire timber industry in the Pacific Northwest. As the summer went on, the strike came to focus primarily on the eight-hour day, with the other demands receding into the background. Both state and federal authorities attempted to arrange a settlement, but without success. In early September the IWW Lumber Workers went back to work but continued their strike through work slowdowns, frequent job changes, and sabotage. The AFL affiliates—the Shingle Weavers and the Timber Workers—allowed their members to return to work shortly thereafter.

8. In June 1917 Amalgamated Association of Street and Electric Railway Employes of America 587 of Seattle began organizing streetcar workers employed by the Puget Sound Traction, Light, and Power Co. The company responded by firing employees who joined the union, and it refused to consider a wage proposal. On July 17, after efforts to meet with company officials failed, some sixteen hundred streetcar workers struck, causing a complete cessation of service in the city. Shortly thereafter, the company began bringing in strikebreakers. With the assistance of federal mediators Henry White and Edgar Snyder, however, an agreement was reached on July 31 and was ratified by the streetcar workers the next day, with the men returning to work on Aug. 2. Under the agreement, Puget Sound Traction agreed to allow streetcar workers to organize, reinstated the discharged men, and fired the strikebreakers. Unresolved issues of wages and working conditions were submitted to arbitration.

9. Members of Street Railway Employes' local 758 of Tacoma, Wash., which was organized in early July 1917, struck the Tacoma Railway and Power Co. on July 16 after the firm refused to consider a wage proposal and fired several union members. The strike ended on Aug. 2, with the company conceding the right to organize, reinstating the discharged men, and agreeing to submit issues relating to wages and working conditions to arbitration.

10. Andrew James Peters (1872–1938), a Boston attorney, served as a Democratic congressman from Massachusetts (1907–14), assistant secretary of the Treasury (1914–March 1917), and mayor of Boston (1918–22).

11. After receiving Wilson's letter, SG wrote to Marsh and, in order to contact Stone and Webster in Boston, to representatives of the Boston Central Labor Union (July 26, 1917, Files of the Office of the President, reel 86, frame 444, *AFL Records*).

From George Creel[1]

Committee on Public Information[2]
Washington, D.C. July 26, 1917.

Dear Mr. Gompers:

This is a memorandum with regard to our talk of yesterday:

I am ready to get behind you and the Central Federated Union in your attempt to Americanize the labor movement.[3] Out of my knowledge of you, and the men associated with you, I have the conviction that it is not necessary to explain that such efforts, in order to have this support, must be open and above board.

As I explained to you, I must insist that the entire movement be governed and directed by organized labor. It is my suggestion that offices be secured on the East Side in New York City and a sound, capable executive chosen. It will be his duty, as a result of conference, to select a committee on publicity and a committee on speakers. I want the meaning of America, and the purpose of America, to be put before the foreign born in all of their languages and in all of their tongues. I contemplate a speaking campaign that will cover the entire East Side. Also literature and posters.

As for the daily paper situation, my talk with Dr. Miller[4] left me profoundly disturbed. He is firmly of the opinion that until a change to Americanism has been brought about, the Jewish dailies will not dare to aid us. If this is the case, we must meet the need in another way. The Government, of course, cannot subsidize papers nor can it start one. I feel certain, however, that we can appeal to a number of rich Jews and get them to start a daily that will serve our purpose.

At your meeting Saturday[5] I beg you to thrash this whole matter out and reach some determination as to organization and procedure. As I told you, I have complete trust in your judgment and am willing to abide by it.

Sincerely, George Creel

TLS, Files of the Office of the President, General Correspondence, reel 86, frames 415–16, *AFL Records*.

1. George Edward Creel (1876–1953), a journalist and writer, served as chairman of the Committee on Public Information during World War I.

2. The Committee on Public Information was created by executive order on Apr. 13, 1917, to supervise voluntary censorship of the press, disseminate news, and mobilize public support for the war.

3. On July 21, 1917, SG met in New York City with Joseph Barondess, Ernest Bohm, Hugh Frayne, and Frank Morrison, as well as Robert Maisel and two other representatives of the National Labor Publicity Organization—David Berry and W. L. Small, the editors of labor papers in Pittsburgh and Newark, N.J.—to discuss how to offset what

they referred to as the "treasonable" activities of "German propagandists and agitators" on New York's Lower East Side and the influence of the Workmen's Council for the Maintenance of Labor's Rights (Files of the Office of the President, Conferences, reel 120, frame 155; "Labor Fights Germanizers," *New York Times,* July 23, 1917). SG suggested setting up a small office and hiring Chester Wright and Louis Miller to prepare articles in English and Yiddish for daily publication. The group voted to meet again on July 28 and invited the participation of a committee from the Central Federated Union of New York City and Vicinity, editors of the Jewish press, and prowar socialists (see n. 5, below).

4. Louis E. Miller (1866?–1927), a New York City journalist and newspaper editor, founded the *Jewish Daily Forward* with Abraham Cahan in 1897 and the *Warheit* in 1905.

5. On July 28, 1917, SG met again in New York City with Barondess, Berry, Bohm, Frayne, Morrison, Maisel, and Small, as well as New York State Federation of Labor president James Holland and a number of prowar socialists, including John Spargo, J. G. Phelps Stokes, and Chester Wright. The meeting adopted a resolution pledging support for the war effort (see "To Charles Moyer," Aug. 6, 1917, below) and directed the Labor Publicity Organization members—Bohm, Maisel, Berry, and Small—to plan a local educational and publicity campaign to counteract antiwar propaganda.

To Daniel Guggenheim[1]

July 30, 1917

Mr. Daniel Guggenheim,
American Smelting & Refining Company.
120 Broadway, New York City.
My dear Mr. Guggenheim:

A letter from your secretary,[2] under date of July 26, informs me that you wish to know the total amount which our Executive Committee desires to raise for the conduct of the work of the Committee on Labor.[3]

Our requirements are problematical at present, in view of the development of the work of the various committees. The Executive Committee decided to raise, as a temporary fund to meet emergency expenses immediately, $10,000. Since that time, requirements from several committees have arisen which, if met, would take us far beyond that sum. This involves the services of experts to assist the chairmen of committees who are giving their time free and meeting their own expenses. For example, Dr. Edward T. Devine has been delegated the work of recommending to the Committee on Labor for the Council of National Defense some method of coordinating social agencies, which requires, because of the exacting demands upon his time in connection with his work in other directions, a secretary with adequate attainments to comprehend the problem assigned to his committee.

I quote this as an illustration merely because you will see that we cannot expect Dr. Devine to meet any such expense or even to raise the money from his committee, in view of the fact that he is obliged to make appeals for his new Institute for Crippled Soldiers and Sailors. This, of course, is for the rehabilitation and reeducation of our men when they come back, with the hope that we may place them upon a self-supporting basis.

The report upon the coordinating of social agencies should indicate to relief organizations throughout the country what they may do to be helpful under war conditions and at the same time reduce the number of duplicating agencies, and hence the appeals for financial aid.

I refer to this because you will see at once the importance of providing adequately to assist Dr. Devine, and we cannot undertake to divert any of our running expense fund for that purpose.

In addition, I am desirous of having had raised a fund for moving pictures. I believe that the quickest method of reaching employers in the interest of the health of wage earners will be the visualization of the reports coming now from the experts in the Committee on Welfare Work. We also intend to have made pictures of prominent members of the Committee on Labor, employers, labor leaders and public men, as the personnel will greatly enhance the interest on the part of the general public. The fund to be required for that work, of course, will be large.*

For the time being, we should like to have a fund of $25,000 placed in the hands of the Treasurer, Hon. Myron T. Herrick,[4] and to be dispensed under the general direction of the Chairman of the Committee on Labor.

Whatever you may feel inclined to give the work, as suggested to me in Washington, will doubtless assist us in securing amounts of similar size from other men. If you care to make a contribution, please forward it to Hon. Myron T. Herrick, No. 1 Madison Avenue, New York City.

Very respectfully yours,   Saml Gompers.
Chairman,   Committee on Labor

*Of course these motion pictures are not intended to be shown for profit, but for general information, education and patriotism.

TLpS, Files of the Office of the President, Letterbooks, Advisory Commission, Council of National Defense, reel 21, pp. 491–92, *AFL Records*.

1. Daniel Guggenheim (1856–1930) served as president of the American Smelting and Refining Co. from 1905 to 1919.
2. F. A. Collins.

3. To augment its limited appropriation from the Council of National Defense, the executive committee of the Committee on Labor voted on June 28, 1917, to raise a fund of $10,000 to cover the cost of additional office staff, investigative work, and printing. SG wrote Guggenheim and other members of the Committee on Labor on July 24, asking them for donations (Files of the Office of the President, Letterbooks, Advisory Commission, Council of National Defense, reel 21, pp. 405–16, *AFL Records*). Guggenheim contributed $1,000 in early August.

4. Myron Timothy Herrick (1854–1929), a Cleveland banker who had served as Republican governor of Ohio (1904–6) and as ambassador to France (1912–14), was a member of the subcommittee on Mediation and Conciliation of the Committee on Labor.

From John Spargo[1]

Old Bennington, Vermont, July 30, 1917.

Dear Friend Gompers:

I want very much to explain to you what was in my mind in formulating the recommendation to the Executive Council of the American Federation of Labor to create some sort of Alliance for Labor and Democracy.[2] I want you especially to know that the suggestion was put forth in no spirit of criticism of your work or that of the Federation. I feel that the stand you have taken throughout is the stand of the wise statesman of labor. Never in all the years of your great leadership of the Federation have you manifested greater gifts of statesmanship than during these past months.

It has been in my mind for some weeks past that instead of leaving the People's Council to assert a monopoly of the work of protecting and furthering democratic interests during the war, the Federation of Labor as the real representative of working-class opinion in this country should take the initiative. We all of us recognize that in these times there are aggressive reactionary tendencies, and that assaults are made upon the democratic rights and institutions of the people. As the People's Council is the only organized body protesting against these things, it wins the support of many people who feel the seriousness of the situation and thus it obtains for its purely obstructive work a power and influence wholly adventitious and unwarranted. It has seemed to me that instead of merely denying their right to speak for labor and democracy, or criticising them, we ought to have some organization of men and women fundamentally loyal to American democracy and to the American labor movement. Naturally the creation of this force ought to be undertaken by the Federation under your able direction. I know that there are a great many men and women in this country who are most anxious for some such organization and who would be delighted to place themselves under your leadership in this crisis.

It is possible for the A.F. of L. to enlist the services of a large number of writers and speakers and so to mobilize the intellectual and moral forces of the labor and democratic movements in the country. I know that men like Matthew Hale[3] of Boston, member of the Constitutional Convention,[4] who is working so loyally with the labor men in that convention; men like J. A. H. Hopkins[5] of New York, and many others would be delighted at the opportunity to serve in such a campaign. Then there are the leaders of the foreign language groups other than the Hebrews—notably the Bohemians and other southern Slavs. A man like Charles Pergler,[6] the well-known Bohemian radical writer, whose position is identical with that of the A.F. of L. would render, it seems to me, quite invaluable service. Then of course there are the American writers such as Ghent, Sinclair,[7] Poole,[8] Leroy Scott,[9] myself and many others who would be delighted to participate in such a movement.

Instead of a few intellectuals getting together and forming a movement and inviting the labor men in, the labor movement itself should, in my judgment, take the initiative and those of us who are privileged to assist in it should be content with the privilege of assisting and not attempt to lead the movement. When I read of great demonstrations being held in various parts of the country, in Philadelphia, Minneapolis, and elsewhere, by this People's Council,[10] capitalizing its interest in democracy in order to more effectively preach its Copperheadism,[11] I long to see counter-demonstrations arranged by the organized labor movement in cooperation with whatever other forces may be available.

May I ask you to be good enough to send me two copies of the legislation program of the Federation.

With warm personal regards, believe me

Very sincerely yours,   John Spargo

TLS, Files of the Office of the President, General Correspondence, reel 86, frames 564–65, *AFL Records*.

1. John Spargo (1876–1966), a socialist reformer and writer, was a member of the national executive committee of the Socialist Party of America (SPA) before breaking with the party when the United States entered World War I.

2. The American Alliance for Labor and Democracy was formally launched in New York City on July 29, 1917, to encourage workers to support the war. During the following weeks it expanded from a local organization to one with a national focus, and on Aug. 15 it issued a circular, signed by SG, Frank Morrison, and Robert Maisel, calling on trade unionists throughout the country to organize local alliances to resist the "pro-German cause" and insure "the future liberty of every workingman" (Files of the Office of the President, General Correspondence, reel 87, frame 250, *AFL Records*). SG served as chairman of the Alliance and Maisel as its director. The organization was financed largely by the Committee on Public Information (see SG to Maisel, Aug. 2,

1917, ibid., reel 86, frame 676; Maisel to SG, Mar. 12, 1918, ibid., reel 93, frame 237; and "To George Creel," July 18, 1918, below.)

3. Matthew Hale (1882–1925), a Boston attorney, served as chairman of the Massachusetts Progressive party in 1912.

4. The Massachusetts constitutional convention, authorized by popular vote in November 1916, held three sessions, June 6–Nov. 28, 1917, June 12–Aug. 21, 1918, and Aug. 12–13, 1919.

5. John Appleton Haven Hopkins (1872–1960), an insurance executive, was a leading figure in the Progressive party in New Jersey.

6. Bohemian-born Charles Pergler (1882–1954) immigrated to the United States in 1890 and subsequently worked in Iowa as an attorney. A proponent of an independent Czecho-Slovak state, he served in 1918 as the diplomatic representative of Czechoslovakia in the United States.

7. Upton Sinclair (1878–1968), a social reformer and writer who was living in Coronado, Calif., was the author of many novels, including *The Jungle* (1906). He resigned from the SPA in 1917.

8. Ernest Poole (1880–1950), a New York City journalist and novelist, broke with the SPA in 1917 over its antiwar policy and subsequently worked for George Creel's Committee on Public Information.

9. Leroy Scott (1875–1929), a New York City journalist and novelist, left the SPA in 1917.

10. The People's Council held rallies during July 1917 in Chicago, Los Angeles, and Philadelphia and scheduled a national convention for Sept. 1 in Minneapolis. That meeting was banned by the governor of Minnesota, however, on the grounds that it would aid the enemy and incite violence. After unsuccessful attempts to find an alternative meeting site in North Dakota and Wisconsin, the national conference eventually met in Chicago.

11. A pejorative term referring to southern sympathizers in the northern states during the Civil War, particularly the peace Democrats who opposed the war policy of the Lincoln administration.

To Robert Maisel[1]

Washington, D.C. July 31, 1917

Mr. Robert Maisel,
Director, American Alliance for Labor and Democracy
280 Broadway, R. 132, New York City.
Dear Sir:

Your favor of the 30th inst. with enclosures came duly to hand and contents carefully noted. Recently I went over the matter again with Mr. George Creel under whose supervision and direction the entire project is to be carried into effect and made effective.

The matters decided, that is, as to personnel, editors, letters to be gotten out, in Yiddish, English, and perhaps Italian and other languages, O.K.[2]

Mr. Creel will send you some pamphlets by tomorrow's mail and he will indicate to me and I shall call your attention which of them should be translated into Yiddish and printed in pamphlet form for general distribution. For matters of this character Mr. Creel will furnish the office with frank so that postage may not be unnecessarily used, it being after all a governmental service which is being rendered.

Going over your budget, it was regarded as indefinite but answers the purpose sufficient to warrant Mr. Creel in saying that there is nothing there violative of what should be done and you are at liberty to go ahead. You may proceed to rent offices in the Stewart building and at the rental stated in the budget, and also to rent a branch office on the East Side. I wish you would consult me first though before you definitely decide upon this latter point as to location and rental. Of course, you will consult me regarding the clerical force to be employed in both offices. You know that I shall not interpose any unnecessary or unavoidable objection.

Can you let me have a list of the personnel on or before Saturday[3] and I shall write you if there be time or otherwise telegraph you.[4]

If you are not too busily engaged on other matters I wish you would try to arrange a programme of procedure and work so that we can take that up at our meeting Saturday afternoon.[5] This applies to the literature and speaking campaign.

Thus far, I have not heard from Chester Wright and I would like him to be at the conference on Saturday ready to proceed with his work. Also try and have Dr. Louis Miller at our Saturday meeting.

You may tell Mr. Wright that he will receive a salary of $50 a week and the same salary will be paid you as director and manager. In the course of a day or so I shall advise you as to office equipment.

Of course, you will understand the necessity of regarding this entire matter as *confidential,* at least for the time being.

Very truly yours,   Saml Gompers.
Chairman

TLS, Files of the Office of the President, General Correspondence, reel 86, frame 573, *AFL Records.*

1. Robert Maisel had worked on the staff of the *New York Call* and was a founder in 1915 and the secretary of the Labor Publicity Organization (from January 1917, the National Labor Publicity Organization). He left the Socialist Party of America because of its opposition to American involvement in World War I and then served as director of the American Alliance for Labor and Democracy (1917–19). He was subsequently the publisher of the *Arbeiter Presse,* a New York City labor weekly, and later founded a New York City labor consulting firm.

2. During August 1917 Maisel hired two or three stenographers, a part-time Yiddish translator, and an office boy.

3. SG left Washington, D.C., on Aug. 2, 1917, for New York City, where he attended a meeting of the advisory council of the Alliance on Saturday, Aug. 4. The meeting appointed David Hermalin and Chester Wright to prepare articles and leaflets in Yiddish and English, established a speakers' bureau, and directed that a circular be sent to AFL affiliates encouraging them to organize local branches of the Alliance throughout the country (Files of the Office of the President, Conferences, reel 120, frame 164, *AFL Records*). SG returned to AFL headquarters by Aug. 6.

4. SG to Maisel, Aug. 2, 1917, reel 224, vol. 236, p. 861, SG Letterbooks, DLC.

5. Maisel wrote SG two letters, both dated Aug. 1, 1917, concerning the agenda for the Aug. 4 meeting (Files of the Office of the President, General Correspondence, reel 86, frames 660–62, *AFL Records*).

From C. O. Edwards

Butte Mont 1917 Aug 2

We respectfully request and urge a speedy investigation of the lynching of Frank H Little[1] in this city this morning and believe it to the best interests of organized labor and the US Government that this be considered at once[2]

Montana State Metal Trades Council
C O Edwards   Secy.

TWSr, AFL Microfilm National and International Union File, United Mine Workers Records, reel 40, frame 1396, *AFL Records*.

1. Frank H. Little (1879–1917), a hard rock miner, joined the Western Federation of Miners as a young man and became an IWW organizer after 1905. He led the IWW free speech campaigns in Spokane, Denver, and other cities, organized agricultural and construction workers, and was active in the 1916 Mesabi Range strike and the 1917 Arizona copper miners' strike. Little served as a member of the IWW general executive board from 1911 until his death. In July 1917 he went to Butte, Mont., after a mine disaster there had killed 164 miners. He was abducted and lynched in the early morning hours of Aug. 1. No one was ever indicted for the murder.

2. SG sent President Woodrow Wilson a copy of C. O. Edwards's telegram on Aug. 2, 1917, expressing his "great anxiety for the consequences if our government does not take immediate steps to maintain justice and constitutional rights [to] all of our citizens" and asking for a prompt investigation of Little's murder (reel 224, vol. 236, pp. 858–60, SG Letterbooks, DLC; quotation at p. 860). SG notified Edwards of his action the same day (ibid., p. 857). Representative Jeannette Rankin telephoned the White House on Aug. 2 to ask Wilson to send federal troops to Butte in response to Little's murder. The president responded that he would not take such a step unless the request came directly from the governor of Montana.

To William B. Wilson

Washington, D.C. August 3, 1917.

Hon. W. B. Wilson,
Secretary of Labor,
Washington, D.C.
Sir:

The Executive Council of the American Federation of Labor instructed that a protest be made against your order[1] of May 23, 1917, temporarily admitting illiterate Mexicans for agricultural purposes.

It is the belief of the Executive Council that the policy you inaugurated is at variance with the purpose and the spirit of the immigration law and constitutes a dangerous precedent which in effect nullifies the law.

You are familiar with the long struggle of the organized labor movement to protect America's wage-earners against unnecessary and harmful competition with lower standards of life and work of illiterate foreign workers. That struggle culminated in the enactment of the Burnett Immigration Law, which was passed by the Congress of the United States over the veto of the President. Perhaps no legislation has ever been more desperately contested in the Congress of the United States. Three presidents vetoed legislation providing a literacy test for immigrants,[2] and only by determined effort was it finally enacted into law.

Yet, as soon as the law became effective, the Secretary of Labor, through executive action, virtually nullified the purpose of the law through an interpretation never intended by Congress and which apparently was not contemplated in the rules established in your Bulletin of May 1, 1917.[3]

The ninth proviso of Section 3, (Provided further, That the Commissioner General of Immigration with the approval of the Secretary of Labor shall issue rules and prescribe conditions, including exaction of such bonds as may be necessary, to control and regulate the admission and return of otherwise inadmissible aliens applying for temporary admission) which is the legal basis advanced as per your special order of May 23, considered under the first rules issued, as obviously authorizing the Secretary of Labor and the Commissioner General of Immigration to make rules to carry out the purposes of the law and not to defeat those purposes. For convenience in considering the whole matter, that part of the rules is quoted here:

["]Subd. 2. Temporary admission of otherwise inadmissible aliens—The ninth proviso to section 3 authorizes the bureau and the department to issue rules and prescribe conditions to control and regulate the admission and return of otherwise inadmissible aliens applying for temporary admission. In cases in which aliens who are mandatorily excluded from permanent entry apply for the privilege of entering the United States temporarily, they shall be required to show that their temporary entry is an urgent necessity or that unusual and grave hardship would result from a denial of their request. A bond, a cash deposit, or other equally satisfactory assurance that such alien will depart in due course from the United States will be exacted by the department in every instance. The submission of an unmounted photograph, in duplicate, may be required when needed as a means of identifying the temporarily admitted alien in connection with his departure at the port of entry or some other port. Ordinarily such cases should be reported as they arise to the department for special ruling. In instances, however, in which the cases fall into regular channels and can be handled under general instructions (for instance, the admission of physically or mentally afflicted aliens from Canada to receive urgent and special treatment or to undergo operations in medical institutions on this side of the boundary) they may be handled under general instructions, which will be issued by the bureau and the department upon request.["]

Evidently this interpretation did not contemplate disregarding the literacy test as well as the contract labor provisions. Under this official instruction application for entrance must come from the immigrant himself and must represent a genuine need of the immigrant, which rendered the provisions of the Immigration Law unjust to him and perhaps to others with whom he had some connection. The initial action in all particulars fell upon the immigrant asking for entrance. Under the later ruling, which nullified the purpose of the Immigration Law, practically all of the activity necessary for the entrance of the immigrant can emanate from some outside person who expects to profit by the entrance of the immigrant. One of the reasons which you assigned for your course in suspending the literacy clause of the Immigration Law was the emergency in which employers in this country found themselves due to the scarcity of workers.[4]

Let me call to your attention that the alleged scarcity of workers, which is assigned as the reason for suspending the Immigration Law, has never been proved by scientific or official investigation and report. On the contrary, recently your department published reports from officials in the middle western states who deny there is a shortage of foreign labor in their respective states. These reports are from Missouri, Oklahoma, Kansas, Iowa, and Nebraska.[5]

John P. McLaughlin,[6] State Labor Commissioner of California, some time ago, declared that there was no scarcity of foreign workers in

California and that the claim of scarcity was caused by failure to mobilize foreign workers and to establish principles and agencies for labor conservation.

Much of the talk about scarcity of workers arose from war hysteria or from the desire of employers to profit through exploitation of illiterate workers whose standards of life and work are lower than those of Americans and who consequently would be willing to work for less wages.

In the opinion of the Executive Council it was unwise for the Government of the United States to yield to this clamor rather than maintain standards of human welfare and protect the rights of citizens in accord with the purpose and intent of the laws of the land.

In the name of the Executive Council of the American Federation of Labor I protest against the continuance of the policy inaugurated by the Department of Labor in the order of May 23, and we ask that the Immigration Law be enforced in accord with the purposes intended by Congress.[7]

Very truly yours,   Saml Gompers.
President,   American Federation of Labor.

TLS, RG 174, General Records of the Department of Labor, DNA.

1. Secretary of Labor William B. Wilson issued an order on May 23, 1917, permitting the short-term admission of aliens, who would otherwise have been barred by the literacy provisions of the Immigration Act of 1917, into the potato growing district of Maine and along the Mexican border because of a shortage of agricultural labor.

2. Presidents Grover Cleveland, William Howard Taft, and Woodrow Wilson each vetoed immigration bills that included a literacy test.

3. "The New Law to Regulate the Immigration of Aliens," *Monthly Review of the U.S. Bureau of Labor Statistics* 4 (Mar. 1917): 487–88.

4. In a letter to SG on June 1, 1917, Wilson said he had been forced to take "prompt action" because growers in Maine and along the Mexican border had threatened to plant fewer crops unless they could "secure farm help from the regular sources" (RG 174, General Records of the Department of Labor, DNA).

5. The reports are summarized in "Grain-Belt Harvest," *Fifth Annual Report of the Secretary of Labor: Fiscal Year Ended June 30, 1917* (Washington, D.C., 1917), p. 74.

6. John P. McLaughlin, formerly a San Francisco teamster, served as commissioner of the California Bureau of Labor Statistics from 1911 to 1921.

7. Wilson acknowledged SG's letter on Aug. 10, 1917, and referred the matter to the U.S. Bureau of Immigration (RG 174, General Records of the Department of Labor, DNA).

To Charles Moyer

August 6, 1917

Mr. Charles H. Moyer,
President Western Federation of Miners,[1]
503 Denham Building, Denver, Colorado
Dear Sir and Brother:

Your telegram of the 4th instant received here this morning. It is as follows:

"Telegram received from Arizona states reported telegram sent by you to Bisbee endorsing Loyalty League and advising working men to join similar leagues being organized in other camps, their purpose to crush and demoralize strike of bonafide unions of Globe and Miami. Four out of five strikes now in progress in southwest in communities dominated by Phelps Dodge interests. They are back of Loyalty Leagues. Can't influence from seat of government be brought to bear on this institution that they owe a duty to the nation at this critical time as well as the working men; will not the President and the Council of National Defense immediately get in touch with Phelps Dodge and urge them to withdraw their opposition to bonafide unionism. Every effort of our people to prove their patriotism, preserve peace and continuous production through agreements is met by a flat refusal by them, wholesale arrests of our members by those under their control and deportation as in case of members of the United Mine Workers in Gallup.[2] Kindly wire me your position in regard to the Loyalty League so that I can put our people right in Arizona."

I have just sent you the following telegraphic reply:[3]

"Telegram received. It is absolutely untrue that I have endorsed so-called Loyalty League or that I have advised working men to join similar leagues. Letter follows."

On July 21 I received a telegram from E. N. Francis,[4] President and Joe Segar[5] of Chauffeurs Local Union[6] of Bisbee, Arizona stating that a petition was being circulated for signatures pledging men as citizens of a Protective League and pledging them further that such a league would practically take no position as to organized labor. To that I sent a telegraphic reply[7] as follows:

"E. N. Francis, President
["]Chauffeurs Local Union #496, Bisbee, Arizona
["]Telegram received. The right of the workers of Bisbee or elsewhere to organize or join a bona fide organization for the protection and promotion of their interests and rights is not only lawful but com-

mendable. The workers of Bisbee should repudiate any organization that pursues an unlawful course or has improper and un-American aims. At the same time all should insist upon the right to extend the field of opportunity and influence of the furtherance of the interests of the workers and aid in promoting general welfare.

["]Samuel Gompers."

It may be interesting for you to know that I received telegrams from several parts of the country, including one from Secretary Green[8] of the United Mine Workers, officially calling my attention to the deportation of law-abiding union workmen and requesting that they be returned to their homes.

Upon being made acquainted of the deportation of men from Bisbee, Arizona I placed the matter[9] in its entirety before the President and Secretary of Labor, Hon. Wm. B. Wilson, and was advised that they had taken the matter under serious consideration and that prompt action would be taken.[10]

Later I received a telegram[11] from Secretary Green of the United Mine Workers stating that union men were deported from Gallup, New Mexico, men who were law-abiding citizens, whose rights had been violated. I immediately[12] brought the matter to the attention of President Wilson and I am sure you will be pleased to know that as a result I received a telegram[13] from Secretary Green two days ago, in which he advised me that the men were being returned to their homes and added "thanks for services rendered."

I know your position clearly as well as that of the men of the bona fide labor movement of our country. Without question the I.W.W., in its propaganda is doing a great deal of injury to the cause of labor and of our country. The good name of our movement is by the I.W.W. brought into disrepute, for the enemies of our movement and those who do not know, just couple us all up together and make no discrimination. But the republic of our country is a government of law and with guaranteed rights and the meanest among our people charged with the most grievous offence cannot legally be deported from his home, from his state and cannot be put into imprisonment or to death without being given a fair opportunity to be tried under the law and by a jury of his peers.

You can rest assured that everything that can be done will be done to protect the rights of all of our people as against injustice and wrong, no matter by whom it may be attempted to be practiced or imposed.

At a recent conference held in New York, after serious discussion, the following declaration was unanimously adopted:

"It is the sense of this conference that it is the duty of all the people of the United States, without regard to class, nationality, politics, or religions, faithfully and loyally to support the Government of the United States in carrying the present war for justice, freedom, and democracy to a triumphant conclusion, and we pledge ourselves to every honorable effort for the accomplishment of that purpose."[14]

I believe this is a good doctrine for American Trade Unionists, American labor men, for American citizenship, and for all those who are living within the confines of our country.

With assurances of best wishes and hoping to hear from you often, I am,

Fraternally yours,   Saml Gompers.
President   American Federation of Labor.

TLpS, reel 225, vol. 237, pp. 29–31, SG Letterbooks, DLC.

1. The Western Federation of Miners was renamed the International Union of Mine, Mill, and Smelter Workers in 1916.

2. In early July 1917 the Gallup-American Fuel Co., a subsidiary of the Phelps Dodge Copper and Coal Mining Corp., purchased the Gallup, N.Mex., copper mines of the Victor-American Fuel Co. Gallup-American promptly announced it would not honor Victor-American's contract with the United Mine Workers of America, and it began firing union members and evicting them from company-owned housing. Some 125 union members called a strike and then set up a tent colony outside Gallup. On the night of July 31 the county sheriff and an armed posse attacked the camp and seized 83 miners, who were loaded in cattle cars and taken out into the southern New Mexico desert. Officers of the United Mine Workers protested to SG and to government officials, threatening a nationwide strike if the situation was not promptly redressed. On Aug. 3 the posse was disbanded, and the deportees were allowed to return. Gallup-American, however, continued to operate with nonunion workers.

3. SG to Charles Moyer, Aug. 6, 1917, reel 224, vol. 236, p. 960, SG Letterbooks, DLC.

4. Earl N. Francis of Bisbee, Ariz., worked as a clerk for the Copper Queen Consolidated Mining Co.

5. Joseph Segar, a resident of Warren, Ariz., ran an auto service in Bisbee.

6. International Brotherhood of Teamsters, Chauffeurs, Stablemen, and Helpers of America 496 of Bisbee.

7. SG to Francis, July 24, 1917, reel 224, vol. 236, p. 357, SG Letterbooks, DLC.

8. William Green was secretary-treasurer of the United Mine Workers (1913–24) and a member of the AFL Executive Council (1914–24) before becoming president of the AFL on the death of SG.

9. "To Woodrow Wilson," July 20, 1917, above; SG to William B. Wilson, July 26 and Aug. 6, 1917, RG 280, Records of the Federal Mediation and Conciliation Service, DNA, and July 30, 1917, reel 224, vol. 236, p. 634, SG Letterbooks, DLC.

10. William B. Wilson to SG, Aug. 6, 1917, RG 280, Records of the Federal Mediation and Conciliation Service, DNA.

11. Green to SG, Aug. 1, 1917, AFL Microfilm National and International Union File, United Mine Workers Records, reel 40, frame 1395, *AFL Records*.

12. SG to Woodrow Wilson, Aug. 2, 1917, reel 224, vol. 236, pp. 858–60, SG Letterbooks, DLC.

13. Green to SG, Aug. 4, 1917, AFL Microfilm National and International Union File, United Mine Workers Records, reel 40, frame 1397, *AFL Records.*

14. This resolution was adopted at a meeting of trade unionists and prowar socialists in New York City on July 28, 1917 (see "From George Creel," July 26, 1917, n. 5, above).

To Thomas Flynn

Washington, D.C., August 7, 1917.

Mr. Thomas Flynn,
408 New Rochelle St., Mt. Oliver Station, Pittsburgh, Pa.

A prominent representative[1] of the War College came to my office just now and conveyed to me information lodged with the college that trouble is expected at McKees Rock steel plants.[2] Let me impress upon you the necessity of endeavoring to maintain production without interruption. The country's needs demand it but this can in nowise interfere with the rights of the workers in making an effort to secure improved conditions and you will undoubtedly do the best you can to aid them as far as you possibly can. The course herein indicated is the policy of the government of the United States and with which the labor movement is in hearty accord.

Samuel Gompers.

TWpSr, Files of the Office of the President, Letterbooks, Advisory Commission, Council of National Defense, reel 21, p. 515, *AFL Records.*

1. SG's appointment records indicate that he met with Henry Lewis Stimson (1867–1950), formerly secretary of war (1911–13), who was now serving as an intelligence officer with the Army War College in Washington, D.C.

2. Thomas Flynn replied on Aug. 8, 1917, that although the International Association of Bridge, Structural, and Ornamental Iron Workers and Pile Drivers and the International Brotherhood of Boiler Makers, Iron Ship Builders, and Helpers of America were organizing there, he anticipated no trouble at the McKees Rocks plants (Files of the Office of the President, General Correspondence, reel 87, frame 14, *AFL Records*). Stimson confirmed Flynn's assessment in a letter to SG dated Aug. 11 (ibid., frame 141).

To William Hutcheson[1]

Council of National Defense
Washington. August 10 [9],[2] 1917

William Hutcheson,
President, United Brotherhood Carpenters and
  Joiners of America,
Carpenters' Building, Indianapolis, Ind.

You know the voluntary agreement entered into between Secretary Baker and me regarding Union scales and standards in cantonment construction work. That agreement has been extended by the War Department to other work. Am advised by high authority that if our voluntary agreement with the Government fails and strikes are inaugurated in establishments to which the agreement applies there is no question that Congress will follow what the English Parliament did under like circumstances and that is to pass a law for compulsory labor and compulsory arbitration.[3] It would be most unfortunate for labor as well as for our country if this were permitted to occur and I appeal to you to avert it. The Government officials will do all they can to have the Situation in New York adjusted.[4]

Samuel Gompers.[5]

TWSr, Files of the Office of the President, Letterbooks, Advisory Commission, Council of National Defense, reel 21, p. 535, *AFL Records.* Handwritten notation: "sent Aug 9."

1. William Levi HUTCHESON served as president of the United Brotherhood of Carpenters and Joiners of America from 1915 to 1952. During World War I he was a member of the National War Labor Board.

2. SG sent this telegram from the War Department on Aug. 9, 1917, after a conference there with Newton Baker.

3. The Munitions of War Act of July 2, 1915 (5 & 6 Geo. V, chap. 54), authorized the Board of Trade (later, the minister of labour) to refer labor disputes in Britain's munitions industries to independent tribunals for binding arbitration and banned strikes or lockouts while such disputes were under review. Further, it empowered the minister of munitions to assign, at his discretion, "controlled establishment" status to any munitions plant, giving him authority to approve wage changes there, limit profits, and ban strikes entirely. Finally, it suspended work rules or customs that restricted production in these establishments and prohibited employers from hiring munitions workers who had left their jobs up to six weeks before unless they could produce a certificate proving they had done so with their employer's consent. The Munitions of War (Amendment) Act of Jan. 27, 1916 (5 & 6 Geo. V, chap. 99), expanded the types of industries included under the provisions of the legislation.

4. A longstanding jurisdictional dispute between the Carpenters and the International Association of Bridge, Structural, and Ornamental Iron Workers and Pile Drivers came to a head in 1917 when the Henry Steers Co., which had a long history of conflict with the Carpenters, hired members of the Iron Workers to do carpentry work

in the construction of navy barracks at Pelham Bay, N.Y. The AFL had suspended the Iron Workers in July 1917 for infringing on the jurisdiction of the Carpenters, and the Brotherhood now threatened to strike cantonment construction sites nationwide if Steers did not discharge these men. With two thousand carpenters already on strike in the New York area, Theobold Guerin, a member of the Carpenters' general executive board, declared: "We do not hit at Steers, for he is only the agent. It is the Government, the real employer in this case, which must agree to our terms. If no agreement is reached, then our men must strike, that is, wherever they are working for the employer against whom we are acting, in this case, as I said, the Government" ("Confer to Avert War Work Strike," *New York Times,* Aug. 10, 1917). After a two-day conference, a settlement was reached on Aug. 10, which required Steers to employ only members of the Carpenters' union to do carpentry work, and the Carpenters to admit members of the Iron Workers' union to the Brotherhood without an initiation fee. The same day, Secretary of the Navy Josephus Daniels agreed to apply the cantonment construction agreement signed by SG and Baker on June 19 to navy construction work.

5. Hutcheson wired SG on Aug. 10, 1917, to say he would defer action on calling a nationwide carpenters' strike. He sent a second telegram the same day indicating that an agreement had been reached in the Pelham Bay matter (Files of the Office of the President, General Correspondence, reel 87, frames 99–100, *AFL Records*). For a third telegram from Hutcheson of that date, regarding the cantonment construction agreement, see "From William Hutcheson," Aug. 10, 1917, below.

To Woodrow Wilson

Washington, D.C. August 10, 1917.

Hon. Woodrow Wilson,
President of the United States,
Washington, D.C.
Sir:—

Late yesterday afternoon, as I was about to attend a meeting of the Council of National Defense, your letter of the 8th instant,[1] together with copy of telegram,[2] was handed me. After my return from the meeting I sent the following telegram:[3]

["]Washington, D.C., August 9, 1917.

"Mr. J. L. Donnelly,[4] President,
["]Convention[5] Arizona State Federation of Labor,
["]Clifton, Arizona.
["]Accept and convey to the officers and delegates of your State Federation Convention the fraternal greetings of the organized labor movement of our country. You may rest assured that every officer of the Federal Government is doing and will do all that lies in their power to see that the great wrong done the deported men shall be

righted and they given an opportunity to return to their homes. In this all may count upon my assistance. In this crucial hour of our Nation's life when freedom and democracy are hanging in the balance and for which all free-men must contend it behooves us all to do our level best in the great cause of labor and for the great principles for which the government and the people of the United States are in this world's struggle.

["] (signed) Samuel Gompers."

I quite agree with you that the tone and the intimation in the telegram you received are harsh, and particularly so when those who know you know your high sense of justice and consuming purpose to protect the rights and the needs of our people.

But sir, is it not right that we sometimes place ourselves in the position of others and take into account their feelings and their indignant resentment of a terrible outrage? You know that the men in the American trade union movement have nothing in common with the so-called I.W.W.; that as a matter of fact they are as antagonistic to the American Federation of Labor, if not more so, than to any other institution in the world. They are opposed to the constructive policy and methods employed by the American trade union movement for the protection and promotion of the rights, interests, and welfare of the workers. So I am justified in saying, that there is nothing in common between the I.W.W. and the American Federation of Labor.

And yet, when we have seen what we have seen, that hundreds of men, citizens of Arizona, nearly all of them law-abiding, rounded up by a group of capitalistic anarchists who have not only taken the law into their own hands but went far beyond any warrant of law and at the point of guns and bayonets driven into cattle cars, deported from their home, city, and state, into a foreign state, carried in such condition for days without food, or drink, or care, or opportunity for rest and left stranded among strangers and their wives and children at home suffering the anxiety of husband and father ruthlessly and without warrant of law abducted from them; when a man in another state is taken from his abode and put to death by another group of capitalistic anarchists,[6] it is no wonder that men will feel deeply at such treatment, at such brutality, with murder in their hearts and carry it into execution and that when expressing themselves honest American citizens, workmen, union men in conventions assembled, will express themselves in terms forceful even though it may be inconsiderate.

Advice reaches me that the State Federation Convention held at Clifton, Arizona, appointed a committee which proceeded toward Bisbee authorized and directed to make an investigation of the outrageous, unlawful deportation and to report to the convention. When that committee were within a few miles of Bisbee they were halted by a group of the character of persons I have mentioned and warned that their entrance into the city would be prevented and if they attempted to enter it would be at the peril of their lives. Of course, the committee could not attempt to proceed further and so returned to Clifton and reported to the convention.

In many parts of the North-west the employers of labor encouraged the so-called I.W.W. for the purpose of breaking up the bona fide trade unions belonging to the American Federation of Labor. They sewed the wind which made for the results which we have witnessed. I wish I could present a picture to you of the situation that exists in several other places of our country, of employers who are taking advantage of the present war situation; employers who have used the soldiers of our government to force the workers into compliance with the employers' wishes; employers who, under the pretext they have contracts for government work have said that unless the workmen yield they will be imprisoned or interned during the war; of employers who have misinterpreted your own declaration and the declaration of the Council of National Defense, that standards of labor should be maintained, into an insistence that no change will be permitted; that notwithstanding the greater profits which employers have been reaping from government contracts insist that the workers shall not share in the slightest but in fact accept lower standards; of employers who have insisted that the labor laws protecting women and children shall be let down and the workers shall be employed for any length of time to suit the employers' convenience; of the legislatures of West Virginia[7] and of Maryland[8] which so recently passed compulsory labor laws. But, sir, neither you nor I have the time to read or to write the details of all this great wrong which in one form or another is being pressed upon the rights, interests, welfare, and safety of the workers of the United States.

A few of the government departments are helping in the effort for the mobilization of the good-will of the workers. With them my associates and I are helping to work out a solution of the various labor problems, but some of the departments and other agencies of the government are either ignoring the situation and in some instances are positively hostile.

It may be said as a truism that either the government and the employers generally will have to deal with the representatives of the bona fide organized constructive labor movement of the country or they will have the alternative of being forced to take the consequences of the so-called I.W.W. with all that it implies.[9] Repression will beget repression and resentment and the repressions and the resentments will find expression in ways which we now know not of.

It is most difficult for me to advise you as to how the telegram from Messrs. Donnelly and French shall be answered,[10] except as this letter may present a thought upon which an answer could be based; to assume a conciliatory attitude; to express the thought that in this republic of American law and order the regular process of law must be maintained; that the rights of the people must be maintained. The commonest, meanest criminal, whose whole life has been one of criminality, if discovered to be guilty of another crime, is charged with the offense by the duly constituted authorities; he is placed on trial, confronted by a jury of his peers, and given an opportunity of lawful defense. A workman, or a group of workmen who, however mistaken or wantonly and illy designed their purpose and course may be, is entitled to the same protection. Only then, can an orderly government be maintained.

I regret that I could not get this letter to you before this.

Very respectfully yours,   Saml Gompers.
President,   American Federation of Labor.

TLS, Woodrow Wilson Papers, DLC.

1. Woodrow Wilson to SG, Aug. 8, 1917, George Meany Memorial Archives, Silver Spring, Md.

2. J. L. Donnelly and Thomas French to Wilson, Aug. 6, 1917, George Meany Memorial Archives. The telegram demanded to know "if you intend to act in restoring law and order in Chochise County, Arizona, and return to their homes the deported men of Bisbee. Are we to assume that Phelps Dodge interests are superior to the principles of democracy."

3. SG to Donnelly, Aug. 9, 1917, Files of the Office of the President, Letterbooks, Advisory Commission, Council of National Defense, reel 21, p. 530, *AFL Records.*

4. John L. DONNELLY served as president of the Arizona State Federation of Labor (FOL) from 1916 to 1917.

5. The Arizona State FOL convention met Aug. 6–10, 1917, in Clifton.

6. A reference to the murder of Frank Little.

7. West Virginia, Acts of 1917, chap. 12, approved May 21, 1917, required that all able-bodied males between the ages of sixteen and sixty resident in the state during the war be regularly employed for at least thirty-six hours a week and earn enough to support themselves and their dependents. Those without such an occupation were to be declared vagrants, fined up to $100, and sentenced to a maximum of sixty day's labor on roads or other public works.

8. Maryland, Acts of 1917, chap. 33, approved June 28, 1917, authorized the governor during wartime to assign unemployed, able-bodied males between the ages of eighteen and fifty to occupations essential for the protection and welfare of the state and the nation. Persons failing to register were subject to a fine. Those refusing to perform assigned work could be punished with a fine of up to $500 and imprisoned for up to six months. The act provided that it was not to apply to workers unemployed because of labor disputes.

9. See, for example, William D. Haywood's telegram to Wilson of July 30, 1917, threatening general strikes among metal miners and agricultural workers unless the Bisbee deportees were returned to their homes (Arthur S. Link et al., eds., *The Papers of Woodrow Wilson*, 69 vols. [Princeton, N.J., 1966–94], 43: 325–26).

10. For Wilson's reply to Donnelly of Aug. 14, 1917, which incorporated some of SG's suggestions, see Link et al., eds., *Papers of Wilson*, 43: 461–62. See also "To William B. Wilson," Aug. 27, 1917, n. 3, below.

From William Hutcheson

Indianapolis Ind Aug 10 [1917]

The understanding reached between Sec of War and yourself included wages hours and conditions Conditions would include that condition under which members of our organization work for employers One of the principal rules of our organization is that they will not work with nonunion men of our craft I trust we will have no difficulty in having the officials of our government to realize that the word condition in the understanding arrived at covers that as described above

Wm L Hutcheson
Genl President

TWSr, Files of the Office of the President, General Correspondence, reel 87, frame 101, *AFL Records.*

William Nee[1] to Frank Morrison

International Brotherhood of Boiler Makers,
Iron Ship Builders and Helpers of America
Subordinate Lodge 298
Portsmouth Va 8-11 1917.

Mr. Frank Morrison
Dear Sir & Bro—
I am useing this means of Bringeing before attention the necesertye of the A.F. of L. by Putting on more Colored Organizer. Now if the A.F. of L. will just open up a Little & get get Busy on the Colored man you can make 1917 the Banner year. in the Organization I understand that they are lots of these men in Raleigh N.C. who wants to Organize & I also Recieved a Letter from Bro Jewell[2] in Jackinvill Fla they have a movent down their to get all of the Colored men Organized. Now

Bro Morrison I have taken a Interest in the Colored man in Regards to getting organized. for. Instinst there is the Coal Trimmer Local #15277³ of Norfolk who I got their contract or agreement drawn up for them & I have attented their meeting Regular. & given them Haelp & hand & advise I was at their meeting last Sunday afternoon. I have been Imformed that they are about twenty five hundred Employees in the Peanut factury in Suffolk Va who wants to get Organized, & I know my Self that they are a Dueal Organization here with a Member ship of Fourteen Hundred Members knowned as the transportation union, Now I want to Recomend to you a good Colored man for a Colored Organizer this man is the farther of the Coal Trimmers Organization here in Norfolk & New Port News and he has been Runed away from all of the three Piers here through the Active Part he taken in getting the Coal Trimmers Organized & I think that Some thing should be done for him along these lines he is a man if you will give him a chance he will bring you Resultz his Name is J C Jones.⁴ #2635 Piedmont Heights Box #208 Portsmouth Va. They are Six Different Rail Roads here who could be Organized on Each whole System Must Close & I would like for you to take this matter up with J. C. Jones.⁵ he is a member of Local #15277. Norfolk Member Ship of twelve Hundred Thanking you in advan for any thing that you may Due for. this man I Beg to Remain your Respt

W. C. Nee
Business Agent & Cor Secty Local #298 Boilermakers
fin Secty & Treasure of the Central Labor Union⁶

ALS, AFL Microfilm National and International Union File, Boilermakers Records, reel 34, frame 2673, *AFL Records.*

1. William C. Nee was business agent of International Brotherhood of Boiler Makers, Iron Ship Builders, and Helpers of America 298 of Portsmouth, Va.

2. Bert Mark JEWELL was an organizer for the Boiler Makers.

3. The AFL chartered Coal Trimmers' Union 15,277 of Sewell's Point and Norfolk County, Va., in 1916.

4. Probably James E. Jones, the treasurer of AFL 15,277.

5. Frank Morrison wrote Nee on Aug. 28, 1917, to ask if he wanted Jones assigned as an organizer in Newport News, Va., where Armistead Goode was already working for the AFL as a salaried black organizer, or if he wanted Jones sent to the other cities mentioned in his letter (AFL Microfilm National and International Union File, Boilermakers Records, reel 34, frame 2672, *AFL Records*). No reply has been found.

6. That is, Norfolk's black central body, chartered by the AFL in March 1917 as the Central Labor Union (Colored).

To Matthew Woll

August 13, 1917.

Mr. Matthew Woll,
President, International Photo-Engravers' Union,
6111 Bishop Street, Chicago, Illinois.
Dear Sir and Brother:—

My relations to the League to Enforce Peace[1] have been unofficial, although last year I prepared a paper to be read at the annual meeting of the League which was held in this city.[2]

When the League was first organized and I was asked to accept membership, I objected to the idea implied by the word "enforce" in the name of the organization. The secretary[3] of the organization sent me literature explaining that the members of the organization were not deluded by the thought that they could establish and maintain peace by force, but that peace must be the result of establishing international agencies to adjust difficulties arising between nations.

International government is naturally the next step in the evolution of political institutions, and will replace the use of force between nations just the same as local and national government has replaced the right and the necessity of individuals to protect their interests by personally resorting to force. Local and national government replaced the right to private warfare between citizens, so in my mind international political institutions will inevitably replace the right of nations to make war upon each other, at least before they have submitted their difficulties to international tribunals. This was the thought underlying the supplementary report[4] which the Executive Council made to the Baltimore convention on international relations. The report, as you will remember, was adopted by the convention.

An international government is a thought that is in the minds of men of all nations. If this International government is to be of a democratic nature, representatives of those who value and need democracy must take part in determining a[nd] organizing this government. There must be a new element dominate in international diplomatic relations. This new note can not come from statesmen and diplomats of the old school. It is expected from that group that has never hitherto been represented in diplomatic relations—from the great masses of all nations. We know that those who control the world's course make their plans and arrange their system of control far in advance of the occasion upon which they will be used. Already the diplomats of the nations are at work upon this problem.

If the workers of the nations now at war are to have any voice in the determination of these methods, they must get to work on the problem now and work out plans and suggestions. In my opinion it is of fundamental importance that the workers of this country formulate definite peace terms for which they think this government and the workers of all countries can stand, and then try to secure the cooperation of every progressive agency that can assist these purposes.

There are men of influence in the League to Enforce Peace. If capable, alert labor men accept membership in that League, and then try to direct its policies in accord with ideals of democratic freedom and democratic international government, great good may result. I hope that you will give considerable thought to the position organized labor must take in the formulation of world peace and world government, and I hope that you will also try to arouse every labor man to the importance of this question.

Since this letter has been written many events have transpired and the League to Enforce Peace is not so active as it was some time ago. And though this letter deals with a specific subject I suppose you have kept yourself somewhat abreast with international situations which have developed in the recent past.

Another thought comes to me in regard to the international relations regarding an international government—a difficult problem—that while maintaining the rights and integrity of each country, yet the question of a large group of small countries dominating the policies of large countries is one which we must receive with very serious consideration.

Enclosed is the letter that you requested be returned to you. With best wishes, I am,

Fraternally yours, Saml Gompers.
President, American Federation of Labor.

TLpS, reel 225, vol. 237, pp. 160–62, SG Letterbooks, DLC.

1. The League to Enforce Peace held its founding meeting in Philadelphia in June 1915, electing William Howard Taft as its president. The organization backed the creation of a league of nations to maintain the peace—by force of arms, if necessary—and the establishment of a world court to adjudicate international disputes. The league supported American participation in World War I and helped draft the covenant of the League of Nations, but it began to fall apart soon after the war's end because of internal partisan disagreements. By late 1920 it had largely ceased to function.

2. The League to Enforce Peace met May 26–27, 1916, in Washington, D.C. SG was unable to attend, but the paper he had prepared, "American Labor and a Constructive Settlement of the War," was read to the conference on May 26. See Files of the Office of the President, Speeches and Writings, reel 112, frames 156–59, *AFL Records*.

3. William Harrison Short.

4. "Supplemental Report of the Executive Council," Nov. 16, 1916, AFL, *Proceedings*, 1916, pp. 256–59.

To Vincent Castelli[1]

August 16, 1917

Mr. Vincent Castelli,
502 Ninth St., NW. Washington, D.C.
Dear Sir:

As you know I have been a regular patron of your establishment for a number of years. I should dislike greatly to have to make any change, but recently I received several communications[2] from the President[3] and Secretary[4] of the Hotel and Restaurant Employes' International Alliance to this effect: that organization is making a special effort to organize the colored waiters of Washington.

Your establishment is a union house with the exception of the head waiter. The fact that this man serves *me and my friends when I come to your* restaurant becomes a matter of general knowledge and retards the progress of the International Alliance in organizing the colored waiters of the city. You see the position in which I am placed.

Is there anything which you can do in the matter?

Awaiting your reply,[5] I am

Very truly yours,   Saml Gompers.
President,   American Federation of Labor.

TLpS, reel 225, vol. 237, p. 305, SG Letterbooks, DLC.

1. Vincent Castelli was the proprietor of Castelli's Restaurant in Washington, D.C.

2. Edward Flore to SG, June 27 and Aug. 14, 1917, and Jere Sullivan to SG, July 2, 1917, AFL Microfilm National and International Union File, Hotel and Restaurant Employees Records, reel 38, frames 2072–73, *AFL Records.*

3. Edward Frank FLORE served as president of the Hotel and Restaurant Employees' International Alliance and Bartenders' International League of America from 1911 to 1945.

4. Jere L. SULLIVAN served as secretary-treasurer of the Hotel and Restaurant Employees from 1899 to 1928 and edited the union's official journal, *Mixer and Server,* from 1900 to 1928.

5. Castelli replied on Aug. 21, 1917, that the headwaiter was willing to join the Hotel and Restaurant Employees (AFL Microfilm National and International Union File, Hotel and Restaurant Employees Records, reel 38, frame 2073, *AFL Records*).

To Frederick Victor Fisher[1]

August 18, 1917.

Mr. Victor Fisher,
Hon. Sec. and Treasurer, The British Workers' League,
31 to 36 Sicilian House, Sicilian Ave., London, W.C.
Dear Sir:

The issues of the British Citizen come to me regularly and bring valuable information of our British fellow-workers. I shall be glad from time to time to send you information and literature that may be of interest to the readers of your paper.

You ask for the names and addresses of members of the Socialist movement in America, who are America first and are not hypnotised by the German propaganda. You evidently do not know that practically all of the prominent Socialists who are Pro-American have been expelled from the Socialist Party. I will, therefore, give you a list of those who are prominent American Socialists even though not in good standing in the Party:

W. J. Ghent, C/O California Out-look, San Francisco, California,
Chas. Edward Russell, Munsey Building, Washington, D.C.,
Arthur E. Holder, #110 F Street, S.E., Washington, D.C.,
Upton Sinclair, Coronada, California,
Jas. G. P. Stokes,[2] #100 William Street, New York City,
Chester M. Wright, #1279 W. Third St., Cleveland, Ohio,
John Spargo, Nestledown Old Benington, Vt.,
Jas. Lord,[3] Pres. Mining Department, American Federation Building, Washington, D.C.,
W. H. Johnson [*sic*], Pres. International Association Machinists, American Federation Labor Building, Washington, D.C.,
John Murray, #1508 Kearney Street, Los Angeles, California,
Robt. Hunter, Highland Farm, Noroton, Ct.,
Frank Hayes,[4] Vice Pres. United Mine Workers of America, #1102–08 Merchants Bank Building, Indianapolis, Ind.
Wm. English Walling, Brookside Drive, Greenwich, Ct.
A. M. Simons, C/o Pearson's Magazine, New York City, New York,
A. W. Ricker,[5] C/o   "

The various nationalities and races that compose the American Republic constitute one of the serious problems that confronted our nation in entering the war; common danger and realization that the war itself was a fight against imperialism have united our people in defense of ideals of humanity and freedom. It is our sincere hope that out of the terrible suffering and sacrifice may come Americanization of all of our people.

Shall be glad to hear from you frequently. With best wi[shes] to all my old friends associated with you, I am

Yours very truly,   Saml Gomp[ers.]

President,   American Federation of L[abor.]

TLpS, reel 225, vol. 237, pp. 369–70, SG Letterbooks, DLC.

1. Frederick Victor Fisher (1870–1954) resigned from the British socialist party in 1914 because of its opposition to the war and in April 1915 founded the prowar Socialist National Defence Committee. He served as honorary secretary of that organization (1915–16) and held the same post (1916–18) in its successor, the British Workers' National League (after March 1917, the British Workers' League).

2. James Graham Phelps Stokes (1872–1960), a wealthy New York City socialist, left the Socialist Party of America in 1917 because of its position on the war. He was president of the Nevada Co. (a mining concern) and the Nevada Central Railroad Co. and was on the board of many philanthropic and educational organizations. Stokes served as treasurer of the American Alliance for Labor and Democracy from 1917 to 1919.

3. James LORD served as president of the AFL Mining Department (1914–22) and as treasurer of the Pan-American Federation of Labor (1918–24).

4. Frank HAYES served as vice-president (1910–17) and president (1917–20) of the United Mine Workers of America and as a member of the National War Labor Board (1918–19).

5. Allen W. Ricker, a socialist writer, was the publisher of *Pearson's Magazine*.

To Newton Baker

Washington, D.C. August 22-1917.

Honorable Newton D. Baker,
Secretary of War,
Washington, D.C.
Sir:

In your letter of August 16, acknowledging receipt of telegrams from labor men in the northwest,[1] you asked for any suggestion as to how the government ought to act in that section. In my opinion, the only effective action that the government can take is action to remedy fundamental wrongs existing in the northwest. The way to protect ourselves against I.W.W'ism. is to remove the causes. It is not necessary to tell you that the American Federation of Labor and the I.W.W. movement have nothing in common in policies or methods. The I.W.W. is destructive in method and in ideal. It seeks to make property holding unprofitable. On the other hand the American Federation of Labor seeks to organize for constructive betterment. The I.W.W. has done everything it could to discredit and minimize the value and the effectiveness of the trade union movement. It is plain that the American Federation of Labor has neither sympathy nor approval for the methods of the I.W.W., but on the other hand, we hold that there are constitutional fundamental rights that can not be denied any citizens or group of citizens under a free government by law. Denial of liberty and rights are not the methods by which abuses of liberty and rights will be corrected.

The I.W.W. movement has been furthered and assisted by arbitrary methods of employers and by arrogant disregard of constitutional and common law. Employers of low ideals who employ despotic methods in dealing with employees have refused to recognize the constructive trade union movement and have fostered the I.W.W. movement, because it opposed the regular labor movement, and attempted to weaken its influence and to disrupt the organization. These employers sowed the seeds of anarchy in order that they might increase their profits. Now, not only these employers, but the state and national governments are confronted with the situation which has been created which threatens serious danger to the whole nation. In several of these western states there have been created, or there are forming, organizations called, "Loyalty Leagues," or similar names. These organizations have as their avowed purpose the furtherance of patriotic purposes and interests. It is regrettable, but true, that the leagues not infrequently bring disrepute to their name. In Arizona, in Cochise County, the Loyalty League has been acting as a revolutionary body in defiance of constitutional and statute law and has been arbitrarily denying or according citizens the right to use public high-ways and to enter towns and to live peacefully in their own homes. Although the Committee claims to be operating against I.W.W'ism. it has deported and arrested citizens affiliated to the American Federation of Labor; men of good reputation and standing who have done their part in service of the nation.

There are many evidences to show that the Loyalty League operating in Arizona has as its fundamental purpose the destruction of the trade union movement in Arizona.

Yesterday I received a letter[2] from North Yakima, Washington, copy of which is enclosed, together with copy of letter[3] received [by] the Secretary[4] of North Yakima Trades and Labor Council. It is difficult to conceive a more offensive tone than that expressed in the letter of the Merchants, Manufacturers and Employers Patriotic League of America. Nothing could be more harmful to national solidarity of interest and purpose than such activities on the part of organizations professedly working for patriotic purposes.

The history of each decade of the world shows that where efforts are made to restrict rights and freedom, these efforts are always applied more drastically and arbitrarily to the poor. I am sure that you will agree with me in the thought that no recourse could be more unfortunate than that; that this war in which our nation is now engaged for the high purpose of human freedom and liberty should be used as a cloak for schemes to deny the masses of the people political and economic freedom and to fasten upon them the most pernicious of all despotisms founded upon economic disorganization and helplessness.

In my opinion the most effective and the most fundamental step for the Council of National Defense and the government of the United States could take in dealing with the situation in the northwest is to provide agencies for considering and adjusting industrial disputes. Such agencies, of course, must have the confidence of the workers or they fail in their purposes. That confidence can only be assured by recognizing those principles of industrial welfare which have been evolved out of the struggles of the workers for industrial protection and welfare. These principles are expressed in the standards established by trade unions in their collective bargainings. To ignore those principles can result only in suspicion and confusion. Trade union standards of work are part of the industrial organization as it now exists. They are facts that must be recognized by employers and the government. To ignore them is to establish a false basis and any plan predicated on such a false basis must be unsound and will inevitably fail of its purposes. There is no one action that would do more to create confidence and to dissipate opposition than the establishment of agencies that will assure to workers engaged in the production of materials and supplies necessary for the conduct of the war, justice and economic protection against exploitation. Any other course would inevitably furnish additional wrongs for the propaganda of the I.W.W. and would add to the confusion, the danger, and the industrial and political anarchy pending in sections of our country.

Very respectfully,   Saml Gompers.
President,   American Federation of Labor.

TLS, RG 62, Records of the Council of National Defense, DNA.

1. Newton Baker to SG, Aug. 16, 1917, Files of the Office of the President, General Correspondence, reel 87, frame 275, *AFL Records*. On Aug. 15 SG had sent Baker copies of telegrams from J. G. Brown and E. P. Marsh, dated Aug. 9, 13, and 14, regarding the situation in the timber industry in Washington state (reel 225, vol. 237, pp. 239, 241–43, SG Letterbooks, DLC).

2. B. M. Williams to SG, Aug. 14, 1917, reel 225, vol. 237, p. 665, SG Letterbooks, DLC.

3. Merchants', Manufacturers', and Employers' Patriotic League of America to Williams, Aug. 11, 1917, reel 225, vol. 237, pp. 666–67, SG Letterbooks, DLC.

4. Herbert "Bert" M. Williams, a carpenter, was secretary (1917–18) of the North Yakima, Wash., Trades and Labor Council. The AFL chartered the organization in 1910.

From Julius Hansen[1]

Idaho State Federation of Labor[2]
Lewiston, Idaho, Aug. 22, 1917.

Dear Sir and Brother:

I am writing you this to let you know how the situation is here in Lewiston. Ever since last summer when I began to organize the workers here, there has been a growing antagonism between the workers and the Commercial Interest and while we have had some and still have traitors in our ranks, we have made some progress up until the war was declared and now it is simply H—2 & 3 because they couldn't run things to suit themselves, openly declared that they would break up the unions, have the sheriff close the hall, etc. this being to the interests of the enemies of Labor. They have made good progress. They have been telling everything that was said and done and then some detectives or Secret Service men have been breaking into our Hall and Lockers and desks and ransacking contents, this for the last three months and now the soldiers are here, broke into the Hall, went through the books, records, etc. without search warrant, giving notice or anything else and the papers boast of it and have arrested three[3] of our most active members and make it common knowledge on the streets that there is six or eight more that they are going to get and that I am one of them. My brother[4] was arrested today working at an addition to the State Normal. We are carpenters.

The charges seem to be treason, I.W.W.'ism and what not. Not a single one of them has done any wrong or committed any crime other than work for the good of labor. This is the crime of the age. There is no I.W.W. here, that is all Bull. What is the game? Have we been completely sold out or has any Government Official gone crazy. This is the federal soldiers making the arrests and it is claimed that it is Government Secret Service men that are making the complaint. How do we know that in breaking into our lockers and desks that they do not place the incriminating evidence there they want and then claim they found it. They arrested the Secretary of the Central Labor Union[5] Monday and then went to his home when his wife[6] was away working, ransacking the house and claimed they found incriminating evidence. Today they arrested my brother and another member of the Central Body. What the charge is, I don't know and don't care. I know they are not true and all this in the name of Democracy and this has been going on and is now more than ever all over the country and nothing appears to have been done but to enter a weak protest.

How long are we to stand this kind of tackle? Now is the time for the A.F. of L. to show if it is worthy of existence or go into history. This thing cannot go on for long. An organization that will not fight for an existence cannot endure for long.

This is a serious affair Mr. Gompers and something must be done before long or Russia will be the place of the universe. Did Mr. Root bring former Russia back with him? If so he is indeed a great man. Will our labor officials do something now or must the sun set on the Stars and Stripes that we have honored so long. Government by secret Service and gunmen cannot endure.

We the workers only have the power and spirit to maintain liberty and democracy. Shall we let it die. Brother Gompers, if ever you did anything for America, do it now; the workers need it.

Hoping to hear from you soon,[7] I am,

Fraternally yours, Julius Hansen

Will answer if at liberty.

TLtpSr, reel 226, vol. 238, pp. 73–74, SG Letterbooks, DLC. Typed notation: "*Copy*." Enclosed in SG to William B. Wilson, Sept. 4, 1917, ibid., p. 72.

1. Julius Hansen was a member of United Brotherhood of Carpenters and Joiners of America 398 of Lewiston, Idaho, and a vice-president of the Idaho State Federation of Labor (FOL).

2. The AFL chartered the Idaho State FOL in 1916.

3. The three men arrested were officers of the Lewiston Central Labor Union (CLU): barber Philip J. Pearl, the secretary; carpenter Ernest Hansen, the treasurer; and painter George A. Parks, the business agent.

4. That is, Ernest Hansen.

5. The AFL chartered the Lewiston CLU in 1916.

6. Emma Pearl.

7. SG wrote Julius Hansen on Sept. 4, 1917, that he had taken the matter up with President Woodrow Wilson, Secretary of Labor William B. Wilson, and the Council of National Defense, which recommended that the president appoint a commission to investigate such violations of workers' rights (reel 226, vol. 238, p. 75, SG Letterbooks, DLC). AFL organizer C. O. Young subsequently reported to SG that the arrests of Pearl, Hansen, and Parks were largely the result of a bitter feud within the Carpenters' local that had spilled over into the Lewiston CLU. According to Young, the Hansens and their supporters had previously brought charges against CLU president John Mulback in order to have him removed from office. The Mulback faction, wanting revenge, had managed to have the three arrested and jailed by accusing them of making unpatriotic statements, which Young dismissed as "foolish talk" and "idle mouthings" (Young to

SG, Sept. 24, 1917, Files of the Office of the President, General Correspondence, reel 88, frames 657–64, *AFL Records;* quotation at frame 661).

From William Johnston

International Association of Machinists.
Washington, D.C. Aug. 22-[19]17.

Dear Sir and Brother:

I desire to call your attention to the undue activity of some of the representatives of the Department of Justice who are going about the country interfering with the normal activities of our representatives.

While we have several cases, I will only recite two for your information, and request that same be presented to the proper officials of the United States Government.

I am reliably informed that a Mr. W. E. Thompson, representing the Department of Justice in Chicago, was sent to Michigan to investigate the activity of Mr. Riley Briggs,[1] business representative of our Association. He visited Muskegon, where Mr. Briggs lives, but on that particular day Mr. Briggs was working in Grand Rapids. Mr. Thompson located him on the evening of August 13.

Mr. Thompson stated that he, Briggs, intended to organize the Lindenman Company of Muskegon and then declare a strike. Mr. Briggs informed him that he was not advocating a strike, and in fact was doing everything to avoid the stoppage of work, but that he did feel as though he had a right to organize men wherever the opportunity offered.

It developed that the Muskegon Employers' Association was responsible for Mr. Thompson's visit to that section of the country.

Now another matter which I desire to call to your attention is the case of James Henderson,[2] our general organizer, who was arrested in Michigan City, Ind. The circumstances are as follows:

The men employed on the Michigan Central were threatening to go out. Mr. Henderson was authorized by me to go over the System and prevail upon the men to remain at work. This he proceeded to do.

On August 6, he arrived in Michigan City. While walking along the street, he was approached by an officer in plain clothes, employed by Michigan City, and was spoken to in the following manner:—"What is your name?" "Why do you ask?" "I am a city officer." Turning up the lapel of his coat he showed his badge. Mr. Henderson replied—"My name is Henderson." "You are the man we are looking for," answered the officer. Continuing he said,—"You are here to make trouble with a meeting tonight, and we want you to know that this will not be stood for here. These are war times, and we have your record, so there will be no meeting." Seeing that the man was excited Mr. Henderson asked,—"Have you anything in writing?" The officer's reply was, "We had better see the Chief of Police."[3]

They arrived at the office of the Chief of Police and found him out. Later he arrived in company with a Mr. Cainey, who, Mr. Henderson was told, was a representative of the Department of Justice. The Chief informed Henderson that he had been followed from Jackson City, and that he was accused of agitating a strike on the Michigan Central Railroad. He further stated that there was more than one officer in the city, in addition to several detectives of the Michigan Central Railroad.

The Federal Officer said the charge was made in Gary, Ind. that Henderson was an I.W.W. and was aiding and abetting the enemy by causing railroad strikes; that his character was well known to the men following him, and that the proof of his mission in that city was very plain,—namely—that of making trouble for the Michigan Central Railroad.

Henderson's reply was,—"I will obey the law, but you had better let this meeting go through tonight or there will be trouble, for the men are demanding some information as to how their representatives are getting along with the officials of the company in their conferences in Detroit."

Mr. Henderson was finally granted permission to hold a meeting with open doors and the right of federal authorities to be present, in addition to representatives of the city police department, and three detectives of the Michigan Central Railroad. Had there been no meeting, and had Mr. Henderson not visited Michigan City, as well as other points, the men would have undoubtedly stopped work of their own volition.

I believe that it is very necessary that an understanding be reached at an early date with the Governmental Authorities to ascertain whether or not the representatives of the Department of Justice are going to be used by the employing interests to intimidate and brow-beat our representatives from pursuing their legitimate business. As stated above, the only mission of Mr. Henderson, in visiting the points in question, was to keep the men at work while a committee of the men, in conjunction with a conciliator from the Department of Labor, were trying to reach an amicable settlement of the differences existing.[4]

Thanking you in advance for any assistance[5] you can render in this matter, I am, with best wishes,

Fraternally yours,   (signed) Wm. H. Johnston,
International President.

TLtpSr, reel 225, vol. 237, pp. 927–28, SG Letterbooks, DLC. Typed notation: "*Copy.*" Enclosed in SG to William B. Wilson, Aug. 30, 1917, ibid., p. 926.

1. Riley R. Briggs was financial secretary of International Association of Machinists 170 of Muskegon, Mich.

2. James "Pitchfork" Henderson, a member of International Association of Machinists 82 of Detroit and an organizer for the international union from 1914 to 1920, had previously served as president of the Columbus (Ohio) Federation of Labor (1909–11) and as an AFL salaried organizer (1912–13).

3. August J. Funk was chief of police in Michigan City, Ind.

4. The controversy, which began in July, was adjusted with the help of three commissioners of conciliation from the U.S. Department of Labor, Robert McWade, J. A. Smyth, and Frederick Feick.

5. SG wrote William Johnston on Aug. 31, 1917, that he had taken the matter up with President Woodrow Wilson, Secretary of Labor William B. Wilson, and the Council of National Defense, which recommended that the president appoint a commission to investigate such violations of workers' rights (reel 226, vol. 238, p. 40, SG Letterbooks, DLC).

A Statement by Samuel Gompers

August 23, 1917.

There was never a war that afforded less justification for war profits than that in which our country is now engaged. The fundamental purpose of this war is to establish *the inviolability of human rights.* For this war our Republic has felt justified in enforcing compulsory military service at the constant hazard of health, body and life; to require the full man power in production and transportation. That corporations, companies and even individuals should have the opportunity to coin the flesh and blood of their countrymen into war profits, is abhorrent to justice and humanity and in conflict with the very ideals for which our people and their allies are contending.

No single determination would do more to unify the nation behind the government's efforts in this war and to establish a feeling of equity and security, than to tax war profits that would virtually wipe out of existence profits resulting from the war. It has long been charged that there are industries and financial interests which have even endeavored to provoke war that they might profit thereby. Even now despite the fact that America has joined in this world struggle for the most exalted fundamental principles and ideals, the false charge has been leveled against us that this is a war for profits. By preventing profits from our present war's necessity nothing would tend so much to enroll the spirit, conscience and activity of our people in one great homogeneous pact to win the war for justice, freedom and democracy the world over.

In recognition of the unusual conditions attending war production, in my opinion the rate of taxation upon war profits should be brought down to nearly normal peace profits and surely the history of industry of the United States demonstrates the fact that those profits are not niggardly to enterprise and wealth.

It is my judgment that it would be extremely unwise for our government to raise all the revenue of this war for democracy and humanity through borrowing and mortgaging the future. Under the borrowing principle safe loans are made to the government for which full compensation is guaranteed.

Interest on loans and often loans themselves must be repaid by taxation levied upon the people, and which of course falls more heavily upon the poor than upon the wealthy.

By taxation on war profits, incomes and inheritance, our country can in large part meet the expenses of the war as we proceed with that great enterprise.

The American Labor movement has officially endorsed[1] the principle of taxation of war profits. Indeed, the justification of the principle cannot be questioned. In defense of the principles of this Republic the government has the right to ask the service of the citizens of the country and to use for defensive purposes all of the resources of the country.[2]

TDc, Files of the Office of the President, Speeches and Writings, reel 112, frames 737–38, *AFL Records*. Typed notation: "Statement Given by President Gompers to the United Press."

1. Probably a reference to "American Labor's Position in Peace or in War," Mar. 12, 1917, above, which condemned profiteering. Also see "Financing the War," *American Federationist* 24 (May 1917): 366–68.

2. The Senate was then debating the war revenue bill (H.R. 4280, 65th Cong., 1st sess.), introduced by Democratic congressman Claude Kitchin of North Carolina on May 9, 1917, and passed by the House of Representatives on May 23. The Senate passed the bill on Sept. 10, and it became law on Oct. 3. Known as the War Revenue Act of 1917, it imposed a graduated excess profits tax of from 20 to 60 percent on corporations, partnerships, and individuals (U.S. *Statutes at Large*, 40: 300–338).

To James Duncan

August 27, 1917.

Personal.

Mr. James Duncan,
First Vice-President, American Federation of Labor,
Hancock Bldg., Quincy, Mass.

Dear Mr. Duncan:

I was really glad to read your letter of the 24th instant. The story you quote is quite apropos.[1] For your information, or for such other purpose as you may care to make of it, I am enclosing to you herein copy of a letter[2] which I have sent to Paul Scharrenberg.[3] I am sure you will read it with considerable interest and satisfaction, and yet all the things enumerated in that letter as agreements reached, are only in part of all that is in the making.

You will observe in the letter that I am assuming that Paul does not know, or it is simply his pure cussedness, and I do not know but that he is really not only German but of that faith and belief.

Yesterday as a member of the Council of National Defense I went down to Mt. Vernon on the government yacht, the Mayflower, with the Secretary of the Navy, the Secretary of State, a number of Naval Officers and members of Congress, accompanying the Japanese Envoys[4] in their pilgrimage to the tomb of Washington at Mt. Vernon, where the Japanese laid a magnificent wreath on Washington's tomb. The address of the Japanese Ambassador[5] was full of the spirit of freedom; it was really a masterpiece.

Both going and returning I had the pleasure of having some interesting talks with General Scott and Admiral Glennon[6] and you can imagine how it tickled the cockles of my heart when I heard them speak of you with such high praise of your work and worth on the commission.

On the trip both ways I was working. One of the things I did was to bring about a meeting between the representatives of the international parliamentary bodies of the allied countries and about ten senators and the Secretary of the Navy Mr. Daniels. It seems that the parliaments of the allied countries about two years ago organized an inter-parliamentary body. The mission of our friend M. Henry Franklin Bouinnon[7] is to invite the Congress of the United States to become part of that international body during the war or perhaps permanently.[8] The French ambassador[9] as well as M. Bouinnon and the senators and Secretary of the Navy expressed their gratitude to me for having brought them together as an initial step in the process of making of the proposition and the advance already made at a time so unexpected by either of them. I assure you I was a pretty busy man.

I am of the opinion that you won General Scott and made a good impression upon the admiral.

Reverting back to Scharrenberg and West's comments and the West article, perhaps they both regard that the agreements reached with the government, the international union officers and myself being "on paper" it is to be regarded as a "scrap of paper" to be destroyed at the first whim or fancy of the government.

Your second letter of the 24th[10] is also at hand and contents noted. I shall send to the Executive Council the correct copy of your cablegram[11] from Petrograd. Of course you understand your cable was put into code at Petrograd, forwarded to the State Department at Washington which furnished me with a de-coded copy, and I suppose the incorrections crept in in that way. I am very glad to get the corrected copy and as you say will ask the members of the E.C. to substitute the corrected copy for the one I sent them.

I am dictating this letter and the telegram[12] I sent you today on the train on my way to New York City, and Miss Guard who is working with me on the trip[13] will get off at Philadelphia, file the telegram to you and return to Washington. At Philadelphia I am to meet a committee who will go from New York to Philadelphia to travel back to New York with me for a conference.

Tonight I will leave New York for Jamestown to attend and address the convention[14] of the New York State Federation of Labor. Labor Day I speak at Erie, Pennsylvania; then I proceed to Buffalo, Chicago and Minneapolis. In the latter city The American Alliance for Labor and Democracy will hold a three days national conference.[15] I do wish that it were possible for you to attend that conference. It may be interesting to say that the declaration adopted by the conference when the American Alliance for Labor and Democracy was formed is as follows:

It is the sense of this conference that it is the duty of all the people of the United States, without regard to class, nationality, politics, or religion, to faithfully and loyally support the government of the United States in carrying the present war for justice, freedom and democracy, to a triumphant conclusion and we pledge ourselves to every honorable effort in the accomplishment of that purpose.

The conference promises to be a great big affair. Of course I know you must be busy in trying to gather up the strings of the work which may have become frayed during your absence. I hope you are standing it well.

With best wishes, and hoping to hear from you whenever convenient,
I am

Fraternally yours, Saml Gompers.
President, American Federation of Labor.

TLpS, reel 225, vol. 237, pp. 795–97, SG Letterbooks, DLC.

1. James Duncan to SG, Aug. 24, 1917, Files of the Office of the President, General
Correspondence, reel 87, frame 624, *AFL Records.* Duncan wrote in reference to an article by George West in the *Coast Seamen's Journal* of Aug. 15, 1917, entitled "A Criticism
of Samuel Gompers: Has the President of the A.F. of L. Outlived His Usefulness?" West
criticized SG for failing to seize the opportunity presented by the war to demand the
"emancipation" of American workers from "exploitation and oppression." Instead of
insisting on "fundamental reforms" and providing "aggressive leadership," he argued
that SG was "complacent and apparently contented with the status quo," with the result that "working-class discontent, robbed of wise leadership and direction, is being
dissipated in I.W.W. upheavals, pacifist obstruction and sullen opposition." Nevertheless, West concluded that "on paper his [Mr. Gompers] stand on the paramount issues
is unassailable." Duncan wrote that West's article reminded him of a story about an
African chief who addressed the sun, saying, "Oh, Thou Glorious Orb, shining like an
old tin pan."

2. In his letter to Paul Scharrenberg of Aug. 24, 1917, SG outlined the original cantonment construction agreement of June 19 and its subsequent extension to other
war work. He went on to quote in full the declaration on labor standards drawn up by
the Committee on Labor of the Advisory Commission of the Council of National Defense as well as its later "Amplification" (reel 225, vol. 237, pp. 703–7, SG Letterbooks,
DLC). Finally, SG sent Scharrenberg a copy of his forthcoming article "War Work and
Union Standards" from the September issue of the *American Federationist* (24: 721–26).
At SG's request, Scharrenberg published SG's letter and article in the Sept. 12 issue
of the *Coast Seamen's Journal.*

3. Paul SCHARRENBERG, a member of the Sailors' Union of the Pacific, was editor
of the *Coast Seamen's Journal* and secretary-treasurer of the California State Federation
of Labor.

4. The Japanese mission, headed by former minister of foreign affairs Kikujirō Ishii,
arrived in Washington, D.C., in August 1917 to resolve disputes with the United States
over China. In November Ishii and Secretary of State Robert Lansing concluded an
agreement that reaffirmed the Open Door policy but recognized Japanese special
interests.

5. Actually Ishii made the address, rather than the Japanese ambassador to the
United States, Aimaro Satō.

6. R. Adm. James Henry Glennon (1857–1940) had served as commandant of the
Navy Yard at Washington, D.C. (1915–17), and was a member of the Root commission to Russia in 1917. Later in the war he was appointed commander of a battleship
squadron in the Atlantic Fleet.

7. Actually Henry Franklin-Bouillon (1870–1937), a member of the French Chamber of Deputies (1910–19, 1923–26) who served briefly as minister of state in charge
of information in the cabinet of Paul Painlevé (Sept.–Nov. 1917).

8. Franklin-Bouillon hoped to persuade the United States to send delegates to interallied parliamentary conferences to be held in the fall, and he met with President
Woodrow Wilson about the matter on Aug. 30. The United States declined to participate, however.

9. Jean-Jules Jusserand (1855–1932) served as the French ambassador to the United States from 1902 to 1925.

10. Duncan to SG, Aug. 24, 1917, AFL Microfilm National and International Union File, Granite Cutters Records, reel 38, frames 1561–62, *AFL Records.*

11. The cable was dated July 7, 1917. SG had forwarded an uncorrected version to the AFL Executive Council on July 18; he sent the Council a copy of Duncan's corrected telegram on Aug. 27 (Executive Council Records, Vote Books, reel 15, frames 428–29, 478, *AFL Records*).

12. SG wired Duncan on Aug. 27, 1917, urging him to accept an invitation to address a mass meeting of the American Alliance for Labor and Democracy in New York City (AFL Microfilm National and International Union File, Granite Cutters Records, reel 38, frame 1560, *AFL Records*).

13. SG's trip, which is described in the next paragraph of this letter, extended from Aug. 27 to Sept. 12, 1917.

14. The New York State Federation of Labor met Aug. 28–31, 1917, in Jamestown, N.Y. SG addressed the convention on Aug. 29. See "An Address before the Fifty-fourth Annual Convention of the New York State Federation of Labor in Jamestown, N.Y.," Aug. 29, 1917, below.

15. The American Alliance for Labor and Democracy convention met in Minneapolis, Sept. 5–7, 1917.

To William B. Wilson

Washington, D.C. August 27, 1917.

Hon. Wm. B. Wilson,
Secretary of the Department of Labor,
Washington, D.C.
Dear Sir:

I take it that one of the first pieces of information which will be brought to your attention after your arrival at your office, is the fact that the Council of National Defense adopted a resolution to create a commission, with the approval of the President, the purpose for the creation of the commission being to make an investigation into the deportation of workers from their homes into different states and imprisonment of workers, and to ascertain the full facts in each instance and to make report to the President or the Council or both.

Early last week I called the matter to the attention of the President in a long interview he accorded me,[1] and he brought the matter to the attention of Secretary Baker who in turn presented the matter to the Council and Advisory Commission in joint meeting last Saturday. I made as full a statement in connection with the case as possible and upon the completion of the discussion it was voted to create a commission. The number and personnel was left to the President's choice, but in the interview the President stated that he would ask you to head the commission and that of course labor should be represented by recommendation from me.

The subject in my mind is as to whether the commission should consist of three or five. In my opinion it should be five. I have just had a conversation over the telephone with Secretary Baker. He suggested my writing to you and I would say that if the commission consists of three, I would recommend the appointment of John H. Walker,[2] President of the Illinois State Federation of Labor as one, and if the commission consists of five that I would recommend the name of Mr. E. P. Marsh, President of the Washington State Federation of Labor as the other.[3] You know Mr. Walker to be a fair man as well as an intelligent man. I do not know whether you know Mr. Marsh as well, but I can stand sponsor for his intelligence and fairness.

If it were not for the fact that I am to leave Washington on an important trip, something of the purpose of which I am sure you know, I would take it upon myself to ask you for the opportunity of talking the matter over with you. However, I present the matter to you for your attention and action on the recommendation of either one or both of these men upon the commission.

Very respectfully yours,   Saml Gompers.
President,   American Federation of Labor.

TLS, RG 174, General Records of the Department of Labor, DNA.

1. SG met with President Woodrow Wilson on Aug. 22, 1917.

2. John Hunter WALKER was president of the Illinois State Federation of Labor from 1913 to 1919 and again from 1920 to 1930.

3. On Sept. 19, 1917, Wilson appointed the commission members, who included William B. Wilson, chairman, Verner Reed and Jackson Spangler, representing business, Ernest Marsh and Walker, representing labor, and Felix Frankfurter, secretary and counsel. Leaving Washington, D.C., at the end of September to investigate and mediate labor unrest in the West and Northwest, the commission visited the copper district of Arizona, the southern California oilfields, the timber region of the Pacific Northwest, and the meatpacking industry in Chicago. Its final report, dated Jan. 9, 1918, was published as *Report of President's Mediation Commission to the President of the United States* (Washington, D.C., 1918).

An Address before the Fifty-fourth Annual Convention of the New York State Federation of Labor in Jamestown, N.Y.

[August 29, 1917]

. . .

Mr. Gompers: Mr. President[1] and Fellow-delegates to this State Federation Convention, Ladies and Gentlemen:

It is indeed a great source of pleasure and gratification to me that I have the opportunity of being with you this morning. Were it possible, did I have the time, did my duties in other directions not forbid, I would much have preferred to sit in the body of delegates at this Convention, rather than to occupy the platform and address you.

I should have been willing and would have much preferred to participate in the discussions upon the various subjects coming before the Convention, and if there be a clash of thought or point of view upon any subject, contend for the principles and the thoughts and the convictions that are in me, with any one who may differ from me.

But I have no choice. I must deal with the situation as I find it, and I am honored indeed by the opportunity of addressing you at all and to address myself to some of the thoughts that are pressing upon my mind for expression.

It is so gratifying to know of the magnificent work and growth and the achievements of the New York State Federation of Labor and the organized labor movement of our state and of our country. There are many who live in the fond hope that regardless of inactivity, that somehow or other improvement will come to the lot and the condition of the toilers of our country. It is good to have optimism. It is good to look upon the brighter side of life; but he who fails to understand, he who fails to take action to remedy existing wrongs and evils, fails in his first duty to himself and to his fellows. And not only now, but for all time to come.

Things do not happen for human betterment in the world of affairs except through the brain and the thought and the devotion and the activity of the masses whom wrongs affect and who aspire for a better life.

The fatalist, the optimist purely who imagines that things happen anyway, reminds me of the story of the hunter who had a companion who was a fatalist and believed that all things would happen regardless of any particular activity.

The hunter and his friend went out one day and into the fields, and after awhile a great flock of wild ducks flew along the horizon, and the hunter levelled his field-piece, shot; when lo and behold, a duck fell to the ground and very nearly before the feet of the hunter and his friend.

The hunter, turning to his friend, said: "You fatalist, I ask you how about this duck lying dead at my feet; [I] shot him."

And the answer came back: "Yes, my good friend, it is true that he is lying dead at your feet, but it wasn't the question of the shot, the fall killed the poor duck." (Laughter.)

The whole history of the world is one of struggle and the written history up to our time fails to record those sacrifices which have been made by the toiling masses that they may be spared some of the burdens of life. The men of means and of title have always been free in every state or country in which they have lived. They have enjoyed privileges and emoluments as well as riches and titles. It has been the poor, the workers, the hewers of wood and the drawers of water upon whose shoulders has been placed the burden to struggle upward and onward. And through all life, in all ages, it has devolved upon the great masses of the people to contend for a larger and better concept of the rights to which the toilers are entitled.

The whole history of the world is marked by the sacrifices which have been made and every movement and every sacrifice which has been made resulted in some distinct improvement in the condition of the toilers, until in our day the world is stirred by the concept as well as the slogan, that the world must be made free for democracy, the people of the whole world. (Applause.)

I am proud to have been permitted to be associated with this wonderful movement of labor of America, for it is my judgment, as the result of long investigation and study, as well as travel and participation in movements, that there is no movement organized in all the world that is comparable with the American trade union movement as represented by the American Federation of Labor. (Applause.) We have indulged ourselves in less fantasy, we have indulged ourselves in less declarations, but we have consecrated our movement to tangible achievements, that shall bring and has brought light into the lives and the homes and the work of the toilers of America. (Applause.)

And it has been our aim constantly to press home the political affairs of our country and the industrial affairs of our every-day lives, a larger participation of labor in all the agencies of government, as well as of industry. (Applause.) So we find now a larger representation and a bigger voice in the determination of the affairs of industry, and of our country.

I would not have any man or woman either understand or infer from what I have said that we—you and I—are satisfied with existing conditions. All our activities—yes, your State Federation Convention—are in themselves the expression of dissatisfaction, of evils and wrongs which have too long existed and the demand for the rights to which the toilers are entitled. (Applause.)

Your meeting and the meeting of the thousands of unions and central bodies, and the conventions of the American Federation of Labor, all of them, almost, or many of them, are in almost perpetual session to devise the ways and means by which we can still further press home upon the political, the industrial, the commercial and intellectual agencies of our country in order that the toilers shall at last come into their own.

But he who realizes the wrongs and the evils still existing and aims to secure improvements in the condition of the toilers, if unwilling to acknowledge that which has been accomplished, will to that same extent minimize and neutralize the things that he would like to do for the betterment of the people and libels the movement and himself included.

Now more than ever is it necessary for the working people to organize more thoroughly in their unions, now more than ever is it essential for the workers themselves to be more completely united in the common welfare of the toilers and to make common cause with every man, with every group of men, with our own country and with all other countries that have the common consent of liberty and freedom and universal democracy. (Applause.)

We in the United States of America felt that the time had passed when any one could think, much less see, a conflict between the peoples of the nations of Europe such as we have seen since August, 1914. By direction of the American Federation of Labor, of which you are an integral and so important a part, I was directed to proceed to Paris, France, in the year 1909, and there participate in a conference[2] of labor of all countries, to carry your mandate to them. Finding there the representative men of the toilers of each country heartened me. It encouraged me in the hope that at last the dream of the poet and philosopher was about to be consummated and the brotherhood of man, of the whole world realized.

As a part of that international labor conference a mass meeting[3] was held at which the representative of each of the labor movements of the countries participating in the congress spoke for the toilers of his country. I have never yet seen a mass gathering more truly sincere, enthusiastic and devoted to a particular cause than I saw at that great mass meeting. And with others I pledged myself and held myself sponsor for the fundamental thought and high ideal that America's workers would stand true to the principle of international peace and for the abolition of international wars.

I had belonged to nearly every one of the peace societies in our country—state, municipal and national. I was on the Board of Directors of them. I was a member of the International Peace Society and found myself so thoroughly in accord with universal peace that perhaps you can imagine my mind and heart and soul racked to the very center when this bloody war was thrust upon the people.[4]

It was some time before I could realize really what had occurred. Men in all of these countries were working for a common uplift, scientists were burning the midnight oil that they might find some relief for the slightest ill that might occur to the most insignificant of the peoples of the world; every one was trying his level best to make of this life a better life when out of the clear sky, this war broke out and at the call of a great autocrat the people who had been trying to do so much for themselves and for the people of the world, were ordered to clutch at the very hearts and the throats of their fellow-men, and the destruction of human life and property going on is unparalleled in the history of the world and staggering to the conscience of decent men and women.

And so we found the world startled and shocked at the beginning of this terrific war and we found the peoples of the other countries responding also to the call to the colors, and the mightiest war of all the world in full swing. We in America, regardless of how our sympathies may have swayed our judgment, maintained a strict and an impartial neutrality.

May I say here, for a moment, something upon the subject of neutrality? I desire to mention it simply because there are some people who have in their minds the thought that, after all, our Government was not neutral. I refer to the charge which has been made that the United States and her people furnished some of the countries at war with arms and ammunition and foods, etc., and that these acts were acts in conflict with the principles of neutrality. Let me say this, that the Government of the United States up to the time of our entrance into the war did not side with any of the contending countries. The people of the United States were engaged in the manufacture and production of certain articles, which, under the laws of the country and under the laws of the world, were perfectly lawful productions. They had the right to sell them to any one who came to the United States and desired to buy.

The American producer and manufacturer sold to those who wanted to buy a lawful product. Now, if one or two of the countries could not buy these products and could not bring them to their own homes, that was not the fault of the United States. And let me say in connection with this, that no country now contending in the war repeats that charge against the United States nor attempts now to argue that the United States was unneutral because it sold its products to those who wanted to buy.

But in addition, during the Spanish-American War the manufacturers of arms and munitions in Germany sold these products both to Spain, as well as to the United States. During the Boer War—a war in which my sympathies went with the Boers—Germany, as well as other countries sold munitions to the Boers, as well as they did to England. No one has—yes, during our Civil War the countries of Europe furnished munitions and supplies to the Southern Confederacy, as well as to the Federal Government.

No one, no nation ever before, attempted to cast a reflection upon any other nation because of the sale of munitions and supplies to any one of the countries, and I want to take cognizance of it and to make this brief explanation of that situation in order to dispel it from the mind, if any one person in this assemblage still holds to that appeal.

But to come to the more vital subject, we are now engaged in war. We have joined the other countries in fighting for democracy and freedom, the world over—not alone for the United States, not for England and France and Russia and poor outraged Belgium, but for the people of Germany and Austria and Hungary as well. (Applause.)

Is it not true that no man in public life was ever more assailed and criticised and denounced than was the President of the United States because he had kept us out of this great war for so long a time; urged on, egged on, ridiculed in every form because he had kept us out of the war and because he declared that sometimes a people may be too proud to fight?

He imagined at that time, he believed at that time that there were some honor and some conscience in the ruling family of Germany. When our people engaged in legitimate travel were by the hundreds sent to an untimely death, when our property was destroyed, property might be made good in some fashion, but for life destroyed there is no compensation—and yet, despite the repeated murdering of our innocent men and women and children, the President declared that there must be some pledge given to safeguard the lives of American men and women and children, and the pledge was given that it would not be repeated.

And then began the warning of a ruthless destruction of all life and property of any people who came within a zone where they had a perfect lawful right to go. That promise and pledge made by the Imperial German Government, like that treaty that held Belgium sacred from invasion, was regarded as a mere scrap of paper and torn into shreds, trodden under foot and the wholesale destruction and murder went on.

Well, men and women, pacifist as I have been from my young boyhood until this war broke out, I am free to say to you this, that I could not blind myself to the altered situation in the world's affairs; that the gauntlet had been thrown down to democracy and that unless the challenge was accepted autocracy would run rough-shod over the peoples of the whole world; and from pacifist, my evolution was into a fighting man.

I hold that in this great time there can be no just foundation for pacifism until militarism is crushed. (Applause.) I could wish that the war would come to an end and human life and suffering be conserved and saved, but a peace at this time without any one thing being determined finally and absolutely to guarantee that a repetition of such a ruthless war can not be again consummated and brought as a curse upon the people of the world is both undesirable and impossible. (Applause.)

When the people of the Colonies of America took up arms for the establishment of this new nation, the Republic of the United States, there could be no ending of that war until either the people of these Colonies were subjugated or freed to enjoy the privileges and the advantages of self-government. It was so determined, and we have won.

During the Civil War, the four years' struggle and sacrifices between the North and the South for the abolition of human slavery and the maintenance of the Union, there could be no compromise, there could be no peace until either dismemberment occurred or slavery was more firmly established, and the two parties were small and at the mercy of an aggrandizing nation of the world.

I saw a few days ago a statement published in a so-called pacifist paper, in which it said, "Why not at this time emulate the good example and the slogan of Gen. Grant, who said, 'Let us have peace'"? But the writer was either ignorant of the facts or purposely misrepresented Gen. Grant and the incident to suit a purpose which is unjustified.

When Gen. Grant uttered that immortal slogan, "Let us have peace," Gen. Lee had surrendered to Gen. Grant more than [thirty-]six months [before] and peace had been established, Gen. Grant had been nominated for the Presidency, and as his slogan for the purpose of helping the people of the South rehabilitate themselves, he said to the people of the North and of the South, "Let us have peace." (Applause.)[5]

As I a moment ago stated as my judgment, we want to fight for the liberation and the democracy of the people of Germany and Austria and Hungary, as well as for the people of the United States, so that after militarism and imperialism and autocracy are crushed, we can say with Grant, "Let us have peace." (Applause.)

We are engaged in war. We are in it. And you and I—members of organized labor, members of our unions—we sometimes enter into contests in which every one is not fully satisfied that it is the best thing to do. In our unions we have rules and laws, among which we prescribe that a strike can only be undertaken when two-thirds of the membership vote in favor of the strike. Some unions have the regulation that it shall be a majority, others three-fourths, etc.

And now, my friends, I want to recall an incident. When I worked at the bench, I was in a number of strikes. (Laughter.) There was one strike in the shop in which I was working, and my judgment was that it was an inopportune time for the men in that shop to go out on strike. I was firmly convinced that they were justified in striking, but I knew that if we went out on strike—I knew as well as I know anything that has not yet occurred—we would be defeated if we inaugurated the strike.

I was the only man in that shop who had that view. I did not vote against it. I expressed my views to the boys, but they did not hold my view and they decided that we should go out on strike. Do you think for a moment that I would remain in that shop and work while they went on strike! (Applause.)

Supposing in any of our unions a question of wages, a wage reduction or a demand for a wage increase came up and the question of striking was adopted by two-thirds of the men, or three-fourths of them—do you think for a moment that the men, the one-third or the one-fourth of them have the right to say that the three-fourths are wrong and that they are going to continue to work and play the part of the scab and the strike-breaker? I hold that the same rule applies to the country, the republic in which we live. (Applause.) I suppose that there is no one, or not many, in our time who will hold that our country can be governed without laws of some kind.

Now, we have a Constitution—the Constitution of the United States. We are living under the Declaration of Independence. The laws and the Constitution of the United States provide that the people of the United States, in the Congress Assembled, the Representatives and Senators, in the regular sessions, shall have the power to declare and make war. In the Senate of the United States, in the House of Representatives of the United States there were not more than two or three who voted against the Government and the people of the United States making war upon the Imperial Government of Germany. In other words, the representatives of the people of this republic, in Congress assembled, under the authority of the constitution of the United States, made that declaration of war, and in the face of the enemy.

Any man living in our country who is unwilling to stand behind that declaration, is unworthy to enjoy the guarantees of peace. (Applause.) I can not carry a gun with the accoutrements of war, I can not fight in the trenches; if I attempted it, after a few days or a week or two, instead of being a help, I would be a burden. And consequently it is no use for me to attempt by braggadocio or any other thought or cause to volunteer my service to enter into the military or the naval force of our Government. But I have done something. They do need in America and in all wars, organizers; and some people have flattered me with being somewhat of an organizer. (Laughter.) They need some administrators, and some have said that I am not such a bad administrator of affairs. They need advice and judgment, and some people have flattered me by saying that I was not much of a damned fool. (Laughter.) So feeling the obligation to give service, I am giving the service, the best that is in me, for the cause in which the labor movement and our country is engaged. (Applause.)

A little bit of an incident, perhaps, to you, but a great big one to me, was that a few days ago I received a letter from my grandson,[6] nineteen years of age, telling me that three months ago he had voluntarily enlisted in the service of our country in the Aviation Corps at San Antonio, Texas. His telling me about his voluntary action made me grow about six feet taller than what I am. (Applause.)

I do know this, that I said to my family group that any one of them who would not serve the United States in this war is not of my blood and I repudiate him. (Applause.) I am in this war with the people behind the President and the Government of the United States. In the meantime, and during the war I propose to see to it as best I can, that the standards of the American workers, the workers in America, shall not be deteriorated. (Applause.) And upon the contrary, that every opportunity shall be given for the working men and women in our country that in the whole industrial and commercial pursuits and activities of our Government, where they bring profit, the toilers shall share in the largest proportion of that profit. (Applause.)

At a conference held in Washington in the Executive Council Meeting Room of our beautiful structure, the officers of nearly all the international unions assembled, adopted a declaration[7] on March 12, nearly a month before the entrance of our country into the war, and insisted upon the maintenance and the improvement of the standards of life of the American working people.

Some time later with the four labor representatives sent to the United States to confer with the labor movement and the labor men of

America, the Committee on Labor was received by the President and I was deputized to make a few remarks, which I undertook to do as best I could, and the President's response was to the effect that the working people engaged in industry and commerce of the United States during this war shall have their rights guaranteed and their standards maintained. (Applause.)

When the Pennsylvania Legislature undertook to repeal the full crew law, the President wrote a letter to Governor Brumbaugh urging him to veto that proposition as against the interests of labor, which interests should be maintained at all hazards. I may say that I have tried to do something in that direction helpful upon that subject. But I want to say to you, my friends, that I think you will be pleased to hear it, that there have been agreements[8] made between the Secretary of War, Mr. Baker, and me, as President of the American Federation of Labor, the terms of which provided that in the construction of cantonments and all appurtenances to them, the union scale of wages, hours and conditions of employment of the union in the vicinity shall prevail as standards in the construction of these cantonments. A committee was created consisting of three men, one of them General Darlington, representing the army, a representative of the public, Mr. Walter Lippmann, and a representative of labor, appointed by me, and the man I appointed was John Alpine, the Vice-President of the National [American] Federation of Labor.

The Secretary of War, by further agreement with me, extended the terms to the aviation plants, to the aviation construction cantonments, and then the Secretary of Navy accepted that same agreement for all construction on land coming under the jurisdiction of the Navy Department.[9]

The same has been introduced, and this morning's Jamestown papers contain the statement of the creation of a similar board[10] under similar conditions for the emergency fleet corporation[11] and for the Navy Department and for the Shipping Board.[12] An agreement was consummated between the Seamen's Union[13] and the vessel owners for improved conditions for the seamen and to stop any agitation for the repeal of the Seamen's Act, making it secure now for all time.[14] (Applause.)

Secretary Baker, for the War Department, cancelled contracts for army clothing to the extent of nearly half a million dollars a few days ago, because this clothing was manufactured in the homes of the workers, and he wanted to abolish the sweat-shop system. (Applause.)

I freely admit that there are still many wrongs prevailing, that many evils still exist in the trades and many misconceptions and many injustices are being inflicted, but we have just declared war. We are really not in it yet, and what other governments have taken three, twenty and forty years to accomplish, cannot be accomplished with a turn of the hand. It takes time.

There is a disposition among the officers of the Government of the United States to deal fairly with labor. I am not going to defend the I.W.W.'s, those who are irresponsible to each other, irresponsible toward labor and irresponsible toward the Government of the Republic of the United States—I am not going to defend them, but I do hold that every man living in our country, no matter what his opinions may be, no matter what is the charge that may be made against him, is entitled to the protection of the laws of our country. (Applause.)

I do not think that there are many men who have been more openly hostile to this gang of industrial free-booters than I have. Well, if men calling themselves labor men undertake by their irresponsive and irrational action to undermine all that we have tried to build up for years, if they then declare that they hold themselves not responsible to any authority or to give an accounting of their conduct to anybody, if there be any other title than that which I have just germinated in my mind and called them, I do not know it. (Laughter.)

The man who is charged with the gravest crime known to the human mind is given the protection of a trial, confronted by a jury of his peers. He has his day in court. Even these industrial free-booters are entitled to that. (Applause.)

It was my pleasure last week to have had the honor of a long conference with the President and this matter was brought to his attention, of the attempt of some employers of labor to take advantage of not only this situation brought about by these so-called I.W.W.'s, but that the employers of labor, with their attorneys and corporations, were making common war upon all organized labor, trade unions, bona fide, constructive, conservative—all of them. I am not violating his confidence, nor would I violate the confidence of the Council of National Defense. I think I am justified in telling you that as a result of that, those incidents, the Council of National Defense adopted and the President approved the creation of a commission to make an investigation of that situation in the West and Northwest and to report to the Council and to the President. Upon that commission labor will undoubtedly have one or more representatives.

All along, in the activities in connection with production, transportation, or war contracts there is the disposition to deal fairly and honorably to the advantage of labor and to see that representatives of labor are on the various boards and agencies.

Now, my friends, that is what we are trying to do. I have had no time to prepare an address to you—indeed I have had little time to give thought to any particular points that I desire to cover in my talk to you this morning. This one thing I know, we are in the war and we cannot get out of it. We dare not get out of it until America and the world is safe, so that you and I and the peoples of the world may each live out their own lives, may each of them evolve and develop as best they can to attain their highest ideals.

As Lincoln said in his time, that "America cannot long remain half slave and half free," so the President of the United States in his great message to Congress on April 2 sounded the keynote for the whole world; and it is the wisdom of his great character, his vision that the world shall be free, and by common consent of the peoples, the democratic peoples of all the world, he is the logical standard-bearer and leader of the war of our time. (Applause.)

With the aid of the Central Federated Union of New York, with the organization of New York State, Pennsylvania, Jersey and a few other places, together with myself, we have organized a movement of trade unionists and men who have declared their unalterable fealty toward the American trade union movement as represented by the American Federation of Labor, accepting these two standards, one and combined. There shall be solidarity in the American labor movement, that the fight against secession and duality in the labor movement must be crushed out, (Applause.) and that with the American trade union movement we shall undertake the campaign for the more thorough organization and the more thorough Americanization of the working people of our country. (Applause.) And standing loyally by our republic that movement has gone on and on, and, as you have heard read, an invitation has been extended to the trade center bodies and state federations to send representatives to a national conference to be held at Minneapolis, Minn., September 5, 6, and 7.[15] It is my earnest hope, as I am convinced it will be to the advantage of the labor movement of the State of New York and of our country itself, that the men of labor shall be at Minneapolis on September 5.

The liberties of many of the people during this war in some of the countries have been taken away from them. In the United States thus far no attempt has been made, and if I read the signs of the times correctly, and I think I do, if the men of labor, of our country will be true to themselves and true to their unions and true to the Republic of the United States and the cause in which we are all engaged, there will be no attempt made to take away any of our liberties. (Applause.)

But on the contrary, that for which we have striven so long, that for which we have given so many hours and years of our lives, will be accomplished, will be maintained forever, except as improvements may come. It is all depending upon us. The course is open for us. We have no choice. I was about to say we must make our choice,—there is no choice. There is only one way, and that is the straight way; not only the straight way to labor patriotism, but to group patriotism, to human patriotism and to the patriotism and loyalty to the cause of labor and cause of our republic for justice and freedom and democracy. (Applause.)

. . .

TDc, Files of the Office of the President, Speeches and Writings, reel 112, frames 743–59, *AFL Records.*

1. James P. Holland.

2. SG is referring to the 1909 conference of the International Secretariat of the National Centers of Trade Unions, which met in Paris from Aug. 30 to Sept. 1.

3. For SG's account of this mass meeting, see AFL, *Proceedings,* 1909, p. 38.

4. For a description of SG's struggle with the issue at a February 1917 meeting of the Advisory Commission of the Council of National Defense, see Franklin Martin, *Digest of the Proceedings of the Council of National Defense during the World War,* 73d Cong., 2d sess., 1934, S.Doc. 193, pp. 97–98.

5. The quotation is from Ulysses S. Grant's letter of May 29, 1868, to Joseph Hawley, accepting the Republican nomination for the presidency (John Y. Simon et al., eds., *The Papers of Ulysses S. Grant,* 28 vols. [Carbondale, Ill., 1967–2005], 18:264).

6. Samuel Harry Gompers (1898–1972), the son of Henry Julian and Bessie Phillips Gompers. He enlisted under the name Harry Boyd Gompers in April 1917 and served in France from August 1918 until the end of the war.

7. "American Labor's Position in Peace or in War," Mar. 12, 1917, above.

8. "A Memorandum of Agreement between Samuel Gompers and Newton Baker," June 19, 1917, above.

9. See "A Memorandum of Agreement between Samuel Gompers and Newton Baker," June 19, 1917, n. 1, above.

10. The Shipbuilding Labor Adjustment Board was created under an agreement of Aug. 20, 1917, to resolve disputes over wages, hours, or working conditions on construction or repair work undertaken at private shipyards for the U.S. Shipping Board, the Emergency Fleet Corporation, or the Navy Department. The agreement directed the board to refer to the wages, hours, and conditions in force on July 15 as the standards for settling disputes. Negotiated by Louis Wehle at the request of President Woodrow Wilson, the agreement was signed by acting secretary of the Navy Franklin Roosevelt, Shipping Board chairman Edward Hurley, and Emergency Fleet Corporation general manager Washington Capps, as well as by SG and officers of the AFL Metal Trades and Building Trades departments and eleven affiliates. The board consisted of three permanent members, representing the public, the Emergency Fleet Corporation, and labor. In addition, two associate members were appointed in each dispute coming before the board—one representing the employer in the controversy and the other the workers—and another member, appointed by the secretary of the Navy, joined the board when it investigated disputes in plants doing work for the Navy. For a copy of the agreement, see AFL, *Proceedings,* 1917, pp. 83–84.

The agreement of Aug. 20 was superseded by a second one, signed on Dec. 8 by representatives of the Navy, the Emergency Fleet Corporation, and officers of the AFL Metal Trades Department and eight unions. It provided for a three-member adjustment board, with one member to be appointed by SG, and a six-member board of review and appeal, three members of which were to be named by SG. Standards for resolving pay disputes under the new agreement were to be the wage rates in the district in question, provided they "have been established through agreements between employer and employes and are admitted to be equitable" (AFL, *Proceedings*, 1918, pp. 56–57; quotation on p. 56).

11. The Emergency Fleet Corporation was established by the U.S. Shipping Board on Apr. 16, 1917, to acquire, build, outfit, man, and operate merchant vessels for the board.

12. The U.S. Shipping Board was established by an act of Congress on Sept. 7, 1916, and formally organized on Jan. 30, 1917, to encourage the creation of a merchant marine and the development of a naval reserve, acquire and allocate merchant shipping, and regulate shipping and shipbuilding.

13. The International SEAMEN's Union of America.

14. The agreement, adopted on Aug. 8, 1917, contained stipulations as to wages, bonuses, and the workforce of seamen in the merchant marine. For the text of the agreement, see AFL, *Proceedings*, 1917, p. 85. Toward the end of August, an additional agreement was made between the U.S. Shipping Board, the International Longshoremen's Association, and representatives of the ship owners providing for a national adjustment commission and local adjustment commissions to resolve disputes relating to wages, hours, or conditions of labor in the loading or unloading of ships. The union scale of hours, wages, and conditions in each port as of Aug. 1 was adopted as the standard for settling disputes. The text of this agreement is printed ibid., pp. 85–86.

15. That is, for the convention of the American Alliance for Labor and Democracy.

To Charles Bottomley[1]

Minneapolis, Minn., Sept. 7, 1917.

Mr. Bottomley,
Secretary Metal Trades Council
Portland, Oregon.

Am advised[2] by Ship Building Labor Adjustment Board that the Portland, Oregon, Metal Trades Council has taken position declining to send committee of council to Washington, D.C., to confer with representatives of that board in an effort to adjust existing differences.[3] Refusal to participate in conference with ship building labor adjustment board at Washington DC on part of Portland Metal Trades Council in an effort to adjust present difficulties is in contravention of a long established policy of the organized labor movement. If Portland Metal Trades Council maintains its attitude and refuses to treat with ship building labor adjustment board then the efforts of the American Federation of Labor to secure justice and recognition for organized labors contention will be immeasurably retarded if not destroyed. My judgment is that the Portland Metal Trades Council cannot afford to take drastic action until every other opportunity has been employed to secure a satisfactory adjustment. I trust that the Portland Metal Trades Council will give most serious consideration to the views herein expressed.[4]

Samuel Gompers,
President American Federation of Labor

TWSr, Files of the Office of the President, General Correspondence, reel 88, frame 112, *AFL Records.*

1. Charles M. Bottomley was secretary of both the executive committee of the Metal Trades Council (MTC) of Portland, Oreg., and Vicinity and the Portland branch of the Pattern Makers' League of North America. He chaired the committee representing the unions involved in the shipbuilding strike that began in Portland on Sept. 24, 1917.

2. The Shipbuilding Labor Adjustment Board wired SG on Sept. 6, 1917, that it had invited the Portland MTC to send representatives to Washington, D.C., to discuss the MTC's wage demands and that Bottomley had replied that no settlement was acceptable unless it guaranteed the closed shop (Files of the Office of the President, General Correspondence, reel 88, frames 96–98, *AFL Records*).

3. On Aug. 3, 1917, the Portland MTC presented a list of demands to local shipbuilding firms that included an eight-hour day, wage increases, and union recognition. When employers rejected the demands, the council authorized a strike to begin on Aug. 22.

4. At the request of federal mediator George Harry, the Portland MTC postponed the strike and sent representatives to confer with the Shipbuilding Labor Adjustment Board in Washington, D.C. When the board was unable to meet with the MTC's delegates, however, because of the resignation of one of its members—Emergency Fleet Corporation representative Edward Carry—they returned to Portland, and some eleven thousand shipbuilding workers left their jobs on Sept. 24. Shipbuilding workers also struck in Seattle and San Francisco, bringing the total number of strikers to about fifty thousand. The board quickly reconstituted itself and went to the West Coast, where it held hearings in Seattle, Portland, and San Francisco in order to fashion an agreement for the entire Pacific Coast. At the urging of President Woodrow Wilson's personal representative, Gavin McNab, San Francisco shipbuilding workers went back to work within a few days, and the strikers in Seattle and Portland did so in October. In its ruling, issued on Nov. 4, the board established the eight-hour day and mandated a pay increase based on wages in effect on June 1, 1916. The shipbuilding workers were dissatisfied with the award, however, since the men in the Puget Sound district were already receiving wages higher than those granted by the board. On the appeal of the unions involved, representatives of the Emergency Fleet Corporation and the Navy authorized a second wage increase on Dec. 10, initially payable as a "war bonus" to the men working full time between Dec. 15, 1917, and Feb. 1, 1918, and then, after Feb. 1, payable to all Pacific Coast shipbuilding workers.

Bottomley wired SG on Sept. 7, 1917, that the Portland MTC had complied with the request to send representatives to meet with the Shipbuilding Labor Adjustment Board and had postponed further action pending the outcome of this conference (Files of the Office of the President, General Correspondence, reel 88, frame 106, *AFL Records*).

The Declaration of Principles Adopted by the American Alliance for Labor and Democracy Convention in Minneapolis

[September 7, 1917]

THE DECLARATION OF PRINCIPLES

The American Alliance for Labor and Democracy in its first national conference, declares its unswerving adherence to the cause of Democracy, now assailed by the forces of autocracy and militarism. As labor unionists, social reformers and Socialists we pledge our loyal support and service to the United States Government and its allies in the present world conflict.

We declare that the one overshadowing issue is the preservation of democracy. Either democracy will endure and men will be free, or autocracy will triumph, and the race will be enslaved. On this prime issue we take our stand. We declare that the great war must be fought to a decisive result; that until autocracy is defeated there can be no hope of an honorable peace, and that to compromise the issue is only to sow the seed for bloodier and more devastating wars in the future.

We declare our abhorrence of war and our devotion to the cause of peace. But we recognize that there are evils greater and more intolerable than those of war. We declare that war waged for evil ends must be met by war waged for altruistic ends. A peace bought by the surrender of every principle vital to democracy is no peace, but shameful servility. Our nation has not sought this war. As a people, we desired peace for its own sake, and we held fast to our traditional principle of keeping aloof from the political affairs of Europe. Our President, with a forbearance and a patience which some of us thought extreme, exhausted every honorable means in behalf of peace; and the declaration of war came only after many months of futile efforts to avoid a conflict. This war, so relentlessly forced upon us, must now be made the means of insuring a world-wide and permanent peace.

We declare that in this crisis the one fundamental need is unity of action. The successful prosecution of the war requires that all the energies of our people be concentrated to a common purpose. After more than two years of exhaustive deliberation, in which every phase of our relation to the great world problem has been thoroughly debated, the constitutional representatives of the people declared the nation's will. Loyalty to the people demands that all acquiesce in that decision and render the government every service in their power.

We strongly denounce the words and actions of those enemies of the Republic, who, falsely assuming to speak in the name of labor and democracy, are now ceaselessly striving to obstruct the operations of the government's purposes, in traducing the character of the President and of his advisors, in stealthily attempting to incite sedition and in openly or impliedly counselling resistance to the enforcement of laws enacted for the National Defense, they abuse the rights of free speech, free assemblage and a free press. In the name of liberty they encourage anarchy, in the name of democracy they strive to defeat the will of the majority, and in the name of humanity they render every possible aid and comfort to the brutal Prussian autocracy. If the sinister counsels of these persons were followed, labor would be reduced to subjection and democracy would be obliterated from the earth. We declare that the betrayal of one's fellow-workers during a strike finds its exact counterpart in the betrayal of one's fellow citizens in time of war, and that both are offenses which deserve the detestation of mankind.

We declare that a sturdy defense of the interests of labor is wholly compatible with supreme loyalty to the government. We fully recognize the many proofs given by the President and the Administration chiefs to the principle that the war shall not be made an excuse for lowering any of the standards which have been established by labor in its long struggle. We declare, however, that predatory influences are at work at all times—and particularly in time of war—to lower these standards. These efforts, wherever made, must be resisted. Not only must all present standards be maintained, but there must be no curtailment of any of the present agencies which make for the betterment of the condition of labor. Our loyalty to the government is the loyalty of free men who will not acquiesce in any surrender of principle.

This war, which on our part is waged for the preservation of democracy, has already set in motion vast forces for the furtherance and extension of democracy. Revolutionary changes have been made—changes which reveal the power and determination of a democratic people to control its own economic life for the common good. We declare that peace shall not be another name for reaction, but that the gains thus far made for labor should be maintained in perpetuity.

We declare that a condition which demands the conscription of men likewise demands the conscription of wealth, and that incomes, excess profits and land values should be taxed to the fullest needs of the government.

We declare that industrial enterprises should be the servants and not the masters of the people; and that in cases where differences between owners and workers threaten a discontinuance of production necessary for the war, the government should assume complete control of such industries and operate them for the exclusive benefit of the people.

We declare that the government should take prompt action with regard to the speculative interests which, especially during the war, have done so much to enhance prices of the necessaries of life. To increase the food supply and to lower prices, the Government should commandeer all land necessary for public purposes and should tax idle land in private possession on its full rental value.

We declare that the right of the wage-earners to collective action is the fundamental condition which gives opportunity for economic freedom and makes possible the betterment of the workers' conditions. The recognition already given to this principle should be extended and made the basis of all relationships, direct or indirect, between the government and wage-earners engaged in activities connected with the war.

We declare that the wage-earners must have a voice in determining the conditions under which they are to give service, and that the voluntary institutions that have organized the industrial, commercial and transportation workers in time of peace shall be unhampered in the exercise of their recognized function during the war: that labor shall be adequately represented in all the councils authorized to conduct the war and in the commission selected to negotiate terms of peace.

We declare our full accord with the declarations agreed upon by the conference of American trade unionists called by the Executive Council of the American Federation of Labor, held in Washington, D.C., March 12, 1917, in which the representatives of affiliated national unions and international trade unions and the railroad brotherhoods participated.

Believing that the material interests of the nation's soldiers and sailors and of their dependents should be withdrawn from the realm of charity and chance, and that health and life should be fully insured, we indorse the soldiers' and sailors' insurance bill[1] now before Congress.

We declare for universal equal suffrage.

Fully realizing that the perpetuity of democratic institutions is involved in freedom of speech, of the press and of assemblage, we declare that these essential rights must be guarded with zealous care lest all other rights be lost. We declare, however, that where expressions are used which are obstructive to the government in its conduct of the war, or are clearly capable of giving aid or comfort to the nation's foes, the offenders should be reprimanded by the constituted authorities in accordance with established law.

Inspired by the ideals of liberty and justice herein declared as a fundamental basis for national policies the American Alliance for Labor and Democracy makes its appeal to the working men and women of the United States, and calls upon them to unite in unanimous support of the President and the nation for the prosecution of the war and the preservation of democracy.

America's Fight for the Preservation of Democracy (n. p., [1917]).

1. The bill, introduced by Democratic congressman Joshua Alexander of Missouri on Aug. 10, 1917 (H.R. 5723, 65th Cong., 1st sess.), was signed into law as the War Risk Insurance Act on Oct. 6 (U.S. *Statutes at Large*, 40: 398–411). It provided compensation for death or disability and insurance against death or total permanent disability to soldiers, sailors, and nurses in the armed forces. It also provided allowances and the compulsory allotment of pay to the families of enlisted men.

From Emmet Flood[1]

General Organizer
American Federation of Labor
Chicago. Sept. 18th, 1917

My Dear Sam:—

I am sure you know of the effort that has been made by the American Federation of Labor to organize the men and women employed in the large Packing Houses, and that you do know that the American Federation of Labor for nearly three years has kept an organizer or interpreter in all of the large Packing House centers, Myself with the assistance of former Vice President Lane, now National Secretary-Treasurer of the Amalgamated Assn.,[2] directing the work. Just now the efforts put forth by the American Federation and its representatives in these packing houses are bringing results.

We discovered in our efforts to organize the Packing Houses in Kansas City and Saint Joseph, particularly, that as soon as we got sufficient number together to call a meeting after the first or second meeting that the group that attended were discharged the following morning, and that all the Companies had to do was to wire in advance for recruits from Denver, Colo.

J. E. Smith,[3] one of our men who spent nearly a year in Kansas City, had on one or two occasions got very well started in the Packing Houses in Kansas City, when matters happened as indicated above.

He wrote me and we decided, Smith and I, to go to Denver and take with us Organizer McCreash[4] of the Amalgamated Association.

We succeeded in organizing, by a careful house to house canvas a Local Union of Packing House workers, and before I left Denver, we had about a 60 per cent of organization among the Retail Market men. we succeeded in organizing two seperate unions[5]

Shortly after my leaving, the packers discharged some twenty men. Smith was there, and succeeded in not only getting the Butcher Workmen to strike in sympathy with the locked out members of the union, but succeeded in getting members of the Building Trades, who were working on new work in the Stockyards to leave their places and finally succeeded in getting a settlement, which provided that all men be returned to their work without discrimination.

This union of Packing House workers, increased very rapidly and soon had a membership of about 70% of all the people working in the Denver Stockyards, and then recently they presented a demand to all the Companies for five cent (?) increase in wages. The Company before getting an opportunity to grant the increase discovered that the Packing House Workers in Omaha and Kansas City had walked out and tied up both industries in those cities, demanding the same increase as the Denver union.

The Company settled with the union in Denver, Colo., with an increase of $2\frac{1}{2}$¢ an hour to all employees and at the same time granted a similar increase to organized and unorganized as well in all their packing houses.

McCreash, the organizer of the Amalgamated Association, demanded for the Kansas City strikers that the Company sign a contract giving recognition to the Amalgamated Assn., and the A.F. of L. The Companies finally conceded and I am enclosing you a copy of the first contract that has been signed between the Amalgamated Assn., and the big Packers for thirteen years.

While it has taken a long time, yet I think the results accomplished has fully justified our efforts.

Lane and myself, who had charge of the work made no exceptions in Chicago, as far as the Packing Houses were concerned, we were giving the same active attention to organizing the workers in these Packing Houses as we did to all the others.

During my absence from Chicago and if I were home, I could not have objected to a delegate in the Chicago Federation of Labor introducing a resolution requesting that all trades represented in the stock yards organize a Packing House conference for the purpose of carrying on a systematic campaign of organizing the workers employed there.

After the thing developed and I saw the men who were in charge of the campaign, I refused to further give a single effort in the direction in which they were going.

The man who was responsible for the resolution in the Federation is a fellow by the name of Foster,[6] who about a year and a half ago appeared in the Chicago Federation of Labor and made a speech, if I remember right alightly condemning some of the actions of the I.W.W. He is now practically in charge of the stock yards campaign with John Fitzpatrick as president of the Packing Trades conference. Foster was formerly a member of the shingle weavers some where in the west now his companions are all as indicated in this letter

Another leading light is an I.W.W., by the name of Johnstone[7] whose present occupation is making speeches at local unions and selling the so-called frame up pamphlet of the Mooney trial. Associated with them is R. T. Sims,[8] the nigger who burglarized and plundered the Office Janitors[9] union out of every dime he could get a hold of.[10]

At the last meeting of the Office Janitors Union, I attended several of the members, who had been arrested as strike picketers and whose trials had not as yet been consummated were left at the mercy of the courts as far as the officers of the Janitors union was concerned without anyone to speak in their defense.

At that meeting I asked the Secretary[11] of the union, who had stolen the pocket book of the scrub woman in our building with forty cents in it, what had become of all the money that was paid by the members of the Janitors Union. He gave me a dirty short curt answer, and I do not think he will ever forget his answer to me for I seriously tried to impress on his mind that a decent civil answer was the best reply to my question.

At that meeting, the printer who did their work, presented a bill for $160.00. I think they owed the Chicago Federation of Labor about six months rent and never paid the lawyer who defended the strikers.

These facts are pretty well known by everybody around the office in Chicago. For some peculiar reason Fitzpatrick, in particular with the partial consent of Edw. Nockels is trying to keep this nigger alive and keep him to the front.

Just prior to Sims entering into the organizing work in the stock yards myself and Secretary Olander, John Walker and Lane had a meeting with a very well recommended intelligent negro doctor by the name of Hall, who seemed to understand that the colored workers were allowing themselves to become discredited in large industrial communities because they could be used by large employers to break down the standards of the workers and agreed to do everything in his power to assist in the organizing campaign in the stock yards. Then came Sims with his fog horn voice and done the very thing, if I know anything about the organizing work, that would prevent complete organization of the stock yards workers.

He called meetings for the negro workers to be organized as Packing House workers in Local unions by themselves. The Chicago Tribune, on the 14th inst., copy of which I enclose printed an article in reference to one of the meetings that was called by Sims.[12] A number of the newspaper boys knowing that I was engaged in the organization of these workers for some time asked me what I thought of the treatment that Sims had received as an organizer for the A.F. of L. In reply I said that Sims was not an organizer for the A.F. of L., and that I was quite sure he was not hooted from the platform because the colored workers did not want to join the union, but the reason might have been that the colored workers knew Sims as well as I do. I said further that Sims had been expelled from the Spanish War Veterans Tanners' Camp because of his unpatriotic utterances in the Chicago Federation of Labor, as a delegate from the Office Building Janitors Union.

Not only did he say that he would be shot before conscription, but advised all the other delegates to do the same. On the same Sunday, he made this statement the union of which he was a member was expelling him for robbing the union.

The President[13] of the former Office Janitors Union was in my office yesterday and he informed me that he was opposed to the strike[14] and that in the presence of John Fitzpatrick Sims pulled out a knife and threatened to cut (Belinsky) the President's belly open unless he stopped agitating against the strike. The strike was called.

One of the first actions of Sims, after the strike was called was to lead this group of strikers through the loop district with their mops and buckets and scrub rags and a negro band leading the parade and Sims the only negro who belonged to the union.

Even after all this, Fitzpatrick and Nockels tried to assist him in a way financially. Nockels wanted me to agree with him that I recommend to you that Sims be employed as a Special Investigator to find out what the influx from the south of so many colored workers, could be for.

My reply to Nockels was, that Sims was a crook and that there was no need of such an investigation. That your office was fully aware of everything in connection with immigration of the negroes to the North.

What prompted me to write you this letter today is that the article in the Daily News of the 14th inst.,[15] copy of which I am enclosing you, caused some comment in the front office of the Chicago Federation of Labor.

A reference was made to me that I was knocking Sims because I did not like him. In reply to that statement, I said I had no quarrel with Sims as a man, but that he was a burglar and a plunderer and for his treason and treachery in the labor movement I would condemn him and ask that he be shunned by all true representatives of the organized labor movement.

Nockels said at no time was it ever shown that Sims books or his accounts were wrong. I told him Yes, that as a matter of fact you had discovered irregularities in his books where he never entered a check for $214.00 that was sent to him by Secretary Morrison until the time you had called his attention to it and that he had charged up to the union at least one item and possibly two for per capita tax that Morrison had already taken out of the check in question, so with a great puff he Nockels dictated a letter to his stenographer, of which you already have a copy.[16]

Sam, I think you know me well enough to know that this long letter is not for the purpose of prejudicing your mind even against this grafting nigger but to let you know the facts and if you remember the occasion of Sims coming to your room in the Morrison hotel I am sure you will agree that his books were irregular.

It might be well to say to you that good big local union of Office Janitors has gone out of business. I cannot see the reason for Fitzpatrick's efforts in trying to keep this nigger alive in the Labor Movement unless that he is afraid that the labor movement around Chicago, may discover that Fitz. committed a serious wrong when he stood by Sims when I was doing everything in my power to get rid of him and that he would now want him to do some thing meritorious in the movement at the present time to justify Fitzpatricks' standing by him. That may be what is in Fitzpatricks' mind.

From what I know about this fellow Sims, something I have not told you in this letter nor that I will not tell you in a letter, proves to me that there is not one spark of decent manhood in his make up. Too often has organized labor suffered as the result of such men as Sims, and too often has organized labor's efforts been defeated in the home of its friends.

I have been fighting for nearly twenty years for the things that are right in the labor movement and a great deal of the time alone. I have often thought my efforts were in vain and I was causing useless worry and hardship for myself trying to set things aright in the labor movement particularly in Chicago. I thought I might stop and let things be as they are, but I find myself in trying to do that rebelling against me, so I expect while God gives me courage and voice and power I shall continue to stand up and fight for the things that appeal to me to be for the best interest of the greatest society I have had the pleasure to know anything about—the Organized Labor Movement of America.

I am sorry I could not attend the Coliseum meeting[17] as I was detained at a conference between two directly affiliated unions one which was on strike and the other actually scabbing the job, the conference lasted until nearly midnight.

I have other matters I wish to write to you about but not now. With best wishes, I remain

Fraternally yours,   Emmet T. Flood

P.S. Mrs Raymond Robins was defeated for a member of the Executive Board of C.F. of L. at regular election Sunday anna Fitzgerald was elected

T and ALS, Files of the Office of the President, General Correspondence, reel 88, frames 324–30, *AFL Records.*

1. Emmet T. FLOOD served as an AFL salaried organizer from 1904 to 1925.

2. Dennis LANE served as secretary-treasurer of the Amalgamated MEAT Cutters and Butcher Workmen of North America from 1917 to 1942.

3. J. E. Smith, a member of AFL Flat Janitors' Union 14,332 of Chicago, served as an AFL salaried organizer from 1916 to 1920.

4. Timothy A. McCreash (1878–1931), a member of Meat Cutters' local 560 of Sioux City, Iowa, served as an organizer (1916–17) and then as vice-president (1917–31) of the international union.

5. Meat Cutters' locals 634 (Butchers) and 641 (Packing House Workers) of Denver.

6. William Z. FOSTER led AFL organizing campaigns in the packinghouse and steel industries between 1917 and 1919. He served as secretary of the Stockyards Labor Council (SLC) in Chicago from its organization in July 1917 until mid-1918.

7. John W. "Jack" Johnstone was an organizer for the SLC. He was a member of the IWW in British Columbia for several years and then was active in Foster's Syndicalist League of North America and, after moving to Chicago, in its successor, the International Trade Union Educational League. Johnstone succeeded Foster as secretary of the SLC in mid-1918, serving in that position until 1920. He later joined the American Communist party.

8. Robert T. Sims served as financial secretary of AFL Office Janitors' Union 15,155 until March or April of 1917.

9. AFL 15,155 was chartered in 1916.

10. Chicago Federation of Labor (CFL) president John Fitzpatrick, on the other hand, wrote SG on Sept. 25, 1917, to say that there was really no discrepancy in Sims's books, only a mix-up caused by Flood, who had refused to turn over the new union's funds to Sims when he was elected financial secretary because he was black (Files of the Office of the President, General Correspondence, reel 88, frames 675–81, *AFL Records*).

11. Walter J. Zukowski was recording secretary of AFL 15,155.

12. The article, entitled "Negroes at Stockyards Refuse to Join Union," reported that a meeting of about a hundred black packinghouse workers on Sept. 13 "hooted" Sims from the platform and unanimously rejected his proposal that they unionize (*Chicago Tribune*, Sept. 14, 1917).

13. Konstanty Belinski was president of AFL 15,155.

14. Several hundred Chicago janitors, window washers, and scrub women struck for higher pay on Feb. 5, 1917. The strike ended in failure.

15. The article, entitled "Labor Leaders Disown Sims," reported on the meeting of black packinghouse workers on Sept. 13. It quoted Flood as saying that because of

Sims's public stance against conscription, Sims had "no authority as an organizer and is discredited in the labor movement" (*Chicago Daily News,* Sept. 14, 1917).

16. Edward Nockels wrote SG on Sept. 17, 1917.

17. An estimated sixteen thousand people attended a patriotic rally held at the Coliseum in Chicago on the evening of Sept. 14, 1917. SG and Elihu Root were the principal speakers at the event.

From Mrs. William Glenning

Philadelphia, Pa. [c. September 18, 1917]

Dear Sir and Brother:

Will you kindly help us organize the lady house workers of the arsenals of the country on house work? I am employed in the Philadelphia Schuylkill arsenal. I believe there is a field for organization here.

Please send an organizer. I know a hundred women who are not satisfied with the treatment accorded them, this is not a woman suffrage proposition. Simply want respect of inspectors and want you please to help us organize. My husband is a union man for 17 years, he tells me without organization we cannot get nothing. His mother received more wages from 1861 to 1865 than we receive today.

My husband met you in Boston in 1905, he tells me we cannot get nothing without organization. We know you are a busy man at Washington, but we are also human beings and cannot stand to be trampled on no longer.

Hoping you will give this letter your earliest consideration,[1]

Respectfully,   (Signed) Mrs. Wm. Glenning

TLtpSr, reel 226, vol. 238, p. 512, SG Letterbooks, DLC. Typed notation: "Copy." Enclosed in SG to Joseph Richie, Sept. 19, 1917, ibid., p. 511.

1. SG referred Mrs. Glenning's letter to AFL organizer Joseph Richie of Philadelphia on Sept. 19, 1917, and informed her of his action the same day (reel 226, vol. 238, pp. 510–11, SG Letterbooks, DLC).

To Woodrow Wilson

Washington, D.C. September 21, 1917

The Honorable Woodrow Wilson,
President of the United States,
Washington, D.C.
Sir:

Several days ago I felt impelled to respectfully call your attention to the action of the Emergency Fleet Corporation and the United States Shipping Board in repudiating and annulling the agreement into which they entered together with the Secretary of the Navy, the responsible officers of 15 organizations of labor, including the undersigned.[1]

This morning Mr. V. Everit Macy,[2] Chairman of the Board, permitted me to see a copy of the letter[3] he addressed to you yesterday in which the situation was more fully set forth.

The purpose of my writing now is to call your attention to the fact of the very precarious position in which the action of the Fleet Corporation and the Shipping Board has placed the representatives and responsible men of the organized labor movement of the country, in annulling the terms of the agreement entered into August 20th.

First the interpretation placed by the Corporation and the Shipping Board upon the Agreement of August 20th is wholly wrong and more than likely unintentionally does the other signators to the agreement an injustice. There is no good reason why the Corporation and the Shipping Board should not determine what part of any award which the adjustment board would make should be borne by the ship yard owners, or by the Government, or by both.

But quite aside from all these considerations, this one fact stands out conspicuously,—that the Secretary of the Navy with the representatives of the Corporation and of the Shipping Board, Mr. Hurley[4] and Admiral Capps,[5] signed the agreement. If there was any provision in the agreement to which they objected they ought to have withheld their signatures until it conformed to their views as to the needs of the Government. But within fifteen days after signing the agreement, important agencies of the Government, the United States Shipping Board and the Emergency Fleet Corporation, nolens volens, broke a solemn agreement. In other words, they have treated it as "a scrap of paper."

You can readily understand the effect and influence of this action upon the minds and actions of the working people of the country. I am free to say that I have grave apprehensions as to the consequences, and I earnestly hope that you may see your way clear to impress upon the Board and the Corporation the need of revising their course and to reinstate Mr. Carey[6] as their representative that Mr. Macy your own appointee and Mr. Berres the man whom I recommended, be brought in to resume their functions under the terms of the August 20th agreement.

Very respectfully yours,   Saml Gompers.
President,   American Federation of Labor.

TLS, Woodrow Wilson Papers, DLC.

1. The U.S. Shipping Board and the Emergency Fleet Corporation were demanding final say in any wage increases approved by the Shipbuilding Labor Adjustment Board. SG maintained that this undermined the agreement establishing the labor adjustment board and made it impossible for that body to function effectively. He met with President Woodrow Wilson on Sept. 17, 1917, to protest and during the following days met repeatedly with labor adjustment board chairman V. Everit Macy, Shipping Board chairman Edward Hurley, and Emergency Fleet Corporation general manager Washington Capps. The dispute was resolved at a White House meeting on Sept. 23 when SG, Hurley, Macy, and Joseph Tumulty, representing the president, agreed that the decisions of the labor adjustment board would be final and not subject to review by the Shipping Board or the Emergency Fleet Corporation.

2. Valentine Everit Macy (1871–1930), president of the National Civic Federation, was chairman of the Shipbuilding Labor Adjustment Board and chairman of the subcommittee on Mediation and Conciliation of the Committee on Labor of the Advisory Commission of the Council of National Defense.

3. Macy to Woodrow Wilson, Sept. 20, 1917, Arthur S. Link et al., eds., *The Papers of Woodrow Wilson*, 69 vols. (Princeton, N.J., 1966–94), 44: 226–29.

4. Edward Nash Hurley (1864–1933), president and later chairman of the board of the Hurley Machine Co. of Chicago, served as chairman of the Shipping Board and president of the Emergency Fleet Corporation from 1917 to 1919.

5. Rear Adm. Washington Lee Capps (1864–1935), the chief constructor of the Navy, served as general manager of the Emergency Fleet Corporation from July to December 1917.

6. Edward Francis Carry (1867–1929), president of the Haskell and Barker Car Co. of Michigan City, Ind., and director of operations for the Shipping Board, had been appointed as the representative of the Emergency Fleet Corporation to the Shipbuilding Labor Adjustment Board but resigned on Sept. 11, 1917. He was replaced by Louis Coolidge.

From Louis Howe[1]

Assistant Secretary's Office,
Navy Department,
Washington. September 22, 1917.

Dear Mr. Gompers:

In conformity with our telephone conversation,[2] the trouble at the Norfolk Yard appears to be a determination on the part of the plumbers, pipefitters, shipsmiths, and boilermakers to insist on the same wages as the machinists.[3] The details are, of course, exceedingly complicated, and I am hardly prepared even to tell you informally what the Department's attitude will be. I am sending you a copy[4] of the notification served by the boilermakers and pipefitters this morning on Naval Constructor Watt,[5] Industrial Manager of the Norfolk Yard. The shipsmiths' note was oral, but of the same nature.

Mr. Daniels is out of town and will not be back until sometime Monday, and Mr. Roosevelt will not be back until Monday night. What I am going to ask you to do is to use your good offices to get the men to postpone their proposed action until at least Tuesday night as there is no one here who could possibly grant their demands, even if such should be the decision. Frankly, I hope you will call the attention of whoever you get on the telephone to the difference in the attitude of these men to that of the men in the other Yards, particularly Philadelphia. I think you will agree with me that a demand which only amounts to four hours' notice involving the complete tying up of our vitally important Navy work at Norfolk, and leaving no alternative for discussion or consideration is not a patriotic thing to do. I am told, informally, that the real trouble is the fixed intention of all the other metal working trades to receive the same wages as the machinists at Norfolk, and that the Metal Trades Council of Norfolk sometime ago agreed to back up the demands of the shipfitters in this matter. This would seem to be carried out by the fact that the shipfitters served the first notice, and that they have been followed during the afternoon by the boilermakers, pipefitters and plumbers. If you can reach the Metal Trades Council, I think you will be able to find some one who can see that this action is delayed until it can be laid before the head of the Navy Department. I would appreciate it if you would let me know what success you have in this matter.[6]

You will understand that at Norfolk we have ships urgently needed for military uses, and under repair, that we are also making mines and other material which must go to the front at once, and that a delay of even a day or two in work will be a very serious military matter. There is probably no Yard where a cessation of work, even for a short time, will be so serious from a military standpoint.

I have just be[en] notified by telephone that an appeal made by Mr. Watt to suspend action until the return of Mr. Roosevelt was met by the shipsmiths with the statement that there would be a meeting tonight at which they would decide the question, and by the boilermakers that they had made up their minds, and that they had no intention of giving us any time whatever. I think if you can get in touch with the Metal Trades Council at Norfolk with an appeal that can be made on the ground of patriotism that the matter can be averted, and eventually adjusted.

Very truly yours,   L McH Howe
Assistant to the Assistant Secretary.

TLS, Files of the Office of the President, General Correspondence, reel 88, frames 601–2, *AFL Records.*

1. Louis McHenry Howe (1871–1936), a close friend and political adviser to Franklin Roosevelt, was an assistant to Roosevelt in the Navy Department.

2. Howe wrote this letter at SG's request after speaking with him by telephone about the situation at the Norfolk Navy Yard.

3. On Sept. 24, 1917, between four and five thousand employees at the Norfolk Navy Yard struck because of dissatisfaction with a new wage scale. The walkout ended on Sept. 27 after the Navy Department agreed to meet in early October with representatives of the men in Washington, D.C., in order to draw up a revised wage scale conforming with prevailing local rates. The Navy also promised that the strikers would be taken back without penalty.

4. The copy of the undated notification may be found in the Files of the Office of the President, General Correspondence, reel 88, frame 604, *AFL Records.*

5. Richard M. Watt.

6. On Sept. 22, 1917, SG wired Joseph Franklin, president of the International Brotherhood of Boiler Makers, Iron Ship Builders, and Helpers of America, and John Alpine, president of the United Association of Plumbers and Steam Fitters of the United States and Canada, appealing to them to contact the locals involved and ask for a postponement of the strike.

From Fred Brown

Bisbee, Arizona, Sept. 25, 1917.

Dear Sir and Brother:

First I want to extend my thanks for having a committee appointed to investigate the conditions that exist throughout this state in regards to labor. A rigid investigation will prove to all the world that the fight that the money barons are making is not against the I.W.Ws. but that it is against all organized labor.

As your representative in this district I want to inform you of my personal experiences on and after July 12th.

July 12th as I was on my way down town to work I was accosted by one H. E. Wootten,[1] a local hardware merchant, and told to get in line with the rest of the agitators and when I asked him what the trouble was he said, "we are going to run every union man out of camp and God help the one of you that ever returns."

I was marched down to the cars and pushed in with the rest of the men and sent to Columbus, N.M. where I stayed until I saw that we would not be sent back to our homes and families by the proper authorities.

I left Columbus June [July] 19th and arrived here the 21st and the next day was informed by one of the Phelps Dodge gunmen that they could get along very well without me in Bisbee. On the advice of our Brothers here I stayed.

On the evening of June [July] 24th as I was on my way to the Post Office I was arrested and kept in jail until the following afternoon when I was taken before the Judge for a hearing on a warrant for vagrancy, charging, "that on or about July 11th, 1917, F. W. Brown did loiter and roam about from place to place without any visible means of support."

I had the trial postponed until tomorrow.

Our Brothers here are putting up the money for me and we will fight the case to the finish.

In regards to the standing of the various unions in this district I will say that they are in a very bad shape with no hopes of improving them so long as conditions remain as they are at this time. The Retail Clerks, Bootblacks and Porters and the Western Federation of Miners have gone out of business entirely and the remaining locals are in a very bad shape as the result of the activeness of the so-called Loyalty League.

Men who do not belong or who will not join this set of outlaws are still being run out of town or sent to jail for 90 days. The Kangaroo court is still in session. Gunmen still guard all entrances to the Warren District and patrol the streets of Bisbee and Lowell.

One of the greatest favors that you can do us at this time is that you insist on the investigating committee coming to Bisbee and meeting with the Warren District Trades Assembly as they will never get the facts as they are from the officials of the State of Arizona or Cochise county or the mining companies.

Hoping that you will do all in your power to help us in this matter,[2] I remain

Fraternally, (signed) Fred W. Brown,
Organizer A.F. of L., Com. 7352.

TLtpSr, reel 226, vol. 238, pp. 965–66, SG Letterbooks, DLC. Typed notation: "*Copy*." Enclosed in SG to William B. Wilson, Oct. 3, 1917, ibid., p. 964.

1. Harry E. Wootton.

2. On Oct. 3, 1917, SG forwarded a copy of Fred Brown's letter to Secretary of Labor William B. Wilson in Phoenix, where he had gone as a member of the President's Mediation Commission (reel 226, vol. 238, p. 964, SG Letterbooks, DLC).

To Robert Maisel

Buffalo Sept. 29, 1917

Mr. Robert Maisel,
Director, American Alliance for Labor & Democracy,
New Morrison Hotel, Chicago, Ill.
My dear Mr. Maisel:

On Tuesday last you made a statement to me at which I was astonished and which has perturbed me ever since. You stated that a number of Socialists who had left the Socialist party by reason of that party's perfidy to the principle of Internationalism and to its Pro-German disloyalty to the United States[1] would hold a conference in Chicago during the coming week for the purpose of forming another Socialist political party.[2]

Since the information you conveyed to me the enormity of the contemplated action has grown upon me, and I determined to write you to Chicago, where I requested you to go, as soon as I could learn where a letter would reach you. I have been traveling[3] somewhat in the past several days and today received a telegraphic reply[4] from Mr. Chester M. Wright, whom I asked[5] to telegraph here, giving me your Chicago address.

For the life of me I cannot understand what good purpose can be accomplished by the Socialists who left the Socialist party and what they can have in view in the effort to establish another political party.

A political party essentially exists to support the administration and government of the country or to oppose it, and, by opposing, wrest the power from the existing administration and government. If the contemplated party is to be organized to support the administration and the government in this present crisis, such a party already exists and therefore a creation of a new party for that purpose is unnecessary, and it must necessarily prove abortive. If the new party is to be organized for the purpose of opposing the Administration and the government, such a party already exists. And, yet, with few exceptions the existing political parties (excepting the Socialist party) are practically united in the support of the President, the administration and the government of the United States in the great enterprise in which we have all entered to crush Imperialism, Autocracy and Militarism and to make it possible for freedom and democracy to live and extend its beneficent influences among the peoples of all the nations of the world.

It is not necessary for me to recount here the history of the formation of how the American Alliance for Labor and Democracy was founded. Suffice it to say that it was through the activity of the President of the American Federation of Labor and the New York Central Federated Union, together with the labor publicity organization, all of whom appreciated the gravity of the situation brought about by Pro-German and disloyal Socialist party propaganda.

Conferences were held at which later a few of the Socialists who left their party were invited to participate. They seemed to be pleased at the opportunity offered them, for they declared their loyalty to the cause to America and her Allies in the war and their fealty to the American Federation of Labor and endorsement of the Labor Conference of March 12, 1917, declaring "labor's attitude in peace or in war."

You will recall that at one of these early conferences you advised me that some of these Socialists had in mind the creation of a new party and, at my request, you conveyed to them my judgment that such a course would at once estrange them from us and that they thereupon abandoned the project.

In the early conferences our Socialist friends indicated and declared their willingness to have the opportunity to co-operate with the American Labor movement and to support it in every effort it made both on the present political or economic and the patriotic grounds it had taken, and you must have noticed that later they grew more insistent upon rights they claimed they were entitled to until specific demands were made for percentages of representation. You know that they represented themselves alone, and while it is true that with others we did not officially represent the American Federation of Labor with its more than two and a half million members, we could not in reality differentiate between the official and unofficial representation of this vast constituency, but, recognizing in these men a willingness to help, together with my other associates, I was willing to give them the fullest opportunity for representation and co-operation. And, now, contrary to all understanding and really in violation of the pledge made by every individual member of the Alliance,—the Socialist members, you inform me contemplate the formation of a new political party at this time.

I do not wish to cast any aspersions upon the motives or the good intentions of those who have the formation of a new party in mind, but someone has said that the road to Hades is paved with good intentions. Nearly all of the great political parties started out with the best of intentions and purposes and either went to rack and ruin or were perverted into channels wholly repugnant to the ideals of their founders.

The Republican party, as all other parties, from the formation of the American government, started out upon a basis of free coinage of silver. The Republican party about twenty years ago suddenly and without warning declared for the gold standard and abandoned the free coinage of silver policy.

The Democratic party for a while longer maintained the principle of the free coinage of silver and then by its silence abandoned that policy.

I am not discussing the wisdom or unwisdom of this course, but merely point out how political parties, formed with the best of intentions, pursued a consistent course for a long period of time and then abandoned that course and assumed quite another. I do not wish to enter into more details of this character, except to remind you of the fact that the Socialist party organized, presumably with the best of intentions, proclaiming lofty ideals and freedom and democracy of internationalism has perverted itself into a political party which might well be described as an American adjunct to Prussian Autocracy, Imperialism and Militarism.

I have already indicated above that the formation of a new party in Chicago at the present time by the Socialists who left their party can be productive of no good results, that it may have baneful influence and effect and that it is violative of the purpose and spirit of the American Alliance for Labor and Democracy, and I am confident that upon such an act no other interpretation can and will be placed.

If there is to be whole-hearted and unreserved co-operation to make the American Alliance for Labor and Democracy the instrumentality for good for the great mass of workers for all of the people of our country for patriotic service to our Republic, and her Allies, in the Titanic struggle in which we are engaged, I urge that the project of forming a new political party at this time be abandoned.

You have my permission to allow a few persons to see this letter, but upon the clear understanding that it is written not for publication.

Please telegraph[6] me to my office at Washington the result of the Chicago conference and later write me a complete report.[7] Very truly yours,

Samuel Gompers. President
American Alliance for Labor and Democracy[8]

TLS, Files of the Office of the President, General Correspondence, reel 88, frames 768–72, *AFL Records*.

1. The 1917 Socialist Party of America convention, which met Apr. 7–14 in St. Louis, adopted a resolution condemning the war and urging workers of all countries to oppose the war effort. The resolution was subsequently approved by a national party referendum. A number of prominent socialists left the party as a result of its position on the war, including William Ghent, Charles Edward Russell, Algie Simons, Upton Sinclair, John Spargo, J. G. Phelps Stokes, and William English Walling.

2. A reference to the short-lived National party, a coalition of progressives, independents, single-taxers, prohibitionists, and prowar Socialists that was organized in Chicago in early October 1917.

3. SG left Washington, D.C., on Sept. 23, 1917, for New York City, where he held conferences on Sept. 24. He then went on to Buffalo for a few day's vacation with his friend Duncan McLeod before returning to AFL headquarters by Oct. 2.

4. Chester Wright to SG, Sept. 27, 1917, Files of the Office of the President, General Correspondence, reel 88, frame 737, *AFL Records*.

5. SG to Wright, Sept. 26, 1917, Files of the Office of the President, General Correspondence, reel 88, frame 706, *AFL Records*.

6. Robert Maisel to SG, Oct. 5, 1917, Files of the Office of the President, General Correspondence, reel 88, frame 924, *AFL Records*.

7. Maisel to SG, Oct. 11, 1917, Files of the Office of the President, General Correspondence, reel 89, frames 82–85, *AFL Records*.

8. On Oct. 2, 1917, SG sent a copy of this letter to the vice-presidents and executive committee of the American Alliance for Labor and Democracy, including John Spargo, who was playing a leading role in organizing the National party (Files of the Office of the President, Letterbooks, American Alliance for Labor and Democracy, reel 23, pp. 143–61, *AFL Records*).

To William Hutcheson

October 2, 1917.

Mr. William L. Hutcheson,
President, United Brotherhood Carpenters & Joiners,
Carpenters' Building, Indianapolis, Indiana.
Dear Sir and Brother:

Two communications from you, both dated September 19th,[1] are hereby acknowledged. In one of these communications you say that, "I am in receipt of information from our representative in Dayton that Capt. Granis, who has charge of the construction work, informed your representative that he has orders from the War Department to make the work on the Aviation Field an open shop, and he claims that same has been agreed to by you" (meaning myself) "and others on all government work and all they are expected to comply with is union wages and hours."

Of course, I am not in possession of any information which would be corroborative of the statement made by you in the above paragraph. However, I have not entered into any agreement with Government officials or anyone else in an effort to establish the open shop, and you, above all others know that the statement made in the above paragraph is entirely at variance with your knowledge of my efforts on behalf of the working people.

There has been no one in the organized labor movement who has fought more insistently than I have to establish contractual relations between employers and our organizations, with the view that when such relations are obtained, the union shop would be the natural result.

You are as familiar as I am with the agreement entered into with the War Department in reference to the construction of the cantonments and the extension of that agreement to cover other construction work now being done and to be done by the Government. From the attitude which has been assumed by the War Department and its performance under the agreement, I question the statement that the War Department has issued any orders directing that a fight be made for the open shop in any of the construction work now going on.

Prior to the declaration of war, the American Federation of Labor made its position clear and after the war had been declared, efforts were made by the American Federation of Labor to secure an understanding between the officials of the Government who were in active charge of war preparation and conduct and the organized labor movement of the country. These agreements must necessarily be in accord with certain fundamentals that have been the basis for all contractual relationship with the Government. For a long period union men and women have been employed in various branches of the Government. For a great many years, the employes of the Government Printing Office have practically all been members of their respective unions; yet there has been no union shop agreement executed between the United States' Government and the International Typographical Union.[2] The same condition of affairs obtains in the Bureau of Engraving and Printing, where practically all the employes are members of the Plate Printers' Union[3] or the Federal Labor Union,[4] consisting largely of plate printers, plate printers' helpers and others. In this Bureau, no union shop agreement has ever been executed between the Government and the organizations involved.

In practically all of the Government's works—navy yards, arsenals and other mechanical institutions—we find also that practically all of the employes are members of their different crafts, yet no union shop agreement has ever existed between the United States' Government and these organizations. In this same category will be found the letter-carriers,[5] the rural route carriers,[6] and other organizations in the service of the Government, and whose members comprise a very large percentage of the working force in the Department in which they are employed; yet none of these organizations have secured a union shop contract with the United States' Government. The Government has taken the position that it cannot legally enter into such agreements. However, it has recognized union representatives as the spokesmen for employes, and has not interposed opposition to the activities of the organized labor movement.

In one of your letters, in relating your interview with Mr. Wehle, a double construction may be put on your language. One, that you have taken the position that while your organization desires to be of assistance to the Government, yet it insists that the carpenters must be under union shop agreement. In another paragraph it is stated that you "insist in localities where work is being performed for the Government, if we have the union or closed shop in effect that it be recognized and enforced."

Surely if all of the carpenters in any given locality are being employed in Government work are members of the union and thus constituting the union shop, the Government should not and I think will not disturb conditions of that character. I would be as much opposed to the Government endeavoring to establish the open shop where union shop conditions prevail as you are, and I would be just as vigorous in my protest.

On the other hand, however, it is impossible to get away from the fact that this country is involved in a serious war, and no one knows as to what the future holds for this Government.

My efforts have been directed towards securing recognition from the Government so as to protect such standards built up by the labor movement—the recognition of union wages, hours and other betterments secured by the organized labor movement. So far we have made material progress along this line.

The men and women of our labor movement have not been called upon to make the sacrifices that the men and women of the labor movement of foreign countries involved in this war were called upon to endure and are now enduring.

As a matter of fact, those who are in active charge of preparation and conduct of this war have been at least fairly disposed to accord to labor that which is rightfully its due.

In view of these facts and with the knowledge which now obtains and with the consciousness of the seriousness of this struggle, if you desire to continue to assume the position stated in your letter, you must do so with the realization that practically all other trades engaged in various capacities for the Government have assumed an entirely different position.

It is not my purpose to attempt to dictate any mode of procedure, but only to lay before you the facts as they exist with the hope that mature judgment will be exercised in dealing with the problems which concern our organizations and our Government in this crisis.

Fraternally yours,   Saml Gompers.
President,   American Federation of Labor.

P.S. As I had occasion to say this afternoon at the conference at which you were present, we have the alternative of working out our industrial relations with the government upon a broad basis and high spirit, voluntarily assuming whatever responsibility may rest upon us, or if refusing to do this, having force of governmental direction and coercion, and I know that you are broad minded and courageous enough to take advantage of the opportunity afforded for voluntary, whole-hearted cooperation and to help secure for the carpenters as well as all other workers the fullest measure of improved conditions, while doing all that can be done to win the war for freedom and democracy.

S. G.

TLpS, reel 226, vol. 238, pp. 925–27, SG Letterbooks, DLC.

1. Files of the Office of the President, General Correspondence, reel 88, frames 417–18 and 419–20, *AFL Records*.

2. The International TYPOGRAPHICAL Union.

3. The International Steel and Copper Plate PRINTERS' Union of North America.

4. The AFL chartered Federal Labor Union 12,776 of Washington, D.C., in 1909.

5. The National Association of LETTER Carriers of the United States of America.

6. The National Rural LETTER Carriers' Association.

From William Hutcheson

Office of Wm. L. Hutcheson, General President
United Brotherhood of Carpenters and Joiners of America
Indianapolis Indiana Oct. 5th, 1917.

Dear Sir and Brother:

Your communication of the 2nd inst.[1] at hand and contents carefully noted.

In reply thereto I again wish to state that the information we received from Dayton in reference to Capt. Granis I have no reason to doubt as being authentic even though you state you have no information to corroborate the statement made by the undersigned and I did not state that you had entered into any agreement with the Government officials or anyone else in an effort to establish the open shop, but the correspondence[2] exchanged between yourself and Louis B. Wehle in reference to the understanding arrived at with Secretary of War Baker shows you as stating that the question of union shop was not included.

I realize full well that it would be asking a great deal from the Government officials to sign an agreement or understanding specifying that nothing but union men would be employed, but it seems rather strange that after coming to an understanding in reference to the basic standards being the union scale of wages, hours and *conditions,* that you should state the understanding of the memorandum signed by yourself and Secretary Baker had reference to union hours and wages, the question of union shop not being included. If there was no intention of coming to an understanding other than in reference to union hours and wages, then what was the necessity of mentioning the word "conditions" as surely any overtime that was provided for is included in hours and wages and the only thing conditions could cover would be the conditions under which the members would work, namely, as to whether they would work with non-union men of their own calling or whether they would work what is usually termed the union or closed shop.

In regards to your statement that I was familiar with the agreement entered into with the War Department in reference to Cantonment constructions will say that I was under the impression at the time, that the word conditions as used would be made appliable to the conditions as outlined above and was not aware that you had made any statement in reference to the understanding referring to union hours and wages, until my last visit to Washington prior to writing you under date of September 19th when I procured copy of the correspondence exchanged between yourself and Louis B. Wehle, representative of the Cantonment Commission. Had I known prior to that time of the interpretation placed on that understanding I would not have gotten into the ridiculous position I was placed in before our membership as on various occasions they were anxious and desirous of ceasing work because of non-union workmen being employed, and through the efforts and instructions of the undersigned were prevented from doing so as I stated to them that there had been an understanding arrived at between yourself and Secretary of War Baker pertaining to hours, wages and conditions and that the hours, wages and conditions in the locality where the work was being performed would be recognized by the Government officials, and then for the Government representatives to come back and state there has been an understanding arrived at between them and yourself as President of the American Federation of Labor whereby it was agreed that the understanding only referred to hours and wages and that the open shop was to be effective on Government work, placed me, as the head of our organization, in anything but an enviable position.

The illustration you draw in reference to the Navy Yards, Arsenals and other mechanical institutions of the Government pertaining to the union shop agreement is not a criterion of the conditions that confront our organization for the reason that the employers of our members who are engaged in doing work for the Government are many times of an unscrupulous nature and while under ordinary circumstances, when there would be no opportunity or chance for them to employ others than members of our organization they would go along, but immediately they get started on Government work they begin to talk emergency work and take advantage of every opportunity to employ non-union workmen and with the conditions that prevail every man that had an idea that he had the ability of a carpenter procured tools and sought employment on Government cantonments with the result that they were placed to work, and not desiring to harass the Government in their War preparations and believing that the word conditions as used in the understanding arrived at between yourself and Secretary of War Baker would apply to the standard under which our members worked, namely, as to whether they worked with non-union men or not, we would not permit our members to cease work because of the employment of these non-union men.

You will understand that on work other than Government work our members would not tolerate non-union workmen coming on the job or being employed by the contractor and if he insisted on employing non-union workmen they would immediately cease work, but this we did not permit them to do on Government work.

As formerly stated the criterion you cite of the Government employes in the Navy Yards and other Government institutions is no comparison with our members working for contractors on Government work, and in my reference to my interview with Mr. Wehle I had no intention of using language on which could be placed a double meaning. My intention was to convey the information that we did not desire to enter into an agreement, the arrangement of which was such that the word conditions was used and that the construction could be put on that word as meaning anything other than the conditions as established in the locality where the work was to be performed, and that to refer to the establishment of the custom as to whether our members would work with non-union men or not, and your illustration that if all the carpenters in a given locality being employed on Government work were members of the union that it would thus be considered a union shop would be correct, but carpenters, like many other human beings, migrate to a large extent, and non-union men do this as well as union and because to-day we have all of the workmen in a given locality in our organization is not saying that tomorrow or the next day (under the present demand) we would not have a number of non-union men put in an appearance, and under my understanding of the terms of the memorandum of agreement that was entered into between the assistant secretary of the Navy, the Shipping Board, yourself and the various organizations, if non-union workmen were put on the work by an employer on Government work and they refused to become members of our organization our members could not cease work for the enforcement of bringing about that result and that right we do not propose to eliminate or waive.

As formerly stated to you we desire to be of assistance to the Government officials but in turn believe we are entitled to some consideration and that organized labor should take a determined stand that the standards as established by them in the various localities be recognized as the standard under which the Government will see that the work is performed, and when I say standard I do not refer to merely hours and wages, and overtime rates but to the standard of the condition under which we work, namely, as to whether we work with non-union men or whether we do not.

I note you state that those who are in active charge of the preparation and conduct of this war have been fairly disposed to accord to labor that which is rightfully its due. I do not desire to criticize any one but I do not believe that simply giving to labor the recognition of hours and wages that they have established is all that they are rightfully entitled to, and even though the other trades engaged in other capacities for the Government may have assumed a different position than that taken by the undersigned, I feel that I am only doing my duty to the members of our Brotherhood and that by taking the stand I have I am not in any way wandering from the path of a trade unionist or American citizen, nor deviating in any manner from the duties I owe this country as a citizen and to the labor movement as a trade unionist and I shall endeavor in the future as in the past to assist the Government in this, the Crisis of our country, but at the same time I shall not overlook or neglect my duty as the head of our organization.

With best wishes, I remain,

Fraternally yours,   Wm L. Hutcheson
General President.[3]

TLS, Files of the Office of the President, General Correspondence, reel 88, frames 917–20, *AFL Records*.

1. "To William Hutcheson," Oct. 2, 1917, above.

2. See "Louis Wehle to Frank Morrison," June 20, 1917, above.

3. SG replied to Hutcheson on Oct. 15, 1917: "I stand as strongly as any man for the thorough organization of all workers, and wherever possible the enforcement of union shop, but I cannot see where anyone can fail to understand this fact, that the government of the United States, representing all the people of the United States, cannot enter into an agreement to employ exclusively members of any one organization. I firmly believe that there are very few men who for conscientious reasons would refuse to become members of a trade union, but even if there be but a few and they are American citizens, the government, as a government of all the people of the United States, cannot be asked to deny these citizens the right to work for the government, or work for government contractors, upon the ground that they are not members of a union" (Files of the Office of the President, General Correspondence, reel 89, frame 160, *AFL Records*).

From John Spargo

Old Bennington, Vermont, October 9, 1917

My dear Mr. Gompers:—

I have your letter of October 2nd.,[1] enclosing your letter of an earlier date[2] to Mr. Robert Maisel. In so far as it is necessary for me to reply to this I shall make my reply very brief and pointed.

You have evidently been misinformed by those whom you have relied upon for advice. There never was any intention of forming a "new Socialist party." Our intention was, and has now been carried out, to form a liberal or radical party by uniting various existing parties and groups. The National Party is now an accomplished fact.

Whether there was need for such a party is a question upon which there must of necessity be a variety of opinion. We could not expect all men to agree either in affirming or denying the proposition involved. Those of us who joined in the effort believed that there was such a need. Having formed the party we naturally must reserve to ourselves the right to define our own position toward the government. We have done that by affirming our unquestioning loyalty to the nation and its allies in a resolution as unequivocal as that of the American Alliance for Labor and Democracy itself. The manifestation of loyalty at our Chicago conference was at least equal to that at Minneapolis.

The Alliance is a non-partisan body. As such I assumed that I could with perfect consistency and honor indulge in any partisan political activity I pleased, so long as it was not contrary to the spirit and the declared policies of the American Alliance for Labor and Democracy. That one of the Vice-Presidents of the Alliance has seen fit to actively participate in the New York City campaign, on the side of the Tammany candidate,[3] must be known to you.

Both Mr. Maisel and Mr. Wright knew a long time in advance of your invitation to me to attend the first conference to consider the state of affairs on the East Side that the movement to bring about the formation of a new party, through a coalition of radical forces, was well under way. I had sent Mr. Wright a circular explaining the movement and he seemed inclined to join it. At least he was on that day, he said, open-minded. At the second conference Mr. Maisel spoke to me about the matter and I told him all that there was to know. At that time he gave me to understand that you would, sub rosa, give the movement your moral support, that you could not actively or openly support it, but that you would pass the word along the line that the time for such a movement was here. It was said that if the prohibition plank could be modified you would encourage a number of the best men in the Federation of Labor to join with us. So definite was that expression of your attitude, made to Mr. Stokes as well as to me, that we discussed together possible modifications of the prohibition plank which the conferees interested in the new coalition party had agreed upon. I reported Mr. Maisel's statements at once to a number of persons, including Mrs. Fels.[4]

Within a very few days, when next I saw Mr. Maisel, he took another tack. His attitude at this time was that the time for a party is not yet here—that you think it a mistake—that a conference is all right, and even a Social Democratic League, but not a party. There were various intimations that if I would throw over my associates with whom for months I had been working I should have a chance to work with you in the formation of a Labor Party on English lines. All this was well ahead of the Minneapolis meeting. I told Mr. Maisel that it was quite impossible for me to "double cross" or throw over my associates in the coalition party movement for any consideration whatsoever, and that I would stay away from Minneapolis if desired and withdraw from the Alliance movement.

In Minneapolis this was substantially repeated, as it has been on three or four occasions since then, the last being at my hotel in Chicago on Monday October first. Each and every time I have told Mr. Maisel that I should loyally stick by the coalition party movement and have told him that it was useless for him to argue against that decision of mine. His suggestions that I "do something" to make the party conference a failure I at all times scornfully rejected. Sabotage is always reprehensible to me, but it is doubly so when directed against one's own colleagues and friends.

In the circumstances, then, I submit that those who have come with me into this Alliance, while remaining faithful to the men and women interested in the new party, have acted in all good faith and have in nowise violated any confidence or trust reposed in them. Whatever duplicity there may have been has been outside of our group. Personally, I have gone to extremes in trying to be absolutely loyal to the Alliance. We had arranged for a delegation of twenty labor men to attend our Chicago conference, but in order that there might be no suspicion that we were using the connections made through the Alliance with the men of the organized labor movement for party purposes, I advised the abandonment of that purpose, which advice was taken.

There is one statement in your letter to Mr. Maisel, referring to the insistence of the Socialist group in the Alliance upon certain percentages of representation, which indicates an entire misconception of the position taken. As I was the one who made the claim, I feel that I am entitled, and in duty bound, to make the explanation. We were all together seeking to plan wisely a mission to the Russian people.[5] I made the suggestion that while the mission must be predominantly composed of actual union men and women there should be a goodly proportion of men and women of the so-called Intellectual groups, naming Frank Walsh and Darrow as typical of the group as a whole. You broke in with "There is no question about that: we are absolutely agreed." I then continued, "To select this mission will take time. We ought to agree in a general way upon the approximate strength of the two divisions of the mission and arrange for the selection of the men. I suggest that Mr. Gompers with the advice of the international officers select approximately seven-tenths and that Mr. Slobodin and myself be permitted to select approximately three-tenths—with the understanding that the selections be submitted to and approved by Mr. Gompers." There was no demand for the representation of our Socialist group, as such, but only a friendly arrangement to divide the labor of selection—nomination, if you please. For example, the first man Mr. Slobodin and I agreed should be asked was Mr. Frank Walsh; the second Mr. Darrow, neither of whom has ever been known as a Socialist; both having been consistent Democrats.

The National Party is a fact. Its declarations on the war and its platform show that it is in no sense an anti-administration party, any more than the American Alliance for Labor and Democracy is anti-administration. The President of the United States himself does not regard the National Party as anti-administration.

As I see it, the question that must be settled now is whether the American Alliance for Labor and Democracy is really a non-partisan organization, as it professes to be. If so, our right to indulge in any political activity—even the creation of a party—which is not demonstrably contrary to the avowed principles of the Alliance cannot be denied. If it is not a non-partisan organization, that fact should be made clear. Perhaps it would be well to have the Executive Committee meet to determine this important question.

With kind regards,

very sincerely yours,   John Spargo

TLS, Files of the Office of the President, General Correspondence, reel 89, frames 43–47, *AFL Records.*

1. SG to John Spargo, Oct. 2, 1917, Files of the Office of the President, Letterbooks, American Alliance for Labor and Democracy, reel 23, p. 155, *AFL Records.*

2. "To Robert Maisel," Sept. 29, 1917, above.

3. John Francis Hylan (1868–1936), a Brooklyn judge, was the Democratic candidate for mayor of New York City in 1917. He was elected in November of that year and served from 1918 to 1925. His candidacy was endorsed by American Alliance for Labor and Democracy vice-president James Holland, the president of the New York State Federation of Labor.

4. Mary Fels (1863–1953) was the widow of Joseph Fels, a soap manufacturer who had made a fortune using the naphtha process. He later turned to social reform activities and, after her husband's death in 1914, Mrs. Fels continued their work in support of reform causes.

5. At a meeting in New York City on Sept. 24, 1917, the executive committee of the American Alliance for Labor and Democracy approved a proposal to send a delegation of American workers to Russia in order to counteract anti-American and antiwar propaganda. Apparently the mission was never sent.

Samuel Gompers, 1918. (National Archives and Records Administration)

SG with his wife Sophia (left) and daughter Sadie (right). (Picture Collection [Collection 99], Department of Special Collections, Charles E. Young Research Library, University of California, Los Angeles)

SG with sons Alexander (left) and Samuel (right), standing in front of SG's home in Washington, D.C. (Collection of Florence Gompers MacKay)

SG and grandson Samuel Harry Gompers, 1918. (Photography Collection, Miriam and Ira D. Wallach Division of Art, Prints and Photographs, the New York Public Library, Astor, Lenox, and Tilden Foundations)

SG with members of his family in London, 1918. Seated front row, from left: Sadie (Mrs. Louis) Le Bosse, SG's cousin Louis Le Bosse, SG's aunt Clara Gompers Le Bosse (1838–1922), and SG. (Photography Collection, Miriam and Ira D. Wallach Division of Art, Prints and Photographs, the New York Public Library, Astor, Lenox, and Tilden Foundations)

Enrico Caruso's 1914 sketch of Gompers, which SG later donated in behalf of children suffering from the war in Italy. (Library of Congress)

A wartime cartoon of SG. (George Meany Memorial
Archives)

The Council of National Defense and Advisory Commission, 1917. Seated, from left: Council members David Houston, Josephus Daniels, Newton Baker, Franklin Lane, William Redfield, William B. Wilson. Standing, from left: Advisory Commission members Franklin Martin, Daniel Willard, Julius Rosenwald, SG, Bernard Baruch, Howard Coffin, Walter Gifford. (National Archives and Records Administration)

SG and members of the British Labor Mission to the United States, 1917. Seated, from left: Ralph Easley, Oscar Straus, Charles Bowerman, August Belmont, James Thomas, SG. Standing, from left: W. S. Carter, William Fellowes Morgan, Joseph Davies, Heathcote Garrod, Elisha Lee, Haley Fiske, Warren Stone. (George Meany Memorial Archives)

THE BIG LITTLE MAN!

Samuel Gompers, leader of American organized labor, returns to America to help labor solve some of its problems.

The High Cost of Living is labor's chief enemy today. Help fight it with Thrift!

Buy **War Savings Stamps** Regularly

A War Savings Stamps poster, 1918. (George Meany Memorial Archives)

SG and members of the AFL mission to Europe, 1918.
Seated, from left: SG and Charles Baine. Standing,
from left: Edgar Wallace, Guy Oyster, William Bowen,
John Frey. (George Meany Memorial Archives)

SG greeting wounded American soldiers at a military hospital near London, 1918. (National Archives and Records Administration)

SG at the front in Italy. (National Archives and Records Administration)

SG greeting Albert Thomas at the
Inter-Allied Labour and Social-
ist Conference in London, 1918.
(National Archives and Records
Administration)

A rare photograph of SG with his personal secretary R. Lee Guard. In back row
are Frank Morrison (center) and George Perkins (far right). (George Meany
Memorial Archives)

A Circular

Washington, D.C. Oct. 12, 1917.

Dear Sir and Brother:

Your attention is invited to the article, "There is no shortage of Labor," in the October Number of the American Federationist.[1]

New and valuable points of information supporting the position of the writer of that article have come to hand since the manuscript was sent to the printer. It is now proposed to collect further data on the subject for publication in an early issue of the American Federationist.[2] If you have within the range of your observation any additional facts serving as supporting testimony in the matter, you would confer a favor on this office by sending to me notes thereon.

Is not the general complaint of a shortage of labor an inspired movement in the interests of a certain group of employers? Among the persons in this group are:

(1) Those who would break through the ten-hour day-work law protecting women, so that a twelve-hour two shift scheme might be established.

(2) Those who would reduce the age line protecting children.

(3) Those who would break down the eight-hour day of the trade unions and of the Government employes.

(4) Those who want to hasten the dilution of skilled labor by unskilled.

It is not to be denied that in a comparatively few instances there is a shortage of the highest skilled mechanics or others possessing technical knowledge. But even in such cases the question remains whether vacancies could not be filled were there systematic methods of distributing labor throughout the country.

The facts as to supply of workers is what this magazine desires to publish. Labor is concerned especially with the general country-wide supply. It cannot permit that an alleged shortage at certain industrial centers or in certain technical occupations can be made the occasion for an alarm throughout the country the consequence of which would be demand for an employing class control of labor and of wages detrimental to the workers.

Fraternally yours,

President,   American Federation of Labor.

Please reply promptly.

TLc, reel 227, vol. 239, p. 343, SG Letterbooks, DLC. Typed notation: "Letter sent to Central Bodies on October 12th, 1917."

1. J. W. Sullivan, "There Is No Shortage of Labor," *American Federationist* 24 (Oct. 1917): 842–45.

2. See "Report of Committee on Alleged Shortage of Labor," AFL, *Proceedings*, 1917, pp. 439–45. The report was reprinted in the January 1918 *American Federationist* ("Alleged 'Shortage of Labor,'" 25: 41–49) and issued as a pamphlet (*The Alleged Shortage of Labor* [Washington, D.C., (1918?)]).

From James Maurer[1]

Headquarters
Pennsylvania State Federation of Labor[2]
Harrisburg, Pa., Oct. 12, 1917.

Samuel Gompers,
President, American Alliance for Labor & Democracy,
Washington, D.C.
Dear Sir:

On October 4th, I addressed a letter[3] to you, in which I asked certain questions of vital importance to the American labor movement, which has honored both you and me with positions of trust. I called your attention to the fact that many trade unionists—men and women who, because of your office as president of the American Federation of Labor, have a right to expect you to deal with them and the public with the utmost frankness—are uneasy as to the source of revenue of the American Alliance for Labor and Democracy of which you are also the president.

In order that you might not misunderstand either my meaning or the nature of the speculations indulged in by those who have a right to your confidence, I asked you specifically whether certain activities of the Alliance for Labor and Democracy have been financed wholly or in part by the widely recognized enemies of labor with whom you have lately been appearing on the platform—such men as Elihu Root and Governor Burnquist[4] of Minnesota. I asked you then and I now ask you, who paid the expenses of the special train[5] from New York to Minneapolis? Who pays the rent for the halls which you have been using in Minneapolis, Chicago, New York and elsewhere? Who paid the tremendous expense of the Minneapolis Convention? And, while you were holding the convention, did or did not the reactionary Civic and Commerce Association, the head and front of the union-crushing forces of Minnesota, give a luncheon at which you and your immediate associates were the guests of honor?[6]

These are questions that are upon the tongues of men and women wherever a few labor unionists are gathered together. You have not seen fit to answer them. As a matter of fairness to the people who have honored you beyond any other man in the American Labor movement, can you remain silent? In these days when motives are constantly questioned and when sources of propaganda funds are constantly being inquired into, is it not imperative that all doubts concerning a movement headed by one who is president of the American Federation of Labor be cleared up at once? As an official of the labor movement of one of the leading states of the nation, I ask these questions. I await your reply.

Fraternally yours, James H. Maurer
President, Pennsylvania Federation of Labor.[7]

TLS, Files of the Office of the President, General Correspondence, reel 89, frames 121–22, *AFL Records.*

1. James Hudson MAURER was president (1912–28) of the Pennsylvania State Federation of Labor (FOL).

2. The Pennsylvania State Branch of the AFL was organized in 1890 and held its last convention in 1893, although a legislative committee continued to function for a time. Its successor, the Pennsylvania State FOL, was organized and chartered by the AFL in 1902.

3. Maurer to SG, Oct. 4, 1917, Files of the Office of the President, General Correspondence, reel 88, frames 883–84, *AFL Records.* Maurer also published the letter in a press release, which was dated Oct. 6 (ibid., reel 89, frames 133–34).

4. Joseph Alfred Arner Burnquist (1879–1961) served as Republican governor of Minnesota from 1915 to 1921.

5. Robert Maisel arranged for a special train to carry delegates to the American Alliance for Labor and Democracy convention in Minneapolis. Dubbed the "Red, White, and Blue Special," the train left New York City on Sept. 2, 1917, amid great fanfare and stopped at major cities as it made its way across the country.

6. On Sept. 5, 1917, SG was the guest of honor at a luncheon for some eight hundred area businessmen hosted by the Minneapolis Civic and Commerce Association and spoke on the subject "Labor and Its Attitude toward the War." Frank Morrison also addressed the gathering.

7. Maurer also gave this letter to the press (Files of the Office of the President, General Correspondence, reel 89, frames 219–20, *AFL Records*). Replying to a query about it from the *Progressive Labor World* in Philadelphia, SG wrote: "I do not think it necessary or fitting that I should take any cognizance of the letter which Mr. Maurer has addressed to me. In the first place it was not a letter deserving an answer. He couched it in language intended to convey insinuations of wrong-doing on my part. He took pains to have it sent to, and it was published by, the 'capitalist' press, which he pretends so much to despise. His letter was prepared, written and sent out by the so-called People's Council. It was undertaken to discredit the American labor movement and to throw odium upon our country in this, its crucial hour" (SG to Royd Morrison, Oct. 13, 1917, Files of the Office of the President, General Correspondence, reel 89, frame 137, *AFL Records*).

From George Perkins[1]

Headquarters
Cigar Makers' International Union of America[2]
Chicago, Ill. Oct. 12, 1917.

Confidential
Dear Sir:

Oscar Nelson,[3] in conversation recently said substantially as follows:

That he went to the office of Mr. Clabaugh (head of the Federal Department of Justice here) in company with Mr. Barrett,[4] one of the federal labor conciliators, and among other things, Mr. Clabaugh said—

That in the raid[5] on the I.W.W. headquarters and the arrest of many of its officers and members, they took to headquarters about three-hundred thousand filled out application blanks;[6] that they have a cart-load of correspondence some of which will be a great revelation and surprise to Samuel Gompers and many others connected with the American Federation of Labor; that this surprise would be occasioned by the revelation that a number of men now prominent in the American Federation of Labor unions were or are members of the I.W.W. and secretly working with them; that the correspondence reveals a scheme of the I.W.W. to bore from within the American Federation of Labor ranks. This and much other matter of a similar nature![7]

Mr. Nelson thinks, and I agree with him, first that you ought to know of this, and second that it might be a good plan for you to get more of this information before it reaches the public press as it will during the trial, in order that you may be prepared to offset any injurious effect it may have on our movement, and that possibly such information if obtainable can be of material use to our movement directly, and indirectly thereby to our government which we are loyally sustaining in this crisis. It is thought that you have a right under these circumstances to know at least some of these things which he (Claybaugh) talked over quite freely with two representatives of the government. Claybaugh probably did not connect Mr. Nelson with the trade union movement. Both Nelson and Barrett saw Claybaugh on a matter connected with the Department of Labor mediation and conciliation work in a strike here in Chicago, and when they entered his office they simply presented their cards as United States mediators and conciliators and were recognized and addressed as such.

I submit this matter without further comment, for your information and such action as your judgment in the matter may dictate.[8] I of course do not expect an answer.

Yours fraternally,   G. W. Perkins

TLS, Files of the Office of the President, General Correspondence, reel 89, frames 129–30, *AFL Records.*

1. George William PERKINS served as president of the Cigar Makers' International Union of America from 1891 to 1926.

2. The CIGAR Makers' International Union of America.

3. Oscar Fred NELSON, vice-president of the Chicago Federation of Labor from 1910 to 1935, also served as a commissioner of conciliation for the U.S. Department of Labor from 1917 to 1922.

4. James J. Barrett was a commissioner of conciliation for the U.S. Department of Labor.

5. On Sept. 5, 1917, agents of the Department of Justice raided IWW offices in Chicago and other cities, as well as the homes of IWW officials, to seize evidence that could be used in prosecuting the organization's leadership. On Sept. 28 one hundred sixty-six IWW members were indicted in Chicago on charges of seditious conspiracy to obstruct the war effort, to discourage recruiting, enlistment, and participation in the draft, and to encourage insubordination and desertion in the military. One hundred of those indicted came to trial in April 1918, and in August all were found guilty. Most received prison sentences of from five to twenty years, and together they were fined over $2 million. Subsequent raids in the fall and winter of 1917 led to additional trials and convictions in other cities. The Supreme Court declined to review the Chicago cases (*William D. Haywood et al.* v. *United States,* 256 U.S. 689 [1921]), but President Warren Harding freed several of the IWW prisoners in 1922, and President Calvin Coolidge commuted the sentences of all remaining wartime prisoners in 1923.

6. In November 1917 Hinton Clabaugh reported to Bruce Bielaski, director of the Bureau of Investigation of the Department of Justice, that he had some seventy thousand IWW membership cards (Bielaski memorandum, Nov. 29, 1917, RG 60, General Records of the Department of Justice, DNA).

7. For Nelson's Oct. 6, 1917, report to John Fitzpatrick regarding his meeting with Clabaugh, see Files of the Office of the President, General Correspondence, reel 89, frames 58–59, *AFL Records.*

8. SG discussed the matter with Attorney General Thomas Gregory on Oct. 17, 1917, and Gregory subsequently sent SG copies of IWW membership cards and other documents. See "A Memorandum Dictated by Samuel Gompers," Dec. 22, 1917, below.

To John Morrison

Oct. 15, 1917.

Mr. John Morrison,
25 Third Avenue, New York City.
Dear Sir:

I have just received a telegram of which the following is a copy:

"Cleveland, Ohio, Oct. 15, 1917.

["]Hon. Samuel Gompers,
["]Washington, D.C.
["]The Cleveland Chamber of Commerce has been asked to verify statement that American Federation of Labor is soliciting funds to assist it in putting out of existence I.W.W. and kindred organizations. Solicitor M. Roberts claiming to represent you asking Cleveland firms for donation. If this appeal is authentic donations will undoubtedly be made. If not shall we try and apprehend Roberts. Please wire at our expense.

["]Signed,　Munson Havens,[1]
["]Secretary."

To this I have made the following telegraphic reply:

"Washington, D.C., Oct. 15, 1917.

["]Mr. Munson Havens, Secretary,
["]Chamber of Commerce,
["]Cleveland, Ohio.
["]You say that M. Roberts is soliciting funds to put I.W.W. and kindred organizations out of existence. Neither Roberts nor any other person has been authorized or is permitted to make any such solicitations on behalf of American Federation of Labor or any of its officers. We would not receive such funds much less permit anyone to solicit for them for any such purpose.

["]Signed,　Samuel Gompers."

If Mr. Roberts has used his credential for any such purpose as indicated in Mr. Haven's telegram, I shall cancel it forthwith. Please advise me promptly, and oblige,

Yours fraternally,　Saml Gompers
President,　American Federation of Labor.

TLpS, reel 227, vol. 239, p. 371, SG Letterbooks, DLC.

1. Munson Aldrich Havens was the long-time secretary of the Cleveland Chamber of Commerce.

To C. O. Young[1]

Oct. 16, 1917.

Mr. C. O. Young,
Organizer, American Federation of Labor,
Box 1066, Boise, Idaho.
Dear Sir and Brother:
Today Secretary Morrison after consultation with me sent you the following telegram:[2]

"Washington, D.C., Oct. 16, 1917.

["]Mr. C. O. Young,
["]Box 1066,
["]Boise, Idaho.
["]Cancel all engagements and arrange to hold conference with organizers Taylor[3] and Brown[4] and others at Seattle Hotel, Seattle, Washington, on October twenty first. Suggest you arrange to reach Seattle on the twentieth. Wire answer.

["]Signed, Frank Morrison."

I should say that we have had several conferences with Major Ledbetter,[5] Colonel Disque,[6] Secretary of War, and others regarding the production of spruce for air craft, and the best means of accomplishing that, as well as securing fair conditions for the workers in the industry.

I can say that it is practically agreed that there ought to be established the basic eight hour workday with time and one-half for overtime beyond eight hours. As to the means of applying it and enforcing it, is a matter that must be worked out, and upon which I cannot give you any definite statement now.[7]

But in addition to this you will find Colonel Disque sympathetic to the idea of organizing the timber and lumber workers whether in the forest or in the plants, and there is unquestionably a splendid opportunity for the organization of these workers.

You will of course consult with Brothers Brown, Taylor and Wheeler with a view of a more thorough organization of these workers, and with them as well as Col. Disque in finding a way out of the present situation, so that the workers may give their best efforts for a spruce production and to secure such other men to help in furnishing the needs of the government in this crucial time of our Republic's history.

Please report as frequently as convenient, giving the results of the movement.[8]

With best wishes, I am,

fraternally yours,   Saml Gompers
President,   American Federation of Labor.

TLpS, reel 227, vol. 239, p. 488, SG Letterbooks, DLC.

1. Charles O. Young served as an AFL salaried organizer from 1904 until around 1933.

2. Files of the Office of the President, General Correspondence, reel 89, frame 205, *AFL Records.*

3. Charles Perry Taylor of Tacoma, Wash., served as secretary-treasurer of the Washington State Federation of Labor (1908–19) and as an AFL salaried organizer (1912–22). He worked as a linotype operator and was a member and at one time president of International Typographical Union 170 of Tacoma. In 1920 Taylor moved to Fresno, Calif., where he organized migrant agricultural workers for the short-lived International Union of Fruit and Vegetable Workers of North America (1921), served as acting president of the union, and edited the *Tri-County Labor News* (1921–23), the organ of the Fresno Labor Council.

4. Jay G. Brown was president of the International Shingle Weavers' Union of America and an AFL salaried organizer.

5. Frederick William Leadbetter of Portland, Oreg., was involved in paper manufacturing and the pulp and lumber business. During World War I he served as the liaison officer for the U.S. Army's Spruce Production Division.

6. Col. Brice P. Disque (1879–1960), a career army officer, had left active service in 1916 to become manager of the Michigan state prison in Jackson which, he boasted, he operated at a profit by providing "gainful employment" for the inmates. Rejoining the army after the United States entered World War I, he directed its Spruce Production Division (1917–19), which was organized in November 1917 to augment the civilian workforce in the production of timber, and served as president of the Loyal Legion of Loggers and Lumbermen, which he established the same month to increase spruce output in the Pacific Northwest by stabilizing labor relations in the timber industry. The Spruce Production Division eventually numbered more than a thousand officers and nearly thirty thousand enlisted men. The Loyal Legion also grew rapidly, with more than a thousand locals and a membership approaching eighty thousand at war's end. Disque left the army in February 1919 and subsequently worked as a business executive.

7. The eight-hour day, with time and a half for overtime, was established in the Northwest timber industry in March 1918.

8. For Young's report to SG of Nov. 3, 1917, which described his meeting on Oct. 23 with Disque, Taylor, and Brown, see Files of the Office of the President, General Correspondence, reel 89, frames 696–98, *AFL Records.*

To Parda Drain[1]

October 23, 1917.

Mr. P. D. Drain,
Manager The Advocate Publishing Company,
409 Sycamore Street, Evansville, Ind.
Dear Sir and Brother:

Your undated letter received. You ask for information regarding the I.W.W. Your attention is called to several editorials which I wrote for the *American Federationist* several years ago, which were afterwards reprinted in pamphlet form. Copy is enclosed herein.

In addition, let me say further that the Industrial Workers of the World, which was organized in Chicago in 1905, represent a very small proportion of the wage earners of this country. It was organized by a group of men connected with the labor movement who had been associated with various discredited plans and visionary theories. In 1908 The Industrial Workers of the World divided into two groups, one having its headquarters at Chicago, and the other at Detroit, fighting each other with the same hostility that they displayed toward employers. The methods and the doctrines of this organization have never found favor and following among workers who had accepted American standards and the American spirit. The I.W.W. can be said to have no real organization in this country; they have organized a local union here and there, but have made no attempt to follow out the pretentious plan which they announce in their constitution and program. Their unions have been formed chiefly where there are colonies of immigrant workers, and where industrial oppression is extreme. These workers, who have not yet learned that industrial welfare must be worked out by following a consistent, definite program, have been incited by the extravagant promises and the wild appeal to violence by the representatives of the I.W.W. to go on strikes. Some of these strikes have involved numbers of workers and have attracted considerable attention. Among them were the strike at Lawrence, Massachusetts; at Paterson, New Jersey; in the hop fields of California; and most recently among the steel workers of Pittsburg, and the iron ore miners of Minnesota.

With the development of war needs in this country the I.W.W. found an opportunity to pursue their predatory tactics of operation and thereby created not only inconvenience to employers but also to the government. When necessary war production was affected the inconvenience grew into a disaster, as interference with the munitions of war meant unnecessary loss of lives of those fighting for our cause. The government felt it necessary to take unusual and drastic steps and legal action was instigated against many of the officials of the organization. However, in many western states unauthorized agencies took "direct action" against workers in their localities and then attempted to justify their course by stigmatizing all of the workers as I.W.W. In some cases, as in the deportations of New Mexico, and Arizona, law-abiding trade unionists were the victims, as well as others who had bona fide I.W.W. cards.

It was to inquire into the situation in the mountain region and western coast that President Wilson appointed a commission to investigate conditions in that locality and to attempt to bring about better relations between employers and employees. The situation and the work of the commission is described in an article published in the October *American Federationist* under the heading, "Law Versus Vigilante."[2]

In conducting these strikes, the I.W.W. leaders have invariably advised workers to use methods that reacted against them, and only resulted in additional victimization. The theory and the purpose of the leaders has invariably been revolution, but they have deceived the strikers by advising them to adopt revolutionary methods instead of methods that would make a strike successful; they have advised against all agreements with employers.

One advantage has almost invariably followed strike movements conducted by the I.W.W. Employers and workers alike have come to have a greater appreciation of the methods and policies of the American trade union movement. In Paterson, New Jersey, a strike of silk workers some years ago was accompanied by violence and suffering on the part of the workers. The strike did not succeed in establishing higher wages or better conditions of work. There were several spectacular methods employed in the strike such as sending the children of the strikers away to neighboring cities to be taken care of by fellow workers, and the production of a play in New York City reproducing strike scenes. However, the strike ended in failure. Since the strike, the silk workers in and around Paterson have been organizing in unions affiliated to the American Federation of Labor, and have been carrying on the constructive work of organization.

Ex[perienc]es in this country have demonstrated again and again that the work of the I.W.W. has brought disaster to the workers involved and has not gained [them any] agency by which to achieve constructive results. The I.W.W. con[tains] but a relatively small number of the wage earners of this country. It has been given considerable prominence in newspapers and in m[agaz]ines because of the sensational characteristics of many of their endeavors. As you know that which is sensational secures much wider publicity than normal constructive work. There are in this country a group of social uplifters who filled the magazines with articles describing the I.W.W. and their tactics; however, even these writers now [seldom men]tion that organization.[3]

Fraternally yours,

President,   American Federation of Labor.

TLp, reel 227, vol. 239, pp. 736–38, SG Letterbooks, DLC.

1. Parda D. Drain, a resident of Evansville, Ind., was manager of the *Advocate*, a weekly Evansville labor paper, from about 1909 until about 1924. He had previously worked as a cooper.

2. *American Federationist* 24 (Oct. 1917): 846–52.

3. The text in brackets in this paragraph is supplied from a transcribed copy of the letter in the Files of the Office of the President, General Correspondence, reel 89, frame 362, *AFL Records*.

From William Carter[1]

Brotherhood of Locomotive Firemen and Enginemen.[2]
Cleveland, Ohio, November 1, 1917.

Dear Sir and Brother:

On my return to the office today after an absence of four months I find your letter of October 13th[3] with regard to the possibility of an affiliation between these organizations and the American Federation of Labor and a suggestion that the matter be discussed at a meeting in Washington in the near future.

This is to advise that I shall be glad to participate in such meeting whenever a date is agreed upon by others.

In the event that such a meeting may not be held before your convention I wish to state that since our Galveston convention in 1896 on many occasions I have attempted to convince our members of the wisdom of such affiliation.

Unfortunately the opinion has become general among our members that an affiliation with the American Federation of Labor would in some manner require them to recognize the negro fireman as representative of firemen, or else admit them to membership. You have explained to me personally that no such result would follow.

It is also the belief of many of our members that an affiliation with the American Federation of Labor would interfere with our contractual relations with the railroad companies to the extent that we would be denounced as scabs should we, after affiliating with the American Federation of Labor continue to haul "scab freight" when the producers of that freight, perhaps in some distant section of the country, were men who had taken the places of organized labor while on legal strike. I know that such a requirement is not included in the laws of the American Federation of Labor, but we have ample evidence that members of unions affiliated with the American Federation of Labor do not hesitate to denounce our members because they do not violate their wage contracts and enter into a sympathetic strike.

I never lost confidence in my belief that affiliation was right for all of these railway brotherhoods until I began to read with careful attention the many jurisdictional fights that take most of the time of conventions of the American Federation of Labor. It seems that there is an insistence on the part of many delegates assembled at conventions of the American Federation of Labor to try to regulate the jurisdiction of other organizations with the result that an organization affiliating with the American Federation of Labor, must submit the internal affairs of that organization to the settlement suggested or demanded by representatives of organizations that have no direct interest in the matter.

I noted with particular interest what was done at your Toronto Convention with regard to the jurisdictional dispute[4] between the Brotherhood of Railroad Trainmen[5] and the Switchmen's Mutual Aid Association.[6] Nothing would give me greater pleasure than to learn that the representatives of these two organizations had come to some mutual understanding over their jurisdictional disputes, which would relieve themselves and their friends of embarrassments that are so pronounced when either of these organizations reach a strike period. It seems that at the Toronto Convention of the American Federation of Labor there were some there who without a just reason attempted to take from the Brotherhood of Railroad Trainmen the right to represent its many, many thousands of switchmen and to transfer the jurisdiction over these many switchmen to an organization that did not represent more than twenty-five per cent of the number of switchmen represented by the Brotherhood of Railroad Trainmen.

This matter came to the attention of officers of our general committees on the different railroads and was a matter of discussion for a considerable period of time and the conclusions reached by our members were that the least these railway brotherhoods had to do with the American Federation of Labor, the better it would be for all concerned.

The old jurisdictional fight between the Brotherhood of Locomotive Engineers[7] and the Brotherhood of Locomotive Firemen and Enginemen has been eliminated largely through the influences of Grand Chief Stone[8] and myself. If either of these organizations now affiliate with the American Federation of Labor, I should not be surprised to hear that some delegate from the "candle-stick makers union" would offer a resolution that all engineers should belong to the Brotherhood of Locomotive Firemen and Enginemen and thus form "an Enginemen's trade union" similar to that of the miners and others of that class. Or, another delegate from some other organization would conceive the idea that the present jurisdictional agreement between the Brotherhood of Locomotive Engineers and the Brotherhood of Locomotive Firemen and Enginemen should be revised and that all engineers should be transferred to the Brotherhood of Locomotive Engineers.

It has been this seeming determination on the part of many delegates at American Federation of Labor conventions to meddle into the affairs of other organizations in jurisdictional matters that has led me to doubt the wisdom of this organization affiliating with the American Federation of Labor.

The two enginemen's Brotherhoods are now at peace and I hope forever, and it would be a dangerous experiment, from my viewpoint, to permit any other organization to assume a semblance of jurisdiction over matters that concern only these two enginemen's Brotherhoods.

Yours fraternally,   (signed) W. S. Carter,
President

Copy to
  W. S. Stone
  W. G. Lee[9]
  A. B. Garretson.[10]

TLtcSr, Executive Council Records, Minutes, reel 5, frames 1443–44, *AFL Records.*

1. William Samuel CARTER was president of the Brotherhood of Locomotive Firemen and Enginemen (1909–22). From 1918 to 1920 he took a leave of absence from the union's presidency in order to serve as the director of the Division of Labor of the U.S. Railroad Administration.

2. The Brotherhood of LOCOMOTIVE Firemen and Enginemen.

3. SG to Carter, Oct. 13, 1917, reel 227, vol. 239, pp. 365–66, SG Letterbooks, DLC. SG sent the same letter to William Lee, Austin Garretson, and Warren Stone (ibid., pp. 359–64). For replies from Lee and Stone, see Executive Council Records, Minutes, reel 5, frames 1442–43, *AFL Records.*

4. The 1909 AFL convention, which met in Toronto, Nov. 8–20, adopted a resolution declaring the Switchmen's Union of North America to be the only legitimate trade union with jurisdiction over switchmen.

5. The Brotherhood of RAILROAD Trainmen.

6. The SWITCHMEN's Union of North America.

7. The Brotherhood of LOCOMOTIVE Engineers.

8. Warren Sanford Stone served as grand chief engineer and then president of the Locomotive Engineers from 1903 to 1925.

9. William Granville LEE served as president of the Brotherhood of Railroad Trainmen from 1909 to 1928.

10. Austin Bruce GARRETSON served as grand chief conductor and then president of the Order of Railway Conductors of America from 1906 to 1919.

To Jay Brown

November 2, 1917.

Mr. J. G. Brown,
President, International Shingle Weavers' Union of America,[1]
202 Maynard Bldg., Seattle, Wash.
Dear Sir and Brother:

Your recent letters dealing with injunction difficulties in your state received. I am glad that you are dealing with the difficulty in a constructive way and are attempting to secure information giving more enlightened understanding of opinions rendered by courts in other sections.

I am sending you a copy of the March 1917 *American Federationist* containing an editorial entitled "Injunctions—A Decision—Press Forward."[2] This decision was handed down by the United States Circuit Court in the injunction case instituted by the American Steel Foundries of Granite City, Illinois, against the Tri-City Central Trades Council.[3] The original injunction I think was granted by Judge Humphrey,[4] who is one of the most bitter adversaries of organized labor. I am also sending you a copy of the Minnesota Supreme Court decision setting aside the injunction which the Grant Construction Company secured against the St. Paul Building Trades Council.[5]

The papers recently contained a report of the decision rendered by Judge Charles Leslie[6] in the District Court of Douglas County, Nebraska, in a suit[7] brought by Attorney General Reed[8] of Nebraska to enjoin the Omaha unions from combination in restraint of trade. The Court's opinion contained the following:

"The Court held that 'there can be no question that the unions have the right to organize or combine for their protection and welfare. And their right to do things in furtherance of their aims, so far as they do not interfere with the rights of others, is clear. Unions not directly involved in a strike may decline, if they so desire, to work on jobs held by them to be "unfair," and may approach non-union men with requests to leave the work or to join the union, so long as they use no violence, make no threats.'"

I have written[9] to Omaha asking for a copy of the complete opinion. As soon as I secure one I will send you a copy. I have also written[10] to the Carpenters for a copy of the decision recently rendered by the New York Court of Appeals in the injunction case brought against the Carpenters in that state.[11] The decision is on very broad lines. I will also send you a copy of that.

In accord with your request I am sending you a copy of the argument of Judge Parker in the Buck Stove and Range case. The principle which Judge Parker emphasizes is freedom of speech and press. I am also sending you a copy of an article written by Andrew Furuseth[12] entitled, "The Essence of Injunctions."[13] In the July, 1916 issue of the *American Federationist* in an article entitled, "Labor's State Legislative Demands,"[14] the origin of the abuse of the injunction is dealt with in considerable detail. I am sending you a copy of that magazine as well as a copy of the March, 1916 [issue] containing an article entitled, "Peaceful Picketing and Two Kinds of Law."[15]

I should be very glad to be of additional assistance to you in this work which you have begun and to consider any new developments in the situation that may arise from time to time.

With best wishes, and hoping to hear from you frequently, I am,

Fraternally yours,   Saml Gompers

President,   American Federation of Labor.

TLpS, reel 228, vol. 240, pp. 79–80, SG Letterbooks, DLC.

1. The International SHINGLE Weavers' Union of America.

2. *American Federationist* 24 (Mar. 1917): 203–5.

3. In May 1914 American Steel Foundries applied for an injunction against members of the Tri-City (Ill.) Central Trades Council, barring them "from doing any acts or things whatever" that interfered with the operations of the company's plant in Granite City, Ill. A federal district court issued the injunction, but in December 1916 the Circuit Court of Appeals for the Seventh Circuit ruled that it was too broad and ordered the district court to modify it, eliminating restraints from the performance of lawful acts (*Tri-City Central Trades Council et al.* v. *American Steel Foundries*, 238 F. 728 [1916]). On appeal, the U.S. Supreme Court in December 1921 ordered a modification of the appeals court's ruling to insure that pickets outside the plant did not act "in a threatening or intimidating manner" (*American Steel Foundries* v. *Tri-City Central Trades Council et al.*, 257 U.S. 184 [1921]).

4. J. Otis Humphrey of Springfield, Ill., served as a judge for the U.S. District Court for the Southern District of Illinois from 1901 until his death in 1918.

5. After the St. Paul Building Trades Council (BTC) put the Grant Construction Co. on the unfair list, BTC members refused to work with subcontractors hired by the firm. The company applied unsuccessfully for an injunction against the BTC in state district court and then appealed the case to the Supreme Court of Minnesota, arguing that while none of the council's acts were illegal in themselves, they were unlawful

when taken together because they constituted "organized economic oppression." In February 1917 the high court rejected this argument and upheld the district court's ruling denying the injunction (*George J. Grant Construction Co.* v. *St. Paul Building Trades Council et al.*, 136 Minn. 167 [1917]).

6. Charles Leslie of Omaha served as a district court judge from 1911 until about 1945.

7. Industrial disturbances broke out in Omaha in May 1917 after employers, backed by the Omaha Business Men's Association, attempted to impose the open shop. The state attorney general sought injunctions in district court against the employers, the members of the association, and most of the city's unions, but was only able to secure them against the owners of coal and building supply yards and the members of one union, International Brotherhood of Teamsters, Chauffeurs, Stablemen, and Helpers of America 211. In November 1918 the Supreme Court of Nebraska upheld the lower court, ruling there was insufficient evidence to sustain such sweeping injunctions as those requested by the attorney general (*State of Nebraska* v. *Employers of Labor et al.*, 102 Neb. 768 [1918]).

8. Willis E. Reed, a Madison, Nebr., attorney, served as the state's attorney general from 1915 to 1919.

9. SG to J. R. Wangberg, Oct. 30, 1917, reel 227, vol. 239, p. 978, SG Letterbooks, DLC.

10. SG to Frank Duffy, Oct. 31, 1917, reel 227, vol. 239, p. 1017, SG Letterbooks, DLC.

11. When the United Brotherhood of Carpenters and Joiners of America refused to handle materials made by Louis Bossert and Son, a Brooklyn millworking company that ran an open shop, Bossert secured an injunction against the union, barring it from taking any action affecting the firm or its products. The injunction was upheld in January 1915 by the Appellate Division of the Supreme Court of New York (*Louis Bossert et al.* v. *Frederick Dhuy et al.*, 166 App. Div. 251 [1915]) but was reversed in October 1917 by the Court of Appeals of New York, which upheld the union's right to prohibit its members from working with nonunion men or handling materials furnished by a nonunion shop (221 N.Y. 342 [1917]).

12. Andrew FURUSETH served as secretary of the Sailors' Union of the Pacific (1891–92, 1892–1936) and as president of the International Seamen's Union of America (1897–99, 1908–38).

13. *American Federationist* 11 (May 1904): 386–91.

14. *American Federationist* 23 (July 1916): 542–58.

15. *American Federationist* 23 (Mar. 1916): 201–3.

To Woodrow Wilson

November 5, 1917.

Honorable Woodrow Wilson,
President of the United States,
Washington, D.C.
Sir:

The Thirty-seventh Annual Convention of the American Federation of Labor will begin its two weeks' session at Buffalo, New York, Monday, November 12, 1917.

The Executive Council at its recent session[1] expressed the hope that it would be possible for you, and, if you could see your way clear, to deliver an address to the officers and delegates to that convention, and through them to express on behalf of our nation a message of good will and encouragement, and the undersigned was authorized and directed and takes pleasure in conveying that invitation to you.

In this crucial hour of the life of our republic, and the cause for which it, together with her allies is contending, such a message as you can deliver would go far to unify the spirit and activity of all of the workers and of all of the people of our country.

Among all our people there are none more loyal in the support of you as President of the United States and the leader of this great crusade, than the great rank and file of the organized workers of America.

Of course if you can, and I feel confident if you can you will, accept this invitation, the opening day of the convention, Monday, November 12th would be the most propitious time, but if that day be not convenient to you, may I suggest Tuesday, November 13th, or Friday, November 16th.[2]

Earnestly hoping that we may have the great pleasure and satisfaction of your acceptance of the invitation, and your inspiring presence at our gathering, I have the honor to remain,

Yours very respectfully,   Saml Gompers.
President,   American Federation of Labor.

TLpS, reel 228, vol. 240, p. 127, SG Letterbooks, DLC.

1. The AFL Executive Council met in Washington, D.C., Oct. 18–27, 1917.
2. President Woodrow Wilson addressed the 1917 AFL convention on Nov. 12 (AFL, *Proceedings,* 1917, pp. 2–4).

From Robert Lansing

November 5, 1917.

Sir:

The President has directed me to reply to your letter addressed to him on October 27th,[1] in regard to the labor situation in Cuba,[2] in which you enclosed a copy of a letter[3] from Vicente Martinez, President of the Association of Machinists and Francisco Domenech, Delegate of the Federation of Labor of Cienfuegos, and at the same time to communicate to you certain information which has been received by the Department of State in regard to this situation.

The Department of State has been informed by the Legation at Habana and by various American Consuls in different parts of Cuba, that the laborers in the sugar mills have been striking for an 8–hour day and that in many parts of the Republic their desires have been complied with. The latest cablegraphic advices state that the strikes have been settled.

In this connection the Department has received reports[4] from different sources to the effect that internal political and also foreign influence appear to be at work in fomenting these strikes and that it is suspected that German agents have been furnishing the agitators with funds. It is also understood that various Spanish subjects who are employed in some of the sugar mills are under German influence and are attempting, by means of strikes, to prevent the sugar crop from reaching the United States and Allied Powers. It is further reported that the President of Cuba issued a proclamation notifying all foreigners who provoked strikes which interfered with the production of sugar that they would be considered pernicious aliens and expelled from the country.

In this connection the President has asked me to put you in possession of the above reports and to state to you, confidentially, that although absolute evidence is not available, indications point to the fact that German influence has a certain amount to do with the present strike situation. Means are being taken to endeavor to investigate the above-reported German activities.

It will give me pleasure to communicate with you further in this connection, as soon as additional reports are received and if at that time it should appear that the strikes have not been settled, I shall be very glad to discuss the matter with you, looking toward the taking of such action as may be consistent.

I am, Sir,

Your obedient servant,   Robert Lansing

TLcSr, RG 59, General Records of the Department of State, DNA. Typed notation: "Confidential" crossed out.

1. SG to Woodrow Wilson, Oct. 27, 1917, reel 227, vol. 239, p. 885, SG Letterbooks, DLC.

2. Cuban sugar mill workers in the provinces of Camagüey, Cienfuegos, and Mantanzas began striking for an eight-hour day on Oct. 1, 1917. Although some employers initially attempted to reach a compromise, Cuban president Mario Menocal warned that the strikes were inspired by pro-German elements and were a threat to the war effort. He ordered the arrest of the strike leaders and the expulsion of "pernicious foreigners" and "agitators" suspected of instigating or encouraging the strikes (*Havana Post,* Oct. 24, 1917). By the last week of October the strikers were returning to work.

3. In their letter of Oct. 21, 1917, Vincente Martinez and Francisco Domenech complained of the Cuban government's repression of the strike and appealed to SG, the AFL, and President Wilson for assistance (reel 227, vol. 239, pp. 886–87, SG Letterbooks, DLC).

4. See, for example, Gustave Scholle to Robert Lansing, Oct. 24, 27, and 30, 1917, RG 59, General Records of the Department of State, DNA. Scholle was the American chargé d'affaires in Havana.

Excerpts from News Accounts of the 1917 Convention of the AFL in Buffalo

[November 18, 1917]

NO POLITICS IN MOVE
TO SHIFT CONVENTION DATE, GOMPERS SAYS

After holding its conventions for 35 years in November the American Federation of Labor hereafter will meet in June. This was decided on at yesterday's session after a long debate on a resolution[1] authorizing the change, during which some of the delegates intimated that there would be a decided advantage to the organized workers of the country in holding the convention before election, as proposed.

Remarks by some of the delegates indicated that in favoring a change in the time of meeting they had in mind the possible political effect as well as their own personal comfort and convenience. It was contended that weather conditions will be more favorable in June than in November. This argument undoubtedly moved many of the delegates to amend the constitution so the convention, beginning next year, can be held earlier than usual.

The change in the meeting time was made after the committee on laws brought in a report recommending that a resolution by John B. Lennon[2] to amend the constitution be adopted. A motion to substitute June for November was carried by a vote of 255 to 21. A motion to make the resolution effective in 1919 instead of next year was lost.[3]

NOT IN POLITICS.

Asked after the session what effect the amendment of the constitution would have on the policy of the American Federation of Labor in considering certain matters, President Gompers said: "The policy of the A.F. of L. with respect to non-participation in partisan politics remains unchanged. We will continue to fight for our friends and try to defeat our enemies."

. . .

Buffalo Express, Nov. 18, 1917.

1. Resolution 1, introduced by delegate John Lennon of the Journeymen Tailors' Union of America on Nov. 13, 1917, was adopted by the convention on Nov. 17. It amended Article III, Section 1, of the AFL constitution to change the meeting date of the annual AFL convention from the second Monday in November to the second Monday in June.

2. John Brown LENNON served as treasurer of the AFL from 1891 to 1917 and as a commissioner of conciliation for the U.S. Department of Labor from 1918 through at least 1920. He represented the Tailors at the convention.

3. The vote on this amendment was 97 in favor to 176 opposed (AFL, *Proceedings,* 1917, p. 267).

[November 20, 1917]

AMERICA FIRST, GOMPERS'S AIM, GETS LABOR O.K.

Union labor yesterday put its stamp of approval on the attitude of Samuel Gompers, president of the American Federation of Labor, in working hand-in-hand with President Wilson and placing the needs of the nation above all other considerations in questions involving the workingman's part in a vigorous prosecution of the war against Germany.[1]

The vote of confidence came after more than three hours of debate in which the pacifist element at the 37th annual convention of the federation was given free range and ample opportunity to express itself. Out of a total of 450 delegates only fifteen were recorded in opposition. The garment workers of New York under the leadership of Rose Shapiro[2] was the only organization refusing to be recorded on the rollcall.

The test of strength came upon a report from the committee on resolutions. The committee reported favorably a resolution indorsing the "patriotic work" of the Alliance of Labor and Democracy which Mr. Gompers took an active part in organizing, as an offset to the People's Council, a pacifist body.

The attack on the resolution was led by Delegate Barnes[3] of Philadelphia. He was supported by Miss Shapiro, Delegate Burke[4] of the sulphite workers, Joseph P. Cannon[5] of the mine workers and a few others. The Alliance and Mr. Gompers were defended by delegates Walker[6] of Illinois, Brown[7] of Washington, Matthew Wall[8] of the photo-engravers, George Berry[9] of the pressmen, Max S. Hayes[10] of the typographical union, and Vice President James Duncan.[11]

OPPOSITION WANDERS.

The opposition frequently wandered from the question before the house, touching upon the high cost of living, the Arizona miners' strike, the Pacific coast shipbuilders' fight, the street railway strike in Springfield, Ill.,[12] and the suppression of foreign language papers, but President Gompers gave them full rein.

The supporters of the resolution did not mince words in condemning the attitude of the pacifists. The words snake, traitor, and sedition were among those hurled at the opposition.

"Labor has a big duty to perform," said Mr. Berry. "We cannot afford to place ourselves in a position that will be misunderstood. If the resolution is rejected it will go abroad to the world that we have turned down the government. It is time we should stand up and be counted.

"If we have traitors in our ranks, I am ready to eliminate them. We cannot take halfway measures. We must show where we stand for the democracy for which we have been fighting for the last 37 years."

Delegate Walker, who was at the Minneapolis meeting of the Alliance for Labor and Democracy, said that the alliance's declaration against treason and sedition seemed to have been unfavorably received by a great many people.

"I have not changed my mind about that," Mr. Walker continued. "Internment should be the fate of those who preach sedition and if that is not sufficient to suppress their advocacy of Prussian autocracy, I am in favor of taking whatever steps are necessary to suppress them.

"Pacifists skulking under the cloak of unionism are going as far as they dare in the way of preaching sedition. This war is no child's play. It means more to us than any issue ever raised in the history of the human race. There isn't a thing that I can do to further the cause of the government in this war that I am not willing to do."

Delegate Brown suggested when the vote was taken that there should be a rollcall. "Let us stand up and be counted," he demanded.

. . .

President Gompers closed the debate in a ringing speech in defense of the alliance and his own position.

"By those who have opposed the report and the recommendation of this committee," he said, "my name has not always been mentioned, but my position was, and there is no difference between the two. For instance, I recall the insinuations made of my hobnobbing with the enemies of labor. Now, I have always said this: I will go anywhere to bring the message of hope to labor—even into the camp of the enemy.

"If there is anyone who can bring one utterance of mine, made anywhere, that has not been in the defense of the rights of the laboring people, let him do so. I dare you! I challenge you!"

Mr. Gompers went into the history of the formation of the People's council, which he said was an offshoot of the Socialist party. He took full responsibility for the calling of the Minneapolis meeting of the alliance.

"The situation demanded," he said, "that there should be a clear cut distinction between what these people represented and what the trades unions stood for. The fact is that the Socialists, since the Detroit convention[13] when they failed to break in,[14] have made war upon the American Federation of Labor. They sought to discredit it. They started the Western Labor Union, the American Labor Union and they started the I.W.W., and finally they started the so-called People's council. In the one instance it was rivalry to the American Federation of Labor and in the last it was hostility to the republic of the United States."

"I do not know how many of you may feel toward me," said Mr. Gompers, "but if I am to continue as president of the American Federation of Labor, it will be by your votes. You may vote against me if you wish, but I must continue on good terms with myself.

"I am not neutral on this war. Pacifist as I have been all my life, when I find a band of murderers abroad and I fail to defend my children, I would not be a pacifist, but a poltroon and a coward.["]

To do a man's duty.

"President Wilson and the members of his cabinet were peace-loving men; I know of no militarist among them, but now they are fighting men. And I publicly declare now that I am a fighting man and will continue to fight for the country to which I owe all; the country I love and in which my hope and aspirations are bound up.

"I purpose to do a man's duty in helping to make this war the last war of this world. All my energies shall be laid at the feet of America and of our Allies to do what I can toward the establishment of democracy throughout the world, even in Germany."

· · ·

ATTACK ON SOCIALISTS.

President Gompers read the declaration that applicants to membership in the alliance signed to show that there was no principle in it adverse to the principles of the federation.[15] He questioned Barnes's loyalty to the organization.

"When the Socialist Trade and Labor Alliance was formed," Mr. Gompers declared, "this Mr. Barnes was quite busy. During that period he attacked the very organization of which he was a member—the cigarmakers—and called its label a dirty rag. That he has not denounced the federation itself in the last few years was not because of his good will toward it."

Referring again to the causes which prompted him to join in the formation of the alliance in opposition to the People's council and the unreasoning attitude of the Socialists, Mr. Gompers said:

"There was lots of agitation, some artificial and some criminal, against the government. Socialists held their convention and declared against the war. A number of members of the party resigned in disgust. Charles E. Russell, an honored member of the Socialist party was sent by President Wilson on a mission to Russia to help the Russians toward their ideals. He was expelled. With him went men and women who were the brains of the Socialist party in America—Stokes, Walling, Spargo, Gaylord[16] and others. They left the party because of the unpatriotic attitude and actions of the Socialist party on the war.

"I read in the Socialist press that conferences were being held by the Socialists. They were going to bring peace. Hillquit promised it in his New York campaign.[17] I saw too that a call had been issued for a conference in New York to take place on June 30th and July 1st to organize the People's council with the object of getting immediate peace.["]

DOESN'T EXPECT CHANGE.

"In that call it was stated that I had sold out the working people to the government and the capitalists; that men could not strike because I was tying their hands.

"You heard Miss Shapiro. She talked about the ideals of democracy. When the secretary read the declaration of the alliance for labor and democracy, showing the principles it laid down, her co-delegates nudged her and she laughed when the remark was made 'Why it contains all your demands.'

"But do you think for a moment that the reading of these declarations or anything that Berry or Wall or I say will change the utterances of those who attack us? If you think it worth while I will send you their publications to show there will be no change. They will say Gompers and his reactionary associates have tied the hands and feet of labor."

The New York meeting at which the People's council was launched was a packed meeting, Mr. Gompers declared. The Socialists were at their old game of playing politics and again attempted to stab the federation in the back.

Replying to another Socialist[18] who attacked his position on the Arizona mine troubles, Mr. Gompers asked what the Socialists had done to clear up the situation there. Not a thing he declared, but to exploit it for votes.

REAL WORK FOR LABOR.

Mr. Gompers then told of his trip to Washington and his talk with the President, after which a commission was appointed to investigate, not only the Arizona trouble, but conditions in California, Idaho and Washington. On that commission were staunch representatives of labor, including John Walker and E. P. Marsh. "I did not shout that from the hilltops," remarked Mr. Gompers.

The first vote was taken on an amendment by the opposition to table the report. It was offered by Cannon, who said the alliance was no concern of the federation. The amendment was defeated. The roll was then called on the adoption of the committee's recommendation and resulted: Yeas, 21,579; noes, 402.

. . .

Buffalo Express, Nov. 20, 1917.

1. On Nov. 19, 1917, the convention endorsed the work of the American Alliance for Labor and Democracy by a vote of 21,602 to 402, with 1,305 not voting.

2. Actually Sarah Shapiro, a member of International Ladies' Garment Workers' Union 25 (Waistmakers) of New York City, who represented the international union.

3. John Mahlon BARNES, a delegate from the Cigar Makers' International Union of America, was a founder and leading member of the Socialist Party of America.

4. John P. BURKE was president-secretary (1917–65) of the International Brotherhood of PULP, Sulphite, and Paper Mill Workers.

5. Joseph D. Cannon represented the International Union of Mine, Mill, and Smelter Workers.

6. John Walker represented the United Mine Workers of America.

7. Jay G. Brown represented the International Shingle Weavers' Union of America.

8. Matthew Woll represented the International Photo-Engravers' Union of North America.

9. George Leonard BERRY was president (1907–48) of the International Printing PRESSMEN's and Assistants' Union of North America and represented the union at this convention.

10. Max Sebastian HAYES, editor of the *Cleveland Citizen* from 1894 to 1939, represented the International Typographical Union.

11. James Duncan represented the Granite Cutters' International Association of America.

12. On July 25, 1917, members of Amalgamated Association of Street and Electric Railway Employes of America division 761 of Springfield, Ill., struck the Springfield Consolidated Railway Co., demanding recognition of their newly-formed union and a pay increase. When the company's response—hiring replacement workers—led to rioting in which one police officer was injured and another killed, Illinois governor Frank Lowden briefly sent in the National Guard to restore order. Division 761 eventually called off its unsuccessful strike—in October 1918—and appealed the dispute to the National War Labor Board, but the board ruled in March 1919 that it did not have jurisdiction and dismissed the case.

13. The 1890 AFL convention met in Detroit, Dec. 8–13.

14. See *The Samuel Gompers Papers*, vol. 2, pp. 386–408.

15. The pledge, written by SG, read as follows: "The undersigned hereby affirms that it is the duty of all the people of the United States, without regard to class, nationality, politics or religion, faithfully and loyally to support the government of the United States in carrying on the present war for justice, freedom and democracy to a triumphant conclusion and gives this pledge to uphold every honorable effort for the accomplishment of that purpose, and to support the A.F. of L. as well as the declaration of organized labor's representatives made March 12, 1917, at Washington, D.C., as to 'Labor's Position in Peace or in War,' and agrees that this pledge shall be his right to membership in this conference of the American Alliance for Labor and Democracy" (AFL, *Proceedings,* 1917, p. 291).

16. Winfield R. Gaylord (b. 1870), a Milwaukee attorney, was a vice-president of the American Alliance for Labor and Democracy. He had served as a Socialist member of the Wisconsin state senate (1909–13) and several times ran unsuccessfully for Congress, losing by a few hundred votes in 1910 and again in 1914. Gaylord left the Socialist Party of America in 1917 because of its opposition to American involvement in the war.

17. That is, Morris Hillquit's unsuccessful campaign for mayor of New York City on the Socialist ticket in 1917.

18. James H. Fisher, a Great Falls, Mont., bookkeeper, who represented AFL Federal Labor Union 14,871 of Great Falls. In 1918 he served as the union's secretary.

[November 21, 1917]

LABOR SUPPORTS U.S. WAR POLICY, NO VOTE AGAINST

. . .

BARNES IS REBUKED.

Delegates to the American Federation of Labor yesterday went on record as unqualifiedly indorsing the conduct of President Samuel Gompers and the executive council in connection with the war.[1] This action was taken on the recommendation of the committee on resolutions shortly before the end of the morning session after Mr. Gompers again criticized Delegate J. Mahlon Barnes, Socialist, of Philadelphia, who on Monday afternoon led the pacifist attack on Mr. Gompers.[2]

Barnes, Mr. Gompers said, must bear the "honor, credit or odium that attaches to his conduct on Monday."

"Time will tell which it is," said President Gompers, "and Mr. Barnes must bear the one or the other."

The subject came before the convention when Barnes, rising to a question of personal privilege, said he wanted to make a statement. He said that the stormy session of the federation on Monday afternoon, when the trades unionists put the stamp of approval on President Gompers and the way he had been co-operating with President Wilson, was the annual escape valve. He contended he was grossly misrepresented. "I have no redress and have nothing to complain of," said he. "I am only a rank and file member of the Socialist party, yet the crimes of this party were heaped on my head."

Denies Gompers's charge.

Declaring that he had no connection with the Western Labor union, the American Labor union, the Socialist Trade and Labor alliance and the I.W.W., Barnes said that he is hated as much by that "coterie as by the person who assailed me on Monday afternoon." The Socialist party, he asserted, did not indorse any of these organizations. The labor organization of which he was a member, he said, was the Cigarmakers' International union. He denied that he called the label of this union a dirty rag, as alleged by Mr. Gompers.

President Gompers, replying to Barnes, suggested that the delegates would appreciate "the handsome compliment paid to them when Barnes described the meeting of last Monday afternoon as typifying the mob spirit. In the mind of this man it is typical of the mob spirit, though there was a full discussion of the question for over four hours. Barnes said that if all the things said about him were true he would be unfit for a seat in the convention. I quite agree with him.

. . .

"Any man who refuses to support the government," said Mr. Gompers, "writes himself down as treasonable to the United States government. Any man who is not loyal to the American Federation of Labor is disloyal to it."

. . .

Buffalo Express, Nov. 21, 1917.

1. The convention voted unanimously to approve the AFL Executive Council's report on its war-related activities, including the declaration on "American Labor's Position in Peace or in War." At the same time, the convention also approved Resolution 150, introduced by George Perkins of the Cigar Makers' International Union on Nov. 13, 1917, which "unreservedly" endorsed the actions of SG and the Council in support of the war effort and the service of "all other labor men" on various "boards,

commissions, and committees" in connection with the war (AFL, *Proceedings,* 1917, p. 318).

2. That is, in the debate on the resolution endorsing the American Alliance for Labor and Democracy. See "America First, Gompers's Aim, Gets Labor O.K.," Nov. 20, 1917, above.

[November 22, 1917][1]

. . .

At the morning session there was another long and at times acrimonious debate favoring the conscription of citizens of allied nations now living in the United States.[2] Thomas Black,[3] a Canadian delegate, brought a storm upon his head by referring to all conscription law as "dastardly," a remark which resulted in a demand for retraction from several delegates.

President Gompers temporarily relinquished the chair to reply to Black and Delegate Cary[4] of Toronto declared that Black's remarks did not reflect the sentiment of union labor in Canada. The demand for a retraction from Black was not put in the form of a resolution and the subject was dropped when the conscription resolution was adopted. The vote was 244 to 20.

. . .

Another question that caused considerable debate was a report by the resolutions committee in favor of a resolution that the A.F. of L. recommend to all affiliated organizations that they provide in their constitutions (if they have not such provisions now) that men coming to the United States and Canada from abroad shall be citizens of the United States or Canada or declare their intention of becoming citizens before they make application for membership or are admitted to membership in unions.[5] The committee's report was not adopted, the subject being referred to the executive council of the federation.

Delegate William Dobson[6] said that if this country is good enough for a man to make a living in he should become a citizen. "There is no room for the man who takes advantage of the opportunities here and will not become a citizen," said he. "My own father could not sit in a union with me if he did not or would not declare an intention of becoming a citizen."

President McClorey[7] of the Bridge and Structural Ironworkers' union pointed out that the I.W.W. is made up largely of aliens.

He was apprehensive that adoption of the resolution might have a tendency to increase the membership of the I.W.W.

Another delegate[8] thought it would render the work of organizing the Mexicans in this country more difficult. The Arizona federation of labor has wired[9] a protest against the resolution.

Delegate Lennon in debating the resolution declared: "If aliens do not want to become citizens they should not be permitted to remain here."

Delegate Woll of the photo-engravers' union feared that adoption of the resolution might lead to industrial difficulties.

Vice President Duncan, who offered the resolution, said that some labor organizations now require their members to be citizens yet "none of these dreadful things has happened that have been spoken of this afternoon."

. . .

Buffalo Express, Nov. 22, 1917.

1. This article describes the proceedings of Nov. 21, 1917.

2. As adopted by the convention, resolution 144, introduced by Edward McGrady of the Boston Central Labor Union on Nov. 13, 1917, called for legislation or treaties to require aliens from allied nations living in the United States to serve in the armed forces either of this country or their own.

3. Thomas Black represented the Toronto District Labor Council.

4. David A. CAREY of Toronto represented the American Federation of Musicians.

5. Resolution 80, introduced by James Duncan of the Granite Cutters' International Association of America on Nov. 13, 1917. The Committee on Resolutions recommended adoption of the resolution, but the convention referred it to the AFL Executive Council with instructions to modify it to address issues raised by the organization of Mexican and Asian workers. At its meeting in May 1918 the Council approved a resolution essentially identical to the one referred to it by the convention.

6. William DOBSON, of the Bricklayers', Masons', and Plasterers' International Union of America, served as secretary of the union from 1900 to 1925 and represented it at this convention.

7. Joseph E. McCLORY, of the International Association of BRIDGE, Structural, and Ornamental Iron Workers, was president of the union from 1914 to 1918.

8. Jay Brown and Joseph Cannon both noted the difficulties this resolution posed for organizing Mexican workers, and John Williams and William Green suggested that it would hamper the organization of foreign-born workers in general.

9. Thomas French to American Federation of Labor Convention, Frank Morrison, Secretary, Nov. 16, 1917, AFL, *Proceedings,* 1917, p. 271.

[November 25, 1917]

FEDERATION MEETING ENDS, ALL OFFICERS BUT ONE RE-ELECTED

. . .

Samuel Gompers, president of the American Federation of Labor for nearly 35 years, yesterday was re-elected, practically without opposition, as was every other officer of the federation, excepting Treasurer John B. Lennon, who was defeated by Daniel J. Tobin, president of the International teamsters and Chauffeurs' union.

. . .

. . . The contest over the office of treasurer was not unexpected. For several years there had been opposition to Mr. Lennon and this year, it is said, the forces that wanted to elect an officer centered on Mr. Tobin as the candidate to oppose him. Delegates who discussed the cause of the contest and the failure of the convention to re-elect Treasurer Lennon after 28 years of service, and admittedly faithful, said that a number of elements contributed to his defeat, among them Mr. Lennon's stand on prohibition, his decisions on jurisdictional questions and disputes between labor organizations, alleged dissensions in the tailors' union,[1] the smallness of this organization as compared with some others affiliated with the A.F. of L. and the fact that he had held the office so long.

. . .

Buffalo Express, Nov. 25, 1917.

1. The Journeymen TAILORS' Union of America.

An Address in Toronto[1]

November 28, 1917.

Mr. Chairman[2] and Friends:

It affords me more gratification to be with you this evening than I can find words to express. Somehow or other there is a destiny which shapes our hands, rough hew them as we will,[3] and it is a pressing thought upon my mind that there is a destiny which is shaping all that we hold dear; that is crystalizing the thought and the activities of the peoples of the democracies of the world, so that the ideals for which we are striving shall find their expression translated into the realities of life. (Applause) There are some people who, touched by the enormity of the sacrifices which are being made and perhaps which may yet have to be made, are horror stricken and terror stricken at it all; and in a large part I share their feelings of horror and terror. It seems to be a fact of life that there is little worth while in the achievements of the human race unless it is sanctified by the blood of man. (Applause) This utterance of mine, I venture to ask you to believe me, would not have passed my lips a little more than three years ago.

From my very earliest young manhood it was my proud boast and it was my intense belief that there would not again occur any large interruption of the international peace of the world. I was a Pacifist "par excellence." I belonged to every peace Society of which I knew anything. I was a member of the Board of Directors and an officer of the International Peace Society and a member of all the State and all the local peace organizations and I enjoyed my tranquility with such passion that I nearly hugged it to death. (Laughter) As a delegate from the American Federation of Labor to the Paris Conference[4] of the organized labor movements of the civilized world—and incidentally I may say that was perhaps the largest public gathering within a hall that I had ever seen in all my life—I heard the spokesmen of the Labor movements of all the respective countries participating in that international conference pledge themselves to eternal international peace. Speaking as far as I had authority to speak in the name of the labor movement of America in all earnestness and sincerity I pledged the all, the thought, feelings and the activities and the hope of American labor against breaking international peace. (Applause) Representatives of the organized labor movement in Germany who were there gave the same pledge to the whole world. Then I came home to the shores of America and conveyed that message to my fellows. We were all encouraged and pleased.

I am taking you into my confidence in telling you that I had been approached on many occasions to have my peace utterances done up in some sort of book form in order that they might be spread throughout America and elsewhere. At last the Carnegie Peace Association prevailed upon me to turn over all that which I had spoken and written upon the subject of international peace and then I turned it over to the printer. I wanted to edit or revise it because there were some thoughts that might have been crudely expressed. The manuscript was now in the hands of the printer. Those who conferred with me told me that it was not necessary to revise it at all because what was there showed "growth and development" and I was again convinced that they were right.

Then, Lo and Behold, in August 1914, I found myself just howling in the wilderness. I had been befuddled and fooled by a schemer and devisor unparalleled in the history of the world, and out of almost a clear sky came the declaration of war by the Imperial German Kaiser. At the command of this militarist, this Imperialist, the peoples of the world were set at each others' throats. I immediately went to the printer and got hold of that damn-fool stuff and took it back. (Laughter and Applause)

I have sometimes a private opinion on certain matters but the man who will not change his opinion when facts are presented to disprove that opinion is very much like the man who said "to argue with a man who has bidden good bye to his reason is like giving medicine to the dead." (Laughter)

These utterances of mine in regard to eternal peace and against international war will have to be revised after the close of the war when victory and triumph has been won. (Applause) For I verily believe that when—mark you, I don't say if—when we shall have triumphed in this war there will be no more great militarist preparations in the great countries of the world (Applause).

Well, his Imperial Majesty who broke all the laws of God and man in inaugurating this war perhaps didn't know the host with which he would have to deal. They had been planning and scheming for nearly half a century. You will remember that the Emperor of Germany had made the people believe that his preparation and his great army was for the purpose of maintaining the peace of the world. When he was called the War Lord he would endeavor to explain and to make the people of the world understand or believe that his whole purpose was that of maintaining international peace. And now, I ask you to consider for a moment, whether it is not true that these false pretences made by him and his underlings were really intended and planned to lull the people of the world into a fancied security so that they would feel that it was not necessary to prepare themselves against any aggression on his part. (Applause)

And I may say in passing that the plan of the whole Imperialist machine of Germany was intended to be conveyed in thought to the people of the whole world. And I want to express this thought, whether there be any member of the Socialist party in this city or this audience. I ask them and you people in this audience to consider this fact: you read of the philosophy of the German Socialist school and you will find that after all it is patterned after the autocratic power of the German Imperial government. (Applause) It is at variance with and in opposition to the great labor movement as expressed by the Trades Unions of the world. (Applause) In our trades unions we represent in fact and in philosophy the fundamental principle of voluntarily and individually yielding a certain amount of our rights in order that all our other rights may be protected and advanced. (Applause) Under the scheme of the German school of socialist philosophy there is a thought that everything must be done by the government and the individual must lose himself.

There has never been a congress of labor into which a representative of the German Socialist party and the German socialist philosophy has not endeavored to break in and break through. There has never been any assemblage of the organized labor movement in America, Canada, England, or any other country, France included, but what an endeavor has been made to foist upon this labor movement the German militarist idea as modified and understood by German socialism.

In all international and national conferences their influences have operated and I freely admit to you that it was impossible for me to make myself proof against the influences they brought to bear—the sophistry they brought to bear in so far as I believed them to be sincere in their advocacy of international peace. So far as their other "bunk" is concerned there is nothing in it for me. (Applause) For there never was more sophistry contained in any pretended philosophy than there is in that which is embodied in German Socialism. It is an effort to hypnotize and chloroform the world into a fancied security and they are playing their part splendidly in support of the militarism of their country in order that it may dominate the world. I ask you whether in the face of all that has been done—the flagrant violation of international law, the violation of every moral law, the violation of every treaty, the violation of every promise and pledge—is it not time for the people yet remaining, the manhood of our countries to rally in the defence of all that is left for manhood and womanhood to revere?

I have heard as you have heard of conscientious objectors. You have heard as I have heard of those who are now pacifists. I want to ask you whether you can transplant your mind—I cannot imagine you transplanting your bodies—to Berlin and then inquire of yourselves what you think his Imperial Majesty, the Kaiser, would say to anyone who declared himself a Pacifist or a conscientious objector. There was one Pacifist, one conscientious objector in Germany, Dr. Carl Leibnicht[5] and the Kaiser and his Government immediately put him in prison. He is there now if he is alive.

Is it possible that we have so far forgotten the spirit of our race or races, have we so far been unable to appreciate the development of the human race, that we cannot or will not do our duty? The ordinary citizen goes home at night and locks the doors and goes restfully to sleep, but when there is a band of murderers who threaten and by physical force endanger the lives not only of himself but of his wife and little ones, when you know that some of your neighbors have been robbed and ravished, who could be the conscientious objector or Pacifist who would not rise with his fellows in the defence of his home and his family? (Applause)

Perhaps I am making an excuse for myself for my change, transition or development from Pacifist to fighting man. (Laughter) Whether I am or not I hold that facts, not theory, have demonstrated the view I held to be unsound, and confronted with the facts of my time I hold that any man in France, England, America, Canada, or any other democratic country which enjoys the freedom and privileges of free institutions who would not fight in defence of them now is a coward and a poltroon. (Applause) I wish I could fight in the fashion that fighting is generally understood, but being 67 years of age they will not let me fight. A man of my years in the trenches would only be a burden on them and therefore they will not have me in the army. But there are other requirements in war. They require organizers, and I have been flattered by people saying I am not a bad organizer. (Applause) They also say in times of war that the services of administrators are required and I have been flattered by being told that I am not such a bad administrator. They also require advisors and no one has yet accused me of being much of a fool. So that in these several directions and to the extent of any powers I possess my services are offered voluntarily without stint to my government in alleging [allying?] itself with the democracies of the world in this fight to a finish.

I have heard some men criticise me rather severely because I have counselled my fellow workers in the United States against participation in international conferences at this time in which representatives of the enemy country would participate. Well, whatever people have said about me no one has accused me of being a blamed fool. It is not easy, I think to catch me napping in any big question. You can perhaps fool me personally quite easily. I hold that when these invitations to the international conference were sent out from Petrograd, or Stockholm or Berne, they were already more or less tainted with German militarist sympathies. (Applause) You never heard any German representative or anyone with German sympathies urge an international conference of labor so long as it seemed likely that the Kaiser's forces were marching triumphantly on Calais or Paris. As soon as the German forces were checked it upset the whole plans of the Kaiser, because there was nothing in their whole plan of forty years preparation but what meant the onward march of the militarist machine over-riding and crushing everything before it like a juggernaut. After the halt that was the beginning of the end the intrigues in the other countries began and international conferences were proposed.

There is not the slightest feeling of bitterness or hatred in my heart or soul against any human being on earth, but for the Kaiser. I would like to see him somewhere so that he could not do any harm again. Probably St. Helena or some such safe place would be quite pleasing. The mischief maker must be guarded over. Speaking of the German people there is no feeling of hatred or bitterness in my soul. Our fight is not alone for the existence of the democracies of the world. The German people must crush militarism and Imperialism from within or the democracies of the world must crush Kaiserism from without and introduce democracies in their country. (Applause)

Look to any of the countries of the whole world, make a mental survey of them and answer yourself the question: are any of the countries

of [the] world neutral? Look to Holland, Switzerland and the Scandi-
navian countries. Awed by the example of the ravishment of Belgium
and with the great military machine of Germany yet to a considerable
extent powerful, Holland, Switzerland, Norway, Sweden and Denmark
have become rich by serving the needs of Germany and have been
paid in the promissory notes of Germany. If Germany wins a plethora
of wealth will flow into these countries. If Germany loses then these
countries are practically bankrupt. Neutral countries! Neutral minds!
There ain't no such animal! (Laughter and Applause) Either fish or
cut bait; either fight or buy Victory Bonds.

The time has gone by when we can view this war as a proposition academic in its character. It is removed from that real[m] and we are now
in the arena of the world's fight for life and decent living. (Applause)
I hope I shall be enabled to avoid and I shall try to avoid any interference in the internal affairs and particularly the internal political affairs
of the Dominion, but I hold it to be a first duty of every Canadian by
birth or by citizenship to do everything within his power to unite the
people in winning this war. (Applause) I know something of the differences of your political parties both of the immediate past and the
distant past. I cannot say that their choice has always been wisest. You
make the same mistakes as we make in the United States but that is
not the question. You may differ on many things when conditions of
peace prevail, and let me say here I am not going to discuss the wisdom or unwisdom of Canada joining in the war. Suffice it for me to
express the opinion that your entrance into the war was wise, patriotic,
and human but whether that is true or not is [not] the question. The
fact is that you are at war and the duly constituted authorities of the
Dominion of Canada have in a lawful way entered into this conflict. It
is no longer, therefore, a matter for academic discussion. It is a matter
of fact with which you have to deal, and having entered the war the
people of Canada without regard to political opinions, without regard
to religion or any other difference, ought to stand united in one solid
phalanx to bring victory and glory to the Dominion [and] every other
nation in the fight for freedom and democracy. (Applause)

In addition to having been a Pacifist I was a believer and am still
a staunch believer in free institutions and the freedom of actions of
men and women. I am opposed to force whenever and wherever it
can be avoided, and when the question of conscription came up as
a practical question in the United States I opposed it. I hold that at
least voluntary institutions should first be put to the final test before
compulsion should be employed, just as exactly as the people of this
Dominion were placed. But the Congress of the United States in its
lawful right ordained that there should be selective draft conscription.

While I used every influence to prevent it I failed in my object. The Congress of the United States, the duly constituted authority of my country decreed otherwise. The decision was made and I held and shall hold it to be the duty of every American citizen in time of war to obey the decision rightfully and lawfully reached. It is all very good when we are at peace to battle with each other for the supremacy of our ideas, but when the duly constituted authority in times of war arrive at a conclusion it is no longer a subject to discuss. (Applause)

A few weeks ago a Russian[6] came to my office in Washington and while we were discussing certain matters he was seriously asked the question whether he approved of the ideas that were being proclaimed by some Russian leaders that there should be a vote by the soldiers whether or not a particular advance should be [made?]. He answered yes. He really believed it. Can you imagine a great army corps covering an area of two, three or four hundred miles and each regiment and each company voting on the question of whether they should advance or retreat? And just imagine a regiment voting aye and the other voting no! What wonderful discipline and effectiveness there would be in such an army! I wonder where General Haig[7] would be if that system prevailed in the forces of the British, Canadian or Australian boys? This is war. This is not playing a game of war, and when the Congress of the United States or the Parliament of Canada has decreed lawfully upon a certain course it is the duty of every man to stand by and see that that policy shall be put into successful operation. (Applause) The same is equally true with the general staff of any army. When the commander in chief issues an order it is the duty of every soldier to obey.

I know some people have criticized my change from Pacifism to the attitude I now adopt in aiding my country in the war and the cause for which we are united. The United States is not and never has been in a war of aggression. It has been altruistic. I think you will agree there is no public man in the world who has been more severely criticized for his actions than the honored head of the American republic, President Woodrow Wilson. Sometimes I have had occasion to be in Buffalo and I have taken advantage of the opportunity to see some old friends on the border. I know they were kindly disposed towards me and they were not hostile to the president but their criticism of Mr. Wilson was severe because he was writing notes and was not doing anything but sending notes. (Laughter) Well, you know that the president declared some time ago that there were some people who felt themselves so justified and morally right that they were too proud to fight. He believed, and I am satisfied he believed sincerely in the honesty of the pledges made by the German Imperial government for reparation and the stoppage of the wholesale murder of innocent women and children. Do you know that Mr. Wilson is a Pacifist? Secretary Lansing is a Pacifist. Secretary of War Baker is a Pacifist. Secretary Daniels of the Navy is a Pacifist. The Secretary of Agriculture Prof. Houston[8] and Secretary of Labor Mr. Wilson are Pacifists. I don't know for certain but I believe Mr. Redfield, secretary of Commerce is also a Pacifist. Just imagine the President and a cabinet of Pacifists at last being driven by their conscience and their duty to take up arms and throw the whole strength of the man power and wealth of the greatest republic in the world into the arena and make this common course successful. (Applause) I suppose it is not necessary to argue the justification of the United States in entering this war. You will remember Bernstoff[9] the German ambassador to the United States published an advertisement in the American papers warning the people of the United States against taking a passage on the ill fated Lusitania. You know that a few days after that warning a German submarine torpedoed that great ship and sent her to the bottom of the ocean with nearly 1500 men, women and children, not one of them combatants. Supposing Ambassador Gerrard[10] representing the United States at Berlin had published similar warning in German newspapers against German men, women, and children taking passage on a merchant vessel unarmed and supposing after the warning had been issued an American man of war or a submarine had sent a German ship to the bottom murdering a thousand of women and children, do you think for a moment that Ambassador Gerrard would have been permitted to live there any length of time? Do you think he would have been given his passports? They would have made short shrift of him and sent him to the great beyond. Patience! There never was in the history of the world so far as my knowledge goes any country which exhibited more patience than the government of my people of the United States. (Applause) Take my word for it men and women, we are in it for fair. (Applause) You know it is not the braggart, it is not the bully who is dependable. It is the man like the nation, patient and forebearing who avoids the contest or conflict but like the advice of Shakespeare in one of his characters: "Avoid conflict but once in it let thine enemy beware of thee."[11] So we are in it.

Mention has been made of Russia. No greater tragedy has ever been enacted than has been and is being enacted in Russia at the present time,[12] and it ought to be a warning to some of our friends in the United States and Canada. See what has happened to the great Russian people. I will go with any man or woman to obtain for labor and for the people the largest measure of return for labor performed and for freedom to be secured but I will not join with any one in so far over running our goal that we lose our venture.[13] (Applause) There are new thoughts, new concepts, and new duties as well as new responsibilities to be met. Don't for a moment imagine that after this war we are going back to the old conditions. There is a responsibility on the part of the employer as well as on the part of the worker. There is a responsibility on the part of the government as well as on the part of the masses of the people. New relations must be established and new understandings reached. Men and women who labor can no longer be disregarded by the powers that be. (Applause) For thousands of years the question has remained: Am I my brother's keeper? The labor movement of the time and the war has crystalized that thought. Yes, you are your brother's keeper, because unless you bear his burdens he will help tear you down. The misery of the world, the degradation of men and women and children will be obliterated; it is now practically obliterated from the concepts and activities of our lives and we must never return to the old conditions of misery, poverty and degradation. (Applause) There must come something out of this war that will compensate the people for the sacrifices that they are making.

I return to Russia because I want to sink into your minds and your hearts that there is no limit to the extent to which I will give my support to secure the best sort of conditions of life and labor for the toiling masses of the world, but I won't permit myself to occupy the position of fools rushing in where angels fear to tread. Under the pretence of securing everything that the human mind can conceive the Maximilists and Bolshevikis of Russia are betraying the people of Russia into the hands of the monster of modern times, the militarist and Imperialistic Government of Germany. Just think of it, the officers of the general staff of the Germans being counsellors and advisors of a pretended Government of Maximilists in Russia to secure a better life for the people of Russia! By God. I have been to Germany and I have seen conditions there and to pretend that there is any hope for the people of Russia while the German Militarist machine remains is preposterous, disgusting, a base fabrication and an intrigue to befool and befog the people of Russia. Imagine the great Russian people on their hands and knees crawling like vipers beseeching his Imperial Majesty for protection and the alleviation of their miserable conditions! I congratulate Britain, Canada, Australia and the United States upon this one fact: If Russia had a well regulated labor movement founded upon evolutionary progress and natural growth you would not find the Bolsheviki or the Maximilist. (Applause) And with all the intrigue of German diplomacy and German money if it had not been for the great trades union movement in Great Britain, Canada, Australia and the United States you would have found some of the German intrigue in all those countries as now represented by the Russian Maximilists.

This war is an indictment of the German Socialist philosophy. Where it has manifested itself at all it has broken down. It has broken down in Germany and it has proven treacherous to the people of the other countries. The Socialist party of America repudiated this war and condemned it just as if it had been made in America instead of in Germany. The Socialist Party broke down in Germany. They had neither the courage nor the understanding to take their stand against the war at the beginning of the struggle. Had they opposed it the sacrifice of ten, twenty, thirty or fifty thousand lives to the German master but a country which at the beginning was compelled to murder 50,000 of its citizens would not likely enter an international conflict. The German socialists failed there. They have been treacherous elsewhere. Some have said, "Why not enter upon a conference for the purpose of ending this war and bringing peace?" It is not everybody who understands this fact that to bring about peace now would install in the minds of the whole world now and ever afterwards that the Germans were the conquerors in this war. She has achieved some of the things which she started out to accomplish. She has crushed Serbia and Roumania; she has ravished and over ran Belgium; she has over ran a large part of France and don't you know that if Germany were to conquer both France and England, including Canada, she would take hold of the British and French navies as a prize for her conquest. Imagine then Germany in possession of two powerful navies in addition to her own! What hope could we have for the safety of Canadians and Americans then?

There can be no peace; not now. They have gone too far. Before we can think of peace much less espouse it the Germans must go back from Serbia; they must go back from Roumania, back from France and back from Belgium, back to their own territory, and then we can talk of peace. (Applause)

This meeting was called primarily as a gathering to impress upon the minds of those here and elsewhere the necessity and the duty of winning this war; by doing either one or the other of two things or both if possible. The men who can fight should give themselves voluntarily if they can. Don't wait for the draft. Volunteer! I have five nephews and seven cousins in the American army. One nephew[14] some months ago was shot and killed in Hayti in the service of the U.S. government. My grandson, nineteen years of age, named after myself, volunteered in the aviation service of the U.S. army. They won't let me fight and there are many men and women who would not be permitted to fight but who can help with money and it is your duty to make it safe for your boys at the front. At today's magnificent parade thousands and thousands of people stood on the sidewalks. I was elated when I looked upon the faces of women and children who were there. Someone by my side said, "Is it not sad to see them?" I said "No." There was no sadness in their faces. It was simply complacence or an acceptance of the situation as they found it and a determination to see this thing through no matter what the cost. Those of you who cannot fight can at least help in the fight by buying Victory Bonds. You are not giving the Government one cent and your investment gives you the best security that any investment in Canada or elsewhere can give you. The whole wealth and assets of this rich Dominion safeguards your investment. In addition you will have saved $50 or $100 or $500 which you would perhaps not have saved if you had not purchased Victory Bonds. If we should fail in this great conflict your fifty or anything else you might have would not be worth a snap of your fingers. If we failed the lights of freedom would go out for the whole world. After all what good would your fifty or hundred be if we lost? Coming over the Border at Niagara Falls we learned that men were near soliciting money for Victory Bonds and to show where my heart was I subscribed for a $50 bond. It was not much but I wanted to show where my sympathies lay. If that fifty goes to help on Victory it's yours with my compliments. And because of the fact that the Canadian labor movement and the American labor movement are one we decided it was our duty to see to it that we would show where our feelings lay and with pride and satisfaction we have invested $10,000 in Victory Bonds. (Applause) I have the pleasure of exhibiting to you now the documents and receipts of the transaction which was made today through Mr. H. H. Williams.[15] (Applause)

I know there has been an effort made, a very narrow and restricted effort, to divide the American and Canadian labor movement. I may say that it would be the gravest error, the biggest mistake in the world to undertake to bring about such a separation. A few weeks ago as a member of the council of National Defence in the United States we were holding a meeting for the purpose of considering the subject of industrial vocation and trade training. Among others a well known Canadian, Sir Charles Ross[16] appeared before our board. He was the owner of a large plant for the manufacture of arms as you know and I believe the Canadian government had taken that factory over. He stated this to the Council "I believe that it is to the best interests of Canadian workers and Canadian employes as well as those in the United States that there should be maintained the best possible international relations between the labor movements of both the Dominion and the republic."

He said further, "I am going upon a tour throughout the United States and Canada and wherever I go I intend to impress upon the minds of employers that it is the best thing for them as well as for the workers to have collective bargaining with the Union of labor. My experience has demonstrated this one fact, that I never got such good service from my employes, I never felt more reliance in their conduct and in their work than when I dealt with them as an entity in an organized capacity.["]

I came here after years of hard work culminating in the convention of the American Federation of Labor lasting two weeks with practically every moment taken up with responsibilities, hard work and great problems. I was asked to come to Toronto to say a word and I accepted the invitation with satisfaction. I came to bring you a message from the workers and the people of the United States to you the people of Canada, all her people with her wonderful past and her great future and my message to all the people of the world is this: Men and women let us be true to ourselves and true to each other. Let us do our whole duty to make it possible that the torch of freedom which has been kept alight for all those centuries in an hour of shame, but kept burning up and up, a flame illuminating the whole world now and for evermore (Prolonged Applause).

TDc, Files of the Office of the President, Speeches and Writings, reel 112, frames 799–813, *AFL Records.*

1. SG addressed this meeting, on behalf of a Canadian Victory Loan Bond drive, at the invitation of Ontario prime minister William Hearst, Toronto mayor Thomas Church, and officers of the Canadian labor movement.

2. Thomas Langton Church, the mayor of Toronto (1915–21), served as chairman of the meeting.

3. The passage, from *Hamlet,* act 5, scene 2, actually reads, "There's a divinity that shapes our ends, / Rough-hew them how we will."

4. See "An Address before the Fifty-fourth Annual Convention of the New York State Federation of Labor in Jamestown, N.Y.," Aug. 29, 1917, n. 2, above.

5. Karl Liebknecht (1871–1919), a German socialist and revolutionary, served as a representative in the Reichstag from 1912 to 1917. An outspoken critic of the war and German militarism, he voted against war credits in 1914 and was a founder of the revolutionary socialist Spartakusbund (Spartacus League) in early 1916 with Rosa Luxemburg. Later that year he was arrested, tried, and imprisoned for advocating the overthrow of the government and an end to the war at a May Day rally in Berlin. After his release from prison in October 1918, Liebknecht was a founder of the German Communist party. He was murdered in Berlin on Jan. 15, 1919, during the Spartacus Revolt.

6. Jacob D. Baum, an envoy from the Council of Workers' and Soldiers' Deputies in Petrograd, met with SG on Oct. 24 and 25, 1917, to discuss possible AFL backing for an international conference of workers and socialists. The AFL Executive Council rejected the proposal on Oct. 25, and SG sent a copy of the Council's decision to Secretary of State Robert Lansing the next day (reel 227, vol. 239, pp. 811–12, SG Letterbooks, DLC).

7. Douglas Haig (1861–1928) was commander-in-chief of the British Expeditionary Force in France (1915–19).

8. David Franklin Houston (1866–1940) served as secretary of agriculture from 1913 to 1920.

9. Count Johann Heinrich von Bernstorff (1862–1939) was German ambassador to the United States from 1908 to 1917.

10. James Watson Gerard (1867–1951), a New York City attorney, served as the U.S. ambassador to Germany from 1913 to 1917.

11. The passage, from *Hamlet,* act 1, scene 3, reads, "Beware / Of entrance to a quarrel, but being in, / Bear't that th'opposèd may beware of thee."

12. A reference to the October Revolution, that is, the overthrow of the Provisional Government in Russia by the Bolsheviks. Lenin issued a proclamation announcing the coup on the morning of Nov. 7 (Oct. 25, Old Style), 1917, after the Bolsheviks seized key transportation and communication points in Petrograd and occupied most of the government buildings. Prime Minister Aleksandr Kerensky left the city in an unsuccessful attempt to secure military support for his government, and the other ministers surrendered. The Bolshevik-dominated All-Russian Congress of Soviets confirmed the transfer of power on Nov. 8 (Oct. 26) and approved a Decree on Peace, appealing for an immediate armistice and a peace settlement without annexations or indemnities, a Decree on Land, calling for the transfer of non-agricultural landed property to peasant communes, and a Decree on the Press, authorizing the closing of newspapers opposed to the new government. Protest strikes among white collar workers in Petrograd and Moscow, of which the most serious were strikes at government fiscal institutions—the State Bank and the State Treasury—were suppressed by the Bolsheviks.

13. A conflation of two passages from Shakespeare, one from *King Henry the Eighth,* act 1, scene 1, which reads, "We may outrun / By violent swiftness that which we run at, / And lose by over-running," the other from *Julius Caesar,* act 4, scene 2, which reads, "We must take the current when it serves, / Or lose our ventures."

14. William Gompers.

15. H. H. Williams was the owner of a real estate and insurance firm in Toronto.

16. Sir Charles Ross (1872–1942), a Scottish-born armaments manufacturer in Canada, was the inventor of the Ross automatic rife, which was used by the Canadian army until 1917. He left the country in 1917 after his factory in Quebec was expropriated by the government, and he later served as an adviser to the U.S. War Department.

From John Fitzpatrick, Dennis Lane, and William Z. Foster

Chicago Ill [November 29, 1917]

Representatives of the international unions interested in the packing industry have exhausted all efforts to get conference with packers but without success Over sixty men discharged for joining our unions This has resulted in unanimous vote by representative of internationals to take strike vote at all points and in all trades in packing industry vote returnable in ten days[1] Similar wire to Secretary Morrison

John Fitzpatrick
Pres   Chgo Federation of Labor
Dennis Lane
Secy Treasurer   Amalgamated Meat Cutters and
Butcher Workmen
Wm Z Foster
Secy   Stockyards Labor Council[2]

TWSr, Files of the Office of the President, General Correspondence, reel 90, frame 293, *AFL Records*.

1. On July 15, 1917, the Chicago Federation of Labor (FOL) approved a resolution introduced by William Z. Foster and Dennis Lane authorizing an organizing campaign in the Chicago stockyards. A week later the Stockyards Labor Council (SLC)—a federation of the various trades working in the yards—was established under the direction of Foster and John Fitzpatrick to carry on the work. Organizing began in September, and in November representatives of the Amalgamated Meat Cutters and Butcher Workmen of North America met in Omaha and drew up a list of demands—including the right to organize, a wage increase, overtime pay, and an eight-hour day—which were endorsed by the other SLC member unions. The "Big Five" meatpacking companies refused to meet with union representatives or consider the demands, however, and packinghouse workers voted to authorize a strike.

To avert a shutdown, both Department of Labor Commissioner of Conciliation Frederick Feick and the President's Mediation Commission were sent to Chicago in an attempt to bring about a settlement, and on Christmas Day representatives of the Big Five and the unions signed an agreement prohibiting strikes and lockouts during the war. Disputes over wages, hours, and other matters were to be settled by negotiation or, if that failed, by binding arbitration. Negotiations between the employers and the packinghouse workers quickly broke down over union recognition, however, and federal arbitrator John Williams resigned. On Jan. 18, 1918, a committee of union leaders, accompanied by their attorney Frank Walsh, SG, Frank Morrison, Secretary of Labor William B. Wilson, and Secretary of War Newton Baker met with President Woodrow Wilson, who referred the matter back to the Mediation Commission. On Jan. 27 the two sides reached a further agreement, under which the employers promised not to discriminate against union members, the unions agreed that the settlement did not imply union recognition, and the questions of wages and hours were referred to a new arbitrator, Judge Samuel Alschuler. Alschuler held public hearings from Feb. 11 to Mar. 7 (SG testified on Feb. 28). The arbitrator's decision, issued on Mar. 30, awarded packinghouse workers an eight-hour day, overtime pay, and a wage increase.

2. In the absence of SG, who was away from the office from Nov. 8 to Dec. 3, 1917, in connection with the AFL convention and other matters, Marion Webster brought Fitzpatrick's telegram directly to the attention of the Department of Labor (Webster to Fitzpatrick, Nov. 30, 1917, reel 228, vol. 240, p. 651, SG Letterbooks, DLC). SG met with Fitzpatrick and other representatives of the Chicago and Illinois State FOLs and Department of Labor mediator Feick after returning to AFL headquarters.

To John Fitzpatrick

December 7, 1917.

Mr. John Fitzpatrick,
President, Chicago Federation of Labor,
166 West Washington St., Chicago, Illinois.
Dear Sir and Brother:

When international relations became extremely critical and before war was declared between this country and the imperial German government, Congress incorporated in the Naval Appropriations' Act, which became law March 4, 1917, the following clause:

"That in case of national emergency the President is authorized to suspend provisions of law prohibiting more than eight hours' labor in any one day of persons engaged upon work covered by contracts with the United States; Provided further, That the wages of persons employed upon such contracts shall be computed on a basic day rate of eight hours' work, with overtime rates to be paid for at not less than time and one-half for all hours worked in excess of eight hours."

In the Federal Eight-hour law of 1912 there was a clause authorizing the President to suspend the law in case of emergency, etc. However, that law did not authorize the time and one half for hours worked in excess of eight. You will see therefore, the significance of the proviso in the Naval Appropriations' Act. Congress thereby strengthened the government's position on the eight-hour principle by providing penalties for overtime. Whenever the President has found it necessary to suspend the eight-hour day in any departments he has invariably cited the proviso in the Naval Appropriations' Act as his authority, although he might have used the emergency provision of the federal law. This in turn demonstrates his adhesion to the eight-hour principle, as he has made it possible for workers to secure the time and one-half for overtime wherever the law has been suspended. These facts make plain the position of the President and Congress. The policies of the various departments which are chiefly concerned in war production are demonstrated by the following incidents:

1. The decision of the Secretary of the Navy in the Ansonia case.[1]

2. The decision of the Secretary of War upon the demand of the leather workers for the protection of the eight-hour workday.[2]

The Ansonia case is described in an editorial in the November, 1917, *American Federationist*, entitled, "Eight Hours Basic in Principle."[3] I am sending you a copy of the magazine containing the article. By extending the application of the eight-hour law to the contracts sublet to the Farrell Foundry and Machinery Company of Ansonia, Connecticut, by the Fore River Ship Building Company of Massachusetts, the Navy Department had made the eight-hour law follow government work even when sub-let.

As you probably know, the leather workers have for years tried to secure the application of the eight-hour law to government contracts on which they have worked. Their long struggle is recounted by W. E. Bryan[4] in the December, 1917, *American Federationist*.[5] Under the ruling of Secretary Baker the leather workers succeeded in establishing their contention that the leather goods they produced were not such as could be secured in the open market. However, the leather workers did not fail to emphasize that part of the eight-hour law which states, "that all classes of work which have been, are now, or may hereafter be performed by the government shall, when done by contract, by individuals, firms, or corporations for or on behalf of the United States or any Territories or the District of Columbia, be performed in accordance with the terms and provisions of section one of the act."

These cases illustrate conclusively the position of the government upon the eight-hour workday.

You will remember that in connection with the efforts of the railroad men to secure the eight-hour workday the President made the statement that society had indorsed the eight-hour principle. In addressing the Committee on Labor of the Council of National Defense on May 15, President Wilson made the following statement:

"I have been very much alarmed at one or two things that have happened: At the apparent inclination of the legislatures of one or two of our states to set aside even temporarily the laws which have safeguarded the standards of labor and of life. I think nothing would be more deplorable than that. We are trying to fight in a cause which means the lifting of the standards of life, and we can fight in that cause best by voluntary cooperation."

Then, as to the second part of your letter,[6] "relative to the preservation of the status quo by employers and unions during the war." By what seemed to be a sinister conspiracy of the press an effort was made to create the impression that I had declared there would be no strikes during the war and that the status quo in industry must be maintained. The following is the origin of that perversion:

You will remember that as soon as war was declared a certain class of employers began an agitation to sweep aside all protective labor legislation during the period of the war. They sought to create the impression that war production made it necessary to cut loose from all moorings and to start pell-mell into a breathless, feverish rush to fill war contracts. There seemed danger that a stampede might result. In order to check such an ill-considered policy and to silence unwise counselors the executive committee of the Committee on Labor of the Advisory Commission to the Council of National Defense drew up a declaration which was afterwards adopted by the Advisory Commission and the Council of National Defense. That declaration is contained in full in an article published in the July, 1917, *American Federationist* entitled, "The 'Drive' On Labor Standards."[7] I am sending you a copy of that magazine. The declaration was published in practically all of the papers of the land and misinterpreted editorially and through glaring headlines in an effort to create the impression that labor meant during war to fore-go strikes. There was absolutely no justification for that interpretation as I said through the press that we could not, and ought not to repress the natural, normal desires of the workers for a better life. What the declaration did state was that the workers would submit to no deterioration of standards of life and work and that there was no justification for the demand for the repeal of labor legislation. To correct this misinterpretation an amplification of the declaration was drawn up and adopted by the Council of National Defense. That declaration makes plain that insistence upon standards of life and work does not mean stagnation but that as costs of living increased it would be necessary to increase wages to enable workers to maintain existing standards.

I am sending you a copy of the declaration adopted by representative spokesmen for national and international organizations who met in Washington on March 12. That declaration contains the following statement:

"War has never put a stop to the necessity for struggle to establish and maintain industrial rights. Wage-earners in war times must, as has been said, keep one eye on the exploiters at home and the other upon the enemy threatening the national government. We maintain that it is the fundamental step in preparedness for the nation to set its own house in order and to establish at home justice in relations between men. Previous wars, for whatever purpose waged, developed new opportunities for exploiting wage-earners. Not only was there failure to recognize the necessity for protecting rights of workers that they might give that whole-hearted service to the country that can come only when every citizen enjoys rights, freedom and opportunity, but under guise of national necessity, Labor was stripped of its means of defense against enemies at home and was robbed of the advantages, the protections, the guarantees of justice that had been achieved after ages of struggle. For these reasons workers have felt that no matter what the result of war, as wage-earners they generally lost."

This entire declaration was approved by the Buffalo Convention.

In his address to the Buffalo Convention President Wilson made the following declaration:

"Now, to stand together means that nobody must interrupt the processes of our energy, *if the interruption can possibly be avoided without the absolute invasion of freedom.* To put it concretely, that means this: Nobody has a right to stop the processes of labor until all the methods of conciliation and settlement have been exhausted. And I might as well say right here that I am not talking to you alone. You sometimes stop the courses of labor, but there are others who do the same; and I believe that I am speaking from my own experience not only but from the experience of others when I say that you are reasonable in a larger number of cases than the capitalists. I am not saying these things to them personally yet, because I haven't had a chance, but they have to be said, not in any spirit of criticism, but in order to clear the atmosphere and come down to business. Everybody on both sides has now got to transact business, and a settlement is never impossible when both sides want to do the square and right thing."

Of course it is preposterous for anyone to believe, much less to state, that the workmen would forego the right to try and organize for their mutual and common protection during any stage of existence, and how anyone could gather the notion that I would make a statement that no effort will be made during the war to organize working people is almost too preposterous to answer. Life, aye, the very elements are naturally attracted toward each other, which is another way of saying they organize. No one thinking clearly can imagine that men with hearts and brains would not follow the natural instinct or intellectual aspiration for association, and organization. Of course the workers will organize, and they will aid very materially in the establishment of the newer concept of mutual rights and duties of the people generally, and a better understanding of the relations between workers and employers.

If there is any other information that I can place at your disposal to help you in arguing this case I shall be very glad to be of any assistance within my power. Do not fail to keep me in touch with the progress in the matter as I should like to know all developments in this most important undertaking.

Fraternally yours, Saml Gompers.
President, American Federation of Labor.

TLpS, reel 228, vol. 240, pp. 1026–29, SG Letterbooks, DLC.

1. The Department of the Navy had awarded contracts for a number of destroyers to the Fore River Ship Building Co., which subcontracted work on the engines for the ships to the Farrel Foundry and Machine Co. of Ansonia, Conn. Iron molders, who worked a nine-hour day at Farrel, claimed the engine work came under provisions of the 1912 eight-hour law and asked for time-and-a-half overtime pay, as stipulated by the 1917 Naval Appropriation Act. The Navy Department turned down this request, however, ruling that engines fell into the category of articles generally available on the open market, which were exempted from the provisions of the 1912 act. SG appealed the case to Secretary of the Navy Josephus Daniels on Aug. 25, 1917, and on Oct. 2 Daniels overturned the department's decision and ruled that the work came under the provisions of the eight-hour law.

2. The United Brotherhood of Leather Workers on Horse Goods had complained that contracts for harnesses and other saddlery were let by the Quartermaster General without regard to the 1912 eight-hour law, even though Ordnance Department contracts, often awarded to the same manufacturers, were governed by its provisions. After Acting Judge Advocate General Blanton Winship ruled that the law did not apply to the saddlery contracts because of the "open market" exemption, Leather Work-

ers' president William Bryan warned Secretary of War Newton Baker that Winship's ruling, which required men in the same shops to work under different conditions, would create serious disturbances and "inevitable disaster" (Bryan to Baker, July 25, 1917, quoted in Bryan, "The Eight-Hour Law," *American Federationist* 24 [Dec. 1917]: 1077–90; quotation at p. 1089). In early August Baker approved the time-and-a-half pay provision for work over eight hours a day in all new saddlery contracts; later in the month he ordered that stipulation inserted into all saddlery contracts with completion dates after Sept. 15.

3. *American Federationist* 24 (Nov. 1917): 994–95.

4. William E. BRYAN was president of the Leather Workers from 1910 to 1938.

5. The article "The Eight-Hour Law," cited in n. 2, above.

6. In his letter to SG of Dec. 4, 1917, relating to the ongoing negotiations in the meatpacking industry, John Fitzpatrick asked for information on the attitude of the government towards the eight-hour day in industries involved in war work and for any statements by SG or the AFL relating to the attitude of labor regarding strikes and wage changes during the war. Fitzpatrick concluded: "Mr. Armour notified us directly through his general superintendent Mr. Ahearn, that his understanding of these statements of yours is that you agreed that there would be no strikes during the war, and more than that, that the unions would make no efforts to organize employees in plants unorganized by the unions previous to the war. We take it for granted that he will present this interpretation as an argument. To combat it effectively it will be necessary that we be in possession of first hand information on the subject" (Files of the Office of the President, General Correspondence, reel 90, frames 371–72, *AFL Records;* quotation at frame 372).

7. *American Federationist* 24 (July 1917): 547–50.

A Statement by Samuel Gompers

Dec. 10, 1917.

It is indeed regrettable that the Supreme Court should have rendered the decision[1] it did in upholding the far reaching and unwarrantable injunction and decision issued and rendered by Judge Dayton[2] of the District of West Virginia. To hold that the United Mine Workers of America is an unlawful organization, or that it is a conspiracy is to hark back to the days when employers were monarchs of all they surveyed, and their employes were servants or slaves. The Miners Union undertook by perfectly lawful methods and means to reach the unorganized and underpaid miners of West Virginia, so that they might be treated as men and as citizens with responsibility of maintaining families upon an American standard.

In its petition the Hichman Coal and Coke Company did not have the temerity to claim that there was any violence or unlawful conduct on the part of the representatives of the union to organize the coal miners. No cognizance seems to have been taken of the fact that in the petition for the injunction the Hichman Company declared "that the Company would not allow any union and that no union man could remain in the employ of the company."

The scale of wages paid the miners in many of the mines of West Virginia is far below that prevailing in the entire competitive field, and the Hichman Company pays the lowest of them all, and yet in its petition the Company said that the Miners Union aimed to have that company "pay such scale of wages as said United Mine Workers of America arbitrarily" fixed.

The Hichman Company in its petition for injunction included portions of the Constitution of the United Mine Workers of America, and in every part of that constitution referring either to strikes or grievances or disputes, this provision runs through all that "when trouble of a local character arises between members of a local union and their employers, the officers of such local shall endeavor to effect an amicable adjustment," and failing in that it shall be referred to the officers of the general organization with the direction to endeavor to bring about an honorable and amicable adjustment. In other words, the officers of the United Mine Workers of America are not empowered with calling or ordering a strike but are directed to avoid one and endeavor by every honorable means to bring about more amicable relations.

When the Clayton Law was enacted, a fact was declared not merely for future guidance of the courts, but one founded upon the fundamental principle, "That the labor of a human being is not a commodity or article of commerce." The declaration of that principle should certainly have had some weight with the court in determining whether a voluntary association of workers organized not for profit, but for their personal protection, should not have been held as a conspiracy in its relations with a corporation or company which assumed a sort of proprietary right in the labor of workers as if that labor and labor power were a commodity or article of commerce.

At the time when the injunction was issued John Mitchell was President and William B. Wilson Secretary-Treasurer of the United Mine Workers of America. The former is now the Food Administrator of the State of New York. The latter is a member of the President's Cabinet. And these men with others of equal standing and character are stigmatized by the court as conspirators. Terms of opprobrium uttered, no matter by whom, will not deter right thinking men from looking with favor upon the unselfish, humane, and patriotic work performed by the organized workers of America.

President Wilson has justly declared that society has given its sanction that the eight hour workday is justified. It is to bring light and hope and patriotism into the life of the workers for which we are organized and are organizing and federating the toilers of America, and we shall go on to reach our goal for a better concept of not only political but industrial democracy.

TD, Files of the Office of the President, Speeches and Writings, reel 112, frames 816–17, *AFL Records.*

1. On Dec. 10, 1917, the U.S. Supreme Court issued a decision in a case involving the Hitchman Coal and Coke Co., a West Virginia mining concern. The company functioned as a union shop from 1903 to 1906 and then, after a strike in the spring of 1906, began operating as an open shop, requiring employees to agree, as a condition of employment, that they would not become members of the United Mine Workers of America. In 1907, after the union began organizing Hitchman miners, the firm secured a restraining order from Judge Alston Dayton to stop such activity. Dayton subsequently granted a temporary injunction against the union in 1908 and a permanent injunction in 1912 on the grounds that it was attempting to induce Hitchman employees to break their labor contracts (*Hitchman Coal and Coke Co.* v. *Mitchell et al.,* 202 F. 512 [1912]). In his 1912 decision Dayton took the opportunity to condemn the union as an unlawful conspiracy to create a monopoly in labor. The injunction was overturned on appeal in 1914 (*Mitchell et al.* v. *Hitchman Coal and Coke Co.,* 214 F. 685 [1914]) but was reinstated with minor changes by the Supreme Court (*Hitchman Coal and Coke Co.* v. *Mitchell et al.,* 245 U.S. 229 [1917]).

2. Alston Gordon Dayton (1857–1920) of Philippi, W.Va., a former Republican congressman from West Virginia (1895–1905), served as a judge in the U.S. District Court for the Northern District of West Virginia from 1905 until his death.

To Woodrow Wilson

Washington, D.C. Dec. 11, 1917.

Honorable Woodrow Wilson,
President of the United States,
Washington, D.C.
Sir:

I am in receipt of authentic information that a most serious and far reaching suspension of coal mining operations is imminent in the State of Alabama.[1] Some two weeks ago Dr. H. A. Garfield,[2] of the United States Fuel Administration,[3] invited representatives of the United Mine Workers and the Alabama Coal Operators to Washington for conference, and urged that all differences be submitted to arbitration with a representative of the Fuel Administration as umpire. To this request the Mine Workers agreed unqualifiedly. The operators asked time to return home for consultation with their associates which was granted and Dr. Garfield fixed Thursday, December 6 as the date for both parties to again meet in Washington.

The Miners' delegation were present on that date and are still waiting, but the Operators have not yet appeared. The latest telegram from their spokesman[4] in reply to a direct telegram from Dr. Garfield sent on Saturday last to be here today, advises he is to be in this city on December 12 on other business and may be consulted at that time.

The Miners of Alabama, feeling further delay intolerable, are on the verge of inaugurating an immediate suspension of mining, thereby curtailing a daily production of 175,000 tons of coal and are already vested with full authority to do so by the International Executive Board of the United Mine Workers of America.

It seemed to me to be my duty to call this critical situation to your attention for such consideration and action which you may deem most wise in the premises. Mr. McCormack, President of the Alabama Mine Operators' Association, is to be in Washington tomorrow, December 12, and Dr. Garfield will be in communication with him.

> Very respectfully yours,   Saml Gompers.
> President,   American Federation of Labor.[5]

TLS, Woodrow Wilson Papers, DLC.

1. In the summer of 1917, representatives of United Mine Workers of America District 20 (Alabama) drew up a list of demands that included union recognition, reinstatement of workers discharged for union membership, an eight-hour day, and a new pay scale, and they set Aug. 20 for a strike if those terms were not met. Although the operators refused to recognize the union or reinstate miners fired for union membership, Secretary of Labor William B. Wilson persuaded the miners to postpone the strike pending mediation. After protracted negotiations, including a three-day conference in December, U.S. Fuel Administrator Harry Garfield proposed an agreement on Dec. 14 that called for recognition of the miners' right to organize, reemployment of discharged union men, formation of grievance committees, use of checkweighmen selected and paid by the miners, and semimonthly pay days. In addition, the agreement urged the implementation of the eight-hour day and postponed the establishment of a new wage scale until July 1, 1918. A special convention of District 20 accepted Garfield's proposal on Dec. 21, and the mine operators agreed to it on Jan. 23, 1918.

2. Harry Augustus Garfield (1863–1942), the president of Williams College in Williamstown, Mass. (1908–34), served as U.S. Fuel Administrator from 1917 to 1919.

3. The U.S. Fuel Administration was created by executive order under authority of the Lever Food and Fuel Act on Aug. 23, 1917, to regulate the production, distribution, and price of coal, coke, natural gas, and petroleum fuel products.

4. George Bryant McCormack of Birmingham, Ala., president of the Pratt Consolidated Coal Co. and of the Alabama Coal Operators' Association.

5. After receiving SG's letter, President Woodrow Wilson contacted Garfield to offer his help. When the mine operators subsequently refused to accept the terms of a settlement negotiated by Garfield, Wilson facilitated a resolution of the matter by warning Alabama senator John Bankhead, whose son was a negotiator for the Alabama Coal Operators' Association, that the government would take over the mines if the owners did not come to an agreement with the miners (Wilson to Bankhead, Jan. 11, 1918, Arthur S. Link et al., eds., *The Papers of Woodrow Wilson*, 69 vols. [Princeton, N.J., 1966–94], 45: 568).

To Woodrow Wilson

35th and Ordway Streets[1]
Washington, D.C., December 14, 1917.

Hon. Woodrow Wilson,
President of the United States.
Sir:

On one occasion I took the liberty of addressing you upon a subject which was then imminent but which is now assuming proportions so threatening and so dangerous that I feel it an incumbent duty upon me, as a man and a citizen, to bring to your attention a thought upon the pending Joint Resolution[2] now before the House of Representatives, being a proposed amendment to the Constitution of the United States, commonly known as the nation-wide prohibition amendment.

Did I for a moment feel that the subject matter were of but passing or momentary interest, or that it did not involve grave injury and dangers, I should hesitate long before asking your consideration of what I hope to present to you; but, because I am so apprehensive of the consequences to our people, our country and the tremendous enterprise in which we are engaged, I feel it incumbent upon me to trespass upon your time so that you might in your own way use your good judgment and great powers to avert what I am fully convinced would be the greatest cause of dissension and discontent among our people, if the pending prohibition constitutional amendment were passed by Congress and submitted for ratification.

The Congress has passed, and you have approved, the law prohibiting the manufacture of spirituous liquors (whiskey, etc.) during the period of the war.[3] Existing law places within your power the modification, limitation and, if necessary, the prohibition of the manufacture of beers and light wines. You have already exercised that power in part, and whenever or wherever it shall appear to you that either of these powers conferred upon you shall be necessary to be exercised, no one whom I know will find the slightest cause of dissent or disapproval.

The advocates of the proposed prohibition amendment have disingenuously declared that the amendment is necessary as a war measure. How fraudulent is this pretense is best understood when it is known that the amendment cannot become effective until after the Legislatures of three-fourths of the States shall have ratified it, and, as is known, it is hoped that the war will have been successfully fought and won and come to an end long before the proposed constitutional amendment could come into operation.

But in the meantime, that is, between the time of the passage of the amendment by Congress (if it should pass) and until its ratification or defeat, covering a period of from six to seven years, and during the time when it is most essential that there shall be unity of spirit and action among the people of our country, the apple of discord will be thrown among them and the minds of the people will be diverted from the essential subject of winning the war to a proposition which can only become operative after the war has been concluded.

Beer is the general beverage of the masses of the people of our country. Light wines are used among large groups of our people. Many of them have acquired the habit by heritage of centuries and generations. The workers—the masses—no more than others in their indulgence in beers or light wines have found them a healthful part of their daily diet, particularly with their meals. With the cosmopolitan character of a large mass of our people, their divers habits and customs, I submit that it is neither wise, practical nor beneficial to divide them into opposite camps upon a non-essential to the winning of the war, when its effectiveness—even if it is advantageous—could only become operative after the war is closed.

In the countries of our Allies liquors—spirits, beer and light wines— are under control and regulation. Not one of our Allies has attempted either during the war or proposed thereafter to prohibit their manufacture or sale. Indeed, the regulations provide as part of the rations to the fighting men some portion of beers or light wines, and in some instances a limited quantity of spirituous liquors.

Upon the proposed constitutional amendment neither the Senate Committee nor the Committee of the House of Representatives having this proposed constitutional amendment under consideration has given one moment of time for the purpose of hearing those who are vitally interested in this question. Requests for hearings of those vitally and primarily interested have been disregarded, ignored and denied.

Hundreds of thousands—aye, perhaps more than two millions of wage earners would be affected and thrown out of employment were nation-wide prohibition forced upon our people. It is not difficult to understand how disaffected would they become during the war when the question would be forced upon their attention that, at some particular time after the war, they would be thrown into a state of unemployment and be bereft of the opportunity of maintaining themselves and their dependents.

Of course you know that the States which have elected to have prohibition within their borders are secured their full right and protection thereunder by State and Federal law, and the Supreme Court of the

United States has recently guaranteed and strengthened that protection.[4] The States, however, which elect and prefer not to avail themselves of that course should not, I submit, be coerced into becoming prohibition territory against their will.

My life has been thrown among the masses of our people. Whatever other characteristic has been developed in me from that mingling with them, I am vain enough to believe that I understand men; and in addition to and quite apart from the direct injury which this proposed prohibition amendment would inflict upon the workers primarily involved, I am constrained to say that the turmoil and dissension which are sure to be generated in the minds of our people as the result of this prohibition proposition causes me great mental and conscious disturbance.

Of course I am conscious of the delicate position in which you are placed in this matter, but the projectors of this scheme of prohibition are neither wise, practical nor patriotic. They are eaten up with egotism and fanaticism. Their project is not calculated to unite our people. They interject a subject calculated to divide and to cause dissension by advocating a measure which could only become operative after the war.

And it is because of the threatened danger which is involved in the entire scheme that I appeal to you as my leader, in common with the leadership of all our people in the great cause of justice, freedom and Democracy, to interpose whatever influence and power you can exert that this imminent danger shall be averted.

Respectfully,   Samuel Gompers.[5]

TLS, Woodrow Wilson Papers, DLC.

1. SG's home address.

2. S.J. Res. 17 (65th Cong., 1st sess.), proposing a Constitutional amendment to prohibit the manufacture, sale, or transportation of intoxicating liquors in the United States and to ban their importation or exportation, was introduced by Democratic senator Morris Sheppard of Texas on Apr. 4, 1917. Approved by the Senate on Aug. 1 and by the House of Representatives on Dec. 17, it completed the ratification process in January 1919 to become the Eighteenth Amendment.

3. The Lever Act.

4. Probably a reference to the U.S. Supreme Court's decision in *Crane* v. *Campbell* (245 U.S. 304 [1917]), handed down on Dec. 10, 1917, which unanimously upheld prohibition legislation enacted by the state of Idaho.

5. President Woodrow Wilson directed Joseph Tumulty to acknowledge SG's letter and say that he appreciated "the very great weight of the arguments" (Wilson to Tumulty, n.d., Wilson Papers, DLC).

From William Appleton[1]

Chief Office
The General Federation of Trade Unions.
London, W.C. 14th December, 1917.

Dear Friend Gompers,

I am sending you some copies of the December "Federationist" which contains an account of my last visit to France.[2] During my visit I met a Mr. J. Smith of Boston, who was securing information in order that he might return to America and lecture. He was a most interesting companion, and I promised that I would write to you in the hope that when he was able to go to Washington, you would see him and obtain from him first hand impressions, not only of France and the war, but of some of the things we discussed while together.

You, of course, will understand that in an article such as the one I have written for the "Federationist," it is impossible to describe everything one saw, or to mention names of places and persons. The Russian soldier to whom reference is made was General Ghurko,[3] whose family have been famous Russian cavalry commanders for three generations. He is an exceedingly able man and was interested to find what to him appeared to be a new type of labour man. The types he had met in his own country had evidently not impressed him, but when he found that I had a record of work, not only for the Labour movement but for the State behind me and that I was not at all affected by shibboleths or commonly repeated phrases, he became very cordial indeed, and discussed with me quite openly many of Russia's problems. He expressed the intention of going to America, though he did not indicate any particular time, and I suggested that if he came your way, he should take the opportunity of going to you and talking to you quite as frankly as he had talked to me.

You will quite understand our sorrow over the turn events have taken in Russia, and much regret that defections in one Italian division has led to such a disaster[4] as the Italians have suffered. Some weeks before the debacle, one of my Italian friends wrote me and told me of the intensity of the German propaganda and of his own fears.

In spite of all the defections, most of which are due to ignorance, we are hoping at least to hold the enemy until America can add her full weight. You can hardly realise, my friend, what the incoming of America has meant to those of us who think seriously. Her incoming has relaxed financial strains, it has increased morales, particularly in France, and it has given us confidence in future settlements that we should hardly have felt had the statesmanlike qualities of President

Wilson been against us or merely neutral. One can feel people everywhere responding to the standards he has set, and one constantly hears expressions of thankfulness that President Wilson's brains and character are on the side of the Allies.

During the dark days that have followed the troubles in Russia and Italy, it has been common to hear ordinary folk saying,—"Ah well, whatever happens, the Americans are not quitters. They'll stick, like us, to the end." You will be interested to know that when the accounts came of the reverse at Cambrai,[5] and it was known that the American train men and engineers had taken up arms and died alongside the British, everybody seemed to take this quite as a matter of course. The greatest eulogy that could be passed upon the men found its expression in this quiet confidence. I have heard quite a lot of good little stories about the men, but stories lose in value when they have to be written, and so I must wait until one of two things happen,—either you come to London, or I go to Washington.

Things are not going altogether satisfactorily in the labour movement here. Ambitions and jealousies are rampant. The new constitution[6] of the Labour Party which Mr. Henderson[7] is rushing through at top speed, will leave the old Trade Union movement helpless. It will become the milch cow of the Party and very little else. The new constitution opens the door to the so-called intellectual, whether he is a prig or a person of common sense, and I look forward with much misgiving to the future of the movement. The Parliamentary Committee of the Trade Union Congress is coalescing with the Labour Party without, I think, realising what the ultimate result of coalition will be. You will remember the story of the lady who rode out on the back of the tiger, but came back inside him. I think this will be another such case.

In the meantime, both the Parliamentary Committee and the Labour Party Executive are doing their best to smash the Federation because they very foolishly and very erroneously think it in their way. The great crime of the Federation is that it has thought quicker, acted quicker, and made fewer mistakes in interpreting the changing situation than has either of the other two bodies. It is also non-political, and is held by the extreme wing of the Labour Party to be out of date. The surprising thing is that in spite of all the hostility and criticism, the Federation is the one organization which is accomplishing things.

We have just, by tact and pertinacity, succeeded in doubling the ordinary soldiers' pay and allowances. Quietly, and without anybody knowing outside our own office, we have secured an enquiry into certain practices in Hong Kong, and we have continued, in spite of attempts to thwart our efforts, to try and steady labour opinion in those allied and neutral countries where the labour movements belong to the International Secretariat.

There are many things, my friend, that you want to know and I would like to tell you. There are many times when I feel the need of advice and counsel such as your wisdom and experience can give, and I shall be glad to hear from you if I cannot see you.

The Committee ask me to say how much they and those whom they represent, value the action of America in coming into the war. It has justified the action that Britain took when Germany determined to pass through Belgium on her projected trip to Paris.

Kindest regards to yourself, to Duncan, Perkins, Golden,[8] Lord and all the other fellows whose ability and comradeship have been helpful to me on various occasions.

Yours faithfully,   W A Appleton

TLS, Files of the Office of the President, General Correspondence, reel 90, frames 639–41, *AFL Records.*

1. William Archibald APPLETON was secretary of the General Federation of Trade Unions (1907–38).

2. "A Visit to France" appeared in the December 1917 issue of the *Federationist,* the official organ of the General Federation of Trade Unions.

3. Vasily Iosifovich Gurko (1864–1937) served as Russian chief of staff (1916–17) before being demoted and then exiled because of his opposition to the Provisional Government.

4. A reference to the Italian defeat at Caporetto (Oct. 24–Nov. 7, 1917). The Italians were forced to retreat some eighty miles, and the combined German-Austrian army took more than 300,000 prisoners.

5. The battle of Cambrai (Nov. 20–Dec. 5, 1917) ended in a draw, with initial British gains offset by German counterattacks. It marked the first significant use of tanks in combat.

6. In September 1917 the national executive of the Labour party authorized Arthur Henderson to write a new party constitution. After the national executive approved Henderson's draft, the document was considered by the party conference at Nottingham in January 1918 and was adopted, with minor changes, by a subsequent conference in February. The new constitution transformed the Labour party from a loose federation of affiliated organizations into a nationally organized and controlled entity, with local branches in every constituency. It provided for individual memberships, revised the election process for the national executive, and called for the common ownership of the means of production, the popular administration of industry, and the political, social, and economic emancipation of the people.

7. Arthur HENDERSON was honorary president of the Friendly Society of Iron Founders (from 1920, the National Union of Foundry Workers) from 1913 to 1935 and general secretary of the Labour party from 1912 to 1934. He served as a Labour member of Parliament, with brief interruptions, from 1903 to 1935.

8. John GOLDEN was president (1904–21) of the United Textile Workers of America and editor (1915–21) of its official journal.

From John Walker

At Seattle, Washington, December 14, 1917.

Dear Sir and Brother:

Since wiring[1] you this morning Colonel Disque had a conference with the Commission[2] and it has developed that on the 6th of November, yourself and Secretary Frank Morrison, Lewis Post, representing the Department of Labor and representatives of the War Department, along with Colonel Disque entered into an agreement[3] covering this situation out here, and that as a result of it, Colonel Disque since then, has been working on the proposition.

Although because of the labor situation here and other red tape and administrative matters, he has been unable to make very much progress. He says that they are getting less than 40% of the output that should be gotten to meet their needs and that can be gotten under anything like the right conditions; and when added to his other troubles, he thought that this Commission was butting in without authority. You can imagine his state of mind; at the same time, you can understand how we felt when we thought that he was butting in without authority, or at least, taking advantage of indirect and partial recognition in the matter to take hold of it entirely.

I regret exceedingly, that this state of affairs has developed. I am finding no fault with what the conference done in Washington at the time that they acted, the need was immediate and vital, and it may have been the best possible thing to do under the circumstances, but it does seem to me that this Commission should have received a copy of that agreement prior to this time, and that we should not, under those circumstances, have been asked to undertake the investigation and adjustment of this situation, and above all, it seems almost a crime for us to have had an agreement establishing the eight hour work day for somewhere in the neighborhood of sixty thousand men (because it was agreed to as stated in my telegram to you, formalities were all that were necessary to conclude it; we had a copy of the proposition they were to adopt; had changed it to meet our views; it was agreed it would go through without any hitch, and we agreed to go through with our part of it; the only thing required of us was that we would recommend to the president that an Executive order be issued requiring all timber and lumber manufactured for the government, to be manufactured on an eight hour day basis.)

And to see that thing upset and the old ten, eleven and twelve hour workday obtain, with not alone what that means to the men involved in the industry, who are doing the work, and the injury that that condition continuing, means to the labor movement, but it means that we are not going to be able to get the needed timber for war supplies, air craft, ships, etc., and the enemies of our government and the labor movement are going to be able to take advantage of the present situation and without question they will too, to more effectively than ever prevent prosecution of the war as it should be prosecuted and as it could be prosecuted. To prevent the getting of needed timber which the Colonel himself said this morning, would mean unnecessary possible prolongation of the war for a year or possibly two, with a cost of possibly millions of lives, and it will also enable them to still further make statements that will discredit and weaken the labor movement here, and strengthen and give prestige to the dual seditious and traitorous organization, the I.W.W.

I have not had a great deal of experience as a diplomat Sam, and this sort of thing makes me feel like *Hell;*—neither am I a quitter, and I do sincerely want, regardless of how it may affect me at all personally, to give all that is in me in every way possible to our country, and the cause of humanity in this crisis,—and, if my staying on in the work of this Commission is going to be more helpful than I can be in Illinois, with the work in that state that there is to do, I want to stay on, but as I see it, unless there is something that I cannot see now, I am rather under the impression that I would be able to do more effective work attending to the regular duties of the president of the Illinois State Federation of Labor than I can in this capacity, and I know that so far as my feelings are concerned, I would much rather do so.

This has been the rottenest experience I have ever had in all my life.[4]

With best wishes I am,

Fraternally yours,   J H Walker
President.   Illinois State Federation of Labor

TLS, Files of the Office of the President, General Correspondence, reel 90, frames 668–71, *AFL Records.*

1. John Walker to SG, Dec. 14, 1917, Files of the Office of the President, General Correspondence, reel 90, frames 665–67, *AFL Records.*

2. The President's Mediation Commission.

3. Walker is referring to the agreement drawn up at a conference at AFL headquarters on Nov. 5, 1917, attended by SG, Frank Morrison, and M. Grant Hamilton for the AFL and Louis Post, Col. Brice Disque, and Maj. Frederick Leadbetter for the Department of Labor and the War Department. The agreement, summarized in a memorandum from Post to Secretary of War Newton Baker on Nov. 6, provided that soldiers could be used for lumbering work in Oregon and Washington to supply the spruce needed for airplane production, that they were to be paid civilian wages, and that they could be employed whenever the requisite number of civilian workers was

unavailable, including times when labor disputes impeded production. The army subsequently created the Spruce Production Division to work in the lumber camps.

4. On Dec. 18, 1917, SG wired Walker in reply: "Absence from the city has prevented earlier reply to your telegram of December fourteenth. I have conferred with the office of the Secretary of War regarding your telegram. I am assured that neither the Department of Labor nor the War Department has taken any action in the matter, both recognizing the fact that Secretary Wilson's Commission ought not to be vexed and troubled by conflicting opinions and orders from Washington during their negotiations" (reel 229, vol. 241, p. 362, SG Letterbooks, DLC).

A Memorandum Dictated by Samuel Gompers

Washington, D.C., December 22, 1917

Some time ago I received a letter[1] from President Perkins of the Cigarmakers' International Union in regard to a confidential piece of information that had come to him regarding the statement made by one of the confidential agents of the Department of Justice regarding the prosecution of the I.W.W.'s in their alleged treasonable conduct toward the government in which it was shown that there was confusion on the part of Mr. Clabaugh of the Department of Justice connecting bona fide unions with the I.W.W. and that Claybaugh asserted that in many instances our prominent trade unionists were members of the I.W.W.

About that same time I received a letter[2] from John Fitzpatrick of Chicago making the same statement and then submitting a copy of a letter[3] addressed to him, Fitzpatrick, under date of October 6 in which Nelson obtained the information as the representative of the Department of Labor of the state of Illinois, and it was not known by Mr. Clabaugh that Mr. Nelson was a trade unionist. The same charge was made in that. Then also a copy of the weekly news letter of the Illinois State Federation of Labor in which the same state of affairs; also copy of a letter sent by a member of the Illinois labor movement to the President in which the situation was presented.

When this matter came to me I had an interview with the Attorney General Mr. Gregory.[4] I wanted to know what information there was in the Department in which that connection or confusion was contained. I insisted that no injustice be done to any man; that no malicious prosecution or persecution should be conducted by the government; that I was opposed to the I.W.W., their tenets, their purposes, and their methods but so long as they were conducting their affairs without being engaged in treasonable conduct they were entitled to as much consideration as any other body. He assured me that there was no such intention on the part of the Department and that great care would be exercised in differentiating the bona fide and normal activities of workers to organize and the evidence that the Department has against the I.W.W. was overwhelming as being treasonable, treacherous to a very marked degree. He said he would give me every opportunity of learning for myself as to the connection between the I.W.W. and active or prominent men in the trade union movement, and that he would let me go through the documents that he had.

Of course, I told him there was no opportunity for me to do that or to have any one else do it. He then said he had cards of membership of the I.W.W.

Yesterday December 21 he called me up over the telephone and asked me to come to see him. I saw him at 1:45 just preceding his going to the cabinet meeting. He assured me that in the prosecution of the I.W.W. and any of them it is not intended at all to be an attack directly or indirectly upon organized labor but the prosecutions against these men is for treasonable conduct toward the government of the U.S. I said that if the prosecution is to go ahead that it was my judgment that the government's attorneys should emphasize that fact; otherwise, it would be likely to be misconstrued or misinterpreted.

He told me that he had card of member in various offices, the cards containing the names and addresses of the men and stated that he would send me either the originals or copies[5] of the originals cards of these names and addresses.

TD, Files of the Office of the President, General Correspondence, reel 90, frames 878–79, *AFL Records*. Typed notation: "Dictated by President Gompers to Miss Guard." Handwritten notation: "These cards are in Mr. Gompers' safe. A large box of documents from Dept of Justice bearing on this case is in basement of Bldg. addressed to Mr. Gompers."

1. "From George Perkins," Oct. 12, 1917, above.

2. John Fitzpatrick to SG, Oct. 10, 1917, Files of the Office of the President, General Correspondence, reel 89, frame 56, *AFL Records*.

3. Oscar Nelson to Fitzpatrick, Oct. 6, 1917, Files of the Office of the President, General Correspondence, reel 89, frames 58–59, *AFL Records*.

4. SG discussed the matter with Attorney General Thomas Gregory on Oct. 17, 1917.

5. Gregory directed Bruce Bielaski, head of the Bureau of Investigation of the Department of Justice, to furnish duplicate copies of the cards to SG (Dec. 21, 1917, RG 60, General Records of the Department of Justice, DNA).

From Clair Covert[1]

Hoquiam, Wash. Dec. 28th, 1917.

Dear Sir & Bro.:—

Relative to the labor unrest in the Lumber industry of the north west; Much has been done by employers, labor leaders, individuals and government representatives to overcome the difficulty and restore the industry to it's normal production, and in many cases it appears that the different factors have worked at cross purposes with one another; Resulting in noneffectiveness.

Secretary Wilson's commission seemingly would have obtained results had it not been for other agencies working, and especially the plan proposed by Colonel Disque of the U.S. Signal Corps which was being put into operation at the time Secy. Wilson's commission was in session investigating the lumber situation.

This Col. Disque scheme will very likely prove to be a failure and will only act as a subterfuge for the lumbermen to get around puting the 8 hours into affect, as it for the most part does not meet with the approval of the men; And too they are appearently missuseing the original plan of leting men voluntaryly sign the pledge to work faithfully and steadily every day they were able, and are now practically forcing all to sign, consequently the effect has failed, for it now comes as the fullfilling of a law and will influence the men just so far as they are unable to evade the law; Every kind of character, anarchist, I.W.W. and all, have freely signed the pledge just because of the position taken against those who refused to sign; Consequently the obligation has very little affect; It has about as much affect on the men as an injunction order from the court. no regard for it[2]

You no doubt have the full text of the Col. Disque plan which is known as the "Loyal Legion of Loggers and Lumbermen" which in it's orignality proposed to have the men sign a pledge to work as steadily as they were able; And they received a badge and membership card; obligation as follows,—This is to certify that —— has become a member of the Loyal Legion of Loggers and Lumbermen for the duration of the war by taking oath to devote his efforts to the production of logs and lumber for army airoplanes and ships, to be used against our common enemy and to do every act and thing within his power to farther the cause of the United States of America in the present conflict. Signed by authority of secretary of war, N. E. Crumpacker[3] first Lutenant of Signal Corpse U.S. Army.

Col. Disque has now arranged to supply soldiers to any employer who professes to be short handed, the buletin of which I am inclosing on cliping, which explains its'self. You will note that from one to four soldiers in each detachment who are required for military reasons, who will draw no pay from the logging company; What does this mean? Is it a fixed plan to suppress all efforts of the Union to organize the men in this industry.

The man detailed, who organized the Legion in the mills of Hoquiam called the men together on the companys time and gave them a lengthy talk on the organization and it's purpose, and during his remarks he spoke against the eight hour day and reflected his opposition to Unions. It appears there is a strong co-operation between these Disque men and the employers, and the men are very suspicious of the whole thing and term it only an employers game under the veil of government supervision, the result will be reversed to what it was origionally planed for; Much discontent will prevail because of it.

The fact is that normal production will not be restored until the eight hours are granted, for thousands of skilled lumber-men and loggers are working at other callings and trades where the eight hours obtain and will not return to ten and twelve hour days. There are skilled loggers working in the ship yards for $3.25 per day and there are common laborers in the woods trying to fall timber, and are in many cases breaking it and otherwise distroying it because of their inability; Now if these men could be changed around it would not particularly hamper the ship building and would speed up the logging. The standard wages for timber fallers are now $5.00 per day so you can see that a man is determined who will work for the $3.25; This is also true to a large extent in the mills, and in fact throughout the industry; There are sufficient numbers of men here if they were at work and were in their proper places.

But there is very little extra labor and as we know men who work those excessive long hours can not work continually the year around, and when they are worn out, there is no one to take their places; Now if we had the eight hours they would be able to work the year around.

However just now owing to the slack season there is considerable extra labor, but within six weeks the descremination against the long hour shops will be something appalling and will actually be dangerous to the wellfare of the government, and it is a shame that these lumber "Kaisers" are alowed to continue to require an impossiability of the men.

The employers are evidently going to contend that the Loyalty Legion is geting the results and continue to protest against the eight hours; It is true just now when labor is so pleantiful that they are geting better results and they are pleased to give the Legion credit for it; Men always work steadily just before the holidays.

The Timberworkers would be glad to have any advice from you in connection with this subject, at any time, for it seems that our very best will have to be applied if we maintain our organization, and if this Disque plan is going to prevent organization work it will be the trial of our lives.

Hoping this finds every thing going well at headquarters.

With best wishes.

Fratternally Yours,   C. Covert

Organizer

TLS, Files of the Office of the President, General Correspondence, reel 91, frames 29–30, *AFL Records.*

1. Clair Covert was president of the International Union of Timber Workers (1918–21) and an AFL salaried organizer (1917–21).

2. This phrase is handwritten in the margin.

3. Maurice Edgar Crumpacker (1886–1927), a Portland, Oreg., attorney, was a first lieutenant—later promoted to captain—in the aviation section of the Signal Reserve Corps and assisted Col. Brice Disque in organizing the Loyal Legion of Loggers and Lumbermen. He later served as a Republican congressman from Oregon (1925–27).

From Eva Gordy

Globe, Ariz., Dec. 29, 1917.

Ladies Auxiliary Globe Miners Union ask relief. Husbands and brothers forced to leave here daily. Twelve hundred men Globe Miami District refused employment. Men brought in from Colorado in violation of the Labor Commission's ruling.

Mrs. Eva Gordy,   Sec'y.[1]

TWtpSr, reel 229, vol. 241, p. 817, SG Letterbooks, DLC. Enclosed in SG to William B. Wilson, Dec. 31, 1917, ibid., pp. 810–11.

1. SG forwarded Eva Gordy's letter to William B. Wilson on Dec. 31, 1917, together with a number of other documents relating to the situation in Arizona (reel 229, vol. 241, pp. 810–22, SG Letterbooks, DLC).

From Emmet Flood

Chicago, January 2nd, 1918.

My Dear Sam:—

Enclosed please find clipping in reference to Frank P. Walsh being here in reference to the stockyards controversy.

There is a great deal of mystery about just what the President's Commission did do in reference to the stockyards matter. Up until today everybody who represented the stockyards workers council and who met with the commission had a different story to tell.

As late as last Saturday, Secretary-Treasurer Lane, was very well pleased because the proposition the packers had presented to the Commission had been turned down by the Commission and the one presented by the stockyards workers council had been accepted and was going to be the agreement which would govern the working condition and wages to be paid by the employers in the stockyards all over the country during the war. I tried to convince Lane, he was mistaken; and that both sides had presented a sort of a proposition that they were willing to concede to; and that these would be presented to the Arbitrator, Mr. Williams[1] and that he would finally reach a decision. However, I could not convince Lane or did I try very hard to my way of thinking.

I understand that Foster the Secty. of the stockyards workers council is of the opinion that the packers have agreed to arbitrate all matters in the controversy and will cover all employees no matter at what trade or calling they may be working in the stockyards, which I think is absurd, although I think both Foster and Lane are sincere in their belief.

Nockels came in to see me today and I think that I got from him nearer the real facts than I did from any of the rest. He said we have the big fellow here to make the packers do business and I said, "Who do you mean?" He said "Frank P. Walsh." So I asked him to give me just the correct information as to what the commission had done with the proposition as presented to them by the stockyards workers council. He said, they had agreed with the commission to arbitrate all matters affecting the stockyards workers and had understood that the packers had agreed to arbitration as well. I said, "Is it the purpose of the stockyards workers council to have Frank P. Walsh present their matter to the arbitrator, Mr. Williams, and is there a set day for your side to present arguments for the things that you demand and is the packer to be represented at the same time to present their side to off-set the claims you make and to argue their side of the case to prevent the workers from getting the things they ask for?" I said, "If this is to be done, you are making real progress, the packers have decided you have a day in court and what is better you have mutually agreed to the Judge who is to hear the case and from all reports, to say the least, he is fair.["]

To this argument Nockels reply was that I did not quite understand what conclusions the commission had reached, but they had today presented their entire case to a representative of the commission and if the packers did not come in with theirs, then the stockyards workers council would demand of the commission that they put in force the agreement which was presented by the workers to the commission.

I said what power has the commission to do any such thing, and I further told Nockels it was my opinion that unless they had the packers tied down to an arbitration agreement with the commission as a third party, that before the government [would] do anything to force the packers into a settlement that they would have to show to the government by a strike tie up that the government itself was in danger of not getting sufficient food stuffs to feed the soldiers at home and assist the allies to feed those at the front; then the government would use its forces and compel both sides to agree on arbitration.

I do not know just what part you and Secty. Morrison took in assisting the last committee who were in Washington on this matter and how the President's commission was injected into the matter.

At the time John Hart[2] and myself were in Washington and had your and Secty. Morrison's co-operation, we left Washington with the understanding that Mr. Hoover[3] and Mr. Gifford and Mr. Post had agreed with you and us that the government ought to get one of its biggest men to go to the Packers and use his efforts and power of the government to force the packer to meet the workers and settle their differences by arbitration and mutual agreement. That plan was never tried out since I returned to Chicago.

Sam, I have no personal feelings in the matter but I know you are interested because they are such a large group of stockyards workers involved and I want to let you know what progress is being made if any, in an adjustment of the entire controversy. I am preparing to go to a hospital tomorrow to have properly diagnosed just what my ailment is. I have been sick since Christmas 1916 with stomach trouble and for the last year I have been treated by five different doctors for chronic gastritis, nervous dyspepsia, ulcers of the stomach, too much acid of several kinds in the stomach and several other things too numerous to mention. Since Christmas this year, I have been suffering intense pain, so I am taking another doctor's advice and am going to the hospital in the morning and for the fourth time I am going to have the contents of my stomach pumped out, tested and have an X Ray picture made and see just what is the trouble. I think myself, I am suffering from gall stones and if my prediction is true I will have them removed before leaving the hospital. I had made up my mind some time ago to go to the Mayo's Hospital at Rochester, Minn., but Mrs. Flood and the children[4] prefer that I be close at home.

With best wishes for a Happy and Prosperous New Year for you and yours, I remain

Fraternally yours,   Emmet T. Flood

p.s. Will you please furnish the information to Secty. Morrison that I am going to be incapacitated for a few days at least, for the reason I may not be able to write him before going to the hospital.

TLS, Files of the Office of the President, General Correspondence, reel 91, frames 144–47, *AFL Records.*

1. John Elias Williams (1853–1919), an industrial mediator and the fuel administrator for Illinois, served from late December 1917 through mid-January 1918 as the federal arbitrator in the labor dispute in the meatpacking industry. After his resignation, he was replaced by Judge Samuel Alschuler (1859–1939), who served on the U.S. circuit court of appeals from 1915 until his retirement in 1936.

2. John F. HART served as president of the Amalgamated Meat Cutters and Butcher Workmen of North America from 1910 to 1921.

3. Herbert Clark Hoover (1874–1964), previously a successful mining engineer, served as chairman of the Commission for Relief in Belgium (1914–19), head of the U.S. Food Administration (1917–19), director of the American Relief Administration (1919) and its privately-run successor organizations of the same name for European children's relief (1919–21) and Russian famine relief (1921–23), secretary of commerce under Warren Harding and Calvin Coolidge (1921–28), and president of the United States (1929–33).

4. Evelyn, Emmet Jr., Anna, Raymond, Marie, Helen, and Rose Flood.

A Memorandum of a Telephone Conversation between Samuel Gompers and William B. Wilson

Jan. 3, 1918.

"This is Sam talking. . . .[1] Oh, not bad. . . . Tell me, how are you? . . . I heard that you were not feeling so well when you returned here. Glad to hear that you are better.

["]I want to talk with you about a matter which is to me exceedingly important. Did you see the article this morning in the Washington Post in regard to that labor program, Brown's article?[2] . . . You saw it? . . . Well, today I had a conference with Dr. Marshall[3] and Mr. Sullivan and they told me, particularly Dr. Marshall told me about the situation as he finds it to exist and developing. The statement that is contained in the article this morning that the American Federation of Labor has given its approval of the proposed coherence of labor and Labor Board,[4] is not true. I know of no one who has had the authority to speak in regard to it, and I know that I have not said a word about it. I am told that it is likely to come up this afternoon at the meeting of the Council of National Defense. Now, the only conference I have had upon the subject at all was this morning with Dr. Marshall and with Mr. Sullivan. Now if you read the article carefully, it speaks of compulsory labor and the prohibition of cessation of labor, and all that sort of thing. You know, of course that that won't go and that no man—. . . . Yes, I know you have been fighting it.

["]I presented to you, I believe it was Saturday, you know that letter[5] in regard to the copper mine situation in Arizona. I also presented to you this morning something in regard to the oil situation[6] there. Now as a matter of fact, so far as I know, whatever cessation of work has seriously occurred and is in vogue now is due to the antagonism and the unwarranted attitude taken by the employers. There are not any very serious strikes now. Your Commission adjusted both those two situations, the copper in Arizona, and oil in Texas and Louisiana. The men have declared their willingness to abide and have accepted without a question, and now they find themselves discriminated against, left without employment and production almost at the lowest possible ebb. My information is that there is not 30% of the copper produced in many of the mines as compared to last year at this time. . . . But there are a large number of men unemployed, the employers refusing to take them back, and the oil situation is exactly in the same condition.

["]Well, coming back to the thought. I do not know whether my presence or advice, either as a member of the Advisory Commission or as President of the American Federation of Labor is worth any consideration, but believe me, sir, that I will never consent to any order or law that shall absolutely prohibit men from in the last resort, striking. To give up that, well, you might as well throw up all hands and quit. . . .

["]Before any action is taken insist that I be given an opportunity to be heard. Now I was going to say. At the conference this morning with Mr. Marshall and Mr. Sullivan, I said that it seemed to me to be too important a matter and too far reaching for me to assume the responsibility alone to determine any course. I said that I was sorry that Secretary Morrison, Mr. O'Connell,[7] and one or two others of the labor men who are in town were not present and hearing the entire conversation and to discuss the proposition, and to consider the plans as well as the charts submitted by Dr. Marshall, as suggestive, and we agreed that we would have a conference here at eight o'clock Monday evening, and I expressed the hope, and the others agreed, that you and Assistant Secretary Post ought to be present by reason of the previous conference, and your absence, and if you can make it for Monday evening, I should be very glad because then we will have a little clearer understanding. Would that be agreeable to you sir? . . . Yes, Monday evening at eight o'clock. . . .

["]Will you please ask Secretary Post to come with you?[8] . . . That will be fine. . . . Indeed. . . . That is fine. . . . That is all right. . . . I will see you then Monday evening if not before."

Secretary Wilson said that he wanted to consult me about a matter. That under the bureau as for labor agencies which the Department has taken over, and has in good swing now, and with the money placed in the hands of the Department by the President, he has thought of having a sort of an advisory commission[9] with someone to aid in its direction, and he said that Mr. Lennon, could be helpful he thought as member of that commission, and he wanted my opinion as to whether that appointment would be agreeable to me. I answered him that it would be entirely.

TD, Files of the Office of the President, General Correspondence, reel 91, frames 199–201, *AFL Records.*

1. Ellipses throughout this document in original.

2. George Rothwell Brown, "Labor Control Looms," *Washington Post,* Jan. 3, 1918. The article discussed the need for the government to develop a uniform national labor policy under the direction of a single labor administrator who could "coordinate the relations with labor of all departments of the government."

3. Leon Carroll Marshall (1879–1966), professor of political economy (1907–28) and dean of the College of Commerce and Administration (1909–24) at the University of Chicago, served as secretary of the advisory council of the Department of Labor, director of industrial relations of the Emergency Fleet Corporation, and economic adviser to the War Labor Policies Board.

4. Brown reported that the Council of National Defense was going to "devise a system for the unification of labor that shall be satisfactory to the government, to industry and to labor itself," and he asserted that all three groups favored the adoption of such a system, including the AFL, which had "approved it in a general way" ("Labor Control Looms," *Washington Post,* Jan. 3, 1918).

5. SG to William B. Wilson, Dec. 31, 1917, reel 229, vol. 241, pp. 810–11, SG Letterbooks, DLC.

6. On Nov. 1, 1917, between nine and ten thousand oil field workers in eastern Texas and northern Louisiana struck for union recognition, an eight-hour day, and a wage increase. After efforts by federal mediators in November and by representatives of the President's Mediation Commission in December proved unsuccessful, the two sides met with Secretary Wilson in Washington, D.C., in January 1918. The subsequent settlement, announced Jan. 30, strongly favored the operators. It made no concessions on wages or hours, did not allow union representatives to attend workers' meetings

with employers or require firing strikebreakers, directed that grievances were to go before complaint committees run by the employers' association, and allowed employers to refuse to rehire anyone they found objectionable.

7. James O'CONNELL was an AFL vice-president (1896–1918) and president of the AFL Metal Trades Department (1911–34).

8. Assistant Secretary of Labor Louis Post attended the conference at AFL headquarters on Jan. 7, 1918, along with Wilson and Wilson's private secretary Hugh Kerwin.

9. Wilson was considering the creation of a three-member advisory committee within the Department of Labor. Following his appointment as War Labor Administrator on Jan. 4, 1918, however, he instead set up a seven-member advisory council and, acting on its recommendation, he established the War Labor Conference Board later in the month (see "From William B. Wilson, Jan. 29, 1918, n. 1, below).

From Gideon Robertson[1]

The Senate,
Ottawa, Can., Jany. 7th 1918.

Dear Mr. Gompers:

Permit me to acquaint you confidentially, with a very acute situation now existing in the Maritime Provinces of Canada, respecting the coal situation.

The amount of coal mined is very much below the normal requirement, and our transportation lines, by rail and water, are living from hand to mouth, with but a few days' supply in advance, and extreme difficulty is being experienced in coping with the situation. In addition to this, some labor disputes are pending, with reference to working conditions and rates of wages as between the miners and the Dominion Coal Company,[2] which however I think can be overcome with reasonable care.

The undersigned, who is a member of the Dominion Cabinet, has been delegated by the Dominion Government to visit Sydney, C.B., with a view of endeavoring to devise some way of increasing the output and adjusting the existing labor difficulties. It has come to my attention today that some representatives of the United Mine Workers of America, which organization you will recall had some very lamentable experiences[3] in Cape Breton in 1909, are due to arrive at Sydney, and it may be that their presence there at this time will be most inopportune, because of the accumulation of difficulties requiring immediate attention, which already exist.

Should it develop that their presence at Sydney at this time is likely to increase the existing difficulties, or foment any further industrial unrest among the miners in this crisis, I shall deem it important in the

National interest, and the efficient prosecution of our war program, to ask you to intercede with the Executive of the United Mine Workers organization for the purpose of with-holding any action on the part of that organization with reference to extending its membership into Cape Breton at this time, knowing that your influence with and advice to them would be respected, especially during this emergency period.[4]

With kind personal regards, I am,

Yours very truly,   G. D. Robertson.

TLS, Files of the Office of the President, General Correspondence, reel 91, frame 268, *AFL Records*.

1. Gideon Decker Robertson (1874–1933) served in the Canadian government as minister without portfolio (1917–18) and minister of labor (1918–21, 1930–32) and was active as a mediator in labor disputes. Born in Welland, Ont., he was a railroad telegrapher by trade and a member of Order of Railroad Telegraphers of North America division 7 (the Canadian Pacific Railway System). He served as the division's chairman from 1908 until 1915 and was a vice-president of the Railroad Telegraphers from 1915 until shortly before his death.

2. In November 1917 the Amalgamated Mine Workers of Nova Scotia demanded a wage increase from the Dominion Coal Co. to offset the rising cost of living. When the operators turned this down, Robertson mediated the dispute, arranging an agreement that gave the miners a 16–percent wage increase effective Jan. 1, 1918, and permitted revision of the pay scale at six-month intervals to compensate for further increases in the cost of living.

3. The United Mine Workers of America began organizing locals in Nova Scotia in 1908 and established District 26 there in March 1909 but met opposition from a rival miners' union—the Provincial Workmen's Association—and from Dominion Coal, which began discharging members of District 26 and evicting them from company housing. The union struck in July 1909 when a government board of conciliation headed by Justice William Wallace of the county court of Halifax ruled there was no evidence of unlawful discrimination by the company. By the end of the year it was evident that the strike was lost, and the executive board of District 26 called it off in April 1910.

4. On Jan. 9, 1918, SG sent a copy of Robertson's letter to United Mine Workers' president Frank Hayes, who replied on Jan. 14 that although the union was conducting an educational campaign among unorganized miners throughout the United States and Canada, it had no intention of doing anything to interfere with coal production (Files of the Office of the President, General Correspondence, reel 91, frames 314, 470–71, *AFL Records*). SG forwarded a copy of Hayes's letter to Robertson, who replied on Jan. 28 to express his government's appreciation (ibid., frame 567; reel 92, frame 48).

To William Appleton

Washington, DC Jan. 9, 1918

Appleton
"Wellwisher Eusquare London"

Am gratified that you and a number of other representatives British Labor men are coming to United States.[1] You and they will find hearty greeting and cooperation.

The declaration of December twenty eighth British labor conference at Westminster[2] is in essential principles identical with declarations of November convention American Federation of Labor at Buffalo.

The Lloyd George declarations last week to the man power conference[3] and those of President Wilson yesterday[4] to the American Congress are in accord upon the vital issues and aims in this war. Thus the official representatives of our governments and of the labor movements of our respective countries have expressed the will and purpose of the people, the governments and the workers of Great Britain and America.

If any call should be issued for an international conference of workers of all countries of the world, the American Federation of Labor will not participate. The people of Germany must establish democracy within their own domain and make opportunity for international relations that life shall be secure that the people of all countries may live their own lives and work out their own salvation and unless this has been accomplished by the German people themselves the allied democracies in this struggle must crush militarism and autocracy and bring a new freedom to the whole world the people of Germany included. Until these essentials are accomplished an international labor conference with the representatives of the workers of all countries Germany included is prejudicial to a desirable and lasting peace.

Gompers.

TWpS, reel 230, vol. 242, p. 167, SG Letterbooks, DLC.

1. The members of the British labor mission to the United States were William Appleton, secretary of the General Federation of Trade Unions, Charles Duncan, secretary of the Workers' Union and a Labour member of Parliament, William Mosses, former secretary of the United Pattern Makers' Association and the Federation of Engineering and Shipbuilding Trades, and Joshua Butterworth of the Shipconstructors' and Shipwrights' Association. The delegation arrived in the United States in February 1918 and together visited Washington, D.C., Baltimore, and Chicago. Duncan and Mosses then toured cities in the West and South, while Appleton and Butterworth went to cities in the Midwest and Northeast. The delegation returned to England in April.

2. On Dec. 28, 1917, some 750 representatives of trade unions, socialist societies, the Labour party, and the TUC, meeting at Westminster, adopted a declaration of war

aims. The statement demanded an end to imperialism, secret diplomacy, and compulsory military service, called for the limitation of armaments, self-determination of peoples, and the establishment of a league of nations, and insisted on an immediate end to the war once the conditions for peace were secured.

3. Prime Minister David Lloyd George summarized British war aims in a speech before labor delegates at a manpower conference in London on Jan. 5, 1918. They included restoration of the sanctity of treaties, a territorial settlement based on the self-determination of peoples, and the creation of an organization to resolve international disputes.

4. President Woodrow Wilson outlined American war aims (the Fourteen Points) in an address before Congress on Jan. 8, 1918. These included an end to secret treaties, freedom of the seas, removal of economic barriers to trade, the reduction of armaments, impartial adjustment of colonial claims, evacuation and restoration of occupied countries, self-determination of peoples, and the establishment of a league of nations.

A Memorandum Dictated by Samuel Gompers

Washington, D.C., January 11, 1918.

Last night I attended a conference called by Herbert L. Carpenter[1] in the office of Senator Wm. E. Borah for the purpose of considering the condition of the Russian people and to devise ways and means by which the serious situation may be relieved by American action. Senators Borah and Owen[2] were present and among others were Senator George E. Chamberlain,[3] John R. Mott,[4] Doctor Billings,[5] John F. Stevens[6] (Mr. Gibbs),[7] Henry L. Slobodin, Edward Filene, Julius Rosenwald,[8] Raymond V. Ingersoll,[9] Oscar S. Straus, Wm. B. Thompson,[10] Samuel N. Harper,[11] Frank A. Vanderlip,[12] John H. Finley,[13] F. C. Porter,[14] Herbert L. Carpenter, and Frank J. Goodnow.[15]

Senator Borah opened the meeting with a statement of the purpose of the conference and Mr. Carpenter then read an extract of suggestions that were made for the relief of the Russian people. Dr. Billings and Mr. Filene spoke and then I was called upon and pointed out that the point had been missed both by the government as well as those who had been speaking to the conference, that is, the failure to bring a message to the Russian workers of the hearty cooperation of America's workers in common sympathy and common union. I pointed out the fact that when the revolution was inaugurated and the Czar deposed, thousands of Russians who had come to the United States fleeing from the tyranny and the persecution of Czardom, returned from the United States to their homes. In the United States they had been exploited when they first came here by their employers; they had gained the notion of their employers as being task masters as well as employe[r]s of the sweat shop. Beneficiaries had become radical solutions in belief and they went back to Russia and there declared that American conditions of workers were worse than that prevailing in Russia. They stigmatized the United States as a Republic for relentless capitalistic oppression and the government and Republic were of a similar character and so circulated among the people of Russia as to the reliability of the American people and the American government in sympathy with Russia and the Allies. At that time a message from the workers of the United States ought to have been sent to Russia but the means to finance such project were not available. This was presented to the authorities of the government and we received no encouragement. The Root Mission, while in itself good, yet, having great respect for Mr. Root, attained much, yet, the fact he was regarded as the representative of Broadway wealth, that is reactionary and had forestalled and anticipated his coming to Russia. The fact that he was the President of the Constitution of the State of New York about a year before his going and the constitution that he prepared for the people was the reactionary document depriving people of democratic freedom, and the fact that the constitution framed under his leadership was submitted to the people, and rejected by them by more than half a million majority, all tended to make the Mission headed by him abortive; that the two men of the Mission who really made an impression upon the working people were Mr. James Duncan, First Vice-President of the American Federation of Labor, and Mr. Charles Edward Russell, and were welcomed wherever they went and invited.

I called attention to the fact what the American Alliance for Labor and Democracy is now undertaking to do, that is, to have Loyalty Week in which all others of the United States could participate and to have demonstrations and mass meetings during that week, that is, on Tuesday, February 12, Lincoln's Birthday and that we would have speakers there at these meetings and that these meetings could be utilized not only for loyalty, but for expressions of sympathy, cooperation and assistance with and for the Russian people.[16]

The thought had occurred to me that those who participated in the conference last night should cooperate in the effort. Also called attention to the fact that I had under consideration the question of sending a delegation of workers from the United States and trying to induce the British and the French workers to also send a delegation of workers to go to Russia for the purpose of spreading the doctrine of good-will and helpfulness.

The entire matter was well received and then further discussion ensued and it was decided that regardless of Russia's continuance in the war, the fact that her people need assistance every effort should be made to help. It was late as I left but it was then contemplated to appoint a committee[17] for the purpose of carrying the suggestion into effect.

TD, Files of the Office of the President, General Correspondence, reel 91, frames 374–76, *AFL Records.* Typed notation: "Dictated by President Gompers."

1. Herbert L. Carpenter (1880?–1963) was a New York City engineer, businessman, and manufacturer.

2. Robert Latham Owen (1856–1947) served as a Democratic senator from Oklahoma from 1907 to 1925.

3. George Earle Chamberlain (1854–1928) served as a Democratic senator from Oregon from 1909 to 1921.

4. John R. Mott (1865–1955) served as secretary of the National Council of the Young Men's Christian Association (1915–28) and was a member of the Root commission to Russia in 1917.

5. Frank Billings (1854–1932), a Chicago physician, headed the American Red Cross mission to Russia in 1917.

6. John Frank Stevens (1853–1943), a civil engineer who specialized in railroads, had served as chief engineer of the Panama Canal (1905–7). Between 1917 and 1923 he headed three railway missions to Russia, the Advisory Commission of American Railway Experts to Russia, which was a body created by the U.S. government to help reorganize and manage the Russian railway system, and the Russian Railway Service Corps and the Technical Board of the Inter-Allied Railway Committee, which worked on reorganizing the Trans-Siberian and Chinese Eastern railways.

7. George Gibbs (1861–1940), a New York City mechanical engineer and railroad consultant, served as a member of the Stevens railway commission to Russia in 1917. He apparently attended the meeting in place of Stevens, who was in Russia.

8. Julius Rosenwald (1862–1932), president of Sears, Roebuck, and Co., served as chairman of the Committee of Supplies of the Advisory Commission of the Council of National Defense.

9. Raymond Vail Ingersoll (1875–1940) was a New York City attorney.

10. William Boyce Thompson (1869–1930), a mining entrepreneur and financier, was director of the Federal Reserve Bank of New York (1914–19) and a member of the 1917 American Red Cross mission to Russia.

11. Samuel Northrup Harper (1882–1943) was a professor of Russian Language and Institutions at the University of Chicago (1905–9, 1915–43). In 1916 he was an adviser to U.S. ambassador to Russia David Francis, and in 1917 he served as an interpreter and guide in Petrograd for the Root commission.

12. Frank Arthur Vanderlip (1864–1937) was president of the National City Bank of New York City (1909–19).

13. John Huston Finley (1863–1940), the state commissioner of education and president of the University of the State of New York (1913–21).

14. Actually Edwards Chappell Porter (b. 1887), executive secretary of the American-Russian Chamber of Commerce in New York City.

15. Frank Johnson Goodnow (1859–1939) was president of the Johns Hopkins University (1914–29).

16. The American Alliance for Labor and Democracy designated the week of Abraham Lincoln's birthday, Feb. 10–16, 1918, as Labor Loyalty Week. SG sent out a cir-

cular on Jan. 4 calling on trade unionists to hold mass meetings during the week to demonstrate labor's loyalty to America. Patriotic rallies and demonstrations were held throughout the country; one of the largest was held in New York City on Feb. 10 and was addressed by William B. Wilson and Hugh Frayne. SG spoke in Washington, D.C., on Feb. 12 and later, in an appearance with Secretary of the Navy Josephus Daniels, made a major address at a "loyalty mass meeting" in New York City on Feb. 22, George Washington's birthday ("Gompers Pledges America's Labor to Nation in War," *New York Times*, Feb. 23, 1918). SG's New York City address was subsequently published by the Committee on Public Information.

17. The American League to Aid and Cooperate with Russia was organized in May 1918. Goodnow served as president of the League, Thompson, Oscar Straus, and James Duncan, among others, as vice-presidents, and Carpenter chaired the executive committee. SG also served on the executive committee, together with a number of others who participated in the conference described in this document.

From Santiago Iglesias

Federacion Libre de los Trabajadores de Puerto Rico
San Juan, Puerto Rico January 11, 1918.

Dear Sir and Brother:

I am in receipt of your letter of December 28,[1] last, quoting a cable-gram[2] sent by you to Governor Yager, through the Bureau of Insular Affairs, in behalf of those workmen who are now imprisoned. The cablegram in question was received by Acting Governor Kern,[3] as Governor Yager was absent in the States, and he informed me that several workers have been pardoned, but that in the case of Bolivar Ochart and others active participants in strikes he had recommended as Attorney General against the granting of such pardon and that he did not feel justified in taking a different action while acting Governor. That the matter will be submitted to the attention of Gov. Yager as soon as he returns. If any future action is taken you will be duly informed. We are sincerely appreciative of the kind support given by you to have these men released.

The war conditions in this Island are affecting the workers generally in a way which it would seem impossible for me to detail. The cost of living here is something unheard of, staples having increased in price in an alarming way whereas the price of Labor has been kept systematically as low as ever. This condition as you will readily understand has brought untold suffering and hardship among the masses and more especially over the agriculture workers whose low wages cannot by any mean cover the cost of his living. The Island is now a huge sugar factory. The National Food Commission[4] has fixed a most encouraging and productive price for sugar. However, the poor field workers are not getting one cent more than what they were getting years ago when food stuff was within the reach of any one no matter how poor he might have been. I sincerely believe that at this war time something may be done by the Federal Administration to improve this condition. Why not have the Administration fix a scale of wages for the agricultural workers here in the same manner that it had fixed the price of sugar? The Administration ought to prevent a strike which will partly affect one of the principal and most necessary staple for war use. The whole situation has been clearly put before you in my letter of December 19,[5] last, and some remedy must be taken. If the agriculture workers are granted an increase to $1.50 per day for 8 hours work the situation will immediately change and there will surely be a boom of new members in our locals. I wish to advise you that I received a cablegram from Secretary Wilson today advising me that Mr. Roberts[6] has been appointed to represent the Labor Department in pending wage dispute between the agriculture workers and their employers.[7] I hope that this first step which is the right direction will follow others in behalf of the starving wage workers of Porto Rico. Federal control, now more than ever justified, over labor matters is paramount to us as a mean of securing those improvement for which we have stand for many years. The local Bureau of Labor cannot be depended upon. It is an absolute failure, hostile to its creation and to serve the purpose and principles which brought it to life. The Department of Labor in some way do a whole lot for us and your sincere and kind cooperation of you, as heretofore, is earnestly solicited.

Another vital point is the establishment of the military camp in San Juan. Thousand of workers and artisans will be employed in the construction of this cantonment for which purpose the recommendations contained in the memorandum of June 19, 1907 [1917], will surely help us a good deal. I am sending herewith a clipping about this matter.

The local representative of the Federal Food Administration who is also a member of the local Food Commission created by an Act of the Insular Legislature, has seen fit to invite me to become a member of the Local Committee in the Porto Rico State Organization of the United States. I have emphatically declined the invitation as a matter of justice and principle. The Federation here when the local Commission was organized was not given, even yet, refused representation in said Commission notwithstanding the fact that such representation was requested from Governor Yager. The work of this Commission was far from satisfactory and criticism was rampant against it. It was a Commission of merchants and business men only. The voice of the people made itself heard in the local Legislature and an investigation was started in which I participated. Now that these charges are pending they invite me to become a member of a Commission which is the lime light of the people, in a secondary position where nothing effective can be done to improve the errors committed in the past.

Mr. Robert has written to me under date of Jan. 2, in regard to some steps in connection with the Democratic Party. This I think can be done and will be of somewhat easier realization if the local elements find that the Federal Administration is really interested in its welfare and supports a number of measures coupled with the necessary action to bring about a general change in our workmen's conditions. More clearly speaking the national Administration has to begin by creating a genuine Department of Labor in Porto Rico, for the well being of the workers and under the direction of true Labor.

I omitted to say that I have been quite interested in the proceedings of the Buffalo Convention and keenly regret that I was not able to attend. It was really a miss on my part although I have tried to keep myself well posted with all the details of this great gathering.

With best wishes and sincere regards, I am

Fraternally yours,   (signed) Santiago Iglesias
Org.   A.F. of L.

TLtpSr, reel 230, vol. 242, pp. 520–21, SG Letterbooks, DLC. Typed notation: "Copy." Enclosed in SG to James Sullivan, Jan. 18, 1918, ibid., p. 519.

1. SG to Santiago Iglesias, Dec. 28, 1917, reel 229, vol. 241, p. 773, SG Letterbooks, DLC.

2. SG's cable to Gov. Arthur Yager was dated Dec. 26, 1917.

3. Howard Lewis Kern (1886–1947), a New York City attorney, was attorney general of Puerto Rico from 1915 to 1919 and served as acting governor of the island in Yager's absence.

4. The U.S. Food Administration was established by executive order on Aug. 10, 1917, under authority of the Lever Act to oversee the production, conservation, and distribution of food. Herbert Hoover served as Food Administrator during the war.

5. In his letter to SG of Dec. 19, 1917, Iglesias reported that sugar prices and the cost of food in Puerto Rico had doubled while wages remained the same, but that sugar growers refused to meet workers' demands or even negotiate. He predicted that more than fifty thousand sugar workers would be forced to strike in early 1918 if no action were taken (Files of the Office of the President, General Correspondence, reel 90, frames 766–67, *AFL Records*). In response to the letter, SG wrote William B. Wilson, Newton Baker, Herbert Hoover, and Frank McIntyre on Jan. 3, 1918, about the situation in Puerto Rico (reel 230, vol. 242, pp. 4–11, SG Letterbooks, DLC).

6. Flournoy C. Roberts of Washington, D.C., was a commissioner of conciliation for the U.S. Department of Labor. After Wilson appointed him to serve as a mediator in the agricultural workers' dispute, SG met with him and Yager on Jan. 16, 1918.

7. A convention of Puerto Rican agricultural workers meeting in Bayamón in September 1917 drew up a list of demands for the 1918 growing season that included an eight-hour day, wage increases, the creation of grievance committees, the institution of written contracts signed by employers, the observance of the laws regulating

woman and child labor, and an end to the persecution of strikers. When the sugar cane growers and the owners of sugar factories on the island refused to consider these demands, strikes began to break out in January 1918 and became widespread in March and April. According to U.S. Department of Labor estimates, the number of striking agricultural workers may have totalled fifty thousand. Few of the strikes resulted in any significant gains.

An Article in the *Washington Evening Star*

[January 18, 1918]

GOMPERS SAYS BURDEN OF ORDER[1] IS ON LABOR

Although the workers of the nation will be the greatest sufferers from the fuel restriction order, they will "maintain their loyal stand despite their suffering and sacrifices which they may be called upon to bear," according to a statement issued last night by Samuel Gompers, president of the American Federation of Labor.

"The shutting down of all industries for five continuous days is only warranted if based upon immediate emergency, and I have some doubt if five continuous days is the best measure," said Mr. Gompers. "It certainly seems a very radical measure to meet the problems of transportation.["]

Protests by Telegraph.

"I am in receipt of a large number of telegraphic protests from workers in several parts of the country, declaring that the effect of the orders will throw their men out of employment; that due to the high cost of living they have been unable to lay anything aside, and that their suffering during this period will be very great.

"In addition to this, I am strongly of the opinion that to place the industries of the country upon an eight-hour basic workday, at least during the war and as a war measure, would have been a much wiser and more practical course than the creation of legal holidays, which will mean holidays from Saturday afternoon until Tuesday morning.

"The workers, the masses of the people will be the greatest sufferers from this new order. Others have been or will be able to hoard their needs and supplies. Of course, the working people of America will maintain their loyal stand despite their suffering and sacrifices which they may be called upon to bear, and yet everything must be done to see that they are not made to suffer unnecessarily.["]

LETTER FROM SECRETARY.

"I have just received a letter from the Executive Secretary[2] of Dr. Garfield, the head of the United States Fuel Administration, in which he says:

"'In connection with the order closing down industry for five days and subsequent Mondays, I am issuing an appeal to industries concerned, asking them not to allow labor to suffer by reason of the shutdown; that this is a war measure which I confidently expect industry will execute without shifting the burden to labor.'

"I prayerfully hope that our captains of industry and business men will show their patriotism by heeding Dr. Garfield's appeal. It would be most unwise did they not heed it."

Washington Evening Star, Jan. 18, 1918.

1. U.S. fuel administrator Harry Garfield issued a fuel restriction order on Jan. 17, 1918. It prohibited burning fuel or using power derived from fuel, between Jan. 18 and 22 and on the subsequent Mondays through Mar. 25, in most factories located in states east of the Mississippi. With some exceptions, the order also prohibited burning fuel on Mondays between Jan. 21 and Mar. 25 to heat wholesale or retail businesses, professional offices, establishments serving liquor, or theaters and other places of public amusement located in states east of the Mississippi, except to prevent damage to property from freezing. Food stores were allowed to remain heated until noon on those days, and drugstores throughout the day. Despite congressional opposition, the order went into effect on Jan. 18; it was suspended on Feb. 13.

2. George Nasmyth to SG, Jan. 17, 1918, Files of the Office of the President, General Correspondence, reel 91, frame 580, *AFL Records.* Nasmyth (1882–1920) served as head of the administrative division of the U.S. Fuel Administration (1917–19).

From William Hutcheson

Indianapolis, Ind., Jan. 18, 1918.

Your wire[1] in reference to Beaumont[2] at hand. As you know the Brotherhood was not a party to understanding or agreement by which wage adjustment commission was created for reasons with which you are familiar.[3] We have endeavored in every way possible to assist the government in all the work required to carry the war to a successful conclusion and believe we are entitled to some consideration. Many ship yard owners feel there should be a representative of our organization on that commission and if their efforts are ever going to be successful in adjusting matters pertaining to our members there certainly will have to be a change made in the personnel of that commission as now constituted. I have already notified our members in various localities to have nothing whatever to do with that commission. I have given approval of movement in Beaumont and will continue to give approval of other movements for the purpose of bringing about a condition for our members to which they are entitled but stand ready to meet with members of the U.S. Shipping Board or other government officials with the object in view of reaching an understanding whereby actions of this kind will be eliminated and unnecessary.

Wm. L. Hutcheson.

TWtcSr, Files of the Office of the President, General Correspondence, reel 91, frame 616, *AFL Records*. Typed notation: *"Copy."*

1. On Jan. 17, 1918, SG wired William Hutcheson that an AFL volunteer organizer in Beaumont, Tex., and a committee from a United Brotherhood of Carpenters and Joiners of America local in nearby Orange had warned him that a ship carpenters' strike was about to begin in the area and had urged that the Shipbuilding Labor Adjustment Board to mediate the dispute. SG went on to say that board chairman V. Everit Macy had told him he would not take up the matter unless the Carpenters' local agreed to abide by the board's decision—as Carpenters' locals in other areas had done when they were involved in disputes involving the labor adjustment board—since the Carpenters were not a party to the agreement establishing the board (reel 230, vol. 242, p. 445, SG Letterbooks, DLC).

2. On Jan. 12, 1918, shipyard laborers in Beaumont and Orange struck for higher wages, an eight-hour day, and overtime pay, and on Jan. 17 they were joined by ship carpenters in the two ports, who struck for a wage increase. Acting on U.S. Department of Labor mediator William Blackman's promise to the shipyard laborers of a retroactive pay increase and, reportedly, Hutcheson's assurance to the ship carpenters that their grievances would be investigated by the Shipbuilding Labor Adjustment Board, the strikers returned to work in Beaumont on Jan. 22 and in Orange on Jan. 23. In February the board met in Washington, D.C., with delegates from ports throughout the Southern and Gulf Coast District—extending from Norfolk to Houston—to draw up a comprehensive settlement covering wages, hours, and working conditions in shipyards doing work for the government. Representatives from Houston, Beaumont, and Orange appeared before the board Feb. 20–23. On Mar. 4 the board issued its ruling, which provided for shop committees to handle grievances, commuting costs for workers unable to find housing near the yards, half days on Saturdays in the summer months, and improved sanitation. The board's wage award granted pay increases but at a rate five to ten cents per hour lower than the rates it had recently awarded workers in the Delaware River District. When this led to considerable dissatisfaction, the board issued a revised scale on Apr. 6 that equalized wages for shipyard workers throughout the Atlantic and Gulf coasts, with the exception of the yard at Newport News, which had a separate agreement.

3. On Sept. 19, 1917, Hutcheson wrote SG that the Carpenters would not become a party to the agreement creating the Shipbuilding Labor Adjustment Board because the document failed to state "specifically and clearly that we as an organization were to have a union or closed shop" (Files of the Office of the President, General Correspondence, reel 88, frame 419, *AFL Records*). Although Carpenters' vice-president Theobold Guerin did sign the agreement, Hutcheson maintained that this was not binding on the union because the Carpenters' general executive board had not ratified the pact and he himself had not signed it. In November, acting with the authorization of the

union's general executive board, he ordered Guerin to withdraw his signature from the document. Local unions, however, were apparently allowed to continue to work informally with the Shipbuilding Labor Adjustment Board.

To Austin Garretson

January 19, 1918.

Mr. A. B. Garretson,
Chief, Order of Railway Conductors of America,[1]
Cedar Rapids, Iowa.
Dear Sir:—

You are doubtless aware that in nearly all of the agencies of the government which deal with the conditions of labor, the unions of the workers of the respective trades or industries are represented so that, insofar, as these are concerned, labor has a voice in determining the conditions affecting the workers, and in at least an advisory if not an executive capacity, are helping to meet the problems with which the government and governmental agencies have to deal. The newspapers of this morning published the names of the men who are to make an investigation and recommendation regarding the wage and other labor conditions affecting the railroad brotherhoods.[2] On not one of these boards can be found the name of a wage worker on or for the railroads.

With the new order of things, that is, with the operation of the railroads under government control, in the determination of wages and conditions of work, the thought has often occurred to me why the railroad brotherhoods have not had some representation either in an advisory or an executive capacity; but in view of the fact that the brotherhoods have in many matters affecting them determined their own policy, I have been loath to make any move without at least having the prior assent of you and the chiefs of the other railroad brotherhoods.

This morning, Miss Rankin,[3] a member of the House of Representatives came into my office and she brought up this very subject. We went over it together and she is very earnestly of the opinion (in which I concur) that the railroad Brotherhoods ought to have a powerful, influential voice in the operation and management of the railroads of the country, and particularly under the new regime of government control. After discussing this further with Miss Rankin, I suggested (and in which she concurred) that a conference should be held at as early a date as possible, in which the four chiefs and Miss Rankin and I are to participate with a view of discussing this subject in all its phases and reach a conclusion that we may jointly press home upon the government.

With the purpose above indicated in view, I ask whether you could not participate in a conference at the American Federation of Labor Building on Saturday, January 26th, when we may go over this situation and give and receive mutual advice and suggestion for practical action in the premises.[4]

I am writing an identical letter to this to each of the other chiefs of the brotherhoods,[5] and shall be very glad if you can send me telegraphic answer[6] as to your concurrence in the proposition made.

I would have asked for a conference at an earlier date but I have an engagement[7] to be at Indianapolis on Tuesday and the early part of Wednesday, and it will be practically impossible for me to return to Washington before Thursday or Friday.

Trusting that the suggestion will meet with your approval and that I may hear from you at your earliest convenience, I am,

Fraternally yours, Saml Gompers
President, American Federation of Labor.[8]

TLpS, reel 230, vol. 242, pp. 511–12, SG Letterbooks, DLC.

1. The Order of RAILWAY Conductors of America.

2. On Dec. 26, 1917, President Woodrow Wilson, acting under a provision in the Army Appropriation Act of Aug. 29, 1916, issued a proclamation authorizing a federal takeover of the nation's railroads and appointing William McAdoo as the Director General of Railroads. On Jan. 18, 1918, McAdoo created the Railroad Wage Commission to investigate the wages and the cost of living of railroad workers. Its members included Secretary of the Interior Franklin Lane, chairman, and J. Harry Covington, chief justice of the Supreme Court of the District of Columbia, Charles McChord, a member of the Interstate Commerce Commission, and William Willcox, a New York City attorney. McAdoo incorporated the commission's report—which was issued on Apr. 30 and which endorsed a pay increase for railroad workers—into his General Order No. 27 of May 25, which created the Board of Railroad Wages and Working Conditions.

3. Jeannette Rankin (1880–1973) served as a Republican congresswoman from Montana (1917–19, 1941–43).

4. On Jan. 26, 1918, SG, James O'Connell, and M. Grant Hamilton met with Rankin and representatives of the railroad brotherhoods, including Austin Garretson.

5. SG to William Lee, to Warren Stone, and to William Carter, Jan. 19, 1918, reel 230, vol. 242, pp. 513–18, SG Letterbooks, DLC.

6. Garretson replied affirmatively on Jan. 23, 1918 (Files of the Office of the President, General Correspondence, reel 91, frame 738, *AFL Records*).

7. SG left Washington, D.C., on Jan. 20, 1918, and on Jan. 21 addressed a meeting in Newark, N.J., of the National Labor Publicity Organization. Later that day he met in New York City with officers of the United Garment Workers of America regarding the army board of control in the clothing industry and with George Creel, Robert Maisel,

and Herman Robinson about the situation in Russia. He then went on to Indianapolis, where on Jan. 22 he met with the general executive board of the United Brotherhood of Carpenters and Joiners of America and addressed the convention of the United Mine Workers of America. SG returned to Washington on Jan. 24.

8. McAdoo's subsequent appointments included a number of labor figures. On Feb. 9, 1918, for example, he named William Carter, president of the Brotherhood of Locomotive Firemen and Enginemen, as director of the Division of Labor of the U.S. Railroad Administration, and his appointments to Railway Boards of Adjustment Nos. 1, 2, and 3 (created on Mar. 22, May 31, and Nov. 13, respectively) were evenly divided between railroad executives and trade unionists.

To Thomas Gregory

Washington, D.C. Jan. 19, 1918.

Hon. Thomas W. Gregory,
Attorney General, Department of Justice,
Washington, D.C.
Sir:

Today I received a letter from Mr. Edwin T. McCoy,[1] of Phoenix, Arizona. He is secretary of the Legal Rights Committee created by the convention of the Arizona State Federation of Labor for the purpose of making secure the rights to which the workers of Arizona are entitled under state law, as well as under the laws of our Government, in an endeavor to help bring to justice the men who were so flagrantly guilty of assuming the functions of a government, functions neither recognized by the laws of Arizona nor of the United States, powers denied to the governments of our country and of that state.

It is not necessary that I should enter into a presentation of these matters. You are fully acquainted with them, and they are more particularly set forth in the findings and recommendations of the Mediation Commission created by the President of the United States, the commission of which the Honorable William B. Wilson, Secretary of the Department of Labor, was Chairman.

Mr. McCoy in his letter to me encloses a copy of the letter he addressed to you under date of January 13th, and which more than likely you have received today by the same mail as his reached me. In this instance I therefore simply desire to supplement and endorse the request made that the subject matter of the President's Mediation Commission's recommendation be given early consideration by your Department. Surely no body of men even in the Vigilante days ever assumed such powers of private invasion of constitutional right, trial and execution, as did the so-called Liberty League of Bisbee, Arizona.

Yesterday when I had the courtesy of your consideration I brought to your attention the charge of Judge Elliott to the jury,[2] sitting in the case[3] against the United Mine Workers of America, and further that after the jury had been out two days without coming to an agreement, that Judge Elliott called for the jury, expressed his opinion that the jury should bring in a verdict for the plaintiff against the miners, and by his statement that he would keep the jury until they reached a verdict, practically sentencing the jurors to permanent imprisonment, the jury under that duress brought in a verdict against the miners, mulcting them in the sum of Two Hundred Thousand Dollars under the provisions of the Sherman Antitrust Law, triple damages, making it Six Hundred Thousand Dollars.

In addition I presented to you the contrast of the treatment accorded by the Supreme Court of the United States in the cases of the International Harvester Company, the Eastman Kodak Company, and others,[4] and the request made that these trusts be not prosecuted at this time.

And on the other hand, the citation by the Supreme Court of the officers of the United Mine Workers to show cause on March 4, 1918, why they should not be punished as for contempt of court.[5]

That all these matters are creating a feeling of unrest, the discriminatory course of the judicial branch of our government when it has to deal with the men of wealth, the corporations, on the one hand, and the workers on the other.

You have done me the honor of expressing your confidence in my desire to be of service to our country, and that confidence simply spurred me to further effort to the very best of my ability. Frankness compels me to say that unless there is fairer consideration given to the workers of our country in this crucial time, it is bound to create discontent and unrest, and the influence I may be enabled to exert to help stabilize that good will, will be greatly minimized.

It has been a great source of satisfaction to me when you have on several occasions expressed your earnest desire to distinguish between the bona fide organized labor movement and its honest effort to promote the rights and interests of the workers, and those elements which make for destructive rather than constructive principles, and I am therefore constrained to place the entire situation as indicated above before you for your consideration and for such action as you may deem wise and necessary in the premises.[6]

Very respectfully yours,   Saml Gompers.
President,   American Federation of Labor.

TLS, RG 60, General Records of the Department of Justice, DNA.

1. Edwin T. McCoy, previously a member of United Brotherhood of Carpenters and Joiners of America 1648 of Bisbee, Ariz., later worked as an examiner for the U.S. Employment Service in Tucson and Phoenix.

2. James Douglas Elliott (1859–1933) of Sioux Falls, S.D., was a judge for the U.S. District Court of South Dakota from 1911 until at least 1930. He took the *Coronado* case after Judge Youmans of the U.S. District Court for the Western District of Arkansas recused himself. For Elliott's statement to the jury, see *United Mine Workers of America et al.* v. *Coronado Coal Co. et al.*, 258 F. 829 (1919).

3. In April 1914 the Bache-Denman Coal Co., which operated eight coal-mining firms in western Arkansas, abrogated the union contracts of two of its subsidiaries—the Prairie Creek Coal Co. and the Mammoth Vein Coal Co. When union miners at another Bache-Denman firm, the Coronado Coal Co., struck in protest, the parent company replaced them with nonunion workers. Union miners rioted at Prairie Creek, shutting down the operation, and in July Bache-Denman went into receivership. In September the receiver sued the United Mine Workers, the union's District 21, twenty-seven locals, and a number of individuals for a total of $740,000 in damages, which would have been tripled under the terms of the Sherman Antitrust Act.

At the first trial of the case, in district court in 1917, the company won a judgment for $600,000 plus legal fees and interest. The circuit court of appeals struck down the interest award (*United Mine Workers of America et al.* v. *Coronado Coal Co. et al.*, 258 F. 829 [1919]), and the U.S. Supreme Court overturned the balance of the judgment, ruling that there was insufficient evidence to prove a conspiracy to interfere with interstate commerce and remanding the case for a new trial (*United Mine Workers of America et al.* v. *Coronado Coal Co. et al.*, 259 U.S. 344 [1922]). At the second trial in district court, held in 1923, the judge ruled that additional evidence brought forward by the company did not demonstrate there had been a violation of the Sherman Act, and he directed a verdict in behalf of the miners. This judgment was upheld in the circuit court of appeals (*Finley* v. *United Mine Workers of America et al.*, 300 F. 972 [1924]) but was overturned by the Supreme Court with respect to District 21, the local unions, and the individual defendants on the basis of the new evidence adduced at the second district court trial, and the case was remanded for still another trial (*Coronado Coal Co. et al.* v. *United Mine Workers of America et al.*, 268 U.S. 295 [1925]). Both a third trial in 1925, and a fourth in 1926, ended in mistrials, and the union and the company finally settled the dispute in 1927, on the eve of a fifth trial, with the union paying the company $27,500.

4. On Jan. 2, 1918, Attorney General Thomas Gregory asked the U.S. Supreme Court to defer argument in seven pending antitrust cases, namely, the suits against the International Harvester Co., the Eastman Kodak Co., the United Shoe Machinery Co., the U.S. Steel Corp., the American Can Co., the Quaker Oats Co., and the Corn Products Refining Co. Solicitor General John Davis noted that "important as the remedy sought in these cases is believed to be, it must give place for the moment to the paramount needs of the hour" (quoted in "Government Defers Anti-Trust Suits," *New York Times,* Jan. 3, 1918).

5. The contempt proceedings were initiated by attorneys for the Hitchman Coal and Coke Co. The company alleged that continued organizing by the United Mine Workers in violation of the injunction banning such activities left the firm unable to hire workers for two of its mines. The contempt proceedings were terminated in April 1918 when the company's attorneys withdrew the petition.

6. On Jan. 21, 1918, Gregory replied that while the Arizona deportations were certainly illegal, it was not clear that they violated federal law. He added that he expected to make a decision on whether to pursue federal prosecutions in the near future. Regarding SG's criticisms of the judiciary, Gregory remarked that his department had no

authority over federal judges (RG 60, General Records of the Department of Justice, DNA).

Cochise County, Ariz., sheriff Harry Wheeler and twenty-four others were eventually indicted in federal district court for the unlawful deportation of more than two hundred Arizona residents, but the charges were dismissed on the grounds that the matter fell under state, not federal, jurisdiction (*U.S.* v. *Wheeler et al.,* 254 F. 611 [1918]). On appeal, the U.S. Supreme Court upheld the district court's ruling (*U.S.* v. *Wheeler et al.,* 254 U.S. 281 [1920]). Prosecution of the case also failed in state court.

From Cyrus Miller

Chicago, Ill. Jan. 20, 1918.

Hon. Sir:

I know that there is a time and place for all things, and feel that now is the time, and the Labor Loyalty Headquarters, the place, that a man of my identity, should speak in defense of a common consideration in the industrial world of men of common fealty.

Tho a Black American of pure African blood, I am not a negro, and when I say a man of my identity, I do not mean a white black man, for such a fellow is at war with himself, in himself, and his most profound sentiments, are but fiction, (so the experience of more than forty years of my life have taught me) but a black, black man of wisdom and integrity as a heritage; American inspiration as environment, knowledge backed by experience that proves to him the necessity of fearlessness in accepting anxiously, duties, obligations as the demands that far transcends the idea of glory as his equipment.

As such a man has not yet appeared, I take the privilege as the time and place demands to call your attention to the great humane appeal that you may not overlook it; that you may bring this Labor Loyalty Week, unfurl a declaration to the world that will emblazon the clear sky, that all laborers 100% American must have a common consideration in the industrial world, that every local in your federation hold open doors for all 100% Americans and that discrimination and segregation be blotted out and you will put in motion an inevetiable accomplishment as your bit, for the world's social democracies, greater than this war can accomplish at this time; such a declaration would regenerate fundamental principles substituting facts for theories.

I do not appeal to you because I had learned of anything in your private or official life that commends itself to me as suggestive along this line but because I feel it to be the only way I can do my bit in this great crisis, and that a word to you might open a debate in your mind as plausible and loyal justice invigorates your humanitarianism.

Our Declaration of Independence says, "All men are created free and equal, endowed with certain inalienable rights, among which are the right to life, liberty and happiness"; yet it was repudiated in the constitution and redeemed by amendments after the Civil War. I'm still impressed that somewhere there is subtilely inscribed or understood "Spurlos Versenkt."[1]

The law that gives a men the right to cage an animal, also gives him a right to protect his captive and tho he does or does not use the necessary precaution for protection of the captive, the law does not avenge the captive, but the one responsible for the captive is held involuntarily.

For the second time Texas advertised herself against colored soldiers (captives) [f]or the second time their helpless captive victims have suffered;[2] for the second time accessors before the fact, have been extold while black 100% Americans have suffered throughout the country; among black Americans there are no pros, spies, traitors, pacifists or I.W.W.'s, but among the accessors before the fact, in Texas, may be any or all the thorns that hamper American solidarity but technically the world of men know, that the part of any federation, that actually deny or challenge the right of its executive head cannot be 100% loyal.

The riot and execution are a fact, but the peculiar questions unanswered are, who is responsible? are the victims (captives) murderers or martyrs? What makes the accessors before the fact immune? Has principle been substituted by vile and wily habits, upon which is built, in sentiment and acts our ideals and maxims? Have we no conspicuous dissenters? Who is responsible?

The world's democracies are not at stake but this crisis is but a necessary evolution, hence, the demand for every influential man and every thinking man to do his bit in the various spheres. I, as a black man, do my bit because I know I am integrant, with or without your recognition, but I feel that you, knowing the test given black men for the past 300 years and yet find them 100% American, demands recognition for you as retribution.

We as Black Men

Stand on this soil thats saturated with blood and tears of ancestors,
Sanctified by martyrdom, romantically awaiting augmenters,
We, with incredible inspiration, seemingly cantagious,
For thoroughly and firm our ideal partiotic ardor rages.

WE NEED,

One Giant essay, one perfect ray, one fact is all that is pleaded,
One center of power, one standard hour, one sentry kept just to lead it.
One grounded right, one beacon light, one duty thats invincible,
One great highway, one right to play, one incontestible principle.

THEN

Strange simplicity and sublime emotion will champion our fate,
No whimsical purpose, nor pretentions, will our history relate,
And, tho hot tears may stream down our cheeks, while our hearts flutter with joy,
'Twill answer harmonious blending sounds with feeling for our boy.

(Signed) Cyrus Miller[3]

TLtcSr, John J. Fitzpatrick Papers, ICHi. Typed notation: *"Copy."* Enclosed in R. Lee Guard to John Fitzpatrick, Jan. 29, 1918, ibid.

1. That is, "sunk without a trace." The German chargé d'affaires in Buenos Aires, Count Karl-Ludwig von Luxburg, used the expression in cables to the German Foreign Office on May 19 and July 9, 1917, which recommended the sinking of Argentinian steamers bound for Europe. The phrase gained notoriety after Secretary of State Robert Lansing released Luxburg's dispatches to the press on Sept. 8.

2. In July 1917 a contingent of black enlisted men from the 24th Infantry moved into an encampment outside Houston. The troops encountered a white population strongly opposed to the posting of black soldiers in their community, and they faced abuse from white residents and police. On the evening of Aug. 23, after two soldiers were attacked and a rumor spread through the camp that a mob was approaching, about a hundred of the troops mutinied, armed themselves, and marched into Houston, firing indiscriminately, killing fifteen people and wounding more than twenty. Two of the soldiers were killed, and two others later died from wounds.

Soldiers involved in the riot were tried in three separate courts martial at San Antonio. The first trial, *U.S. v. Sgt. William Nesbit et al.*, which involved sixty-three defendants, was held in November. All but five of the men were found guilty—thirteen were sentenced to death, forty-one to life at hard labor, and four to shorter terms. The verdicts and sentences were kept secret while they were reviewed by Maj. Gen. John Ruckman, commander of the army's Southern Department. With his approval, and with the army still acting in secret, the thirteen sentenced to death were hanged on Dec. 11.

The second trial, *U.S. v. Cpl. John Washington et al.*, took place in December and involved fifteen defendants, all of whom were found guilty. Five were condemned to death and the others received sentences of seven to ten years at hard labor. Ruckman announced the sentences on Jan. 2, 1918, but because of the outcry from the black community after the earlier, secret executions, their implementation was delayed. A third trial, *U.S. v. Cpl. Robert Tillman et al.*, involving an additional thirty-nine defendants, was held in February and March. Eleven of these men were condemned to hang, twenty-six were sentenced to prison, and two were acquitted.

The judge advocate general and Secretary of War Newton Baker reviewed the verdicts in the *Washington* and *Tillman* trials and in late August, on Baker's recommendation, President Woodrow Wilson commuted the death sentences of ten of the men but let them stand for the other six. Their executions took place in September. Many of the life sentences were later reduced by presidential action; the last of the men was paroled in 1938.

3. On Jan. 29, 1918, R. Lee Guard sent John Fitzpatrick a copy of Cyrus Miller's letter and asked for more information about him (John J. Fitzpatrick Papers, ICHi). Fitzpatrick's reply has not been found.

To William B. Wilson

Washington, D.C. January 23, 1918.

Honorable W. B. Wilson,
Secretary of Labor,
Washington, D.C.
Sir:

Last summer I had an interview with Mr. Giles B. Jackson[1] and three other negro men in regard to a proposal to establish a Bureau of Negro Economics.[2] I was very much impressed with the sound basic sense of the proposition these men submitted, and with the seeming integrity and intelligence of the men themselves.

Mr. Jackson submitted to me his plan which was to secure government aid for their proposed bureau, although retain the bureau under private control. I suggested to him that in order to secure the advantage of federal funds, it would be necessary to establish some official connection with the government. If you could find opportunity to consider Mr. Jackson's plan, and perhaps to have a personal conference with him, I think it would be of value.

Respectfully,   Saml Gompers.
President,   American Federation of Labor.

TLS, RG 174, General Records of the Department of Labor, DNA.

1. SG had met with Giles Beecher Jackson (1853–1924), a Richmond, Va., attorney, on July 20, 1917. Jackson became director of the Negro Division of the U.S. Employment Service in the Department of Labor when it was created in February 1918 and served in that post until mid-1919.

2. The Division of Negro Economics was established by William B. Wilson on May 1, 1918, to advise the Department of Labor on matters relating to black workers. George Haynes was appointed director.

To Joseph Dehan[1]

Jan. 25, 1918.

Mr. Joseph Dehane,
811 Kelly Street, New York City.
Dear Friend:

Last night I returned from trip to Indianapolis, where I worked very hard but think I did a pretty good job. This morning your two letters[2] awaited me. I read them with a great deal of interest. I want to first speak of a personal matter, that is your description of Mrs. Dehan's[3] condition and how she is affected by your son's[4] departure for the other side. You know my great affection for Mrs. Dehan and the regard and esteem in which I hold her, but despite her great mother love I hope you will impress upon her the necessity of just gritting her teeth, and to manifest and be under self-control. The son is doing his duty, [not on]ly to his country as a country, but in defense of the honor and the life and the safety of the women and the girls of the whole country. Let us hope that but few of our boys shall be hurt or make the supreme sacrifice. Let us hope that they may all come back with triumphant shout and safety for manhood, womanhood and childhood, the world over accomplished. No sacrifice is too great in the struggle for its achievement, and I may say that this applies to you too, as well as to Mrs. Dehan.

In addition let me say that when writing to your son, see to it that not a depressing word or expressions of sympathy are contained in the letters. Write to the boy as you would talk in ordinary conversation—talk of interesting events. Do not make him homesick. It is the worst evil of a soldier's life. Write him frequently. A message from home of love and affection will make him feel that his father and mother, his brothers and friends who write him are happy in the conception that he is doing a man's duty.

When you learn where a letter will reach him, I shall be very glad to send him even a word,[5] and I want to express to him my appreciation for his sending to us his splendid photograph in uniform, and he looks better than I have ever seen him in all his life, clean cut, intelligent, and fit.

I think that your work[6] with those Italian cigarmakers was splendid and the results commendable. I felt sure that in your hands the problem would be worked out to good advantage, even to the men who were so stubborn and hid themselves behind a pretense. I thank you for the comprehensive statement you made in regard to that situation.[7]

Now regarding the circular you sent me issued by the Secretary[8] of the New York State Federation of Labor for a proposed act for state health insurance,[9] I have written a letter to Brother Fitzgerald, at Albany, who asked my opinion upon it.[10] I regard the matter as exceedingly serious and fraught with great dangers. If you attend the conference to be held at Albany February sixth, I think you might get from Brother Fitzgerald a copy of my letter to him, or he might let you see it when you get to Albany.

Were you present at the last conference[11] at Albany? I was asked my opinion upon the propositions that were to be considered, and I entered into the subject fully.[12] I see by the subjects adopted that some of my suggestions were approved and incorporated, while others were not regarded favorably. I am sure that my suggestions were appropriate and advantageous to our cause and our movement.

No I have not seen or heard from Mack.[13]

I am going to try to get a seat on the train leaving Washington at eleven o'clock in the morning, due Pennsylvania Station at 4:45.[14] If I cannot get a seat on that train, I shall come on the train leaving 2:40, due Pennsylvania Station 8:07 in the evening. I should like you to meet me.

I return one of the circulars herein, keeping the other for my files.[15]

Sincerely yours,   Saml Gompers.

P.S. Since dictating the above letter, I find that there is not a seat obtainable on the 11 A.M. train Monday, and shall therefore come over on the 2:40 train. due 8.07.

S. G.

TLpS, reel 341, vol. 357, pp. 312–13, SG Letterbooks, DLC.

1. Joseph Dehan, a member of Cigar Makers International Union of America 251 (Packers) of New York City, served as a vice-president of the New York State Federation of Labor (FOL) from 1915 to 1921.

2. Dehan's letters to SG, dated Jan. 14 and Jan. 21, 1918, are in the Files of the Office of the President, General Correspondence, reel 91, frames 452–58, 678–80, *AFL Records*.

3. Sophia Dehan.

4. Lewis Dehan served in France for thirteen months.

5. SG to Lewis Dehan, June 5, 1918, Files of the Office of the President, General Correspondence, reel 96, frames 44–45, *AFL Records*.

6. SG is referring to Dehan's assistance in organizing a cigar shop in New York City in the face of opposition from Italian cigarmakers.

7. That is, Dehan's letter to SG of Jan. 14, 1918 (see n. 2, above).

8. Edward Bates.

9. On Feb. 6, 1918, a conference in Albany called by the executive council of the New York State FOL unanimously approved legislation to create a state health insurance system for industrial workers and dependents not covered by the state's workmen's

compensation law. The measure was introduced in the state senate on Feb. 18 but died in committee.

10. SG's letter to Thomas Fitzgerald of Jan. 22, 1918, warned that a system of state health insurance could pose "grave dangers" to the basic liberties of workers and urged further careful consideration of the measure rather than "hasty action" (reel 230, vol. 242, pp. 611–12, SG Letterbooks, DLC; for a more legible copy, see Files of the Office of the President, General Correspondence, reel 91, frames 709–10, *AFL Records*).

11. A reference to a conference held in Albany on Jan. 8, 1918, under the sponsorship of the executive council of the New York State FOL, which approved the legislative program for 1918. Dehan did not attend the meeting.

12. SG to Fitzgerald, Jan. 2, 1918, reel 229, vol. 241, pp. 978–80, SG Letterbooks, DLC.

13. John A. McDermott.

14. SG left Washington, D.C., for New York City on Jan. 28, 1918, where he made arrangements for the American Alliance for Labor and Democracy's Labor Loyalty Week and met with committees from the Central Federated Union of Greater New York and Vicinity and the United Hebrew Trades in an attempt to reconcile the two organizations. He returned to Washington by Feb. 4.

15. Dehan had sent SG two circulars, one regarding the health insurance act proposed by the New York State FOL and the other pertaining to the cigar shop Dehan had organized.

From Hugh Frayne

New York, January 28, 1918.

Dear Sir and Brother:—

In compliance with instructions contained in your letter[1] of January 18th in which you enclosed copy of letter from George W. Harris,[2] editor of the New York News, 135 West 135th Street, relative to organizing and affiliating the colored workers of the country with the American Federation of Labor,[3] I beg to say that I had a conference in this office on Saturday morning, January 26th, with Mr. Harris, at which time we discussed this matter in detail and I was able to make him understand that contrary to the belief of some, the A.F. of L. had given in the past and were giving at the present, a great deal of time and effort to organizing the colored workers throughout the country.

As a preliminary to taking up this work I suggested that Mr. Harris and a few other prominent colored men of the country would appear[4] before the Executive Council some time during its next session,[5] the time to be mutually agreed upon, when a better understanding might be reached and a plan made whereby a campaign for organizing the colored workers could be worked out. He suggested the names of the following colored men to be present with him:

Emmet J. Scott,[6] Assistant to the Secretary of War,

Major Robert R. Moton,[7] Principal of Tuskegee School, the position formerly occupied by Booker T. Washington.

While I have in mind that former delegations of colored men have appeared before the Executive Council presuming to represent the colored workers, I am satisfied that they were not of sufficient prominence and standing to interest the colored workers of the country, hence the suggestion that these men who are the foremost men of their race be asked to appear and if they can be made to understand, which I believe will be an easy matter, the importance of organizing and affiliating the colored workers and they will be willing to give their assistance to that end, the undertaking will be a success from the beginning.

In line with the above, I suggest that you communicate with Mr. Harris, setting a time for him and the others whom I have mentioned to appear before the Council some time during the next session.[8]

Hoping these suggestions will meet with your approval, I beg to remain,

Fraternally yours,   Hugh Frayne

General Organizer   American Federation of Labor.

TLS, AFL Microfilm Convention File, reel 28, frame 2246, *AFL Records.*

1. SG to Hugh Frayne, Jan. 18, 1918, reel 230, vol. 242, p. 544, SG Letterbooks, DLC.

2. George Wesley Harris (1884–1948) was editor of the *Amsterdam News* (New York City) from 1910 to 1913 and editor and publisher of the *New York News* from 1913 to about 1937. He served as a New York City alderman from 1920 to 1923.

3. Harris wrote SG on Jan. 12, 1918, expressing interest in cooperating with the AFL in organizing black workers and requesting a meeting with SG to discuss the subject (AFL Microfilm Convention File, reel 28, frame 2246, *AFL Records*). SG replied on Jan. 18 that he would be happy to meet with Harris when he came to Washington, D.C., but suggested that in the interim he meet with Frayne in New York City. He sent Frayne a copy of Harris's letter and his reply the same day and asked Frayne to give the matter his attention (reel 230, vol. 242, pp. 530, 544, SG Letterbooks, DLC).

4. See "Excerpts from the Minutes of a Meeting of the Executive Council of the AFL," Feb. 12, 1918, below.

5. The AFL Executive Council met in Washington, D.C., Feb. 10–17, 1918.

6. Emmett Jay Scott (1873–1957) served as a special assistant to the secretary of war from 1917 to 1919 on matters relating to black soldiers and civilians. He had previously served as private secretary to Booker T. Washington (1897–1915) and was later secretary-treasurer (1919–33) and secretary (1933–38) of Howard University.

7. Robert Russa Moton (1867–1940) was principal of the Tuskegee Normal and Industrial Institute from 1915 to 1935.

8. On Feb. 7, 1918, SG sent letters of invitation to Harris, Moton, and Scott to meet with the AFL Executive Council during its February meeting (reel 231, vol. 243, pp. 252–54, SG Letterbooks, DLC).

To John Frey[1]

January 29, 1918.

Mr. John P. Frey,
Editor, *Iron Molders Journal*
Commercial Tribune Building, Cincinnati, Ohio.
Dear Sir and Brother:—

You have, no doubt, learned through the newspapers that upon my invitation,[2] four leading labor men of Great Britain will shortly visit the United States to make a tour of the country to bring about a better understanding among the workers and all of our people and to solidify the action of the workers of both Great Britain and the United States. You also know that I have been urged to go to England with that same purpose in view but I have thus far found it impossible to make the trip.

What the representative British Workers will do in bringing the message to the workers of America cannot be compared in importance with the message of good will and encouragement from the workers of America to those of Great Britain, particularly in this crucial hour.

Colonel A. C. Murrey[3] and Mr. Arthur Willert,[4] representing the British Government, called upon me. We had a conference, the purpose of which was to take into consideration an invitation which these gentlemen tendered for a small delegation of representative workers of America, in company with a small group of men and women of other walks of life to visit Great Britain[5] and bring a message of hope and encouragement that shall hearten the workers and the people of Great Britain in the terrific conflict in which they, with the allied countries of France, Italy and the United States are engaged.

In the conference with Colonel Murrey and Mr. Willert, the names of many were considered. It was finally concluded that an invitation should be extended to you to serve upon the mission as indicated above. A formal invitation will be sent you in due course.

The primary purpose of my writing you is to acquaint you with the above facts and to press upon you the importance of favorably considering and accepting the invitation when it reaches you.[6]

Insofar as publicity is concerned, I trust that you will regard this letter as confidential, at least, for the time being.

Fraternally yours,   Saml Gompers.
President,   American Federation of Labor.

TLpS, reel 230, vol. 242, pp. 969–70, SG Letterbooks, DLC.

1. John Philip FREY served as editor of the *International Molders' Journal* (to 1907, the *Iron Molders' Journal*) from 1903 to 1927.

2. SG to George Barnes, Jan. 5, 1918, Files of the Office of the President, General Correspondence, reel 91, frame 238, *AFL Records*. SG issued the invitation at Barnes's suggestion.

3. Arthur Cecil Murray (1879–1962) was a military attaché at the British embassy in Washington, D.C., from mid-1917 until March 1918.

4. Arthur Willert (1882–1973), chief American correspondent for the *Times* (London) from 1910 to 1917 and again from 1918 to 1920, was the Washington representative of the British Ministry of Information (1917–18).

5. An American labor mission, headed by James Wilson of the Pattern Makers, visited England, France, and Ireland in April and May 1918. The other members of the labor mission included Frey, William Johnston of the Machinists, George Berry of the Printing Pressmen, Martin Ryan of the Railway Carmen, Melinda Scott of the Straw Hat Trimmers, Agnes Nestor of the Glove Workers, William Short of the Washington State Federation of Labor, and Chester Wright, publicity director of the American Alliance for Labor and Democracy.

6. Frey replied on Jan. 31, 1918, that he would accept the appointment provided it was approved by the president and executive board of the Molders (Files of the Office of the President, General Correspondence, reel 92, frames 131–32, *AFL Records*). SG met with Frey and the other members of the American labor mission on Mar. 25 and again on June 1 (ibid., Conferences, reel 120, frames 232–50, 304–26). For his instructions to the delegation, see SG to Wilson, Mar. 26, 1918, reel 233, vol. 245, pp. 206–8, SG Letterbooks, DLC.

From William B. Wilson

Office of the Secretary
Department of Labor
Washington January 29, 1918

My dear Mr. Gompers:

The President of the United States has placed upon the Secretary of Labor the responsibility of formulating and administering, in the present emergency, a National Labor Program.[1]

The present emergency demands the most effective utilization of the productive resources of the nation. The National Labor Program must be administered with that goal in mind. It will greatly assist in that administration to have representatives of employers and of employes meet in conference with the view of reaching agreements on principles and policies which should govern their relations.

I am, accordingly, taking the liberty of requesting the American Federation of Labor to designate five persons who will adequately and appropriately represent the workers of the country in such a conference. These five persons will be asked to name a sixth who will represent the general public, and these six persons will meet six others selected in a similar manner by the National Industrial Conference Board, which has been asked to represent for this purpose the employers of the country.

It is desirable that the conference be called at the earliest possible moment. There should, of course, be no time limit imposed upon the selection of representatives which would operate to cause a hasty choice, but it is earnestly hoped that your list of five representatives may be in my hands within a very few days.[2]

Yours very sincerely,   W B Wilson
Secretary of Labor

TLS, Files of the Office of the President, General Correspondence, reel 92, frame 92, *AFL Records.*

1. On Jan. 4, 1918, President Woodrow Wilson, acting on the recommendation of the Council of National Defense, appointed Secretary of Labor William B. Wilson as War Labor Administrator, with responsibility for creating federal agencies to maintain a stable workforce for war production, safeguard the working and living conditions of workers in war-related industries, and promptly and equitably resolve labor disputes. Secretary Wilson appointed a seven-member advisory council to outline a plan of organization, and the council in turn recommended the creation of the War Labor Conference Board to develop uniform standards and procedures to guide the government's labor policy. Wilson asked SG (in the letter printed here) and the National Industrial Conference Board, an employers' organization, for nominations to the new board, which was to consist of five labor members and five employers, with each side choosing a representative of the public to serve as chairman on alternate days. The board's report, dated Mar. 29, recommended the creation of the National War Labor Board to oversee the adjustment of labor disputes in war-related industries. (See "To the Executive Council of the AFL," Mar. 30, 1918, below.)

2. SG submitted the names of Frank Hayes of the United Mine Workers, William Hutcheson of the Carpenters, Joseph Franklin of the Boiler Makers, Victor Olander of the Lake Seamen, and Thomas Rickert of the Garment Workers (SG to William B. Wilson, Feb. 4, 1918, reel 231, vol. 243, p. 173, SG Letterbooks, DLC). Franklin was unable to serve and was replaced by William Johnston of the Machinists. The labor representatives chose Frank Walsh to serve as joint chairman with William Howard Taft, who was named by the employers.

From Bernard Larger

Office of B. A. Larger General Secretary
United Garment Workers of America
New York, February 1st, 1918.

Dear Sir and Brother:—

I am enclosing a copy of an article published in today's issue of the "Times.["][1] I was called on the 'phone, and my attention directed to it, and was therefore compelled to send out and buy the paper. Doubtless you are aware that the news-dealers in this city are on strike.[2]

The article explains itself. Kirstein[3] will retain the offices of the former Board of Control,[4] in New York City, and as long as he is there, you might just as well have Mrs. Kelley.[5]

Secretary Baker has determined to take the side with the secession movement, against organized labor, and I think that right out of his own office there are other things going out relative to the eight hour day—decisions being made that will affect all the firms manufacturing goods for the government.

We are in the same position we were before the change. The man[6] who was fair and wanted to treat everybody right has been detailed to Omaha, Nebr. This does not speak volumes for the fairness of Secretary Baker toward organized labor, by recognizing the representatives of the secession movement. Kirstein was one of the their representatives in Boston and took an active part in having the clothing manufacturers recognize the secession movement.

In the firms, manufacturing government work in this city, where the seceders have been on strike[7] for some time past, nothing has been done by the Secretary of War to control the situation—they have the right to call a strike whenever they please, and I presume that Kirstein will read the Riot Act to the manufacturers for not recognizing them.

We have a large number of manufacturers in this city who are perfectly willing to recognize the Garment Workers, or the American Federation of Labor as they put it, but when they see that the American Federation of Labor has so little influence with Secretary Baker, I venture to say that a conference which is now being determined on, will be called off and they will simply tell us, as they have done before, that the Secretary of War does not recognize the American Federation of Labor, and so why should they.

Fraternally yours,   B. A Larger
General Secretary,   United Garment Workers of America.

TLS, Files of the Office of the President, General Correspondence, reel 92, frames 179–80, *AFL Records.*

1. The article, "Post for Dr. E. M. Hopkins," reported that Louis Kirstein had been retained as "administrator to enforce labor standards in the manufacture of army clothing" (*New York Times,* Feb. 1, 1918).

2. On Jan. 26, 1918, members of the New York News Dealers' and Stationers' Protective Association began boycotting most of the city's major dailies in protest against a new price scale. The newspapers countered the boycott by setting up their own newsstands and increasing home delivery service, and newsdealers who were not members of the association simply refused to honor it. The association officially ended the boycott on Feb. 7.

3. Louis Edward Kirstein (1867–1942), vice-president and manager of William Filene's Sons Co. of Boston, was chairman of the board of control established by Newton Baker in August 1917 to oversee labor standards in the manufacture of army clothing. Bernard Larger accused him of prejudice in favor of the Amalgamated Clothing Workers of America.

4. The War Department dissolved the board of control for labor standards in army clothing on Jan. 23, 1918, on the grounds that the standards had been incorporated into army contracts so the board's functions could be handled directly by the army through the Quartermaster General. Kirstein, however, was appointed administrator of labor standards in army clothing and continued the work he had done as head of the board of control.

5. Florence KELLEY, secretary of the National Consumers' League, also served as a member of the board of control. Larger charged that she was a pacifist who opposed the war effort.

6. Probably a reference to Walter Kreusi, the only member of the board of control about whom Larger had not voiced objection.

7. On Sept. 10, 1917, the Amalgamated Clothing Workers struck Mark Cowen and Co., a manufacturer of army clothing, in a dispute over wages and working conditions that involved some seven hundred workers. The firm eventually hired members of the United Garment Workers of America to replace the strikers and was gradually able to resume production in December. At the time Larger wrote this letter, the Clothing Workers were also on strike against the F.B.Q. Clothing Co. That strike, which began on Jan. 10, 1918, when the firm locked out about a hundred employees who made uniforms, eventually involved the company's entire workforce—nearly three thousand workers. It ended on Mar. 9 under the terms of a settlement arranged by a federal mediator.

From Edwin McCoy

Legal Rights Committee
Arizona State Federation of Labor
February 1st, 1918.

Dear Sir and Brother:

I am in receipt of your letter of Jan. 19th[1] with reference to action by the Department of Justice in the Bisbee affair and also a letter from the Attorney General a copy of which is enclosed herewith.

From this reply it would seem that the Attorney General was considering prosecutions for the actual deportations. This we are advised by Mr. Felix Frankfu[r]ter and numerous other attorneys was not a violation of any Federal statutes.

The report of the President's Mediation Commission called attention to numerous violations however, to-wit:

On the morning of July 12th Mr. ____ Stout,[2] Supt. of the Copper Queen Smelter and Mr. ____ Rae,[3] Auditor of the Phelps-Dodge Co. (Copper Queen Branch) assumed control of the Douglas office of the Western Union Telegraph Co. and exercised a complete censorship over all outgoing messages. The Douglas office appears to be the relay office for that part of Arizona and the control over messages from Bisbee was as effective as if control had been exercised in Bisbee. At the same time representatives of the Sheriff's office of Cochise County, Arizona,[4] attempted and did with considerable success exercise a censorship over the local telephone office of the Mountain States Telephone Company at Bisbee. Almost seven months have elapsed since these arbitrary and unlawful acts were committed and it would seem that the Department of Justice had had sufficient time to complete any investigation required and be in a position to act.

At the time the President's Mediation Commission was in Bisbee Mr. Felix Frankfurter informed me that the violation of the draft laws in this district were the most flagrant and extensive that he was aware of in the United States. Mr. Harry Wheeler,[5] Sheriff, was chairman of the Local Exemption Board and Mr. G. H. Dowell,[6] General Manager of the Phelps-Dodge Co. (Copper Queen Division) was a member of the District Exemption Board. Among the men deported on 12th July were several hundred who were registered and were under legal obligation to report to the Local Exemption Board. In addition a large number of men who were subsequently deported by the "Kangaroo Court" were registered under the draft law.

In view of the fact that these men had been forcibly ejected from the state and armed guards posted to prevent their return, a number of these men, on receipt of notice to appear before the exemption board for examination failed to appear. According to the local press of the Warren District these men were certified direct into the army without medical examination or the right to present any claim for exemption and have it legally passed upon as provided by the draft law. In this case the case of Chas. N. Cavis[7] is worthy of notice. Mr. Cavis was a member in good standing of the Bisbee painters union. Shortly after July 12th he was produced by the Sheriff's office before the "Kangaroo Court" and forcibly deported from the district. He failed to appear before the local exemption board for examination and was included in the Cochise County contingent sent from Douglas. At the time it was well known among his friends that he was suffering from consumption, but no medical examination was had and he was sent to Camp Funston. Some time thereafter he was discharged for physical disability and soon after his return to Arizona he died and was buried by the Tucson painters union.[8] This is an extreme case but his untimely death is a direct result of the unlawful actions of the local authorities, several of whom were members of the U.S. Exemption boards.

Other men who returned to the district in compliance with notices to appear before the Local Exemption Board were arrested and thrown into jail without legal charge or warrant. Under arrest they were produced before the local board and if accepted were sent to Camp Funston, but if rejected for any reason or presented legal claim for exemption they were immediately deported.

It would seem to a layman that the Department of Justice had had ample time to thoroughly investigate these patent violations of the law and that the long and inexcusable delay in prosecuting the offenders was due to political and corporate influence rather than from lack of sufficient information.

At the time the President's Mediation Commission was in Arizona the settlement it made provided that no discrimination should be shown in the employment of men, except that those guilty of disloyal utterances should not be employed, and provided machinery for enforcing their agreement.

Immediately after the Commission left the State the "Loyalty" League took it upon itself to determine who were loyal citizens qualified for employment by the mining companies. In direct violation of the agreement with the Commission the companies have made it a fixed rule not to employ any person who does not present the written approval of the local branch of the "Loyalty" League, but up to the present time the officials designated by the President's Mediation Commission to enforce that Commission's agreement have taken no action to stop this unlawful practice. At the same time the "Loyalty" Leagues were used as a means of blacklisting men, as they could ask questions which are unlawful for an employer to ask in this state. Of late, I am advised, that among the numerous questions asked of men applying for work concerns their political beliefs, especially with reference to their stand with reference to how they will vote for Governor, Hunt[9] or Campbell.[10]

The officials of these "Loyalty" Leagues are the same men who conducted the deportations and other unlawful acts last summer and you can readily see that the findings and settlement of the President's Mediation Commission is very much of a farce as long as the Government permits these men guilty of deporting thousands of men and interfering with the operation of the draft laws to virtually enforce the findings of the President's Mediation Commission according to their own ideas and impose such additional requirements and conditions as they see fit.

No relief can be expected through the local Federal officials. The Phelps-Dodge Co. has been in politics in this district for many years and all local Federal officials have been appointed through its influence or are at least not offensive to this corporation.

I trust that you can bring sufficient pressure to bear on the Department of Justice to secure an early decision as to its intention and am thoroughly convinced that procedure through the regular officials of that department will not be received with any degree of confidence, but that the situation is of sufficient importance to warrant the appointment of a Special Agent who will be free from suspicion of being subject to Phelps-Dodge influence.

Until I hear from you[11] I will make no reply to the letter of the Attorney General.

With all good wishes and kindest regards, I remain,

Fraternally yours,   (signed) E. T. McCoy
For Legal Rights Committee of
Arizona State Federation of Labor.

TLtpSr, reel 231, vol. 243, pp. 336–38, SG Letterbooks, DLC. Typed notation: *"Copy."* Enclosed in SG to Thomas Gregory, Feb. 7, 1918, ibid., p. 335.

1. SG to Edwin McCoy, Jan. 19, 1918, reel 230, vol. 242, p. 528, SG Letterbooks, DLC.

2. Harry H. Stout of Douglas, Ariz. The Copper Queen works was a division of the Phelps Dodge Corp.

3. Robert Rae of Douglas.

4. Both Douglas and Bisbee are located in Cochise County, Ariz.

5. Harry C. Wheeler was sheriff of Cochise County.

6. Grant H. Dowell of Douglas.

7. Charles N. Cavis (or Cavins), a sign painter, was a member of Brotherhood of Painters, Decorators, and Paperhangers of America 983 of Bisbee. He died in late 1917.

8. Painters' local 596.

9. George Willey Paul Hunt (1859–1934), a Democrat, served seven terms as governor of Arizona (1912–17, 1917–19, 1923–29, 1931–33). In the 1916 election he was apparently defeated by Thomas Campbell, but Hunt contested the result and, after a lengthy recount, was declared the winner.

10. Thomas Edward Campbell (1878–1944), a Republican, served as governor of Arizona from Jan. 1 to Dec. 25, 1917, and from 1919 to 1923.

11. SG had already sent a letter to McCoy regarding Gregory's reply to SG's letter of Jan. 19 (SG to McCoy, Jan. 25, 1918, reel 230, vol. 242, p. 938, SG Letterbooks, DLC). See "To Thomas Gregory," Jan. 19, 1918, n. 6, above.

To Joseph Franklin

Washington, D.C., Feb. 6th, 1918.

Mr. Jos. A. Franklin,
National Hotel, Washington, D.C.
You have no doubt seen the indiscriminate charges made against the
workers in the shipyards charging them with shirking and slacking in
their work. It is of the utmost importance that you and a committee
having knowledge of the situation come to Washington the earliest
possible time to refute the charges before the Senate Committee.[1] If
the charges are untrue and I believe them to be, there seems to be a
disposition to discredit labor over the whole country. If on the other
hand the charges have any basis at all arrangements should be made
to change the situation as soon as possible. Please telegraph reply.

Samuel Gompers.

TWpSr, reel 231, vol. 243, p. 223, SG Letterbooks, DLC.

1. Joseph Franklin testified before the Senate Committee on Commerce on Feb.
14, 1918, during its hearings on the Emergency Fleet Corporation, in order to refute
charges that workers engaged in ship hull construction were slowing down their work
and interfering with production.

To H. C. Frank

February 6, 1918.

Mr. H. C. Frank,
801 E. 4th St., Brookings, S.D.
Dear Sir:
The American labor movement has never regarded government
ownership an[d] operation in itself as a solution of industrial problems. Government ownership and operation may retain all of the defects and injustices of private ownership and operation. Whether either system has advantages over the other depends entirely upon the
principles upon which operation is based. Either system may provide
democratic conditions under which workers have an opportunity to
present and to maintain their rights and best interests. Government
ownership, which establishes all the evils of bureaucracy may deny
employes the essentials of justice and freedom. The welfare of employes always depends upon their self-interested knowledge of their

own business interests and their ability to forward these interests. Industrial organization must be flexible so as to meet new situations and of such a character that those affected can make necessary provisions to continuously safe-guard their rights and welfare.

The American labor movement has indorsed government ownership of railroads and agencies for communication, as well as municipal utilities, but it has always insisted that government ownership and control as well as private ownership and operation shall be safe-guarded by the right of employes to organize. Government operation of railroads as a war measure was a necessary short cut to eliminate the evils that have resulted from legislation that prevented the railroads of the country from operating as a unified continental system as well as from the mischief resulting from the control which the banking interests have established over railroads.

Very truly yours,   Saml Gompers.
President,   American Federation of Labor.

TLpS, reel 231, vol. 243, p. 473, SG Letterbooks, DLC.

To Woodrow Wilson

Washington, D.C. February 9, 1918.

Honorable Woodrow Wilson,
President of the United States,
Washington, D.C.
Sir:—

Mr. William English Walling and I have had several conferences, particularly in these past few days, at which was discussed the situation as it exists in Russia and Germany.

As a result, he has prepared a statement which I have gone over with him. It fully represents our views of the situation. It is our opinion that the statement should be presented to you for your consideration and I, therefore, take the liberty of enclosing it herein in the hope that it may be a contribution of some helpfulness to your thoughts on the subject.

Respectfully yours,   Saml Gompers.
President,   American Federation of Labor.

[ENCLOSURE]
THE CHIEF DANGER OF REVOLUTIONS AND REVOLUTIONARY
MOVEMENTS IN EASTERN EUROPE: REVOLUTIONS IN WESTERN
EUROPE.

Revolutions can succeed or cause serious trouble more easily in free countries than in military autocracies. Hence, free countries have more to fear than military autocracies from international revolutionary movements like that of the Bolsheviki or the German Minority Socialists.[1]

The Governments of America and Great Britain are doing everything possible to encourage the German Minority Socialists and are apparently inclined to recognize the Bolsheviki as the de facto Government of Russia, which they undoubtedly are. But such recognition, or any friendly steps, would be taken by the Bolsheviki in Russia and all other countries as an acknowledgment of partial defeat by the "imperialist" governments of Great Britain, France and America, against which they have declared a world wide class war (with violence and a reign of terror, according to Lenine's last speech to the Soviet).[2]

The German and Austrian pseudo-revolutionary strikes[3] in reality proved the helplessness of the German and Austrian workers unless aided by widespread military revolt. But, occurring as they did at the same time with the Bolshevik conquest at Kiev, Odessa and Orenburg,[4] they have immeasurably strengthened Bolshevik confidence—until the slightest concession, or anything but a continuation of complete outward indifference, would be taken by them as showing that they are conquering the Entente countries also, and that we are becoming afraid of pacifist strikes similar to the Austrian and German ones.

The direct objective of our government in "establishing a better understanding" with the Bolsheviki is not to encourage them either in their home or their foreign policy but solely to delay and restrict their approach to Germany and above all to encourage their efforts to revolutionize the peoples of Central Europe. We are also endeavoring to appeal directly to these peoples to revolt. Both policies have the over-whelming approval of the Entente peoples. But we forget that the continuing success of Bolshevism in Russia and the growing strength of pacifist strikes in Germany and Austria immensely aid the already dangerous pacifist movements among the working-men of France, England, and Italy—movements united in the demand for a Stockholm conference to bring about "an immediate democratic peace." As we have seen with the Bolsheviki, the emphasis is on the "immediacy" which involves a recognition of the war map and of the military situation at the time the conference is held. This is proved nearly every time a Stockholm advocate gets up to speak or write. "This awful war must end at once." That is the avowed purpose of the Conference, which proposes to deal with "realities."

Entirely independently of German victories, brutal German peace terms, Bolshevik surrenders, or other events, the Stockholm movement grows—without the slightest check or interruption. I have watched carefully for the influence of events. It is nil. No German victory or ultimatum can affect the underlying cause, war weariness—accompanied by Utopian dreams fanned into new life by the Russian revolution.

The Stockholm movement grows apace. Sooner or later delegations may steal from the Entente countries (or be chosen from persons residing abroad) and the conference will occur—or an agreement will be reached without it. The conference will contain one minority demanding German peace terms and another standing for the equal rights of all peoples, but the overwhelming majority will be for those terms upon which an immediate peace can be obtained. And if the conference is not held a Labor and Socialist entente, including all the parties of Europe will probably soon be formed and will reach the same conclusion.

The current in this direction is steady and rapid, and is accelerating. The French Socialists are unanimous and the labor unionists nearly unanimous for Stockholm, while a clear majority have already subordinated the question of peace terms to the proposition that an immediate peace can and should be attained. In Italy the situation was similar until the great defeat. After that there was a short revival of the fighting spirit; all later reports indicate a rapid tendency for Socialists and unionists to resume their previous revolutionary pacifist activities. The situation in England is not very much better. For the first time a full third of the labor unions have adopted the whole pacifist program, while Henderson, a leading spokesman of British Labor repeats almost daily that an international Socialist and Labor conference can bring an early end to the war. There is no danger that an international revolutionary strike to end the war will begin in England, but there is a very grave danger that such a movement may spread to England from Italy or France. The danger is not immediate. But if Bolshevism continues to succeed, and the German Socialists' strikes become more prolonged and menacing, a few months more may produce movements far more threatening to the French and Italian armies than are Bolshevism and German Socialism [to] the armies of Germany and Austria. Such a general European movement would almost certainly spread to England. Nor could it fail to have an effect on Chicago, New York, San Francisco and our other foreign industrial centers in this country.

Even if—in the midst of such a crisis—the German government were overthrown and the war brought to an end, Germany would keep a very large part of the advantages she has won.

For the danger is that these widespread strikes will begin before the power of America has been fully developed, that is before Germany has lost anything whatever of her conquests. The German Socialists might voluntarily and magnanimously surrender a certain part of the German gains. But even the Haase[5] and Liebknecht programs do not offer to relinquish German domination over Germany's present allies, nor her economic domination over Russia and all surrounding small nations. Nor does the Haase program offer any solution of the questions of German and Austrian Poland and Alsace-Lorraine or propose any compensation for the vast destruction done by the Kaiser—except very vaguely—and insufficiently—in the case of Belgium.

But it is far more probable that any revolutionary movement in Germany, before her military defeat—would prove either partial or abortive. The result would then be that Germany would have been less weakened by her own upheaval than Italy, and France—and, perhaps, less weakened than England.

The peace then offered would be even worse than that of Haase, namely, Erzberger's[6] and Czernin's[7] Teutonic adaptation of the status quo ante and "no annexations, no indemnities" formula, with neighboring nations bound by coerced economic treaties and "readjustments of the frontiers."

To aid the German Socialists (positively) and the Bolsheviki (negatively) is not only playing with fire, it is almost certain to end the war before German defeat or American victory—with all the consequences that must inevitably follow such an indecisive outcome.

TLS and TD, Woodrow Wilson Papers, DLC.

1. That is, the Unabhängige Sozialdemokratische Partei Deutschlands (USPD; Independent Social Democratic party) of Hugo Haase and the Spartakusbund (Spartacus League) of Karl Liebknecht and Rosa Luxemburg.

2. Vladimir Ilich Lenin (1870–1924) was a founder of the Russian Communist party, a leader of the Bolshevik Revolution, and head of the Soviet government from 1917 until his death. He made these remarks in an address before the Third All-Russian Congress of Soviets in January 1918 after the Bolsheviks had dissolved the Constituent Assembly.

3. A wave of strikes began in Berlin on Jan. 28, 1918, triggered by the harsh German territorial demands on Russia at Brest Litovsk, which indicated to war-weary Germans both the inflexibility of the country's military leaders and the likelihood of a lengthy continuation of the war. Three to four hundred thousand strikers took to the streets in Berlin, and the strikes soon spread to other large cities and eventually involved over a million workers. Facing severe shortages of food, fuel, and clothing, the strik-

ers demanded immediate peace negotiations based on the formula of no annexations and no indemnities, an end to autocratic rule and military repression in Germany, and amnesty for political offenders. The strikes were put down quickly and with great severity, and thousands of the strikers were arrested and drafted into the army.

4. The Bolsheviks captured Kiev, Orenburg, and Odessa in late January and early February 1918.

5. Hugo Haase (1863–1919), a delegate to the Reichstag (1897–1907, 1912–18, 1919), was a critic of German annexationist war policies and an opponent of the government's requests for war appropriations. Expelled from the Sozialdemokratische Partei Deutschlands (Social Democratic Party of Germany) in January 1917, he was subsequently a founder of the USPD. Haase condemned the German demands at Brest Litovsk and called for an immediate end to the war with the right of self-determination for the peoples in the occupied territories. He died on Nov. 7, 1919, from wounds suffered during an assassination attempt the previous month.

6. Matthias Erzberger (1875–1921), a delegate to the Reichstag (1903–18, 1919–21) and a leader of the Zentrum (Center party), headed the German armistice commission at Compiègne in November 1918 and served as Germany's finance minister from June 1919 to May 1920. Although he sponsored a peace resolution approved by the Reichstag in July 1917 that called for peace without annexations or indemnities, freedom of the seas, economic harmony, and international courts of arbitration, he endorsed the German demands at Brest Litovsk. Erzberger was assassinated on Aug. 26, 1921.

7. Count Ottokar Czernin (1872–1932) served as foreign minister of Austria-Hungary from 1916 to 1918.

Excerpts from the Minutes of a Meeting of the Executive Council of the AFL

Tuesday, February 12, 1918

AFTERNOON SESSION.

. . .

In accordance with previous arrangement upon request from representatives of colored workers, a hearing was granted with the following representatives present:[1]

R. R. Moton, Principal Tuskegee Institute.

John R. Shillady,[2] Secretary National Association for the Advancement of Colored People.

Fred. R. Moore,[3] Editor New York Age.

Archibald Grimke,[4] Washington Association for the Advancement of Colored People.

Emmett J. Scott, Special Assistant to the Secretary of War.

Eugene Kinckle Jones, Executive Secretary, National League.

Thomas Jesse Jones,[5] Educational Director Phelps Stokes Fund.

In the course of the hearing President Gompers made the following statement:

Meeting Executive Council, Feb. 12, 1918.

"Mr. Gompers: Before you leave I think I should indulge myself in an observation or two in connection with the purpose of your coming to us and presenting the matters you have.

["]First, I am confident that I express the opinion of each and every member of the Executive Council of the American Federation of Labor that we welcome your call, and that the subjects matter which you submit to us for consideration will receive due attention.

["]I may say that among the earliest declarations of the American Federation of Labor was a resolution reading something like this. I won't trust my memory to assert that it is verbally accurate, but essentially it is:

["] 'That it is the duty of the working people of the United States to organize and cooperate for the protection and the promotion of the rights and interests of all the workers and without regard to nationality, sex, politics, color or religion.'[6]

["]The American Federation of Labor publishes a whole lot of literature. In one or more of the leaflets or pamphlets issued, that resolution and declaration has a conspicuous place, and in the years which have passed such circulars have been printed and distributed by the millions.[7]

["]As has already been stated by a number of the members of the Executive Council that in their respective trades and organizations colored workers are received with the same welcome and receiving the same support as are white workers. Among those organizations is my own trade union.[8] For many years a colored man[9] was the treasurer of our International Union. At one of the conventions of the American Federation of Labor held at Birmingham, Alabama,[10] we went so far, probably further than we had a right to go or that it was practical to go, but we declined to participate in a banquet which was prepared for us, for the officers and the delegates of that convention, because the colored delegates to that convention were not invited. That was in 1891. The banquet was abandoned because of our refusal to participate in it under those circumstances.[11]

["]At every convention of the American Federation of Labor in the past thirty years there have been colored men, and they have received at our hands the same treatment of courtesy and cordiality and fraternity as any white man could expect. At the last convention of the A.F. of L. held at Buffalo in November, there were a number of delegates of colored workmen there and they had certain propositions which they submitted for consideration of the convention. There were some of them acting rather diffidently and all too modestly, and because of the realization of that fact, as presiding officer I asked them to come from the far part of the convention hall right to the center so that they might be seen and heard, and have the advantage of talking to and being heard by all the delegates at the same time, and the resolutions they offered were of a practical character and were adopted.[12] Also resolutions offered then and at other times for the purpose of organizing colored workmen. It is a self-evident truth which Mr. Harris uttered that unless we help the negro workmen to help themselves to raise their standards they will inevitably help to either check or break down the standards of the white workers. So if it be not a question of humanity, if it be not a question of consideration for the colored workers it is a question of self-protection at least. The barest, crudest manifestation of the facts warrant us in doing all that we possibly can in trying to encourage and help to organize the colored workmen of America.

["]At the convention of the United Mine Workers of America, held ending about two weeks ago,[13] I had the pleasure of being in attendance personally at that convention. I there saw quite a respectable number of colored delegates in attendance at that convention and accorded every right and courtesy. I may say with some pardonable pride that at the conclusion of my address to that convention, it was a colored delegate[14] who arose and moved that my address be printed for distribution to the delegates and for general distribution to the delegates, and that the motion of that colored delegate was adopted by unanimous vote.

["]Now the American Federation of Labor, realizing the situation as it exists, particularly in the south, has gone so far that whereas there are a number of central labor unions in the south composed of delegates from the trade unions and who are prejudiced to that extent that they will not sit in the same hall with colored delegates, the American Federation of Labor has provided that when in the judgment of the Executive Council the circumstances shall warrant, an exception shall be made and that a charter to an additional central labor union may be issued when it is composed of delegates from the negro workers' unions. That is something which we do not tolerate in any other instance.

["]The fact of the matter is, and I am going to try to speak as plain to you as a man ought to men. That is my characteristic. Sometimes I say things that are not always congenial. But in many instances the conduct of some of the colored workmen, and those who have spoken for them has not been in asking or demanding that equal rights be accorded to them as to white workmen, but somewhat conveying the idea that they are to be petted and coddled and given special consideration and special privilege. Of course that can't be done. And then I want to make another observation, which in my several years of experience has come to me. The colored workers have been the victims of many of the colored misleaders who have sought advantage to themselves at the sacrifice of the interests of the rank and file of the colored workmen, to ride into power, to ride into position, to ride into emolument or advantage. More instances of that class of action have come under my observation than I care to mention even approximately.

["]Several members of this Executive Council have had conferences with the late Mr. Washington,[15] and there is considerable correspondence. There was one great difficulty, and I say it with all respect to the wonderful work which Mr. Washington has done for his people during his great life, and that was that we could not get anything like an expression of hearty accord with our movement. To my mind an educational institution such as Hampton and Tuskegee ought to concern itself with something more than this super-education, this academic education, something even additional to manual training, and that is to meet the real facts of life, not in the theory of this academic learning. I think that the institutions of learning throughout the whole world are emerging from and developing into the understanding that the prime duty of man is to be of value to society, to his fellow man. The old concept of teaching was that the dignity and the advantage and the emoluments that would come from a university education would be in the professions and the professions are largely parasitical; the emergence from that and the development into the concept that to do work and service to society and to contribute to the health and the comfort of the people is of primary importance and carries with it greater dignity and honor and service. The duty which the students owe to society after they have graduated, their duty in their every day walk of life is to associate themselves with their fellows in so far as it is possible for them to associate. It has been well said by a number of you delegates, that the American Federation of Labor is in addition to being an idealistic organization, a practical organization and undertakes to deal with the practical questions of the day, never losing sight of the ideal of the hope, of the aspirations for a higher and a better life for all. It is only of recent times that we hear what I interpret and what I see as manifested here this afternoon, a sincere desire on the part of the representatives of colored workers to seek the assistance and the cooperation of the organized labor movement of America in order that the best interests of the colored workers may be protected and promoted. I have seen it growing and I am free to say to you that to me it is very, very welcome.

["]You must have in mind this fact, gentlemen, that this is a Federation of organized workers, and is a voluntary body, that is, its existence depends upon the good will, the desire, the cooperation of the workers organized in their unions. We have all sorts of men to deal with. We have, I think, among the brainiest in all the country, and we have some not quite so brainy. We have enlightened men, and some not quite so enlightened. We have unselfish and altruistic men, and some who are not quite so. We have every element to contend with. We must maintain our Federation and we cannot always do that which we would like to do and yet maintain our Federation, which as you have said has grown into power and influence. It is because we have tried to keep abreast and perhaps a little ahead of the great mass of workers. We can't rush too far ahead and then find ourselves high and dry without a Federation, without a following, without anything of the support for the existence of which we can only continue.

["]The suggestion which you make for the appointment of a committee will receive the consideration of the Executive Council during the course of our sessions here. . . .[16]

["]The Executive Council thanks you for your presence, for coming here, and for the lucid manner in which the entire subject has been presented to us."

Thomas J. Jones, Educational Director Phelps Stokes Fund, submitted the following resolution or declaration:

We wish especially to address ourselves to the American Federation of Labor which at its recent convention in Buffalo, N.Y. voiced sound democratic principles in its attitude toward Negro labor.

We would ask the American Federation of Labor, in organizing Negroes in the various trades, to include: (1) Skilled as well as unskilled workmen; (2) Northern as well as Southern workmen; (3) Government as well as civilian employees; (4) Women as well as men workers.

We would have Negro labor handled by the American Federation of Labor in the same manner as white labor: (1) When workmen are returning to work after a successful strike; (2) When shops are declared "open" or "closed"; (3) When Union workers apply for jobs.

We would have these assurances pledged not with words only, but by deeds—pledged by an increasing number of examples of groups of Negro workmen given a "square deal."

With these accomplished, we pledge ourselves to urge Negro workingmen to seek the advantages of sympathetic co-operation and understanding between men who work.

It was suggested by the delegation that a committee be appointed to meet with them to work out a plan for organization.[17]

. . .

TDc, Executive Council Records, Minutes, reel 5, frames 1485–87, *AFL Records.*

1. Not listed here but also in attendance at the meeting was George Harris, editor and publisher of the *New York News.*

2. John Shillady (1875–1943) served as secretary of the National Association for the Advancement of Colored People (NAACP) from 1918 to 1920.

3. Frederick Randolph Moore (1857–1943).

4. Archibald Henry Grimké (1849–1930), a Washington, D.C., attorney, helped found the NAACP and served as president of its Washington, D.C., branch from 1913 to 1925.

5. Thomas Jesse Jones (1873–1950) was a specialist in education for the U.S. Bureau of Education (1912–19) and education director of the Phelps-Stokes Fund (1913–46).

6. Probably a reference to Resolution 160, adopted by the 1893 AFL convention in Chicago, which affirmed the AFL's commitment to organizing all workers "irrespective of creed, color, sex, nationality or politics" (AFL, *Proceedings,* 1893, p. 56).

7. An 1896 circular describing the objectives of the AFL declared: "The American Federation of Labor endeavors to unite all classes of wage-workers under one head, through their several organizations . . . that class, race, creed, political and trade prejudices may be abolished" (*The Samuel Gompers Papers,* vol. 4, pp. 119–20).

8. The Cigar Makers' International Union of America.

9. William T. Jones, financial and corresponding secretary of Cigar Makers' local 219 of Mobile, Ala., from about 1890 to 1897, served for at least two years as treasurer of the international union.

10. The 1891 AFL convention met in Birmingham, Ala., Dec. 14–19.

11. See *The Samuel Gompers Papers,* vol. 3, pp. 133–34.

12. The 1917 AFL convention referred two resolutions (58 and 166), regarding the appointment of black organizers in the South, to the AFL Executive Council for action, depending on the availability of funds. A third resolution (36), introduced by the San Francisco Labor Council on behalf of the International Negro League, called on President Woodrow Wilson, Congress, and "all executive and judicial officers of the land" to do all in their power to remove "the political, civil and economic disabilities, so offensive and destructive to the rights of negroes as human beings and American citizens" (AFL, *Proceedings,* 1917, p. 177). The convention referred the portion of the resolution dealing with the organization of black workers to the Executive Council for action. The *New York Age,* the black weekly published by Moore, editorialized that "by making special provision for the formation of unions among Negroes," the AFL had admitted that the black worker "must be counted as a legitimate labor asset at his true value" (Dec. 29, 1917).

13. The 1918 convention of the United Mine Workers of America was held in Indianapolis, Jan. 15–26. SG addressed the convention on Jan. 23.

14. Probably George H. Edmunds, a United Mine Workers' organizer from Des Moines.

15. Booker T. Washington.

16. Ellipses in original.

17. The AFL Executive Council directed SG to appoint a committee to discuss the

matter further with representatives of black workers. For an account of the resulting joint conference at AFL headquarters, see "Excerpts from the Minutes of a Conference between Committees Representing Black Workers and the AFL," Apr. 22, 1918, below.

To David Kreyling[1]

February 13, 1918.

Mr. David Kreyling,
Secretary, Central Trades and Labor Union,
2228 Olive St., St. Louis, Mo.
Dear Sir and Brother:

The decision referred to in your letter of January 31 is evidently that of the Supreme Court of the United States in the Hitchman Coal and Coke Company versus United Mine Workers of America. That decision is one of the most far reaching ever handed down by the Supreme Court. The decision if rigidly and scrupulously adhered to would mean the destruction of the organized labor movement. However, the position taken by the court is out of harmony with the thought and tendencies of the present times. The decision [i]s reached through legalistic argumentation and with reference to former legal decisions. The decision however, is industrially unjust. The majority opinion concurred in by six Justices of the Supreme Court leaves out of consideration conditions and forces in the industrial world and reasons that make necessary collective action in order to assure workers their rights as individuals. The majority opinion wrongfully presupposes that employers and employes are equal in so far as ability to exercise their individual rights are concerned. Workers very well know that it [i]s frequently impossible for them to exercise their theoretical rights.

Since the opinion of the Supreme Court is at variance with the facts in the case and is opposed to present tendencies and thought, it can not stand as final. However, effort will be made to have the decision reversed by the Court. If that is not done then other steps must be taken. Freedom and opportunity for improvement mean too much to wage earners for them to permit such a barrier to stand. However, you will remember that the case of the Hitchman Coal and Coke Company versus United Mine Workers was begun in 1907 and therefore the rights and freedom accorded wage earners under the labor provisions of the Clayton Anti-trust Act were not involved. Future cases begun will have to take into consideration the broader vision and thought of this new legislation which declares that the labor of a human being is not a commodity or article of commerce. I see no reason why this decision of the Supreme Court should interfere with the making of new agreements and the progress of the organized labor movement.

Fraternally yours,   Saml Gompers.
President,   American Federation of Labor.

TLpS, reel 231, vol. 243, pp. 667–68, SG Letterbooks, DLC.

1. David J. KREYLING was secretary-organizer of the St. Louis Central Trades and Labor Union from 1901 to 1933.

Excerpts from the Minutes of a Meeting of the Executive Council of the AFL

Saturday, February 16, 1918.

AFTERNOON SESSION.

. . .

The following was adopted:

We are face to face with a world crisis. We are in a world struggle which will determine for the immediate future whether principles of democratic freedom or principles of force shall dominate. The decision will determine not only the destiny of nations but of every community and of every individual. No life will be untouched.

Either the principles of free democracy or of Prussian militaristic autocracy will prevail. There can be no compromises. So there can be no neutrality among nations or individuals—we must stand up and be counted with one cause or the other. For Labor there is but one choice.

The hope of Labor lies in opportunity for freedom. The workers of America will not permit themselves to be deceived or deceive themselves into thinking the fate of the war will not vitally change our own lives. A victory for Germany would mean a pan-German Empire dominating Europe and exercising a world balance of power which Germany will seek to extend by force into world control.

Prussian rule means supervision, checks, unfreedom in every relation of life.

Prussianism has its roots in the old ideal under which men sought to rule by suppressing the minds and wills of their fellows; it blights the new ideal of government without force or chains—political or industrial—protected by perfect freedom for all.

Unless the reconstruction shall soon come from the German workers within that country it is now plain that an opportunity to uproot the agencies of force will come only when democracy has defeated autocracy in the military field, and wins the right to reconstruct relations between nations and men. The peace parleys[1] between Russia and Germany have shown the futility of diplomatic negotiations until Prussian militarists are convinced they cannot superimpose their will on the rest of the world.

Force is the basis of their whole organization and is the only argument they will understand.

Spontaneous uprisings in Germany in protest against the militarist government have shown that the German government is still stronger than the movement for German emancipation. German freedom is ultimately the problem of the German people. But the defeat of Prussian autocracy on the battlefield will bring an opportunity for German liberty at home.

We have passed the period when any one nation can maintain its freedom irrespectively of other nations. Civilization has closely linked nations together by the ties of commerce, and quick communications, common interests, problems and purposes. The future of free nations will depend upon their joint ability to devise agencies for dealing with their common affairs so that the greatest opportunity for life, liberty and pursuit of happiness may be assured to all.

This matter of world democracy is of vital interest to Labor. Labor is not a sect or a party. It represents the invincible desire for greater opportunity of the masses of all nations. Labor is the brawn, sinews and brains of society. It is the user of tools. Tools under the creative power of muscle and brain shape the materials of civilization. Labor makes possible every great forward movement of the world. But Labor is inseparable from physical and spiritual life and progress. Labor now makes it possible that this titanic struggle for democratic freedom can be made.

The common people everywhere are hungry for wider opportunities to live. They have shown the willingness to spend or be spent for an ideal. They are in this war for ideals. Those ideals are best expressed by their chosen representative in a message delivered to the Congress of the United States January 8, setting forth the program of the world's peace. President Wilson's statement of war aims has been unreservedly endorsed by British organized labor. It is in absolute harmony with the fundamentals endorsed by the Buffalo Convention of the American Federation of Labor.[2]

We are at war for those ideals. Our first big casualty list has brought to every home the harass and the sacrifices of war. This is only the beginning. A gigantic struggle lies just ahead that will test to the uttermost the endurance and the ability and the spirit of our people. That struggle will be fought out in the mines, farms, shops, mills, ship yards, as well as on the battle field. Soldiers and sailors are helpless if the producers do not do their part. Every link in the chain of the mobilization of the fighting force and necessary supplies is indispensable to winning the war against militarism and principles of unfreedom.

The worker that fastens the rivets in building the ship is performing just as necessary war service to our Republic as the sailor who takes the ship across or the gunner in the trenches.

This is a time when all workers must soberly face the grave importance of their daily work and decide industrial matters with a conscience mindful of the world relation of each act.

The problem of production indispensable to preventing unnecessary slaughter of fellow men is squarely up to all workers—aye, to employes and employers. Production depends upon materials, tools, management, and the development and maintenance of industrial morale. Willing cooperation comes not only from doing justice but from receiving justice. The worker is a human being whose life has value and dignity to him. He is willing to sacrifice for an ideal but not for the selfish gain of another. Justice begets peace. Consideration begets cooperation. These conditions are essential to war production. Production is necessary to win the war.

Upon the government and upon employers falls the preponderance of responsibility to securing greatest efficiency from workers. Standards of human welfare and consideration of the human side of production are part of the technique of efficient production.

Give workers a decent place to live, protect them against conditions to take all their wages for bare existence, give them agencies whereby grievances can be adjusted and industrial justice assured, make it plain that their labor counts in the winning a war for greater freedom, not for private profiteering—and workers can be confidently expected to do their part. Workers are loyal. They want to do their share for the Republic and for winning the war.

This is Labor's war. It must be won by Labor at every stage in the fighting and the final victory must be to count for humanity. That result only can justify the awful sacrifice.

We present these matters to the workers of free America, confidently relying upon the splendid spirit and understanding which has made possible present progress, to enable us to fight a good fight and to establish principles of freedom throughout the whole world. We regret that circumstances make impossible continuous close personal relations between the workers of America and those of allied countries, and that we cannot have representation in the Inter-Allied Labor Conference about to convene in London.[3]

Their cause and purpose are our cause and purpose. We cannot meet with representatives of those who are now aligned against us in this world war for freedom, but we hope they will sweep away the barriers which they have raised between us. Freedom and the downfall of autocracy must come in Middle Europe. We doubly welcome the change if it comes through the workers of those countries. While this war shall last, we shall be working and fighting shoulder to shoulder with fellow workers of Great Britain, France and Italy. We ask the workers of Russia to make common cause with us, for our purpose is their purpose, that finally the freedom lovers of all countries may make the world safe for all peoples to live in freedom and safety.

. . .

TDc, Executive Council Records, Minutes, reel 5, frames 1498, 1502–4, *AFL Records.*

1. Peace negotiations between Russia and the Central Powers opened at Brest Litovsk in December 1917 and continued, with interruptions, until Mar. 3, 1918. Under the harsh treaty terms imposed by Germany, Russia relinquished Poland, Finland, the Baltic provinces, and Ukraine, which together accounted for over a quarter of its population and industry, a third of its agricultural land, and more than half its iron and coal deposits. Russia also agreed to demobilize its army and navy and surrendered extraordinary commercial and financial privileges to citizens and corporations of the Central Powers.

2. The 1917 AFL convention adopted a statement, submitted by the Executive Council, on the principles that should govern the peace negotiations: "1. The combination of the free peoples of the world in a common covenant for genuine and practical co-operation to secure justice and therefore peace in relations between nations. 2. Governments derive their just power from the consent of the governed. 3. No political or economic restrictions meant to benefit some nations and to cripple or embarrass others. 4. No indemnities or reprisals based upon vindictive purposes or deliberate desire to injure, but to right manifest wrongs. 5. Recognition of the rights of small nations and of the principle, 'No people must be forced under sovereignty under which it does not wish to live.' 6. No territorial changes or adjustment of power except in furtherance of the welfare of the peoples affected and in furtherance of world peace." The convention also adopted the Council's declaration of the fundamental points to be incorporated in the peace treaty: "1. No article or commodity shall be shipped or delivered in international commerce in the production of which children under the age of 16 have been employed or permitted to work. 2. It shall be declared that the basic workday in industry and commerce shall not exceed eight hours. 3. Involuntary servitude shall not exist except as a punishment for crime whereof the party shall have been duly convicted. 4. Establishment of trial by jury." In addition, the convention recommended that "the governments of the various nations shall exchange labor representatives, according to them the same authority and honor that is given to any other diplomat" (AFL, *Proceedings,* 1917, pp. 451–52).

3. The Inter-Allied Labour and Socialist Conference on war aims and peace negotiations, attended by members of the Labour party and the TUC Parliamentary

Committee as well as British, French, Italian, and Belgian socialists, met in London, Feb. 20–23, 1918. It endorsed the declaration of war aims adopted by the Westminster conference on Dec. 28, 1917, proposed an international conference of labor and socialist organizations to meet in a neutral country and to include representatives from all belligerent nations, and authorized sending a delegation to the United States to secure the endorsement of its actions from American socialists and representatives of the American labor movement.

Arthur Henderson cabled SG on Jan. 10, inviting the AFL to send delegates to the conference, and he reiterated the invitation by letter on Jan. 16. SG replied by cable on Feb. 18, making no mention of Henderson's cable and saying the letter had not reached him until Feb. 9, too late for the AFL to send a delegation. He expressed regret, conveyed fraternal greetings to the meeting, and indicated that an AFL delegation would visit Great Britain and France later in the spring. To Henderson's query about AFL participation in an international conference—that is, a meeting in a neutral country that would include socialist and labor delegates from all belligerent powers—SG replied: "Executive Council in declaration unanimously declared 'We cannot meet with representatives of those who are aligned against us in this world war for freedom but we hope they will sweep away the barriers which they have raised between us'" (Files of the Office of the President, General Correspondence, reel 92, frame 641, *AFL Records*).

From William English Walling

Greenwich Connecticut February 19, 1918.

My dear Mr. Gompers:—

I am sure you do not read such a pro-German organ as The New Republic. I also find it very painful, but the publication has a very wide influence and I feel it necessary to read it.

The last issue publishes a supplement,[1] the new program of the British labor party now under discussion. And The New Republic endorses[2] this program as a suitable basis for a new progressive political movement in this country. At the same time The New Republic repeats its infamous attacks[3] on The Federation of Labor which you will also find enclosed.

I believe all thoughtful persons will agree with The New Republic that the time is ripe for a program somewhat along the line of the British Labor Party and I believe that they are also justified in their feeling that the American Federation of Labor would naturally lead this movement. I wonder if you have yet had time to give your attention to this problem: would it not be worth while to have formulated for the June convention of the A.F. of L. a program[4] which would get together in a compact form the present position of the A.F. of L., and add to it any new planks that seem fully justified by the war? While the A.F. of

L. would certainly not proceed along identical lines with the British laborites, it does seem to me that they have taken up several lines of reform hitherto neglected by the A.F. of L. The point is that they have been three and a half years in the war, while we have been in it only one year. As a consequence they have thought out some problems of reconstruction during and after the war to which we have given less attention.

I believe that a combination of the present reforms endorsed by the A.F. of L., together with a few of those now being taken up by the labor party would make a program as strong or stronger than that of the laborites.

Naturally I am not suggesting any radical departure in policy. It is chiefly a question of getting the present federation policy into a shape that will appeal more strongly to the public and also secure support from all the genuine democrats. I believe the general principles laid down by yourself and the Federation since the beginning of the war, together with the platform of the Alliance for Labor and Democracy, give a sufficient foundation for such new measures as might be proposed. It would only remain to apply these principles in a somewhat more concrete and definite way in order to get a wider and more enthusiastic public support.

Finally I fear that if the Federation does *not* proceed actively along these lines we shall have some kind of a half-baked radical movement which will take a similar course. This would be deplorable, as such a movement would probably be pacifist, more or less pro-German, and objectionable from every standpoint. So far, fortunately, the National Party has failed, but I fear that either it may come to life again or have a more damaging successor. For example, there is already a movement for the non-partisan party support for pacifist candidates in the Fall elections.

Sincerely yours,   Wm English Walling

TLS, Files of the Office of the President, General Correspondence, reel 92, frames 659–60, *AFL Records.*

1. The supplement was published as part two of the *New Republic's* Feb. 16, 1918, issue under the title *Labor and the New Social Order—A Report on Reconstruction by the Sub-Committee of the British Labor Party.*

2. The *New Republic* endorsed the program in a Foreword to the supplement.

3. "British and American Labor," *New Republic,* Feb. 16, 1918, pp. 69–71, criticized the AFL's policy of political non-partisanship and advocated the creation of an American labor party.

4. The 1918 AFL convention, which met in St. Paul, June 10–20, amended and adopted Resolution 62, which instructed the Executive Council to set up a committee to investigate the problem of postwar reconstruction. The Council appointed John Frey

of the Molders, B. M. Jewell, acting president of the AFL Railway Employes' Department, John Moore, president of United Mine Workers of America District 6 (Ohio), George Perkins, president of the Cigar Makers, and Matthew Woll, president of the Photo-Engravers to serve on the committee. The committee reported to the Council in December, and its report was printed in January 1919 as a pamphlet entitled *American Federation of Labor Reconstruction Program* ([Washington, D.C., 1919]).

An Article in the *Chicago Defender*

[February 23, 1918]

COME NOW, LORD GOMPERS!

It was good news and better that informed us of the advent of Doctor Moton into the sanctum of Samuel Gompers, the labor tyrant of the United States.[1] Gompers has long been the one lion whose den the Race has not dared. Doctor Moton, filled with grace and wisdom, and full to heaping measure of suavity and human kindness, led a responsible delegation from a respectable organization to treat with the czar upon matters affecting Negro laborers.

After almost fifty years of bitter opposition to Race laborers, skilled and unskilled, the American Federation capitulates to the wisdom of unionizing them. The increasing numbers and importance of Race workers in the North, in the free states as against the slave states—as slavish now as when Jeff Davis cussed the moon and turned his back on the sun—force the white labor trust to throw down the bars and seek still greater power through embracing those heretofore spurned and rejected on no other ground than that they belonged to the race of Booker T. Washington and not to that of Robert E. Lee.

We claim no confidential relation with Mr. Gompers, the body Doctor Moton speaks for, or the American Federation of Labor. But we claim closest relation with the Race for which Doctor Moton's committee speaks, and to which in a moment of distress Mr. Gompers now eagerly turns.

It is for that race, and no other organization, that the Defender speaks.

To the manner born, true in every test, loyal through three hundred years of uninterrupted residence upon this continent, and claiming the brawniest arm that ever raised an implement of labor, the American Negro deserves the protection which organization secures, and merits such consideration with which Lord Gompers may now stoop to flatter him.

If the union labor badge marks the American white man freeman, that is the very badge to be worn by the Race upon whose labor such civilization as the semi-barbarous South may boast was built and upon which it is now maintained!

That much we all of us are in agreement upon.

The parting of the ways now comes, if it comes at all—a consummation devoutly to be hoped against—when the proposition is advanced to organize the Race into separate unions. That is, when Union No. 3 of bricklayers and plasterers is composed of white laborers, and Union No. 4 of bricklayers and plasterers is composed of Colored men.

That is the spirit and the essence of Jim Crow; and Jim Crow, in any form or by any faith, is our cup. We are resolutely opposed to its infamy in church and state, and we are immovably pledged against it in the labor unions, whether North or South.

If that is the proposition as made by Gompers and accepted by any league or by Doctor Moton—the honesty of this man is not here questioned—the issue is joined and the fight is on.

There is no color line in the handiwork of labor, and there should be none in the councils of labor. Whatever progress the Race has made in the world of labor in the free states has been made in spite of and not because of the American Federation of Labor. Thus far the Negro has come alone, and alone he can go still farther, until the politics of American labor is taught the theory of "the sweat of the brow."

Only a few hours ago the New York Times felt impelled to rebuke Mr. Gompers for sustaining the Brotherhood of Carpenters in its persistence in embarrassing the government at a time when every saw and hammer is needed.[2] Mr. Gompers may properly sustain the Brotherhood of Labor and Man without fear of rebuke from any source.

The Race will refuse the union until the union accepts and considers the Race man at least as much of [a] citizen and man as the foreign laborers in the unions whose particular mark is their universal apprenticeship and their inability to speak the English language. These are plain facts; likewise these are plain times.

Before the terms of the American Federation of Labor to Jim Crow the Race are accepted, let a conference be called in Chicago. Let a committee of two be chosen by the people meet in Chicago, and let Mr. Gompers come or send a representative, and let these three select two men like Dr. George Hall[3] and Robert McCurdy for referee.

Then we can know what we are doing. As it is, the laborer is being fed from a spoon, the bowl of which no one can tell from the handle!

Chicago Defender, Feb. 23, 1918.

1. See "Excerpts from the Minutes of a Meeting of the Executive Council of the AFL," Feb. 12, 1918, above.

2. "What Is the Answer?" *New York Times*, Feb. 17, 1918. For a discussion of the strike, see "To Albert Berres," Feb. 25, n. 4, below.

3. George Cleveland Hall (1864–1930) was a Chicago physician.

To Albert Berres

Feb. 25, 1918.

Mr. A. J. Berres,
Secretary-Treasurer, Metal Trades Department, A.F. of L.,
A.F. of L. Building, Washington, D.C.
Dear Sir and Brother:
Today I sent you the following telegram:—

["]Washington, D.C., Feb. 25, 1918.

"Mr. A. J. Berres,
["]A.F. of L. Building,
["]Washington, D.C.
["]You are urgently requested to attend conference of great importance American Federation of Labor Building, Washington, D.C., ten o'clock Tuesday morning, March fifth.[1] Am mailing to you letters and other documents setting forth the cause and need for the conference. Am sending identical telegrams[2] to the signatories to the Wage Adjustment Board Agreement[3] so that you and they may be advised in sufficient time to so arrange your and their affairs as to attend the conference March fifth.

["]Samuel Gompers."

You are doubtless aware of the unfortunate situation as it developed in some of the shipbuilding yards within the recent past.[4] The correspondence[5] between the President of the United States, Edward N. Hurley, Chairman United States Shipping Board, Emergency Fleet Corporation and President Hutcheson of the United Brotherhood of Carpenters and Joiners reveals the critical situation as it exists.

At Washington last week President Hutcheson, Secretary Duffy,[6] Board Member Guerin[7] and Mr. Brindell representing the United Brotherhood of Carpenters and Joiners had a conference[8] with Chairman Hurley and Mr. Charles Piez,[9] Vice-President and General Manager, United States Shipping Board, Emergency Fleet Corporation, and

Mr. V. Everit Macy, and Mr. A. J. Berres of the Wage Adjustment Board of the United States Shipping Board,—Secretary Frank Morrison and I participating. An effort at adjustment of the misunderstanding was made but a definite conclusion has not been reached.

Enclosed you will please find copy of a memorandum which Mr. Hutcheson of the Carpenters and Joiners submitted as his proposal for the adjustment of the differences. The memorandum is marked "A."[10]

I transmitted[11] this memorandum to the wage Adjustment Board of the United States Emergency Fleet Corporation through its Chairman Mr. V. Everit Macy. To this I received a reply from Mr. Macy, copy of which is enclosed, marked "B."[12]

Later conferences were held between President Hutcheson, Mr. Piez of the Shipping Board of the Emergency Fleet Corporation and Secretary Frank Morrison of the American Federation of Labor.

Enclosed, you will please find copy of a letter addressed to Mr. Hutcheson by Honorable Franklin D. Roosevelt, Assistant Secretary of the Navy and Mr. Charles Piez, Vice-President and General Manager of the United States Shipping Board, Emergency Fleet Corporation, marked "C."[13]

Further you will find enclosed copy of the proposal made by President Hutcheson as a memorandum for agreement or for amendment of the existing memorandum of agreement, marked "D."[14]

In addition you will find enclosed copy of a written statement made by Mr. Blackman,[15] a representative of the Shipping Board, Emergency Fleet Corporation, marked "E."[16]

With all these documents before us, I had a conference yesterday, Sunday, February 24th, at the Continental Hotel, New York City, with President Hutcheson, Mr. E. Featherstone[17] and Mr. John Flynn, of the Brotherhood of Carpenters and Joiners and there and then it was understood that I would telegraph to you as I have and which is quoted in this letter.

On Saturday, February 23rd, over long distance telephone, I submitted that Assistant Secretary of the Navy, Mr. Franklin D. Roosevelt, should issue an invitation to you and to the other signatories of the memorandum of agreement to attend the conference. Mr. Roosevelt expressed the opinion that the invitation should be extended by me and I have complied[18] and now again urge that you and the other signatories to the memorandum of agreement attend the conference at ten o'clock Tuesday morning, March 5, 1918 to take into consideration and endeavor to determine the best course which can be pursued in order to bring about unity of spirit and action that the shipbuilding program of our country may be carried to a successful completion and if possible, without the cessation of work.

Kindly telegraph me that you will attend the conference.

Fraternally yours, Saml Gompers
President, American Federation of Labor.

P.S.

New York, N.Y., Sunday, Feb. 24th, 1918.

I have dictated the telegram above and this letter in this city[19] today to be carried to Washington and put into effect tomorrow, Monday, February 25th.

S. G.

TLpS, reel 231, vol. 243, pp. 978–79, SG Letterbooks, DLC.

1. The day-long conference, held Mar. 5, 1918, discussed and then rejected William Hutcheson's demand for a revision of the agreement creating the Shipbuilding Labor Adjustment Board.

2. See, for example, SG to James O'Connell, Feb. 25, 1918, Files of the Office of the President, General Correspondence, reel 92, frame 774, *AFL Records*.

3. For the agreement creating the Shipbuilding Labor Adjustment Board, see "An Address before the Fifty-fourth Annual Convention of the New York State Federation of Labor in Jamestown, N.Y.," Aug. 29, 1917, n. 10, above.

4. On Feb. 11, 1918, between seven and eight hundred carpenters in five Staten Island, N.Y., shipyards went on strike, demanding the same wage scale as that awarded on Feb. 1 to Pacific Coast shipyard workers by the Shipbuilding Labor Adjustment Board. On Feb. 14 between five and six hundred carpenters in several Baltimore shipyards joined the strike. Faced with severe criticism in the press and appeals for an end to the strike from President Woodrow Wilson and U.S. Shipping Board chairman Edward Hurley, Hutcheson persuaded the strikers to go back to work on Feb. 19 in expectation of a wage decision from the Shipbuilding Labor Adjustment Board. On Mar. 1 the board issued wage awards for the Delaware River and Baltimore districts, mandating pay increases in those ports, and on Apr. 6 it issued its North Atlantic award, which created a generally uniform wage scale for most Atlantic and Gulf coast shipyards.

5. Much of this correspondence was published in the press. See, for example, the coverage in the *New York Times*, Feb. 15–18, 1918.

6. Frank Duffy was secretary of the United Brotherhood of Carpenters and Joiners of America (1903–48) and editor of the union's official journal (1901–41).

7. Theobold M. Guerin (1867–1944), a member of Carpenters' local 78 of Troy, N.Y., served the Brotherhood as vice-president (1900–1909) and then as a district representative to the union's general executive board (1913–44). He was also a vice-president (1912–22) of the New York State Federation of Labor and served as an alternate for Hutcheson on the National War Labor Board (1918–19).

8. The conference was held on Feb. 19, 1918.

9. Charles Piez (1866–1933), president (1906–24) and later chairman of the board (1924–32) of the Link-Belt Co. of Chicago, was general manager of the Emergency Fleet Corporation from December 1917 to December 1918 and its director general from December 1918 through April 1919.

10. Hutcheson's memorandum proposed that a member of the Carpenters sit on the Shipbuilding Labor Adjustment Board "with full authority and voting power" whenever the board was considering "matters pertaining to hours and wages in reference to construction of wooden ships or work affecting the wood working craft" (Proposed Memorandum, n.d., reel 231, vol. 243, p. 934, SG Letterbooks, DLC).

11. SG to V. Everit Macy, Feb. 13, 1918, reel 231, vol. 243, p. 547, SG Letterbooks, DLC.

12. Macy informed SG that the Shipbuilding Labor Adjustment Board had unanimously rejected Hutcheson's proposal (Feb. 13, 1918, reel 231, vol. 243, p. 935, SG Letterbooks, DLC).

13. Franklin Roosevelt and Charles Piez wrote Hutcheson on Feb. 21, 1918, informing him that they were willing to submit his proposal to a conference of representatives from the Navy, the Emergency Fleet Corporation, and the AFL "for discussion and determination" (reel 231, vol. 243, pp. 936–39, SG Letterbooks, DLC; quotation at p. 938).

14. Hutcheson's memorandum repeated his earlier proposal (see n. 10, above) and added two new sections. The first of these would have required employers to procure the labor they needed "through the offices of the Department of Labor." The second called for referring disputes that could not be resolved between the workers and management directly to the president of the Carpenters and the U.S. Shipping Board and stipulated that no cessation of work would occur while an adjustment was pending (Proposed Memorandum, Feb. 21, 1918, reel 231, vol. 243, p. 940, SG Letterbooks, DLC).

15. William BLACKMAN was a commissioner of conciliation for the U.S. Department of Labor (1915–17) and head of the labor division of the Emergency Fleet Corporation.

16. Mr. Blackman's Statement, Feb. 23, 1918, reel 231, vol. 243, p. 941, SG Letterbooks, DLC.

17. Probably Daniel F. Featherstone.

18. The other letters of invitation may be found at reel 231, vol. 243, pp. 932–33, 942–72, 974–79, SG Letterbooks, DLC.

19. SG was in New York City, where he held a number of conferences between Feb. 21 and 24, 1918, and addressed a labor loyalty meeting on Feb. 22. On Feb. 26 he appeared before a joint session of the state legislature in Albany regarding a prohibition amendment, and from there he went to Chicago to testify in the meatpacking arbitration hearings on Feb. 28. He probably returned to AFL headquarters on Mar. 2.

To Newton Baker

February 26, 1918.

Honorable Newton D. Baker,
Secretary of War,
Washington, D.C.
Sir:

The following statements were embodied in letters from union men received at this office. The first is from Arthur S. Froats, member of Local Union 1668, United Brotherhood of Carpenters and Joiners of America, 60 College Street, Buffalo, New York:

"On February 5th, I applied at the Works for a job—long lines of men in waiting on the same errand. I was ushered into the office of the man in charge of the Company's Employment Department, who asked me to file a written application. I said—'I have already filed three such applications, and in each case been assured I should hear from it soon.' He professed not to find them on file, so I made out application, as requested. He said—'You are a Union man?' I replied 'Yes.' 'Oh, you are high-priced man—60¢ an hour,' said he—'That is why you have not heard from your application.['] I said—'Why not tell me that when I first applied?' He went on—'We are paying 45¢ an hour—if you would like to go to work for that, you can do so at once.' I replied—'No! it is understood that the prevailing rate of wages in the district shall be paid on Government work for skilled workmen.' He said—'As you qualify, you will be paid more.' I said, 'I do not ask you to keep me on if I do not qualify, but how long would a man be required to work at that wage to prove himself qualified?' He 'could not say—did not know, could promise nothing.' I said—'You cannot keep good men at that pay, it is not a living wage, and no real mechanic is going to put his skill, his labor and his expensive tools in for 45¢ an hour, when he can earn so much more outside your factory.' He replied—'Oh, we may have to pay more by and by. If you can live through the winter, all right.' I said—'Your competent men will leave you in the spring.' He said—'That's just the way with you fellows—you are not patriotic.'

["]He renewed his offer of 45¢ per hour. I refused to accept such wages, with no definite standard and no real assurance of advancement—only the strong probability that as soon as I claimed higher wages, I would be discharged, for the Curtiss Corporation is weekly hiring men, and discharging men (by no means always for inefficiency). Applicants here have been kept waiting from month to month with excuses of necessary delay in material and equipment, while the persistent advertising of the Curtiss Corporation throughout the country has brought many men from outside quarters to the city, expecting that ability and willingness to work and learn would insure reasonable wages. Some are receiving even less than the minimum wage. Men are stranded here, to work until they can earn enough to get away, or are discharged, to walk the streets of Buffalo. Does not the situation spell trouble?

["]I object to being told I am not patriotic. I am a tax payer, owner of a liberty Bond and a true American citizen—more than willing to serve my Country and my Government to the best of my ability. I am also a competent mechanic—a skilled workman, as Carpenter, Millwright and Shipjoiner."

This was received from H. J. Conard,[1] Secretary of the Detroit Metal Trades Council, 346 Randolph Street, Detroit, Michigan:

"In regard to violations of the basic 8 hour day, Ford Motor Co. pays the regular hour rate for hours worked over eight. Nearly all the motor companies work nine hours a day with five on Saturday. Work is coming thru different departments of these plants with the drawings plainly marked 'Ordnance Dept., U.S.A.' or similar titles that show the work is for the government; or with a red, white and blue tag bearing a like marking.

["]Some of the shops are Packard, Hupp, Maxwell, Lincoln Motor Companies, Dodge Bros., Aluminum Castings Co. that all work the nine hour day without paying time and one half for the ninth hour."

Representatives of the organized labor movement of Massachusetts came to this office to see if something could not be done to secure the enforcement of the eight hour day on war contracts in Massachusetts. The situation in Massachusetts has been made very difficult by an opinion written by Samuel J. Rosensohn,[2] a copy of which is enclosed. This opinion is in marked contrast to the position you took in regard to the eight hour day for the Leather Workers.[3]

These incidents which I am bringing to your attention are only representative of many other situations throughout the country. In connection therewith, I wish to present for your consideration the following:

Do you not think it would be well to provide trouble departments for dealing with these causes of friction before they result in a situation that would delay production? It is not necessary to present details to you only to remind you that injustice is the cause of practically all labor troubles. I am sure we are all anxious that the industries of this country shall produce continuously and effectively munitions and not Bolsheviki. Do you not think it is high time that we take up at once the matter of providing a labor adjustment board for munition workers? Some agreement, essentially similar to that under which cantonments are being constructed, would enable the government to go forward with its war program to the greater satisfaction of all. Then, in addition, it will be necessary to take up the matter of providing similar boards for other groups of workers. May I not hear from you in regard to this matter at an early date?

Very truly yours,   Saml Gompers.
President,   American Federation of Labor.

TLpS, reel 232, vol. 244, pp. 64–66, SG Letterbooks, DLC.

1. Harry James Conard was a Detroit pattern maker.
2. Samuel J. Rosensohn (1880–1939), a New York City attorney, was a labor adviser

to Secretary of War Newton Baker during World War I. On Oct. 29, 1917, Rosensohn wrote Edwin Mulready, chairman of the Massachusetts War Emergency Industrial Division, that the time-and-a-half provisions of the 1917 Naval Appropriation Act did not apply to government contracts for products available on the open market and that the eight-hour-day guideline, where applicable, included weekend work, regardless of the custom of half days on Saturday.

3. See "To John Fitzpatrick," Dec. 7, 1917, n. 2, above.

From Giles Jackson

Department of Negro Economics.
National Civic Improvement Association
Richmond, Va., March 2, 1918.

Dear sir:

I am writing to thank you for your interest manifested in the cause I represent; I refer to the Bureau of Negro Economics.[1] I received your letter of February 12[2] enclosing copy of letter from Mr. Oscar A. Price,[3] containing information that the Director General would see me at any time when I came to Washington.

Upon receipt of this letter I proceeded to Washington. Being unacquainted with the Director-General, I secured a letter of introduction from Senator Martin,[4] which letter is here enclosed.[5] I accordingly met the Director-General on February 14th and went into the discussion of my plans for establishing a Bureau of Negro Economics. At the close of my conference, the Director-General gave me a letter to the Honorable W. B. Wilson, endorsing my proposition, which letter I am also enclosing.[6]

I called at the office of Secretary W. B. Wilson but was unable to see him, therefore, I have never delivered to him the letters referred to. I am sending them to you and would respectfully ask if you would transmit[7] them to the Secretary of Labor with such comment that you may feel justified in making in behalf of creating this Bureau. I would respectfully submit that ninety-nine percent of the people of the South are of the opinion that this Bureau should be created. The Chamber of Commerce of the City of Richmond has sent two or three delegations to Washington, urging upon Senator Martin the importance of having this Bureau created, and having Your Humble Servant put in charge.[8] The City Council of this city sent a delegation to Washington urging upon Secretary Wilson the importance of creating this Bureau. This, however, was sometime last fall. A delegation from Atlanta, Georgia, headed by the Honorable W. Schley Howard[9] also called upon the

Secretary last fall and urged that this Bureau be established, with your Humble Servant in charge.

The industrial centers of the South are suffering on account of the shortage of labor, and I am satisfied that the plans contemplated by the promoters of this Bureau would mean an immediate relief of this situation. I believe our plans would relieve both the agricultural and industrial centers.

Should the Secretary create this Bureau, and should I be in charge of the same, I would, of course, submit my plans to you for your consideration. I feel that this Bureau would, in a great measure, be a relief to you in handling the Negro labor question.

I shall be in Washington on the 6th and would like very much to have a conference with you with respect to the propositions herein referred to.

Now I would be indeed grateful to you if you would take this matter up with the Secretary in person, asking him to create this Bureau and make the appointment that we may get to work at once, in order that our work may be a relief to the situation confronting the early planters of crop in the South.

As to my fitness and qualification for handling this Bureau, I would respectfully refer you to the Honorable Thomas S. Martin of Virginia; the Honorable W. Schley Howard, of Atlanta, Georgia. I will not refer you to the thousands of Virginians who would not only give testimony in my behalf, but would come to Washington, if necessary, to give evidence concerning me. I am touching on this point because I feel it is important that I should do so.

Thanking you for past favors and for an early reply,[10] I am

Respectfully yours,   Giles B. Jackson.

TLS, Files of the Office of the President, General Correspondence, reel 93, frames 33–34, *AFL Records.*

1. See "To William B. Wilson," Jan. 23, 1918.

2. SG to Giles Jackson, Feb. 12, 1918, reel 231, vol. 243, p. 652, SG Letterbooks, DLC.

3. Oscar Price to SG, Feb. 7, 1918, reel 231, vol. 243, p. 653, SG Letterbooks, DLC. Price was private secretary to William McAdoo, Director General of the U.S. Railroad Administration.

4. Thomas Martin of Virginia.

5. Martin to McAdoo, Feb. 14, 1918, Files of the Office of the President, General Correspondence, reel 92, frame 567, *AFL Records.*

6. McAdoo to Wilson, Feb. 14, 1918, Files of the Office of the President, General Correspondence, reel 92, frame 564, *AFL Records.*

7. SG to Wilson, Mar. 5, 1918, reel 232, vol. 244, p. 344, SG Letterbooks, DLC.

8. Jackson was not appointed as director of the Division of Negro Economics; George Haynes served in that position from 1918 to 1921.

9. William Schley Howard (1875–1953) served as a Democratic congressman from Georgia (1911–19).

10. SG replied on Mar. 3, 1918, that he had transmitted copies of Jackson's letter and the letters from Martin and McAdoo to Wilson (reel 232, vol. 244, p. 347, SG Letterbooks, DLC).

From Jennie Newman[1]

Cereal Mill Employes #15403,[2]
March 3, 1918.

Dear Sir:

Just dropping you a line asking advice on what can be done in regards to our union here. We organized a little over a year ago[3] as fast as we elected officers they would fire them, then they would drop the union, we would put in others and the same thing happen. We let it run slowly along so finally they thought we were all gone and in fact we were few in number, only about fifteen out of a little over seven hundred, so we got busy and have a few new members already in and a couple of hundred ready to reinstate, but they got wind of it and have begun the same old thing and fired several of the union members, telling them no fault in their work but because they belong to the union and the rest are afraid to belong as some are people with dependents and need the work. The union is badly needed and the Employees would readily respond if they could see their way clear they know it has done a great deal of good so far but how we are going to make a success when we were out on the second strike we would of made a success of it if we had waited a day or two longer, but there is three other unions in the mill the electricians,[4] sheet metal workers[5] and millwrights,[6] and they got an agreement with Laid[7] and told us they would stay by us but they haven't.

Now what is the thing I to do it had tried all the old heads to know what is best before the government took control of the railroads the men on the roads said if we pulled all union people out of there they would discontinue their services, would take no cars out and place none in and then the government could take it over, but we don't know what is the proper thing to do at this time they are sure the lowest type of humans they only think of an employe as a dog. Mr. Laid told us last spring he would lose his place before he would let a union come in there, it is far worse than a penitentiary and surely there is some way to come out ahead if you would like further information write me, but please let me hear from you by return mail as this is a serious condition and needs prompt attention.

Please answer by return mail,[8] and oblige,

(signed) Mrs. Jennie Newman
Sec. of Cereal Mill Employes Union #15403

P.S. We did hear once the government was going to take the Quaker Oats over, if not is there any way we could place it so they would?

TLtpSr, reel 232, vol. 244, p. 589, SG Letterbooks, DLC. Typed notation: *"Copy."* Enclosed in SG to F. A. Canfield, Mar. 9, 1918, ibid., p. 588.

1. Jennie Newman, who worked at the Quaker Oats plant in Cedar Rapids, Iowa, served in 1918 as the secretary of AFL Cereal Mill Employes' Union 15,403 there.

2. AFL 15,403 was chartered in 1917.

3. On Jan. 9, 1917, some seventy-five men struck the Quaker Oats plant in Cedar Rapids demanding a wage increase and an eight-hour day. The next day around seven hundred additional workers, many of them women, joined the walkout. Representatives of the Iowa State Federation of Labor (FOL) and the Cedar Rapids FOL organized the strikers into AFL 15,403 and arranged a compromise that ended the two-day walkout, by which the workers' demands were submitted to company officials in Chicago. While the company's response was still pending, Cedar Rapids plant manager George Laird began firing union members, triggering a second walkout on Jan. 31 that involved over a thousand workers. Within a few days, representatives of the skilled crafts at the plant arranged a new settlement ending the second strike. Although the agreement established a grievance committee and pledged the company not to discriminate against union members, it did not require Quaker Oats to rehire workers who had been discharged. Further, the company received the assurance that employees would not stage another walkout without a week's notice, and it issued a public statement insisting that the settlement did not entail union recognition. During the course of the year, the company continued to fire active union members.

4. International Brotherhood of Electrical Workers 405.

5. Amalgamated Sheet Metal Workers' International Alliance 263.

6. United Brotherhood of Carpenters and Joiners of America 1039.

7. J. George Laird was manager of the Quaker Oats plant in Cedar Rapids.

8. On Mar. 9, 1918, SG asked AFL organizer F. A. Canfield of Cedar Rapids to assist AFL 15,403, and he notified Newman of this the same day (reel 232, vol. 244, pp. 588, 590, SG Letterbooks, DLC).

From Frank Ryan[1]

Leavenworth, Kansas March 10th. 1918

Dear Sir & Bro

You no doubt are fully informed of the various efforts made by my friends to secure my release, so far as I am aware all efforts have failed.

On Sept 18th 1916. I was Elegible for Parole. haveing qualified in accordance with the provisions of the Parole Law, I made application for Parole and was denied. So I have decided to make a personal appeal to you "as one Father to another," you being a Father of a Family. Can no doubt more readily understand my present feelings.

I have two motherless boys. all the children I have and who are now in the military service of our Country. The Eldest F. J. Ryan recently promoted to a Sergeant in Co. C. 311th Field Signal Bn. stationed at Camp Grant, is a Graduate Electrical Engnr. the 8[6]th Division of which his Company is a part are to depart for Europe May 15th next. My youngest son Edwin S. Ryan, didnot wait to complete the last semester of his four year. U. course as a Civil Engnr. He enlisted in the Naval Aviation Corps and is stationed at Camp Farragut. Co. 19. Barracks [948] W. Great Lakes, Ills. I have made many sacrifices in an effort to properly educate these boys, devoted my whole life so to speak, toward this one purpose they were to be my sole dependance in my declining years.

they are now called to their countries service to make the supreme sacrifice if need be.

I have too much respect for their mothers memory to have them visit me while in Prison, and in prison Garb. On the 25th of this month I will have served three years and ten months. In a letter dated sept 4th 1917, addressed to our Prest McClory. Mr Walter Drew. made this statement. quote (personally I believe no especial good will come from Mr Ryans further confinement) Being in full accord with the Governments war policies. I am confident I can be of greater service to my two soldier boys and to my country if given my freedom at this time, when such a great sacrifice is required and readily given by my children all the earthly ties I have, it does seem reasonable to expect that some concession could be made at this time to enable me to visit my boys as a free man, before they are shipped to Europe.

I am sure the boys can fight more valiantly and die if need be more contentedly in the interest of a Government that will temper its Justice with Mercy. As May 15th is close at hand quick action is necessary.

It would be differcult for me to understand and believe, that an earnest appeal made to Prest Wilson in my behalf by you, on the grounds herein set forth would be denied.

In conclusion permit me to most heartily commend and endorse. the cooperation given by yourself and the A.F of L. to Prest Wilson and his war Policies. Tho overburdened as you must be, I trust you will find time to make a personal appeal in my behalf.[2]

thanking you in advance

        I am sincerely and Fraternally Yours   Frank M Ryan

ALS, AFL Microfilm National and International Union File, Bridge and Structural Iron Workers Records, reel 35, frames 2093–94, *AFL Records.*

1. Frank M. RYAN, formerly president of the International Association of Bridge and Structural Iron Workers (1905–14), was convicted in 1912 in connection with the dynamite conspiracy case brought against members of the union and imprisoned in the federal penitentiary at Leavenworth, Kans.

2. SG replied on Mar. 23, 1918, that he had discussed the matter with Woodrow Wilson on Mar. 21 and had left a copy of Ryan's letter with the president (reel 233, vol. 245, p. 678, SG Letterbooks, DLC). Wilson commuted Ryan's sentence to time served on Apr. 6.

From Edward Thompson[1]

Executive Board of the Southeastern Railroads of
Colored Helpers & Laborers
Jacksonville, Fla Mar 10th 1918

Dear sir

We feel it is our duty to write you to let you know that we feel that we are now and will bee in the future greatly benifited by having attended the labor conference at Washington, D,C Feb 12th

Not only do we feel benifitted directly but we feel that mass of colored Helpers and Labors employed by the Railroads in the Southeastern District will be benifited by our efforts to get fair play

And we take this oppertunity to express our verry high appraciation of the assistance you rendered us in getting us into the conference we thank you most heartily for any effort put forth by you on our behalf Now Mr, Gompers i have been before Mr, Robert Mc,Wade[2] U,S, Cinciliation Commissioner and have been apointed to repersent all of the Helpers and Labors of the southeastern district through this Executive Board we are ware the fact that we have a broad field to work in and we feel equal to the tast and with the assistance of your council we feel that in a short time we shall have all the roads thouroughly Organized and in the American Federation Of Labor

Therefore we feel that we may with some degree of assurance call upon you the President of the greatest Labor Organization on Earth and your Executive council for advice and assistance in our infancy now in order that we may go on with the Organization we ask you will you kindly have mr Frank, Morrison, Sect Of A,F, of L, to notify the sevral Locals in this district that you concur and Recognize this Executive Board of colored Helpers And Labors of the Southeastern

Railroads we will highly appreciate it and can go on with the Organization without a hitch[3]

hoping that you will grant my request

> Respt,   E, D, Thompson,
> General Chearman,

TLSr, AFL Microfilm Convention File, reel 28, frame 2250, *AFL Records.*

1. Edward D. Thompson, a Jacksonville, Fla., railroad laborer, was the founder and chairman of the Executive Board of the Southeastern Railroads of Colored Helpers and Laborers, an independent union.

2. Robert M. McWade, a former journalist and newspaper editor, was a commissioner of conciliation for the U.S. Department of Labor from 1914 to at least 1920.

3. Apparently neither SG nor Frank Morrison answered Thompson's letter. In response to an inquiry from David Gatewood, president of AFL 15,854 (Railroad Helpers and Laborers) of Savannah, Ga., who Thompson had written claiming to be the official representative for all railroad helpers' and laborers' organizations, Morrison replied on Mar. 7, 1918, that Thompson had been given no authority over AFL affiliated locals. That same day Morrison also wrote C. M. Battle, secretary of AFL 15,680 (Railroad Helpers and Laborers) of Rocky Mount, N.C., where Thompson had scheduled a conference for Mar. 20, asking for additional information on the man and his organization (vol. 500, pp. 648–54, Frank Morrison Letterbooks, George Meany Memorial Archives, Silver Spring, Md.).

To John Frey

March 11, 1918.

Mr. John P. Frey,
Editor, International Molders' Journal,
Lock Box 699, Cincinnati, O.
Dear Sir and Brother:

Some time ago you wrote[1] me relative to your editorial policy in regard to the Supreme Court decision in the Hitchman Coal Company's case. I have participated in several conferences with the officers of the United Mine Workers in regard to this matter and at their request assisted in securing the services of Judge Alton B. Parker in the case.[2] After mature consideration it was determined that there were not proper grounds for requesting a re-hearing. Therefore, on March 4 a brief was filed with the Supreme Court. The brief had previously been carefully considered by President Hayes and Secretary Green of the Miners, Judge Parker and Professor Hogg[3] and me. In dealing with the case editorially, I am sure you can render invaluable assistance by presenting all phases of the fundamental principles involved.

The decision does not affect the labor provisions of the Clayton Anti-Trust Act, and I do think that any interpretation discounting the value of those provisions ought not to come from organized labor. Our best method, I think, lies in an educational campaign, as intensive and extensive as possible, to educate public opinion to such a degree that the federal court must necessarily follow. It is part of legal history that courts do follow public opinion. The acceptance of economic facts by the courts can be accelerated by self-interested activity on the part of those concerned. With practical gains in organization, in addition to education of public opinion, opinions like that expressed by the Supreme Court in the Hitchman Coal Company case can be nullified and made impossible in the future.

I shall be glad to see all that you write on this matter,[4] as I know the thoroughness with which you are accustomed to deal with this subject.

With best wishes, I am,

Fraternally yours,   Saml Gompers

TLpS, reel 232, vol. 244, p. 755, SG Letterbooks, DLC.

1. John Frey to SG, Jan. 26, 1918, AFL Microfilm National and International Union File, Molders Records, reel 40, frames 2024–25, *AFL Records.*

2. SG to Alton Parker, Feb. 6, 1918, reel 231, vol. 243, pp. 227–28, SG Letterbooks, DLC.

3. Charles Edgar Hogg (1852–1935) served as one of the attorneys for the United Mine Workers of America in the Hitchman Coal and Coke Co. case. He had previously served as a Democratic congressman from West Virginia (1887–89) and as dean of the College of Law at West Virginia University (1906–13).

4. The April 1918 issue of the *International Molders' Journal* published an editorial entitled "The Hitchman Coal Co. Decision," which denounced the Supreme Court's ruling in the case.

From James Duncan

The Granite Cutters' International Association
of America[1]
Quincy, Mass. March 11, 1918.

Reference Resolution No. 37.[2]

Dear Sir & Brother:

Yours of March 9 is received. I have not yet received the minutes of the E.C. meeting held in February, but I am of the opinion that the intention of the Council in authorizing you to correspond with affiliated organizations for the purpose of securing their views for the formation of a needle trades department was that you should correspond with organizations in the clothing industry, they being directly affected, and whether this would also include the Boot & Shoe Workers, who in their machines use needles somewhat similar to what tailors and garment workers use, may be a question. Replying in the broader sense will say that it does not appear to me to be necessary to have a needle trades department of the A.F. of L., for if there is need of a combination of the kind then the so-called needle trades should be amalgamated into one association under the caption of the Clothing Trades Association, or some caption having the same meaning.

I have the same opinion with reference to the mining department. Really and truly, as there needs to be joint action by those occupations the different kind of miners should be in one organization and the different kinds of needle workers should be in one organization. There is danger in too many departments and there should only be a department formed or maintained in my opinion in the A.F. of L. when said department would have enough to do to attend to special lines of co-ordinate duty which could be better transacted in that way than in a general way by the A.F. of L. Perhaps the whole process of departments is still on trial or in the experimental position, for while much is done in their discussions to get a better understanding, too frequently the methods and forms of appeals they have leave a loophole for the organization not doing the right thing to still look for a chance to hold on to its wanton aggressiveness.

You have the data before you, but really other trades cannot give much of a practical expression upon the need for a needle trades department other than the organizations whose members are needle workers, so from a practical standpoint the investigation or recorded expression of opinion should be more particularly provided by the representative officers of those employments.

Fraternally,   James Duncan
Int'l President.

TLS, AFL Microfilm Convention File, reel 28, frame 2272, *AFL Records.*

1. The GRANITE Cutters' International Association of America.

2. Resolution 37, introduced by representatives of the International Ladies' Garment Workers' Union at the 1917 AFL convention, called for the formation of an AFL Needle Trades Department. The convention referred the resolution to the AFL Executive Council for investigation, and on Mar. 9, 1918, SG sent a letter of inquiry to AFL national and international unions soliciting their views on the matter (reel 232, vol. 244, p. 586, SG Letterbooks, DLC). Fewer than half replied and, of these, most were opposed to the idea. The Council subsequently recommended against the establishment of such a department, and its report was approved by the 1918 AFL convention.

From Brice Disque

Spruce Production Division
U.S. Signal Corps
War Department
Portland, Ore., March 12th, 1918

My dear Mr. Gompers:

Possibly you are familiar with the recent developments in the lumber industry in the Northwest. Briefly, the operators and employees in the lumber industry having placed the matter entirely in my hands for decision, I decided that they go on a basic eight hour day on March 1st, with the understanding that no man's daily wage would be reduced and that all would receive for the eight hour day what they had been receiving previously for ten hours work.

I will not burden you with the reasons why I made the decision, but I believed then, and continue to believe, that it was the best thing for the Government, operators and employees and to date I have had no reason to regret my action.

There are some sixty five thousand laborers in the lumber industry who have joined our Loyal Legion of Loggers and Lumbermen under a pledge to support the Government's war program in every possible way. The conduct of these men has been such that employers are learning to appreciate them and for that reason are willing to go much further in granting concessions.

The purpose of this letter is to advise you that recent developments indicate an attempt on the part of the shingle weavers and timber workers union labor organization to unionize membership of the Loyal Legion. You, I believe, know that I have no personal objection to union labor. I stated to you frankly in our conference at Washington that I had seen the benefits of union labor in more than one instance, but I feel that it would be a fatal error to permit the unionizing of lumber camps or mills through the medium of this Loyal Legion at this time. Almost without exception the operators in this territory will resist to the limit any attempt along this line. They feel that they have generously met the fair requirements of their employees and a great many of them have cheerfully accepted my decision with reference to the eight hour day through patriotic and other laudable motives, but, having placed all these matters in my hands and agreeing to act upon my decisions, they feel that it would be taking unfair advantage of them to use the war conditions or the Loyal Legion, which was organized because of the war emergency, to unionize their operations and I agree with them.

I believe that you can assist me and that you will see that it would be wrong for union labor to do anything in this matter during the period of the war and it is now my hope that you will address a communication to such representatives as you may have in this section of the country urging them to discontinue such efforts as are now being contemplated and as outlined above.

In addition to deciding that the industry should go on a basic eight hour day, I have decided that they should equip their lumber camps with complete bedding facilities and my medical officers are making frequent sanitary inspections so that I have every reason to believe that the conditions of the laboring men in the lumber industry are rapidly improving and soon will be the equal of any in this country and I am sure that you will approve of everything we have done in this matter. Enclosed you will please find copy of my bulletin 31 which covers the matter in detail.

With great respect, I am

Very sincerely yours,   Brice P. Disque
Colonel,   Signal Corps.[1]

TLS, Files of the Office of the President, General Correspondence, reel 93, frames 211–12, *AFL Records.*

1. For SG's reply, see "To Brice Disque," Apr. 11, 1918, below.

From Burnice King[1]

Metal Trades Council of Birmingham, Alabama
and Vicinity
Birmingham, Ala. March 12th, 1918.

Dear Sir & Brother:—

By direction of the Executive Board of the local Metal Trades Council, I desire to bring to your attention the following facts, and to urge your immediate action along the lines suggested.

The Metal Trades of the Birmingham and Bessemer Ala. Districts, have been on strike for three weeks for an eight hour day.[2] No other consideration enters into the controversy. We are not asking for a closed shop, union recognition or anything but an eight hour day, with overtime pay for work in excess of eight hours.

The Department of Labor had a Conciliator[3] in here for several weeks previous to the strike and he has made active efforts before and since the men quit work to secure an adjustment. He has held conferences with the heads of the U.S. Steel Corporation in Washington and New York and expects to have another soon.

The Steel Corporation is the largest employer involved and the Government Conciliator Mr. Fairley and all of the International Representatives of the different crafts handling the strike are of the firm opinion that the success or failure of the movement depends on what we are able to get from this corporation. Practically every plant in the entire district does a large amount of overflow work for the Steel Corporation that they cannot find room for in their own shops and for that reason the policy of the independent shops is absolutely dictated by the Steel Corporation. In fact one employer who has always been fair with us, closed down his plant when the strike was called and has since told his men that he would gladly settle with us but cannot do so on account of the attitude of the Steel Corporation.

There are approximately five thousand metal trades mechanics on strike or locked out of the different plants and it is conservatively estimated that at least twelve thousand unskilled laborers and miscellaneous labor are thrown out of work on account of the controversy. Practically all plants are doing some form of government work and the eight hour law is being absolutely ignored. The hours in the independent plants are in some instances nine, others ten; the steel corporation hours are from ten to thirteen per shift, straight time.

We keenly appreciate what the Conciliator has done, but we are convinced that the corporation officials are merely stalling in the hope that the men will become discouraged and give up the fight.

Monday morning March the 11th, the local officials of the Steel Corporation, sent their private police out of the plant on the public street of the city to mingle among the pickets for the deliberate purpose of provoking trouble. All of the well known tactics of these thugs and gun-men were resorted to in an effort to start a riot. There were at least two hundred special gun-men lined up inside the plant armed with rifles and revolvers in readiness to start a general killing in the event the ones who had gone among the men outside could provoke a fight.

This morning we saw the same thing repeated and one of our pickets was actually assaulted by one of the company thugs on the public street some distance away from the plant.

We feel that the Department of Labor has probably done all that it can and pressure should be brought to bear by stronger Government Departments to force a settlement of this controversy before serious trouble develops. We think the situation is such as will warrant the attention of President Wilson himself.

In view of the foregoing, you are urgently requested to immediately invoke all possible influence in the interest of securing the eight hour day for the men. As nothing but the eight hour day is involved, we do not think any long investigation necessary, especially so in view of the fact that the Department of Labor has made a thorough investigation and is in possession of the data on the subject.

Please advise by wire at once of your action in this matter. Our Congressman Geo. Huddleston[4] from this District is in hearty accord with us and if you can use him in any manner he will be delighted to have you call on him.

With kindest personal regards, I am,

Fraternally yours, B. W. King

Secty. Metal Trades Council of Birmingham

Alabama & Vicinity.

TLS, Files of the Office of the President, General Correspondence, reel 93, frames 234–35, *AFL Records*.

1. Burnice W. King, a member of International Association of Machinists 7 of Birmingham, Ala., was secretary of the Birmingham Metal Trades Council and business agent for the three Machinists' locals in the city (7, 271, and 359). In August 1918 he was elected president of the Birmingham Trades Council and in 1919 served as a vice-president of the Alabama State Federation of Labor.

2. On Feb. 20, 1918, some five thousand Birmingham metal trades workers struck for an eight-hour day. More than twenty firms in the area were affected, with the Tennessee Coal, Iron, and Railroad Co., a U.S. Steel Corp. subsidiary, being the largest. The Department of Labor estimated that some sixteen thousand workers were eventually involved. Department of Labor commissioner of conciliation William Fairley was unsuccessful in his attempt to mediate an agreement, and in April the dispute was referred to the National War Labor Board. The board heard testimony on the strike on May 9 (see "Excerpts from the Minutes of a Hearing before the National War Labor Board," May 9, 1918, below), but in July voted that it lacked jurisdiction in the matter. The strike ended in failure during the summer. In September U.S. Steel announced it would voluntarily adopt an eight-hour workday but would continue its open-shop policy.

3. William R. Fairley of Pratt City, Ala., served as a commissioner of conciliation for the Department of Labor in 1914 and from at least 1916 to 1919.

4. George Huddleston (1869–1960) served as a Democratic congressman from Alabama from 1915 to 1937.

From Benjamin Schlesinger[1]

President's Office
International Ladies' Garment Workers Union
New York, N.Y. March 12, 1918.

Dear Sir and Brother:—

Replying to your favor of March 9th, in which you request our views on Resolution #37, introduced at the Buffalo Convention of the American Federation of Labor, I beg to say that the question of forming a Garment Trades Department has been a subject of intense discussion at every convention of our International Union.

During recent years the various organizations in the garment industry have had to carry on bitter and costly struggles to improve the conditions of the workers in their respective trades. As soon as the I.L.G.W.U. was through with a gigantic strike, during which its members were called upon to make immense sacrifices, another organization in the industry immediately afterward took the field to fight for the same improvements, with the result that the garment industry was always in a state of disturbance and turmoil. The fact of the matter is that all trades in the garment industry suffer largely from the same defects, and there is no reason why the organizations in this industry should not be united into a department, to remedy the defects in all trades by coordinated effort at the same chosen time.

Another point to consider is the organizing work. At the present time each and every organization in the industry carries on organizing work on its own resources. To find four organizers in a city with no more than three or four hundred garment workers, is a very common occurrence. By establishing a Garment Trades Department this duplication of effort and waste of money would be eliminated, as one organizer working under the auspices of that Department, would be able to attend to the needs of cities with a limited number of garment workers even though employed in four different trades.

Besides, the officers and delegates of our conventions seem to feel, and rightly so, that in view of the fact that most trades in our industry are subject to long periods of idleness, many workers by reason of their ability to make all kinds of garments, look for and find work in other garment trades that happen to be busy during that time. These temporary influxes have always been a source of dissatisfaction and irritation to the workers in the garment trades. The officers and delegates of our conventions are convinced that the formation of a Garment Trades Department would not only do away with this irritation and dissatisfaction, but would also tend to bring about the proper brotherly spirit among the workers in the entire industry.

Hoping that the Executive Council will take favorable action on Resolution #37 and will recommend to the next Convention of the American Federation of Labor the formation of such a Department, I am

Fraternally yours,   Benj. Schlesinger
President.

TLS, AFL Microfilm Convention File, reel 28, frames 2272–73, *AFL Records.*

1. Benjamin SCHLESINGER was president of the International Ladies' Garment Workers' Union (1903–4, 1914–23, 1928–32).

To Paul Vaccarelli[1]

March 13, 1918.

Mr. Paul Vaccarelli,
Vice-President, International Longshoremen's Association,
1475 Broadway, New York City.
Dear Sir and Brother:

Since I reached headquarters I have taken up the matter which you presented to me[2] regarding the Longshoremen in and around New York,[3] and I am impressed with the necessity of writing you upon the subject. You informed me that the men were pleased and enthusiastically accepted the suggestion I made to you, and that is that they should continue work without interruption so that the interests of our people and of our Republic in this crucial time may be fully protected and that we may carry on the program of America supported by labor to carry the war to a triumphant conclusion.

Of course you are aware that in accordance with the agreement entered into referring to the work of the men employed in the operation of tugs, barges, lighters, ferry boats, and other harbor marine equipment in the Port of New York, also river vessels engaged in carrying on the commerce of the Port of New York, an award was made November 16, 1917.[4] I have been furnished with a copy of that award and I find it exceedingly interesting and advantageous. It is quite true that the award made is not all that one could desire, but that it has been of material advantage to all the workers involved goes without question.

Under the award the Shipping Board has compelled employers to pay workmen back wages amounting in many instances to between $30. and $40. It has made companies, particularly the Jay Street Terminal Company, live up to the conditions of the award, and are making all the companies carry out the award under the threat that unless they do the government will take them over.

In view of all these circumstances and many others which might be related, I am appealing to you and through you to the membership of the organizations involved to do everything within your and their power so that the work may go on without interruption and in doing so to do it voluntarily rather than as we know some countries, particularly Germany and Austria, have enforced compulsory labor. We are Americans and free men, and we want to give service as free men. Let us follow the discipline we impose upon ourselves to do the right thing rather than have service made compulsory.

When all the employers and companies have fully carried out the awards and complying with them the question of a revision of the rates and conditions may well be a step for consideration, discussion and possible presentation. I am writing you thus fully upon this subject in order that we may act cooperatively both in spirit and in fact.

Counting upon your cooperation as I feel I am justified from what you have stated to me, I am, with best wishes,

Yours fraternally,   Saml Gompers
President,   American Federation of Labor.

TLpS, reel 232, vol. 244, pp. 753–54, SG Letterbooks, DLC.

1. F. Paul A. Vaccarelli served as a vice-president of the International Longshoremen's Association from 1914 to 1919 and was president of Longshoremen's local 738 (River Front Workers) of New York City. He was also president and manager of the Packard Transportation and Repairing Co. and the Santaro Construction Co.

2. SG probably met with Vaccarelli between Mar. 8 and 12, 1918, while in New York City. After returning to AFL headquarters he met with Longshoremen's president T. V. O'Connor on the day he wrote this letter.

3. On Nov. 16, 1917, the three-member New York Harbor Wage Adjustment Board of Arbitration, composed of representatives of the U.S. Shipping Board, the Department of Labor, and the Department of Commerce, issued a wage award for some fifteen thousand workers engaged in operating tugs, barges, lighters, ferries, and other marine equipment in New York harbor. In the weeks that followed, however, it became evident that many owners of boats operating in the harbor were refusing to abide by the terms of the award, leading to widespread complaints from their employees, warnings of strikes, and threats by the Shipping Board to seize the boats in order to compel compliance. In February 1918 the harbor boatmen's and tidewater boatmen's unions—both of which were affiliated with the Longshoremen—as well as the lighter captains' union and International Union of Steam and Operating Engineers 379 compounded the problem by making new wage demands and threatening to strike if these were not met. When the harbor wage board issued a new award on Mar. 20, granting

them only minor concessions, the four unions rejected the decision and a strike again seemed imminent. (See "To Stephen Condon," Apr. 23, 1918, below.) The unions took their case to the newly-organized National War Labor Board, which referred the matter back to the harbor wage board but increased that body's membership to five, to include representatives of employers and employees. On May 22 the harbor wage board drew up another wage scale, but before it could be issued another complication arose, when the Director General of Railroads issued new wage scales for all railroad workers, including those working in harbors. This award affected about 40 percent of the workers awaiting the harbor wage board's decision and would have resulted in two different scales. After meeting with the Board of Railroad Wages and Working Conditions, the harbor wage board finally issued its award on June 8, and it was confirmed by the Railroad Administration on June 18, making it applicable to railroad employees in the port of New York. After the harbor wage board was further enlarged, to include representatives of railroad employers and employees, the agreement was modified and was reissued on July 12, again with the approval of the Railroad Administration.

4. For the text of the award see "Award of Board of Arbitration in New York Harbor Wage Adjustment," *Monthly Review of the U.S. Bureau of Labor Statistics* 6 (Jan. 1918): 230–33.

To Robert Maisel

March 14, 1918.

Mr. Robert Maisel,
Director, American Alliance for Labor and Democracy,
51 Chambers Street, New York City.
Dear Sir:

Your several letters[1] came duly to hand and contents noted. I read them with great interest and partly on my own desire for a conference with Mr. Creel, as well as your suggestion on that subject, he and I had quite a lengthy conference, when the entire subjects matter of your communications were discussed.

I find that Mr. Creel is not averse to bearing legitimate expenses of any particular campaign in furtherance of the purposes of the American Alliance for Labor and Democracy in its work to bring about the greatest degree of unity and solidarity among the working people and others of our country for the support of the government of the United States and its Allies for victory in this great world war.

But Mr. Creel insists and I am in entire accord with him that there is entire failure in your letters to suggest campaigns and plans to the achievement of a specific object.

Mr. Creel stated that if you will devise plans for campaigns going into detail as to first what is to be accomplished, and how it is to be accomplished, if he approves them he will authorize that they be carried into effect and in any matter in which he has any doubt he will consult me in regard to it and accept my judgment whether the suggested plan or campaign and its details ought to be carried out.

I am writing to you to say candidly that there is considerable adverse criticism in regard to you upon these points. Mr. Creel believes that for the expenditure of the money there ought to be practical plans devised and when approved put into effect. You will find it advantageous to give this matter your immediate and thoughtful consideration.[2]

Very truly yours, Saml Gompers.

President, American Alliance for Labor and Democracy.

TLS, Files of the Office of the President, General Correspondence, reel 93, frame 295, *AFL Records.*

1. Robert Maisel to SG, Mar. 8 and Mar. 12, 1918, Files of the Office of the President, General Correspondence, reel 93, frames 124–25, 237–38, *AFL Records.*

2. For Maisel's reply to these criticisms, see his letter to SG of Mar. 15, 1918, Files of the Office of the President, General Correspondence, reel 93, frames 332–34, *AFL Records.*

From Florence Gompers

The American Red Cross
Washington, D.C. March 14, 1918.

Dearest Grandfather:

Following up our 'phone conversation of the other evening, I wonder if you will think me impertinent if I should, from time to time, mail you some such material as the enclosed with a view to educating you along the line of Red Cross activities?

This ambition of mine has *absolutely* no connection with your *public* attitude towards this organization; I have no idea of endeavoring in my feeble way to influence your views of the proper use of your *name* as an endorsement. I am simply keenly anxious that *you,* with your broad and clear insight of most every "big" thing which affects our country, should have a clearer conception of the magnitude of the American Red Cross, and *not* think of it as merely an agency for furnishing nurses, and knitted goods and surgical dressings.

We have "reams" of more readable and descriptive material than this, but knowing how busy you are, I thought you *might* find time to read this short statement on the way to one place from another.

The *"Government" might* undertake to furnish dressings & knitted goods for *our men,* although they thereby would lose millions' of dollars worth of *volunteer effort* but *obviously* one government couldn't go into other bruised countries and do the work the American Red Cross is doing.

Now, be a dear, good Grandfather and promise to make a *sincere* effort to read some of the "stuff" I send you. *I* promise to make it light—but it's hard because it's "oozing" out of my finger-tips![1]

With lots of love,

Your Granddaughter, Florence

ALS, Files of the Office of the President, General Correspondence, reel 93, frames 289–91, *AFL Records.*

1. SG released a statement on Mar. 22, 1918, endorsing the work of the American Red Cross (Files of the Office of the President, Speeches and Writings, reel 113, frame 92, *AFL Records*).

From James Howey[1]

Superior, Wisconsin Mar 17-1918

Dear Sir

Mr Gompers, with your Permission, I I wish to ask you a fiew questions I am an Old Union Labour Member I have a Union Card signed by T. V. Powderley[2] I am 65 years of age at Present I am Employed at the Superior Termanal & Transfer Rail Road Round House and Shops The Only Union men Reckonized by the Co is the machinest who work 9. Hours 8. Hours is their regular time but they work the Extra Hour making a 9. Hour Day and get time and a half for the Extra Hour They get $5.00 for a Day of 9 Hours

all the Others get $2.50/100 a Day of Ten Hours of very hard & heavey work some are Painting Enjins others Corking flues Others are helping make general Repairs Ect none are Reckonized as union men Except the Machinist

the Rail.Road men generally believe that they are working for the U.S. Government since the Government are Operating the Roades *is that* Right

and we believe that the Government intended that 8. Hours constitued a Days work in the Rail.Road. servis we are all willing to work 10 Hours if the Termanal syston will Pay us for the Extra 2. *Hours*

we fully beliave that the Government that the U.S. Government intended that Eight. Hours should Constitute a Days work

it is Galling to us men to see a third of our comrads wash up and go Home after they have worked 8. Hours or 9. Hours with Time and a

Half for the Extra Hour Pleas Tell me does *8.* Hours Constitute a Days work in the Government Controled R.R. shops Pleas write me and Tell me what our Rights are and if we are intitled to more Pay than $2.50 for 10. Hours hard work

mr Gompers I am writing this with my Diner Pail by my side killing Two Birds with one stone and it is Sunday the 17th of march

Samuel Please write me and Tell me what our Rights are and may God Bless you Samel it would be harder for the Labouring man to loose you than any U.S President we have Ever had Saml we cannot live on $2.50 a Day and support our Familyes

I Pray that God will Bless you and President Wilson you are two of the Greatest men the world has Ever Seen Hoping to Here from you soon[3]

Yours Truly   Capt J. W. Howey

ALS, Files of the Office of the President, General Correspondence, reel 93, frames 377–79, *AFL Records.*

1. James W. Howey was employed as a car repairer in Superior, Wis.

2. Terence Vincent POWDERLY was grand master workman (later general master workman) of the KOL from 1879 until 1893 and served as chief of the Division of Information in the Bureau of Immigration and Naturalization from 1907 until 1924.

3. On Mar. 27, 1918, SG referred Howey's letter to Arthur Wharton, president of the AFL Railway Employes' Department and an adviser to the U.S. Railroad Administration's Railroad Wage Commission; SG informed Howey of his action the same day (reel 233, vol. 245, pp. 252–53, SG Letterbooks, DLC).

To Elbert Gary

Washington, D.C., March 18, 1918.

Honorable Elbert E. Gary,
71 Broadway, New York City.

A committee representing the more than five thousand workmen in the metal trades of Birmingham and Bessemer District of Alabama in conference with me today reported that the dispute between them and the metal trades employers in Alabama is for the recognition of the basic eight hour day. I am advised that a conference has been called by you with the representatives of subsidiary companies or companies allied with your corporation to discuss the situation. The men sought an opportunity for conference with their employers but without avail. Later they submitted a statement to the companies that unless within a reasonable period a conference was held or the basic eight hour demand accorded, the men would quit work, and that no attention was paid to this communication, and that since then, that is since February twenty approximately five thousand skilled men have quit work and between eleven and twelve thousand semiskilled and unskilled have been affected thereby. Of course it is unnecessary for me to impress upon you how great are our country's needs in this crucial time and how necessary it is that at least the basic industries shall be in continuous operation. It has been my purpose as well as that of the entire labor movement to bring about that much desired purpose. In view of the fact that the Congress of the United States has enacted and the President approved and proclaimed the necessity of establishing the eight hour work day as a basic principle and that in case of emergency such as now exists when more than eight hours are worked in a given day at least time and one half should be paid therefor, may I not with all seriousness impress upon you and your associates the industrial, economic and patriotic service to declare and put into operation the basic eight hour day as herein indicated so that the industry in Alabama and elsewhere may be resumed and continued without further interruption.

Samuel Gompers.[1]

Note.
If Judge Gary is not at the office please repeat this telegram to him wherever he may be.

TWSr, Files of the Office of the President, General Correspondence, reel 93, frames 398–99, *AFL Records.*

1. For the reply, see "From Elbert Gary," Mar. 19, 1918, below.

From Elbert Gary

New York March 19 1918

Your telegram[1] just received. I am not prepared to answer it in full without further inquiry as to facts concerning which I have the impression you are misinformed in some respects. There has been no failure on our part to consider everything which has been presented. You are correct in assuming that we fully realize our country's needs. We have done and will continue to do our part in serving the Government.

E H Gary.

TWSr, Files of the Office of the President, General Correspondence, reel 93, frame 421, *AFL Records.*

1. "To Elbert Gary," Mar. 18, 1918, above.

A Memorandum Dictated by Samuel Gompers

Washington D.C. March 21, 1918

MEMORANDUM.

Last evening as per arrangements made with Secretary Tumulty, I had a conference with the President, at the White House, from six o'clock until six-forty, and I brought to his attention and we discussed a number of questions. I informed him that I received a large number of letters and telegrams from various parts of the country, including the Chicago Federation of Labor, in which either directly or indirectly, I was asked to inaugurate a general strike of all workers of the country should Tom Mooney be executed.[1] I expressed my great apprehension of what results might be should he be executed. I stated to him that the Chicago Federation of Labor had under consideration a resolution to declare a general strike and to demand that I should declare one, but that better judgment prevailed in that body, who referred the entire subject to me for advice and suggestion as to the best course to pursue, and that I advised self-control first and then persistent effort in the endeavor to secure a new and a fair trial for Mooney, and I would give my full support to that proposition.[2]

I called to his attention the report of the commission appointed here.[3] The President expressed his great regret at failure to secure a new trial by the highest court in California; urging action to prevent the execution of Mooney, but he said as I knew, he had no power in the premises; the matter was entirely within the state, but that he was doing all he could to prevent Mooney's hanging.[4]

TD, Files of the Office of the President, General Correspondence, reel 93, frame 487, *AFL Records.* Handwritten notation: "Dictated by Mr. Gompers."

1. After the California Supreme Court upheld Thomas Mooney's conviction in early March 1918, he was again scheduled for execution. In July Gov. William Stephens granted him a temporary reprieve, and in November, after the U.S. Supreme Court refused to review the case, Stephens commuted his sentence to life imprisonment.

2. SG to Edward Nockels, Mar. 16, 1918, reel 232, vol. 244, p. 880, SG Letterbooks, DLC.

3. The President's Mediation Commission report on the Mooney case, dated Jan. 16, 1918, recommended that if the California Supreme Court sustained Mooney's conviction, Woodrow Wilson should "use his good offices" in an attempt to secure a new trial for him ("Report on the Mooney Cases by the President's Mediation Commission to the President of the United States," Arthur S. Link et al., eds., *The Papers of Woodrow Wilson*, 69 vols. [Princeton, N.J., 1966–94], 46: 68–74; quotation at p. 73).

4. President Woodrow Wilson wired Stephens on Mar. 27, 1918, asking him to consider commuting Mooney's sentence.

To John Spargo

March 22, 1918.

Mr. John Spargo,
Old Bennington, Vt.
Dear Sir:

I thank you most earnestly for sending me a copy of your letter of the 18th instant[1] which you addressed to Mr. Paul Kellogg,[2] Editor of the Survey. I have read it with keenest interest and satisfaction, and I say this, without any references which you have made in the letter about me.[3] The whole spirit of your letter is good, and it ought to have some influence on the mind of Mr. Kellogg and his future course.

You have perhaps heard or read in part in the newspapers that I have had rather a pretty good "run in" with him last Saturday in New York.[4] His articles in the Survey have been most unwarranted and misinterpreted the heart and spirit of the American labor movement.

The address which I delivered was impromptu. I understand it was taken down stenographically and if I have the chance I shall be very glad to furnish you with a copy of it.

The Washington Post of today publishes a telegram from New York[5] stating that Mr. David C. Coates,[6] Chairman of the new National Party, announced last night that he would send an invitation[7] to Mr. Arthur Henderson, Chairman of the British Labor Party, to send one or two representatives of that organization to this country at the expense of the National Party, to tour the United States and interpret the labor program of the British Labor Party to the laboring masses of this country.

I am in entire accord with your expression regarding the reconstruction program[8] discussed by the British Labor Party. Much of it I endorse. From some of it I dissent, but the spirit of it is not bad. Is it not the best course for us to pursue to secure the greatest possible unity and solidarity of spirit and action, at least for the present, rather than discussing a series of subjects which after all can only find free expression after the war has been triumphantly closed? Ought we have our minds diverted from the will to fight and to win for freedom?

When I read your letter to Mr. Kellogg I felt impelled to write you even though crowded with other important work. When I read the telegram from New York, the substance of which I have given you above, I felt that I ought not to delay.[9]

Very truly yours,   Saml Gompers.
President,   American Federation of Labor.

TLpS, reel 233, vol. 245, pp. 135–36, SG Letterbooks, DLC.

1. John Spargo to Paul Kellogg, Mar. 18, 1918, Files of the Office of the President, General Correspondence, reel 93, frames 413–15, *AFL Records*. Spargo's letter was deeply critical of Arthur Henderson's proposal for an international conference involving labor and socialist delegates from all belligerent powers.

2. Paul Underwood Kellogg (1879–1958) served as editor of the *Survey* from 1912 until 1952, when the journal ceased publication.

3. Spargo wrote Kellogg: "I believe that the position taken by Mr. Gompers and his associates in the American Federation of Labor is absolutely sound and represents the best interest of the working class in all countries. Never at any time has Mr. Gompers shown greater wisdom or statesmanship in his leadership of the labor movement than in the position he has taken toward the repeated suggestions to send delegates to so-called peace conferences. Of course, I am not unaware of the fact that a number of radical intellectuals like yourself have been severely criticizing that position. But, then, I remember that practically the same group has given its sympathy and more or less open support to every freak movement within the ranks of organized labor, and to every disruptive element that has arisen within the labor movement in the last fifteen or twenty years. If I am not mistaken, you gave the I.W.W. more support and encouragement than you had ever given the bonafide labor movement of the country, notwithstanding the fact that the I.W.W. was intended to be a dividing force in the labor movement. Personally, I have long entertained a profound distrust of the criticism of the labor movement by so-called radical intellectuals. . . . My experience has led me to believe that no good ever came to the labor movement from the criticisms of those whose knowledge of the movement is purely academic and theoretical" (Files of the Office of the President, General Correspondence, reel 93, frame 414, *AFL Records*).

4. On Mar. 16, 1918, SG, Kellogg, and William English Walling delivered addresses at a National Civic Federation luncheon in New York City held in honor of the visiting British labor delegation. Their talks were later published in *Addresses by Paul U. Kellogg . . . Samuel Gompers . . . and William English Walling . . . on the British Labor Party's Program of Reconstruction after the War and the Stockholm Conference . . .* (n.p., [1918]).

5. "Invites British Labor Men," *Washington Post*, Mar. 22, 1918.

6. David Courtney COATES was a member of the Committee on Labor of the Advisory Commission of the Council of National Defense and chairman of the National party.

7. Coates and J. A. H. Hopkins to Henderson, Mar. 20, 1918, Files of the Office of the President, General Correspondence, reel 93, frame 444, *AFL Records*. The invitation was issued by direction of a resolution introduced by Spargo and adopted by the first National party convention, held in Chicago in March 1918.

8. A draft of the Labour party's reconstruction program was published in January

1918 under the title *Labour and the New Social Order: A Report on Reconstruction.* After it was submitted to member organizations for consideration, a revised version was adopted by the Labour party conference held in London in June. The program called for a minimum standard of living, nationalization of industry and common ownership of the means of production, institution of a highly progressive tax system, and use of surplus wealth for the common good. Spargo told Kellogg he was "in cordial sympathy" with the program and "in entire agreement with most of it" (Files of the Office of the President, General Correspondence, reel 93, frame 414, *AFL Records*).

9. Spargo replied on Mar. 27, 1918, that the newspaper account of Coates's invitation to Henderson was correct (Files of the Office of the President, General Correspondence, reel 93, frames 721–22, *AFL Records*).

To Joseph Tumulty

Washington, D.C. March 23, 1918.

Hon. J. P. Tumulty,
Secretary to the President,
The White House, Washington, D.C.
My dear Mr. Tumulty:

Permit me to acknowledge receipt of your favor of the 22d instant with enclosed resolution[1] adopted by the Texas State Federation of Labor and transmitted to the President by Mr. Geo. H. Slater,[2] its Secretary. The language employed in the second Whereas, is that well known to the men in the labor movement, and hence when many bodies employ these terms they erroneously imagine that all are familiar with the situation.

Perhaps the recital of a few instances may be helpful. For years the Los Angeles Times and a few newspapers of the same caliber have attacked, abused, and denounced the labor movement and its men, stigmatizing both in vilest terms and opposing every species of legislation asked by the workers at the hands of the government of the United States, of the several states, and municipalities. Not a measure demanded or method employed but has received the same treatment at the hands of these publications.

The magazine American Industries, later The Square Deal, issued monthly by the National Association of Manufacturers, pursued the same course as did the Los Angeles Times and other newspapers of that ilk.

The National Erectors' Association is founded principally upon antagonism to union labor and its activities are directed to the accomplishment of that purpose.

The National Association of Manufacturers conducted a system of espionage and secret lobbying against the workers' interests, the expose of which you know at least in part through the Congressional Committees.

The National Industrial conference declared by themselves to be an Eight Billion Dollar concern, started last year upon a campaign of "extermination" of organized labor.

The United States Steel Corporation is pronouncedly and openly anti-labor, and is closed to the employment of any worker who may be a member of an organization.

The overwhelming preponderance of the work of the various detective agencies throughout the country is a system of espionage upon workers who may join unions, to report them to the employers for dismissal, and in many instances where organization has not been entirely prevented, to provoke the workers to premature strikes and to defeat them and to trump up charges against innocent defenseless workers.

I am just reciting a few of these instances. They will give an insight of what workers of Texas in the State Federation convention[3] know by experience and by authentic information they have.

Of course the President in his reply will express in the warmest terms his appreciation of the resolution of loyalty and devotion. He could make some reference of his understanding and gratitude for this position of the workers that they need fear no enemies or antagonists as to what hurt or injury they could do to the great humanitarian cause of labor, so long as they pursue the course which American labor has outlined for itself and that the efforts of the enemies of labor must and will prove abortive so long as the rational, natural and loyal course is faithfully adhered to and that he is persuaded and convinced that the toilers in this crucial time will give a good accounting of themselves.[4]

With kindest personal regards, I am,

Sincerely yours,   Saml Gompers
President,   American Federation of Labor.

TLS, Woodrow Wilson Papers, DLC.

1. In his letter to SG of Mar. 22, 1918 (Files of the Office of the President, General Correspondence, reel 93, frame 538, *AFL Records*), Joseph Tumulty conveyed President Woodrow Wilson's request for advice on how to respond to a telegram from George Slater transmitting a resolution adopted by the Texas State Federation of Labor (FOL). The resolution read: "Whereas organized labor affiliated with the Texas State Federation of Labor has evidenced its loyalty to our government by its men in the trenches and the opening of its treasuries in the support of the war against autocracy and Whereas in spite of all we have done and are doing the enemies of labor would have the public believe that organized labor is not doing its full duty in this hour of our nation's crisis be it Resolved as further evidence of our loyalty that the Texas State Federation of Labor in its 21st annual convention assembled in the city of San Antonio March 18 1918

pledge its members to any sacrifice needed be it our lives the lives of our loved ones or our treasuries and in the conduct of our affairs to exhaust every means to avoid cessation of labor in any branch during the war and in every way to prove by our acts that our members are loyal to President Woodrow Wilson and his administration fully realizing the responsibility resting upon organized labor" (Slater to SG, Mar. 21, 1918, ibid., frames 536–37).

2. George Henry SLATER served as secretary-treasurer of the Texas State FOL from 1914 to 1919.

3. The Texas State FOL convention met in San Antonio, Mar. 18–23, 1918.

4. For Wilson's reply to Slater of Mar. 26, 1918, which utilized SG's suggestions, see Arthur S. Link et al., eds., *The Papers of Woodrow Wilson*, 69 vols. (Princeton, N.J., 1966–94), 47: 144.

To Ernest Bohm

March 25, 1918.

Mr. Ernest Bohm,
Secretary, Central Federated Union,
243 East 84th St., New York City.
Dear Sir and Brother:

For confirmation I quote to you herein telegram[1] I sent to you under date of March 22nd. It is as follows:

["]Washington, D.C., March 22, 1918

["]Mr. Ernest Bohm, Secretary,
["]Central Federated Union,
["]Labor Temple, 243 E. 84th St., New York City.
["]Permit me to extend to the Central Federated Union my hearty appreciation and congratulation for the splendid resolution unanimously passed at your last meeting, in insisting that the struggle for world freedom and democracy may go on to a triumphant conclusion. In addition I should add that Socialist and other pro-German anti-American propaganda and its attacks, and slurs upon the American Labor Movement and myself will not divert us from our duty in this crucial time of the world's history, or at any other time.

["]Samuel Gompers.["]

This morning I received a letter of which the following is a copy:

"The Teachers Union.[2]
["]#70 Fifth Avenue
["]New York, March 23, 1918.

"Mr. Samuel Gompers,
["]Washington, D.C.
["]My dear Mr. Gompers:

["]As the delegate of the Teachers' Union to the Central Federated Union of New York City, I was astonished to hear a telegram read bearing your signature which contains these words: 'In addition, I should add that Socialist and other pro-German anti-American propaganda and its attacks upon the American labor movement and myself will not divert us from our duty in this crucial time of the world's history or at any other time.'

["]Surely you cannot mean what the telegram states. I am a Socialist but not a member of the Socialist Party as I am unalterably opposed to its attitude on the war and am unqualifiedly behind the President in this war for the liberation of mankind from a militaristic, autocratic Prussian yoke. Your telegram stigmatized me and thousands of other loyal Socialists as disloyal. Why? Can't a man be a believer in Socialism and be intensely loyal? I have done my bit and am still doing it and therefore resent being classed among the disloyal. If it was not your intention to so stigmatize loyal Socialists, why did you not add these words after the word Socialist, 'who are disloyal' in that case no characterization of the disloyal would have been severe enough to meet with my disapproval. Moreover, would not your telegram have been stronger and more in harmony with the dignity of the office you hold if you had omitted the word 'Socialist' because it assumes that disloyal individuals are only to be found among the Socialists and not among the Democrats and Republicans?

["]Of course, it is probable that the wording of the telegram was inaccurate or else it did not properly express the idea that you had in mind. Will you, therefore, before I have my organization take action, please let me know if the telegram was correctly worded and if it conveyed your real meaning? Trusting to hear from you, I remain

["]Fraternally yours
["](A[b]r. Lefkowitz) ["][3]

For your further information I quote to you a copy of my reply[4] as follows:

["]Washington, D.C., March 25, 1918.

["]Mr. A. Lefkowitz, Member,
["]The Teachers' Union of New York City,
["]70 Fifth Avenue, New York City.
["]Dear Sir:

["]Your favor of the 23rd instant came duly to hand and contents noted. In reply I should say that there may be a Socialist here and there who declares his loyalty to the American government and to the labor movement, but as the term is generally understood it is expressed in Socialist Party organization. I have heard and seen some Socialists mouthing a declaration of loyalty and yet in their every utterance attacking, their action belying their lip service. I have seen published and I have heard you in the Central Federated Union meeting unwarrantably attack the American labor movement and without the slightest basis of truth or justification.

["]The delegates and other attendants at the meetings of the New York Central Federated Union know how much higher conception you have of the dignity of the Presidency of the American Federation of Labor than I have.

["]I thank you for your suggested advice contained in your question why I did not add after the word Socialist in my telegram 'who are disloyal,' but as a matter of fact, Socialists are so generally disloyal that it is the exception when we find one here and there who is loyal and one who merely declares his loyalty upon the principle of 'safety first.' My particular purpose in sending the telegram I did was not only to convey my sincere congratulations and appreciation to the Central Federated Union for its splendid resolution adopted the meeting before the last, but to take cognizance of the malicious attack[5] published in the Socialist publication, the New York Call, in which the honor, honesty of the American Federation of Labor and I were attacked in the most brutal and lying manner.

["]You say that you want me to answer you whether the telegram correctly conveys what I had in mind. The above will answer that question, but you add, using your own language, 'before I have my organization take action.' The natural inference from that declaration is that at your whim and fancy you can have your organization 'take action.' My understanding of the trade union movement is that a man may advise his organization to take action upon a certain situation, but to have the organization take action implies that one carries the will of the organization in his vest pocket, and yet if you propose to 'have your organization take action' as a threat to me, you have this my letter to practically advise you to go as far as you like.

["]Yours, etc., (signed) Samuel Gompers.
["]President, American Federation of Labor."

It seemed to me that inasmuch as the entire subject matter concerns the C.F.U. as much as any other body or person the entire matter should be placed in your possession to be presented to the C.F.U. at its forthcoming meeting for the information it contains as well as for the archives of your central body.

With best wishes, I am

Fraternally yours, Saml Gompers
President, American Federation of Labor.

TLpS, reel 233, vol. 245, pp. 233–35, SG Letterbooks, DLC.

1. SG to Ernest Bohm, Mar. 22, 1918, reel 233, vol. 245, p. 9, SG Letterbooks, DLC.

2. American Federation of Teachers 5 of New York City.

3. Abraham Lefkowitz, a New York City high school teacher, was a founder of Teachers' local 5 and served on the editorial board (1918) and as business manager (1918–19) of its official journal, *The American Teacher.*

4. SG to Lefkowitz, Mar. 25, 1918, reel 233, vol. 245, pp. 231–32, SG Letterbooks, DLC.

5. "C.F.U. Aims Puny Blow at World Congress," *New York Call,* Mar. 17, 1918.

To William B. Wilson

Washington, D.C. March 25, 1918.

Hon. Wm. B. Wilson,
Secretary, Department of Labor,
Washington, D.C.
Sir:

When I had the pleasure of conference[1] with you last Saturday among other things presented to you for consideration was the case of Thomas Mooney, who as you know has been sentenced to death and in whose case the highest court in the state of California decided that it could not go outside of the record, notwithstanding the tremendous amount of evidence which has been discovered since the trial that much of the testimony upon which Mooney was convicted was manufactured and perjury.

When I had the honor of an interview with the President last Wednesday evening I brought the same state of facts to his attention and he was very much interested. But quite apart from the case itself, I mentioned to the President as I did to you that from many quarters come insistent demands upon me that I should call or order a general strike of all the workers of the country in protest against the execution of Mooney. I have endeavored by everyway in my power to placate our fellow workers at the same time assuring them all that every effort would be made to secure some relief from the execution of the sentence and that Mooney's life may be spared.

In addition to this state of affairs, the fact should be stated that the Mooney case has attracted such wide spread feeling among the people of many other countries. You know of its effect in Russia some months ago and also in Mexico.[2] A well informed woman has just returned from France and England and she reports that the Mooney case has a meaning among the great mass of the people of both these countries which is not understood in the United States.

With all these facts in mind, knowing what the President has done, I feel it absolutely necessary to lay the facts before you, and to ask you in turn that you may present them to the President and endeavor to prevail upon him to go to extraordinary limits in order to prevent Mooney's execution.

Of course, I could address my letter directly to the President, but because he is so extraordinarily engaged in the manifold and important duties of his office, I have written this to you in order to have the essentials of this matter brought to the President's attention again with the sincere hope that everything may be done to avoid an injustice as well as a very serious situation.

Today I sent a telegram[3] to Governor Stephens[4] of California, of which the following is a copy:

["]Washington, D.C.
["]March 25, 1918.

"Governor William D. Stephens,
["]Sacramento, California.
["]With all the facts of the mistrial in the case of Tom Mooney before you, much of which I have had before me, and inasmuch as the entire situation is in your hands to dispose of as your judgment directs in the cause of justice, fair dealing and mercy, I appeal to you in the name of the American Federation of Labor to exercise the great power which is vested solely in you. The highest court in California has declared that it could not go outside of the record in the case. When almost incontrovertible evidence has been discovered since the trial that con-

viction was had largely upon manufactured and perjured evidence, if the courts cannot or do not take cognizance of these facts, certainly you, as the governor of the great state of California, have the right, the jurisdiction and the power and I trust you will exercise it."

["]Samuel Gompers.["]

Feeling sure that you will do your level best to accomplish the de-sired result,[5] I have the honor to remain

Yours very respectfully,   Saml Gompers.
President,   American Federation of Labor.

TLS, RG 174, General Records of the Department of Labor, DNA.

1. SG met with William B. Wilson on the afternoon of Saturday, Mar. 23, 1918.
2. Protests against the impending execution of Thomas Mooney were held in St. Petersburg and Tampico in April 1917 (see "To John O'Connell," May 9, 1917, n. 3, above). Mooney also figured in protests in St. Petersburg in September of that year, although Alexander Berkman was the principal focus of those demonstrations.
3. SG to William Stephens, Mar. 25, 1918, reel 233, vol. 245, p. 150, SG Letterbooks, DLC.
4. William Dennison Stephens (1859–1944) served as governor of California from 1917 to 1923. He had previously been a Republican congressman from that state (1911–16).
5. Wilson replied on Apr. 5, 1918, that he had brought the case up for consideration at a Cabinet meeting on Mar. 26, and he assured SG that the president was doing all he could to persuade Stephens either to pardon Mooney or give him a new trial (RG 174, General Records of the Department of Labor, DNA).

From William Short[1]

Washington, D.C., March 26, 1918.

Dear Mr. Gompers:—

In line with our conversation this afternoon, I am herewith submit-ting to you a brief statement of the facts in the case of Hulet Wells vs. The Federal Department of Justice,[2] as I understand them:—

Mr. Wells[3] was recently convicted in the District Court at Seattle of conspiracy to obstruct the draft law. His conviction was secured at the second trial held in connection with his case.

At the first trial the Jury disagreed, holding that there had not been sufficient evidence presented to justify conviction. Mr. Hulet Wells is a former president of the Seattle Central Labor Council[4] and is a mem-ber of the International Brotherhood of Electrical Workers.[5] He has been active for many years in affairs of the Seattle labor movement and is now a delegate to the Central Labor Council. He was present as a delegate to a meeting called by the State Federation of Labor at Seattle, shortly after the declaration that a state of war existed between our country and the Imperial German Government. This meeting was called by the State Federation of Labor and there were delegates present representing most of the organizations affiliated with it.

At this meeting, the position of our government in declaring that a state of war existed was endorsed by the meeting but the meeting also adopted a resolution condemning and opposing the draft law which was then being considered by Congress. The position of yourself and many other prominent men of our labor movement was quoted in connection with their opposition of the labor movement to the principles of conscription. The Seattle Central Labor Council, later, by almost unanimous vote adopted a similar resolution. There was found in Seattle, about this time, a branch of the American Union against Militarism. There were quite a number of the members of organized labor affiliated with this organization. The branch also included the present Chairman[6] of our State Public Service Commission, also several Clergymen and attorneys.

It was at one of the meetings of this organization that the circular was drafted and plans made for its distribution on which the charge of conspiracy to obstruct the draft law on which Mr. Wells was convicted was based. The evidence developed during the trial to show that Mr. Wells had nothing to do with the drafting of or distribution of this circular but had left the meeting prior to this action having been taken by the branch but had later agreed to provide for the printing of the circular.

The only charge in addition to this brought against Mr. Wells was his connection with the drafting of a resolution opposing conscription which was introduced and adopted by the Seattle Central Labor Council. The Jury in the first trial held disagreed and during the course of the trial Mr. Wells had made the statement to the court that now the purposes for which America entered the war had been made public by our President, that he was no longer in opposition to our prosecution of the war but was in full accord with the purposes laid down by President Wilson.

The feeling was general at this time among our people that no further good could be accomplished by a further prosecution of the case inasmuch as no guilt had been established and the danger of further opposition on the part of Mr. Wells to the policies of our government had been removed by his declaration to the court.

It was not until the District Attorney, Mr. Clay Allen[7] moved for a new trial and imported from Portland, Oregon, Mr. Clarence Reames,[8] the District Attorney for Oregon, to prosecute the case in the second trial, that any general sympathy had been expressed for Mr. Wells by our people. The case then seemed to have taken on the air of persecution rather than prosecution. The fact that he had lost his position in Seattle as a result of his former activities and was still and is still unable to secure employment, also the fact that he had mortgaged and lost his home in Seattle and that his family was in destitute circumstances, has aroused a general feeling of sympathy for him among a large majority of the workers of Seattle and vicinity who were not in accord with his former actions as they related to our war program. The sentence of the court in imposing a sentence of two years in the penitentiary has entered fuel to the fires of dissatisfaction that are growing as a result of the impression created by the court at the second trial of persecution.

Mr. Wells is out on $10,000.00 bail furnished jointly by his father and Mr. Doyle,[9] the Business Agent of the Seattle Central Labor Council. Steps are being taken now to appeal against the decision of the court but in the meantime a strong disaffection is growing up between the workers of Seattle and this branch of our Federal Government that may possibly endanger the war program. There is a general feeling among even the most conservative members of our movement that the policy pursued by the District Attorney has at least been very unwise if not totally unjust.

I have personally known Mr. Wells for a number of years and while he is a Socialist, he differs in a large measure from most of the men connected with that organization inasmuch as he has always tried to work in harmony with the policies of the legitimate trade union movement. He is a man of very high character and absolutely honest and sincere in his convictions. I have never seriously disagreed with him on any question except the question of lending the full support of our trade union movement to our government in this world crisis and since talking this matter over with him recently, I am honestly convinced that he has been converted in a large measure to our view point.

I am also honestly convinced that the best interests of our government would be served by executive clemency in his case because even if the case is appealed and the decision reversed in a higher tribunal, it would only tend to encourage those who are desirous of opposing the war policies of our Government, while the confidence that an over-whelming majority of our members have in the liberal and just policies of the Wilson Administration would be restored by some such executive action on his part. However, this is a matter that can be left much better to your own personal judgment. I have merely tried to recite to you the facts in the case as I understand them and know them to be.

Fraternally yours,　William [M.] Short,

President,　Washington State Federation of Labor.

P.S. Herewith is attached the statement of Mr. Wells to the Jury in his first trial which was published in the newspapers of our city.

W. S.[10]

TLtcSr, RG 60, General Records of the Department of Justice, DNA.

1. William Mackie SHORT served as president of the Washington State Federation of Labor from 1918 to 1927.

2. On May 28, 1917, Hulet Wells and three other Seattle antiwar activists were arrested for distributing a circular urging resistance to the draft. They were charged with conspiracy to incite murder and assassination and conspiracy to resist by force and violence enforcement of the laws of the United States, in particular the Selective Service Act. In September, at the first trial of their case (*U.S. v. Wells et al.*), the charges were dismissed against one defendant, a second was acquitted, and the jury deadlocked on the verdict for Wells and codefendant Samuel Sadler. The prosecution immediately announced it would retry the case and brought charges against Wells, Sadler, and two additional men, Joseph and Morris Pass. The four were tried in February 1918, convicted of seditious conspiracy, and sentenced to prison terms.

3. Hulet Martell Wells (1878–1970) was editor of the *Socialist Voice* (Seattle) in 1911, Socialist candidate for mayor of Seattle in 1912, chairman of the Washington state Socialist party in 1913, and president of the Central Labor Council of Seattle and Vicinity (CLC) from 1915 to 1916. Arrested in 1917 and charged with conspiracy, he was convicted in 1918 and imprisoned from June 1919 to November 1920 at McNeil Island Penitentiary and then at Leavenworth. After his release from prison, Wells returned to Seattle and resumed his activity in the labor movement, joining the Farmer-Labor party and serving as its state chairman in 1925 and then as editor of the *Vanguard,* a publication of the Unemployed Citizens League of Seattle and the Seattle Labor College (1932–33). Subsequently an aide to congressman Marion Zioncheck, he moved to Washington, D.C., and after Zioncheck's death in 1935, he worked as a post office clerk.

4. The Western Central Labor Union was reorganized in 1905 as the Seattle CLC, and the new organization was chartered by the AFL the same year.

5. The International Brotherhood of ELECTRICAL Workers.

6. Elbert F. Blaine, a Seattle attorney, was president of the Okanogan Power and Irrigation Co. and manager of the Washington Irrigation Co. He served as chairman of the Public Service Commission of Washington from 1916 until at least 1919.

7. Clay Allen was U.S. district attorney for the Western District of Washington from 1913 to 1918 and served as a judge in the Superior Court of King County, Wash., from 1918 to 1920.

8. Clarence L. Reames served as a special assistant attorney general in the War Emergency Division of the Department of Justice.

9. Charles W. Doyle, a member of Brotherhood of Painters, Decorators, and Paperhangers of America 300 of Seattle, served as business agent (1908–28?) and secretary (1923–57) of the Seattle CLC.

10. SG sent a copy of Short's letter to Attorney General Thomas Gregory on Apr. 3, 1918 (Files of the Office of the President, General Correspondence, reel 94, frame 83, *AFL Records*).

To Bernard Larger

March 29, 1918.

Mr. B. A. Larger,
General Secretary, United Garment Workers of America,
Rooms 116–122, Bible House, New York City.
Dear Sir and Brother:

Your letter of March 28[1] enclosing copy[2] of letter received from the National Women's Trade Union League received. There is a federal eight hour law applying to government employes, whether men or women. Now that the National Women's Trade Union League, as well as every other progressive women's organization are supporting the proposed federal amendment[3] which gives equal suffrage to women, it is hardly consistent to ask for a federal eight hour law applying to women only. If there is a desire to make the present eight hour law more comprehensive, the effort should take the form of an attempt to perfect the present law, and that action should not be taken without the consent and approval of the organized labor movement.

As a result of war conditions there is a constant increase in the number of women coming into industry and entering trades and callings hitherto closed to them. This tendency makes the problem of economic organization of women increasingly important and urgent. The problem of protecting women against exploitation and maintaining their welfare can not be solved by political methods and legislation alone. The fundamental move must be in the economic world so that women will be in a position to control and utilize their economic power and deal with economic problems through economic means.

I heartily indorse the eight hour workday as the maximum that ought to be worked by men or women, but I sincerely regret any effort to mislead women into thinking that they can trust their economic welfare to legislation. Economic welfare of women wage earners is an economic problem differing in no essential principle from the economic welfare of the men. That agency which has demonstrated greatest effectiveness in dealing with men's problems is the agency that will also prove most effective in establishing and protecting the economic welfare of women wage earners.

Fraternally yours,   Saml Gompers
President,   American Federation of Labor.

TLpS, reel 233, vol. 245, p. 434, SG Letterbooks, DLC.

1. Bernard Larger's letter to SG of Mar. 28, 1918, asked for information on the AFL's position on an eight-hour law for women (AFL Microfilm National and International Union File, United Garment Workers Records, reel 37, frame 2560, *AFL Records*).

2. National Women's Trade Union League to Larger, Mar. 25, 1918, AFL Microfilm National and International Union File, United Garment Workers Records, reel 37, frame 2561, *AFL Records.*

3. Several resolutions introduced in the Sixty-fifth Congress proposed a woman suffrage amendment, but none of them were adopted. The following year, however, the Sixty-sixth Congress did pass a resolution providing for woman suffrage. It was ratified as the Nineteenth Amendment to the Constitution in 1920.

A Statement by Samuel Gompers

[March 29, 1918]

America is in this war because the mailed fist of militarism is gripping the throat of freedom. America is more than a name, more than a country or even continent. It is a symbol, the meaning of America is epitomized in the word freedom. It is that which has brought to our shores the oppressed, those who vainly sought opportunity in other lands. That which is America to Americans by adoption as well as our native born has become an issue in a war precipitated by German autocracy.

Never before was a war waged as this one. The contending forces consist not only of enlisted men, whole nations are mobilized. Each and every man, woman and child has a responsible duty necessary to the success of America and our Allies winning this war. It is a war in which the man power, financial and national resources, industries, transportation systems, intellectual abilities of one group of nations is pitted against another group. So fundamental is the issue there can be no neutrality for nations or individuals. The countries of the world are too closely bound together for autocracy and democracy to exist longer side by side.

Because the freedom gives life, meaning and hope, America's Labor is whole-heartedly behind our Republic. The trade union movement is the product of freedom and the hand maid of democracy. Labor knows that the authority which German imperialism seeks to impose upon the world would deny workers the right to control and direct their associated activities.

The trade union movement represents the aspiration of men and women for a better life—it is part of the age-old struggle for human freedom. It is the agency through which workers can put their abilities at the service of our democratic nation.

Because they grasp the fundamentals involved, the workers are giving it their full support, moral, financial, service.

They will fight to the end and give their all in this war for freedom, the results of which will be translated into oppression or opportunity in every day of their lives and work.

America's workers have made their choice, they stand true under their banner on which are emblazoned the watchwords, "Justice freedom and democracy."

TD, Files of the Office of the President, Speeches and Writings, reel 113, frames 93–94, *AFL Records.* Typed notation: "Statement prepared by President Gompers, March 29th, 1918, for publication in the books 'Why We Must Win the War' which are to be published by the Committee on Public Information."

From Dennis Lane

Chicago Ill 1918 Mar 29

Through press reports and other information we have learned that our first vice president brother Fred D Schmidt[1] is in custody of the federal authorities at St Louis on a technical charge of entering a barred zone without a permit Schmidt was born in Germany took out his first papers and has an honorable discharge for services in the US Army dated May 18 1911 You know that our international stands with you and President Wilson [f]or a successful termination of this war for a worlds democracy and I am positive sure that the independent packers of St Louis where we have organized their plants nearly one hundred percent within the last ninety days are being permitted to use the government to discredit our international union and first vice president Fred D Schmidt The general press reports are that he is also being held [f]or fermenting strikes at Omaha[2] Kansas City[3] and other places In Omaha and Kansas City he acted with mediators Fike[4] and Patrick F Gill[5] and settled strikes in these two cities in a few days All of the organizers for the American Federation of Labor who are working in the packing house districts have been in the custody of the police som[e f]or days and others for a few hours You remember the deportation of organizer Ball[6] [f]rom Oklahoma City by the chief of police[7] who claims and it has never been denied that when he deported Ball he done so at the request of representative of the Department of Justice in that particular city May I urge you in the name of our international union that you request the Department of Justice at Washington to make immediate investigation and report so that we may know in reality who is responsible for the incar[c]eration of vice president Schmidt

Dennis Lane.[8]

TWSr, Files of the Office of the President, General Correspondence, reel 93, frames 865–67, *AFL Records.*

1. Frederick "Gus" Schmidt, a member of Amalgamated Meat Cutters and Butcher Workmen of North America 88 of St. Louis, served as a vice-president of the international union from 1917 to 1920. Born in Prussia, he immigrated to the United States in 1904 and served in the U.S. Army from 1908 to 1911. He had not become a citizen, however, so on Mar. 25, 1918, he was arrested as an enemy alien and forbidden to travel outside the St. Louis area. SG and Meat Cutters' president Dennis Lane protested his case to Secretary of Labor William B. Wilson, and in May the Department of Justice was persuaded to allow Schmidt to make a short trip to Ft. Wayne, Ind., to deal with labor difficulties there. As late as July, however, SG was still attempting to have Schmidt's travel restriction lifted completely.

2. Some five thousand Omaha packinghouse workers struck for a wage increase in early September 1917. Department of Labor commissioner of conciliation Frederick Feick arranged a settlement by mid-month, which included a 2½-cent-per-hour pay increase, reinstatement of the strikers, an end to discrimination against union members, and the right of workers to form grievance committees.

3. Nearly three thousand Kansas City, Kans., packinghouse workers struck in early September 1917, demanding an eight-hour day and a wage increase with time-and-a-half for both overtime and Sunday work. By mid-month Department of Labor commissioner of conciliation Patrick Gill arranged a settlement, with terms similar to the Omaha agreement—a 2½-cent-per-hour wage increase, the rehiring of strikers, an agreement by employers not to discriminate against union workers, and the right to form grievance committees.

4. Frederick L. Feick served as a commissioner of conciliation for the U.S. Department of Labor from 1917 until at least 1920.

5. Patrick Francis Gill, former Democratic congressman from Missouri (1909–11, 1912–13), was a commissioner of conciliation for the Department of Labor from at least 1916 until at least 1920.

6. Elmer E. Ball, who lived in the vicinity of Ft. Worth, Tex., was a member of the Meat Cutters and served as an AFL salaried organizer. The Oklahoma City incident mentioned by Lane took place in November 1917.

7. William B. Nichols was the Oklahoma City chief of police.

8. SG replied to Lane on Mar. 30, 1918, that he had taken up the matter with government officials, and R. Lee Guard subsequently wrote Lane that it had been referred to the Department of Labor (reel 233, vol. 245, pp. 436, 762, SG Letterbooks, DLC).

C. Bethuel Young[1] to Frank Morrison

Pacific Coast District Council 38–A, I.L.A.
Ship Yard Laborers, Riggers and Fasteners
National Hotel, Washington, D.C. March, 29th. 1918.

Mr. Frank Morrison,
Secretary, American Federation of Labor,
Washington, D.C.

Dear Brother Morrison:—

I have gone over very carefully the communication[2] with enclosures; which you handed to me to-day; and while I believe that after our conversation you have all of the vital points yet I believe that the[re] is an answer due you which will probably refresh your mind of a few facts existing.

In the first place be it known that there was no other place except the I.L.A. that would give to our application for affiliation any consideration, and that being chartered as Shipyard Labors we were common tramping ground and trading property for the craft which was so disposed to use us.[3]

In answer to the claim of the Building and Common Laborer for their right to the Laborer in the Shipyard for the reason that his men are going into the Shipyards to work; let me say that if such a plan as he suggests were carried out on a large scale it would eventually work out as follows:—Some of his men might shift to the saw mill, woods, the steel plant and the shop, some might go to the farm and others to the mines and if his theory carried out eventually he would have a very large industrial organization. After the I.W.W. theory.

The Structural Iron Worker says the Rigging is his for the reason that he does the Rigging on construction work. Now as a matter of fact the I.L.A. is the only International that has ever had jurisdiction over or done the ships rigging and they have given us that Jurisdiction.

The carpenter says that the Fastening work is his, and while this is the case we have tried for a year to break down his doors for admission and he has positively refused to admit to membership this class of workers.

We have largely organized ourselves by the efforts of our active members. We have laid hold of an oppertunity to fill a very large gap in the Labor Movment. We are composed of men from many walks of life, men who are in the changing scenes of this worlds economy are brought to face what every man faces if he has to deal with the Boss as an individual and not as an organization.

Having grasped the oppertunity to become a part of the great labor movment of the country this orphan child finds that some of his big brothers are not willing to associate with him but rather want to stack the cards so that the proggress that he hoped to make in wage and working conditions are almost as remote as when he was in a single state.

Then comes the possibility of affiliation with the I.L.A. as the dawn of a new morning and who is there that shall say that in this time of great need, in this time when every individual as well as organization shall not do his best and take advantage of every oppertunity to be a living factor in the proggress of our country.

T'is not the man who claims to be but the man who is who is needed to-day. Not the man to tear down, but the man to build that we need at this time, and *We Are Building Ships.*

We are also building in the minds of our members the advantage to be gained by organization. We are building *Union* men, not *Scabs.*

We are not asking for anything but fair play and we have a right to ask for that, and we are willing to give fair play in return.

According to your suggestion I am willing to meet any one and go over the claims that they may have in this matter, and if at any time while I am here you wish to go into this matter further I will be glad to meet at your suggestion.

Sincerely yours,   C. B. Young

TLS, AFL Microfilm Jurisdiction File, Hod Carriers, Building and Common Laborers Records, reel 51, frame 1206, *AFL Records.*

1. C. Bethuel Young was president of International Longshoremen's Association Pacific Coast District Council 38–A (Ship Yard Laborers, Riggers, and Fasteners), which had its headquarters in Seattle. He was in Washington, D.C., for a conference with Frank Morrison regarding jurisdictional questions relating to his union.

2. Morrison to Young, Mar. 23, 1918, AFL Microfilm Jurisdiction File, Hod Carriers, Building and Common Laborers Records, reel 51, frame 1205, *AFL Records.*

3. Early in 1918 the Longshoremen began chartering AFL directly affiliated locals of shipyard laborers as the "Ship Yard Laborers, Riggers, and Fasteners" subdistrict on the Pacific Coast, and by mid-March they had a dozen local affiliates with some thirty-five hundred members. When several AFL internationals objected on jurisdictional grounds—Morrison's Mar. 23 letter to Young mentioned complaints from the Hod Carriers and the Carpenters—an agreement was reached in May 1919 among the Longshoremen, the Hod Carriers, the Carpenters, the Sheet Metal Workers, the Boiler Makers, and the Bridge and Structural Iron Workers giving each union jurisdiction over the shipyard laborers of its own craft.

To the Executive Council of the AFL

Washington, D.C. March 30, 1918.

Document No. 27.
Executive Council, American Federation of Labor.
Colleagues:—

By the President's order, the Secretary of Labor took over many of the functions performed by the Committee on Labor of the Council of National Defense, the Committee of which I am chairman. The Secretary of Labor, Honorable Wm. B. Wilson, communicated with the Association of Employers and me,[1] as President of the American Federation of Labor, and asking of me that I appoint a committee of five labor men to meet with a like committee of the employers, to be appointed by the Employers Association, jointly to form a commission for the purpose of endeavoring to devise a plan and agree upon principles for labor standards, the avoidance and adjustment of labor disputes during the war. I appointed the following representatives of labor to act upon the commission:

Frank J. Hayes—President, United Mine Workers of America,

Wm. L. Hutcheson—President, United Brotherhood of Carpenters and Joiners of America,

Wm. H. Johnston—President, International Association of Machinists,

Victor Olander—Member of the Executive Council of the International Seamen's Union of America, and Secretary of the Illinois State Federation of Labor,

T. A. Rickert—President, United Garment Workers of America.

The commission met several days each week for the past month. For the employers the Honorable Wm. H. Taft was selected as legal representative. Honorable Frank P. Walsh was selected as the legal representative of the labor members of the commission.

The commission finally reached an agreement, of which the enclosed is a copy.[2] It is transmitted to you for your information and archives. The entire document will be published in the newspapers tomorrow, Sunday morning. It is a wonderful achievement.

With best wishes, I am,

Fraternally yours,   Saml Gompers.
President,   American Federation of Labor.

TLcS, Executive Council Records, Vote Books, reel 15, frame 590, *AFL Records*. Typed notation: *"Enclosure."*

1. "From William B. Wilson," Jan. 29, 1918, above.

2. SG enclosed a copy of the Mar. 29, 1918, report of the War Labor Conference Board (WLCB) to the Secretary of Labor. The report recommended creating a National War Labor Board (NWLB) to settle labor disputes in war-related industries through mediation and conciliation, and it outlined principles to govern employer-employee relations during the war. The statement of principles opened with the stipulation that there should be no lockouts or strikes while the war was in progress but went on to affirm the right of workers to organize in trade unions, to bargain collectively, and to earn a living wage. It called for maintenance of existing standards of wages, hours, and other conditions in union shops, equal pay for women performing the same work as men, and observation of the eight-hour day where required by law.

Secretary of Labor William B. Wilson appointed the members of the WLCB to serve on the NWLB, and on Apr. 4 he sent Woodrow Wilson a copy of the Mar. 29 report. President Wilson issued a proclamation on Apr. 8 confirming those appointments and approving the WLCB report, thereby formally constituting the NWLB. For the genesis of the WLCB, see "From William B. Wilson," Jan. 29, 1918, n. 1, above; a copy of the Mar. 29 report may be found in the Executive Council Records, Vote Books, reel 15, frames 591–94, *AFL Records*.

To Edward Doyle

April 2, 1918.

Mr. E. L. Doyle,
Post Office Box No. 1493, Denver, Colorado.
Dear Sir:

Your letter of the 21st ultimo[1] received and contents noted. On behalf of an "Independent Union of Mine Workers of America,"[2] you make application for a charter of affiliation to the American Federation of Labor.

In reply, permit me to call your attention to the fact that under the laws of the American Federation of Labor, no charter can be granted to an organization of workers who come under the jurisdiction of an existing organization except with the full consent and approval of that organization.

Of course, I have some understanding of the situation as it exists and some of the reasons assigned for the action in the effort to establish an independent or dual organization, but the trade unionism recognized by the American Federation of Labor, the trade unionism for which we have all fought all these years, is that there shall be unity and solidarity in spirit and in fact among the workers of a given trade, industry or calling, and I would rather fight within the ranks of my union for a cause in which I believed and be defeated my whole life than to attempt to form and foster a dual and rival union to an organization particularly as the United Mine Workers has done so much for the workers in that industry. Of course under the laws and the policies and principles of the American Federation of Labor a charter such as the one for which you apply cannot be granted. I therefore, transmitted[3] copy of your letter together with carbon copy of my reply thereto, to President F. J. Hays, United Mine Workers of America and will advise you upon receipt of reply from him.[4]

Very truly yours,   Saml Gompers.
President   American Federation of Labor.

TLpS, reel 233, vol. 245, p. 645, SG Letterbooks, DLC.

1. Edward Doyle to SG, Mar. 21, 1918, AFL Microfilm National and International Union File, United Mine Workers Records, reel 40, frame 1637, *AFL Records.*

2. In April 1917 the executive board of the United Mine Workers of America suspended the charter of District 15 (Colorado) for reasons of financial insolvency and low membership. Doyle, the district's secretary-treasurer, and John Lawson, its president, were removed from office, and the district was placed under the International's oversight. After Doyle and Lawson were defeated for reelection in early 1918, they founded the Independent Union of Mine Workers of America, with Lawson as president and Doyle as secretary. The new organization soon collapsed.

3. SG to Frank Hayes, Mar. 28, 1918, reel 233, vol. 245, p. 643, SG Letterbooks, DLC.

4. Hayes replied on Apr. 8, 1918, approving SG's course of action in refusing the charter (AFL Microfilm National and International Union File, United Mine Workers Records, reel 40, frame 1637, *AFL Records*).

To William Hutcheson, John Hynes,[1] and Thomas Savage

Washington, D.C., April 2, 1918.

William L. Hutcheson, President of the Carpenters.
J. J. Hynes, President of the Sheet Metal Workers.
Mr. Savage, Acting President of the I.A. of M.[2]
The strike[3] of the carpenters and incidentally other trades in the ship building plants at Norfolk and the Ham[p]ton Roads District of Virginia has created the deepest impression and expressions of indignation among Senators and members of the House. Even among those always taking a friendly attitude toward organized labor. One friendly Senator[4] expressing the views of many today publicly declared that unless strikes in ship yards are voluntarily abandoned during the war he would favor and press home the enactment of a law making it a criminal conspiracy to strike in the ship yards. Such a law would in-

volve large fines and long terms of imprisonment. I appeal to you to use your best effort promptly and effectively to have the men in the Hampton Roads District of Virginia resume work and by negotiation adjust whatever differences exist.[5]

Samuel Gompers.

TWSr, Files of the Office of the President, General Correspondence, reel 94, frame 46, *AFL Records.*

1. John Joseph HYNES, of the Amalgamated Sheet Metal Workers' International Alliance, served as president of the union from 1913 to 1938.

2. Thomas Savage served as acting president of the International Association of Machinists while William Johnston was in Europe.

3. On Apr. 1, 1918, some four thousand building trades workers employed on government contracts in the Norfolk area struck for a wage increase, demanding pay equivalent to that awarded on Mar. 7 to workers at the Newport News Shipbuilding and Dry Dock Co. by the Shipbuilding Labor Adjustment Board. Although the carpenters were the largest group of workers involved, the strike also involved plumbers, electricians, sheet metal workers, painters, engineers, and dock builders. The men were persuaded to return to work on Apr. 3 on patriotic grounds and the promise that the government would promptly attend to their demands.

4. Probably a reference to James Alexander Reed (1861–1944), a Democratic senator from Missouri (1911–29), who announced in the Senate on Apr. 2, 1918, that he was ready to vote for a law to punish any employers or employees who conspired to interfere with the American shipbuilding industry during the war.

5. For William Hutcheson's reply, see "From William Hutcheson," Apr. 3, 1918, below.

From William Hutcheson

Indianapolis Ind Apl 3 [19]18

Replying to your wire[1] will say if you recall the undersigned spent a great deal of time in Washington endeavoring to reach an understanding whereby a cessation of work by our members might be prevented You know the result of those efforts and incidently I might say that the matter might have been brought to a final conclusion at that time had the representatives of other trades and yourself rendered some assistance I have no desire for our membership to in any way be a hindrance to the progress of work but I realize that under the existing circumstances and unless an understanding is reached between our organization and the representatives of the government that there will no doubt be periodical strikes such as just occurred in Norfolk and while I can no doubt be able to assist in getting the men to return to work yet had we some understanding with the representatives of the government I would then be able to prevent the men from ceasing work I have already wired our membership at Norfolk advising them to return to work If the representatives and senators desire to advocate the enactment of a law along autocratic lines making it a criminal offense for men to cease work then I fail to understand where in we are fighting for world democracy as a law of that nature would take from the workmen their guaranteed rights as citizens of the United States

Wm L Hutcheson

TWSr, Files of the Office of the President, General Correspondence, reel 94, frames 94–95, *AFL Records.*

1. "To William Hutcheson, John Hynes, and Thomas Savage," Apr. 2, 1918, above.

From Robert Bruère

Bureau of Industrial Research
Washington, D.C. April 6, 1918

My dear Mr. Gompers:

Thank you for your letter of April 3.[1] I am sorry that the notice of the second conference which was held at your office on March 22[2] did not reach me for I should have been greatly interested in the discussion.

Sir Charles Ross's memorandum, which you were good enough to send me, is an extremely interesting document; but I fear that it does not take sufficient account of the existing boards, divisions and the like, that are handling the government's labor problems. Does it not seem to you that any centralized arrangement of production and labor control ought to be based on the recommendations which Secretary Wilson's Advisory Council made to him on January 22?[3] The plan of the Advisory Council admirably supplements existing machinery without breaking down what has already been built up.

What I had in mind when I first spoke to you about this matter was that the supplementary war labor administration which Secretary Wilson's Council devised, might be transferred as a whole to the War Industries Board[4] and put under the single-headed direction of a competent engineer acceptable to labor. Such a transfer could only be made by an order from the President, since the President has appointed Secretary Wilson Labor Administrator. As long as the Secretary remains in this position, the machinery should be built up under him as already planned, and any attempt to duplicate its work under the War Industries Board will merely bring confusion and delay. Unless Secretary Wilson's proposed labor administration can be transferred as a whole by a presidential order, it should be developed as already planned, and do its work in coordination with Mr. Baruch. And, of course, it should be remembered that such a transfer if ultimately made would not take away from the Department of Labor any of the functions which it ordinarily exercises.

Would it not be a misfortune if such machinery as has already been built up under the Shipping Board and the War Department were dislocated at this critical time? And is not the problem one of integration and development rather than a problem of making a clean sweep and building anew from the bottom? Now that we have had some weeks to consider the matter I hope that it may be possible for you to call another conference to go over the entire situation and clear it up.

In any case I am afraid that this whole problem of centralized labor and production control cannot be effectively solved until Congress has granted the President the power for which he asks in the Overman[5] bill.[6] You have no doubt noticed that Senator Reed opened the attack upon the Overman Bill in the Senate on Thursday. It is obvious that in spite of the President's particular request for its enactment the bill is going to have hard sledding. I still feel most earnestly that it would be a great thing for the country and for labor if you could find your way to make a public declaration in support of Senator Overman's measure. Given the freedom to act which the Overman Bill is designed to confer, President Wilson could confidently be relied upon to make the readjustments essential to the best interests of the country.

Cordially yours,   Robert W. Bruère.

TLS, Files of the Office of the President, General Correspondence, reel 94, frame 191, *AFL Records*.

1. SG to Robert Bruère, Apr. 3, 1918, reel 233, vol. 245, p. 602, SG Letterbooks, DLC.

2. SG's appointment records indicate that he met on Mar. 22, 1918, with John Donlin, Frank Morrison, Charles Ross, William Spencer, William Johnston, and Stanley King at AFL headquarters regarding munitions.

3. A reference to the advisory council's recommendation to William B. Wilson—actually dated Jan. 19, 1918—regarding the creation of the War Labor Conference Board.

4. The War Industries Board was established by the Council of National Defense in July 1917 as an advisory body to coordinate industrial production during the war. President Woodrow Wilson enlarged its functions in March 1918, giving it wide authority over the manufacture, pricing, and purchase of war materials. It became an independent agency by executive order in May 1918.

5. Lee Slater Overman (1854–1930) served as a Democratic senator from North Carolina from 1903 until 1930.

6. S. 3771 (65th Cong., 2d sess.), introduced by Overman on Feb. 6, 1918, authorized the president to coordinate or consolidate executive bureaus, agencies, and offices. It became law on May 20, 1918 (U.S. *Statutes at Large*, 40: 556–57).

A Circular

Washington, D.C. April 8, 1918.

Dear Sir and Brother:

Several requests have been made from international officers that I send a succinct statement of the principles involved in the present war. These trade union officers wanted the statement to send out to their organizers and representatives to assist them in interpreting war problems and conditions to the workers generally. As I thought the statement may be of general utility, I am sending you a copy also.

Fraternally yours,   Saml Gompers.
President,   American Federation of Labor.

[ENCLOSURE]

April 8, 1918.

To the Toilers of America.

Brothers:

Will the battle line of freedom hold against the onslaughts of autocracy's military machine?[1] Upon that line hangs the destiny of the world for decades to come. The line can hold back the offensive and drive the invaders out of the Republic of France only if it is the concentrated expression of national determination unfailingly supplying men, munitions, food, and every accoutrement required.

Workers of America, the safety of that battle line in France depends mainly now upon us. We must furnish the majority of those in the trenches. We must build the ships that carry the troops and munitions of war. Regardless of hidden dangers we must maintain the life line of ships on the high seas which connect the fighting front with our national bases of supplies. We must make the guns, the munitions, the aeroplanes. We must have ready food, clothing, blankets. We serve in the great industrial army that serves overseas with the fighting forces.

We must do all these things because a principle is involved that has to do with all we hold dear.

We are fighting against a government that disregards the will of the governed—a government that pries into intimate relations of life and extends its supervision into smallest details and dominates all of them. We are fighting against involuntary labor—against the enslavement of women and the mutilation of the lives and bodies of little children. We are fighting against barbarous practices of warring upon civilian populations, killing the wounded, the agents of mercy and those who bear the white flag of truce.

We are fighting for the ideal which is America—equal opportunity for all. We are fighting for political and economic freedom—national and international.

We are fighting for the right to join together freely in trade unions and the freedom and the advantages represented by that right.

Our country is now facing a crisis to meet which continuity of war productions is essential. Workers, decide every industrial question fully mindful of those men—fellow Americans—who are on the battle-line, facing the enemies' guns, needing munitions of war to fight the battle for those of us back at home, doing work necessary but less hazardous. No strike ought to be inaugurated that cannot be justified to the men facing momentary death. A strike during the war is not justified unless principles are involved equally fundamental as those for which fellow citizens have offered their lives—their all.

We must give this service without reserve until the war is won, serving the cause of human freedom, intelligent, alert, uncompromising wherever and whenever the principles of human freedom is involved.

We are in a great revolutionary period which we are shaping by molding every day relations between man and man. Workers of America as well as all other citizens have difficult tasks to perform that we might hand on to the future the ideals and institutions of America not only unimpaired, but strengthened and purified in spirit and in expression—thus performing the responsible duty of those entrusted with the high resolve to be free and perpetuate freedom.

Fraternally yours,   (Signed) Samuel Gompers.
President,   American Federation of Labor.

TLpS and TLpSr, reel 234, vol. 246, pp. 131–32, SG Letterbooks, DLC. Handwritten notation: "To the Presidents of Nationals."

1. SG is referring to the German spring offensive on the Western Front, which opened on Mar. 21, 1918.

James Duncan to Frank Morrison

The Granite Cutters' International Association
of America
Quincy, Mass. April 9, 1918.

Mr. Frank Morrison,
Secretary American Federation of Labor,
Washington, D.C.
My dear Frank:

I suppose you saw in the "Survey" Mr. Kellogg's story under the cap-tion "American Labor Out of It."[1] In any event Mr. Kellogg sent me a letter calling my attention to it, and I sent him a reply[2] and am herewith enclosing a copy of it in case you may not have seen the copy of same I sent to President Gompers, and which I had intended to be also for you, but I am of the opinion at the present time I did not mention same to Pres. Gompers. You will find my letter self-explanatory. Since then I have received a statement from Mr. Kellogg in which he tries to have me believe that his statement to which he had called my attention was not intended to bear the meaning which I took out of it.

I am also at this time again mentioning that Pres. D'Alessandro[3] is expecting you to be present at the official opening of the Building Laborers' headquarters. You may have other things about that time, and all of them important, but really because of the importance of the event, namely, a headquarters being established for so-called unskilled labor, organized in and affiliated to the American Federation of Labor, there is need for a representative from the headquarters of the A.F. of L. to be here, and which means either President Gompers or yourself. You will have in mind that many of those who have tried to severely criticize us, such as certain socialists, I.W.W.s, intellectuals, capitalis-tic employers, magazine writers, have tried to show to an indulgent public, that the American Federation of Labor is more concerned in the organization of mechanics or so-called skilled workers than they are in common or building laborers, and who are usually classed as so-called unskilled workers.

It is quite a substantial building for any organization to have, as its headquarters, and, therefore, of more importance in that it has been erected by the money of a laborers' union, and which adds stability as well as an appearance of continuance of organization which per-haps nothing else in the way of tangible argument could present. Of course, I will be present, but that will be in the capacity of President of my own trade Association, and as our headquarters are now located in the Building Laborers' new official home, I could not be said to be a visitor, nor could I add anything to the celebration equal to either Pres. Gompers or you being present. It is not merely an instance of being present for the short time that the ceremony will take up, nor the mere opening or dedication of a building, it is an instance of the American Federation of Labor being officially represented at an International Headquarters of an unskilled line of employment, and which will forever put a quietus upon the line of argument indulged in during many years past that the A.F. of L. pays little attention to that kind of employment.[4]

Fraternally, James Duncan
Int'l President.

TLS, AFL Microfilm National and International Union File, Granite Cutters Records, reel 38, frame 1570, *AFL Records.*

1. *Survey,* Mar. 9, 1918, pp. 617–26. The article reported on the January 1918 Labour party conference at Nottingham and focused in particular on the addresses of the fraternal delegates from Belgium, Russia, and France. The piece was sharply critical of the AFL for not sending fraternal delegates of its own, either to the Nottingham meeting or to the subsequent Inter-Allied Labour and Socialist Conference, held in London in February.

2. James Duncan to Paul Kellogg, Mar. 23, 1918, Files of the Office of the President, General Correspondence, reel 93, frames 547–48, *AFL Records.*

3. Domenico D'ALESSANDRO, of the International HOD Carriers', Building and Common Laborers' Union of America, served as president of the union from 1908 to 1926.

4. Neither SG nor Frank Morrison were able to attend the dedication of the Hod Carriers' new headquarters in Quincy, Mass., which took place on Apr. 20, 1918. Duncan spoke at the ceremony.

To Brice Disque

April 11, 1918.

Colonel Brice P. Disque,
U.S. Signal Corps, Spruce Production Division,
Yeon Building, Portland, Oregon.
My dear Colonel:

Permit me to assure you that I regret more than I can find words to express that circumstances were such, duties and obligations so portentous and immediate that I could not make earlier reply to your letter of the 12th ultimo.[1]

I read your letter with the deepest interest and satisfaction, and I think that not only you but the country is to be congratulated upon the decisions which you have reached regarding the establishment of the basic eight hour day and other matters too numerous to mention in this letter,—yes, the organization of the Loyal Legion of Lumbermen and Loggers for service in spruce and other timber production for our country's war needs.

There is not one thing which you have done so far as I learn, in all these matters, to which I would enter one word of dissent, but on the contrary, my strongest endorsement.

I also have before me a copy of a letter you addressed to the Editor of the Evening Journal, and which was published in its issue of March 25, 1918.[2] I quite agree with you in the statement which you make in your letter that it might have taken an exceedingly long time before the organized labor movement would have established the eight hour basic day in the spruce and lumber industry; but I think you will agree that during the conferences which you and I have had in the office of the American Federation of Labor and later participated in by Major Ledbetter, that the question of the establishment of the eight hour day in the lumber industry by either your order or proclamation by the President of the United States, was one of the things we agreed should be put into operation as the most potent factor to bring about an end of the then existing strike and to accomplish hearty co-operation of the loggers and timber workers for the nation's war program.

Mr. C. Covert, President of the International Union of Timber Workers, has forwarded to me a copy of his letter to you dated March 30th, 1918.[3] I have also read that letter carefully and I cannot but feel that Mr. Covert presents to you matters which are deserving of your serious and favorable consideration. I quite agree that the Loyal Legion which you have organized, as such should not be made the ground upon which the timber workers' union should recruit its membership, but surely no one can seriously object to the timber workers' union extending its membership from among timber workers, any more than the timber workers' union would have the right to enter serious objection to the employing lumbermen's association from extending its membership to those employing lumbermen who are not yet members thereof.

In Mr. Covert's letter to you he practically pledges his organization, (as did Mr. C. O. Young, the general organizer for the American Federation of Labor) to whole hearted support of your program, and to encourage to the fullest extent the support and co-operation of the Loyal Legion. It is my earnest wish that that shall be done, and I shall be very glad to be helpful in every way within my power to aid in its fullest accomplishment.

With your understanding of industrial affairs, you know that after we all shall have helped to bring about a triumphant conclusion of the war for our great cause and country, we shall have great industrial, economic and sociological problems to meet. The Loyal Legion will have then spent its usefulness, for it will have accomplished the purpose for which it has been organized. What then is to take its place to meet the new problems which will be imminent and prodigious? If there be a well organized body of workers in the Timbermen's international union, such an organization in that industry as organizations of workers in the various industries, will be in a position to function and to help the solution of the problems to which I have referred and by which we shall inevitably be confronted.

I am in so hearty accord with all the things you have done and with all of the things for which you have declared except this one, that I ask you to give very serious consideration to this subject matter and to the thoughts expressed by Mr. Covert as well as those contained herein.

With every wish for your success and hoping to hear from you at your early convenience,[4] I am

Very truly yours,   Saml Gompers.
President,   American Federation of Labor.

TLpS, reel 233, vol. 245, pp. 959–60, SG Letterbooks, DLC.

1. "From Brice Disque," Mar. 12, 1918, above.

2. "Disque Reproves Bellingham Men," *Oregon Journal* (Portland), Mar. 25, 1918.

3. Clair Covert to Disque, Mar. 30, 1918, Files of the Office of the President, General Correspondence, reel 93, frames 913–15, *AFL Records.*

4. In his reply to SG of Apr. 20, 1918, Disque warned it would be against the best interests of the government for the International Union of Timber Workers to attempt to organize during the war and stated that the Loyal Legion of Loggers and Lumbermen was the most suitable organization for maintaining the steady production of timber (Files of the Office of the President, General Correspondence, reel 94, frames 643–44, *AFL Records*).

From David Coates

Headquarters
The National Party
Chicago April 11, 1918.

Dear Friend Sam,

My duties as National Chairman of the National Party have occupied my time away from Headquarters much of late, and therefore I have been delayed in writing you and sending you a copy of our letter[1] to the British Labor Party, as promised in my recent interview[2] with you in Washington. A copy of the invitation to our brothers and comrades in the British Labor Party is herein enclosed; also copy of a statement[3] to the men and women of America for whole-hearted support of the administration in the prosecuting and winning of the war, in which you may be interested.

I enjoyed the chat I had with you in Washington as I have always enjoyed personal contact with you for many years. While you deprecated the building of the National Party at this time, I was very glad indeed to hear you say what you did concerning the possibilities after the war was over. As I recall your statement, it was about as follows:

"Most people believe I am opposed to partisan political action, but that is not altogether true. I believe the past policy of the American Federation of Labor along non-partisan lines has done more for labor in the enactment of laws for its protection and benefit than has been accomplished by any political labor party in the country. But, if after the war is over, it appears that a more definite policy shall be pursued along political party lines, I shall not hesitate to aid in the building of a labor party in America, and shall be with it body, soul, and breeches."

You will never find me misinterpreting you in the slightest degree, and I trust our relations will continue as friendly as they have been in the past. While our work may be in different channels, I am sure you appreciate that I am trying to work to the same common end with you. My whole heart and desire is bound up in the common good for all our people.

With best wishes from Mrs. Coates[4] and myself to Mrs. Gompers[5] and yourself, I am,

Yours fraternally and sincerely,   The National Party,
D. C. Coates   National Chairman.

TLS, Files of the Office of the President, General Correspondence, reel 94, frame 346, *AFL Records.*

1. See "To John Spargo," Mar. 22, 1918, n. 7, above.
2. SG met with David Coates at AFL headquarters on Mar. 23, 1918.
3. Coates to the Men and Women of America, Mar. 30, 1918, Files of the Office of the President, General Correspondence, reel 93, frames 911–12, *AFL Records.*
4. Sarah Pearce Coates.
5. Sophia Julian GOMPERS.

An Article in the *New York Times*

Washington, April 22.-[1918]

GOMPERS DENOUNCES PLAN.

Announcement in the Senate today by Senator Poindexter[1] that labor leaders were proposing a general strike in protest against the conviction of Thomas Mooney and others[2] resulted in a statement to-night by Samuel Gompers, President of the American Federation of Labor, declaring that any attempt to incite such a strike would be in violation of union laws and repugnant to the rights and interests of workers themselves, and would react against Mooney. Mr. Gompers's statement follows:

"The machinations of the prosecution in the Mooney trial justify the judgment that he was found guilty on perjured evidence. It is greatly regrettable that the California courts refused to consider this claim which was discovered since the trial. Every legal action has been and will be taken by the bona fide labor movement of the United States to secure justice for Mooney. Any attempt to incite a strike of the work-ers of a trade or industry of a locality, State, or of the nation, is not only violative of the laws of the national and international unions of America, but is repugnant to the rights and the interests of the work-ers themselves.

"Such an attempt either to incite or order a local or general strike is unjustifiable and dangerously prejudicial to the lives of our sons and brothers fighting in France for the safety of the homes, freedom, and democracy the world over. In addition, such an agitation as has been inaugurated can only react against Mooney.

"Men of labor, let us with all fair-minded citizens endeavor to secure justice for Mooney, but let us put forth our efforts on a line that will insure commendation, not condemnation coupled with failure."

New York Times, Apr. 23, 1918.

1. Miles Poindexter (1868–1946) served as a Republican congressman (1909–11) and senator (1911–23) from the state of Washington.

2. Poindexter charged that organized labor in his state was holding a referendum on the question of calling a general strike on May 1, 1918, to support Mooney. He accused the IWW of instigating the idea, which he denounced as "moral treason . . . deserving of death" ("Charges I.W.W. Plot to Strike on Coast," *New York Times,* Apr. 23, 1918).

Excerpts from the Minutes of a Conference between Committees Representing Black Workers and the AFL

Washington, D.C., April 22, 1918.
11 A.M. Executive Council room.

CONFERENCE, WITH COMMITTEE REPRESENTING AMERICAN FEDERATION OF LABOR, AND COMMITTEE OF COLORED WORKERS.

Committee for American Federation of Labor:
  Samuel Gompers,
  Frank Morrison,
  James O'Connell.
  (Mr. Alpine, Mr. James[1] and Mr. Donlin[2] absent.)
Committee for colored workers:
  Mr. R. R. Moton, Principal Tuskegee Institute,
  Mr. John R. Shillady, Secretary National Association for the Advancement of Colored Workers, (white)
  Mr. Fred R. Moore, Editor New York Age.
  Mr. Archibald Grimke, Washington Association for the Advancement of Colored People.
  Mr. Emmett J. Scott, Special Assistant to the Secretary of War,
  Mr. Eugene Kinckle Jones, Executive Secretary, National Urban League.
  Mr. Thomas Jesse Jones, Educational Director Phelps Stokes Fund.
  Dr. James H. Dillard,[3] President, Jeannes Fund. (white)
  Dr. Geo. E. Haynes, Educational Secretary, National League on Urban Conditions among Negroes.
  Mr. Gompers: Gentlemen: In accordance with the action of the Executive Council of the American Federation of Labor and in compliance with the request made by the committee of five of you gentlemen who appeared before the Executive Council, I appointed a committee of five to represent the American Federation of Labor, Mr. O'Connell, Mr. Morrison, Mr. Donlin, Mr. Alpine, and Mr. James. Mr. O'Connell and Mr. Morrison are here. Mr. Alpine is absent. Mr. James has been here this morning and can be reached again. By reason of the fact that there are only two of the members of the committee here, I deemed it prudent and just to leave other work and sit with you, at least for a while until a majority of the committee appointed appear.
  I do not think it necessary to recount the purposes of the history

of the development of this effort at unity and cooperation except to say that the convention of the American Federation of Labor at Buffalo last November passed a unanimous resolution to make a more thorough effort for the organization of the colored workmen, but I ought to say in passing that it is not a new departure for the American Federation of Labor, for we have always held to the necessity of organizing the colored workmen. We have not been as successful in that work as we would like to have been, but that was not our fault. We devoted as much of our time and our energy and of our meager funds as was at all available, and utilized it for the accomplishment of that purpose, that is, the organization of the colored workmen. There are more colored workmen organized than is generally known, and there is not any fault or criticism that we have to make upon their loyalty and their devotion and their willingness, if necessary, to make sacrifices in order to further the common good. The fact is of course that there are so many of them who are unorganized.

Nor shall I attempt to indicate, much less point out, some of the causes that they are not as well organized as is desirable. We are going to try our level best, and your offer to cooperate in that effort is commendable and welcome and we shall do our level best. The question is as to how. . . .

. . .

. . . I do not think it needs either a question or an answer as to whether the negro workmen should be organized. That ought to go without saying. The negro worker has his rights and interests and he should employ the normal agencies to protect and promote both. As to the question of his remaining in the south, that may be desirable and preferable, but I am not quite so sure that this is a subject with which this conference should concern itself. At any rate, I could not refrain from bringing the matter to your attention, and I think we had better apply ourselves anyway to a statement just as concise and brief as we can of what we can do in furtherance of the common purpose, that is, the organization of the colored workers.

. . .

Mr. Dillard: I was not going to say anything except this. My own impression is that there is not going to be near as much trouble as some people think. I lived in New Orleans twenty years. I had an addition built to my house just before I left there. The men who put the slate on the roof, and the bricklayers, were colored. The carpenters were white and the painters were white. They worked together in perfect harmony. There was not any friction at all. Now if anybody had gone there and raised some question, why may be there would have been some trouble, but things just go along naturally and I do not think there is any friction. In New Orleans I was asked by the carpenters union to represent them in trying to get an interview with the architects and boss contractors and I went and attended a joint meeting of the bricklayers and carpenters union, about half and half, and they were in the hall, and all conferring together in perfect harmony. I do not believe there is any trouble or going to be any trouble. I think the matter will be much more plain sailing than any of us suppose.

Mr. E. K. Jones: There is going to be some difficulties such as you suggested might occur when someone raises the question. It seems to me that that is the time when this committee, or one member from each side, can come in and offer their services to some local group to adjust differences that may occur. For instance you probably know here, that is the trouble now in Newark, N.J., where in the building trades certain colored officers were elected. The white members of the group objected to having such a large number of colored officers and refused to consider the officers as elected. The matter was referred to the Executive Council of that district or trade, and the organization in which the trouble was had sent the colored President to the Central Labor Union[4] as their delegate. The Central Body refused to recognize this colored man and seat him. Now the matter is still pending. Now it seems to me that in a case like that where just a little tact is necessary to adjust the thing rather than have strained relations follow because of misunderstanding, if say, one of the group of the A.F. of L. and one of our group should offer their services to the local people there for conference and adjustment we could get further along and some practical, definite steps than we ever could by conferring here occasionally on the general situation. Now it seems to me that that is one definite thing which this committee can decide, to offer their services in some constructive way to local communities where such differences are arising and in no other way can we gain and hold the confidence of the colored working men in that community where the trouble has arisen, except by handling concrete cases to the satisfaction of both races.

Mr. Morrison: I will say this, that nobody outside of a member of a union will be able to handle any differences in an organization. We will have to work that out. The machinery we desire to get is to organize the colored workers into unions. Now you are not going to have any more harmony among colored workers when they are organized than among the white when organized, or any other organization, political or otherwise. There are different views about what should be the policy and there are very bitter fights. Those same things occur in local unions. There are fights about officers in the white unions. But the majority rules. Now if they do not want a certain policy carried out and the fight is made on them, it will be made whether they are colored or white. The chief thing is to get the machinery back of the colored workers to have them organize and then the proposition that you raise will work itself out gradually. You are going to have those differences. You must expect them, but they will work out all right.

. . .

Mr. O'Connell: It seems to me that there is a much deeper proposition than some little dispute arising. I have been dealing with this colored question for years. You seem to confine your opinions as to the building trades situation. The number of colored people employed in the building trades is very small. It is not the fundamental situation because the building trades as a rule have organized the colored men either in their unions or in separate unions, and in the building industry they have been organized or they could not work on the buildings. In the great industries of the country, however, they have not. The shipping industry for one. The great munitions industry, the steel industry, the miscellaneous industries have not been organized at all, comparatively speaking.

I attempted for fifteen years to organize the colored people at the Newport News shipping yard, where about 60% are colored. There are now about 8,000 colored men employed there. I have gone there personally. I have had the Federation keep an organizer[5] on the payroll for about two years. We have had a man[6] stationed at Newport News for nearly a year, not steadily, but three or four months at a time, and with all of the effort we have put forth there we have not succeeded in organizing probably more than 100 men in all, that is, in the shipyard. He has organized locally some of the building trades men, in the Tidewater district, etc. Now for the reason.

Below all this situation of organizing the colored people and I am going to be very frank with you, is another situation. Newport News is a pivotal point and a typical situation that covers the colored situation all over the country. To get at the Newport News colored people you have got to go through all sorts of agencies down there from the preacher in the church, to the insurance man, cooperative societies of various kinds, savings societies of all kinds, societies that have no meaning or name except what they may choose to give it themselves, and has no purpose in view that I can see other than to bleed and fleece these colored people. These organizations dominate the situation down there. They get to these people and prevent them from organizing. They go to their fraternal societies and their political societies, and they dominate them politically and the moment you get a few of them together to try to organize them and you get the machinery moving and explain things to them, get rid of their doubts and the skeptical ideas they have about getting in with the white men, instilled into them by a few of the grafters down there among the colored people, and they are apparently unlimited, living well and getting good returns, and I am talking from personal observation and investigation of the things down there. For many years Mr. Booker Washington, before he died, issued a circular statement and it was construed and put into the minds of these men down there discouraging them from organizing with the white men or organizing at all, and set forth many reasons why they should not do it, and owing to the fact that some international unions did not organize the colored men, some of them allowed separate unions by themselves. Some of them did not object to their being organized into federal unions coming under the Federation direct, but all these things were misrepresented to the men. We could not get one thing straightened out in their minds before there would be half a dozen more things put into their minds. The employers were anxious to keep them from organizing and helped to circulate all these things and that situation still prevails, not so much as it did, because we have driven it into cover, but it is still there. Now that state of affairs has got to end before we can organize these men. They have fear, first, as to their jobs if they organize. They have fear, second, if they join an organization of the white men and are not in the international union, that if their wages are brought up that they will be displaced and the white men given the work. That is the thing that is put into their minds, and that is the furthest from the organized man's mind. The same thing prevails in other localities, and that can be remedied by such men as you with standing and influential connections with the colored organizations, giving a broad, liberal explanation of your view of the necessity of the colored men organizing, and organizing under the conditions as laid down by the American Federation of Labor. They can't expect to come into the organized forces and change these conditions to their liking after we have spent a century of time and trouble and expenditure of funds in laying down a basis of what we believe to be the best plan upon which people should organize. We are not attempting to organize the colored men upon any different basis from the white men, only we have had our troubles in getting the white organizations to recognize the right of the black men to organize. Some will issue charters direct and others will issue them for auxiliaries. The Federation itself has organized them direct into the A.F. of L. and pay them regular strike benefits if involved in strikes. We have explained that all to them, but somebody gets to them after we have explained and the last fellow gets them and holds them. . . .

. . . And where they are organized and they understand the situation and are not dominated by outside influences which are very strong and hard to overcome by us, because of the influences in the localities which make it very difficult for these men to exist there unless they go along with them. They find it difficult to get houses, and credit in the stores, and difficult almost to do anything unless they go along with these people who are dominating and I think that is the big thing which you men as leaders in this movement have got to help straighten out. Make them understand that they are being organized for their own benefit, not for ours, because while we benefit indirectly, yet it is not for our benefit at all. We want them organized and we are doing all we can but having to fight an opposition underneath. The cards were not on the table, to use a poker expression, and you do not know who you were fighting. We knew we were fighting the boss, but as for the outside influences, we had to dig those up. . . .

. . .

Mr. Moore: Would not a general statement of the policy of the Federation, promulgated to the masses of the colored people, work out and explain your attitude, and cause them to think about either coming in or organizing? Your attitude is not thoroughly understood by the masses of the colored people. But there has never been any known policy, for instance, published through the negro press as to the attitude of the organized labor toward the negro.

. . .

Mr. Scott: I was very much interested in Mr. O'Connell's description of the situation at Newport News, yet I wonder if that would not apply to any body of people who are undisciplined. The colored people, like anyone else, have been up against bitter and dear experiences, and naturally they are suspicious and when it comes to grafters I do not think that is confined to any one race.

Mr. O'Connell: Oh, undoubtedly, there are as many white grafters for that matter. When we put Goode to work at Newport News we brought him up here, and talked the matter over. We wanted to put a colored man in there. I tried white men by the dozens. And I got the Federation to agree to put a colored man in if we could locate one who would fill the job. Finally we got Mr. Goode, who is a local preacher down there, and able to make a good talk, etc. Now he, without any questioning from us, said, "the first thing I have got to do is to talk with the preachers, and then with the lawyers, the doctors, etc." He had all those influences in mind.

Mr. Scott: It seems to me you took a big fundamental step when you took a colored man to do the work. Now, if they are standing off, without confidence, whether it is a white man or a colored man, it seems to me the first thing necessary to be done is to make the colored people feel that there is a desire on the part of the American Federation of

Labor that they should be organized and affiliated with the organization. They have not felt this heretofore.

. . .

[Mr. Gompers:] . . . I may call to your attention something I asked to be sent to me, and it is a list of organizations which have been formed within about a year and a half and that is about from the beginning of the Railroad Helpers and Laborers Unions. Most of them, I think, have been organized within this past six or eight months. There are 71 local unions up to last Saturday, and among them eleven are of colored workmen as follows:

West Virginia, 2
Texas, 3
Oklahoma, 1
North Carolina, 2
Mississippi, 1
Alabama, 1
Georgia, 1

These are local unions directly affiliated to the American Federation of Labor, who will be organized into a International Union with the government of their own affairs. I had several conferences with Mr. Morrison, Mr. O'Connell, and later with Mr. A. O. Wharton, a most capable man, President of the Railway Employes Department, and Mr. Donlin, President of the Building Trades Dept. of the A.F. of L. and at the last I asked Mr. Davison,[7] the Secretary-Treasurer of the International Association of Machinists, to sit with us. We went over the entire matter and it was agreed that it ought to be done, and I issued a circular[8] to these local unions to send delegates to a convention[9] to be held in St. Louis for the purpose of putting them on their own feet and for the first opportunity of self-government, and then with the aid which the American Federation of Labor, its officials, its influences, its organizations, can give to help build up a new industrial organization composed of the railroad helpers and laborers unions of the United States. The convention is to be held May 27, and I have made arrangements with Mr. Wharton, who is a very fine type of man, brainy and full of ideas and ideals, to take charge of the convention and preside. Perhaps he may have some other assistants, but you may rest assured that these colored workers sending delegates from their unions are going to receive as good treatment as any white man there. I mention this to show the practical work that is going on, without any advertising. It is not sensational. It is the ordinary character of our every day work. That which does not look sensational does not seem to interest anybody. It is so normal that it attracts but very little attention, and so to prevent an epidemic, that is, so good that nobody pays any attention to it. But let there be an incipient epidemic and the whole world runs amuck. The things that go right do not seem to interest people at all.

Dr. Moton: I have since our meeting here realized, what had not been in my mind clearly before, and that is, that the A.F. of L. is not hostile to negro organization, but this is true generally that the general feeling is that there is no particular cordiality or no particular desire on the part of organized labor for negroes to affiliate with them. . . .

. . .

Dr. Haynes: Could we not have a statement in which we could join as to this conference and the attitude of the A.F. of L. that can be given the widest publicity, a general statement as to organizing, and we join in with you in the statement?

Mr. Morrison: I think the whole thing hinges on the active, influential forces that control in a measure the minds of the colored people, particularly the preachers and doctors and other influences. They should issue a statement calling upon the colored people to organize, and organize in affiliation with the American Federation of Labor, just simply to do it, and that is their salvation to secure improved conditions.

Dr. Moton: On practically the lines of the statement Mr. Gompers gave us.

Mr. Morrison: And then say that the A.F. of L. has for years favored such organization.

Dr. Moton: If we issue such a statement there should be some definite follow up plan for organization. We may issue all the statements we want, and we may say to the colored people you ought to organize but they do not know what to do or how to do it, and it seems to me that if we are going to follow it up with something tangible there ought to be an arrangement whereby a competent, intelligent negro organizer may be maintained on the field.

Mr. Morrison: Well the Federation has one or two in the field now. But after those people get organized they will have their own organizers and carry on their own movement the same as the white people do. . . .

. . .

Mr. Gompers: In the industrial centers in the south the workers in industry are as fully organized as anyone in the country. Except as Mr. Morrison points out, in the Textiles comparatively the organization is not so strong as in the east.

Now the agricultural workers and there is one of the big things. The agricultural workers of the United States, both white and black, have failed for some reason or another that takes too long a time to explain, if explainable, to organize. In nearly every country on the face of the globe, there is some form of organization among the agricultural workers. I do not mean the farm owners, who are the employers of the farm laborers. I mean the laborers themselves. In other countries you find the agrarian movements: the peasants' movements: but in the United States, whether it be that there is still some land to be gotten for nothing, and the hope in the minds of all of them, or a large number of them that they will some time be land owners, but no one can tell exactly what it is. The colored agricultural workers of the south have no semblance of organization, no movement of any kind.

. . .

Mr. Moore: . . . The fundamental thing is confidence in you and we can't work on any basis of organization unless we can instill in the minds of the black people that the Federation means exactly what it says, and you can get all the organizers you want, until you take the fundamentals, that is, the policy, which is not now known by the masses of the people.

. . .

Mr. Shillady: I want to make a statement. I have been summing up as to the attitude of the most intelligent writers upon this subject, and this expresses I think, the difficulties that stand in the way. . . . Now for the statement of what the colored people say, that is, the best informed of them. That certain unions exclude colored men, as follows:

Wire weavers,[10]

Boilermakers,

Switchmen's union, etc.

I appreciate the fact that the international unions have local autonomy, but this is what is in the minds of the colored people. Certain unions in certain localities do decline to organize them as members.

. . .

Then certain unions do admit colored men but thereafter these men have found it difficult to get jobs. . . . Then at times white men have objected to working with colored men. . . . There are a great many occasions arising when colored men are discriminated against. However, the discrimination may have occurred just the same regardless of their color, and it may be only that the discrimination may be such as any union would have to make in order to maintain its own standards, and I think that is one distinction that has to be made clear, the difference between. Of course in order to meet that more than a verbal statement is necessary. There would have to be a willingness to take these men in if they are qualified workers in their craft.

Mr. Gompers: That is the desirable thing to do, but you cannot always achieve that which you desire. There is no power vested anywhere by which a local union can be compelled to accept any people for membership. Where such a condition exists that a local union, say by indirection, excludes men of certain faith, if you please, or color, or politics, the thing is to do the next best thing when you can't do the thing you desire, and the right thing to do, do the best you can. . . .

. . .

Mr. Dillard: What amount of opposition is there in the south toward a separate organization of negro workers?

Mr. Gompers: Very little.

. . .

If you would say this: In three weeks the Executive Council of the American Federation of Labor is going to convene here.[11] In addition to the other business that will come before the Council will be to go over a tentative draft for the report of the Council to the convention of the Federation, which is to be held in June at St. Paul. We shall undoubtedly make report on this subject,[12] and I have not the slightest doubt but what the convention will give its wholehearted endorsement to any recommendation that the Executive Council of the A.F. of L. will make to that convention, because of its fundamental character and this is the course from which there has been no deviation, as I tried to indicate in the declarations made in the beginning of our conference. The reaffirmation of it, the organization of workers, the insistence upon equal treatment in so far as we had the power to insist and enforce, the evidence which I showed you in one small instance of these new unions, and the issuance of a call for an international union so that they shall be self-governing. If you felt after conferring with us, and we with you, and talking this matter over, and you believe that we are sincere that what we stand for is what we are doing, if you believe that we are sincere in that, and you will make some statement to the men whom you can reach through your avenues and channels better than we can. We can reach them at work. We can break through the barrier of the employer. Leave him to us. We will deal with him. But the other agencies that stand between the employer and us and behind the workmen, we can't reach them. If the employer is the only barrier we will get at the men. There is something in this human element that no amount of money and no amount of other barriers are invented by the employer except those who stand between as the guide, as the leaders of the men.

Mr. Morrison: There is one proposition this committee should understand. We have got a colored organizer, Goode, at Norfolk. We have an organizer working in Chicago,[13] colored. We are paying part expenses of an organizer in Birmingham[14] at the present time. The Mine, Mill and Smelter Workers and the Mine Workers, and many other international organizations have colored organizers. There are a great many colored organizers working in the labor movement, besides the three of them under direct pay from the American Federation of Labor, and it is contemplated by President Gompers if we can get a good man to select that will be put to work in the south.

Mr. Gompers: You report our attitude and you can just imagine then that that is a real, red blooded movement. If we have a statement from you to report to our Executive Council and in turn reported by our Executive Council to the convention, I tell you, gentlemen, in my judgment this organization of the negro workmen will go on and gain such an impetus and tremendous force. We gather strength continually from each other's cooperation.

TD, AFL Microfilm Convention File, reel 28, frames 2257–64, *AFL Records*.

1. Newton A. JAMES of Hyattsville, Md., was secretary of the Maryland State and District of Columbia Federation of Labor and of the Washington, D.C., Central Labor Union.

2. John H. DONLIN, a member of the Operative Plasterers' and Cement Finishers' International Association of the United States and Canada, served as president of the AFL Building Trades Department from 1916 to 1924.

3. James Hardy Dillard (1856–1940) of Charlottesville, Va., was director (1907–31) of the Anna T. Jeanes Foundation, established in 1907 to assist rural black schools.

4. The AFL chartered the Essex Trades Council, the central body of Newark, N.J., in 1901.

5. Armistead Goode, a resident of Portsmouth, Va., served as an AFL salaried organizer from 1916 to 1920.

6. Possibly James E. Jones, secretary of AFL 15,277 (Coal Trimmers) of Norfolk, Va., James H. Wilson, a Portsmouth machinist, or J. H. Gilmour, who had worked as an organizer in Newport News, Va., for the International Association of Machinists in 1917. Jones was black; Wilson and Gilmour were white.

7. Emmett C. DAVISON served as secretary-treasurer of the International Association of Machinists from 1917 to 1944.

8. SG to Railroad Helpers' and Laborers' Locals, Apr. 19, 1918, reel 234, vol. 246, pp. 525 (verso)-26, SG Letterbooks, DLC.

9. A convention of directly affiliated AFL local unions of railroad helpers and laborers was held in St. Louis in late May 1918 to consider forming an international union. David Kreyling, secretary-organizer of the St. Louis Central Trades and Labor Union, represented the AFL at the meeting. The 1918 AFL convention voted against a resolution calling for the chartering of a black railway employees' union, both on jurisdictional grounds and because it was against AFL policy to grant charters on racial lines. In July the AFL Executive Council voted to transfer its directly affiliated local unions of railroad helpers and laborers to the United Brotherhood of Maintenance of Way Employes and Railway Shop Laborers, which had recently altered its bylaws to permit black workers to become members in segregated "allied" lodges. In September Frank Morrison notified these locals of this decision.

10. The American WIRE Weavers' Protective Association.

11. The AFL Executive Council met in Washington, D.C., May 13–20, 1918.

12. The AFL Executive Council report to the 1918 convention outlined the actions taken at the February and April conferences with representatives of black workers and

indicated that the black representatives had agreed to issue a statement urging blacks to organize in affiliation with the AFL (AFL, *Proceedings,* 1918, pp. 130–31). The convention endorsed the report and recommended that SG and the Executive Council give special attention to organizing black workers. See also "From Eugene Kinckle Jones and Fred Moore," June 6, 1918, below.

13. John Riley, who served as an AFL salaried organizer from 1918 to 1920.

14. Ralph Clemmons, who served as an AFL salaried organizer in Alabama in 1917 and 1918.

To Stephen Condon[1]

April 23, 1918.

Mr. Condon,
President,[2] Lighter Captains Union Local 847, Series 2,
International Longshoremen's Association,
1142 49th St., Brooklyn, N.Y.
Dear Sir and Brother:

I am writing to you in response to a letter[3] received by me today without signature, but as you are the President of the union it is fair to assume that the absence of signature was due to oversight. If the matter with which your letter deals were less important, I would inquire whether you had written it, but I will assume that you have, hence reply thereto.

I have not the slightest doubt but that there is merit in the complaints which you make. In a telegram to Brother Paul Vaccerelli I said that I would submit the complaints to the War Labor Board at their meeting today. Much to my regret I learned that it was impossible for the Board to meet today but that the meeting had been deferred until Monday, April 29th.

It was my hope also to personally present the grievance and make such argument as might be necessary. That of course is now out of the question, for I must leave early Thursday morning upon an important mission[4] which I can neither postpone nor neglect.

One thing I desire to impress upon your mind and the minds of all those good men you represent. It would be a great wrong to inaugurate a strike at this time in the affairs of our country, particularly if there is the slightest avenue open for the adjustment of any grievances which may exist. I repeat that there must be merit in the grievances presented, but bear in mind that they are capable of being adjusted and that our first duty in this critical time of our nation's history, yes, in the life of civilization itself, is that it behooves us to continue our services so that we shall not be overwhelmed and the men who stand for freedom, justice and right may not have their lives crushed out.

You know the propaganda and some of the forces that are at work to make for the undoing of the American Republic in the present conflict. They consist of all kinds of methods. Do not, I beg of you, be led into a false position, or lead others into a false position which you cannot justify, and not only before our fellow workers but our fellow citizens at home, and the fighting boys at the front.

In addition let me call your attention to the situation as it presented itself in the Congress of the United States within this past few days. If we had not been active, alert, and insistent, there would now have been upon the statute books of the United States a law that would have made a strike criminal and seditious and subjecting those participating in it or projecting it to large fines, long terms of imprisonment, and possibly death.[5] There is little doubt in my mind that the American people and particularly our legislators who represent the people, the men and women of the United States who have brothers and sons on the firing lines of France and who are going there, will not tolerate a condition by which these fighting boys will lack the means to fight and of subsistence due to a grievance which could be righted without a cessation of work; yes, even if the grievance is required to be adjusted at a later date. The dangers which are avoided are not sensational and sometimes not interesting, but it is good for thinking men to bear in mind the dangers which are averted and not wait for dangers to arise and then regret that they have been allowed to occur.

I regret too that you should have allowed any personal matter to have crept into your letter. It does good to no one. You express confidence in me, and I assure you that I am proud and grateful, but I can assure you that it is a mistake for anyone to suppose that President O'Connor[6] has failed in any particular to be of service to you, to your fellow workers, and to all the members of your International Association, but in any event I appeal to you, to your associates, and to all our fellow workers and fellow union men to stand faithful to the true cause of trade unionism, and the great cause in which our country is engaged.

At the meeting of the War Labor Board on Monday I have asked Secretary Morrison to appear and make the argument, and I have also communicated with President O'Connor and he too declared that it was his purpose to appear before the War Labor Board in furtherance of the consideration and the hopes for adjustment of the claims presented.

With best wishes, I am,

Fraternally yours,　Saml Gompers.
President,　American Federation of Labor.

·

TLpS, reel 234, vol. 246, pp. 387–88, SG Letterbooks, DLC.

1. Stephen J. Condon was the business agent of International Longshoremen's Association 847, Series 2 (New York Harbor Lighter Captains).

2. Actually, James McGuire was the local's president.

3. President, Lighter Captains' Union, to SG, Apr. 20, 1918, Files of the Office of the President, General Correspondence, reel 94, frames 660–63, *AFL Records.* The letter complained that the Nov. 16, 1917, New York harbor wage award was not being observed and that wages and working conditions in the port were intolerable, and it urged prompt action by the government to avert a strike. (See "To Paul Vaccarelli," Mar. 13, 1918, n. 3, above.)

4. SG left AFL headquarters on Apr. 25, 1918, for Ottawa and Montreal, and then visited Boston and New York City before returning to Washington, D.C., on May 6. He addressed a joint session of the Canadian Parliament in Ottawa, a mass meeting in Montreal, and a joint session of the Massachusetts legislature in Boston and met with a number of labor and government officials in these cities.

5. S. 383 (65th Cong., 1st sess.), to punish willful injury or destruction of war-related materials, premises, or transportation facilities with fines of up to $10,000 and/or prison terms not to exceed thirty years, was introduced by Democratic senator Charles Culberson of Texas on Apr. 4, 1917. On Mar. 6, 1918, Republican congressman Joseph Cannon of Illinois proposed an amendment extending the provisions of the act to anyone who interfered with or obstructed the war effort, including war construction or the production of war materiel. When the AFL objected, Democratic congressman George Lunn of New York offered another amendment, declaring that nothing in the act made it unlawful for employees to strike for better wages or conditions of employment. The House adopted both amendments, but the Senate disagreed, and both were eventually eliminated from the legislation. Known as the Sabotage Act, it became law on Apr. 20 (U.S. *Statutes at Large,* 40: 533–34).

6. Thomas Ventry O'CONNOR served as president of the International Longshoremen's Association from 1909 to 1921.

Ralph Van Deman[1] to Frank Morrison

April 24, 1918.

Mr. Frank Morrison,
Secretary of American Federation of Labor,
Washington, D.C.
Dear Mr. Morrison:

I appreciate that to-day all that the Government need do to secure the full cooperation of the American Federation of Labor is to ask for it, and that the only question of the American Federation of Labor will be as to the feasibility of the plan proposed. With this in mind, I propose the following plan for utilizing your organization as an aid to Military Intelligence in gathering information:

I must explain the function of Military Intelligence in order that you may appreciate the importance of the service that the American Federation of Labor can perform. In order to combat and counteract the activities of German agents, Military Intelligence is engaged in gathering information relative to such activities as evidenced by (1) attempts to secure and communicate information of military value, including army, navy, and commercial secrets; (2) dissemination of hostile propaganda; (3) acts of violence; (4) the creation of dissatisfaction and discord among the civil population. We desire all possible information from every possible source relative to the above and kindred matters, whether it is in the form of legal proof or mere rumor or mere suspicion. Each informant serves as a check upon each other informant, and each rumor or suspicion is subject to careful scrutiny and investigation. By this laborious process of separating the wheat from the chaff, we are able to secure accurate information which enables us to guard the safety of the forces in the field and the civilians at home, and to maintain their respective morale.

The American Federation of Labor, thru its extensive local, district, and national organization, could gather a very great amount of valuable information relating to these matters. Much of this information would seem unimportant and valueless to those who are not in a position to collate and piece together this information with other informations such as we possess, and, to be frank, much of it would probably be valueless even to us. However, in the ultimate analysis, the benefit to Military Intelligence and to the country at large from the collection and transmission of such information would be almost incalculable. We desire, therefore, that each local union constitute itself an unofficial branch of Military Intelligence and forward to us, thru its secretary, all information that its members have or may hereafter learn relative to disloyalty or hostile activities, and any persons suspected thereof, and relative to labor conditions in their vicinity. In this latter connection, you appreciate that unsatisfactory labor conditions, whether due to conflict between employer and employee, or due to the influence of I.W.W. or Bolshevikism, is a fertile field for German propaganda, and even tho no enemy activity is actually manifest, it is a potential menace to the successful prosecution of the war. Military Intelligence would further desire permission to communicate with the various local and district officers in order to secure definite information relative to general conditions or specific individuals.

To indicate in a general way the enlargement of our organization thru the utilization of yours, the list of the Executive Board and District Secretaries of the United Mine Workers alone discloses twenty-one towns or cities in which we have no representatives and no expeditious means of securing information.

If this general plan meets with the approval of the Federation, I shall be glad to have Captain Schmuck,[2] of this office, confer with you as to the details of manner in which it will be put into effect.[3]

Very truly yours,   R. H. Van Deman,
Colonel, General Staff,
Chief, Military Intelligence Branch,
Executive Division.

TLtcSr, Military Intelligence Division, RG 165, Records of the War Department General and Special Staffs, DNA.

1. Col. Ralph Henry Van Deman (1865–1952), a career army officer, served as chief of the U.S. Army's Military Intelligence Division from April 1917 to June 1918. He rose to the rank of major general before his retirement in 1929.

2. Thomas K. Schmuck. For Schmuck's role in creating the plan for working with the AFL and his authorship of this letter, see his memorandum for Major Hunt, June 27, 1918, Military Intelligence Division, RG 165, Records of the War Department General and Special Staffs, DNA.

3. Schmuck and Eugene Kinkead of the Military Intelligence Division subsequently discussed the matter with SG and Frank Morrison, and on May 27, 1918, Morrison sent Kinkead a list of AFL affiliates, giving the names and addresses of the unions' secretaries (Frank Morrison Letterbooks, vol. 502, p. 364, George Meany Memorial Archives, Silver Spring, Md.). There is no indication of further action on SG's or Morrison's part, despite subsequent requests (see Kinkead to Morrison, June 7, 1918, Military Intelligence Division, RG 165, Records of the War Department General and Special Staffs, DNA).

To Woodrow Wilson

Washington, D.C. May 6, 1918.

Honorable Woodrow Wilson,
President of the United States,
Washington, D.C.
Sir:

I feel it my unescapable duty to present to you certain facts in regard to conditions in Porto Rico in the form of charges against Arthur Yager, Governor of Porto Rico. These charges, signed and specified by Santiago Iglesias, President of the Free Federation of Workers of Porto Rico, show that Governor Yager has been derelict in cooperating with national war policies; that he has not performed his duties as an administrator with impartiality and equity to all; that he has knowingly or unknowingly used the high power of his office to interfere with constructive efforts of Porto Rico's workers to better their conditions of life and work, and that his policies and acts have been at complete variance with those high ideals and standards of human welfare and value that are essential to democratic institutions. A statement has been made out to accompany these charges describing conditions in Porto Rico and embodying documentary evidence proving the charges.[1]

The agricultural workers who are now on strike in the sugar plantations of Porto Rico have been denied political, legal, and industrial justice. The United States government, which is now in a war against the principles of autocracy and denial of human right, cannot longer remain responsible for a condition in territory over which it has jurisdiction, which is totally at variance with the ideals and institutions for which our government and nation have declared.

The situation in Porto Rico, which is inducing and leading the working people to the verge of a revolution, is being used to the discredit of our Republic in Spanish speaking countries. The story of injustice in Porto Rico has already been carried to the Spanish speaking people of North and South America, and even to Europe. The people of those countries value the declarations of our government and our people by the results they are able to achieve.

I feel very keenly that a condition ought not longer to remain which I am sure you, and all other right thinking citizens, would not approve or sanction if the facts were known. I therefore, am bringing to your attention the following charges and supplementary information in order that steps may be taken to remedy a situation which is totally at variance with the desires of our people and which is being used to discredit the high aims and desires of our Republic.

Conditions in Porto Rico have in years past been presented to you personally and to various governmental agencies, especially to the Federal Commission on Industrial Relations. It is my purpose at this time not only to make charges against Governor Yager, but to suggest that a commission ought to be sent to the Island to make an investigation and a report with recommendations. The evil that exists there is in the main economic. For years, the workers of Porto Rico have been underfed, practically starving. Something practical ought to be done to better such a condition among workers in an Island rich in many valuable products. A practical effort ought to be made to give these people of Porto Rico the real opportunity which democracy implies, and with which I know you have the most sincere and practical sympathy.[2]

Respectfully,   Saml Gompers.
President,   American Federation of Labor.

TLS, Woodrow Wilson Papers, DLC.

1. Santiago Iglesias to Woodrow Wilson, Apr. 30, 1918, Woodrow Wilson Papers, DLC.

2. Wilson replied on May 20, 1918, that after taking up the issue with Secretary of War Newton Baker he believed the charges were unfounded, but he suggested that SG meet with Baker to discuss the matter. SG and Iglesias met with Baker and Gen. Frank McIntyre in July and agreed with Baker's suggestion that a commission be appointed to study labor conditions in Puerto Rico. Iglesias reported to the 1919 AFL convention that no such commission had yet visited the island, and the convention authorized an AFL investigation of living and working conditions there. The report of that commission, which visited Puerto Rico in 1920, is printed in AFL, *Proceedings*, 1920, pp. 236–45.

From Clara Stutz[1]

Grade Teachers' Union of Washington, D.C.[2]
May 6, 1918.

My dear Mr. Gompers:—

I wish to acknowledge the receipt of your letter[3] dated May 4, 1918 in which you ask for reasons for making the minimum wage for school-teachers in Washington $1000, especially why the $500 minimum should be raised to $1000.

Since 1906 when the present salary schedule was made effective the value of the dollar has shrunken to 50 cents, according to some estimates to as little as 40 or 33⅓ cents, so that substituting a $1000 for a $500 salary is really no increase; it is merely the restoration of the value of the dollar.

The $750 minimum proposed by the new House bill[4] is not sufficient to maintain a teacher at anything like her maximum efficiency. Teaching is not an art that can be acquired once and for all time. A teacher must be continually spending her salary to keep herself efficient enough to earn it. Study, some travel, a broader experience than can be obtained with a salary so low as to forbid the refinements of life are essential. The board and room which last year cost the teacher $35. have risen to $50. Clothing has soared so tremendously that in order to dress as well as is expected of her she will be forced to cut down magazine subscriptions and lectures (all items taken into account in her rating.) The expense budgets of last year showed teachers earning $900–$1000 having dependent relatives were in debt. One hospital experience wipes out a teacher's entire savings.

The Government is paying $1100 and $1200 to clerks, some of them with less than a grammar school education, most of them without high school education. This sort of thing is stripping the teaching profession of its best material. Young women with the character and qualifications to make good teachers, for economic reasons cannot afford to spend the years of training in High and Normal schools when six months of stenography and typewriting fit them to earn a higher salary. It takes longer to train a teacher than a soldier. Normal schools all over the country are suffering. Our own Normal[5] shows a decrease of more than 50%.

The question of justly compensating a teacher is of minor importance. The welfare of the Public Schools is at stake. We are at a crisis. All over the country teachers are being forced to give up the profession for which they were trained to take positions for higher wages, which others could fill, while there are no trained women to take the places they leave vacant. For years the school teachers have been underpaid. Though their work has been eulogized on public platforms, and they have been told, that the very fate of the Republic rests upon their shoulders, the lowest salaries have been considered sufficient compensation. If there has been even so much as a grain of truth in the assertions of the value of the calling then the country cannot afford to lose her trained teachers. It is said that Germany boasts of spending more on education now than she did before the war. England recognizes the importance of education in war time, and is strengthening instruction. A Democracy can least of all save on its schools. Are we not running the risk of a fatal blunder if we allow the exodus of teachers to other industries to continue?

These are the facts as I see them. If they are strong enough to enlist your interest,[6] I shall feel that our cause has won a brilliant champion.

> Very respectfully yours,   Clara K. Stutz,
> President,   Grade Teachers Union.

TLS, AFL Microfilm National and International Union File, American Federation of Teachers Records, reel 45, frame 2169, *AFL Records.*

1. Clara K. Stutz was president of American Federation of Teachers 16 of Washington, D.C., and served as a vice-president of the national union from July 1918 until late 1920.

2. The Grade Teachers' Union (also known as the Grade School Teachers' Union) of Washington, D.C., was chartered as Teachers' local 16 in February 1918.

3. SG to Stutz, May 4, 1918, reel 234, vol. 246, pp. 771–72, SG Letterbooks, DLC.

4. H.R. 11,692 (65th Cong., 2d sess.), the District of Columbia appropriations bill for the fiscal year ending June 30, 1919, was introduced by Democratic congressman Thomas Sisson of Mississippi on Apr. 25, 1918, and became law on Aug. 31 (U.S. *Statutes at Large,* 40: 918–54). The act provided for teachers' salaries ranging from $750 to $1,900.

5. Probably the James Ormond Wilson Normal School, founded in 1873 as the Washington Normal School and renamed in 1913.

6. On May 14, 1918, SG wrote John Walter Smith, chairman of the Senate Commit-

tee on the District of Columbia, quoting extensively from Stutz's letter and asking him to consider an increase in the minimum salary proposed in the appropriations bill. He informed Stutz of his action the same day (reel 235, vol. 247, pp. 122, 168–69, SG Letterbooks, DLC).

Excerpts from the Minutes of a Hearing before the National War Labor Board

Washington, D.C. May 9, 1918.

BIRMINGHAM CASE

Mr. Taft: Mr. O'Connell, this meeting was—this meeting was [called] at your instance and by your written communication on behalf of the Metal Trades and we would be glad to hear either you state it or Mr. Gompers if he is here for that purpose.

Mr. Gompers: I prefer that Mr. O'Connell proceed.

Mr. O'Connell: I will briefly state the case to the Board and later want him to say something to the Board. There is involved in a strike and a lockout in Birmingham, Alabama and that district several hundred Metal Trades men employed in the Commercial shops at Birmingham, the steel mills in that district. The strike does not involve the steel mill workers proper, only the mechanic trades such as Machinists, Boiler Makers, Blacksmiths, etc. In the city of Birmingham, in the Commercial shops it involves the men in the Metal Trades, the skilled trades to the extent of several hundred. In Birmingham is formed a Local Metal Trades Council of our department which is a department of the Metal Trades of the American Federation of Labor, having jurisdiction over the Metal Industry. We form local metal trades councils in the various cities throughout the country, and the Local Unions of Metal Trades, such as Molders, Machinists, Blacksmiths, Boilermakers join the Local Council and that becomes the central body from which they deal collectively. In Birmingham we have such a body. These representatives of the Local Unions in Birmingham meeting jointly in this Council decided to ask the employers for an Eight hour day, without reduction in the day's earnings. In other words if they were getting Five dollars a day for Ten hours, they would get Five Dollars a day for Eight hours. The hours have varied, running all the way from Eight to Thirteen and the days running from Five and one-half to Seven, some of them working Sundays in the mills, etc. A communication was addressed by the section of the Local Metal Trades Council to all the employers in the district.

Mr. Taft: To all the companies whose names you gave the Commission?

A. Yes,—asking them for the inauguration of the Eight hour day with the necessary compensation provided for the reduction in the hours. No reply was received from any of the employers to that notification. About a week later another notification was sent out setting forth that if a reply was not received by a certain date that the men would cease work. Meantime some of the shops closed down and upon the date set for the notice given by the men that if the eight hour day was not granted, they would cease work, on that morning they ceased work, those who had not been locked out or shops closed down. The strike involves several hundred tradesmen and that strike has been on since that time.

. . .

Mr. Gompers: I should like the opportunity to say a word supplementing that which Mr. O'Connell has presented, to say that after the strike occurred, I learned that the president and the board of directors of the United States Steel Corporation had invited the president[1] of the subsidiary companies to meet the board in New York, and being in touch with the men engaged in the strike and endeavoring to be somewhat helpful in cooperating with the Governmental agencies through the Department of Labor, I addressed a communication[2] to Judge Gary and urged that the Board of Directors of the United States Steel Corporation should make some definite declaration upon the subject of the basic eight hour day—regard it as one of the big things to be considered and to the determination of the policy for that great big industrial institution, that would have such a—well, I was going to say tranquillizing effect, that at any rate, it would have a great influence on the minds of the great mass of the workers of the country, that it would go far to drive any delusions away from the workers themselves, or any conflict on the part of the employers and workers. I received a reply[3] from Judge Gary in which he said that the company could not or would not inaugurate the eight hour day. . . .

Mr. Taft: Really, as you state it, Mr. Gompers, it is an issue between you and the steel company, is [it not], as to the eight hour [day], I mean this having or being a local case, but one in which you seek to raise the general issue?

A. Yes, that is, we hope that the U.S. Steel Corporation, under the enlightened management, shall take this view and act upon the situation, but while we would like that to be done, it is not an issue before your Board. If the Board shall make a declaration that the basic eight hour day should apply in the plants of these gentlemen, I haven't the slightest hesitancy in believing that it is going to have a wide spread influence in the entire steel line and steel industry. A few months ago there was a great industry involved in the very same issue. I think it took all the ingenuity of the labor men, of the Secretary of Labor, Secretary of War, of the President of the United States, to avert what would have been a calamity to the industry particularly, but to the country and to our cause, but it was averted because it was taken up in time and the matter presented to the President of the United States. It was before the creation of the Labor Conference Board, but it was the beginning, and the basic eight hour day is now in operation in the great packing houses of Chicago and nearly entirely throughout the country, and I venture to say, if I may—I am impelled to go on for just a moment—the employers do not know of the great advantage of an eight hour day. I mean those who haven't gone through the experience, and to these as to their industry, to their workers, they don't know it. They place themselves in the position that to concede anything as a demand by labor, is a surrender of their position. That is the great mistake. They do not want to meet that new concept that the worker is in addition a citizen and a man and giving important service, not as a mere machine, but as a man and that he is entitled to the consideration of equal standing in the discussion of the problems of the relations between employer and employee. They are no longer master and man, or master and servant, or owner and slave. They are men, and in America particularly are we men and we insist upon being considered and discussed and discussed with, the problems, the greatest problem ever confronted or presented to the people of the whole world. The rightful relations between employee and employer. And we propose to have a voice in determining what those relations shall be, and if men, employers will not concede that position. Well, there is going to be the dickens to pay, that is all. I am not ready to concede it, that is all, but for the sake of our consideration, for a moment, concede that the employer has whipped these men, and that most of them are unemployed. Others have gone elsewhere. That has not settled it and it is not going to settle it. The problems of controversies between employers and employees are not settled that way. They may for a time being squelch either the one side or the other, but the discontent and resentment will exist and grow and it is not good. We are trying to do our level best, and I think when I say we, I am speaking now generally as citizens of the Republic, the men of labor doing everything that they possibly can that the individual group thought should not prevail at this time, during the period of this war, but that the aggregate thought and activities should be unified in the one great overtowering question of affecting and producing and transporting to win the war. That is the first thing, and if men won't take that position, I hate like the mischief to attribute any ulterior motives to any man, but it is the failure to understand the duty of the time. The masses of men are workers, laborers, mechanics and they have got to furnish the majority of the men to do the fighting and to make the supreme sacrifice if necessary. They have got to do the great work of production, manual labor as well as intellectual labor. Whether the employers will accept the position or not, this war is going to have a wonderful influence in the remaking of the world, and the introduction of new rules and regulations, and there will be new concepts of the rights of man and the relations between man and man, whether they be employer or employee, and it is to make for that great one common purpose for which I am pleading, have pleaded, and particularly pleading and emphasizing since the war. That thing to me, to our cause and to our men is more sacred than winning the war, and while fighting for the safety of the concepts and principles of justice and freedom abroad, we do not lose it at home during the time of the conflict. I do hope that the Board will favorably consider the question of taking cognizance of the case. . . .

. . .

. . . I am appealing to the employers. You just look at us square in the eyes as men to men and we are not going to try to fool you or hurt you, but we are looking out for our people, because if we don't, someone may sympathize with them and they will walk upon the other side. It is our business, it is our job to see that the men of labor are receiving fair consideration and fair treatment and fair pay, and a work day that does not undermine their health and their strength and their ability to produce. I will wait. You just meet us halfway, you will find that we are not quite as black as we have been painted.

. . .

. . . We believe in the eight hour work day and as a basic principle for a basic day. We have secured that by economics. There are many industries we have secured it in, legislation of the United States and the several states and municipalities and the provisions in the law, in all the laws guaranteed this one fact that in case of emergencies, such as the loss of life, or the involving of fire or pestilence or war or the imminence of war, that the eight hour law could be suspended by the proclamation of the President. Now, with our entrance into the war, a new situation was presented us. We were in war and if the emergency, having presented itself and come upon us the President suspended the operation of the eight hour law, there would be no penalty, no check for employers to work their employees more than eight hours. An amendment was passed to the law providing that when the President of the United States shall declare that the eight hour work day is suspended—the suspension of the eight hour work day—that in such cases the employers having contracts or sub-contracts with the Government shall pay not less than time and a half for such overtime beyond eight hours. Now just this word. We want the eight hour day. We do not want the extra pay for the sake of the extra pay, but our experience has shown us that if there is not a penalty of some sort, the employers will [think] anything is a proper time to require work beyond the eight hour day, and the time and a half is intended to be a penalty.

Mr. Taft: That is what the Supreme Court—

A. Yes. It is intended to be a penalty and so that only when great emergencies exist, will the employer have his employees work more than eight hours a day. That is the idea. We want the eight hour day for the conservation of the human side of the work. It is not the question of the compensation, except that is just about as good of a check as can be had for the employment of workers beyond the eight hour day.

. . .

TD, RG 2, Records of the National War Labor Board, DNA.

1. George Gordon Crawford (1869–1936), the president of the Tennessee Coal, Iron, and Railroad Co. from 1907 to 1930.
2. See "To Elbert Gary," Mar. 18, 1918, above.
3. Apparently a reference to Gary's telegram to SG of Mar. 19, 1918, printed above.

To the Editor of the *Boston Post*

May 15, 1918.

Editor, The Boston Post,
Boston, Mass.
Dear Sir:

My father[1] sent me part of the Sunday issue of the Boston Post containing what is supposed to be an interview[2] with him. In the letter of transmission he says that there are many things in the interview attributed to him which he did not say and others which were distorted.

As a matter of fact the whole story is a reflection upon the man interviewed. Your representative gained entrance into a private home in which the inmates were unaccustomed to protect themselves from newspaper publicity and misrepresentation. I wonder whether you think it fair to send a sharp witted reporter to interview an old man of nearly 92 years of age, blind at that, incapable of defending himself in any way. In my opinion it was contemptible to the last degree.[3]

> Very truly yours,   Samuel Gompers.
> President,   American Federation of Labor.

TLpS, reel 235, vol. 247, p. 167, SG Letterbooks, DLC.

1. Solomon GOMPERS.
2. "Sam Gompers' 91-Year-Dad Reminisces," *Boston Post,* May 12, 1918.
3. C. B. Carberry, the managing editor of the *Boston Post,* wrote SG a letter of explanation on May 21, 1918, which SG acknowledged on May 31. SG declared himself satisfied with Carberry's account and stated that a printed apology in the *Post* was unnecessary (reel 235, vol. 247, p. 718, SG Letterbooks, DLC).

From William Appleton

Chief Office
The General Federation of Trade Unions
London, W.C. 1. 15th May, 1918.

My dear friend Gompers,

Great efforts have been made by the Defeatists in this country and in France, first, to win over the American delegation to their views concerning Stockholm and Bern,[1] and secondly, to discredit them everywhere, but it became clearly apparent that nothing could move them from their loyalty to the United States Government and to the American Federation of Labor. Macdonald[2] has publicly insulted them in the Glasgow "Forward." The "Labour Leader" has vilified them in a most vulgar manner and Henderson himself has written to the Trades and Labour Councils in such a fashion as to seriously prejudice the position of the delegates in the minds of those who only read Henderson's statements. I have not seen a copy of the letter he sent, but I have seen its effects. To appreciate the extent of the damage that he might have done, had other steps not been taken, you have always to remember that for some years it has been the policy of the I.L.P. to secure all the official positions on the trades councils. Henderson appears to have made special efforts in Swansea with results that he hardly would have expected, for although the trades councils have declined to participate in the welcome, the Mayor[3] and the citizens are hoping to give a welcome which I am sure will reflect honour upon the principality of Wales.

In Bristol, Ernest Bevin[4] used all his influence to prevent a real successful public meeting. The Mayor[5] who is largely under the influence of Bevin, was willing to give a civic reception, but not willing to undertake the promotion of a public meeting. I, at once, took upon myself the responsibility of cutting Bristol out of the programme. I could not agree to permit any of the delegates of the American Federation of Labor to go into a city and run the risk of insult.

On Monday night we had a very happy gathering. The delegates dined with me at the House of Commons and I invited a number of friends who represent all kinds of interests. We had a very happy evening.

On Sunday, we had a meeting in the People's Palace, Mile End Road. The spirit of this meeting was magnificent; the people rising and cheering again and again.

In France, I know that the delegates have had a very serious time, for the greatest efforts were made by the Defeatists to prevent Wilson and his colleagues reaching the real democracy of France. The groups of Defeatists had conspired together. They had passed resolutions that no one but the appointed speakers should say a word, that no opinions should be expressed except it was the opinion agreed upon by the majority of the Defeatists themselves. It was only with very great difficulty that the patriotic socialists broke through the barriers that the Defeatists had erected. Some of my friends write to say that the success of our men was impaired in France by the action of the Defeatists. Others, however, who read French papers, have come to me almost daily with expressions of delight on their faces, saying that the utterances of the American delegates made grand and encouraging reading for Frenchmen.

You will know that I have done what I could here, but owing to the fact that most of the arrangements had been made in my absence and most of the dates filled up, my opportunities have been limited. I am sure, however, that the great blow has been struck at our own Defeatists. Henderson has already paved the way for a volte-face.

Kindest regards.

Yours faithfully,   W A Appleton

TLS, Files of the Office of the President, General Correspondence, reel 95, frames 462–64, *AFL Records.*

1. That is, the proposal to hold a conference in a neutral country that would include socialist and labor delegates from all belligerent powers.

2. James Ramsay MacDonald (1866–1937), founder and secretary of the Labour Representation Committee—the organization that became the Labour party in 1906, was secretary (1906–12) and then treasurer (1912–24) of the Labour party and a Labour member of Parliament (1906–18, 1922–35, 1936–37). He later served as prime minister and foreign secretary in the first Labour government (1924) and as prime

minister in both the second Labour government (1929–31) and the national coalition government that succeeded it (1931–35).

3. Benjamin Jones, a haberdasher and draper, was mayor of Swansea, Wales, from late 1917 through late 1918.

4. Ernest Bevin served as a national organizer for the Dock, Wharf, Riverside, and General Labourers' Union from 1914 to 1920.

5. Frank Sheppard (1861–1956), a member of the National Union of Operative Boot and Shoe Riveters and Finishers, was the mayor of Bristol from late 1917 through late 1918.

Frank Grimshaw[1] to Frank Morrison

Stove Mounters' International Union[2]
Detroit, Mich. May 16, 1918.

Mr. Frank Morrison,
Secretary A.F. of L.;
Washington, D.C.
Dear Sir & Brother:—

Our organization is desirous of securing information as to the scope of an act of Congress, approved April 20, 1918, commonly known as the "Sabotage Act"[3] and entitled:

"An Act to punish the wilful injury or destruction of war material, or of war premises or utilities in connection with war material, and for other war purposes." (copy Enclosed)[4]

The facts in connection with the case on which we are asking information are as follows:

The members of our organization have been on strike at Detroit, Mich. in the shops of the Michigan Stove Company, Peninsular Stove Company and Detroit Stove Works since February 8, 1918,[5] and these firms have contracts for certain lines of stoves and ranges for the United States government, one of the firms is also making shells for the government, but the entire output of these plants *is not* for the government, only a very small portion being government work.

In connection with our strike our members have been very successful in inducing men employed as strike breakers to quit work in these shops, but have been very careful not to induce men employed on government work to quit.

On May 14th one of our members[6] engaged in inducing men not employed on government work to leave the employ of the Michigan Stove Co. was arrested upon complaint of this firm by a United States officer but was released after being questioned, and also warned by the government agent that if he again attempted to induce any work-men in the employ of the Michigan Stove Co. to quit work he would be tried under the "Sabotage Act," and that his arrest would follow regardless as to whether the party he was attempting to induce to quit was employed upon work for the U.S. government or not.

In fact the statement was made by the government agent that an attempt to induce any man in the employ of the Michigan Stove Co. to quit work on account of our strike, regardless of whether such person approached was employed upon government work in this shop or not, would be a violation of the act of April 20, 1918.

We have endeavored to secure legal advice upon this matter from the United States Attorney of this district and have been advised that the matter should be presented to the United States Attorney-General at Washington, D.C. for an opinion, and for this reason we are requesting the A.F. of L. to submit the matter to the Attorney General and secure a ruling upon the following questions:

Can any attempt by workmen on strike to induce men employed as strike breakers to quit work, be construed as a violation of the act in question, when such men it is proposed to induce to quit work are in the employ of a firm making goods or munitions for the government, the men in question not in any manner whatever being employed in the production of work for the government by such firm?

In other words does the fact that a firm may have a government contract for goods that are produced by a part of the workmen in their employ place the entire plant under the jurisdiction of the government?

Could the words "war premises" as defined in the act, be construed as applying to the entire plant of such concerns and their employees, or would it apply only to such buildings, or parts of buildings in which work is being made for the government, and could any action in attempting to induce workmen employed in such buildings, but not directly employed in producing war material for the government, to quit work be construed as a violation of this act?

The entire matter as it appears to us is that the Michigan Stove Company is making an effort to use this law and the government agents for strike breaking purposes by advancing the claim that their plant is "war premises" as defined in the act, when but a very small percentage of the goods they are producing are being made for the government or can be classed as war material.

We can not believe that such was the intention of the law and for this reason would request that the A.F. of L. refer the matter to the Attorney General and secure an opinion upon the case at as early a date as possible, because as the situation now stands it will practically mean the arrest of any of our members should they attempt to induce strike breakers to quit work on work that is not being made for the government.

Thanking you for an early reply[7] upon this matter, I remain,

Yours fraternally,
Secretary Treas.

TL, AFL Microfilm National and International Union File, Stove Mounters Records, reel 42, frame 1014, *AFL Records.*

1. Frank GRIMSHAW served as secretary-treasurer of the Stove Mounters' International Union of North America from 1913 to 1932.

2. The STOVE Mounters' International Union of North America.

3. See "To Stephen Condon," Apr. 23, 1918, n. 5, above.

4. AFL Microfilm National and International Union File, Stove Mounters Records, reel 42, frame 1014, *AFL Records.*

5. After their contract negotiations with leading stove making firms in Detroit broke down, Stove Mounters' local 1 of that city struck the companies on Feb. 8, 1918. Since three of the manufacturers had contracts to supply stoves to the army, they were able to enjoin the strikers from picketing or speaking with strikebreakers. The strike continued into the summer of 1919 but ended in failure.

6. Edward Lipke.

7. Frank Morrison took up the matter with the Attorney General's office, which declined to give an opinion on the scope of the Sabotage Act. The Department of Justice asserted that Lipke had not actually been detained but had come to the department's office in Detroit voluntarily, in response to a request for an interview.

To W. G. Hudson

May 20, 1918.

Mr. W. G. Hudson,
District Supervisor Second District, United States Shipping Board,
   Emergency Fleet Corporation,
115 Broadway, New York, N.Y.
Dear Sir:

Your letter of May 13th received and contents noted. You say that the local shipyards foremen of foreign birth give preference to workmen of foreign birth—members of the Brotherhood of Painters, Decorators and Paperhangers,[1] which frequently results in men, who otherwise should be employed, standing around idle while men of foreign birth are taken on. You request my advice.

In reply let me say that undoubtedly work men native born American and naturalized citizens should be given the preference.

> Very truly yours,   Saml Gompers.
> President   American Federation of Labor.

TLpS, reel 235, vol. 247, p. 257, SG Letterbooks, DLC.

1. Brotherhood of PAINTERS, Decorators, and Paperhangers of America.

To Newton Baker

May 22, 1918

Honorable Newton D. Baker,
Secretary of the War Department,
Washington, D.C.
Sir:

Of course it is generally known that the regulations[1] for the selective draft were to be issued soon. I have today been advised that they are to be issued tomorrow, May 23rd.

In regard to the subject matter of idle persons, I have had several conferences with Col. Wigmore,[2] Col. Johnson,[3] Dr. E. Stagg Whitin[4] and others, and I have urged that some cognizance should be taken and regulations made affecting those who may be unemployed by reason of disputes with employers.

My information is that a conclusion has been reached omitting such proviso in the selective draft regulations, and the fact perturbs me considerably for I am sure that the issuance of such regulations without the proviso I have indicated will arouse considerable resentment and protest.

Of course I know how busily engaged you are with the tremendous important duties devolving upon you and the problems you have to meet. I tried to get into telephonic communication with your office several times today and was advised that it was utterly impossible to break in upon your time. It was my intention to as briefly as possible present this matter to your attention in time before the regulations were issued.

However I take this opportunity of presenting this matter to you in this form, and trust that it may receive your early and favorable consideration and action.[5]

> Very respectfully yours,   (Signed) Samuel Gompers.
> President,   American Federation of Labor.

TLtpSr, reel 235, vol. 247, p. 471, SG Letterbooks, DLC.

1. On May 23, 1918, Provost Marshal General Enoch Crowder issued a directive, known as the "Work or Fight" order, which required all men of draft age either to engage in some useful or essential occupation or serve in the military.

2. John Henry Wigmore (1863–1943), dean of the law school at Northwestern University from 1901 to 1929, served on the judge advocate general's staff during World War I, rising to the rank of colonel.

3. Hugh Samuel Johnson (1882–1942) served in the army from 1903 to 1919. In 1917, while deputy provost marshal general, he wrote significant portions of the Selective Service Act, and he was subsequently in charge of its implementation. In 1918 he was promoted to the rank of brigadier general and served as chief of the army's Bureau of Purchase and Storage and then as assistant director of the army's Purchase, Storage, and Traffic Division. He was also a member of the War Industries Board.

4. Ernest Stagg Whitin (1881–1946), chairman of the executive council of the National Committee on Prisons and Prison Labor (1908–46), served as a member of the Prison Labor and Waste Reclamation Section of the War Industries Board during World War I.

5. On May 25, 1918, Secretary of War Newton Baker issued a statement explaining that Crowder's order was not intended to affect labor controversies and maintaining that "unemployment by reason of strikes will not . . . cancel either exemption or deferred classification" ("Denies Draft Order Is Aimed at Labor," *New York Times*, May 26, 1918).

A Statement by Samuel Gompers

May 22, 1918.

The accompanying sketch of the undersigned was made by Enrico Caruso[1] in Mr. Caruso's dressing room of the Metropolitan Opera House in New York City one evening in April, 1914. I had met Señor Caruso several times and a mutual, friendly relation sprang up between us. He often invited me to his dressing room and from the wings I heard his interpretations of the great operatic arias.

He asked my permission to make a sketch which I readily gave and he took his pencil and drew on an ordinary piece of paper a few lines at the time in between the singing of his great parts. When it was completed, he asked me to come often and sometime when he could give his whole attention to drawing a better sketch of me. However, I valued the sketch just as it was and although I have met him several times since, the subject has never been broached.

I have been requested to donate the sketch so that someone who might be interested to purchase it might do so, the proceeds to go in aid of the suffering children of Italy's fighting men. I regret to part with it but I contribute it for the good that the proceeds may do.

Saml Gompers.

TDpS, reel 235, vol. 247, p. 376, SG Letterbooks, DLC.

1. The celebrated Italian tenor Enrico Caruso (1873–1921) sang with the Metropolitan Opera in New York City from 1903 through 1920. A noted caricaturist, a collection of his portraits was published in 1922.

To Edward Hurley

Washington, D.C. May 24, 1918.

Mr. Edward N. Hurley,
Chairman, United States Shipping Board,
Washington, D.C.
Dear Sir:

May I add to the protest already lodged with you by the Building Trades Department of the American Federation of Labor? It is the earnest desire of all the workers of this country that contracts shall not be let by the government to those firms and employers who have maintained policies antagonistic to the best interests of workers and who have opposed standards and conditions of work conducive to the development of the best citizenship. As you know, the Building Trades Department protested against letting the contract for the construction of several hundred houses in Camden, New Jersey, to a contractor hostile to the principles of organized labor, but the Department withdrew its protest when given the assurance that future work would be let under different conditions. However, almost immediately afterwards nine hundred and sixty, (960), houses were let in Philadelphia to a firm equally antagonistic.

Representatives of the Building Trades were told by those entrusted with the housing program of the Shipping Board that Admiral Bowles[1] had been given blanket authority to let the work.

For years, organized labor has been contending for principles which experience has demonstrated are essential for the welfare and protection of workers. The standards which organized labor seeks to establish and maintain are not arbitrary measures, but are the result of years of experience which has determined methods and principles most conducive to efficiency and to conservation of labor power. Organized labor is contending for principles which underlie the vitality and virility of the nation. We are not contending for measures that can be discarded without injury to the whole race.

As you know, the Administration has issued regulations affecting construction industries which practically confine building operations to government contracts. The housing program of the Shipping Board will constitute a considerable portion of the building work done in the country. To continue the policy inaugurated by the Shipping Board of giving contracts to those firms who are antagonistic to the principles of organized labor would result in taking advantage of the war emergency to strengthen the opponents of trade unionism. The organized labor movement, including all of the building trades, have declared their desire to cooperate with the government to win the war. It would be indeed regrettable for the Shipping Board or any other government department, to maintain a policy that would obstruct the work of mobilizing labor of this country in support of the administration war program.

Where the government has given the workers opportunity for expression of judgment in letting contracts, construction work has been swift and sure—as in the building of vast cantonments and camps last year.

May I not urge that you take up the matter at your earliest convenience and secure the adoption of policies in harmony with the best interests of the nation and the workers concerned?[2]

Very truly yours,   Saml Gompers.
President,   American Federation of Labor.

TLS, RG 32, Records of the U.S. Shipping Board, DNA.

1. R. Adm. Francis Tiffany Bowles (1858–1927), formerly the president of the Fore River Shipbuilding Co. in Quincy, Mass. (1903–13), served as manager of the division of construction (1917–18) and assistant general manager (1918–19) of the Emergency Fleet Corporation.

2. Edward Hurley replied on June 17, 1918, that he had referred the matter to Howard Coonley, vice-president of the Emergency Fleet Corporation (RG 32, Records of the U.S. Shipping Board, DNA).

From Thomas Blanton[1]

House of Representatives U.S.
Washington, D.C., May 24, 1918.

My dear Mr. Gompers:

I am just in receipt of your favor of the 22d instant,[2] and I am afraid that I am losing a life time faith in the cause of organized labor. When I came to Washington at the convening of the sixty-fifth Congress, organized labor had no better friend anywhere, and I had been its friend and active supporter for twenty years, but the unreasonable and baseless fight it is now making against the Borland[3] Amendment[4] has thoroughly disgusted me.

One of the planks in the platform of organized labor has been, and still is, having an eight-hour work day. There is but one thing required in the Borland Amendment, and that is to make Government clerks work eight hours a day. Every member of Congress who has given the matter any investigation at all knows conclusively that there are several thousand clerks here in Washington now who are working only seven hours for the Government, and they further know that of the 240,000 Government employes, there are quite a number who are absolutely inefficient, who are time killers and clock watchers; and every time Congress makes an attempt to weed out these inefficients, and to grant increases in salary only to the deserving, organized labor rushes to the rescue and demands increases for all alike.

I represent fifty-eight counties in Texas, representing a territory of five hundred sixty-six miles east and west, and four hundred miles north and south, and there is not a single man in my district who works less than eight hours a day, and it is absolutely ridiculous for any man to try to uphold an organization that insists upon letting Government employes during this war crisis continue to work only seven hours a day. It isn't fair to the members of organized labor who are working eight hours a day. And I won't be honest with you if I do not tell you that I believe that Congress will disgrace itself if it refuses to pass this Borland Amendment, thereby still permitting thousands of Government clerks to work only seven hours a day.

This is not a question of paying employes for overtime, because the overtime question is not involved here. It is simply and solely a question of requiring employes who now work seven hours to work eight hours.

I sincerely hope that you will withdraw your opposition to this legislation.[5]

Very sincerely yours,   (Signed) Thomas L. Blanton.

TLtcSr, AFL Microfilm National and International Union File, National Federation of Federal Employees Records, reel 45, frame 2367, *AFL Records.* Typed notation: *"Copy."*

1. Thomas Lindsay Blanton (1872–1957) served as a Democratic congressman from Texas (1917–29, 1930–37).

2. SG's circular letter of May 22, 1918, evidently sent to the members of the House of Representatives, urged either the defeat of the Borland amendment (see n. 4, below) or that additional legislation provide for a basic eight-hour workday and payment of time-and-a-half for overtime (AFL Microfilm Convention File, reel 29, frame 1469, *AFL Records*).

3. William Patterson Borland (1867–1919) was a Democratic congressman from Missouri (1909–19).

4. Borland unsuccessfully attempted to add an amendment to various appropriation bills in 1916, 1917, and 1918 to increase the minimum workday of federal employees from seven hours to eight. He finally succeeded in having his amendment added to H.R. 10,358 (65th Cong., 2d sess.), an appropriation bill for the fiscal year ending June 30, 1919, which was approved by the House and the Senate in June 1918. President Woodrow Wilson vetoed the measure on July 1, and the House sustained the veto.

5. See "To Thomas Blanton," June 4, 1918, below.

To Leonard Hatch[1]

May 27, 1918.

Mr. L. W. Hatch,
Chief Statistician, State of New York Dept. of Labor,
Office of State Industrial Commission,
Capitol, Albany, N.Y.
Dear Sir:

Your letter and copy of the plan of shop organization for the promotion of safety and sanitation proposed by the Industrial Commission received. The fundamental principle upon which the plan is based is admirable. Safety and sanitation ought to be dealt with in a constructive preventive manner as a supplement to our compensation legislation. Indeed, it would be wiser if preventive policies preceded remedial.

I have not time to examine in detail the plan you submit but there is one suggestion I would like to offer for consideration. In suggesting composition of workmen's committees the wording is such as to create the impression that the workers have not an inherent right to voice and representation in matters which vitally concern them. The day is past when the viewpoint and the wishes of workers can be debarred from a part in management. The plan reads, "the management may allow wage earners of each department or occupation to select their representatives." This wording is based upon the hypothesis that the management is granting a concession to wage earners. Quite the opposite is true. Wage earners have a right to select their own representatives. While I recognize that for practical purposes the Industrial Commission may deem it expedient to urge shop committees even though not selected along democratic lines, yet I think that the alternative suggestion of the Commission ought to contain no intimation that democracy in industry comes as a favor of the management. A slight change in wording making the suggestion read, "the wage earners of each department or occupation should select their representatives," would inject a very different tone.[2]

I am glad that the Industrial Commission has taken up this work in such a practical way. It cannot help but be beneficial.

Very truly yours,   Saml Gompers.

President,   American Federat[ion of Labor]

TLpS, reel 235, vol. 247, p. 714, SG Letterbooks, DLC.

1. Leonard Williams Hatch (1869–1958) served as a statistician with the New York State Department of Labor (DOL) from 1897 to 1920 (from 1907, chief statistician).

2. The New York State DOL's Bureau of Statistics and Information subsequently revised the wording of the document in accordance with SG's suggestion.

To Thomas Blanton

June 4, 1918.

Hon. Thomas L. Blanton,
House Office Bldg., Washington, D.C.
Dear Sir:

Your communication of May 24th[1] in answer to mine relative to the Borland Amendment, is hereby acknowledged.

While I have no desire to enter into a personal controversy over the Borland Amendment, yet the context of your letter indicates that either you have not carefully read my communication or that you have failed to grasp the meaning contained therein. You have fallen into an error in discussing the eight hour day with reference to the Federal employes.

If the Borland Amendment should prevail, it will not be an eight hour day any more than the present law is a seven hour day. Existing law requires that Federal employes shall work seven hours per day, with the express provision that the heads of departments may require overtime *ad libitum* without any extra compensation for extra hours of service performed. That is not a seven hour day.

If the Borland Amendment prevails, the law will require Federal employes to work a minimum of eight hours per day, with the same express provision that department heads can require any number of hours in excess of eight without any extra compensation for overtime. This is not an eight hour day. When we want an eight hour day, it ought to be an eight hour day in fact, not in fiction.

On the other hand, the Federal employes are now being employed in excess of seven hours a day and some of them in excess of eight hours per day, yet there has been no complaint upon their part in working this extra time, even though they are receiving no extra compensation therefor.

Your attention is called to this fact; that no head of any department of the Government, nor the President, nor the Council of National Defense, nor any other Government body having to deal with this question has asked or approved the Borland Amendment or given it any support whatsoever. As shown above, the department heads are now authorized by law to require the employes to work any number of hours *ad libitum*. What, after all, is the motive of the supporters of the Borland Amendment? Are they out of harmony with the President, the Secretary of the Department of State, the Secretary of the Department of Treasury, the Secretary of the Department of War, the Attorney General, the Postmaster General, the Secretary of the Department of the Navy, the Secretary of the Department of the Interior, the Secretary of the Department of Agriculture, the Secretary of the Department of Commerce, and the Secretary of the Department of Labor?

If those who support the Borland Amendment feel that the officials mentioned above are not performing the service to our Government that is demanded of them, then it occurs to me that charges out to be made direct; for, under the law, as I have already pointed out, they have the power within their hands to compel these employes to work any number of hours, as well as require them to work on Sundays and holidays.

You say that, "When I came to Washington at the convening of the sixty-fifth Congress, organized labor had no better friend anywhere, and I had been its friend and active supporter for twenty years, but the unreasonable and baseless fight it is now making against the Borland Amendment has thoroughly disgusted me."

Of course, no one can question your right to take any position you desire and to criticize as severely as you care any action taken by the labor movement, but when you state that we are making a baseless fight, you are wide of the mark. While you apparently desire to have your letter construed that you are a champion of the eight hour day, yet the positive declaration of that policy is conspicuous by its absence in your letter. You have not stated that you are in favor of an eight hour day and I take it that your letter means just what it says, that you are perfectly willing that the Government shall establish by law a minimum eight hour day and with the provision added thereto that there shall be no limit to the number of hours worked.

Your attention is also called to the fact that immediately after the United States declared war, there arose a wild cry from employers throughout the country that all labor laws be suspended and that everything for which Labor had fought in the last fifty years be thrown in the scrap heap. This became so insistent that the Council of National Defense on two occasions issued a statement in which it advised that no change of the standards of labor be made until a thorough investigation had been made and the Council of National Defense approved the requested changes. Up to this time there has been no investigation made by the Council of National Defense because it has not been asked to make that investigation, and it has made no recommendations changing any of the standards except where the present law has lodged discretionary power in the hands of the officials of our Government.

At the time when it was being insistently demanded that the hours of labor be lengthened despite the law, I had the honor to address a communication[2] to the Congress of the United States pointing out that the present Federal eight hour law contained a provision whereby the eight hour law could be waived in cases of great emergency by the President of the United States. On March 4, 1917, the Naval Appropriation Law was approved, and a provision in that law specifically states that the eight hour day should prevail upon work covered by contracts with the United States Government, and further that all hours worked in excess of eight shall be paid for at not less than time and one-half. The eight hour law has been waived in a number of instances by the President of the United States and all these waivers have been specifically based upon the provision incorporated in the Naval Appropriation Law just quoted.

As you have occupied the position of Judge of the 42d Judicial District of Texas, you must be aware of the fact that any law without a penalty attached is incapable of enforcement. With the Borland Amendment adopted without the usual penalty, the eight hour day cannot be enforced and will not be even a basic eight hour day any more than the present law is a real seven hour day.

You are quite right when you say that "one of the planks of the platform of organized labor has been and still is having an eight hour workday," but you would not want to interpret that demand as a minimum working time for each day. It is intended to be and practiced as a maximum workday, only in case of extraordinary emergency to be departed from, and then the overtime to be paid for at least time and one-half.

Further on you say that "there are quite a number (of employes) who are absolutely inefficient and who are time killers and clock watchers." Of course you know how serious a charge is the one you have made, and if true, the heads of the departments in which such inefficients, time killers, and clock watchers, are employed, are subject to grave charges. It is quite true that when the Government employs workers for the performance of Government service, they ought to be paid a living minimum wage, a wage upon which they can live and support themselves and their dependents upon a standard of life consistent with American manhood and womanhood.

More than likely, after you have read the above, you will find that your position upon the Borland Amendment is not quite so justified as you have expressed yourself in your communication to me of the 24th ultimo. At least I hope so, and in the light of that fact you will support the position which the organized labor movement has taken and which the United States Senate represents upon this measure.[3]

I regret that owing to pressing important duties, it has been impossible for me to reply to your letter at an earlier date.

Very respectfully yours,   Saml Gompers
President,   American F[ederation of Labor]

TLpS, reel 235, vol. 247, pp. 818–21, SG Letterbooks, DLC.

1. "From Thomas Blanton," May 24, 1918, above.

2. See "To the Executive Council of the AFL," Feb. 10, 1917, nn. 4 and 5, above.

3. Blanton replied on June 6, 1918, that he favored a fixed rather than a minimum eight-hour day for federal employees, with additional compensation for overtime (AFL Microfilm National and International Union File, National Federation of Federal Employees Records, reel 45, frame 2366, *AFL Records*).

From J. E. Harrison et al.

International Longshoremen's Association.
City of New Orleans, La., June 4, 1918.

Dear Sir:—

We, the undersigned members of Local 979 International Shipworkers Union engaged in boiler and vessel scaling and repairing respectfully represent to you the following facts: The grievance committee of the above named union has been blacklisted by the metal trade association of this city, the president of which is Mr. Tod[1] residing at 4007 Dumaine St., N.O. La., who says that if we get a letter from Mr. Gompers stating that we are affiliated with the A.F. of L., they will recognize our charter, otherwise, they will do nothing.

We have been engaged in this line of work since 1903 and experienced no trouble until a union was formed for the expressed purpose, it seems of freezing us out on account of race. We applied to them for membership and were refused, we then applied to Mr. T. P. Woodland,[2]

Vice-President of the I.L.A. and organizer and we unionized accordingly. The other unions refused to work with us and the metal trades
association supported them. We have no trouble with the bosses and
can work but everytime we get a job, the metal trades threaten to
walk off the job because they claim that we are not affiliated with the
American Federation of Labor. Our charter was taken through the
I.L.A. because the I.L.A. has granted charters for this class of work to
unions in several cities and it was our opinion that they had a perfect
right to do so.

We are asking, now, for the assistance of the A.F. of L. to help us out
and straighten the matter for us. Notify us of our status and advise us
if we are right, for we have been idle since February.

The charter we hold is properly signed by Mr. T. V. O'Connor and Mr.
J. J. Joyce,[3] and our local is affiliated with the Central Trades Union of
the A.F. of L. United Labor league and in order to justify ourselves we
have tried every fair and honorable means to get this matter straightened.

We have the honor, now, to appeal to you for a ruling as to our right
to work and enjoy the benefits of organized labor. Begging a prompt
reply and favorable consideration,[4] we are,

                          Respectfully,   (Signed) J. E. Harrison
                                                    Jos. Butler,
                                           Geo. Buffurton
                                             Allen Reed,
                                             A Belliare[5]

TLtpSr, reel 235, vol. 247, pp. 987–88, SG Letterbooks, DLC. Typed notation:
"Copy." Enclosed in SG to T. V. O'Connor, June 13, 1918, ibid., p. 986.

1. Wilmer L. Todd, a New Orleans machinist.

2. Thomas P. Woodland, a New Orleans screwman and a member of International
Longshoremen's Association 237 of New Orleans, served as a vice-president of the
international union from 1911 until his death, around 1924.

3. John Joseph Joyce was secretary-treasurer of the Longshoremen from 1906 until
his death, around 1937.

4. On June 13, 1918, SG sent a copy of Harrison's letter to Longshoremen's president T. V. O'Connor, and he informed Harrison of his action the same day, noting
that within the AFL "each organization has complete autonomy over its membership"
(reel 235, vol. 247, pp. 985–86, SG Letterbooks, DLC; quotation at p. 985).

5. Arthur Bellaire.

From Eugene Kinckle Jones and Fred Moore

New York, June 6th, 1918.

My Dear Mr. Gompers:

We write to present suggestions for further cooperation between our committee and the American Federation of Labor as growing out of our recent conference[1] in Washington:

First, we wish to place before you our understanding of your statement to us at the conclusion of the meeting. We quote you as follows; and will be glad for you to make any changes in the text as will make the statement more nearly conform to the ideas which you have in mind relative to the connections that should be established between white and Negro workingmen:

"We, the American Federation of Labor, welcome Negro workingmen to the ranks of organized labor. We should like to see more of them join us. The interests of workingmen, white and black, are common. Together we must fight unfair wages, unfair hours and bad conditions of labor. At times it is difficult for the national organization to control the actions of local unions in difficulties arising within the trades in any particular community, inasmuch as the National body is made possible by the delegates appointed by the locals; but we can and will use our influence to break down prejudice, on account of race, color or previous condition of servitude, and hope that you will use your influence to show Negro workingmen the advantages of collective bargaining and the value of affiliation with the American Federation of Labor. But few people who are not thoroughly acquainted with the rapid growth of the Federation of Labor know of the large numbers of colored people who are already members of our organization. The unpleasant incidents in connection with efforts of colored men to get recognition in trades controlled by the American Federation of Labor have been aired and the good effects of wholesome and healthy relationship have not been given publicity; and for that reason, a general attitude of suspicion has been developed towards union labor on the part of colored working people; but I hope that out of this conference will spring a more cordial feeling of confidence in each other on the part of men who must work for a living."

We are willing to cooperate with the American Federation of Labor in bringing about the results of the recent conference, and would make the following suggestions and recommendations which, with your approval, we shall proceed to carry out to the best of our ability.

First, we suggest that you prepare a statement, along the lines of the quotation from you given above, and send it to us for approval and then to be given to the Negro press throughout the country as expressing your position on matters connected with the relationship between Negro and white workingmen.

This statement, in our judgment, should contain a clear exposition of the reasons why certain internationals may exclude colored men as they do by constitutional provision and still be affiliated with the A.F. of L. whose declared principles are opposed to such discrimination. This we think necessary because the stated facts above alluded to will be familiar to the leaders among the colored people, particularly to editors and ministers whose cooperation it is essential to secure if the best results are to be obtained.

We would suggest further that you consider the expediency of recommending to such Internationals as still exclude colored men that their constitutions be revised in this respect.

Second, that a qualified colored man to handle men and organize them be selected for employment as an organizer of the American Federation of Labor, his salary and expenses, of course, to be paid by the American Federation of Labor.

Third, that for the present we meet at least once a quarter to check up on the results of our cooperative activities and to plan for further extension of the work, if satisfactorily conducted.

Fourth, that you carry out your agreement to have your Executive Council voice an advanced position in its attitude towards the organization of Negro workingmen and have these sentiments endorsed by your St. Paul convention in June, and this action be given the widest possible publicity throughout the country.

We should be glad to hear from you at your earliest convenience as to the action taken by your Council on these recommendations with such other suggestions or recommendations as may occur to you.[2]

Sincerely yours,   Eugene Kincale Jones,
Fred R. Moore.

For the following committee:

Dr. R. R. Moton, principal of Tuskogee Institute.

Mr. John R. Shillady, secretary of National Association for the Advancement of Colored People.

Mr. Fred R. Moore, editor of New York Age.

Mr. Archibald Grimke, Washington Association for the Advancement of Colored People.

Mr. Emmett J. Scott, special assistant to the Secretary of War.

Mr. Eugene Kincale Jones, executive secretary, National Urban League.

Mr. Thomas Jesse Jones, educational director Phelps Stokes Fund.

Dr. James H. Dillard, president of Jeanes Fund.

Dr. George C. Hall, vice president of the executive board, Chicago Urban League.

(P.S. Please address all communications care of E. K. Jones, 200 Fifth Avenue, Room 1120, New York City, N.Y.).

PLSr, AFL, *Proceedings*, 1918, pp. 198–99.

1. See "Excerpts from the Minutes of a Conference between Committees Representing Black Workers and the AFL," Apr. 22, 1918, above.

2. The 1918 AFL convention referred this letter to the AFL Executive Council, which, at its July 1918 meeting, directed the officers at AFL headquarters to give every assistance in organizing black workers.

Excerpts from News Accounts of the 1918 Convention of the AFL in St. Paul

[June 11, 1918]

Socialists and political theorists in today's session of the American Federation of Labor were told to keep hands off while organized labor is helping the United States to win the war. The report of the federation's mission of conference with labor leaders of Allied counties, when read, proved to be a notable document.

The commission said the Teutonic workingmen have built up their own barriers between themselves and their brothers in labor's ranks elsewhere, and that the only thing that will right matters and restore the workingmen to their rightful status will be the absolute crushing of the Teutonic military power.

The federation meanwhile will not treat with the Teutonic workingmen, the report declared, until the sinister militant power which controls them, has been broken.

POLITICAL PRESSURE CONDEMNED.

"It is unsafe and unsound passively to contemplate the influence exerted upon the trade union movement in the great industrial nations of the world by political leaders whose viewpoint and experience are those of theorists and politicians," the report said, and throughout it emphasized that organized labor, both here and abroad, is capable of taking care of itself.

"While the socialistic groups work with the trade unions politically, they maintain their separate affiliation with the international socialistic organization," the report said.

PRESIDENT'S MESSAGE RECEIVED.

Enthusiasm marked the session, when, in addition to the strong tone of patriotism that was sounded in the mission's report, President Woodrow Wilson sent a message asking new pledges of loyalty.[1] The outburst that followed the reading of the message left no doubt that the federation, already pledged with all its strength to the maintenance of American ideals and their preservation by fighting for them, again will put itself on record before it adjourns.

Following President Wilson's message, came one from the Council of National Defense congratulating the federation on the stand it has taken and expressing hope and confidence that it would reaffirm its principles and continue to make the stand effective.[2]

WILSON PRAISED IN EUROPE.

The report of the mission of the American Federation of Labor sent to Europe described a severe storm and an attempt at torpedoing their vessel. James P. Frey[3] read the report for James Wilson,[4] chairman of the mission, which was in part as follows:—

"During our trip through France and the British Isles, nothing was more often or more forcibly borne in upon us than the high esteem and respect universally felt in those countries for our own president, Woodrow Wilson. It was a source of great gratification to note the position of world leadership which our president occupies. Wherever the mission went, it found the same generous measure of praise and the same high degree of admiration and confidence expressed. In public meetings everywhere mention of President Wilson's name and his war aims always brought forth a spontaneous and prolonged demonstration.["]

LOOK TO AMERICA WITH CONFIDENCE.

"The actions and utterances of President Wilson have immeasurably heartened the people of the countries of our Allies and have inspired them to a lofty and abiding faith in the triumph of democracy. It is to President Wilson that millions of our brothers across the sea look with confidence as the great leader who will bring the world to peace through victory on the same high plane that so strikingly characterized America's entry into the conflict.["]

WILSON WAR POLICY ACCEPTED.

"In discussion with the various sections of the labor movement abroad, one of the notable features was the unanimity with which all agree in support of the war aims set forth by President Wilson and indorsed by the American Federation of Labor. It is President Wilson's interpretation of the war and his declaration of his purposes that has made it in reality among all people, what Samuel Gompers so graphically termed it, 'A crusade for human freedom.'"

AMERICAN VIEW PREVAILS.

The report then took up the divergence of opinion among British and French labor circles as to the wisdom of holding an international labor conference at which representatives of the Central Powers should be present. Throughout its visit abroad, the American mission stood out firmly against allowing German delegates to be present at any such conference, a view to which the Allied representatives finally came around.

"The mission," said the report, "justifies in assuming that the leaders of Great Britain are far from unanimous as to the advisability of holding an international conference. Many of those who believed in the holding of an international conference were vigorous in their belief that the German military machine must be defeated, their opinion being that such a conference would assist in bringing about such results through its influence upon the workers in Germany and Austria."

"HANDS OFF" TO POLITICS.

After outlining the group, socialistically and otherwise, which forms labor parties in England and France, the report said:

"It is unsafe and unsound passively to contemplate the influences exerted upon the trade union movement in the great industrial nations of the world by political leaders whose viewpoint and experiences are those of the theorists and politicians. The policies and program of the workers must be formulated by the workers themselves, acting through their industrial organizations, if their best interests are to be conserved."

NO "PACIFIST VIRUS" IN EUROPE.

Of the attitude of the workers toward the war, the report says:

"Your mission was given exceptional opportunities to observe the attitude of both organized and unorganized labor. All of the chief industrial centers of England and Scotland were visited. A careful and extended observation leads us to report that the working people in the mass have not been infected with the pacifist virus and that there is among them no wish to falter in the course that must be run to win the war.

"Shortage of food in France and the British Isles impressed us as being of prime interest to Americans. Rationing is universal. In both countries the civilian population willingly sacrifices the food of normal times in order that the men at the front may be supplied.["]

War Weary but Determined.

"The scale of war preparations as we saw them indicate no fixed stopping point, but a determination to plan for any eventuality and never to count the war won or the ground safe until the fact of victory itself has been achieved."

The mission found a certain war weariness among the people of France and England. "But," said the report, "despite the burden, the will to win remains unshaken. The deep meaning of the war is graven into the hearts of the people in all walks of life, and there is an unmistakable and profound conviction that, to quote an American, 'the only way out of this war is through it.' Beneath the care and weariness that is all but hidden, there is a serenity that betokens confidence. It is an unshakable confidence."

Closer Touch Proposed.

An important recommendation made toward the end of the report was as follows:

"While there exists free intercommunications between the trade union movement of the allied nations, it has in our opinion, proved insufficient to keep in as close touch with what is transpiring and developing abroad as was essential to our mutual welfare. We therefore recommend that, during the period of the war, the American Federation of Labor maintain one or more direct representatives in Europe."

"We left for home with the definite knowledge that our declarations had penetrated into Germany and Austria with sufficient depth to give to large sections of those countries a knowledge of the spirit and determination of the American trade union locals.

"It is fair to assume, in a light of this knowledge, that at last the German and Austrian leaders of the misguided population know that in America the workers understand that the barrier between us and them has been built by their own actions and must be destroyed by the Teutonic people themselves or by the weight of our armed forces before there can be any discussion with them relating to peace or international fellowship."

. . .

Minneapolis Journal, June 11, 1918.

1. AFL, *Proceedings,* 1918, p. 134.
2. AFL, *Proceedings,* 1918, pp. 134–35.

3. Actually John Frey, who represented the International Molders' Union of North America.

4. James Wilson represented the Pattern Makers' League of North America.

[June 12, 1918]

. . .

Miss Malinda Scott[1] of New York of the United Hat Trimmers, was the first signer of the resolution filed with the federation secretary at today's session, seeking representation on the executive council.[2] Miss Alice Scott[3] and Miss Minnie Tritelbaum[4] of the same organization also signed, as did Mrs. Sara Conboy,[5] New York, of the textile workers, Miss Rose Yeats,[6] Worcester, Mass., of the railway mail clerks, Miss Alice Nestor,[7] Chicago, of the glove workers, and Miss Anne Weinstock,[8] Boston, of the glove workers.

The demand came in the form of a resolution that the bylaws be changed to provide for an executive committee of 10, instead of 8, which would mean the addition of two vice presidents. Not less than two of the 10 members shall be women, the resolution reads.

WOMEN THE "SECOND LINE."

In a written statement the women stated their position.

"Women are now a vital factor in industry, especially in war industry," the statement read. "With millions of the men of the nation going to France, it is possible that women soon will be the largest factor in the industrial army—the second line of defense.

"At present the women's point of view is not represented on the executive council of the American Federation of Labor, which never has had a woman member. Justice and foresight demand that the women now be recognized and given position and the vote in the councils of the federation."

Miss Malinda Scott, speaking of the increasing number of women who are entering industrial life and of the necessities that call them in, said care must be taken lest the compensatory scales be affected adversely to labor. It is essential, she said, that women be safeguarded against possible exploitation of their work in a manner to reduce the wage scale. Women who do men's work and do it as well as men do, should not receive less than the men receive, she said.

. . .

Minneapolis Journal, June 12, 1918.

1. Melinda Scott represented the National Women's Trade Union League at the convention.

2. Resolution 132, introduced on June 13, 1918, would have amended the AFL con-

stitution to increase the number of AFL vice-presidents from eight to ten, of which at least two would be women. The convention did not adopt the resolution.

3. Alice Scott of Irvington, N.J., represented AFL 15,850 (United Felt, Straw, Panama, and Velvet Hat Trimmers' and Operators' Union) of Newark, N.J. She served as that union's secretary from 1917, when it was chartered by the AFL, until at least 1920.

4. Minnie Teitelbaum (variously Teitlebaum) of Brooklyn represented AFL 14,569 (United Felt, Panama, and Straw Hat Trimmers' and Operators' Union of Greater New York). She served as the union's secretary from about 1915 until at least 1923.

5. Sara Agnes McLaughlin CONBOY was secretary-treasurer of the United Textile Workers of America (1915–28) and represented her union at the convention. During World War I she served on the subcommittee on Women in Industry of the Committee on Labor of the Advisory Commission of the Council of National Defense.

6. Rose A. Yates, a Worcester, Mass., railway freight house clerk, represented the Brotherhood of RAILWAY Clerks. By 1919 she had married James Forrester, the union's president, and in the early 1920s she was president of the Washington, D.C., branch of the National Women's Trade Union League.

7. Actually Agnes Nestor.

8. Anna Weinstock of Boston represented AFL 15,200 (Neckware Workers' Union) of Boston. She served as the union's secretary from at least 1918 through 1926.

[June 13, 1918][1]

. . .

GOMPERS URGED TO VISIT ITALY.

As a result of the beneficial results obtained by the American labor mission to Great Britain and France, Delegate D. D'Alessandro, president of the International Hod Carriers' Building and Common Laborers' union, submitted to the convention resolutions recommending that President Gompers visit Italy to bring American labor's methods to the Italians, and that our Allies may not lose sight of the cause for which we are struggling.[2]

A plea that Mooney, sentenced to death at San Francisco for alleged participation in the bomb plot which cost many lives, be given a new trial in the interest of justice and humanity,[3] was placed before the convention by Delegates Dan P. McKillop,[4] boilermakers' and shipbuilders' and helpers' union, and William B. Foster, Chicago Federation of Labor.

MISCARRIAGE OF JUSTICE SEEN.

The resolution said that the Mooney case is generally accepted among men as an example of miscarriage of justice, and is attracting international attention because such a thing is possible in the country famous as the "land of equality, freedom and justice for all."

The records in the case indicate, the resolutions said, that it was decided on evidence since found to have been perjured, which was so reported by a commission appointed by President Wilson and headed by Secretary of Labor Wilson, which recommended that in the interests of justice a new trial be granted.

Resolutions[5] requesting that women industrial workers, equipped to do the same quality of work as men, be organized in their respective crafts to insure retention of present wage standards and working hours, were submitted by Delegates P. Harry Jennings,[6] of the Massachusetts state branch, and Martin T. Joyce,[7] of the International Brotherhood of Electrical Workers. It was pointed out that unscrupulous employers are taking advantage of war time conditions to lower wages and pay women less wages than they paid men whose places they are taking, believing that many thousands of these women will remain for an extended period in industry.

A request[8] was made yesterday by Delegate J. E. Giles,[9] of the Stenographers', Bookkeepers' and Assistants' union that the federation issue to the union an international charter, in resolution submitted.

Resolutions[10] requesting that the federation go on record as advocating women's suffrage were also submitted.

. . .

SOCIALISM VS. PATRIOTISM.

Socialism and patriotism squared off in battle at the morning session when Frank Duffy,[11] fourth vice president and chairman of the committee on organization, declared he would resign from his committee if B. Schlesinger of New York, representing the Garment Workers' union, did not apologize to the convention.

Apology was demanded because Schlesinger and three other members of his union voted against the adoption of the American Labor Mission's report, on the ground that it designated Socialists as politicians.[12]

"I have a son in the navy,"[13] said Mr. Duffy, "a nephew in the army, and I have five other sons all still under age,[14] but ready to go as soon as they reach their majority.

"As a patriot I cannot and I will not sit in convention with a man like Schlesinger unless he apologizes to this convention."

"It is not necessary for the chair to defend Delegate Schlesinger, nor does the chair propose to do so," said President Gompers, "but I think it is a misunderstanding, which when smoothed out will result in delegates withdrawing their action."

President Gompers then stated the facts in Tuesday's debate, but, still unwilling to sit with Schlesinger as a member of his committee, Mr. Duffy attempted to ask Schlesinger if he would null his vote on the labor report. He was, however, ruled out of order by President Gompers.

Schlesinger was given the floor, and in his statement to the delegates declared he was as much of a patriot as anyone.

Meet without Socialist.

President Gompers here declared the incident closed, but it was not closed, for upon adjournment of the convention until 9:30 A.M. today, the committee on organization met, with Schlesinger absent. Schlesinger's attention was called to the fact that the committee was in session.

"I don't give a damn," he replied. "I won't sit with them."

The committee adjourned, but before adjournment each member declared his and her intention of resigning unless Schlesinger resigned or apologized to the convention.[15]

. . .

Minneapolis Tribune, June 13, 1918.

1. This article summarizes several of the resolutions presented to the convention on June 11, 1918, and the proceedings of June 12.

2. Resolution 130, introduced by Domenico D'Alessandro on June 11, 1918, called on SG to go to Italy. The resolution was adopted on June 20 with the suggestion that SG arrange the visit to coincide with his forthcoming trip to Great Britain and France, which the convention had approved just before turning to consideration of Resolution 130. SG sailed from New York on Aug. 15 or 16 aboard the *R.M.S. Missanabie.* The ship was sunk by a German submarine off the coast of Ireland on her return voyage to the United States. He was accompanied by Edgar Wallace, editor of the journal of the United Mine Workers' of America, Charles Baine, secretary-treasurer of the Boot and Shoe Workers' Union, William Bowen, president of the Bricklayers', Masons', and Plasterers' International Union of America, John Frey, editor of the journal of the International Molders' Union of North America, and Guy Oyster, secretary of the mission. They arrived at Liverpool on Aug. 28. During the course of the trip, SG visited England, Scotland, France, and Italy, attended the meeting of the TUC at Derby and the Inter-Allied Labour and Socialist conference in London, and inspected sectors of the front in Belgium and France as well as in Italy. He sailed for home from Brest on Oct. 21 and arrived back in New York on Nov. 3.

3. On June 19, 1918, the convention adopted a substitute for this measure (Resolution 131) and a similar one (Resolution 82), which had both been introduced on June 11. The substitute expressed the hope that the governor of California would pardon Thomas Mooney and asked President Woodrow Wilson to use any power vested in him that could prevent Mooney's execution.

4. Daniel McKillop, a member of International Brotherhood of Boiler Makers, Iron Ship Builders, and Helpers 104 of Seattle, represented the Boiler Makers at the convention.

5. Three resolutions calling for the organization of women workers who were replacing men because of the war were introduced on June 11, 1918—Resolution 92 by P. Harry Jennings and Martin Joyce, Resolution 98 by James Brock of the Laundry Workers' International Union, and Resolution 9, which the convention adopted on June 13, by A. J. Linck of the Racine (Wis.) Trades and Labor Council.

6. Patrick Harry Jennings, the business agent of the International Brotherhood of

Teamsters, Chauffeurs, Stablemen, and Helpers of America 379 of Boston, represented the Massachusetts State Federation of Labor at the convention.

7. Martin T. JOYCE, a member of International Brotherhood of Electrical Workers 103 of Boston, served as secretary-treasurer of the Massachusetts State Federation of Labor (1911–31). He represented the Electrical Workers at the convention.

8. Resolution 94, introduced on June 11, 1918, proposed that the AFL issue a charter to an international union of office workers. The convention did not adopt the resolution.

9. J. Edwin (or Edward) Giles, a bookkeeper in the AFL offices, represented AFL 11,773 (Stenographers', Typewriters', Bookkeepers', and Assistants' Union) of Washington, D.C.

10. Four resolutions supporting the woman's suffrage amendment (42, 57, 95, and 127) were introduced on June 11, 1918. In lieu of these, the convention on June 14 adopted a substitute, which endorsed H.J. Res. 200 (65th Cong., 2d sess.), introduced by Democratic congressman John Raker of California on Dec. 18, 1917, to amend the Constitution to extend the right of suffrage to women. The House of Representatives approved that measure on Jan. 10, but the Senate rejected it Oct. 1 and again Feb. 10, 1919.

11. Frank Duffy represented the United Brotherhood of Carpenters and Joiners of America at the convention.

12. Benjamin Schlesinger seems to have objected to the section of the American labor mission's report which stated that "In Great Britain and upon the European Continent there exists today among the workers more or less joint industrial and political movements. . . . While these Socialist groups work with the trade unions politically they maintain their separate affiliation with the International Socialist organization. Our European trade union brothers are the best judges of what their political activities should be and what affiliations, political or otherwise, which this should include, but the existing condition tends nevertheless to emphasize the urgent necessity for a purely international trade union federation at which the industrial problems can be given ample consideration entirely apart from any political movements or considerations" (AFL, *Proceedings*, 1918, pp. 141–42).

13. Frank Duffy, Jr.

14. The three who can be identified were Joseph, William, and George Duffy.

15. When Schlesinger made no attempt to meet with the rest of the committee, the other members eventually decided not to resign.

[June 15, 1918][1]

. . .

DEBATE REHABILITATION.

Industrial rehabilitation after the war was the subject of lengthy debate following the committee's report on a resolution[2] providing:

That the A.F. of L. urge on the government the necessity for immediately evolving a program for re-adjustment of industry after the war in order to avoid the chaos, suffering and friction which will otherwise result and in order for the present to encourage enthusiasm and hearty co-operation on the part of the workmen which will naturally result from the knowledge that they will get a square deal and will, therefore, result in increased production; and

Resolved, That we recommend that a commission of five members be appointed, connected with the Department of Labor, on which commission union labor shall predominate, whose duties it shall be to consider and recommend to the President, through the Secretary of Labor, and to execute, as directed by him, means whereby the readjustment may be accomplished, and that we particularly recommend that the excess labor provided be used to reduce hours of work without deduction of pay, to provide greater comfort and safety in carrying on the work; that the government and employers recognize seniority rights in employment and assist in restoring temporary employes to their former occupations and that public works be undertaken and other means be found to provide means of making an honest, comfortable living for these workers and the returning soldiers, if necessary by taking over the industries by the people and operating them for the public welfare.

President Gompers assured the delegates the question is not being neglected, and he told of several conferences in that regard already under way. The committee's recommendation that the question receive the careful consideration of the executive council and, if necessary, be recommended for action by Congress, was adopted.

. . .

St. Paul Pioneer Press, June 15, 1918.

1. This article describes the convention proceedings of June 14, 1918.

2. Resolution 62, introduced on June 11, 1918, by delegates James Taylor of the International Association of Machinists and Daniel McKillop of the International Brotherhood of Boiler Makers, Iron Ship Builders, and Helpers of America. On June 14 the convention adopted a substitute resolution instructing the AFL Executive Council to appoint a committee to investigate the problem and recommend appropriate legislation to Congress. The committee reported to the Council on Dec. 28, 1918, and its report was subsequently published as a pamphlet entitled *American Federation of Labor Reconstruction Program* ([Washington, D.C., 1919]).

[June 16, 1918]

PEACE BY VICTORY, NO NEGOTIATIONS, IS "PEACE TERMS" SLOGAN OF LABOR

Peace by victory and no negotiations with labor representatives of Germany and Austria while war continues, will be the gist of the report on "peace terms" by the American Federation of Labor's committee on international labor relations. George W. Perkins,[1] chairman of the committee, made this statement yesterday and will so report early next week.[2]

. . .

The committee will also report that the federation still stands firm on the declaration adopted at Buffalo, in the following terms:

A league of the free peoples of the world in a common covenant for genuine and practical co-operation to secure justice and therefore peace in relations between nations.

No political or economic restrictions meant to benefit some nations and to cripple or embarrass others.

No indemnities or reprisals based upon vindictive purposes or deliberate desire to injure, but to right manifest wrongs.

Recognition of the rights of small nations and of the principle, "No people must be forced under sovereignty under which it does not wish to live."

No territorial changes or adjustment of power except in furtherance of the welfare of the peoples affected and in furtherance of world peace.

No article or commodity shall be shipped or delivered in international commerce in the production of which children under the age of 16 have been employed or permitted to work.

It shall be declared that the basic workday in industry and commerce shall not exceed eight hours.

Involuntary servitude shall not exist except as a punishment for crime whereof the party shall have been duly convicted.

Interest was added to the consideration of peace terms yesterday by word from Washington, that Secretary of Labor William B. Wilson and members in Washington of the American Federation of Labor heartily favored sending Samuel Gompers to Europe on a mission for the further cementing of international labor relations. A resolution asking that Mr. Gompers be sent to Italy on such a mission is before the present convention.

Asked yesterday if he would go to Italy on such a mission if the convention so voted, the labor chief said: "I would go to Italy or anywhere else that the American Federation of Labor or the government of the United States might consider desirable during the war. And I would do anything else that might in any way advance the cause of democracy and freedom and militate for victory in this struggle."

. . .

Minneapolis Journal, June 16, 1918.

1. George Perkins represented the Cigar Makers' International Union of America at the convention.

2. The Executive Council's report on "Peace Terms" reiterated the declarations of previous AFL conventions and endorsed the peace program outlined by President Woodrow Wilson in his address to Congress of Jan. 8, 1918. The convention's Committee on International Relations endorsed the report and added the declaration that

"no just nor lasting peace can be obtained by negotiations until victory is achieved" (AFL, *Proceedings*, 1918, p. 334). The convention adopted the committee's report unanimously.

[June 18, 1918]

A.F.L. HAS FIRST REAL DEADLOCK

The first deadlock, and the first real battle for votes on the convention floor of the American Federation of Labor, took place yesterday, starting at the morning session, and coming to a climax late in the second session of the day.

Before the fight could be settled amicably, roll had to be called, the vote resulting in a verdict of 17,735 against 7,675 votes in favor of accepting a committee report, which declined to "remove all barriers to the fullest freedom of movement (consistent with the best interests of labor) from one craft union to another."[1]

REFUSES CLAIMS.

The fight started when the committee on organization, declining to interfere with the autonomy rights of international unions, refused to recognize claims that during the stress of war, members of certain craft unions, joining other craft unions for the purpose of helping out in war production, thereby forfeited their claims to benefits accruing through membership in the unions which they deserted.

Charges were made that when boilermakers left their trade to assist in the shipbuilding industry, they were forced by the shipbuilders' union to cancel their membership in their own union, thus relinquishing all claim to any benefits which would have belonged to them had they not, through patriotism, gone to assist in the making of ships.

ROLL CALL DEMANDED.

Failing to get at the wishes of the delegates through an aye and nay vote, counting of hands was resorted to, but this, being close, was contested. It was then a roll call was demanded, the majority favoring the committee's refusal to interfere with the jurisdictional rights of international unions.

. . .

St. Paul Pioneer Press, June 18, 1918.

1. Resolution 109, introduced by James Duncan of the Seattle Central Labor Council on June 11, 1918, called on the AFL Executive Council, national and international affiliates, state federations, and city central bodies to undertake an intensive organizing campaign and urged national and international affiliates to remove barriers restricting the freedom of workers to move from one union to another. The Committee on

Organization endorsed the first proposal but recommended rejecting the second on the grounds that it interfered with the autonomy of affiliated unions. The convention adopted the committee's report by a vote of 17,736 to 7,675, with 1,207 not voting (AFL, *Proceedings*, 1918, pp. 268–69).

[June 21, 1918]

GOMPERS AGAIN IS MADE PRESIDENT OF LABOR FEDERATION

Delegates who attended the 38th annual convention of the American Federation of Labor were on their way home today, following adjournment of the convention late yesterday. Atlantic City was chosen as the next convention city.[1] As forecast by The Journal, Samuel Gompers, president, Frank Morrison, secretary, and Daniel Tobin, treasurer, were re-elected without opposition.

THREE CORNERED FIGHT.

In a brisk three cornered fight, Jacob Fischer,[2] Indianapolis, delegate from the barbers union, won the vice presidency left vacant by the retirement after 23 years of service of James O'Connell, Washington. James Wilson of Cincinnati, representative of the Patternmakers, and William H. Johnston, Washington, International Association of Machinists, were his chief opponents. Johnston was beaten on the first ballot. He represented the socialist element in the convention. Thomas A. Rickert, Chicago, won the vice presidency formerly held by H. B. Perham.[3]

. . .

Other re-elections were: First vice-president, James Duncan of Quincy, Mass.; second, Joseph F. Valentine,[4] Cincinnati; third, John R. Alpine, Chicago; fourth, Frank Duffy, Indianapolis; fifth, William Green, Indianapolis; sixth, William D. Mahon, Detroit.

. . .

Minneapolis Journal, June 21, 1918.

1. The 1919 AFL convention met in Atlantic City, June 9–23.

2. Jacob FISCHER served as secretary-treasurer of the Journeyman BARBERS' International Union of America from 1904 to 1929 and as an AFL vice-president from 1918 to 1929.

3. Henry Burdon PERHAM served as president of the Order of Railroad Telegraphers of North America (1901–19) and as an AFL vice-president (1909–18). He represented the Telegraphers at the convention.

4. Joseph F. VALENTINE represented the International Molders' Union of North America at the convention. He served as president of the union (1903–24), as an AFL vice-president (1906–24), and as vice-president of the AFL Metal Trades Department (1908–24).

To Robert Bass[1]

St. Paul, Minn., June 15, 1918

Hon. Robert P. Bass,
Labor Adjustment Board, U.S. Shipping Board,
Washington, D.C.

Your telegram to J. A. Madsen addressed to him at Seattle, was repeated to him by telegraph this morning and he submitted it to me. I cannot refrain but interpose a protest against the suggested action of the National Adjustment Commission to reopen the case which had been adjusted, particularly upon the point which formed the preliminary cause of the dispute. The award rendered provided that the employment halls created by employers associations should be abolished July 1, 1918, and now, when we are within a few days of the time when the provisions of the agreement are to be carried into effect, the whole question is proposed to be reopened. How can we expect large bodies of workmen to give whole hearted support to our program when comparatively small numbers on the other side refuse to comply with the award rendered by the official representatives of our government?[2]

Samuel Gompers

TWcSr, Files of the Office of the President, General Correspondence, reel 96, frame 142, *AFL Records*.

1. Robert Perkins Bass (1873–1960) chaired both the U.S. Shipping Board's Marine and Dock Industrial Relations Board, which had oversight over labor problems concerning seamen, dock, and harbor craft workers, and the National Adjustment Commission, an independent agency associated with the Shipping Board, which had oversight over the wages, hours, and working conditions of longshoremen. A former governor of New Hampshire (1911–13) and member of the subcommittee on Mediation and Conciliation of the Committee on Labor of the Advisory Commission of the Council of National Defense, he also served as a member of the War Labor Policies Board.

2. On Dec. 18, 1917, the National Adjustment Commission ruled that hiring halls operated by employers in the Puget Sound region were to be abolished by July 1, 1918. The commission apparently then agreed to hold additional hearings on the matter, but Bass wrote SG on June 18 that these had been called off (Files of the Office of the President, General Correspondence, reel 96, frame 163, *AFL Records*). The commission subsequently directed that the halls were to be turned over to the U.S. Employment Service.

To Robert McCabe

St. Paul, Minn., June 17, 1918

Mr. R. C. McCabe,
Managing Editor Boston America[n],
Boston, Massachusetts.

As it becomes necessary for men to leave industry and commerce to serve at the front, production essential for the military and civilian necessities must be maintained by women and such men as can be released from dispensable activities. Women coming into industry must receive the equal pay with men who have been displaced or who are doing the same work. These standards would constitute safeguards against unnecessary supplanting men by women or their exploitation. Those who come into war work should understand their responsibility for maintaining the standards of civilian life which rest upon economic standards. We must not fail in our patriotic duty of maintaining the rights and institutions of freedom which constitute our Republic. Women must give service to win this war. That service must be given as members of society responsible for better conditions and higher standards for all, not as substitutes for men but as free women mindful of their rights and duties, fighting a war for democracy and human justice shoulder to shoulder with men.

Samuel Gompers.

TWpSr, reel 236, vol. 248, p. 38 verso, SG Letterbooks, DLC.

William Z. Foster to John Fitzpatrick

Headquarters
Stockyards Labor Council
Chicago, Ill. June 22nd 1918

Dear Friend Fitzpatrick;—

I just got back to Chicago today all tired out from my strenuous work at the convention. For days there I fairly sweat blood trying to get something done. I believe I lost ten pounds in weight. I never want another job as hard. I am a damned poor lobbyist.

Yet I think I had fairly good success. The response I got far exceeded my expectations. I honestly believe a big movement has been set on foot to organize the steel industry. The resolution[1] went flying thru the committee without opposition. Then it came to the convention and went thru there like greased lightning. I didnt even speak on it, nor did any one else. I figured that you would be there in a day or two and that I could stand in the background and let you handle the heavy weights and get them interested. Imagine my disappointment and dismay when word came to me that you were not coming to St. Paul. I felt almost like giving up in depair.

However I decided I wouldnt be licked without a struggle and finally had a conference[2] called by Gompers. But it was called at an almost fatally inoportune time, during the noon recess of the convention. All I had time to do was to take the names of thos present and make arrangements for a further conference[3] the following night. At this meeting, which was well attended by a representative and influential gathering I managed to have Sam Gompers act as Chairman. He gave the steel move his official blessing in this meeting, saying that the A.F. of L. was prepared to go down the line on the proposition. Then after a long discussion, we did about the only thing we could do, appointed a committee of ten to submit a program to a meeting[4] to take place the next night. This committee recommended that, among other things, a conference[5] be called within thirty days in Chicago of international presidents, or their duly authorized representatives equipped with full power to act, for the purpose of launching the campaign. Morrison was at the meeting when this was adopted. He seemed enthusiastically in favor of the whole movement and assured all present that he would do his utmost to make it a success.

At our conferences there were 21 internationals (from the metal mines right thru to the finished product), 7 state federations and 14 city central bodies represented. Most of the delegates present were men prominent in their organizations, fully a dozen being general presidents. The sentiment was fine. It was absolutely unnecessary to make any argument as to the need and opportunity of organizing the steel mills at this time. Everybody seemed to realize that now is the appointed time to do this big job. Nor was it neccasry to urge upon them that the best way to do it was by all the organizations to make a common fight of it. Everybody seemed to realize that too. Past experience in the steel industry had made it plain as day that it is folly for any one organization, however powerful, to make a fight alone. The only question was how best to jump into the work. I was most delighted and surprised at the businesslike and determined spirit shown.

Without a doubt a big movement has been started. I am sure the A.F. of L. will make a big effort, as will at least a dozen powerful international unions out of those represented at the conferences. Now all that is needed to bring the organization of the steel mills strictly within the realm of probability is that the right man be put in charge of the work of organization. Frankly I dont know of another man in the country qualified to do this, with any reasonable hope of success, outside of yourself. It seems to me that you are not only confronted with the most splendid opportunity ever presented to any labor man in this matter but also with the most solemn duty. If this campaign goes over it will be the greatest boon ever won by working men any-where. It will put labor over the top once and for all and forever out of danger of serious defeat. If it is lost, as it can most easily be by some incompetent getting at the head of it (which may well happen if you decline to take charge of it) it will by the same token be the most serious calamity that has ever overtaken the American working class. With whatever earnestness I may possess I would urge you to take this matter up seriously with Sam Gompers and Frank Morrisson and see that the movement takes the right course. I have done all in my power to make the thing a success. But now I have reached about the limit of my resources. I need help. When that conference convenes, if the matter is left to me to put over I feel reasonably certain that the whole thing will fail. but if you will go to bat on it as you did in the Stockyards project then I am positive that it will succeed. To make the thing go there absolutely must be someone at the head of it who will back up the organizing force to the limit in the drastic and unusual methods necessary. If it is some conservative or pussyfooter, then good night. It will be a noble cause ignobly lost.

As Sam Gompers has said the stockyards movement has blazed the way and shown labor how to organize the basic industries. In this big movement everybody is looking to us in Chicago to take the lead. It would be worse than folly for us to refuse to do it.

How soon will you be back in Chicago? I hope that when you do come back you will have the proposed movement in good hands. Be-lieve me I will lose no time mapping out an effective program for the conference. Write me as soon as you can and tell me when you will be back

Yours. Wm Z Foster.

TLS, John J. Fitzpatrick Papers, ICHi.

1. Resolution 29, adopted by the 1918 AFL convention, directed the Executive Coun-cil to hold a conference during the convention, attended by delegates from interna-tional affiliates, state federations, and city central bodies with members involved in the steel industry, "for the purpose of uniting all these organizations into one mighty drive to organize the steel plants of America" (AFL, *Proceedings*, 1918, p. 163).

2. For the minutes of this meeting, held June 17, 1918, see AFL Microfilm Conven-tion File, reel 29, frame 1128, *AFL Records*.

3. For the minutes of the June 18, 1918, meeting, see AFL Microfilm Convention File, reel 29, frames 1128–29, *AFL Records.*

4. For the minutes of the June 19, 1918, meeting, see AFL Microfilm Convention File, reel 29, frame 1129, *AFL Records.*

5. See "Excerpts from the Minutes of a Conference on Organizing the Iron and Steel Industry, Held in Chicago," Aug. 1–2, 1918, below.

A Report by Joseph Joyce[1]

[June 23, 1918]

Report Made by: Joseph J. Joyce
Place Where Made: St. Paul, Minn.
Date When Made: June 23, 1918
Period for Which Made: June 11, 1918
Title of Case and Offense Charged or Nature of Matter under Investigation:
    In re: Hon. Samuel Gompers, Protection of at St. Paul, Minn.
    Convention of A.F. of L.
Statement of Operations, Evidence Collected, Names and Addresses of Persons Interviewed, Places Visited, etc.:
At St. Paul, Minn.

Agent Campbell[2] received the following message from chief *Bielaski*,[3] Washington, D.C.:

"Understand report being circulated effect persons opposed to *Gompers* President Federation Labor who now in St. Paul may attempt to harm him. Suggest you see that proper precautionary measures are taken. *Bielaski.*"[4]

Agent *Campbell* being out of the City when the message was received late yesterday, employee called on *Mr. Gompers* Secretary at the St. Paul Hotel, and discussed the matter with her of looking out for Mr. Gompers while he was in the City, but not conveying to her that any danger was anticipated. She stated that in other cities Agents of this department and the Police Department has guarded him and remained close to him to see that no harm came to him from his enemies, of whom he admittedly has many. Employee thereupon decided to go with Mr. Gompers wherever he went outside of the hotel, and to stay close to him when he was around the public parts of the hotel, and in the Convention Hall.

Employee was with him last night until after midnight, and m[et] him this morning at nine oclock when he came from his room and was with him at all times when he was not in his room, or in the hotel dining room, during which time a certain amount of protection was given by the house detective, to whom employee had the management suggest that he look out for any cranks or radicals who might attempt to approach Mr. Gompers in the hotel.

Employee left Mr. Gompers after one oclock this evening.

The matter was handled in this manner all the time he was here.[5]

TW, RG 65, Records of the Federal Bureau of Investigation, DNA.

1. Joseph J. Joyce was an agent with the Bureau of Investigation in the Department of Justice.

2. Thomas E. Campbell was an agent with the Bureau of Investigation, stationed in St. Paul.

3. Alexander Bruce Bielaski (1883–1964) served as chief of the Bureau of Investigation from 1912 to 1919.

4. Bielaski's telegram to Campbell was dated June 10, 1918 (RG 65, Records of the Federal Bureau of Investigation, DNA).

5. Joyce's subsequent daily reports, spanning the period from June 12–22, 1918, can be found in RG 65.

From Austin Joyner[1]

Atlanta, Ga. July 2-,1918

Dear Sir:

Herewith sworn statement about which Jerome Jones[2] wired you.[3] Principal points as we see them are that even the paid defenders of the Western Union's policies are disgusted; that the so-called "Union"[4] formed by the Western Union was formed, as stated frankly to its secret agents, only as a temporary expedient to get by the War Labor Board's principles; that the men as a whole, desire to join the CTUA[5] but are prevented by Co-ercion and by the propaganda spread by Western Union secret agents that "the Western Union has bought out the War Labor Board; the president is afraid of the W.U. and that the W.U. and allied Companies dominate Congress."

The affiant has other information of a more vital nature but fears to give it until the Gov't takes over the telegraph lines—he will then appear before an investigation committee, with others, under oath and reveal the whole amazing story.

The strike[6] scheduled for July 8 will be successful in Atlanta in tieing up the wire service. For God's sake strive to get some action before then.[7]

Very respectfully   A. F. Joyner

ALS, Files of the Office of the President, General Correspondence, reel 96, frame 340, *AFL Records*.

1. Austin F. Joyner was a district organizer for the Commercial Telegraphers' Union of America. In early 1918 he was president of Telegraphers' local 122 of Jacksonville, Fla., and then, moving to Atlanta, he served briefly as president of Telegraphers' local 60 of that city.

2. Jerome JONES was the editor of the *Journal of Labor* in Atlanta (1898–1940) and president of the Southern Labor Congress (1912–19).

3. Jones to SG, July 2, 1918, Files of the Office of the President, General Correspondence, reel 96, frame 538, *AFL Records*.

4. Association (variously, Associated) Western Union Employees.

5. The Commercial TELEGRAPHERS' Union of America.

6. In April 1918 the Western Union Telegraph Co. began firing employees who had joined the Commercial Telegraphers, and by mid-May over eight hundred telegraphers had lost their jobs nationwide. To avert a strike, the National War Labor Board proposed a compromise allowing workers to join the union but not obligating the company to recognize it. When Western Union refused to accept this proposal, the Commercial Telegraphers, who insisted that their members be reinstated, set July 8 as a strike date. After appeals by SG and Secretary of Labor William B. Wilson, union president Sylvester Konenkamp agreed on July 7 to postpone the strike. On July 16 Congress authorized the president to take control of the telegraph, telephone, and marine cable systems, and on July 23 Woodrow Wilson issued a proclamation placing all telegraph and telephone systems in the United States under control of Postmaster General Albert Burleson as of midnight July 31.

7. R. Lee Guard acknowledged Joyner's letter on July 5, 1918, saying that SG was doing all he could to assist the telegraphers (reel 236, vol. 248, p. 469, SG Letterbooks, DLC).

From Mary Van Kleeck[1] and Mary Anderson

Office of the Chief of Ordnance
Production Division
War Department
Washington July 5, 1918.

My dear Mr. Gompers:

In accordance with your request in our conversation this morning, we take this opportunity to outline to you some of the problems now presented in plants for training women workers. Miss Anderson and I have just returned from a trip which included visits to the cities where district offices of the Ordnance Department are located, and in our journey we had occasion to note the present tendency to believe that active campaigns should be conducted to bring women into positions hitherto held by men. Although it is evident that an increasing shortage of skilled labor will make necessary an increase in the employment of women, it is of course obvious that their introduction into men's work should be carefully guarded, both for the sake of the women themselves and in order that there may be no lowering of the standards already attained by the men. We have therefore viewed with some apprehension plans for publicity campaigns to encourage the employment of women. Whereas these campaigns may not actually increase greatly the number of women employed, there is danger that the publicity with its emphasis on wholesale recruiting for patriotic reasons, may cause a great deal of restlessness among the men in the industries, which would be likely to interfere with production.

So far as we have discovered, the only specific plans for training which are now being put forward by anyone with official authority are those of the Committee on Training, of which Mr. Miles[2] is Chairman. Although it has seemed to us that in many of its aspects Mr. Miles' plan has practical value, the effect of the luncheon conferences with business men which have been held in some of the cities which we have later visited seems to have been to stimulate campaigns such as we have described for the introduction of women.

Of course one of the most crucial questions in connection with the training of women for men's work is the rate of pay. The representative of the Women's Branch in the Philadelphia District office has discussed this matter with Mr. Miles, who while endorsing the principle of equal pay, seemed inclined to believe that in many concrete instances it would probably be necessary to readjust existing rates of pay in case they seemed too high for the women who are to be trained for the work.[3] According to our representative's impression, Mr. Miles seems to think that the Vestibule School[4] could be used as a place for determining rates. The first danger in this plan would be that the employees would not be represented, and moreover the rate-fixing would be done under conditions likely to be more nearly ideal as to conditions of machinery and scheduling of work than prevail in an ordinary shop.

As the whole question of the training of women has such an important bearing on the labor problem, it seemed to us desirable to bring these facts to your attention for such action as may be thought advisable.

Sincerely yours,   Mary Van Kleeck
In Charge of Women's Branch
Industrial Service Section.
Mary Anderson
Supervisor in Women's Branch
Industrial Service Section.

TLS, Files of the Office of the President, General Correspondence, reel 96, frames 402–3, *AFL Records*.

1. Mary Abby Van Kleeck (1883–1972), a social researcher and reformer, was the long-time director of the Russell Sage Foundation's department of industrial studies. A specialist in the field of women's employment, she took a leave of absence from the foundation in early 1918 to serve as director of the Women's Branch of the Industrial Service Section of the U.S. Army Ordnance Department, where she drew up standards for the employment of women in war industries. Van Kleeck also served as a member of the War Labor Policies Board (1918–19) and as the first director of the Department of Labor's Woman-in-Industry Service (1918–19), which in 1920 became the Women's Bureau.

2. Herbert Edwin Miles (1860–1939) of Racine, Wis., served as chairman of the subcommittee on Industrial Training for the War Emergency under the Committee on Labor of the Advisory Commission of the Council of National Defense. A retired businessman, he had previously served as president of the Wisconsin State Board for Vocational Education (1911–17).

3. Miles subsequently wrote SG that he had been misunderstood, and he met with Van Kleeck on July 12, 1918, to clarify his position (Miles to SG, July 12 and July 13, 1918, Files of the Office of the President, General Correspondence, reel 96, frames 539–40, 547, *AFL Records*).

4. A type of industrial training shop that became widespread during World War I. Vestibule schools served as a means of rapidly instructing new workers in manufacturing processes deemed vital to the war effort.

To John Morrison

July 6, 1918.

Mr. John Morrison,
25 Third Avenue, New York, N.Y.
Dear Sir:—

Your letter of June 28th[1] was received and contents noted. You say that Mr. Leon R. Whipple[2] representing the National Civic Liberties Bureau,[3] #70 Fifth Avenue, had written to you as to securing copy of a booklet containing the names of labor papers, as he is sending out material which is of considerable importance to labor circles. You advise me that the material he is sending out is to solicit funds for defending the members of the I.W.W. now on trial in Chicago. I have had no communication from Mr. Whipple regarding this matter and you can rest assured that the National Civic Liberties Bureau will not be furnished with any lists or other documents by my office.

Very truly yours,   Saml Gompers.
President   American Federation of Labor.

TLpS, reel 236, vol. 248, p. 513, SG Letterbooks, DLC.

1. Actually, John Morrison to SG, June 26, 1918, Files of the Office of the President, General Correspondence, reel 96, frame 220, *AFL Records*.

2. Leonidas Rutledge Whipple (1882–1964), a New York City journalist and educator, worked on publicity and research for the National Civil Liberties Bureau in 1918 and 1919.

3. Actually the National Civil Liberties Bureau, which was established as a branch of the American Union against Militarism in 1917 to protect constitutional liberties and the rights of conscientious objectors during World War I. It was the predecessor of the American Civil Liberties Union, which was founded in 1920.

From C. O. Young

General Organizer for
American Federation of Labor
Seattle Washington. July, 8th, 1918.

Dear Brother Gompers:

I note that you joined with Secretary Wilson in request to President Konenkamp[1] to avoid Telegraphers strike at this time, to "avoid hinderance to our government," Etc.[2]

I wish to say, that I have been with the lockedout Telegraphers here,[3] since the beginning some ten weeks ago. Two-Hundred and Thirty men and women, a Hundred and Thirty of them women. These people have been for the last Ten Weeks on the charity of the other organizations for funds to enable them to live, and keep shelter over their heads. Yet, when I attended the Telegraphers Union meeting last night; and President Konenkamp's telegram was read asking that the strike be postponed at the request of Secretary Wilson and yourself, they heartily agreed, although the fact of the postponement will mean that there will be little more funds forthcoming to provide food and shelter for the lockedout people.

I note the promise that the interests of these lockedout workers is to be looked after to the utmost in the adjustment of this matter. I trust that in the adjustment that the time lost by these people will not be overlooked; I know that the individual sinks into insignifficance in times like these. But may I appeal to you, that in the interest of future harmony in the great task before our nation, little things like justice to a groupe of citizens like those Telegraphers who have been locked out, is essential to the future harmony of these people and the Sixty thousand onlooking unionists in this vicinity.

Some assurance that the matter of lost-time would be considered would be of great comfort to the lockedout people, whom I have been able to satisfy that our President would take care of their entire interests though they were just an insigniffant groupe. I have been able to convince them that the principle of the right to organize, is not an insigniffant matter, or, item; but the most vital of all principles to labor; and from that fact we could rest assured that the President of the U.S., sensible to this fundamental right, would not let Mr Carlton,[4] or any one else to defeat his purpose after declaring that the right to organize should not be violated.

I have been able to keep our people here, in an optomistic mood, by useing the argument that the President could not afford to allow Carlton to defy the War Labor Board at this time; for if he did, he had just as well desolve the board as far as its effectiveness was concerned—if Carlton could defy it, then, others could and would do so, and then the full force of the Presidents contention of the workers right to organize and to bargain collectively would fall to the ground.[5]

In connection with the right to organize I wish to call to your attention, to matters in connection with our attempts to organize in the lumber industry. Colonel Disque of whom you wrote me on about the 16th, of last October,[6] as being a sympathetic soul, is cutting quite a swath in this part of the country. As per your request I have tried in every way honorable way to co-operate with him; but find that the only way to co-operate with him is to go into his camp soul and body and comply with all of the fool things that he cooks up; setting at naught all of the things that we have held as fundamental throughout time. He organized his Loyal Legion of Loggers and Lumbermen, as he said, in order to be helpful to spruce production, and assurance of loyalty of the men in the camps and mills—that this organization in no sense, would interfere with the men's civil rights; yet, he now claims that the Loyal Legion does interfere with those rights, as he considers that when a man takes the pledge of the Loyal Legion that he is virtually an enlisted man. He denies that our organization of Timber-workers can exist where the Loyal Legion exists. He urges that if any man in the camp or mill where the Loyal Legion is organized, refuses in a limited time to join the Loyal Legion, that he be told to "beat it," (his language in address at Spokane two weeks ago). He also tells the members of the Loyal Legion that they should not belong to a union, and that if they did he would withdraw his help in any particular. His officers who organized the Loyal Legion tells our people that they are not acting as loyal men and that it will count against them after the war if they belong to the union in preference to the Loyal Legion. These same officers have broken up our meetings, tried to desolve our unions, urged men to throw away their union cards. Through such influence it has developed that local defense councils and mayors of certain small towns in Idaho have refused our organizers the right to hold meetings etc. Colonel Disque told me in the Presence of President Covert of the Timberworkers Union and President Hartwig[7] of the Oregon State Federation of Labor,[8] that we should cease organizing for the period of the war. He also told us at the same meeting that because the men in the Shipyards had organized that it had been a great handicap to our government. He claims that he and he alone secured the Eight-hour day in the lumber industry; Yet, I have a clipping from the Portland Oregonian in an issue before the eight-hour day was granted, wherein he said thet any one who said that he had or would advocate the eight-hour day during the war was not telling the truth. But still, he says that he admires you and the principles for which you stand. He stands for a maximum wage; I hardly think you have ever said you did. He says we should not organize during the war; I have never seen where you advocated such thing. He says that labor should be content with a bare living during the war; though throughout time labor has received less than a living wage, and though at this time wages are somewhat increased, it is but little above the bread line, I have never heard you advocate that labor should be content with a bare living in time of peace, or war.

He tells the men of the Loyal Legion that they have been given a square deal through the efforts of the Loyal Legion (Colonel Disque), yet the wages in the camps and mills are much below any other war industry. He says that the workers are favored just as much as the employer. He claims that the employer must toe the mark as well as the workmen; Yet he has not ventured to break up any of the lumbermen's Associations. A short time ago a number of them met here in the City of Seattle, and formed an organization[9] which had for its purpose the protection of their financial interests in government contracts; and sent a delegate or delegates back to Washington City in the interest of a raise in the price of lumber. The delegates have recently returned and announced with much noise in the papers that they had been successful in their mission, and yet, the Colonel has not made manifest audibly at least, his disapproval. In Spokane Washingtom Two weeks ago at a loyal Legion convention[10] called by the Colonel where the workmen who come to that convention had their expenses paid by their employers; committees were appointed for various purposes, one, committee (Committee to discuss and report on wages), reported; recommending that a minimum wage be established. In the midst of that report, they were notified by the Colonel that no minimum wage would go, and that it would not be discussed in the convention. He reminds me of a mormon Conference which I visited in Salt Lake last year, and is about as democratic. There, the head of the church is supreme and has full charge of all things literal and spiritual. In this conference the head of the church announces the appointments of the verious heads and departments of the church. The names of the appointees of the departments are read to the conference; then, the chairman of the conference or some potentate of the church, would say: "All who favor, manifest." A perfect sea of hands would go up. Then he would say: "all opposed manifest," but not a visable hand. I was curious to know why a motion was not made and matters discussed, and was informed as intimated that the head of the church was the whole show, and that to take issue with him in his appointments or orders was to fly into the face of God. I was told that one fellow tried it but was followed persistently till he was nomore. So with the Colonel, I feel that if you desire his good will and approval that every time he says: "All who are in favor manifest"; that hands must go up or forever be under his ban. I made an address at the Washington State Federation of Labor Convention[11] held in Aberdeen Washington a couple of weeks ago wherein I discussed the matter of our right to organize; citing the atitude of the Telegraph companies who had lockedout their employes because they attempted to organize unions. I also spoke of the fact that Colonel Disque had been attempting to destroy the Timberworkers Unions, and that when we protested to him he had told us that he had no legal right to break up the meetings but that we should not attempt to organize during the war; and that he did not stop the work of his men that were then in Idaho breaking up our meetings untill some time afterwards, when all the damage possible could be done. Then he gave his orders in such manner that it practically will prevent organization in that district. He then held the Loyal Legion Convention at Spokane Washington and dictated resolutions which was addopted that further made organization in the Inland Empire (the pine district, of Eastern Washington and Idaho), impossible at this time. He at that meeting again told the convention how he admired you and your principles; but still took the position that you have never taken, and can not take.

Yesterday, or, day before, I received a letter from the Colonel criticising what I had said in the Aberdeen convention of the Washington State Federation of Labor, calling my attention to certain sentences which appeared in the public press (you can guess how acurate usual reporters are, careful as they may be). I answered him calling his attention to the inacuracy of some of the statements purporting to come from me. Then I proceeded to pan the gentleman for his unfair atitude in all of his dealings with the subject under discussion. If he replies, I shall not be atall considerate with his feelings. I have been patient with his idiotic antics upon your assurance that he appeared to be in sympathy with our principles. In my dealings with him he has not confined himself to the truth; nor, has he demonstrated that he is sympathetic with any-thing accept that which he cungers up in his dreams of great glory he will attain for the part he plays in his efficiency programma in winning the war. He imagines that the lumber industry is of such peculiar nature that he can fix a particular programme, out of touch with the other industries economic conditions, and put it into operation and if allowed to be dictator can prove that he can force men to work for a lower wage and thus prove to the government his great efficiency.

In the matter of the Eight hour day which he claims that he himself secured in the lumber industry, he now is allowing ten hours to be worked, and declares that no over-time rate shall be paid. In one mill that had been shut down for a considerable length of time, has been allowed it, and his proclamation hangs on the wall of the mill, to run ten hours per day, with no overtime wage allowance. The man who has charge of the Loyal Legion of Loggers and Lumbermen in the Seattle District, has his headquarters in the Employers Association offices in Seattle. In Tacoma the headquarters of the Loyal Legion is with the office of Colonel Griggs[12] (Not a real Colonel) who is one of the worst union haters in the lumber industry, and they are many. When he was at Aberdeen Washington some time ago he came in a private Pulman car and after holding a meeting with the Loyal Legion Members (Failed to tell you that both employers and workmen belong to the Loyal Legion) on matter of wages, we found him at the home of one Cooney[13] of the Grays Harbor Commercial Company, a large lumber concern over which slave driver Coony is manager, having dinner with him. The first time we called for him at Mr Cooney's they told us he was not there, but we used a camouflage afterwards, calling for a certain Lieutenant that was with his party and found that he was with "Lagree" Cooney. We asked the Lieutenant if we could have a conference with the Colonel on an important matter, and was informed that the Colonel said that he could not meet us; asking that we come to Portland at a later date and then he would talk over the matter with us.

This may seem to you a rather extended letter, and may not be of vital interest as it seems to me; but I contend that the right to organize is in jeopardy and to me, that is the principle of all principles.[14]

Pardon the length of this letter.

Address me, #207. Maynerd Building, Seattle, Washington.

Yours fraternally.   C. O. Young

P.S. Secretary Morrison, has on file a number of letter which I have written from time to time on this question discussing Colonel Disque, which you nodoubt have seen. Note Clippings enclosed.

C. O. Y.

TLS, Files of the Office of the President, General Correspondence, reel 96, frames 461–67, *AFL Records.*

1. Sylvester J. KONENKAMP served as president (1908–19) and acting secretary-treasurer (1916–19) of the Commercial Telegraphers' Union of America.

2. SG to Konenkamp, July 7, 1918, reel 236, vol. 248, p. 644, SG Letterbooks, DLC.

3. On Apr. 29, 1918, more than a hundred telegraphers in Seattle were fired by the Western Union Telegraph Co. after they attended a Commercial Telegraphers' organizing meeting, joined the union, and then wore red, white, and blue union ribbons to work. By mid-May more than two hundred operators in the city had been locked out. (See "From Austin Joyner," July 2, 1918, n. 6, above.)

4. Newcomb Carlton (1869–1953) was president (1914–33) of the Western Union Telegraph Co.

5. A reference to President Woodrow Wilson's proclamation of Apr. 8, 1918, approving the creation of the National War Labor Board and endorsing the War Labor Conference Board's statement of principles, which included the right of workers to organize and to bargain collectively with employers.

6. See "To C. O. Young," Oct. 16, 1917, above.

7. Otto Robert HARTWIG served as president of the Oregon State Federation of Labor from 1916 to 1925.

8. The AFL chartered the Oregon State Federation of Labor in 1902.

9. Seattle lumber wholesalers organized a local dealer's association there in June 1918.

10. The Inland Empire Division of the Loyal Legion of Loggers and Lumbermen held a convention in Spokane on June 22, 1918.

11. The 1918 convention of the Washington State Federation of Labor met in Aberdeen, June 24–28.

12. Everett Gallup Griggs (1868–1938) of Tacoma, Wash., was president of the St. Paul and Tacoma Lumber Co. (1908–33) and manager of fir production in the Spruce Production Division under Col. Brice Disque, serving with the rank of major.

13. Neil Cooney of Cosmopolis, Wash., was manager of the Grays Harbor Commercial Co. and president and manager of the Chehalis County Logging and Timber Co. and the Cosmopolis Water Co.

14. For SG's response to the various complaints about Disque, see "To Brice Disque," Aug. 5, 1918, below.

To Samuel Harry Gompers

A.F. of L. Building.
July 11, 1918.

Private Samuel Gompers,
1st Lt. Sig. R.C.O.S.,
American Expeditionary Force, England.
My dear Grandson:

Your letter of June 6th enclosing your portrait and papers all came to hand. We were all glad to get a word from you and to know that you are in good health. In spite of the fact that you are nearly bursting into a laugh the picture is very good and we appreciate it very much. It was also very fine to know that you are well and like your work.

In regard to the papers,[1] I must say that I have already begun upon them and shall hasten them as much as I possibly can.

Pardon brevity, but I am so awfully crowded with work. Don't fail to write when you can. Grandmother and Aunt Sadie[2] join me in love to you.

Affectionately, Saml Gompers.

TLpS, reel 236, vol. 248, p. 728, SG Letterbooks, DLC.

1. SG may be referring to papers relating to Samuel Harry Gompers' enlistment under the name of Harry Boyd Gompers and his efforts to obtain a commission. For Henry Julian Gompers' affidavit of this date regarding the matter, see Files of the Office of the President, General Correspondence, reel 96, frame 503, *AFL Records*.

2. Sadie Julian GOMPERS was the younger daughter of SG and Sophia Julian Gompers.

Maurice Welch[1] to Frank Morrison

Grand Sec'y and Treas
Switchmen's Union of North America
Buffalo, N.Y. July 11, 1918.

Frank Morrison,
A.F. of L. Bldg.,
Washington, D.C.
Dear Sir & Brother:—

I have your favor of July 8th enclosing an item for instructions to organizers which you desire revision and return which I am herein enclosing and I make the same notation as I did on former occasions which you have persistently left out the word White Male person. Now this omission has caused the organization a considerable expense responding to requests of the colored switchmen of the South who on reading the instructions have written in for an organizer to visit various locations only to find their prospective members composed of colored gentlemen. The organization will not admit to membership that race of people and I will request that if the word White is not included that you might leave the entire item out of your instructions to organizers and oblige[2]

Yours in B.H. & P.

M. R. Welch
G.S. & T.

TLS, AFL Microfilm National and International Union File, Switchmen's Union of North America Records, reel 45, frame 1228, *AFL Records*.

1. Maurice R. "Mike" Welch served as secretary-treasurer of the Switchmen's Union of North America from 1901 to 1929.

2. On July 17, 1918, Frank Morrison replied to Welch, indicating his willingness to leave out the paragraph altogether (vol. 502, p. 763, Frank Morrison Letterbooks, George Meany Memorial Archives, Silver Spring, Md.).

From William Appleton

Chief Office
The General Federation of Trade Unions
London, W.C. 1. 12th July, 1918.

Dear Gompers,

The cables[1] that we have sent you will be in your hands long before this letter can reach Washington. Havelock Wilson[2] and myself with one or two others, have talked over the advantages and disadvantages of your coming to Great Britain at the present time. I have also personally consulted Spargoe[3] and Wallace.[4] Spargoe, with the consent of his colleagues, and Wallace on his own initiative, each think that you might render service and help to consolidate those Trade Unionists who are out to win the war.

In the memorandum which I have drafted and which Havelock Wilson has taken charge of, because I am going to France, we suggest that you shall not allow yourself to be prejudiced by any party nor any policy. It is necessary however, that you should know that already efforts have been made to weaken your own influence and that of the American Federation of Labor.

J. H. Thomas had suggested to W. M. Hughes,[5] Prime Minister of Australia that he should call an inter-Empire conference. When Hughes mentioned the matter to me, I told him that there was a possibility of you calling a conference on behalf of inter-Allied Labour and I was certain that you would not repeat the mistake of the Labour Party by ignoring the Colonies. He at once said that he was not only prepared, but anxious, to leave the matter entirely in your hands.[6]

The other bodies, i.e., the Labour Party and the Parliamentary Committee of the Trade Union Congress, are issuing statements concerning the formation of a new International and these statements rather complicate the situation, but many of us are satisfied that if you come over here and investigate the situation for yourself, you would be able to call into conference, not only the Trade Unions of Great Britain with Colonial representatives, but you would also be able to attract to such a conference representatives from France and Italy.

You may rest assured that if you come this side, every effort will be made to promote the success of your visit. A week should enable you to size up the situation here, and another three weeks should suffice for the convening and holding of an inter-Allied conference.

Spargoe will, I am sure, have kept you in touch with what is happening and Wallace, who sails in a day or two, may be able also to give you valuable information.

Yours faithfully,   W A Appleton[7]

TLS, Files of the Office of the President, General Correspondence, reel 96, frames 516–17, *AFL Records*.

1. William Appleton and J. Havelock Wilson cabled SG on July 12, 1918, urging him to visit Great Britain (Files of the Office of the President, General Correspondence, reel 96, frame 517a, *AFL Records*).

2. Joseph Havelock WILSON was the president of the National Sailors' and Firemen's Union of Great Britain and Ireland and a member of Parliament (Liberal/Labour, 1892–1900, 1906–10; Coalition Liberal, 1918–22).

3. John Spargo, who was a member of a prowar Socialist delegation headed by Algie Simons that visited Great Britain, France, and Italy in the summer of 1918.

4. Edgar Wallace of the United Mine Workers of America was in Europe in 1918 as a correspondent for the labor press.

5. William Morris Hughes (1864–1952) served as prime minister of Australia from 1915 to 1923.

6. SG cabled William Appleton, Charles Bowerman, and Léon Jouhaux on Aug. 6, 1918, to say that if a conference of bona fide labor representatives from the allied countries was called for the middle of September, the AFL would send a delegation (Files of the Office of the President, General Correspondence, reel 97, frame 117, *AFL Records*). Bowerman and Arthur Henderson replied on Aug. 9 that the Parliamentary Committee of the TUC and the executive committee of the Labour party had set the conference for Sept. 17–19 (ibid., frame 200).

7. SG replied on Aug. 9, 1918, that Appleton's proposal to invite representatives of the British colonies to attend the Inter-Allied conference met with his approval but

that he had no influence in the matter (Files of the Office of the President, General Correspondence, reel 97, frame 212, *AFL Records*).

From W. M. Henderson

Hamlet, N.C. 7-15-[19]18.

Dear Sir:

Referring to a letter written by Mr. McAdoo some time ago giving notice that all R.R. Employes regardless to race or color were to receive an increase in wages including back time as far back as 1915. Therefore we have been looking for our increase pay but up to this writing nothing has showed up in our favor. Therefore it makes us very dissatisfied. We understand the white men are all receiving theirs, but nothing has been done for us. We all took *Liberty Bonds* and contributed to the Red Cross and buying W.S.S.[1] and we are unable to meet our obligations and live at the present prices of provisions and at the present pay for our work, so I would be pleased to hear from you along this line that I may break the news to my brothers just what you say about the future. We are not contending for back time but we feel like we ought to have some consideration when it comes to being paid for our services.

We close thanking you in advance for your advice along that line, I await your reply,[2]

W. M. Henderson,
Member of Union No. 15899.[3]

TLtpSr, reel 237, vol. 249, p. 82, SG Letterbooks, DLC. Typed notation: *"Copy."* Enclosed in SG to G. H. Sines, July 19, 1918, p. 81, ibid.

1. War savings stamps.

2. SG replied on July 19, 1918, that he was referring Henderson's letter to G. H. Sines of the Board of Railroad Wages and Working Conditions, and he sent Sines a copy the same day (reel 237, vol. 249, pp. 80–81, SG Letterbooks, DLC).

3. The AFL chartered Railroad Helpers' and Laborers' Union 15,899 of Hamlet, N.C., in December 1917.

To George Creel

July 18, 1918.

Mr. George Creel,
Chairman Committee on Public Information,
10 Jackson Place, Washington, D.C.
Dear Mr. Creel:

I am just in receipt of your letter of the 17th instant and I confess my astonishment and disappointment in perusing its contents, particularly as you say that the Committee on Public Information can no longer extend financial aid to the American Alliance for Labor and Democracy.[1]

I am aware that Congress appropriated the meager sum of $1,250,000.00 for the activities of your Committee and it is really regrettable that this should have been done, but the facts are as they are consequently the situation as presents itself must be met, but I admit that the taking away of the financial aid to the Alliance is in my judgment the most impracticable and calculated to prove the most injurious.

In my opinion you are not completely informed as to the work and the influences which the Alliance has promoted and has exerted. It is not generally known, but it is nevertheless a fact, that in ninety six cities of the Union the mass meetings last Sunday, July 14th, as a tribute to France on the anniversary of her Revolutionary Day was due to the work primarily of the Alliance and the tremendous success of the meeting at Madison Square Garden in New York last Sunday evening[2] is generally attributed by those who know to the work and the cooperation of the Alliance, and it is not amiss to say that these widespread activities and these widespread influences culminating in such demonstrations throughout the country cannot be brought about by a mere request or appeal made upon the spur of the moment or with a few weeks preparation. It requires the activities and the central offices stirring the Alliance branches in the various localities to action. The organizations of the Alliance having continuous existence will always be ready to do what may be necessary to meet any given emergency is the thing which counts.

Yesterday, Mr. Byiro[3] and Mr. Sisson[4] were here in conference with several other gentlemen and the undersigned (you were invited but could not attend) and in the course of personal conversation with Mr. Byiro and Mr. Sisson they both declared that the work gotten out by the American Alliance is of the first importance to our country and our cause. That statement was made to me evidently without the knowledge of Mr. Byiro or Mr. Sisson or me that you had contemplated discontinuing the assistance to the Alliance by reason of the cut in the appropriation of your Committee's work.

My information is that the cost of maintaining the Alliance activities approximates about $5,000 a month or about $60,000 a year, and I am wondering by which other agency that amount of money can be expended by your Committee with such advantage to our country's cause.

At the beginning and for several months after the Alliance was formed a number of us contributed from our meager incomes in order to carry on its initial work. We then undertook to secure contributions from private sources but they were totally inadequate and that project was abandoned. It will be impossible to continue the work either from our own personal contributions or from contributions of others.

As to your suggestion of having Mr. Babson[5] taking care of the financial affairs of the Alliance, permit me to say that so long as I have anything to do with the Alliance either as its President or as a member, the organization will accept neither financial aid, assistance nor direction from Mr. Babson.

Unless you decide upon retrenchment in another direction and afford the necessary aid to the Alliance, I think it will be necessary to wind up its affairs.

Please advise me of your decision[6] and oblige

Yours very truly,
President   American Alliance for Labor and Democracy.

TLc, Files of the Office of the President, General Correspondence, reel 96, frames 680–81, *AFL Records.*

1. On July 17, 1918, George Creel wrote SG that because of a reduction in his congressional appropriation, the financial support from the Committee on Public Information to the American Alliance for Labor and Democracy would end on Aug. 1 (Files of the Office of the President, General Correspondence, reel 96, frame 616, *AFL Records*).

2. A meeting attended by some twelve thousand people was held in Madison Square Garden on July 14, 1918, in celebration of Bastille Day. Among those who addressed the meeting were SG, Secretary of the Navy Josephus Daniels, who also read a statement from President Woodrow Wilson, and the French, Italian, and British ambassadors to the United States. Similar celebrations were held in more than two hundred U.S. cities and many small towns.

3. Carl Byoir (1888–1957), a newspaper editor and reporter, served as an associate chairman of the Committee on Public Information from 1917 to 1918.

4. Edgar Grant Sisson (1875–1948), a newspaperman and magazine editor, served as an associate chairman and general director of the foreign section of the Committee on Public Information from 1917 to 1919.

5. Roger Ward Babson (1875–1967), a statistician and investment analyst, served as

director general of the Information and Education Service of the U.S. Department of Labor from 1918 to 1919.

6. Creel wrote SG on July 19, 1918, after consulting with Chester Wright, to assure him of his belief that the matter could be adjusted to SG's "absolute satisfaction." Creel concluded: "I want you to be assured now, as at all times, that your wish is very nearly law to me, and that I will do everything in my power to carry forward your desires" (Files of the Office of the President, General Correspondence, reel 96, frame 699, *AFL Records*). An Aug. 9 letter from SG to Creel indicated that an arrangement had been made to continue the work of the Alliance (ibid., reel 97, frame 215).

To Woodrow Wilson

Washington, D.C. July 19, 1918

Hon. Woodrow Wilson.
The White House,
Washington, D.C.
Sir:

Of course it was my fault that I did not in advance ask you whether you could spare some time yesterday for the presentation to you of other important matters than the question of prohibiting child labor,[1] and I readily realize that your engagements forbade my even suggesting that you would give me more time than you had at your disposal yesterday.

And yet the matters which I desired to submit to you for consideration were of prime importance and I feel that it is my imperative duty to bring them to your attention in this form.

From many sections of the country there come to me resolutions, telegrams, in the form of petitions and protests regarding the Mooney case, one cablegram from the Secretary of the Parliamentary Committee of the British Trade Union Congress, the Right Honorable Charles Bowerman, all of them urging, even protesting. I know of no one particular thing that is calculated to do the cause of America and the cause of our allies greater injury than the execution of Tom Mooney. I am exceedingly apprehensive of its consequences if it should be permitted to take place. The Mooney case is now and for months has been an international and a political issue, rather than a local or judicial state issue in California, and as the days go on I am sure that feeling and that issue will become intensified. If Mooney should be executed with the general knowledge or belief that his conviction was had upon manufactured or perjured evidence, and of that there is little or no doubt, I repeat that I am apprehensive of the consequences.

Enclosed you will please find copies of a few of the telegrams and a copy of the cablegram which I have received within the recent past, and to which your attention is respectfully called.[2]

Enclosed you will please find a copy of the confidential report made by the American Labor Mission[3] which by direction of the American Federation of Labor I sent to Mexico. It throws a great light upon the situation in Mexico.

You will observe that the American Labor Mission made some recommendations.

1. The plan for the education of the Mexican people as to the cause for which the United States entered into the world war against Germany and Austria.

2. That the best agency to help stabilize relations between the Mexican and the United States governments is the organized labor movement of the two countries.

3. The American Federation of Labor has not the means to conduct such a campaign. Because the Congress has cut the appropriation made for the Committee on Public Information it is practically impossible for that committee to bear the expense.

It has been suggested that it might be borne by the fund which the Congress has placed at your disposal for the purpose of helping to win the war. This fact, as I had the opportunity of saying to you yesterday, was concurred in by Honorable William B. Wilson, Secretary of Labor, Mr. Buyor and Mr. Sisson of the Committee on Public Information, (Mr. Creel at the last moment being unable to attend the conference). Secretary Wilson will beyond doubt place the matter before you for consideration and action in more concrete form. I have absolute confidence in the official whose name you suggested that I should present this matter to, but I am convinced that these things should receive your careful consideration.

Another phase of the Mexican situation and the relations between it and the United States has come to me in another form and which, as I took occasion to say yesterday, must be presented to you if presented at all.[4] I am under word of honor to convey it to no one but you. I hope that I may have an opportunity of conveying this information to you some time in the late afternoon Monday July 29th, or any hour which may be convenient to you Tuesday July 30th.[5] The Executive Council of the American Federation of Labor will hold a week's session[6] outside of Washington, hence it will be necessary for me to be in attendance with my associates; therefore the suggested dates.

I am very anxious to aid in all things that will benefit our country and our cause, so anxious that I am impelled to present these matters to you for your consideration and action.[7]

I have the honor to be

Yours very respectfully,　Saml Gompers.

President,　American Federation of Labor.

TLS, Woodrow Wilson Papers, DLC.

1. On June 3, 1918, the U.S. Supreme Court struck down the Keating-Owen Act, which prohibited the interstate transportation of goods produced with child labor (*Hammer* v. *Dagenhart,* 247 U.S. 251 [1918]). The Child Labor Tax Act, passed in early 1919, attempted to sidestep the court's ruling by imposing a 10–percent tax on the net profits of firms producing goods with child labor for interstate commerce. In 1922 the court also declared this statute unconstitutional (*Bailey* v. *Drexel Furniture Co.,* 259 U.S. 20 [1922]). SG met with President Woodrow Wilson to discuss the matter on the afternoon of July 18, 1918.

2. The copies are filed with SG's letter in the Woodrow Wilson Papers, DLC.

3. An American labor mission consisting of James Lord, president of the AFL Mining Department, Santiago Iglesias, president of the Federación Libre de los Trabajadores de Puerto Rico (Free Federation of the Workers of Puerto Rico), and John Murray, secretary of the Pan-American Federation of Labor (FOL) Conference Committee, visited Mexico in May and June 1918. The mission's confidential report described the pro-German attitude of Venustiano Carranza's government and the Mexican press but noted that the Mexican labor movement was generally pro-Ally and was the "only trustworthy source for spreading the truth throughout Mexico." The report also included resolutions adopted on July 3 at an AFL-sponsored conference in Washington, D.C., that was attended by SG and representatives of the Mexican labor movement, AFL affiliates, and the Pan-American FOL Conference Committee. These called for the establishment of the Pan-American FOL and urged the labor press of the two countries to carry publicity promoting the new Federation. The mission's confidential report is printed in Arthur S. Link et al., eds., *The Papers of Woodrow Wilson,* 69 vols. (Princeton, N.J., 1966–94), 49: 26–36, quotation at p. 29. The mission also issued an official report, which is printed in AFL, *Proceedings,* 1918, pp. 248–53.

4. A reference to a proposal by John R. Phillips, described as a large property owner in Mexico, that he serve as an unofficial U.S. representative to Carranza.

5. SG met with Wilson on July 29, 1918.

6. The AFL Executive Council met in Atlantic City, July 23–28, 1918.

7. Wilson agreed to help support a bilingual newspaper published under the auspices of the American Alliance for Labor and Democracy, with the money channelled through the Committee on Public Information. The *Pan-American Labor Press: El Obrero Pan-americano,* under the principal editorship of John Murray, began publication on Aug. 28, 1918. The Committee on Public Information also allotted $25,000 in behalf of the founding meeting of the Pan-American Federation of Labor held in November 1918 at Laredo, Tex.

Excerpts from the Minutes of a Conference on Organizing the Iron and Steel Industry, Held in Chicago[1]

[August 1–2, 1918]

FIRST DAY.

. . .

The Secretary[2] read the minutes of the three conferences held June 17 to 20[3] at the St. Paul convention, at which the representatives of 21 international unions, 14 city centrals and 7 state federations deemed the time appropriate to start a campaign to organize the iron and steel industries and provided for the present conference as the means to start it off.

On motion the minutes were approved as read.

In formally opening the conference President Gompers stated that already the steel corporations are interested in our campaign. He had been visited recently by two men, who had in their possession a copy of the letter of invitation to this conference. They did not deny it when he charged that they had gotten it from sources hostile to labor. He warned of the danger of letting such things get into unfriendly hands.

President Gompers also reminded the delegates present of their patriotic duty in this great crisis in the struggle between the irreconcilable forces of democracy and autocracy. He reviewed this struggle in the past, pointing out the foundation of our government on the principle of the rights of man, [and] how this principle was rapidly spreading all [ov]er the world when the proponents of autocracy, feeling their rule menaced, released the present world storm to head off if possible the advance of [th]e people. He advised that every effort should [be] exhausted before any strikes are allowed to [oc]cur in the present movement, so that under no circumstances should our boys at the front be denied the fullest and best opportunity to make an effective fight for democracy.

President Gompers stated that the steel magnates are already taking steps to defeat our efforts, even as big employers always do in similar circumstances, by increasing wages. . . .

. . .

President Gompers said that the steel companies cannot make us angry by giving their employes better wages. In fact we welcome them as bringing to the workers a better life, more education, and a greater interest in their own welfare. The old relation in industry of master and slave is giving way to new ones where employer and employe meet on a basis of equality as parties having problems to solve. We have established democracy in politics, now we must establish democracy in industry. Too long did autocracy reign in the packing industry, and among the telegraphs. But this is all changed now. And our present purpose is to establish industrial democracy in the iron and steel industry.

After these remarks President Gompers called for suggestions as to the course to be pursued.

· · ·

At this point in the conference the Secretary submitted a proposed order of business, which took up the problem in hand under three heads, viz.: (1) Organizing force; (2) Finance; (3) Recruiting Organizers. Moved that the proposed order of business be accepted and that its various propositions be taken up seriatim. Adopted.

Moved that this conference create a national committee to carry into effect Resolution No. 29, adopted by the St. Paul convention. Adopted.

Moved that this national committee have full charge of the organizing work; that it consist of one member of each of the co-operating international unions, and that it meet at stated intervals, at such other times as it may deem necessary, or upon call of the Secretary with the approval of the representative of the A.F. of L. Adopted.

Moved that the chairman of the national organizing committee be a representative of the A.F. of L. Adopted.

Moved that local organizing committees be established in the principal steel centers.

Amended that this motion be understood as an instruction to the national committee. Motion adopted as amended.

· · ·

SECOND DAY.

· · ·

Moved that the National Committee to handle the campaign be now organized. Adopted.

· · ·

In accordance with previous action taken, President Gompers assumed the chairmanship of the National Committee.

Wm. Z. Foster elected Secretary-Treasurer.

· · ·

Moved that the organizations present make an initial contribution of $100.00 each to the organizing fund of the National Committee, and that the Secretary-Treasurer request those not present to do likewise. Adopted.

Moved that a uniform initiation fee be charged during this campaign by all the organizations involved. Adopted.[4]

. . .

Moved that the next meeting of the National Committee be held in the headquarters of the Chicago Federation of Labor, 166 West Washington street, Chicago, Ill., on August 16th, at 10 A.M. Adopted.

Moved that steps be taken at once to establish local organizing committees of all co-operating organizations in the following steel districts: Pittsburgh, Cleveland, Chicago, Bethlehem, Youngstown, Buffalo, Alabama, Minnesota.

Amendment, that these committees also be set up, if possible, in all other big steel centers. Motion adopted as amended.

In the consideration of this motion a long discussion took place, shared in by all the delegates present, upon the question of whether the organization work should be concentrated upon one point or carried on simultaneously at many points. From this discussion the opinion prevailed that inasmuch as the steel industry is national in scope, it can be best handled on a national basis.

Moved that a letter be sent to the central bodies in all steel centers advising them of the proposed movement and asking their co-operation. Adopted.

Moved that the Secretary-Treasurer of the National Committee be instructed to draft a set of simple rules to serve as the basis for the organization of local organizing committees in the various localities. Adopted.

Moved that the matter of appealing to the general labor movement for financial assistance be left to the Secretary-Treasurer, who shall act in the matter with the approval of the chairman of the National Committee. Adopted.

. . .

PD, Executive Council Records, Vote Books, reel 16, frame 69, *AFL Records.* Enclosed in SG to the AFL Executive Council, Aug. 13, 1918, ibid., frame 68.

1. Representatives of the Blacksmiths, Boilermakers, Electrical Workers, Iron, Steel, and Tin Workers, Machinists, Mine, Mill, and Smelter Workers, Molders, Plumbers, Quarry Workers, Railway Carmen, Seamen, Stationary Firemen, Steam Engineers, Steam Shovel and Dredgemen, Structural Iron Workers, the Chicago Federation of Labor, and the Chicago Building Trades Council attended the conference.

2. William Z. Foster.

3. Actually, the conferences were held June 17–19, 1918. See "William Z. Foster to John Fitzpatrick," June 22, 1918, nn. 2–4, above.

4. The conference agreed to a uniform initiation fee of $3.00, of which $1.00 would be contributed to the organizing fund of the national committee.

To Brice Disque

Washington, D.C., Aug. 5, 1918.

Col. Brice P. Disque,
Spruce Production Division, United States Signal Corps,
Seattle, Washington.
Dear Sir:

Information reaches me[1] that you have interfered with and prohibited the formation of legitimate, constructive unions of lumbermen. While no objection can be interposed against your formation of the Loyal Legion, I urge upon your consideration that you have no right to prevent the organization of legitimate constructive unions.

You know that I have helped you and Major Ledbetter in reaching the conclusion which you and he have declared to be practical and helpful.

If you persist in the course against which protest is made, whatever ill consequences may result will rest upon your shoulders alone.

Samuel Gompers.

TWtpSr, reel 237, vol. 249, p. 530, SG Letterbooks, DLC.

1. See "From C. O. Young," July 8, 1918, above, and Clair Covert et al. to SG and Young to SG, both Aug. 1, 1918, Files of the Office of the President, General Correspondence, reel 97, frames 1–4, 26–31, *AFL Records*.

To the Executive Council of the AFL

Washington, D.C., August 8, 1918.

Confidential.
Document No. 69
Executive Council, American Federation of Labor.
Colleagues:

Additional urgent requests have come within the past two days for representation of the American Federation of Labor in a labor conference of the Inter-Allied Countries, and I have replied that if the conference is held about the middle of September the American Federation of Labor will be represented.[1] I assume that Fraternal Delegates Bowen[2] and Gompers (the latter of whom you have selected to fill the vacancy caused by Brother Franklin's resignation) will be in Europe about that time and that they could act in part as representatives of the American Federation of Labor.

Insistent demands have been made within the same past few days to have a labor mission go over to France, England and Italy. The expenses are not to be borne by the A.F. of L., but the source similar to that which bore the expense of the Labor Mission which we sent to Europe a few months ago.[3]

I have been in telegraphic and telephonic communication with a number of active and faithful American trade unionists, with a view of their acceptance as members of the mission. A few have already accepted and I am expecting definite replies so that the number of the mission shall be filled within twenty-four hours.[4] You can understand how exceedingly difficult it would have been to act otherwise by reason of the fact that the labor commissioners must leave within the course of the week and it is necessary for them to not only arrange their affairs but to secure passports and attend to all matters which an overseas voyage of a few months may involve.

I therefore ask the members of the Executive Council to return their votes by telegraph on the following:

Resolved, That the trade unionists selected by the Executive Council and by President Gompers to proceed to Europe, including the British Trade union Congress,[5] be constituted a Mission and representatives in any Inter-Allied labor conference.[6]

Again I ask that the Executive Council will please return their votes promptly and by telegraph. You will of course observe how essential it is for safety's sake to regard these entire matters in the strictest confidence.

Fraternally yours, Saml Gompers.
President, American Federation of Labor.

TLcS, Executive Council Records, Vote Books, reel 16, frames 65–66, *AFL Records.*

1. SG sent this cable to William Appleton, Charles Bowerman, and Léon Jouhaux on Aug. 6, 1918 (Files of the Office of the President, General Correspondence, reel 97, frame 117, *AFL Records*). The Inter-Allied Labour and Socialist Conference met in London, Sept. 17–20, 1918. It was attended by delegates from Great Britain, France, Italy, Belgium, the United States, Canada, Greece, and Serbia, and by consultative delegates from Rumania and Russia. The conference adopted an amended version of a resolution on war aims introduced by SG and a resolution urging that Allied efforts to assist Russia should be influenced by a desire to preserve liberty, democracy, and the beneficial results of the revolution.

2. William J. BOWEN, of the Bricklayers', Masons', and Plasterers' International Union of America, served as president of the union from 1904 to 1928.

3. The expenses of the Gompers mission were borne largely by the U.S. government. See SG to R. Lee Guard, Aug. 2, 1918, Files of the Office of the President, General Correspondence, reel 97, frame 40, *AFL Records;* Guard memo, Aug. 11, 1918, ibid., frame 274; and Robert Lansing to Walter Hines Page, Sept. 14, 1918, RG 59, General Records of the Department of State, DNA.

4. For the members of the American labor mission, see "Gompers Urged to Visit Italy," June 13, 1918, n. 2, in "Excerpts from News Accounts of the 1918 Convention of the AFL in St. Paul," June 11–21, 1918, above.

5. The 1918 conference of the TUC met in Derby, Sept. 2–7.

6. The AFL Executive Council voted in favor of this proposal.

From Charles Trobitz[1]

Railroad Helpers and Laborers Union, No. 15920,[2]
American Federation of Labor,
Grand Junction, Colo. August 9th, 1918.

Dear Sir:—

Official notice has been received by the local machinist from their grand lodge to the effect that the engine inspectors tool room men and cellar packers are to come under the jurisdiction of the machinist helpers,[3] and these jobs will be filled by machinist helpers. In our local shops the cellar packers job is held by Mr. E. A. Campbell,[4] a colored man, he is also secretary to our local union. I understand that he is to be supplanted by a machinist helper. Now if Mr. Campbell is to lose his job on account of his color, this union will make a hot protest against it. Mr. Campbell would join the machinist helpers union, but is barred from it, on account of color.

I sincerely hope to hear from you in regard to this matter.[5]

Respectfully yours,   (Signed) C. T. Trobitz, Pres.

TLtpSr, reel 238, vol. 250, p. 167, SG Letterbooks, DLC. Typed notation: "*Copy.*" Enclosed in SG to William Johnston, Aug. 19, 1918, ibid., p. 166.

1. Charles T. Trobitz of Grand Junction, Colo., was an engineer for the Denver and Rio Grande Railroad.

2. The AFL chartered Railroad Helpers' and Laborers' Union 15,920 of Grand Junction in December 1917.

3. Supplement No. 4 to General Order No. 27, issued by Director General of Railroads William McAdoo on July 25, 1918, dealt with the classification of employees in the mechanical departments of railroads under federal control and specified that toolroom attendants, box packers, and oilers, among others, were to be classified as machinists' helpers.

4. Earl A. Campbell of Grand Junction was a box packer and oiler for the Denver and Rio Grande Railroad and served as secretary of AFL 15,920 in 1918.

5. On Aug. 19, 1918, SG sent a copy of Trobitz's letter to William Johnston, president of the International Association of Machinists, who confirmed that Campbell's job now came under the jurisdiction of his union; R. Lee Guard informed Trobitz of this response on Aug. 30 (reel 238, vol. 250, pp. 166 and 479, SG Letterbooks, DLC). By month's end Campbell had lost his job. He subsequently worked as a janitor and as a clerk at a lower rate of pay.

To William Stephens

August 10, 1918.

Confidential.
Honorable William Stephens,
Governor of California,
Sacramento, California.
Dear Sir:—

I am writing this letter a few days before my departure from the United States to head a labor mission to Great Britain, France and Italy in the hope of cementing the masses of the workers of these countries with our own in a solid phalanx to stand faithful and true behind our allied governments in the momentous struggle in which we are all engaged.

For reasons which are obvious I have asked my secretary to withhold the mailing of this letter until news shall reach here of my arrival on the other side; but whether I shall reach there or fail, I am prompted to present to you, perhaps the last word that I may have an opportunity of submitting to you, an appeal that you may exercise the great power vested in you in behalf of Thomas J. Mooney.

From information which I have, and of a most authentic character, I can say to you that there is no case of which I have any knowledge in my long life, which has attracted such universal attention as the case of Tom Mooney, and there is a deep feeling manifested among the workers of France, England, Italy and of Russia, that a gross miscarriage of justice has taken place in the Mooney trial.

It is not possible for me now to indicate the seriousness of the situation, should the sentence imposed upon Mooney be carried out, but I am apprehensive as to its consequences. The Mooney case has passed from the Judicial stage; it rests primarily now in your hands. It has become not only a national but an international issue, and regardless of all other opinion, its international aspect deserves very serious and [sym]pathetic consideration and action at your hands.

In the name not only of labor but [of] Justice, and of the cause for which we are all so stoutly standing and making sacrifices to win this universal struggle, I appeal to you to exercise your prerogative in behalf of Thomas J. Mooney.[1]

Very respectfully yours,
President,   American Federation of Labor.

TLp, reel 238, vol. 250, pp. 374–75, SG Letterbooks, DLC.

1. Gov. William Stephens replied on Sept. 11, 1918, that he had already granted Thomas Mooney a reprieve until Dec. 13 and that Mooney's attorneys were preparing an appeal to the U.S. Supreme Court. He promised to give the case his full consideration, however (Executive Council Records, Vote Books, reel 16, frame 88, *AFL Records*).

Excerpts from the Minutes of a Conference of the League to Aid Russia at the Headquarters of the National Civic Federation in New York City

August 13, 1918, 8 o'clock P.M.

Mr. Samuel Gompers, presiding.

. . .[1]

Chairman Gompers: Ladies and gentlemen: For some time the situation as it applies to the conditions of the government and the people of Russia has occupied a large part of the attention of the people of our country. About January last a meeting in the City of Washington, at which were a number of men taking part in the leading events of our country and of our relations, was held in the office of one of the leading United States Senators, and after a general discussion at which the condition of the people of Russia and the governmental conditions were related, it was decided to organize a league for the purpose of helping the people of Russia.[2] At that time it was not known whether Russia was to remain in the war or whether a final military collapse would ensue, but the conclusion was reached that whatever betide the Russian activity or inactivity, that the considerations of humanity demanded that the people of the United States should do all that they possibly could to help the people of Russia in their great stress and demoralized financial, economic and material condition. Events came fast and thick, and Russia ceased to be a factor in the Allied cause against German and Austrian militarism and autocracy. But the activity of the League which we had formed continued, not so much in its material assistance direct, but in its effort to direct the attention of the American people and the American government, to be of some substantial aid in assuaging the poverty and misery and demoralization of the Russian people. The establishment of the powers that existed, that is the Bolsheviki government, the so-called government of the Soviets, called the direct mandate of the Soviets, the dissolution of the first directly elected representative of the people of Russia in constituent assembly,[3] the dissolution of it at the point of the bayonet, by the power of force, seized by the Bolsheviki—there seemed to be no other governmental authority in Russia known that could speak either by authority of the mandate of the people of Russia—no one seemed to be able to speak for Russia and her position in the war, or in her own economic, political and social life but the Bolsheviki as represented by Lenine and Trotsky.[4]

. . .

I want to make my position clearly understood. I don't want any man or woman to believe that I am unwilling to go the full limit of the ideals of democracy and justice. The only limit to my activities is the practical application of the highest ideals, and if the high ideals do not and cannot conform to practical application, to that degree I will either discard them or wait for a better time. (Applause.) My intense desire, and I think I interpret the American labor movement accurately—that we want to establish the very best possible conditions for the masses of our country and the masses of every other country on the face of the globe. We realize that its achievement is a matter of development and not of cataclysmic eruption, and we must not imagine that a transition from infancy to full-grown manhood, from peasantry and slavery, can be transformed overnight into a full-fledged co-operative commonwealth. And, in passing, I don't want anyone to infer for a moment that I am committed to a co-operative commonwealth. I believe in democracy, in justice, in fair dealing and opportunity for the development of the best that is in the human, and to make for a social conscience and for social justice and the attainment of the best conditions consistent with the intellectual development of the people of our country. I offer that thought to Russia, as well. To think that Russia from her condition of impoverished peasantry, with little industry, can be transformed from a subjugated people into a condition where the highest concepts, the highest ideals of human justice, of human relations, can be established by mere proclamation, is idle, is impotent—must be impotent and ineffective. Just as Germany, with her imperialist government undertook to prepare the military arm of her government for world conquest, she suborned and she propagated this idea among the German workers as represented by the socialists of that country, that internationalism, international brotherhood should be the dominating cries and watchwords of the world's affairs; and while Germany and German socialism undertook to chloroform the people of the other countries of the world in perverting the ideals of internationalism and of human brotherhood in all the countries of the world, the idea of nationalism and of Germanism was impregnated in the minds of the people of Germany—so much so that many of us were infected with this beautiful thought and ideal of international-ism, and many of them carried along with them until long after the time when that ideal had been dispelled.

So, coming back to Russia and the Russian situation: Lenine and Trotsky—and I know Trotsky; I have met him and had to contend with him here—the agents of Germany consciously or unconsciously, theo-retically or practically, or, as some one has said, that they are money honest, and my answer was that if they are money honest they have missed their calling and their opportunity, for their work was worth much to Germany. However, just a word and I shall finish. Having this matter in mind—all these matters in mind—a few weeks ago I saw in the newspapers that Mr. Raymond Robbins[5] had just returned from Russia and that he represented the idea of the Bolsheviki government. By pure coincidence he called me up on the telephone and inquired whether he could not see me. I had already decided upon the course which I shall indicate in a moment. He came to see me[6] and spoke to me for fully an hour and a half, without one word of interruption on my part. At its conclusion I showed him a copy of one of the letters that I had already directed should be prepared and sent to a number of men in Washington to consider what the condition and situation of the Russian people and the Russian government were, and to see in which way we could be helpful.[7] Mr. Robbins was delighted, and so expressed himself, by the invitation that I had extended, and I informed him that he was one of the gentlemen to whom I had ex-tended an invitation. The meeting was held. There were about twenty representative American citizens present. We held a meeting from about eight o'clock until nearly one in the offices of the American Federation of Labor, and Mr. Robbins occupied about two-thirds of the time, and the statement that he made in his direct address was almost letter perfect, accurate, a repetition of the statement he had made to me a few days before. I shall not at this time undertake to give even a summary of what he said. I shall prefer that we may enter into a pre-sentation of what we understand the situation to be now. This I may say, that—yes, two points. One was that he read a document written by one of the British Consuls at Moscow, Mr. Lockhart,[8] in which Mr. Lockhart supported Mr. Robbins' view that the Bolsheviki was the only government which ought to be recognized because it had all power, and Mr. Lockhart expressed the view that it was a mistaken course for the Allied governments not to give credit to the Bolsheviki for the power and their willingness to aid the Allied cause. Within this past few days I have seen published in the American newspapers the fact that the Bolshevik government has arrested Mr. Lockhart, and that he has only been released upon the compulsory protests of the allied governments.[9] I don't know—I am not quite so sure that Mr. Lockhart has that very kindly understanding of the power and the sympathy of the Bolshevik government that he had at the time he addressed this letter to Mr. Robbins, and Mr. Robbins said that Mr. Lockhart and he had had breakfast for about three months every morning. The other is that Lenine and Trotsky, as published in today's papers, are no longer the power in Russia;[10] that, after all, there is coming a reaction among the people of Russia, to realize the situation—the world situation and the world opportunity—to choose between the intention and purpose and the high ideals of the allied countries, not followed but led by idealism of America, or to submit to the yoke imposed by the imperial government of Germany; and it is gratifying to every man and woman who believes in this great cause in which we are engaged, that the time is near at hand when Russia, with the help of America first, and the help of the allied countries as can be given—that Russia, proud, big, noble-hearted Russia, will again rise and in her strength and in her moral and physical power, take her stand among the great democracies of the world. (Applause.) We are in this war. There can be no compromise upon the issues involved. Either we are going to establish the opportunities for justice and freedom for all the world, or we will prove ourselves poltroons and cowards, unfit to have the great privilege of self-government and self-determination. (Applause.)

. . .

. . . I have tried to indicate in my opening remarks that the German socialist philosophy is in entire harmony with the German militarist, imperialist thought and theory. No one can dispute, no one wants to dispute the fact that the ideal and the idealism of human brotherhood of internationalism is subscribed to by every earnest, honest lover of the human kind, but it is the perversion of that idea which has been part of the German propaganda, hand in hand with the socialists and the government. As, for instance, in the United States we have had what was called an American Socialist Party. As a matter of fact, we find that the groups in that party are made up such as, for instance, of the German socialists in the United States, the Austrian socialists of the United States, the Hungarian socialists of the United States, the French socialists of the United States, the American socialists of the United States, the Jewish socialists of the United States, and so forth and so forth. Well, each of these groups of nationality or race have their representative in the administration of the affairs of the American Socialist Party. Each of these groups selected their own representative in the administration of the affairs of the American Socialist Party. And then all of the groups selected the American representative of the entire Socialist Party, and the joint representative of the American Socialist

Party is a German.[11] I have said this: That the socialist parties and the socialist propaganda are British, American, French, Italian, Spanish agents of branches of the German Socialist Party and propaganda. I am not going to attribute any improper motives to any man or any woman, but the fact is that when we are won over to a theory of deep sentiment and high idealism, it is difficult for men to understand the conditions which come about that—well, I was going to say disembowel the very thought and the fundament and ideals of such a movement. It has been the American labor movement that has always exposed—understood and exposed this situation, and it has been the refusal, much to the disgust of German socialists—the German socialist party and the American branch of the German socialist party, that they could not capture the American labor movement to their propaganda, and make of it a tail to the kite of their schemes. We realize what is here and we are going to make our fight here and over there, and it is not good and won't be good for any man or any group of men to stand in the way of this onward march of the Twentieth Century Crusaders. (Applause.)

. . .

Mr. Gompers read the following:

That it is the sense of this conference that the first duty of the people and the Republic of the United States and her allied democratic nations is to concentrate every energy and make every essential sacrifice that the cause of justice, freedom and democracy shall find its triumphant conclusion; that every effort should be made by our peoples and the governments of our country and of our allies to materially and morally support the people of Russia first to sustain themselves in their great stress so that they may have the opportunity of working out their own life, freedom, democracy and destiny; and to these high purposes we pledge our earnest and unlimited support.

Mr. Easley: I move that that be made the sense of this meeting. (Seconded.)

Chairman Gompers: You have heard the motion which has been duly seconded, that this expression be adopted by this conference. Are you ready for the question? All who favor the adoption will please signify the same by saying Aye. Contrary, No. It is a unanimous vote.

. . .

Mr. Gompers: I want to carry the message of America—of American manhood and American womanhood, American hopes and principles and idealisms to the people on the other side; and if I get there, that job will be done, or count me as an exile from the United States. (Applause.)

I thank you very much for your attendance and for your intelligent and patient consideration of the subject.

. . .[12]

TDc, Files of the Office of the President, Conferences, reel 120, frames 411–18, 442–44, 456–57, 461, *AFL Records*.

1. Ellipses in original.

2. See "A Memorandum Dictated by Samuel Gompers," Jan. 11, 1918, above.

3. The Bolsheviks dissolved the Constituent Assembly on Jan. 19 (Jan. 6, Old Style), 1918.

4. Leon Trotsky (1879–1940), a leader of the October 1917 Bolshevik Revolution and a founder of the Comintern in 1919, served as commissar of foreign affairs (1917–18) and commissar of war (1918–25) in the Soviet government. Defeated in a power struggle with Joseph Stalin after the death of Vladimir Lenin in 1924, he was removed from office and expelled from the Communist party. In 1929 he was exiled from the Soviet Union and found refuge in Mexico, where he was murdered by Stalin's agents.

5. Raymond Robins (1873–1954), a social economist and reformer, was a member of an American Red Cross mission to Russia in June 1917 and head of a second Red Cross mission, Nov. 1917–May 1918. After his return to the United States he argued for American recognition of the Bolshevik government.

6. SG's appointment records indicate that he met with Robins on July 16, 1918.

7. Invitations to a July 18, 1918, meeting to consider the situation in Russia, were sent on July 16 and 17 to Herbert Carpenter, William English Walling, William Thompson, Ralph Easley, Raymond Robins, Louis Brandeis, William B. Wilson, Chester Wright, George Creel, Frank Morrison, and Frank Goodnow (reel 236, vol. 248, pp. 927, 938, 940–46, 952, SG Letterbooks, DLC; Files of the Office of the President, General Correspondence, reel 96, frame 657, *AFL Records*).

8. Robert Hamilton Bruce Lockhart (1887–1970) served in Russia as British vice-consul (1912–15), acting consul-general (1915–17), and then as an unofficial British diplomatic agent to the Bolshevik government (1918).

9. On Aug. 10, 1918, the *New York Times* reported Lockhart's arrest in Moscow and on Aug. 13 reported his release.

10. On Aug. 13, 1918, the *Washington Post* reported that the Bolshevik government was to be transferred from Moscow to Kronstadt, and that Lenin and Trotsky had already left the city, because of the threat from a military unit known as the "Czech Legion." The Legion, consisting of some thirty to forty thousand rearmed Czech prisoners of war who had resisted the Bolsheviks' attempt to disarm them, had seized important towns in the central Volga region east of Moscow and along the Trans-Siberian Railroad in an effort to secure their route to Vladivostok, where they had been told they would be evacuated from Russia.

11. Possibly a reference to German-born Adolph F. GERMER, who served as national secretary of the Socialist Party of America from 1916 to 1919.

12. Ellipses in original.

To Woodrow Wilson

Washington, D.C., August 14, 1918.

Honorable Woodrow Wilson,
President of the United States,
Washington, D.C.
Sir:—

The Senate Committee on Military Affairs has incorporated a provision in the new draft act stipulating that those registrants who are placed in exempt or deferred classes shall become subject to military draft if they do not remain steadily at work when physically able.[1] The amendment in this respect reads as follows:—

"Persons engaged in occupations or employments found to be necessary to the maintenance of the military establishment, or the effective operation of the military forces, or the maintenance of national interest during the emergency, provided, that, when any person shall have been placed in a deferred or exempted class for any of the reasons in this paragraph set forth, he shall not be entitled to remain therein unless he shall in good faith continue, while physically able to do so, to work at and follow such occupation, employment, or business, and if he fails so to do shall again become subject to the draft; the President shall make regulations for enforcing this provision."

This provision clearly means that the Act will provide not military draft alone, but draft for all labor in occupations at home.

The membership of the American Federation of Labor has but one purpose in this war—to win the war. Its purpose is to so conduct itself as to give the greatest possible strength to our country.

The American Federation of Labor has given every service at its command to make the military draft a success thus far, and it will continue to do so. It has voluntarily rendered full and unselfish service in industry. It has taken great pride in giving freely its best service to the Republic.

The American Federation of Labor must, however, protest most emphatically against any measure which aims to place the working people of the country under draft compulsion in industry. American labor would at once regard such a measure as a direct attack upon its integrity, and affront to its pride in past achievement and a suspicion concerning its motives for the future.

It will be unnecessary for me to recall to you the record of conduct and achievement made by American Labor since our country entered the war, but may I call to your attention the fact that in England where there exists legislation affecting Labor in a much more compulsory manner than in the United States, there has been a record of more wide-spread dissatisfaction and stoppage of work.

American Workers ask but one thing and that is that they may have the opportunity to work under conditions that will permit them to give their best service to the country. They are ardent in their desire to serve fully and continuously. They recognize fully what is at stake in this great struggle. They need no compulsion, and I am sure I voice their views when I say that they will feel the keenest resentment at any attempt to compel them to give that which they are already giving gladly in a cause which they hold more sacred than life.

It seems to me improbable that this proposed compulsory legislation meets your conception of what needs to be or ought to be done and I express to you the protest of Organized Labor against the contemplated compulsory provision in the belief that it will find agreement in your own view of what is just and right.[2]

Respectfully yours,　Saml Gompers.
President,　American Federation of Labor.

TLS, Woodrow Wilson Papers, DLC.

1. The new draft act, which became law on Aug. 31, 1918, extended the Selective Service Act of 1917 to include men between the ages of eighteen and forty-five (U.S. *Statutes at Large*, 40: 955–57). The final version of the act did not include the provision to which SG objected.

2. President Woodrow Wilson sent a copy of SG's letter to Secretary of War Newton Baker on Aug. 20, 1918, asking his opinion of the objectionable provision. Baker replied on Aug. 22 that the amendment simply stated the policy that was then in operation. Since the government already had the authority to act along those lines, Baker said he was indifferent as to whether or not the provision was included in the bill.

From Percy Thomas[1]

The Commercial Telegraphers' Union of America
August 14, 1918.

Dear Sam:—

I would like to find out what Burleson intends doing.

We have made substantial progress, but many many still are on the pendulum. Burleson's failure to definitely announce his policy is retarding our growth and costing support.

Unless the Postmaster General recognize the right of the Telegraphers to organize and affiliate with a union of their craft, and do so soon, he will have the fight of his life on his hands, and although our means may seem to him negligible, I think they will prove sufficient to focus the attention of the country on his part in the issue. He can have the real support of all engaged in the Telegraph industry; through that support can make Government control a success, can demonstrate the wisdom of Government Ownership of the wire systems, and he can refuse it and thereby justify at least, in part, the impression that Theodore N. Vail[2] was indirectly his sponsor, is his master and that his advocacy of Government Ownership is as sincere as his desire is to help men to a higher state. . . .[3]

Clowry,[4] Carlton and their subordinates for years have made Americans blush for themselves in Western Union offices. It will not look well after the President's Proclamation[5] for Mr. Burleson to imitate them. Nor can we permit him to refuse us organization and equal rights for men and women. It would mean, at the close of the war, if the wires were returned to private control, the driving out of the business of all who had opposed Vail and Carlton's will. We must protect those who have shown enough of the milk of human bravery to fight official oppression . . .[6] I am thoroughly rebellious at this delay, and think the Proclamation should go as it lays.[7]

Sincerely and Fraternally,   Percy Thomas.

TLS, Files of the Office of the President, General Correspondence, reel 97, frame 357, *AFL Records.* Handwritten notation: "Aug 16 Answered by Mr. Konencamp."

1. Percy THOMAS was president of New York District Council 16 of the Commercial Telegraphers' Union of America (1917–19, 1921, 1923) and deputy international president or organizer for the union (1907, 1918–19).

2. Theodore Newton Vail (1845–1920) was a founder, president (1885–87, 1907–19), and chairman of the board (1919–20) of the American Telephone and Telegraph Co.

3. Ellipses in original.

4. Robert Charles Clowry (1838–1925) served as president and general manager of Western Union from 1902 to 1910. American Telephone and Telegraph acquired control of the company in 1909.

5. That is, President Woodrow Wilson's proclamation of Apr. 8, 1918, endorsing labor's right to organize. See "From C. O. Young," July 8, 1918, n. 5, above.

6. Ellipses in original.

7. On Aug. 7, 1918, Postmaster General Albert Burleson, director general of the U.S. Telegraph and Telephone Administration, agreed to reinstate Western Union employees discharged for union membership and assured Commercial Telegraphers' president Sylvester Konenkamp there would be no further discrimination against union members. On Aug. 14 Burleson directed Western Union to take back any employees dismissed for union affiliation, but the company would only agree to "rehire" the workers—not "reinstate" them—thus stripping them of their seniority, and it refused to take all the men back. Konenkamp protested the matter to the National War Labor Board at the end of August and again in October. The following April, after lengthy negotiations, the Telegraph and Telephone Administration ordered Western Union to restore seniority rights to the telegraphers rehired by Dec. 31, 1918. Although some

seven hundred workers benefited from this decision, the Commercial Telegraphers charged that many more should have been covered, that Western Union was still hostile toward the union, and that their wage demands were not being met. These problems culminated in an unsuccessful strike by the telegraphers, June 11–July 2, 1919.

From Charles Moyer

International Union of Mine Mill and Smelter Workers
Denver, Colo., August 28, 1918.

Dear Sir and Brother:

In answering your favor of the 21st.[1] permit me to say in re the deportation of A.F. of L. organizers at Birmingham, Alabama that while in attendance as a delegate on the A.F. of L. convention at St. Paul, I received through the mails, first, the enclosed resolution; third [second], a letter from Ed. Crough,[2] general organizer of the International Union of Mine, Mill and Smelter Workers, also I believe, a voluntary organizer of the American Federation of Labor.

The letter was in part as follows:

"Last Friday night, June 7th. I went to North Birmingham with negro Hale[3] to attend a mass meeting; he informed me he had distributed hundreds of circulars among the negroes that day yet when we arrived at the hall there were no negroes in sight. We were there about thirty minutes and no negroes had arrived and the hall was not lighted. About this time a white man came and asked for the proprietor whose name was Taylor; he was told Taylor was gone after ice, he then walked away. I was informed that he was a plumber working for the city. We then noticed an auto loaded with Company bosses drive up and stop at the upper side of the place, the men not getting out of the machine. After a few minutes more, two machines came up from the other side, a number of men jumped out of them and rushed over to where I was sitting. The plumber was with them and he pointed to Hale and myself saying we were the ones. Then three men told me they had a warrant for me. I demanded to see the warrant, they seized me and forced me into an auto where one man kept a gun on me while the other drove the machine out into the country about twenty miles. They then placed a cloth over my eyes tying it tight and took me out of the machine; in a few minutes I heard another machine drive up and then I was handcuffed to another man whom I afterward found was Hale. After having us sit on a bench for a long time while they entered into a discussion among themselves they came over to us and told Hale to make a statement which he did. I was then asked for a statement after which they took some letters and two rituals from me. Two of the letters were from you, the others were from my wife,[4] nephew and brother. They kept all of the correspondence. In my statement I told them my mission in Alabama, and from whom I carried credentials. They then began to argue with me saying that I did not understand the South or the negro that the negro could not be organized except through the Southern white man and advised me to have nothing more to do with them. They said Flynn[5] and others had come to North Birmingham and preached "Social Equality" between the races and they would not stand for it and that I had better stay away from Birmingham. One of them cursed me, saying I should be in Hell. He appeared to be the leader of the mob.

["]After about an hour of arguing, they took us across the road saying they were going to tar and feather us. They tore off my tie and collar then my coat but finally said they would direct me to the next depot if I would promise to take a train from there. Being uncertain as to what they might do I promised to take the train. They then stripped the negro and put something on him, it looked like tar; they then plastered him with feathers. I was taken up the road again, blind-folded and turned loose. After they had told me every turn in the road so that I would not go astray. After hearing them leave I returned to look for the negro but could not find any trace of him. Later I found a place called Republic where I succeeded in getting a man out of bed to drive me to Birmingham, reaching there about seven o'clock in the morning. I later went to the office of the machinists and found Hale there; he said he got back about four o'clock, that they took him back with them within six miles of town. That he went to a coal mine, got some gasoline, paid two men to rub off the tar and walked into town."

["] (Signed) Edward Crough."

Later developments in this case are explained in the following copy of a letter from Mr. B. W. King.

["] (LETTER HEAD)

["]International Association of Machinists
["]Lodges No. 7, 271, 359.
["]Birmingham, Alabama.
["]August 24th, 1918.

["]Mr. Chas. H. Moyer,
["]Itl. Pres. M.M. & S.W.
["]#503–511 Denham Bldg., Denver, Colo.

"Referring to our previous correspondence and telegrams in reference to the grand jury investigations of the outrage against Organizer

Edward Crough near this city, beg to further advise that the grand jury summoned and heard a large number of witnesses in this case on August 7th. However they did not complete the case, but recessed until September 9th, at which time they will hear any additional testimony that we can produce and ballot on the indictment.

["]I have conferred with the Circuit Solicitor who is prosecuting the case and he advises me to get in touch with you and have Crough here on September 9th. Both the Solicitor and the Attorneys for the State Federation of Labor are of the opinion that we will be able to complete an excellent case against the guilty parties if we can get Crough here on Sept. 9th.

["]We are going the limit in this case and we would thank you very much to get in touch with Crough and have him make arrangements to be on hand in Birmingham at the time specified.

["]Thanking you to give this matter your immediate attention and advice, I am with best wishes, fraternally yours,

"(Signed) B. W. King
["]President　Birmingham Trades Council.["]⁶

I advised Mr. King by wire that Mr. Crough is at this time in Russellville, Alabama.

Hoping that the foregoing will be helpful to you in presenting this case to the proper Government officials and that they may be interested to the end that a full and complete investigation⁷ shall be had, I am,

fraternally yours,　Chas H. Moyer
President　I.U. of M.M. & S.W.

TLS, AFL Microfilm Convention File, reel 29, frames 1393–94, *AFL Records*.

1. The letter of Aug. 21, 1918, asked Charles Moyer to provide any relevant information or documents relating to the recent deportation of organizers from Birmingham, Ala. (SG to Moyer, reel 238, vol. 250, p. 247, SG Letterbooks, DLC). Moyer had brought the issue to the attention of the 1918 AFL convention, which directed the Executive Council to demand a federal investigation of the matter.

2. Edward Crough (1874–1951) was an organizer for the Western Federation of Miners (from 1916, the International Union of Mine, Mill, and Smelter Workers) from about 1905 until 1918 and served as a vice-president of the union from 1918 until 1926.

3. William W. Hale, an AFL salaried organizer in 1918.

4. Katherine Dye Crough.

5. Thomas H. Flynn, an AFL salaried organizer from 1900 to 1923.

6. The Birmingham, Ala., Trades Council was founded in 1890 and chartered by the AFL the same year.

7. On Sept. 3, 1918, acting president John Alpine sent a copy of Moyer's letter to William B. Wilson (reel 238, vol. 250, p. 577, SG Letterbooks, DLC). Wilson replied on Sept. 12 that the Department of Labor was looking into the matter (AFL Microfilm Convention File, reel 29, frame 1395, *AFL Records*).

From Samuel Harry Gompers

On Active Service with the American Expeditionary Force
Sept 1 1918.

Dear Grandfather;

I am very glad to know that you have arrived safely in London, and only wish that I were in England so that I could spend a few days with you.

I understand that you are to visit Paris before you return, if this is so, let me know, and we will see if we can make some arrangement to get together.

We are located about—[1] miles behind the lines, and in the zone of advance, waiting for equiptment. I am writing two letters one to London & one to Paris, and hope that you will receive one of the two. my address at present is

Priv. Harry B Gompers
185 U.S. Aero Squadrin
A.P.O. 731 A.
A.E.F. France
No. 253043.

Would like to know if you have done anything about my re-instatment & commission, have not heard from you for over three months.

Will close now hoping to hear from you very soon; I remain

Your Grandson   Sam Gompers.

ALS, Files of the Office of the President, General Correspondence, reel 97, frames 671–72, *AFL Records*.

1. Blacked out.

To John Alpine

Derby, England, September 4 [3], 1918.

Mr. John R. Alpine,
Acting President A.F. of L.,
Dear Sir and Bro.

First let me say that I am considerably disappointed in not having received a letter from you. However, I suppose I should not complain because everything must be regarded as secondary to bringing over here our fighting boys and men who are engaged in this great war, together with the munitions and supplies.

Since my arrival here I have been busy every hour. On the trip over I delivered three addresses: one evening to the soldiers in the stern of the vessel, again to the soldiers in the bow and another evening to the officers and civilian passengers in the lounge or saloon, and of course discussions and conferences with several of the officers and passengers.[1] In addition there were almost daily conferences with the men composing our mission.

On the ship's arrival the Mayor of the city gave us a royal reception and we then went on our way to London.[2] A number of men came to see me from the Government, American Embassy and labor organizations as well as a number of personal friends. The British Government tendered us a luncheon[3] at which Mr. George Barnes,[4] of the British War Labor Cabinet presided. It was attended by men in the labor movement as well as representatives of all shades of opinion, governmental and private groups. I sat between Mr. Barnes and the Prime Minister, Lloyd George. Addresses were made by Mr. Barnes, the Prime Minister, another labor member of the Cabinet Mr. George Roberts,[5] and the British Ambassador to Washington, Lord Redding,[6] who is now in London. Of course I had to respond.[7] Perhaps you may have seen something of it in the American newspapers.

The press and newspapers here have been very kind in their treatment of our mission and myself. Of course we paid our respects to the American Embassy,[8] to the officers in command of our Army and Navy in England, and had conferences with the representatives of the British Government.

We paid a visit to Dartmouth Hospital,[9] which is the American base hospital near London for wounded American soldiers. It was a wonderful reception they gave me and of course I had to talk to them collectively, as well as going through several of the wards and shaking hands with the men and saying a word of cheer to them. It was wonderful to see how courageous they are and hopeful that they may soon again be fit to re-enter the ranks.

You know that Mr. Page,[10] the American Ambassador to Great Britain just tendered his resignation because of broken health, but Mrs. Page tendered us a luncheon at the Embassy and it was most interesting and charming.[11] In the evening there was a conference with some officers of the American Army located here and it too was exceedingly interesting and important.

On Sunday[12] I visited members of my family that I had never known before and from whom I had received letters in London. The American Government placed several automobiles at the disposal of our mission and I took one of them to carry me around as quickly as possible. I made an appointment for all of them to meet me at my cousin's home, Mr. Louis LeBosse,[13] 37 Merchant St., R3, London and I have set aside Monday morning at 11 o'clock for that purpose. They were delighted to meet me and declared that I had brought them much happiness by coming to see them.

Sunday afternoon we travelled from London to Derby. We had a special car reserved for us as well as seats in the restaurant car. We arrived here in a chilling down pour of rain, and because of such meagre hotel accommodations with three others I was taken to the mansion of the Mayor[14] and Mayoress,[15] Mr. and Mrs. Hulse, where we spent the night. They are typical English, and did all they could to make us comfortable. However, on Monday it was decided that we should stop at the St. James Hotel. Some of the members of the Parliamentary Committee gave up their rooms and doubled up in order that we might be accommodated at the hotel. Monday morning, Labor day, the Trade Union Congress opened in the Central Hall and a splendid reception was accorded us by the delegates to the Congress. We have been in constant attendance at the Congress. The sessions were interesting but the whole method of procedure is perceptibly different from the Conventions of the American Federation of Labor. In so far as procedure is concerned there is much room for improvement and it is not at all comparable to our conventions of the A.F. of L. at home.

Yesterday at noon there was a luncheon held in a tremendous tent. I estimate that there were 1200 persons present and of course I had to deliver an address.[16] It was given under the auspices of the Seamens League, of which J. Havelock Wilson, M.P. is General Secretary. The Prime Minister of Australia, Mr. Hughes was present and also delivered an address. In the afternoon the Congress met again and in the evening the Executive Committee of the General Federation of Trades Unions gave a dinner. You remember Mr. Appleton. He is the Secretary

September 1918

and he presided. As you can understand I was required there also to make an address. After the dinner and speeches were over there were no means of conveyance (street cars stop running at 9:45 pm) and we had to walk through the dark narrow streets from the hotel where the dinner was given to our hotel. In addition, it was again raining. This morning we again attended the Congress where an exciting discussion upon the important question of trade union jurisdiction.

I forgot to mention that the President of the Trade Union Congress delivered his address[17] and I refrain from discussing it for I do not know where it would lead me, and I should prefer not to discuss it in this letter.

At noon today on returning to the afternoon Congress I met the representative of the New York Tribune here who is covering the Congress and incidentally yours truly, and he informed me that he had just received the news of the tremendously important victory which the allied forces had achieved today in the capture of Lens.[18] On arrival in the hall I wrote this information on a piece of paper and handed it to the Chairman[19] and when "in good turn" he made the announcement to the delegates it seemed as if every[one] was aflame with glorious enthusiasm. It gave quite a set back to the feeling of pacifism which it has been endeavored to impregnate in the minds of some of the delegates. I was very much gratified at being the means of giving that piece of information.

This evening, thank goodness, I am free from meetings and conventions and so I am again at work with the assistance of my Secretary, Mr. Oyster,[20] and am taking advantage of it to get out some little work, as well as this letter.

I met a number of our friends who wanted to be remembered, among them Appleton, Tillet,[21] Siddons,[22] Gosling,[23] Bellemy[24] and Davis[25] and others, and those who know you wanted me to convey their very best wishes. In spite of the continuous important and pressing work, I am feeling quite well.

I met Arthur Henderson, Ramsay MacDonald and they were surprisingly cordial. There are many things which convey to me of their utterances that I prefer also not to write but which I shall take pleasure in mentioning when I get the opportunity after my return.

Wednesday evening I have a conference with the Parliamentary Committee of the British Trade Union Congress and the Executive Committee of the General Federation of Trade Unions, and thereafter I shall know more definitely as to the Interallied Labor Conference—whether London or Paris or both.

I am informed that the French Socialist Party have decided that if the General Federation of Trade Unions are represented at the inter-allied labor conference they will insist upon the American Socialist Party being represented. I have answered that I will refuse under any circumstances to participate in any conference at which the so-called American socialists are represented.

Mr. Stead[26] has asked me to have a conference upon the subject to draft a constitution or laws or rules for a proposed league of nations. I have expressed to him the view that we should favor such a proposition.

It is impossible to enumerate, much less comply with the requests made by the newspaper men and others to write articles, messages etc., for them, and the appeals which are made to me for conferences and for financial contributions are tremendous. I suppose they think that I am a man of means with unlimited funds at my command. I am not criticising them but simply mention it to show the notion which takes possession of some people. I expect to leave here Saturday morning in order to be in London that afternoon.

On the night we reached London I went out of the hotel intending to take a little walk, but the city was almost absolutely in darkness and one could not see an approaching person of which there were quite a number until within about two or three feet away, so I determined to return to the hotel and then went to work with Mr. Oyster.

One thing I think should be said and that is I am gratified at the unity of our own mission and the general feeling of cheer and confidence among the people of England whom I have met. They are tremendously grateful and appreciative of America's entrance into the war, of the large number of men and supplies sent over and of the spirit as represented by our great President and by the American Labor movement.

You will note that I have avoided as far as possible mentioning specifically dates and places and facts. This is followed not only as a matter of necessity but because it is of practical importance.

Kindly remember me to all of my friends. With best wishes,

Yours fraternally,   (signed) Samuel Gompers.

TLtcSr, Files of the Office of the President, General Correspondence, reel 97, frames 735–37, *AFL Records.* Typed notation: *"Copy."*

1. For one of SG's addresses aboard the *R.M.S. Missanabie,* delivered on Aug. 18, 1918, see Files of the Office of the President, Speeches and Writings, reel 113, frames 269–72, *AFL Records.*

2. On their arrival at Liverpool on Aug. 28, 1918, the members of the American labor mission were welcomed by the deputy lord mayor, Archibald Tutton James Salvidge (1863–1928) and by the American consul. SG and his party were escorted to London later that day by American naval officers.

3. The luncheon was held on Aug. 30, 1918.

4. George Nicoll BARNES, a member of Parliament from 1906 to 1922 (Labour, 1906–18; Coalition Labour, 1918–22), was minister without portfolio (1917–18) in the British War Cabinet.

5. George Henry Roberts (1868–1928) had served successively as president and secretary of the Norwich, England, branch of the Typographical Association, as president of the Norwich Trades Council, and, between 1904 and 1906, as a national organizer for the Typographical Association. From 1906 to 1923 he was a member of Parliament (Labour, 1906–18; Coalition Labour, 1918–22; Independent, 1922–23), serving as a party whip (1907–14; chief whip, 1912–14), parliamentary secretary to the Board of Trade (1916–17), privy councillor (1917), and minister of labour (1917–18).

6. Rufus Daniel Isaacs, Lord Reading (1860–1935), served as the British ambassador to the United States from January 1918 until May 1919. He was also lord chief justice (1913–21).

7. The address is printed in SG, *American Labor and the War* (New York, 1919), pp. 227–36.

8. On Aug. 29, 1918, the members of the American labor mission visited the American embassy and then went to the Spitalfields district of East London, where they saw the house in Fort Street where SG was born and the neighborhood where he grew up.

9. SG visited U.S. Army Base Hospital No. 37 at Dartford, Kent, on Aug. 30, 1918.

10. Walter Hines Page (1855–1918) served as U.S. ambassador to Great Britain from 1913 to 1918.

11. Alice Wilson Page (1858–1942) hosted the luncheon at the American embassy on Aug. 31, 1918.

12. That is, Sept. 1, 1918.

13. Louis Le Bosse, a printer, was the son of François and Clara Gompers Le Bosse.

14. E. J. Hulse (1874–1920), managing director of the clothing manufacturing firm of J. Smith and Co., served as mayor of Derby from 1917 to 1918.

15. Mrs. H. Hulse, who on Sept. 25, 1918, was elected as the first woman member of the Derby Town Council.

16. An account of SG's address at the luncheon, held on Sept. 2, 1918, was printed in the *Times* (London) on Sept. 3.

17. John William OGDEN, president of the Northern Counties' Amalgamated Weavers' Association (1911–30), served as president of the 1918 meeting of the TUC. He addressed the congress on Sept. 2.

18. Press reports of the capture of the French city of Lens in September 1918 were incorrect. The Germans did not evacuate the city until early October.

19. That is, John Ogden.

20. Guy Harrison Oyster (1879–1928) continued to serve as SG's traveling secretary until early 1923.

21. Benjamin TILLETT served as secretary of the Dock, Wharf, Riverside, and General Labourers' Union of Great Britain and Ireland from 1889 to 1922 and as a Labour member of Parliament from 1917 to 1924 and from 1929 to 1931.

22. Probably James Andrew SEDDON, president of the National Amalgamated Union of Shop Assistants, Warehousemen, and Clerks (1902–19), who served as a member of Parliament (Coalition National Democratic and Labour) from 1918 to 1922.

23. Harry GOSLING was secretary of the Amalgamated Society of Watermen and Lightermen (1893–1921) and president of the National Transport Workers' Federation (1911–21).

24. Albert BELLAMY served as president of the Amalgamated Society of Railway

Servants (1909, 1911–13) and its successor, the National Union of Railwaymen (1913–17).

25. William John DAVIS was secretary of the National Society of Brassworkers and Metal Mechanics.

26. Francis Herbert Stead (1857–1928), a socialist and a pacifist, was superintendent (1894–1921) of the Browning Hall Settlement House in London and in 1916 was a founder of the League to Abolish War, which supported creating an international organization equipped with a peacekeeping army.

Excerpts from a News Account of an Address by Samuel Gompers at the 1918 Trades Union Congress in Derby

Derby, Sept. 5. [1918]

MR. GOMPERS AT THE CONGRESS.

Mr. Samuel Gompers, President of the American Federation of Labour, gave an address to the Trade Union Congress this morning. . . .

It would be untrue to say that the speech of Mr. Gompers quite fulfilled the expectations of many members of his audience. It was long and discursive, and failed, except at intervals, to grip and rouse the delegates. The Congress likes to be taken, as it were, by assault. Mr. Gompers just moved quietly from topic to topic, making no appeal to the emotions except, curiously enough, when he digressed from his theme. One received the impression that he was suppressing his instincts and picking his way cautiously, for fear lest he should shock or offend one section or another of his hearers. In spite of this the message which he brought was both heartening and instructive. . . .

. . .

MR. GOMPERS' MESSAGE FROM AMERICA.

Mr. Samuel Gompers was received with enthusiastic cheers. He was proud, he said, to appear, for the third time, before the British Trade Union Congress. He had been with them before at Cardiff in 1895[1] and at Ipswich in 1909.[2] Now he was with them on their golden anniversary. They represented four-and-a-half million wage-earners. The American Federation of Labour represented three-and-a-half millions. When they bore in mind the vastness of America and the diversity of race and tongue among its people, when they remembered that many of these people came to America in bitterness against their own countries, when they remembered that slavery had only been abolished for a little more than 50 years, and when, with those facts in mind, they saw three-and-a-half million trade unionists in America united in spirit and in fact, they must realize that the movement was a tribute to the genius of American manhood and character. The American Labour movement had undergone many of the same trials as the British movement. As a result of one such trial they had secured the enactment of a declaration that the labour of a human being was not a commodity or article of commerce. (Cheers.) In addition, a law had been passed giving the seaman the right to quit his vessel when it was in safe harbour, and it was his hope that at an early date the democratic countries of the world would pass a similar law.

Referring to the agreement with the War Department and the Navy Department in America, whereby trade union rates, hours, and conditions prevailed on all war work, Mr. Gompers said:—"That agreement was accepted by several Departments, including the Shipping Board engaged in the construction of ships. Thank God they are being turned out at a rate never dreamt of in the philosophy or imagination of America. You have heard, no doubt, of a great ship being turned out in one of our shipyards in 27 working days. Just before I left the other side for England I learned that a 12,000–ton steel ship was launched within 24 working days from the time when the keel was laid. (Cheers.) During the days of the Civil War in America the cry went up for men, and the men of the North sent back the message to Abraham Lincoln: 'We are coming, Father Abraham, five hundred thousand strong.' America says to Great Britain, France, and Italy, and her other Allies: 'We are coming, men of the democracies, five million men strong.' (Loud cheers.) I may, in passing, quote the remark made by that great leader of the democrats of the world, President Wilson (cheers), who said: 'Why stop at 5,000,000?'" (Cheers.)

There was now entire agreement between the Government of the United States and the Labour movement, Mr. Gompers continued. He had not always been in accord with Governments, either in the United States, or here in the country of his birth. He had not been in accord with the British Government at the time of the Boer War. He had not agreed with the policy of the old Governments towards Ireland. (Cheers.) But the Albion of the old day was not the Britain of to-day. The American Federation of Labour had laid down certain fundamental principles of right and justice, and pledged themselves to support the Government of the United States in meeting its enemies for the maintenance of those principles. . . .

No Peace with a Ruthless Marauder.

Mr. Gompers next described the constitution and work of the Labour Policies Board in America.[3] The American trade union movement, he went on, is all its own. We will not yield to any body or group the leadership of our movement, whether it be the Democratic Party, the Republican Party, the Socialist Party, or any other party. We stand by ourselves. We make no pretence to being brainy, intelligent, or even idealist. We simply know that we are wage workers. Our movement is of the working people, for the working people, by the working people. In this world crisis our movement has stood unswervingly for international peace. None was stronger in its declaration than our movement, but how many of us could believe in international peace when a ruthless marauder set his hordes on peace-loving peoples, aimed at the destruction of democracy and freedom, and aspired to world domination? How anyone can continue longer to entertain thoughts and ideals of international peace while this is going on is far beyond my ken. (Loud cheers.) Labour is not in this war because of love of war. The men in uniform in Great Britain and France are not the representatives of militarism. (Cheers.) I hate the thought of killing, but unless we defend our wives and our children, unless we are willing to fight in defence of the ideals and the democracy for which the men of long ago and the men of the recent past have dared to suffer, then we shall be unworthy of our great heritage. I would not prolong the war one minute longer than is necessary to achieve the aims of the democracies of the world, but I should be unwilling to shorten it by one hour if it meant that the militarist machines are to be continued as they are now, and to bring us within the next decade into another war. (Loud cheers.)

. . .

Times (London), Sept. 6, 1918.

1. For a summary of SG's address before the 1895 meeting of the TUC, see *The Samuel Gompers Papers*, vol. 4, pp. 59–60.

2. For a summary of SG's address before the 1909 meeting of the TUC, see *The Samuel Gompers Papers*, vol. 7, pp. 489–90.

3. Secretary of Labor William B. Wilson established the War Labor Policies Board on May 13, 1918, to standardize the labor policies of government agencies relating to wages, hours, working conditions, and the distribution of labor. It consisted of representatives from the departments of Labor, War, Navy, and Agriculture, the Food, Fuel, and Railroad Administrations, the War Industries Board, the U.S. Shipping Board, the Emergency Fleet Corporation, and the Committee on Public Information.

James Duncan to Frank Morrison

Office of First Vice-President
Quincy, Mass., Sept. 13, 1918.

Mr. Frank Morrison,
Washington, D.C.
Dear Sir & Brother:

Your favor of Sept. 7 is received. If you do not have some idea of the personnel of the "Laboring Men's Council" referred to by Major E. F. Kinkead,[1] it would be a good idea to have some of our local or general organizers look into it, so that it might be known who the men are, but if you have an idea who they are let me know sometime when you are writing.

Bill Hayward[2] and the I.W.W.s connected with him had a speedy trial and their trip to Leavenworth was arranged without much ostentation and which will have burned into the heart of Mr. Hayward, for so strong was his ego that no doubt he expected there would be a great demonstration and which did not materialize.

And, now comes the alleged defence of Debs. As I am writing to you his case is not settled, but as he while not pleading guilty pleaded guilty, very likely he too will be locked up or fined, or both, for his wild ravings.[3] In the plea on his own behalf, he fought for free speech, but then like his earlier life he did not understand the difference between free speech and license. He had a wonderful, active brain and it is too bad it has been so misapplied. His erraticism was as much in evidence in the sensational ending of the trial as had been his course in earlier life. He evidently had four lawyers[4] selected by himself to take care of his case and who pleaded not guilty for him; then when the time came for him to put in defence he had none, brushed his lawyers aside and addressing the judge and jury admitted everything as charged against him. Evidently the freedom of speech and press he claimed for himself was utilized by the reporters present, for in describing the closing scenes they said of him that he had a tall, gaunt form, clothed in a well worn grey suit of clothes, which hung on him as if the clothes had been made for a man several times his size. Again his erraticism you see is in evidence, for if he could afford to have four attorneys taking care of a case in court in which he was to admit the full truth of the charges against him, a small part of the fees to the lawyers could have been well applied in getting him a union made suit of clothes, fitting him and looking neatly; but then, an up-to-date appearance of that kind would not perhaps have had the same effect upon the jury.

Fraternally,   James Duncan
First Vice-Pres.

TLS, AFL Microfilm National and International Union File, Granite Cutters Records, reel 38, frame 1574, *AFL Records.*

1. Eugene Francis Kinkead (1876–1960), a former Democratic congressman from New Jersey (1909–15) and sheriff of Hudson County, N.J. (1915–17), was a major in the military intelligence division of the U.S. Army, stationed in Washington, D.C. He later became a banker. Kinkead had written Frank Morrison to warn him that an organization known as the "Laboring Men's Council" had recently been formed "out of the very radical elements of the industrial workers of the world" to take over or subvert the AFL (Morrison to Kinkead, Sept. 7, 1918, vol. 503, p. 708, Frank Morrison Letterbooks, George Meany Memorial Archives, Silver Spring, Md.).

2. William Dudley HAYWOOD, secretary-treasurer of the IWW, was convicted of conspiracy to interfere with the war effort in August 1918 and sentenced to twenty years in prison. Released on bail pending appeal, Haywood fled to the Soviet Union in 1921.

3. Eugene Victor DEBS was arrested in June 1918 under provisions of the Espionage Act for a speech he gave in Canton, Ohio, at the state convention of the Socialist party. He was tried in September on charges of attempting to incite insubordination and mutiny in the armed forces and seeking to obstruct recruiting and enlistment. At his trial Debs admitted making the speech but denied he was guilty of the charges, claiming his right to freedom of speech. He was convicted and sentenced to ten years in prison and began serving his sentence after the U.S. Supreme Court upheld his conviction in March 1919 (*Debs v. United States,* 249 U.S. 211 [1919]). His sentence was commuted to time served by President Warren Harding in 1921.

4. Debs was represented by attorneys Seymour Stedman, William Cunnea, Joseph Sharts, and Morris Wolf.

An Excerpt from an Account of the Inter-Allied Labour and Socialist Conference in London

[September 20, 1918]

· · ·

Mr. Frey (United States) presented the following report of the Commission on war aims:—

The Conference welcomes the participation of the American Federation of Labour, and recognises, in agreement with the Federation, in this world war a conflict between autocratic and democratic institutions; the contest between the principles of self-development through free institutions and that of arbitrary control of government by groups or individuals for selfish ends.

The Conference agrees that, after four years of war, it is essential that the peoples and the Governments of all countries should have a full and definite knowledge of the spirit and determination of this Inter-Allied Conference, representative of the workers of the respective countries, with reference to the prosecution of the war.

In accordance with the declaration of the previous Conferences of the 14th of February 1915,[1] and 20th to 24th[2] February, 1918, the Conference declares it to be its unqualified determination to do all that lies within its power to assist the allied countries in the marshalling of all their resources, to the end that the armed forces of the Central Powers may be driven from the soil of the nations which they have invaded and now occupy; and, furthermore, that these armed forces shall be opposed so long as they carry out the orders or respond to the control of the militaristic autocratic Governments of the Central Powers which now threaten the existence of all self-governing people.

The Conference, further, welcomes the confirmation in all essential features, which the 14 propositions laid down by President Wilson, and presented to the Conference by the American Federation of Labour, give to the proposals contained in the Memorandum on War Aims, agreed to by the Conference of 20th to 24th February, 1918, and appended hereto. The conference accepts these 14 propositions as a concise summary of the main principles which the Memorandum of War Aims expounds in detail to the various questions to be dealt with; and agrees that only in these principles can the groundwork for a lasting peace be found.

The Conference accordingly calls upon the several Governments of the allied nations unequivocably to adopt these principles, as formulated by President Wilson and expounded in the Memorandum of War Aims, in a Joint Declaration of Allied Policy; and the Conference recommends the representative organisations of the workers in each country to bring pressure to bear upon the Government, in order to induce it to adopt this course.

The Conference once more takes note of the tremendous sacrifices which the world is requiring from the mass of the people in each country. It declares that because of their response in defence of principles of freedom the peoples have earned the right to wipe out all vestiges of the old idea that the government belongs to or constitutes a "governing class." In determining issues that will vitally affect the lives and welfare of millions of wage-earners, justice required that they should have direct representation in the agencies authorised to make such decisions. The Conference, therefore, declares, in confirmation of the demand of the Inter-Allied Conference of 20/24th February, that:—

1. In the official delegations from each of the belligerent countries

which will formulate the Peace Treaty the workers should have direct official representation.

2. A World Labour Congress shall be held at the same time and place as the Peace Conference that will formulate the Peace Treaty closing the war.

The Conference further welcomes the declaration by the American Federation of Labour of the fundamental principles to be included in the Peace Treaty, as being in substantial agreement with those applied in detail in the Memorandum of War Aims of 20th-24th February appended hereto, and also with the 14 propositions of President Wilson, namely:—

1. A league of the free peoples of the world in a common covenant for genuine and practical co-operation to secure justice, and, therefore, peace in relations between nations.

2. No political or economic restrictions meant to benefit some nations and to cripple or embarrass others.

3. No indemnities or reprisals based upon vindictive purposes, or deliberate desire to injure, but to right manifest wrongs.

4. Recognition of the rights of small nations and of the principle, "No people must be forced under sovereignty under which it does not wish to live."

5. No territorial changes or adjustment of power except in furtherance of the welfare of the peoples affected and in furtherance of world peace.

The Conference further expresses its general sympathy with the aspirations of the American Federation of Labour expressed in the following propositions which that Federation desires to see incorporated in the treaty which shall constitute the guide of nations in the new period and conditions into which we enter at the close of the war as being fundamental to the best interests of all nations and of vital importance to wage-earners:—

(a) That in law and in practice the principle shall be recognised that the labour of a human being is not a commodity or article of commerce.

(b) Involuntary servitude shall not exist except as a punishment for crime whereof the party shall have been duly convicted.

(c) The right of free association, free assemblage, free speech and free press shall not be abridged.

(d) That the seamen of the merchant marine shall be guaranteed the right of leaving their vessels when the same are in safe harbour.

(e) No article or commodity shall be shipped or delivered in international commerce in the production of which children under the age of 16 years have been employed or permitted to work.

(f) It shall be declared that the basic work day in industry and commerce shall not exceed eight hours per day.

(g) Trial by jury should be established.

The Conference notes that most of these aspirations find expression in general terms in the Memorandum of War Aims of 20th/24th February, whilst others—such as those relating to trial by jury and the restriction of the industrial employment of children under 16—are not universally applicable in all countries, and require adaptation to the circumstances of each nation. The Conference accordingly invites the special consideration of these aspirations by the Labour and Socialist Movements of the several allied nations. The Conference places special importance on paragraphs (a) and (c), which provide for an advanced conception of the right of the worker to complete self-control, and for the unabridged freedom of association and expression.

In pursuance of the policy of the Memorandum of War Aims of 20–24 February, the Conference declares its objection to all treaties and agreements purporting to bind nations, which have been or may be concluded by their Governments without immediate publicity and without Parliamentary authority or ratification; and protests against the continuation for a single day of the present war for the purpose of obtaining any objects aimed at by any of the secret treaties or agreements which are not in accord with the 14 propositions of President Wilson or the Memorandum on War Aims appended hereto.[3]

. . .

Proceedings of the Inter-Allied Labor Conference . . . (Washington, D.C., [1918?]), pp. 31–33.

1. See *The Samuel Gompers Papers,* vol. 9, pp. 239–40, n. 2.

2. The conference actually concluded on Feb. 23, 1918.

3. The conference adopted the report of the Commission on War Aims later the same day.

An Address before the Inter-Allied Labour and Socialist Conference in London

September 20, 1918.

(Replying to Mr. Kneeshaw,[1] Scotland)

Mr. Gompers: Perhaps I might have avoided arising and addressing myself to the question under consideration if it had not been for the challenge offered by the delegate who says he comes from Scotland, but inasmuch as he has put forth the challenger I cannot refrain from speaking and taking cognizance of his challenge, and at the same time discussing some of the matters which have been presented upon this floor today.

First let me say that anticipating the challenge of the delegate I did go to Scotland[2] (Applause) (Interruption by Kneeshaw) (Hold your tongue, sir: I did not interrupt you.) and within 24 hours of the time it was known that I was to come to Edinbourgh—the information was given through a simple announcement made—Usher's Hall was filled to its capacity. My associates and I delivered addresses upon what we believed to be the war situation and the manner in which the workers and the masses of the people of our democratic country and the allies considered it, and I did not hesitate to present fully and frankly the American labor position and the position of the American people and the Government upon the real issues. And I may say that my associates and I were rewarded with a reception and approval of our remarks by a unanimous vote of that great meeting, and the President[3] of the Edinbourgh Trades Council with the other officers of that Trades Council were upon the platform, and with the President of the Trades Council moved a vote of thanks to my associates and myself for the presentation of our position. The motion was passed unanimously. I may say too, that the President of the Trades Council informed my associates and me that late on the previous evening while that council was in session the information was conveyed to that body that my associates and I were coming to Edinbourgh the following evening, and the motion was made that the officers should not attend. More than likely the delegate would associate himself with the one who made that motion, too. Of course he would. Oh! these ultra goody-goody men; I trust them not.

Kneeshaw—interrupting. What's the use of arguing—

Gompers. I am not arguing with you—I am simply telling you. I might say that the Chairman of the Trades Council informed me that a motion was passed authorizing and directing them to appear at the meeting which we were to address.

The gentleman to whom I am replying spoke with regret that the American nation did not enter the war before the time it did. How can he consistently express regret that we entered the war too late and be himself opposed to the war.

He spoke of Debbs, Haywood and Mooney. That is a most delicate subject to have brought up here, but I am willing to meet it. Now, in the case of Mooney, there was a parade in the City of San Francisco with the purpose of urging the Government and the people of the

United States to prepare in the event that they were to be dragged into the war, and during that parade 22 people were killed by a bomb. The charge was made that Mooney was guilty of placing that bomb. I do not stand for that charge but I do believe that in civilized life there must be some one responsible for the placing of that bomb and that whoever is responsible should be punished in some form. The American Labor Movement has expressed the belief that there is sufficient doubt as to Mooney's guilt upon the evidence presented and demands at the hands of our government that he be given a new trial. The President of the United States has urged his great influence with the Governor of California that Mooney might be given the opportunity of a new trial. I do not know whether the delegate knows that in the United States in the matter of crimes, trials and the exercise of police powers there are 48 separate governments each of them in its own right and in its own way determining the trials of offenders or alleged offenders and that the President of the United States has no more power to order a new trial than has the premier of Great Britain or the King of England. So we have done our duty so far as Mooney is concerned and will continue to do so. No man, if we suspect him of being an unjust victim of greed or oppression can fail to receive our fullest support and cooperation. So you do not have to worry about what you call class conscience.

As for Haywood and Debbs perhaps the delegate would associate himself with them, too. Of course he would—he said so here, and my American understanding of that is this. Mr. Haywood and his associates in the I.W.W. have been the greatest enemies to the trade union movement of America—greater than any capitalistic combination of that country. I wish I had with me at this moment a pamphlet published in America—upon the activities of that character of men. Now the charge against him and his associates was not that he is against the organized labor movement of the United States but that he entered into a conspiracy with others for the purpose of bringing the authoritative action of the American Government into disrepute and to thwart the American Government's decision to carry on this war. I wonder how the delegate can consistently express regret that we came into the war so late and then sympathize with the men who conspired to defeat and overthrow the purpose to prosecute the war. Mr. Kneeshaw this morning spoke upon this subject declaring that there was no difference between the aims and purposes of what I believe he termed the imperialistic governments of Germany and Austria [and those] of the Allies. I do not want to misquote him—I want in substance to be substantially right.

Voice. That was right.

Well, I am glad that I asked the question. I never want to mis-state the position of another. Here we are in session in this conference and each giving expression to his views.

I wonder whether there is any difference in the holding of a conference of this character with the free expression of every man, in England, in France and in Germany. Perhaps Mr. Kneeshaw has been in Germany—I have, on two occasions, and how any man can express the thought that there is no difference between the democratic institutions of Great Britain, France and the United States on one hand and Germany and Austria on the other more than passes my understanding.

Kneeshaw, interrupting. Insofar as the purposes of the governments on both sides are concerned they are both imperialistic insofar as the war is concerned. I object to your putting words into my mouth.

Gompers. Believe me, if it were in my power, I would not put words into your mouth.

Let me call attention to a few incidents which may be a slight contribution to the discussion and understanding.

When the Government of Great Britain declared a proposition calling for what was then termed a "Naval Holiday,"[4] an effort to curtail the building of tremendous fleets and the reduction of the production of armaments, the American Federation of Labor, in Convention[5] soon after, took cognizance of that declaration and passed unanimously a resolution calling upon the Government of the United States to second the proposition and do everything within its power in furtherance of it. Due to our activity we succeeded in having the House of Representatives—on a par with your House of Commons—adopt the resolution[6] seconding the proposition. The Convention of the American Federation directed that I should communicate with the labor movements of all the countries for the purpose of having them prevail upon their respective governments so as to put that proposal into effect. Complying, I communicated with Mr. Carl Legien, President, International Federation of Trade Unions, conveying to him the action of our convention,[7] and requested him, as the President and the proper medium to communicate with the labor movements of the various countries and I asked him to convey this information and request to the labor movements of the countries with the result that he informed me that under German law he had no right to communicate such a resolution to the labor movements of the other countries.[8] Rather a big difference in the democracies of Great Britain and France and the United States and that of Germany. The American Federation of Labor passed a resolution calling upon the labor movements of the countries of the world to hold a peace conference at the same time and place where the conference of the official delegates of the various countries would meet.[9] Mr. Legien informed[10] me when I conveyed[11] that request to him that it would be utterly ridiculous and no influence could be had upon the Government of Germany. The day before the President of the United States appeared before the Congress of the United States I sent a cablegram[12] to Carl Legien asking him to do anything that he could to prevail upon his government or to give some utterance so that America might be kept out of the war. What was his answer? That he could not and would not, and directed me to appeal to Great Britain to stop the blockade of Germany because it was starving men and women and children in Germany[13]—forgetting that after all a blockade is only a siege—forgetting the siege of Paris in 1870 when they starved out the people of Paris. I wonder what the consequences would be to the democracies of Great Britain and France and the United States, what the opportunities for the labor movements of these countries would be if it were possible for Germany to win.

Since my associates and I have been in Great Britain we have talked and talked freely. We have not undertaken to criticize the labor movement of England or Scotland or Wales—we have presented our views and those views we shall continue to present—the criticism of the gentleman to the contrary, notwithstanding.

I hold in my hand a clipping from a German labor paper. The name of it I do not know. It gives a verbatim report of an address delivered by Mr. Legien, President of the German Federation of Trade Unions. I shall not burden you with reading all that it contains but just to give you a few of the salient points. In it Mr. Legien says every effort that the German labor movement has made in the interest of peace has been without result. You know and I have indicated in a way what efforts were made by the German labor movement in the interests of peace. Then it goes on to say that President Gompers came to Europe not to fulfill his duty as a leader to bring the war to a conclusion, but on the contrary to squelch the flame now so manifest among the workers of England. Well, I have been in England now for a little more than three weeks and I have not seen the flame. I have seen a spark here and there but far removed from the torch that is burning in the hands of British labor and the labor of France to light our way to the victorious and glorious peace by which we shall win the opportunity and right to live our own lives and work out our own salvation.

I could not help from making these observations. I came to England, not of my own volition, not of my own initiative at least, but upon the invitation of the men active in the labor movement of Great Britain, their fraternal delegates which they sent to our annual conventions, the delegates of the British labor movement who came to the United States, the Secretary of the Parliamentary Committee, our honored Secretary Right Honorable Mr. Thomas, Mr. Duncan,[14] Mr. Butterworth,[15] Mr. Appleton, each one of them, they did not give me an official invitation, but they said come to us, to meet our men and talk with them, your influence can do nought but good and we came here to try to help in the cause in which we are engaged with the instructions of the conventions of the American Federation of Labor repeatedly made, directing [and] requesting and authorizing our commission to come with the direct mandate of our people, 100%, not a dissenting view, the American people are determined that they are not going to permit this menace of militarism and autocracy to overwhelm the world. We recognize, the labor movement recognizes that this conflict is one between democracy and autocracy and that the only opportunity we shall have of working out our own salvation and destiny even with all the wrongs which exist in democratic countries is that we stand as a solid phalanx behind our respective countries until the battle flags of the allies are adorned with immortal wreaths of victory. The masses of the people, particularly the workers, in fact no one who has any understanding of the rights to which the workers are entitled and which has been to them now too long denied, can fail to see and understand that we are going to carry on—that we are going through. The Government of our country is in entire accord with the trend and the work and the understanding of the labor movement of our country; that we stand behind our rights as workers, as citizens, and we in turn, having confidence in the integrity and the high purpose of the men in control of our government, that we are going to stand as a unit behind the allies and are going to fight with them until the end, until democracy and the opportunity for emancipation shall have been secured.

TD, Files of the Office of the President, Speeches and Writings, reel 113, frames 283–89, *AFL Records.*

1. J. W. Kneeshaw (b. 1878) served on the city council of Birmingham, England, from 1911 to 1919 and was a member of the executive committee of the Labour party from 1918 to 1919. He was a conscientious objector during the war.

2. SG and the other members of the American labor mission left London for Scotland on Sept. 10, 1918. SG made addresses in Edinburgh on Sept. 11 and Glasgow on Sept. 13.

3. Andrew Eunson.

4. In March 1912 Winston Churchill, First Lord of the Admiralty, proposed a one-year naval holiday between Great Britain and Germany, during which no capital ships would be built by either nation. He reiterated the proposal the following year in March and again in October, suggesting that, in addition to halting naval construction themselves, Germany and Britain should attempt to persuade the other major European powers, the United States, and Japan to join in the agreement. Germany rejected the 1912 offer and failed to respond to the subsequent proposals.

5. The 1913 AFL convention adopted a resolution introduced by SG endorsing Churchill's proposal for a naval holiday, urging labor movements in other countries to support it and other governments to adopt it, and calling on the U.S. government to encourage the proposition.

6. H.Res. 298, introduced by Democratic congressman Walter Hensley of Missouri on Oct. 31, 1913, and passed by the House of Representatives on Dec. 8, asked President Woodrow Wilson to use his influence to bring about the one-year naval holiday agreement.

7. SG to Carl Legien, Dec. 19, 1913, reel 177, vol. 189, pp. 402–3, SG Letterbooks, DLC.

8. Legien replied on Jan. 21, 1914, that he preferred not to send the AFL resolution to other national trade union centers because it would introduce the discussion of highly divisive political questions into the International Federation of Trade Unions (AFL Microfilm Convention File, reel 27, frame 1022, *AFL Records*). He also noted that some national trade union centers, such as his own, were legally barred from adopting such a resolution.

9. The resolution was adopted by the 1914 AFL convention. See *The Samuel Gompers Papers,* vol. 9, p. 226, n. 4.

10. Legien to SG, Apr. 2, 1915, *The Samuel Gompers Papers,* vol. 9, pp. 263–65.

11. SG to Dear Sir and Brother, Dec. 10, 1914, AFL Microfilm Convention File, reel 27, frame 2082, *AFL Records.* SG sent the cable to some three dozen international trade union leaders.

12. "To Carl Legien," Apr. 2, 1917, above. The cable is dated the same day President Woodrow Wilson addressed Congress.

13. SG seems to be referring to Legien's reply to an earlier cable SG had sent him, dated Feb. 4, 1917 (see "To the Executive Council of the AFL," Feb. 4, 1917, n. 5, above). No reply to SG's cable of Apr. 2 has been found.

14. Charles DUNCAN was secretary of the Workers' Union and a Labour member of Parliament.

15. Joshua Butterworth, a member of the Shipconstructors' and Shipwrights' Association, served on the British labor mission to the United States in the spring of 1918.

John Voll[1] to Frank Morrison

Glass Bottle Blowers' Association
of the United States and Canada[2]
Philadelphia, Pa. Sept. 23, 1918.

Mr. Frank Morrison,
Secretary, American Federation of Labor,
Washington, D.C.
Dear Sir & Brother:

On September 11th[3] I wrote you regarding the action of the Local Draft Board at Tarentum, Pa., in ordering two members of our Association, who were picketing the Flaccus Glass plant, to either go to work or fight and requested that you take the matter up with the War Department, which you did, and in reply[4] sent me a statement, facsimile taken from the New York Times[5] from Secretary Baker of the War Department's position relative to the Work or Fight order which involved a dispute between capital and labor. This statement had been shown to the draft board but without avail. They exercise authority and power that has not as yet been exercised by the War Department and which Congress refused to put in the draft law.

The men who were ordered to work or fight are not claiming exemption nor do they ask to be placed in the deferred class. They are ready when their time comes to do their full and whole duty. However, it is not fair, not just, nor right that an employer, who has refused to pay the wage scale that 98% of the skilled men in the industry receive and who has refused to accept mediation and arbitration through government agencies after government investigation has been made, is given the opportunity by the government or by the War Department to fill up his plant at will with men who might be ready to accept the conditions which he prescribes through depriving our Association and our members from safeguarding our interest by informing the men who may be employed by the Flaccus Company of the conditions that prevail and the contention as between the company and the men who formerly worked in the plant. This order of the Local Draft Board simply means, if put into practice and carried out, an agency for breaking strikes and industrial disputes as between capital and labor.

As stated in my previous letter, we have advised every one of the men formerly employed in the Flaccus plant to obtain employment elsewhere[—]this they have done[—]and many of them are now working in plants in and around Tarentum on direct war orders for the government. It is necessary, tho, to leave one or two of our members on duty so that our interests might be protected and that we may be informed at all times as to any move the company may make for continuing the conditions which were so unfair and unjust previous to the men leaving their employ.

If this ruling or decision is to stand as made by this Local Board at Tarentum organized labor may as well resolve itself into a mutual admiration society, because so far as its activities are concerned in protecting its legitimate rights and interests they will be null and void and I am sure that our government or any governmental department does not want to abrogate or smother the rights of citizens who have contributed so much towards the successful preparation and prosecution of the war, who have sacrificed and are ready to sacrifice their all. So if this order is to stand at Tarentum then the Flaccus firm should be given orders from the War Department, that they must not, in any way or manner try to operate their plant so long as the workmen are prohibited from safeguarding their interest at that place.

Sincerely trusting you will give this your earliest attention,[6] I am, with kindest regards and best wishes,

Fraternally yours,   John A. Voll
President.

TLS, AFL Microfilm National and International Union File, Glass Bottle Blowers Records, reel 38, frame 1160, *AFL Records.*

1. John A. VOLL was president of both the Glass Bottle Blowers' Association of the United States and Canada (1917–24) and the Ohio State Federation of Labor (1909–18).

2. The GLASS BOTTLE BLOWERS' Association of the United States and Canada.

3. Voll to Frank Morrison, Sept. 11, 1918, AFL Microfilm National and International Union File, Glass Bottle Blowers Records, reel 38, frames 1159–60, *AFL Records.*

4. Morrison replied on Sept. 13, 1918, that he had taken the matter up with the War Department, and that in view of the Secretary of War Newton Baker's position on the "Work or Fight" order, the action of the Tarentum, Pa., draft board was unwarranted (AFL Microfilm National and International Union File, Glass Bottle Blowers Records, reel 38, frame 1160, *AFL Records*).

5. For the article in the *New York Times,* see "To Newton Baker," May 22, 1918, n. 5, above.

6. On Sept. 25, 1918, Morrison sent a copy of Voll's letter to Provost Marshal General Enoch Crowder's office, and on Oct. 4 he sent Voll a copy of the reply, which stated that the Tarentum draft board would be notified that selective service regulations were not to be used against persons involved in industrial controversies (AFL Microfilm National and International Union File, Glass Bottle Blowers Records, reel 38, frame 1161, *AFL Records*).

An Item in the *New York Times*

Paris, Sept. 24. [1918]

GOMPERS PARTY IN PARIS.

Samuel Gompers, President of the American Federation of Labor and his party of American labor leaders arrived in Paris today. They were received cordially by representatives of the Government and the Workers' Federation.[1] The Americans were entertained today by the federation and will have luncheon[2] at the Foreign Office tomorrow.

Mr. Gompers was met on his arrival by Arthur Hugh Frazier,[3] Secretary of the American Embassy, Captain Jackson,[4] the Naval Attaché, and other naval and army representatives. Mr. Gompers's grandson, an aviator in the American Army, who has just reached Paris from active service, awaited his grandfather at the hotel at which the labor leader will stop.

New York Times, Sept. 25, 1918.

1. On Sept. 24, 1918, the members of the American labor mission visited the head-quarters of the Confédération générale du travail (CGT; General Confederation of Labor), where SG addressed a group of striking dressmakers and seamstresses who were holding a mass meeting; that evening they were entertained by the CGT executive board at a dinner and reception. The next evening the mission visited the offices of the Fédération française des travailleurs du livre (the French typographical union), where SG made a short address and the group dined with officials of the union. On Sept. 26 SG addressed a mass meeting arranged by the CGT.

2. SG and the other members of the American labor mission attended a luncheon hosted by the French foreign minister, Stéphen-Jean-Marie Pichon, on Sept. 25, 1918.

3. Arthur Hugh Frazier (b. 1868), a career diplomat, was first secretary at the U.S. embassy in Paris (1916–18) and served on the staff of the Supreme War Council.

4. Richard Harrison Jackson (1866–1971), a career naval officer, served in 1917 and 1918 as naval attaché and special representative of the Navy Department to the Ministry of Marine in Paris.

Frank McCarthy[1] to Frank Morrison

General Organizer
American Federation of Labor
Boston, Sept. 26, 1918

Mr. Frank Morrison,
Secretary American Federation of Labor.
Dear Sir:—

In further reply to yours of August 13th[2] relative to unorganized laborers in Fore River and Squantum shipyards, I wish to say, since my report to you on the matter of August 16th I took up the question with Organizer Dick[3] of the International Boiler Makers Union and officers of the local[4] Boiler Makers Union whose members are employed in the shipyards named and found that the laborers that Organizer Dick had in mind was a great number of colored men employed in the yards as bolters, reamers and rivetters, lines of work coming within the jurisdiction of the Boiler Makers International Union, but which workers the Boiler Makers refused to admit to membership on account of their color. With the assistance of Organizer Dick and local Boiler Makers officers, I started to work in an effort to get these men into organization using the Boiler Makers Hall as a headquarters which they gave without charge. I organized a half a dozen of the men employed in the yards into a working committee, supplied them with printed matter for the meetings. At the first meeting which was attended by about forty, (all colored) it was clearly demonstrated that these men could not be organized into any but a Boiler Makers Union, as immediately after the speakers had made their various statements, the question of color was raised and a number of those in attendance who appeared to be trained for the purpose demanding to know why the white men employed in the same line of work as themselves and by whose side they were working every day, were taken into the Boiler Makers Union and they (the colored workmen) were denied admission to that organization. Organizer Dick, local Boiler Makers officers and myself endeavored to clearly outline and explain to them the situation and while we succeeded in convincing the majority of those in attendance of the advisability of their organizing into a A.F. of L. Federal Union, the noisy and apparently trained minority refused to be convinced and continued their pretense of believing as they expressed it, that the proposed organization was to be only a "nigger union" to be used by the white men to keep the colored men under control and have carried on that line of propaganda in the yards since that time. Since then we have held four meetings, all of which were worked up by a number of men employed in the yards aided by printed matter and all the assistance we could give but to no purpose, each meeting being smaller than the one preceding it, caused by the active opposition in the yards of those apparently trained opponents referred to above.

While I am of the opinion that the only way these people can be organized is by opening the doors of the Boiler Makers local to them, I am keeping at the work and am receiving very earnest assistance from the local officers of the Boiler Makers Union employed in the yard, the results of which work I will keep you informed.[5]

Yours respectfully,   Frank H. McCarthy
General Organizer   American Federation of Labor

TLS, AFL Microfilm National and International Union File, Boilermakers Records, reel 34, frames 2587–88, *AFL Records.*

1. Frank H. McCarthy served as an AFL salaried organizer from 1903 to 1932.

2. On Aug. 13, 1918, Frank Morrison wrote McCarthy that there were about a thousand unorganized black shipyard laborers in and near Quincy, Mass., and he instructed McCarthy to meet with international union organizers to consider the best course of action (vol. 503, p. 70, Frank Morrison Letterbooks, George Meany Memorial Archives, Silver Spring, Md.).

3. John Dick.

4. Possibly International Brotherhood of Boiler Makers, Iron Ship Builders, and Helpers of America 33 of Quincy.

5. The Boiler Makers did not establish a local union for these workers. In November 1918 the AFL chartered Federal Labor Union 16,354 in Boston, a union composed of black workers; McCarthy served as its secretary.

From R. Lee Guard

Washington, D.C. Oct. 7, 1918.

Mr. Samuel Gompers,
President American Federation of Labor,
c/o American Express Company, Paris, France.
Dear Mr. Gompers:

Today I received a note from Mr. Dehan asking me to send you the enclosed as he did not have your address. He also asked that I should send you his very best wishes. I am sending this to you to the Paris address although according to the cable reports you left for Italy, but probably you will get this on your return to Paris on your way home.

The Kaiser's peace proposal has just been made. Everybody is on an edge for the President's reply, but I think we can all anticipate with much certainty what will be the tenor of that reply.[1]

Your declaration that "Those who live by the sword must die by the sword"[2] has been widely commented upon by the papers here.

We are in the midst of the Fourth Liberty Loan drive. Mr. Alpine secured the approval of the Executive Council for the purchase of bonds to the amount of $10,000.[3] Needless to say the rest of us individually have done our duty in this respect.

I had a long talk this morning with Miss Melinda Scott who came in my office to see me. She is very anxious for your return for she is having troubles of her own in the new obligations she has assumed.[4]

I trust that you are keeping up to the mark physically. I am just as happy that you are not in Washington at the present time as there is a terrible epidemic of Spanish Influenza raging now.[5] Not only is this true of Washington but in the whole east and middle west. This morning's paper reports 10,000 cases in the city and there have been hundreds of deaths. The schools, churches, libraries and theatres are all closed. I fancy that the crowded housing conditions as well as crowded conditions in business and government offices do not help in the least to lessen the plague. Thus far no one in our office has been ill. I hope we will escape it.

With sincere good wishes, in which all of your friends here join, I am

Very truly yours,

TLc, Files of the Office of the President, General Correspondence, reel 98, frames 445–46, *AFL Records.*

1. The "Kaiser's peace proposal" was actually a note from German chancellor Max von Baden, addressed to President Woodrow Wilson and delivered to the White House on Oct. 6, 1918, by Swiss chargé Frederick Oederlin. It asked Wilson to call for an ar-

mistice and initiate peace negotiations based on the Fourteen Points and subsequent pronouncements. Wilson replied on Oct. 8, asking for a clarification of the note and demanding German withdrawal from all occupied territory as a precondition for a cease-fire. The two governments subsequently exchanged additional notes outlining the conditions for an armistice.

2. SG made this statement at a luncheon at the American Club in Paris on Sept. 26, 1918. It was quoted in newspapers in the United States the next day.

3. John Alpine to the AFL Executive Council, Sept. 27, 1918, Executive Council Records, Vote Books, reel 16, frame 93, *AFL Records.*

4. In August 1918 Melinda Scott was appointed a special representative of the U.S. Employment Service in the Department of Labor. She was granted a leave of absence from her work as an AFL salaried organizer in order to take the position.

5. An estimated thirty to fifty million people died worldwide in the influenza pandemic of 1918–19, well over half a million of them in the United States.

John Alpine to the Executive Council of the AFL

Washington, D.C. October 14, 1918.

Document Number 92.
Executive Council, American Federation of Labor.
Colleagues:

With profound regrets I am advising you that news was received at this office early this morning of the death of Miss Sadie Gompers, beloved daughter of President Gompers. Miss Gompers had been ill but a few days and her death was occasioned because of influenza, which disease as you know is exceedingly prevalent here. The sad news was cabled by the State Department to President Gompers, who at this writing to the best of our knowledge, is in Italy.[1]

You are aware of the proposed public demonstration which was to have been tendered Mr. Gompers at Chicago on November eighth, and in this connection let me advise that after consultation with Messrs. John B. Lennon, James O'Connell and Frank Morrison, and after having talked with First Vice-President James Duncan by telephone, I have assumed the responsibility of advising[2] Mr. Wright, of the American Alliance for Labor and Democracy, that the reception proposed to be held at Chicago on the eighth of November should be postponed until Mr. Gompers has been consulted with and after which a date may be determined upon.[3]

I feel that the members of the Executive Council will quite agree that this action is advisable.

The earthly remains of Mr. Gompers only daughter will be placed in a receiving tomb until the arrival of her father and definite arrangements then completed for final interment.[4] This reference is made in order that the Council may more fully understand the objections which must be presented and which should prevent the necessity of having Mr. Gompers leave his home for Chicago so soon after his arrival under such sad conditions. While Mr. Gompers has all the parental love of a father for the remaining members of his family, I feel it is not assuming too much authority if I say that the departed daughter occupied a little more than a proportionate share of his heart and affections. All in all, as stated, I believe the Chicago meeting should be deferred.

Just a word as to the meeting of the Executive Council at Laredo, Texas on November eleventh. Because of the reasons advanced for the deferment of the Chicago reception, I am in doubt as to the propriety of adhering to the original date set for the Laredo meeting.[5] There are, of course, different principles involved. The Chicago meeting is of the character of a personal demonstration given in honor of the President of the American Federation of Labor, while the effect of such a meeting would have a very distinct advantage with regard to the affairs of our nation and the war in which we are so vitally concerned. The Laredo meeting is of a different character; it is a meeting of the Executive Council of the American Federation of Labor held at Laredo primarily because of the Pan-American labor project. Invitations have been extended to President Woodrow Wilson and to President Carranza; to the Mexican Federation of Labor and to the governors of the border states of Mexico and of the United States. It is very unlikely that either President Wilson or President Carranza will attend the meetings referred to, but this council meeting will of necessity be of the utmost importance. Mr. Duncan has suggested in my telephonic conversation with him of today that the Laredo meeting might be postponed for one week, making the substitute date November eighteenth.

Of course President Gompers may arrive at a sufficiently early date to advise in person as to a change of date concerning the Laredo meeting, but then his arrival is not at all definite. It seems to me there are two or three suggestions that are quite applicable at this time:

First: Shall the Executive Council meeting at Laredo, scheduled for November eleventh be postponed one week or until November eighteenth and those interested and invited to attend be advised of the change in date of the meeting?

Second: Will you place the matter in the hands of Secretary Morrison and the writer, awaiting such further information as may be received, and after which you will be advised by wire of our proposed action in this matter?

Third: Shall we postpone the meeting indefinitely and wait until Mr. Gompers returns?

If I may be permitted I would say that the second proposition appeals to me as being preferable since there may be some developments within the next few days that may serve as a guidance.[6]

Kindly return your vote by wire as quickly as possible.

Fraternally yours,   John R. Alpine.
Acting President,   American Federation of Labor.

TLcS, Executive Council Records, Vote Books, reel 16, frame 112, *AFL Records*.

1. William B. Wilson cabled the news of Sadie Gompers' death to John Frey via the American embassy in Rome, which forwarded the message to SG's party in Turin: "Please break news to Mr Gompers that his daughter Sadie died this morning from influenza Remains will be interred temporarily until Mr Gompers return Mrs Gompers will go immediately to New York after interment" (undated cable, Samuel Gompers Papers, NN). SG's children also cabled, sending their message to reach their father in Paris, his next stop: "Sadie died double bronchitis from influenza Everything possible done Body held Washington Mother well Atlantic City with Emily Tyler Dad be brave" (undated cable, ibid.).

2. John Alpine contacted Chester Wright by telephone.

3. After subsequently hearing from SG's physician and other friends, Alpine and Frank Morrison were persuaded that arrangements for the Chicago meeting should go forward. A two-day reception for SG and the other members of the American labor mission to Europe was held in Chicago on Nov. 8 and 9, 1918, attended by representatives of ninety-six national and international unions, twenty-five state federations of labor, twelve state councils of defense, eight branches of the American Alliance for Labor and Democracy, as well as twelve governors and a number of other prominent individuals, including Felix Frankfurter, Edward Hurley, William McAdoo, and William B. Wilson. For SG's speech at the event, see "An Address at a Reception in Chicago Honoring the Members of the American Labor Mission to Europe," Nov. 8, 1918, below.

4. Funeral services for Sadie Gompers were held on Nov. 5, 1918, in New York City, with Rabbi Stephen Wise presiding.

5. Alpine and Morrison also decided to proceed with this meeting, and the AFL Executive Council met in Laredo and San Antonio, Tex., Nov. 11–21, 1918. While in Laredo the members of the Council attended the founding meeting of the Pan-American Federation of Labor, held Nov. 13–16.

6. The AFL Executive Council voted in favor of the second proposition.

John Alpine to James Duncan

Washington, D.C. October 18, 1918.

Mr. James Duncan,
First Vice-President, American Federation of Labor,
25 School Street, Quincy, Mass.
Dear Friend Jim:—

I have wanted to write you for several days but have been pulled here and there and everywhere, night and day, so that there has been no opportunity for a quiet talk with you. Yesterday our telephone operator tried all day to get you over long distance but failed. Then I sent you and the other members of the Executive Council the telegram[1] which, of course, you have before this.

My mind has not changed one iota from the first position I took as regards deferring the Chicago meeting and possibly the one at Laredo. Miss Guard and I hold that position. Sam's physician and other friends who have spoken, written or wired me upon the subject maintain that the meeting should not be called off. His physician, speaking as his medical adviser, expressed the belief that it would do Sam more harm to know that his friends felt that he might not be able to "carry on" than would the effort to address the meeting, no matter how great the strain, etc. If it had been Sam's son who was killed in service, it would be a different matter but his only daughter, his baby, who was also his companion, friend, pal and chum—the one whom he loved best of all his family—a strong, healthy young woman who had never been ill in her life—for her to be taken so suddenly, to me it seems inhuman to expect from him, what everyone else seems to expect, that it will be a relief to his feelings to address the Chicago meeting. As I say, I have not changed my mind. I have simply waived my position in the face of such insistent demands and the physician's opinion that the arrangements for the meeting should go on.

Of course the date for the Chicago meeting is tentative. The epidemic that is making such awful ravages may result in its indefinite postponement. In any event, I am advised by the officers of the Alliance that the sending out of cards with the definite date will be postponed as long as possible. In the meantime, there may come a message from Sam or John Frey or Charlie Baine[2] giving us some idea as to how he is standing the shock.

Of course, if the meeting does take place, you will be in Chicago prepared to make the welcoming address as originally planned. I hope though in the meantime you will have some care for yourself. Miss Guard and I have spoken of you frequently. We both realize that you did not have sufficient stay away from your office. She told me of her personal letter to you in which she related some of her personal experiences when she broke down three years ago—that she wrote you in the hope that what she said might have some influence in having you take sufficient time really to recuperate.

I have wished for you frequently. I have felt the need of your counsel and advice but I have tried as best I could to meet the emergency of the situation caused by President Gompers' absence. Aside from my personal desire for your good health and well being, Jim, I feel that in these troublous times, as never before, the labor movement needs more than ever, the help and close cooperation of every loyal, true, clear-thinking man and our country needs them and if possible, they will be even more needed during the reconstruction period which will follow the war. It is glorious to realize that one can serve one's fellowmen, one's country and I know you share that sentiment.

So I again urge you to have some care for yourself that you may be fully fit and ready for whatever may be before you and whatever may be required of you.

With the best of good wishes, I am,

Sincerely yours,

Acting President,   American Federation of Labor.

TLc, Files of the Office of the President, General Correspondence, reel 98, frames 576–77, *AFL Records*.

1. John Alpine to the AFL Executive Council, Oct. 17, 1918, Executive Council Records, Vote Books, reel 16, frame 113, *AFL Records*.

2. Charles L. BAINE, a member of the American labor mission, served as secretary-treasurer of the Boot and Shoe Workers' Union from 1902 to 1931.

To Sophia Julian Gompers

October 19, 1918

PARAPHRASE OF TELEGRAM

Confidential
From: Jackson, Paris
To: Navintel.
129. For Mrs. Sophia Gompers,
Care of John Morrison
318 West 51st St. New York City:
"Will leave on first available ship from France or England. Be courageous. Take heart. Dont you come to meet me. I will come direct to you wherever you are.

["]Samuel Gompers."

TWSr, Naval Historical Center, Washington, D.C.

William Buckler[1] to Irwin Laughlin[2]

London, October 29, 1918.

Irwin Laughlin, Esq.,
American Chargé d'Affaires,
London.
Sir:

On September 23, acting under your instructions, I started from London with Mr. Gompers and his five colleagues of the American Labor Mission who were about to visit France and Italy. I was their escort during this journey, and on October 21 I took leave of Mr. Gompers and three members of his party on the U.S. transport anchored in Brest harbor which was to convey them to the United States.

At Mr. Gompers' request, and with your approval, I remained in France one week longer with Messrs. J. P. Frey and C. L. Baine, the two members of the Mission designated by Mr. Gompers to represent the A.F. of L. at an Executive inte-rallied conference called by Mr. Arthur Henderson to meet in Paris on October 26. This conference, however, was made impossible by the Seamen's Union embargo[3] on October 25, and did not after all take place.

On October 27 at 8 P.M. I left Messrs. Frey and Baine in the train which was to take them from Paris to Brest, and on the same evening I started for London, which I reached yesterday afternoon.

As to the details of the Mission's activities, during the two weeks spent in France and the ten days in Italy, Mr. Gompers himself will doubtless give full information as soon as he arrives in Washington this week. I will therefore merely summarise here such impressions as I have been able to gather respecting the results accomplished by the Mission.

1. Honors paid to the Mission unique.

As a token of the respect paid to Labor and its representatives in European countries the reception everywhere given to this Mission was absolutely without precedent. No group of non-official persons has ever before been received with such public honors and high official marks of distinction as were lavished on Mr. Gompers and his colleagues. A list of these would be tedious. It is enough to mention that they included an informal open-air luncheon near the battlefield of Cambrai with Sir D. Haig,[4] the British Commander-in-Chief; a State luncheon at the French Ministry of Foreign Affairs and a luncheon at the Elysée with the President[5] of the French Republic; a dinner with General Diaz,[6] the Italian Commander-in-Chief, and a dinner with the King[7] of Italy at the Royal Villa near Padua. Wherever the Mission went it was received by the highest personages almost exactly as though it had been officially representing the Government of the United States.

These facts are likely to be of no little importance in the future, since labor men will not soon forget that in these critical times they have even without credentials been recognised as representatives of a great democratic state. It was indeed evident that French and Italian Socialist labor leaders appreciated the honors paid to the American Labor Mission as reflecting upon themselves and their own class. When the American delegates went from luncheon at the Quai d'Orsay palace of the Ministry of Foreign Affairs to confer with the Confédération Générale du Travail at its offices in the working-class quarter of Paris, the French laborer naturally felt that he was receiving a share of the honors paid to his American colleagues.

2. Direct Results Achieved.

The good effects produced by the Mission were partly, perhaps mainly, indirect and of a kind not susceptible of being catalogued. Among its direct achievements, however, the following are conspicuous:

(a) Proof that organised Labor in the U.S. is solidly supporting the Government.

This was particularly valuable in France and Italy, where pacifist Labor and socialism have declared in favor of President Wilson's policy. The fact that American labor said "we support the President and we are with him in pushing the war to complete victory," made it difficult for the pacifists to criticize the American labor attitude, since to do so would have stultified their own claim to being loyal supporters of the President.

The same good effect was produced in England, especially during the Inter-Allied Labor and Socialist Conference which met at Westminster on September 17 to 19. There can be no doubt that by securing publicity of the proceedings and moving their declaration on war-aims,[8] which included an endorsement of the President's "14 points," coupled with the vigorous prosecution of the war, the American delegates forced Henderson, Thomas and other British delegates to assume a vigorous pro-war attitude, and to dissociate themselves from the views of men like Longuet,[9] leader of the French majority socialists. Had Henderson and Thomas not assumed a distinctly anti-pacifist attitude, they would have placed themselves in the foolish position of openly antagonizing Mr. Gompers, the ardent supporter of President Wilson whom Henderson and Thomas are constantly extolling.

(b) Attacking the policy of the "official" Italian Socialists, and contradicting their misrepresentations of the A.F. of L.

In several of his Italian speeches, notably at Rome, Milan and Turin,[10] Mr. Gompers denounced the false statements issued by the "Avanti"[11] regarding himself and the policy of the A.F. of L. He showed that the "official" socialists were afraid to meet the American Mission at a conference[12] which had been arranged in Turin, and attacked their tyrannical dictation under which the Mayor of Milan,[13] the Confederazione Generale del Lavoro[14] of Milan and three labor representatives in Turin had been compelled to avoid all contact with the Mission. Mr. Gompers' speeches received wide publicity through the Italian press.[15]

(c) Establishing friendly relations with the French Confédération Générale du Travail, with the French socialists, and with the pro-war Labor and Socialist groups in Italy.

The Mission made it clear that, while strongly opposed to Internationalism of the German type, they look forward eagerly to promoting after the war cordial international relations between all organisations of working men which sincerely endeavor to improve the conditions of labor. The Mission showed itself ready to confer with all the Socialist members of the French Chambers, and even with the anti-war Socialists in Italy. These latter, however, did not have the courage to face such a meeting.

(d) Forestalling certain Italian proposals for permitting the emigration to the U.S. after the war of invalid and disabled soldiers.

These important proposals were, without previous notice, submitted in outline to the American Mission at a conference with the Italian Commissariat on Emigration and with certain socialist deputies held in Rome on October 10th.[16] While disclaiming all official knowledge on the subject and making clear that his views were personal and expressed on the spur of the moment, Mr. Gompers informed the Conference as to what he felt sure would be the attitude of the A.F. of L. and of American working men in general. This frank statement is believed to have practically killed these proposals, and if they are revived through diplomatic channels it will doubtless be in a much modified form.[17]

3. INDIRECT RESULTS ACHIEVED.

(a) Strengthening the hands of the pro-war socialists and labor men in France and Italy at the critical moment when the possibility of peace came suddenly into view and when firmness among the Allies was of special importance.

In this respect the Mission performed in France and Italy the same function which it had already carried out in England, especially at the Inter-Allied Labor and Socialist Conference of September 17 to 19; that is, it gave backbone and encouragement to the pro-war socialist and labor elements which are prepared to back their respective Governments in insisting upon complete victory over militarism.

Signor Bissolati,[18] the Socialist member of the Italian Cabinet, on three occasions expressed his personal feeling of gratitude to Mr. Gompers and to the Mission for having come to Italy at precisely that moment. The same thought was voiced in different ways on many occasions within my hearing, and there can be no doubt that, although no Pacifists may have been actually converted by the Mission its visit had a most valuable effect in upholding the hands of pro-war Italians and in determining doubters to assume a pro-war attitude. It is a remarkable fact that at none of the Mass Meetings addressed by Mr. Gompers was any dissent expressed among the audience. The only exception was at Turin, (the centre of Italian pacifism and "giolittism"[19]), where about 1,500 people listened to Mr. Gompers in an open gallery similar to the London "Burlington Arcade," because all theatres and halls had been closed on account of the "grippe." Even in this audience, to which hostile pacifists might easily have had access, there was only a slight outburst of hissing which lasted not more than a minute, and the audience, which stood patiently for over an hour closely packed together in the gallery, cheered all the pro-war sentiments uttered by

Mr. Gompers and Mr. Frey. It is also remarkable that the official socialists were so afraid of the Mission that they forbade their supporters,
as mentioned above, to have any contact with Mr. Gompers or his colleagues. These facts show with what salutary respect the Mission was
regarded by pacifist elements in Italy.

The news of the first German Note, requesting an armistice and
intimating an agreement with the President's "14 points," reached
Rome at noon on October 6, the very day on which the Mission arrived there. From that moment Mr. Gompers devoted an important
part of all the speeches which he delivered in Italy to warning the
Italian public against showing weakness or undue anxiety for peace.
The fact that the mere announcement on October 6 of the German
peace-move produced strikes and disorder in Milan, Turin, and Florence, shows that these warnings of the American Mission were much
needed.

(b) Demonstrating that the attitude of vigorous and militant labor
leaders need not necessarily be hostile to the Government of their
own country.

Colonel Grossi, head of the Press Section of the Italian General Staff,
remarked to me that in his opinion one of the most permanent and
valuable results of the Mission would be to show in a striking way to the
Italian working man that representatives of labor, who had achieved
great victories for the class which they represented, were sufficiently
broad-minded and statesmanlike to support the Government of their
country when they believed its policy to be sound. He said that to Italian labor, which was apt to believe only in revolutionaries, iconoclasts
and enemies of its own government this demonstration could not fail
to be extremely instructive.

(c) Showing that the U.S. Government honors the representatives
of its labor organizations and regards them as worthy of every official
support.

The fact that the Mission was not only accompanied by a diplomatic
agent sent by the Embassy in London, but everywhere received the
most marked assistance and courtesies from the American diplomatic
missions and from representatives of the U.S. Army and U.S. Navy, was
doubtless one of the reasons for the honors paid to the Mission by
Foreign Governments as described above under the first heading. It
had also, however, a wider importance than this, as was several times
remarked to me by representative Italians. In view of the confidence
felt among Italians in the influence of the U.S. Government upon
the coming peace settlement, these gentlemen said that it was most
valuable to have it thus publicly advertised that the American Mission,
although unofficial, had the fullest approval and backing of the U.S.

Government. A favorite device among Italian pacifists had been to suggest that the Mission did not agree with the views of President Wilson, and the fact of this official support was the best means of scotching that lie.

October 31, 1918.

I find that the views above expressed, as to the achievements of the Mission in France and Italy, resemble those set forth by Captain W. S. Sanders,[20] (British officer attached to the Mission) in his report to the War Cabinet on the visit of the Mission to Great Britain. While I have not seen that report, I gathered yesterday, in conversation with him, that it makes several of the points above outlined.

I am, Sir,

Your obedient servant,   W. H. Buckler.

TLtcSr, RG 59, General Records of the Department of State, DNA.

1. William Hepburn Buckler (1867–1952), an attorney, diplomat, and archeologist, was a member of the staff at the U.S. embassy in London (1914–18) and served with the American delegation to the 1919 Paris peace conference. He was assigned to accompany the American labor mission at SG's request and in response to the requests of the American ambassadors in Paris and Rome.

2. Irwin Laughlin (1871–1941) served as secretary (1912–17), chargé d'affaires (1912–13, 1916, 1918), and counselor (1916–19) at the U.S. embassy in London.

3. On Oct. 25, 1918, members of the National Sailors' and Firemen's Union at Folkestone refused to transport Arthur Henderson and his secretary across the English Channel to attend the Inter-Allied executive committee meeting scheduled for the next day in Paris.

4. For a description of SG's informal lunch with Gen. Douglas Haig and his tour of the battlefield at Cambrai on Oct. 2, 1918, see Files of the Office of the President, General Correspondence, reel 98, frames 393–400, *AFL Records*. SG and the other members of the American labor mission visited the American lines Sept. 27–29, the Belgian lines Oct. 1, and the British and Canadian lines Oct. 2.

5. Raymond Poincaré (1860–1934) was president of France from 1913 to 1920. He and his wife hosted a luncheon for the members of the American labor mission on Oct. 19, 1918, but SG did not attend because he was mourning the death of his daughter.

6. Gen. Armando Diaz (1861–1928), chief of staff and commander of the Italian army, gave the dinner for SG and the American labor mission on the evening of Oct. 11, 1918. The group visited the Italian front Oct. 11–12.

7. Victor Emmanuel III (1869–1947), king of Italy from 1900 to 1946. SG probably dined with the king on Oct. 10, 1918.

8. See "An Excerpt from an Account of the Inter-Allied Labour and Socialist Conference in London," Sept. 20, 1918, above.

9. Frédéric Jean Laurent Longuet (1876–1938) led the faction of the Section française de l'internationale ouvrière (the French Socialist party) that had gained majority control of the party in early October 1918. This group opposed French war policy and called for a negotiated peace. Longuet, a grandson of Karl Marx, served in the French Chamber of Deputies from 1914 to 1919 and from 1932 to 1936. A journalist, he wrote

for many socialist publications and served as editor of, among others, *L'Humanité* and *Le Populaire*.

10. SG delivered major addresses in Rome, Milan, and Turin on Oct. 8, 14, and 16, 1918, respectively.

11. *Avanti!*, the official journal of the Partito socialista italiano (Italian Socialist party), opposed socialist participation in the war effort and called for peace without territorial annexations, self-determination of peoples, and international mediation to end the war.

12. The socialists in question had declined SG's offer to meet with them, saying any discussions with him would be "impossible," given his views. SG, in turn, dismissed them as an organization of "serfs," more interested in "chasing votes" than dealing with questions of concern to Italian workers (SG remarks quoted in Thomas Nelson Page to Robert Lansing, Oct. 17, 1918, RG 59, General Records of the Department of State, DNA).

13. Emilio Caldara (1868–1942), a socialist, served as mayor of Milan from 1914 to 1920.

14. The Confederazione generale del lavoro (General Confederation of Labor) was organized in 1906.

15. North Winship, the U.S. consul in Milan, expressed a similar opinion in his report to the State Department on Oct. 17, 1918, which summarized SG's visit to the city and included transcripts of several of his speeches: "The visit of Gompers Commission to Milan on Monday, October the 14th, left a very good impression among all circles except that of the Official Socialist Party. He and his commission were received not only by the Civil and Military authorities, but by all the patriotic and labor organizations except the Confederazione del Lavoro. . . . At noon, a lunch was given by the Associazione Irredenti which was largely attended. . . . In the afternoon a rather remarkable official reception was given at which every political party was represented except the Official Socialists; and all of the authorities including Senators and Deputies were present, all expressing in sincere and cordial terms their greeting to Mr. Gompers. . . . In the evening a Conference was held at the Conservatorio arranged by the Unione Italiana del Lavoro. Mr. Gompers' speech . . . was excellently translated into Italian by an interpreter Mr. Gompers brought from Rome, and was one of the best pieces of American propaganda that has been delivered in this city, for he attacked fearlessly the Official Socialist Party and the 'Avanti' and he was absolutely justified in all he said. The 'Avanti' in defence has published yesterday a long article. . . . The other papers of Milan gave Mr. Gompers' speech in full including the 'Popolo d'Italia' which is edited by Mussolini. It is interesting to know also that Mussolini who is a patriotic socialist attended the official reception on Monday afternoon making an excellent address of greeting to the Gompers' Commission, and of praise to the American people" (RG 59, General Records of the Department of State, DNA).

16. The meeting actually took place on Oct. 9, 1918. Among others, SG met with Angiolo Cabrini (1869–1937), director of the Italian branch of the International Labor Office, and Filippo Turati (1857–1932), a founder of the Partito socialista italiano.

17. The proposals called for the modification of U.S. laws barring contract laborers and the readmission to the United States of Italians who had repatriated in order to serve in the Italian armed forces. The U.S. military attaché at the American embassy in Rome felt that SG's rejection of these proposals had an unfortunate effect on Italian public opinion. In his confidential report of Oct. 12, 1918, he wrote: "Mr. Gompers and the A.F. of L. stand in the view of Italian opinion as the intransigent opponents of Italian migration to the U.S., as the strenuous upholders of the contract-labor provision in our immigration statutes and as the men who have created the distinction between

desirable and undesirable Italians. Obviously Italians resent, have resented and will always resent this, no matter how right is our own point of self-defense. Mr. Gompers' visit has only re-opened an old, deep and widespread Italian wound" (Military Intelligence Division, RG 165, Records of the War Department General and Special Staffs, DNA).

18. Leonida Bissolati (1857–1920) was a founder of the Partito socialista italiano and the first editor of *Avanti!*. Expelled from the party in 1912 because of his support for the government and his conviction that war between Italy and Austria-Hungary was inevitable, he founded the Partito socialista riformista (Reformist Socialist party) and served as editor of its journal, *Azione Socialista*. He supported Italian entry into World War I and, at the age of fifty-eight, enlisted in the army and saw combat duty. He served in the Italian cabinet as minister without portfolio (1916–17) and minister of war pensions and army welfare (1917–18).

19. In this context, a reference to the non-interventionist position espoused before Italy's entry into World War I by Giovanni Giolitti (1842–1928). Giolitti served five times as prime minister of Italy (1892–93, 1903–5, 1906–9, 1911–14, 1920–21).

20. William Stephen Sanders (1871–1941), a leading figure in the socialist Fabian Society in England, serving as a member of its executive committee (1904–21), as organizing secretary (1907–13), and as general secretary (1914–20), was a captain in the British army during World War I.

An Address at a Reception in Chicago Honoring the Members of the American Labor Mission to Europe

[November 8, 1918]

ADDRESS OF PRESIDENT SAMUEL GOMPERS

Mr. Chairman,[1] My Fellow-countrymen, My Fellow-workers: I am more profoundly impressed than I can well express in words by all that is implied as well as demonstrated in this great gathering tonight. An over attempt at modesty is in itself a species of vanity and I would not have you believe for a moment that I lack appreciation of all that has been said and all that is implied in so far as I may be concerned, but I would prefer, much prefer, that at least the main part of all this great gathering and the sentiment which has produced it shall be interpreted as the tribute to the great labor movement of which I am proud to be one. (Prolonged applause.)

Men in their own lives have attempted to do and to give the best that was within them. Time, opportunity and circumstance were lacking. But I hold that the man who has done his level best in the cause of righteousness and of justice and of freedom and who failed in his attempt is entitled to as much profound gratitude as the man who has had the greatest success in his life. (Applause.) For no man can do better than his best!

And so it has been my aim, so it has been my purpose, to endeavor to help bring up a spirit of democracy among my fellow workers that the great tributes shall not go to any one man but to the great mass and thought and movement of which we are a part. (Applause.)

Perhaps one of the circumstances causing adverse criticism more than any other during the recent trip of my associates and myself was the fact that the people on the other side of the Atlantic have not yet learned the meaning and to have practiced the principles of democracy. (Applause.)

I have reference particularly to the fact that they have been so accustomed to pay tribute to the man or woman actually or figuratively at the head of their governments, that even in the civil and civic life the man at the head of a mission was accorded all the honors to the neglect of the men forming part of that mission. (Applause.) And it was necessary for your humble servant, as the chairman of the mission, to practically hold on to my associates in order that they might not be shoved out of the gathering. (Laughter.)

I did not intend to even privately, much less publicly, make mention of this typical fact, except that I now want to emphasize with whatever power that is in me, the thought and the fact that the principles of democracy do not flash in the air, they are not fanciful, they are not theoretical, for if they are thought of in that fashion, they lose their potency and virility and effect. (Applause.) Democracy must be practiced and acted every day of our lives to be true. (Applause.)

I wouldn't want any of you ladies and gentlemen to imagine that I have in my mind the possibility that leadership can be dispensed with, that leadership carries with it no responsibility, as well as dignity and respect. On the contrary, I believe now more than ever that the men placed in responsible positions are moving true to the trust imposed in them, are deserving of the respect and of the gratitude of a loyal democratic people, and I want to call to the attention of my fellow countrymen the fact that unless the principles of democracy are practiced in our every day lives we shall assuredly as the sun rises and sets, lose the power of democracy because we have not used that function in our lives. (Applause.)

Mr. Chairman, Brother Duncan (Jim), the men and the women who sent their messages here, the rank and file of our people who may have their vision directed here tonight: I want you to believe me that I feel all that has been said and all that is implied and left unsaid, that I have a profound appreciation and gratitude from the innermost recesses of my soul more deeply than I can express. I can only hope that what of life may be left to me will give you and them no cause for regret for the respect and the confidence you have expressed for and in me, for it is, after all, all that one can do—to try and give service to his fellows, and if the trying is worthy of appreciation, I have tried. (Applause.)

It was a great mission entrusted to my associates and myself, a mission to convey the message of fraternity and good will and cooperation and sacrifice, that the opportunity to live the lives of free men and women shall not be crushed from the face of the earth (applause) the message that America had arisen to the stature of her greatness and thrown herself across the path of the conquering Hun. It was a message that if need be our America would sacrifice and die rather than live the ignominy of cowardice.

America is more than a country. America is more than a continent. America is more than a name. America is an ideal. America is the apotheosis of all that is right. (Prolonged applause.)

Some people would have gladly—well, if not gladly, quite sadly—yielded to this great threatening power of the monarchical military autocratic machine of Germany. It is so easy, it is so comfortable not to get into the conflict. It is the character and the willingness of a people to strive and to sacrifice that makes happiness and peace possible. (Applause.)

Paraphrasing a couplet of some years ago I say that in a great struggle it is better to fight and to lose than not to fight at all. (Applause.)[2]

Where a great principle is involved and men fail to defend it, where a great principle is involved and men refuse to make a sacrifice to preserve it, there is no hope for them or for those who come after them. Fight for the right and even though you are defeated, the spark is still in the heart and the brain, handed down from father to son, from mother to daughter and to the generations after that until finally that spark bursts into a flame and the torch of liberty is again alight. (Applause.)

I say this as a man of 68 years of life and who for more than fifty years of that life has been one of the most active pacifists in the world, belonging to all the peace organizations of America and of the world.

That was a pacifist who was giving his assistance to the movement of labor, to the movement of the men and women of other walks of life to maintain the peace of the world. It did not imply that when a marauder with his band of militant assassins went abroad to kill, to ravage, to destroy, that my pacifism need consistently shield the man or the men who would not fight to defend their wives and their little ones.

The man or the men who would not fight in defense of freedom—the men who would not fight in defense of their country engaged in a righteous cause, are unworthy to live and enjoy the privileges of a free country. (Prolonged applause.)

And so, whining, cowardly, beaten Austria asking for peace and getting it, (laughter) the puppet of Germany, the puppet of the kaiser, that demanded the extermination of Serbia, while the Serbians, driven out of their country, have come back, and Austria-Hungary is an imperial government of the past. (Applause.)

It was a great privilege and a pleasure to be upon the Belgian front in Belgium and to find the Belgian army having that very morning captured five thousand German soldiers. (Applause.) When that demand was made by the German imperial government ostensibly upon Serbia but actually, knowing the conditions and situations, upon England and France and Russia, there was this one great mistake which autocracy and imperialism always makes. Like a criminal planning a crime, robbery or murder, with all the ingenuity of these people, they always leave something without their reckoning, some trail which proves their undoing, so with the imperialistic machine of Germany; they, with their preparation for half a century to perfect the greatest scientific military machine that the world has ever known, they took for granted that Belgium, small; France, frivolous; Russia, a weakling; England indifferent and money-making—that they would not respond to the principles of justice and of right; and it never entered into the minds of the autocrats of Germany that America, this easy-going people of ours, the people engaged in labor, in business, in politics, with this vast country of ours with more than a hundred millions of people made up of all nationalities—that there could be anything like a united spirit and a willingness to serve and to sacrifice.

It was one of those great mistakes in the calculation of autocracy which believes nothing is efficient except power. (Applause.) The autocracy of Germany could not understand or feel what is meant by the practice of freedom and democracy and that once the soul of the people of our democracy was touched, they would stand united more thoroughly than the people of any country on the face of the globe; united and determined that, come what may, that spirit of freedom proclaimed in the Declaration of Independence, for which our forefathers gave up their lives and their possessions, in order that America might not only be a new nation, a republic, but with the new meaning of the rights of man.

The autocracy of Germany failed to understand what was meant by the struggle of our Civil War to maintain the Union and to abolish human slavery. (Applause.) They did not know; the autocracy of Germany could not comprehend a war undertaken by the United States against Spain for the liberation of Cuba.

The autocracy of Germany could not understand that a hundred millions of people in the confines of the United States of America could be or would be united to make safe for our people the traversing on the seas and to avenge the lives of those who had been murdered on the Lusitania. (Applause.)

We had been too often described as the nation whose ideal was the dollar mark. Never in the history of the world has a people responded with such alacrity, with such earnestness and willingness to serve and, if need be, to die, as the people of our republic in this cause. (Applause.) I am more proud today in my righteous claim as an American citizen after my return, after all that I have seen, than ever before in my whole life. (Applause.)

In the work of our American Federation of Labor Mission to England, to France and Belgium, our conferences with our men there, our public discussions with the men of labor and of other affairs there, we predicated our position upon the declared basis of the American labor movement and we put forth our position not only upon the righteousness of our cause and our stand but upon the further fact that we had two million of our own American boys over there, (applause) flesh of our flesh and blood of our blood. (Applause.)

We were giving, if need be, our boys and our women and the production of wealth with our hands and brain and we had the right to have a say-so in every detail in which we were involved in this struggle. (Applause.)

Before the United States entered into the war it might have been regarded as gratuitous for us to even suggest a thing to any of the democratic nations involved in the struggle, but now that we were in the war up to the hilt—well, nothing could be done by kings or cabinets or men of labor without the full consent of the representatives of our republic. (Applause.) And it was with no mealy mouths that the American Labor Mission expressed their firm convictions.

I call your attention to part of the declaration adopted by the conference of America's workers at Washington, the capital of our nation, on March 12, 1917, where the Executive Council had summoned representative labor men and a declaration adopted worthy of serious consideration in every line and every word even now and for the future insisting upon conditions of labor and freedom during any war which may come or during the times of peace, if peace should prevail, upon the basis of an American standard of life and work. American labor, American workers, stood 100 per cent behind the government and the President of the United States. (Applause.)

I commend this to your serious thought. I am quite confident that as time goes on the utterances in this declaration will become more and more important. I refrain from reading it because it is too lengthy. I will not even read the declaration made by the London Inter-Allied Labor Conference of September.[3] I wish merely to call your attention to the fact that the American Labor Mission proposed and the conference adopted, not in the same words but in the same sense and purpose and meaning, the declaration of organized labor of America of more than a year and a half before. (Applause.)

That conference which in secrecy has declared its pacifism and some other things (applause) was held in executive, or secret session, but at the demand of our mission and at the proposal of our mission, that conference in which we participated was had with the searchlight of public opinion right upon every delegate present.[4] (Applause.)

We held that we could not be consistent in denouncing secret diplomacy and at the same time hold executive, secret sessions ourselves. (Applause.) Whether they liked it or not, they voted for open sessions. From that time we knew that America's position was right and would be endorsed. Men can't help being a little more decent in public than they may be in secret and private. (Laughter and applause.)

The conditions which we found to exist in our Allied countries was something to give us all concern. Every attempt that we made was combated by the pro-Germans, by the propagandists, by the pacifists and by the French and Italian bolsheviki. The socialist bolsheviki press of those countries endeavored to forestall every move we made or were about to make. (Applause.)

In Italy, for instance, we were represented by this press as fakes and frauds and all that sort of thing, that we were not representing American labor, that we didn't speak for them nor in their name. Our answer was—the difficulty with these people is that whatever of a labor movement exists there is usually dominated by some professor, some failure in professional life (laughter) who had got his fangs into the labor movement and usually poisoned it and destroyed it—that the American labor movement was composed of working men and working women and that the men in the official positions of our movement were the men who had been taken from the mine, from the shop, from the building, and said, "Now, you don't build any more, you don't mine coal any more, you don't make brick any more; we want you to be our spokesman, our defender, our advocate," and that doesn't sit well in the crop of the so-called intellectuals of England or France or Italy or even in the United States.

Our labor movement is conducted for the working people, is composed of the working people and administered by the working people. (Applause.) We said that we had fully four million organized workers in America, and the Avante, literally translated into English, the Advance, a Bolsheviki organ, pretended Italian official socialist paper, came back and said, "Well, Mr. Gompers may represent four million workmen in the United States, but he represents more millions of dollars."

I mentioned each member of the mission and referred to the trade at which they'd given the major portions of their lives, mentioning my own as a cigarmaker who worked at his trade for 26 years, and I said there was not any member of our mission who if he left the position he occupied and did not earn anything in three or six months, would not have to go to the poorhouse. (Applause.)

And as an interesting incident, when I got that far Mr. William Bowen, President of the Bricklayers,[5] interrupted me and said, "You are mistaken, sir. I can live a year without it." (Laughter.)

But I made this remark—I intended to refute, to repudiate and condemn the statement made that we represented money of any character, but I did try to say something like this: "If I represent dollars, no one has yet accused me of having received German dollars." (Applause. Prolonged applause.)

And I made this general inquiry, whether the publishers of the Avante, the official socialist organ of Italy, could make the same claim honestly. (Laughter and applause.)

I shall not pay too great a tribute to my associates nor make any claim for myself. All I think I should say and what I am justified in saying is that we did try like the mischief and succeeded to some degree in putting some stiffening into the backbone of the people of the countries which we visited to stand behind their countries at least until after the war was won.

We have come back to our country more thoroughly American than ever, (applause) more thoroughly convinced that our people and our government stand out as a wonderful object lesson to the peoples of the whole world. (Applause.)

We visited the fronts, the battlefields where shot and shell and deadly gas was thick; we were within the firing lines, in trenches, on ramparts, in the open field with the whizzing and the screaming of shells bursting in the distance upon enemy soil and right within a radius of a few feet of where we stood. We saw the flames of Cambrai lighting the sky; we saw the great Monte Grappe[6] which the valiant French soldiers were for more than four years endeavoring to reconquer and retake without effect, and our boys, American boys, just took it, with one thousand prisoners from the German militarists. (Applause.) On the Piave, on the firing line within 350 yards from the lines of the Austrian soldiers, we saw the battles; we saw men falling from the clouds, their balloons or machines having been destroyed. Some of them, I don't know whether it was for their best, with their parachutes over them, fell within the lines of the German army. We saw the German dead on the battlefields; we saw their horses, we saw their cannon abandoned; we saw cities and towns and villages destroyed, annihilated, nothing left except crumbled stone and brick to testify that a living human being ever occupied it.

No mind can conceive the actual facts and conditions we saw. Nine years ago in connection with a mission for labor, by direction of the American Federation of Labor I incidentally went to Naples and then to Pompeii and there I saw what the world called the City of the Dead. No living human being was there. There are evidences in some of the available picture books that define the magnificent art and architecture. There are evidences of amphitheatres, of great public market places, of the racing of the chariots and the horses, and of the slaves. But in the cities and towns and villages we saw there was not the slightest evidence that ever a human being trod upon that soil. You may see in pictures, you may read in stories, or you may have described to you by a tongue more eloquent and capable of description than my poor powers will permit, but it is not given to human kind to understand all of the awful destruction and devastation, the havoc wrought by the brutal German militarist machine. (Applause.)

We went to the hospitals, the first aid units, and we saw Americans, not only lacerated and wounded and bereft of limbs; we not only saw all the horrors of it, we also saw men who were gassed in the hospitals and Hell in Dante's fertile mind contained nothing to equal the horrors of the men gassed by German kultur.

Time and circumstances prohibit an attempt at detail. The men of America, our country, our republic—our people and our country—are not merely respected by the people of our allied countries of Europe, they are venerated.

The name of America and the name of Wilson are constantly upon the lips expressing the deepest sentiment of the people of all classes in the democratic Allied countries of ours, all except the pro-Germans and the Bolsheviki which are one and the same.

America is acclaimed by the king[7] and queen[8] of England, by President Poincare, by Clemenceau,[9] Viviani,[10] Joffre[11] and the great mass of workers, by the workers of Belgium and of France, by the workers and the masses of the people of Italy, by King Albert[12] (applause) of reviving Belgium, by Victor Emmanuel, the King of Italy (applause), by her prime ministers, by all the great men, by all the leading spirits, by the rank and file of the masses of the people of this generation—"Vive la America! Vive Wilson!" on the tongues and the lips of all. (Applause.)

There is not in all France or Italy any city or town or village in which you can not find a street, a boulevard or a park named after Wilson. (Applause.) Traversing twenty miles of road uphill to reach the top of Monte Grappe, only a mile and a half high but by the devious rising, winding course about the middle of that mountain, Monte Grappe, is a little station where our boys get their coffee and sandwich and once in a great while a piece of pie—there on that mountain is Via Wilson. (Applause.)

We must be worthy of battle, we must be true to the altruism and to the sense of justice of the republic of the United States. One of the greatest mistakes of Germany was that she mistook her own position and she believed that she was profound when she was merely ponderous. (Laughter.) Might and power and force were the only elements which could decide. Perhaps one of the greatest mistakes which German kultur and diplomacy has made since the beginning of the war has been her treatment of Russia since Russia went out of the war. If Germany had entered into a treaty with Russia upon fair, liberal, generous terms, she would not only have won the respect of the people of Russia but it would have made a profound impression upon the peoples and the governments of all the countries of the world, and more than likely would have made her the dominant figure and factor in the lives of the nations of the world.

It wasn't necessary for her to regard such a treaty with Russia with any more respect than she regarded the treaty with Belgium—simply as a scrap of paper. She then could have gone in and whipped Russia and in turn taken all the generous provisions away. It is the idea of brute force, that nothing can win except power. The nation which has lived by the sword must and will perish by the sword. (Applause.)

One of perhaps the greatest master strokes of all that has been said during this war in the many wonderful utterances of our great President, was the answer which he made in that very brief note to Austria.[13] It broke the backbone of their morale. The hope was that labor would be divided in the United States, that labor would be divided in the other Allied countries and that the President and the governments of our Allied countries would be forced to make a premature peace favorable to Germany and to Austria.

And our own wonderful Pershing[14] when standing before the tomb of Lafayette, called upon for an address, delivered himself thus: "Lafayette, we are here!" (Applause.)

That phrase, that declaration, is also on the tips of the tongues of the people of France. It was not my good fortune to have been a participant in the luncheon given to the American Labor Mission by President Poincare of France and Mme. Poincare.[15] The incident which forbade my being there is probably known to you, but at that luncheon my associates told me not only the President, but Mme. Poincare, with unbidden tears falling upon her cheeks, expressed her great appreciation and gratitude to the soldiers and the manhood and womanhood of America, not only for what we were now doing but for our first contribution that changed the tide of battle at Chateau Thierry last July.[16] (Applause.)

Ours was the only force, the only power left to save France and England. We were gratified with assurances of the same character, expressions of the same feeling of gratitude and veneration by the Cabinet of Great Britain and that great democrat Lloyd George. (Applause.)

We, in our land, expect to live our own lives and work out our own problems. As a result of this war there must come a new understanding of the rights of man. As a result of this war there must come new relations not only between nation and nation but between man and man. (Applause.)

Our men and women have bent and are bending their backs to the task of production of the things upon which the armies and navies depend. Men and women of labor of America have done their full duty and will continue to do their full duty and for the sacrifices which they have made out of their strength and health, for the sacrifices they have made upon the battlefields, freedom must not be lost to them in times of peace. (Applause.) They want an accounting of the stewardship of our people, of what we have done and what we have failed to do to maintain the standard of life, the American standard of life, that no pauperization of the sisters and brothers and fathers and mothers shall occur while our boys are at the front mingling as they do, ditch-digger and the son of millionaire and businessman, all of them in the same trench, in the same tent, sharing the same fare, the same hardships and the same risks—these men will come back to our country with glory and victory written into their very souls and they shall want an accounting of our stewardship while they have been over there. (Applause.)

They know now that the peoples of the world, regardless of where their countries may be, are now so much nearer than before. Our American soldier boys are speaking French, are speaking Italian, and they will have a new lingo in which they can question us. (Laughter.)

They have gotten a broader vision and understanding. Their own lives and minds will have become broadened. They have mingled with the English Tommies, the French Poilus and Italians, who have given them a new thought, and the man or woman who can't answer straightforwardly to her boy or his boy when he comes back here will have a hard row to hoe, believe me.

The war is nearly over, men and women. (Applause.) It was my great privilege to say, almost at the beginning of the war, that we hoped and expected that the German people themselves would crush militarism and autocracy from their country, but if they failed—by the gods, we would crush it for them. (Applause.)

The alternative was either inside or outside. Instead of their crushing their autocratic militarist machine themselves we have done it—are doing it—will continue to do it from the outside while some spirit of German democracy, or German desperation against the failure of that militarist machine will help to establish democracy in Germany. (Applause.)

We want to see this world governed by the peoples of the land, by the people who must work and serve and pay, and they shall have a voice in determining finally and once and for all what the condition of service shall be.

We want the [D]eclaration [of Independence][17] to defend us, the right to life, liberty and the pursuit of happiness not to be mere generalities but the rules of every-day life where every man shall be a king and every woman a queen by her own fireside. (Applause.)

In the time now near at hand we have yet much to do. The war work campaign about to begin, is just as essential now and for the future as has been any preparation for the military side of the war. Service, contributions, payment, anything and everything for labor, for freedom, for justice, for democracy. (Applause.)

Thus when this war shall finally have been triumphantly closed, there will come the problem of reconstruction and rehabilitation. With the demobilization of our army and the men of our great fleets into their civic life, it will mean either intelligent demobilization, or rampant demoralization. (Applause.)

To meet the new problems after the war will take the best thought of our best men and our best women, unselfish and true, with high consciences and high resolves, determined to do it right.

It has been a terrible war, men and women. It has cost more lives and more sacrifice than any previous struggle in the history of the world; it involved more.

The crusade was for an ideal. What was contained in our Revolutionary War, what was contained in Lincoln's immortal proclamation of freedom for the black slave—all of these thoughts and ideals made for a time or for a nation are all intended and will, with the intelligent cooperation of our people, be the rules and regulations and the constitution of the nations of the whole civilized world.

You and I who have given our flesh and blood as a contribution and as a sacrifice to this world struggle, may feel our losses keenly, but in the time that shall come and when the story shall have been written, those generations of men and women, yet unborn, will just as we praise and glorify the sacrifices of those who have gone before and made possible the life of the American people as we see it and understand it, so will the future rise up and call us blessed for the service which we have done, for the sacrifices which we have made for glorious America, for the glory and the civilization and the freedom and the justice of the peoples of the whole world, and then the song of the poet and the dream of the philosopher shall have been realized in the universal brotherhood of man. (Applause.)

American Federationist 25 (Dec. 1918): 1081–88. An edited transcript of this address can be found in Files of the Office of the President, Conferences, reel 120, frames 499–515, *AFL Records*.

1. James Duncan.
2. The passage, from the poem "Peschiera" by Arthur Hugh Clough (1819–61), reads: "'Tis better to have fought and lost, / Than never to have fought at all."
3. See "An Excerpt from an Account of the Inter-Allied Labour and Socialist Conference in London," Sept. 20, 1918, above.
4. On Sept. 17, 1918, at the first session of the Inter-Allied Labour and Socialist Conference, John Frey proposed that the meetings be open to the public and members of the press. Frey's proposal was adopted the same day.
5. The Bricklayers', Masons', and Plasterers' International Union of America.
6. Monte Grappa, to the northwest of Venice, was the scene of fierce fighting on the Italian front in late 1917 and 1918. The combat in October 1918 involved the American 332d Infantry Regiment, which was sent to Italy in July.
7. King George V (1865–1936) reigned from 1910 to 1936.
8. Mary of Teck (1867–1953), queen consort of King George V.
9. Georges Clemenceau (1841–1929) served as premier of France from 1906 to 1909 and again from 1917 to 1920.
10. René Viviani (1863–1925) served as premier of France from 1914 to 1915.
11. Joseph Jacques Césaire Joffre (1852–1931) served as commander in chief of the French armies on the Western Front from 1914 to 1916.
12. Albert I (1875–1934) reigned as king of the Belgians from 1909 to 1934.
13. Probably a reference to President Woodrow Wilson's Sept. 17, 1918, note rejecting Austria-Hungary's proposal of a confidential, non-binding conference of representatives from the belligerent states to discuss peace terms. Wilson's note, communicated by Secretary of State Robert Lansing, declared that the United States had already laid out the terms upon which it would consider peace. The following month Austria-Hungary accepted the Fourteen Points and Wilson's subsequent pronouncements as the basis for peace negotiations. A subsequent exchange of notes clarified the conditions for an armistice, which was signed on Nov. 3.
14. John Joseph Pershing (1860–1948) commanded the American Expeditionary Force in Europe (1917–19) and later served as army chief of staff (1921–24).
15. Henriette Benucci Poincaré (1858–1943).
16. Two American divisions were instrumental in stopping a German offensive at Château-Thierry, on the Marne to the east of Paris, in early June 1918.
17. The text in brackets is supplied from a transcript of the address printed in SG, *American Labor and the War* (New York, 1919), p. 282.

To Woodrow Wilson

Laredo, Texas, Nov. 11, 1918.

Honorable Woodrow Wilson,
President of the United States,
Washington, D.C.

   With the war's triumphant close today,[1] the cause of justice, freedom and democracy has not only been vindicated but made safer for all time. In this beautiful dawn of this new era in the life of the peoples and nations of the world, the Executive Council of the American Federation of Labor, in official session at Laredo, Texas, on behalf of the wage workers of our beloved Republic express to you, to our people and to the peoples of all democratic countries our heartiest felicitation upon the consummation of this most momentous epoch of the world's history.

By Order of the Executive Council of the American Federation of Labor,

Samuel Gompers,   President.

TWtcSr, Files of the Office of the President, General Correspondence, reel 98, frame 799, *AFL Records*.

   1. German representatives signed an armistice before dawn on Nov. 11, 1918, and a cease-fire took effect on the Western Front at eleven o'clock that morning. Bulgaria, Turkey, and Austria-Hungary had already capitulated, on Sept. 29, Oct. 30, and Nov. 3, respectively.

GLOSSARY

The names of individuals and unions included here are rendered in CAPITAL LETTERS at their first annotation in this volume.

INDIVIDUALS

ALPINE, John R. (1863–1947), was born in Maine and worked as a gas fitter in Everett, Mass., and then in Boston, where he was president of United Association of Journeymen Plumbers, Gas Fitters, Steam Fitters, and Steam Fitters' Helpers of the United States and Canada 175 (1904–5) and of the Boston Building Trades Council (1905). Alpine served as special organizer, vice-president (1904–6), and president (1906–19) of the international union (from 1913, the United Association of Plumbers and Steam Fitters of the United States and Canada) and as an AFL vice-president (1909–19). During World War I he was appointed to the Cantonment Adjustment Commission that supervised labor relations on military construction jobs. He lived in Chicago from 1906 until 1920, when he moved to New York City, where he was employed by the Grinnell Co. as assistant to the president for labor relations. In 1931 President Herbert Hoover appointed him assistant secretary of labor in charge of the Federal Unemployment Service.

ANDERSON, Edward E. (1869?–1937?), was born in Michigan and by 1903 was working as a barber in Pueblo, Colo. He served as secretary of Journeymen Barbers' International Union of America 219 of Pueblo (1904–15) and as vice-president (1911–15) and secretary-treasurer (1916–22) of the Colorado State Federation of Labor. He also served for a time as president of the Pueblo Trades and Labor Assembly and the Pueblo Union Label League and was editor and publisher of the *Pueblo Labor Press*. Anderson moved to Denver in 1916 and from 1929 to 1932 was secretary-treasurer of Barbers' local 205 of that city.

APPLETON, William Archibald (1859–1940), was born in Nottingham, England, where he worked as a lacemaker. Moving to London, he served as secretary of the Amalgamated Society of Operative Lace-

569

makers (1896–1907), secretary of the General Federation of Trade Unions (1907–38), and president of the International Federation of Trade Unions (1919–20).

BAINE, Charles L. (b. 1870), was born in Canada and immigrated to the United States with his family in 1880. He settled in Chicago where he worked as a shoe cutter and served as business agent of Boot and Shoe Workers' Union 133. He was elected to the executive board of the Boot and Shoe Workers in 1899 and served as the union's secretary-treasurer from 1902 to 1931.

BARNES, George Nicoll (1859–1940), was born in Lochee, Forfarshire, Scotland, went to work in a jute mill at the age of eleven, and began his apprenticeship in a woodworking machinery firm in 1872. In 1879 he moved to London, where he joined the Amalgamated Society of Engineers. He subsequently served as the union's assistant secretary (1892–95) and secretary (1896–1908). Barnes served as a member of the Parliamentary Committee of the TUC (1906–8) and as a member of Parliament (Labour, 1906–18; Coalition Labour, 1918–22). In December 1916 he became minister of pensions, and in 1917 he replaced Arthur Henderson in the War Cabinet as minister without portfolio. Barnes was the Labour representative of the government to the Paris peace conference and a signatory of the peace treaty. A proponent of international organizations aimed at preventing future conflicts, he drafted the proposals for the creation of the International Labor Organization (ILO) and in 1919 chaired the British delegation at the first ILO conference in Washington, D.C.

BARNES, John Mahlon (1866–1934), was born in Lancaster, Pa., and became a member of the KOL in the 1880s. He joined the Cigar Makers' International Union of America in 1887, serving as secretary of local 100 of Philadelphia (1891–93, 1897–1900) and local 165 of Philadelphia (1903–4), and was elected a vice-president of the Pennsylvania State Federation of Labor in 1902. He joined the Socialist Labor party in 1891 and was corresponding secretary of the Philadelphia Central Committee and an organizer for the party's Philadelphia American branch in the 1890s. A founder of the Socialist Party of America in 1901, he was secretary of its Philadelphia branch and the Pennsylvania representative on its national executive committee in the early years of the decade. He served as the party's national secretary from 1905 until 1911 and as its campaign manager in 1912 and 1924.

Baroff, Abraham (1870–1932), was born in Russia and immigrated to the United States around 1890, obtaining work in the women's garment industry in New York City. He was a leader of the 1909–10 shirtwaist and dress makers' strike in New York City and was a founder of International Ladies' Garment Workers' Union 25 (Ladies' Waist and Dress Makers) of New York City, serving for several years as its manager. Baroff became a vice-president of the Ladies' Garment Workers and a member of the union's general executive board in 1914, and he served as the union's secretary-treasurer from 1915 until 1929.

Bellamy, Albert (1870–1931), was born in Wigan, England, became a railway engine cleaner in 1887, and eventually rose to the positions of locomotive engineer and traveling locomotive inspector. From 1908 to 1920 he was chairman of the workers' committee of the London and Northwestern Railway's conciliation board. Bellamy served as president of the Amalgamated Society of Railway Servants (1909, 1911–13) and its successor organization, the National Union of Railwaymen (1913–17). He was a member of the first War Pensions Appeal Tribunal (1917–19) and later a member of the tribunal staff (1919–27). From 1928 until his death he served as a Labour member of Parliament.

Berres, Albert Julius (1873–1940), a longtime resident of Washington, D.C., served as chairman of the executive council of the District of Columbia branch of the Pattern Makers' League of North America (1906–10) and as a member of the union's executive board (1909–14). Berres also served as secretary-treasurer of the AFL Metal Trades Department (1908–27), resigning that position to become secretary in charge of industrial affairs for the Motion Picture Producers' Association in Hollywood, Calif.

Berry, George Leonard (1882–1948), was born in Tennessee. After serving in the Spanish-American War, he took a job as a press feeder for the *St. Louis Globe-Democrat* and joined the International Printing Pressmen's and Assistants' Union of North America in 1899. About 1902 he earned his pressman's card and moved to San Francisco, where he was an active member of Printing Pressmen's local 24, serving as its president (1906) and then as business agent. Berry was president of the international union from 1907 until his death, moving to union headquarters in Cincinnati in 1907 and then to Rogersville, Tenn., in 1911. He served in the army during World War I, taking a leave of absence from his union responsibilities, and in 1921 helped organize the American Legion. He founded the International Playing Card Co. in 1926 and was the owner and publisher of the *Rogersville Review,* a weekly paper. He later served as an AFL vice-president (1935) and as a Democratic U.S. senator from Tennessee (1937–38).

BEVIN, Ernest (1881–1951), was born in Winsford, Somerset, England. He left school at the age of eleven and about 1894 moved to Bristol, where he worked as a mineral water delivery man. He formed a Bristol carters' branch of the Dock, Wharf, Riverside, and General Labourers' Union in 1910 and from 1914 to 1920 served as a national organizer for the Dockers' union. Bevin was secretary of the Transport and General Workers' Union (1922–40), a leader of the 1926 general strike, and a member (1925–40) and chairman (1936–37) of the General Council of the TUC. In 1940 he was elected as a Labour member of Parliament and became part of Winston Churchill's wartime coalition government, serving as minister of labour and national service (1940–45). After the war he served as foreign minister in the Labour government (1945–51).

BLACKMAN, William (b. 1861?), was born in New York and by 1890 was working as a locomotive engineer in Seattle, where he served as master (1890–93) of Brotherhood of Locomotive Firemen 407 and secretary (1895–97) of American Railway Union 98. After moving to Olympia in 1897, he served as president of the Washington State Labor Congress and its successor, the Washington State Federation of Labor (1898–1906), and as the factory, mill, and railroad inspector for the Washington State Bureau of Labor (1897–1900) and then as commissioner of the bureau (1901–5). Blackman moved to Washington, D.C., about 1915 to work as a commissioner of conciliation for the U.S. Department of Labor (1915–17). In September 1917 he joined the staff of the Emergency Fleet Corporation, serving as head of its labor division from December of that year until July 1918, when he became a field representative for the U.S. Railroad Administration. Blackman continued to work as a labor mediator until at least 1931.

BOHM, Ernest (1860–1936), was born in New York, worked as a compositor, clerk, and manager of a cloak operators' union early in his career, and became secretary of the Excelsior Labor Club of the KOL in 1881 and corresponding secretary of the New York City Central Labor Union in 1882. During the 1880s and 1890s he was active in the organization of the brewery workers, serving briefly in 1888 as an editor of the *Brauer Zeitung,* the official journal of the National Union of the United Brewery Workmen of the United States. He was later secretary of Brewery Workmen's local 31 (Ale and Porter Brewers) and of the New York City Brewery Workmen's local executive board. He supported Henry George's 1886 mayoral campaign and in 1887 participated in founding the United Labor party and served as secretary of the Progressive Labor party. Bohm was a member of the Socialist Labor party and, from 1896 to 1898, secretary of the executive board of the Socialist Trade and Labor Alliance. He served as secretary of the Central Labor Federation of New York City (1889–99) and of the Central Federated Union (CFU) of New York City (by 1913, the CFU of Greater New York and Vicinity) from 1899 to 1920. From 1919 to 1921 he was secretary of the New York City branch of the National Labor party (from 1920, the Farmer-Labor party), and from 1921 until his death he was a leader of AFL Bookkeepers', Stenographers', and Accountants' Union 12,646, holding several positions, including the presidency.

BOWEN, William J. (1868–1948), was born and attended grammar school in Albany, N.Y., and at the age of thirteen apprenticed there as a bricklayer. In 1890 he joined Bricklayers' and Masons' International Union of America (from 1910, Bricklayers', Masons', and Plasterers' International Union of America) 6 of Albany, serving over the following years as its business manager and president. Bowen also served as a vice-president (1901–4) and president (1904–28) of the Bricklayers.

BOWERMAN, Charles William (1851–1947), a London typographer, was secretary of the London Society of Compositors (1892–1906) and a member (1897–1923) and secretary (1911–23) of the Parliamentary Committee of the TUC (from 1921, the General Council). He served as a Labour member of Parliament from 1906 to 1931.

BROWN, Jay G. (1874–1942), was born in Minnesota and by 1903 was working as a shingle weaver in Hoquiam, Wash., where he joined International Shingle Weavers' Union of America 21. Brown served as president (1907–9, 1912–18) of the Shingle Weavers (from 1913 to 1914, the International Union of Shingle Weavers, Sawmill Workers, and Woodsmen; from 1914 to 1916, the International Union of Timberworkers; and from 1916, the International Shingle Weavers' Union of America). While in this office he moved to Seattle. He was an AFL salaried organizer in 1907 and again from 1915 to 1918 and was involved in the AFL-supported iron and steel organizing campaign of 1918–20, becoming secretary of the National Committee for Organizing Iron and Steel Workers after William Foster resigned in early 1920. From 1920 to 1924 Brown also served as secretary-treasurer of the Chicago-based

Farmer-Labor party. He then returned to the Seattle area, working first in the lumber mills and then as a motion picture operator.

BRYAN, William E. (1858–1938), was born in Middleport, Ohio. After attending high school and, briefly, a business college, he worked as a steamboat clerk, railroad passenger agent, and traveling salesman before joining his father in the harness trade in 1895. Moving to Kansas, he joined United Brotherhood of Leather Workers on Horse Goods 44 of Wichita and served as secretary-treasurer of the Kansas State Federation of Labor (1907–9) and chief clerk of the Kansas Bureau of Labor and Industry and Factory Inspection (1909–10). In 1910 Bryan was elected president of the Leather Workers and moved to Kansas City, Kans. He continued as president when that union merged with two others in 1917 to form the United Leather Workers' International Union, and he remained in office until his death. In the 1930s Bryan moved back to Middleport.

BURKE, John P. (1884–1966), was born on a farm near North Duxbury, Vt., moved with his family to Franklin, N.H., when he was twelve, and went to work in a hosiery mill there at the age of thirteen. Within a few years he began working at the Franklin plant of the International Paper Co., and in 1905 he joined the pulp and sulphite workers' local of the International Brotherhood of Paper Makers, Pulp, Sulphite, and Paper Mill Workers at Franklin. The next year, when pulp and sulphite workers seceded from the Paper Makers to form the International Brotherhood of Pulp, Sulphite, and Paper Mill Workers, he became a member of that union's local 9 in Franklin. Burke was a vice-president of the New Hampshire State Federation of Labor (1914–16?), was the Socialist candidate for governor of New Hampshire in 1914, and served as a vice-president (1914–17) and president-secretary (1917–65) of the Pulp and Sulphite Workers, moving to the union's headquarters at Ft. Edward, N.Y., upon becoming its president.

CAREY, David A. (1859?–1927), was born in Ireland and by 1890 was living in Toronto. He was active in the Toronto Trades and Labor Council and the Trades and Labor Congress of Canada, serving as president of the congress from 1896 to 1898. Carey joined the Toronto Musical Protective Association (American Federation of Musicians 149) in 1898 and served the Musicians as a district vice-president (1902–15) and executive board member (1915–27).

CARTER, William Samuel (1859–1923), a native of Austin, Tex., worked as a railroad baggageman, fireman, and engineer from 1879 to 1894. He edited the official journal of the Brotherhood of Locomotive Firemen (1894–1904) and later served the union (from 1906, the Brotherhood of Locomotive Firemen and Enginemen) as secretary and treasurer (1904–9) and president (1909–22). From 1918 to 1920, he was director of the Division of Labor of the U.S. Railroad Administration and took a leave of absence from the union's presidency.

CHRISTMAN, Elisabeth (1881–1975), was born in Germany, came to the United States with her family as a small child, and settled in Chicago, where she went to work in a glove factory at the age of thirteen. Christman joined a local glove workers' union in Chicago in 1901 and became a member of International Glove Workers' Union of America 18 in 1902, serving as treasurer (1905–11) and president (1912–17). She served the international as secretary-treasurer (1913–31)—taking a leave of absence in 1918 to serve as head of the Women's Field Division of the National War Labor Board—and as vice-president (1931–37). Christman was a member of the executive board of the Chicago Women's Trade Union League from 1910 to 1921 and secretary-treasurer of the National Women's Trade Union League from 1921 to 1950.

COATES, David Courtney (1868–1933), a native of Durham, England, immigrated to the United States in 1880 and settled in Pueblo, Colo., where he became a printer. After living for several years in Denver, where he was a member of International Typographical Union 49 and worked on the staff of the *Rocky Mountain News,* he returned to Pueblo in 1895. The following year he founded the *Pueblo Courier* with Otto Thum, serving as its business manager until 1901, and he published the *Colorado Chronicle* with Thum in 1902 and 1903. Coates was a founder of the Colorado State Federation of Labor in 1896 and served as its secretary (1897–99) and president (1899–1901). He was later lieutenant-governor of Colorado (1901–2), elected on a fusion ticket supported by "silver" Republicans, Democrats, and the People's party. Moving to Wallace, Idaho, in 1904, he became a member of Wallace Labor Union 150, a local of the American Labor Union, and published and edited the *Idaho State Tribune* (1904–6). Coates was elected vice-president of the American Labor Union in 1903 and became its president in 1905, representing it at the founding convention of the IWW. Moving to Spokane, he served as a member of the city charter commission in 1910 and as commissioner of public works from 1911 to 1914, and he published the *Labor World.* From 1915 to 1917 Coates was editor of the *Nonpartisan Leader* in Fargo, N.D. SG appointed him to the Committee on Labor of the Advisory Commission of the Coun-

cil of National Defense in 1917, and in 1918 he served as chairman
of the National party. In the early 1920s Coates moved to southern
California, where he was publisher of the *North Hollywood Sun* and a
member of Typographical local 174 of Los Angeles. He died in North
Hollywood.

CONBOY, Sara Agnes McLaughlin (1870–1928), was born in Boston.
A candy worker by age eleven, she later worked in a button mill and
then in a carpet mill, where she became a highly skilled weaver. Conboy was a young widow working in Roxbury, Mass., in 1909 when she
successfully led a strike that resulted in the organization of the carpet
weavers in that city and her appointment as a United Textile Workers
of America organizer (1910–15?). She subsequently served the Textile
Workers as acting secretary (1915) and secretary-treasurer (1915–28),
moving to Brooklyn where the union's offices were located. She was
also a vice-president of the National Women's Trade Union League
(1911–13) and an AFL salaried organizer for women (1914–15). During World War I she served on the subcommittee on Women in Industry of the Committee on Labor of the Advisory Commission of the
Council of National Defense.

COVERT, Clair (b. 1880?), was born in Texas and by 1915 had moved
to Washington state, where he worked as a carpenter and a sawyer and
lived in Aberdeen, Hoquiam, and finally Seattle. He served as president
of the International Union of Timber Workers from 1918 to 1921 and
as an AFL salaried organizer from 1917 to 1921.

D'ALESSANDRO, Domenico (1869–1926), was born in Italy and immigrated to the United States in 1895. A day laborer in Boston, he was
president of AFL Laborers' and Excavators' (Italian) Union 11,679
from 1904 until it joined the International Hod Carriers' and Building
Laborers' Union of America in 1906 as local 209. D'Alessandro served
the international union (from 1912, the International Hod Carriers',
Building and Common Laborers' Union of America), as organizer
(1907), vice-president (1907), and president (1908–26). He lived in
Albany from 1910 until he moved to Quincy, Mass., around 1918.

DAVIS, William John (1848–1934), was born in Birmingham, England, went to work as a printer's errand boy around the age of nine,
and in 1861 entered the brass trade, working as a chandelier maker
for various Birmingham firms and eventually becoming a foreman. In
1872 he was a founder of the Amalgamated Society of Brassworkers
(from 1873, the National Society of Amalgamated Brassworkers; from

1905, the National Society of Amalgamated Brassworkers and Metal Mechanics; from 1911, the National Society of Brassworkers and Metal Mechanics; and from 1920, the National Society of Brass and Metal Mechanics) and served as secretary of the union from 1872 to 1883 and again from 1889 to 1921. He was a member of the Parliamentary Committee of the TUC (1881–83, 1896–1902, 1903–20), serving twice as its chair (1898–99, 1912–13). During World War I he served on several government advisory committees connected with national service and munitions. After his retirement from union office, he moved to France, living outside Paris.

DAVISON, Emmett C. (1878–1944), was born in Chesterfield County, Va., attended school in Richmond, and served in the Spanish-American War. After completing his apprenticeship, he joined International Association of Machinists 10 of Richmond, becoming its business agent around 1910. Davison served as secretary-treasurer (1911–12) and president (1912–15) of the Virginia State Federation of Labor and as organizer (1913–17) and secretary-treasurer (1917–44) of the Machinists. Around 1923 he moved to Alexandria, where he served as a member of the city council (1932–34) and mayor (1934–37).

DEBS, Eugene Victor (1855–1926), born in Terre Haute, Ind., entered railroad work as an engine-house laborer and became a locomotive fireman. Elected secretary of Brotherhood of Locomotive Firemen 16 of Terre Haute in 1875, he became grand secretary and treasurer of the Locomotive Firemen and editor of the union's official journal in 1880. Debs resigned as an officer of the brotherhood in 1892 to begin building a single union for all railway workers and resigned the editorship of the journal in 1894. He founded the American Railway Union in 1893 and led it in the successful 1894 Great Northern Railroad strike. Imprisoned for six months in 1895 for his role as president of the union during the Pullman strike, he turned his energies to political activity after his release. In 1896 he supported the People's party campaign; in 1897 he was a founder of the Social Democracy of America, a socialist communitarian movement; and in 1898 he participated in founding the Social Democratic Party of the United States, running as the party's candidate for president in 1900. He was a founder of the Socialist Party of America in 1901, and he was its candidate for president in 1904, 1908, 1912, and 1920. In 1905 Debs participated in founding the IWW but left the organization three years later. During World War I, he was prosecuted under the Espionage Act and sentenced to ten years in prison. SG supported the campaign for clemency that culminated in a presidential pardon for Debs in 1921.

DOBSON, William (1864?–1953?), was born in England where he became a bricklayer. He emigrated in the 1880s, living first in Toronto and then in Buffalo, where he was secretary (1893) of Bricklayers' and Masons' International Union of America 36. In 1895 he moved to North Adams, Mass., where he served as corresponding secretary (1896–1901) of Bricklayers' and Masons' local 18. Dobson served as secretary (1900–1925) of the international union (from 1910, the Bricklayers', Masons', and Plasterers' International Union of America), moving with the union headquarters to Indianapolis in 1905. After leaving union office, he remained in Indianapolis, working as vice-president of the United Labor Bank and Trust Co. until 1934.

DONLIN, John H. (1868?–1952), was born in Illinois. He worked as a plasterer in Chicago and was a founding member of Operative Plasterers' International Association of the United States and Canada 5 of Chicago. In 1908 he became president of the international union, serving until 1912. Donlin was president of the AFL Building Trades Department (1916–24) and served on the Committee on Emergency Construction of the War Industries Board during World War I. From 1927 until his death he was editor of *The Plasterer*, the international union's official publication.

DONNELLY, John L., was a member of International Union of Mine, Mill, and Smelter Workers 70 of Miami, Ariz., and served as vice-president (1915–16) and president (1916–17) of the Arizona State Federation of Labor. He was chair (1916–17) of the Arizona state district of the Mine, Mill, and Smelter Workers, which was involved in the union's "New Blood" movement, that sought to radicalize the organization and replace its president, Charles Moyer.

DUFFY, Frank (1861–1955), was born in County Monaghan, Ireland. At the age of two he immigrated with his family to England, and in 1881 he came to the United States, settling in New York City. There he joined United Order of American Carpenters and Joiners 2 and served as the first president of the order's executive council for Greater New York. In 1888, when the order merged with the Brotherhood of Carpenters and Joiners of America to form the United Brotherhood of Carpenters and Joiners of America, Duffy became a member of Carpenters' local 478. He served as president of the local's executive council (1888–1901) and as its business agent (1896–98), and for four terms he was financial secretary of the brotherhood's New York district council. He was an organizer for the Carpenters in 1896 and four years later was elected to the union's executive board. Duffy served the brotherhood as secretary-treasurer (1901–2), secretary (1903–48), and editor of the union's official journal (1901–41). He moved to Philadelphia in 1901 and then to Indianapolis in 1902 when the union changed the location of its headquarters. Duffy served as an AFL vice-president from 1914 to 1939. He was also a board member of the National Society for the Promotion of Industrial Education (1912–20), served on the Indiana State Board of Education (1915–19), and was a member of the American labor mission to the 1919 Paris peace conference.

DUNCAN, Charles (1865–1933), was born in Middlesbrough, England, where he attended school until the age of sixteen and then apprenticed at an iron works. He joined the Amalgamated Society of Engineers around 1888 and served as the union's district secretary. In 1898 he became a member of the newly created Workers' Union (from 1919, the National Amalgamated Workers' Union), serving as its president (1898–1900) and secretary (1900–1929). Duncan served on several government commissions during World War I and became involved with the prowar British Workers' League. He served several terms as a Labour member of Parliament (1906–18, 1922–33) and was a member of the Labour party executive committee from 1920 through 1922.

DUNCAN, James (1857–1928), was born in Scotland and immigrated to the United States in 1880. He joined the Granite Cutters' National Union of the United States of America in 1881 and during the early 1880s served as an officer of the union's locals in New York, Philadelphia, Richmond, and, finally, Baltimore, where he settled in 1884. He was Maryland state organizer for the Granite Cutters, organizer for the AFL, and president of the Baltimore Federation of Labor (1890–92, 1897). Duncan served the Granite Cutters (from 1905, the Granite Cutters' International Association of America) as secretary (1895–1905), secretary-treasurer (1905–12), and president (1912–23) and edited the union's official journal from 1895 to 1928. He was an AFL vice-president (1895–1928) and acting president of the Federation during President John McBride's illness in 1895. He was also a member of the National Civic Federation Industrial Department (1901–2) and executive committee (1903 to at least 1923). President Woodrow Wilson appointed him a member of the Root mission to Russia in 1917, and he also served as a member of the American labor mission to the 1919 Paris peace conference.

EASLEY, Ralph Montgomery (1856–1939), was born in Browning, Pa., founded a daily newspaper in Hutchinson, Kans., and then moved to Chicago to work as a reporter and columnist for the *Chicago Inter Ocean*. In 1893 he helped organize the Chicago Civic Federation, leaving the *Inter Ocean* to serve as the federation's secretary. He resigned from that position in 1900 and moved to New York City to organize the National Civic Federation, bringing together prominent representatives of business, labor, and the public in cooperative reform efforts and in the settlement of labor disputes. Easley served as secretary of the National Civic Federation (1900–1903) and as chairman of its executive council (1904–39). In his later years he increasingly devoted himself to opposing radical labor organizations and social movements.

FISCHER, Jacob (1871–1936), was born in Osborne, Ohio, and at the age of sixteen moved to Indianapolis, where he lived the rest of his life. He served the Journeyman Barbers' International Union of America as a vice-president (1894–98), president (1898–1902), organizer (1902–4), and secretary-treasurer (1904–29). Fischer was also an AFL vice-president (1918–29) and a vice-president of the AFL Union Label Trades Department.

FITZPATRICK, John J. (1871?–1946), was born in Athlone, Ireland, and, after the death of his parents, was brought to Chicago by his uncle. He worked in the Chicago stockyards and in a brass foundry and then took up horseshoeing and blacksmithing, joining Journeymen Horseshoers' National Union of the United States (from 1892, International Union of Journeymen Horseshoers of the United States and Canada) 4 in 1886—and over the years serving as the local's vice-president, treasurer, business agent, and president—and then joining International Brotherhood of Blacksmiths, Drop Forgers, and Helpers 122 around 1921. Fitzpatrick was an executive committee member (1899–1900), organizer (1902–4?), and president (1900–1901, 1906–46) of the Chicago Federation of Labor and an AFL salaried organizer (1903–23). He played a major role in the 1917 meatpackers' organizing campaign and the 1919 steelworkers' organizing campaign, ran unsuccessfully for mayor of Chicago on the Labor party ticket in 1919, and served on the National Recovery Administration Regional Labor Board (1933–35).

FLOOD, Emmet T. (1874–1942), was born in Illinois and worked as a teamster in Chicago, where he joined International Brotherhood of Teamsters 715 (Department Store Drivers). He served as an AFL salaried organizer from 1904 to 1925, organizing, among others, a nurses' and attendants' union in Illinois state hospitals. Flood retired from the labor movement after SG's death and worked in the trucking business.

FLORE, Edward Frank (1877–1945), was born in Buffalo and began working in his father's saloon about the age of fourteen. He joined Hotel and Restaurant Employees' International Alliance and Bartenders' International League of America 175 of Buffalo in 1900 and soon became its recording secretary and then its financial secretary and treasurer. Flore became a vice-president of the Hotel and Restaurant Employees in 1905. Defeated in a bid for the union's presidency at the 1909 convention, he returned to his job as a bartender, but he was elected president of the union in 1911 and served in that position until his death. Flore also served as an AFL vice-president (1936–45).

FOSTER, William Z. (1881–1961), born in Taunton, Mass., was a member of the Socialist Party of America from 1901 to 1909, joined the United Wage Workers' Party of Washington in 1909, and became a member of the IWW in 1910, participating in the Spokane free-speech campaign. He then traveled to Europe, where he became a convert to the strategy of "boring from within" existing trade unions. After unsuccessfully contesting the AFL's right to represent the American labor movement at the 1911 meeting of the International Secretariat in Budapest, he returned to the United States and settled in Chicago. He left the IWW in 1912, joined the Brotherhood of Railway Carmen of America, and organized and was a member of the Syndicalist League of North America (1912–14) and the International Trade Union Educational League (1915–17). Between 1917 and 1919 he led AFL organizing campaigns in the packinghouse and steel industries, and in 1920 he founded the Trade Union Educational League. The following year he went to Moscow and, upon his return, joined the American Communist party. He was the party's candidate for president in 1924, 1928, and 1932 and served as the party's longtime chairman (1930?–44, 1945–57) and chairman emeritus (1957–61). He died in Moscow, where he had gone for medical care.

FRANKLIN, Joseph Anthony (1868–1948), was born in Sedalia, Mo., and took up the boilermaking trade in 1892. A charter member of Brotherhood of Boiler Makers and Iron Ship Builders of America 221 of Pittsburg, Kans., he served the Boiler Makers (from 1906, the International Brotherhood of Boiler Makers, Iron Ship Builders, and Helpers of America) as vice-president (1906–8) and president (1908–44).

FRAYNE, Hugh (1869–1934), was a member of Amalgamated Sheet Metal Workers' International Association (from 1903, Alliance) 86 of Scranton, Pa., and a vice-president of the international union (1901–2, 1904–5). He was an AFL salaried organizer from 1902 until his death and beginning in 1910 was in charge of the AFL's New York City office. During World War I, Frayne chaired the labor division of the War Industries Board.

FRENCH, Thomas A. (b. 1880?), was born in California and later moved to Phoenix, Ariz., where he served as secretary-treasurer of the Arizona State Federation of Labor (1916–17, 1920–21).

FREY, John Philip (1871–1957), was born in Mankato, Minn., and moved to Montreal in 1878, where he lived until the age of fourteen. He worked in a Montreal printing shop and on a farm and lumber camp in Upper Ontario before moving with his family to Worcester, Mass., in 1887. After finding work first as an errand boy and then in a grocery, he apprenticed as a molder. In 1896 he helped organize Iron Molders' Union of North America 5, serving as the local's president until 1900 and as vice-president of the Molders from 1900 to 1903. Frey moved to Bellevue, Ky., in 1903 after he was appointed editor of the union's official journal, which was published in Cincinnati, and about 1909 moved to Norwood, Ohio. He served as editor of the journal until 1927 and was president of the Ohio State Federation of Labor from 1924 to 1928. Frey moved to Washington, D.C., to serve as secretary-treasurer (1927–34) and president (1934–50) of the AFL Metal Trades Department.

FURUSETH, Andrew (1854–1938), was born in Furuseth, Norway, and went to sea in 1873. He immigrated to California in 1880, making his home in San Francisco, and in 1885 he joined the Coast Seamen's Union, serving as secretary from 1887 to 1889. He later served as secretary of the Sailors' Union of the Pacific (1891–92, 1892–1936) and president of the International Seamen's Union of America (1897–99, 1908–38) and was a legislative representative in Washington, D.C., for the AFL (1895–1902) and for the Seamen.

GARLAND, Mahlon Morris (1856–1920), born in Pittsburgh, served as president of the Amalgamated Association of Iron and Steel Workers of the United States (from 1897, the Amalgamated Association of Iron, Steel, and Tin Workers) from 1892 to 1898 and as a vice-president of the AFL from 1895 to 1898. An iron puddler and heater, he joined the Iron and Steel Workers in the late 1870s. He was fired in 1878 for union activities and worked in several midwestern cities before returning to Pittsburgh in 1880. There he joined Iron and Steel Workers' South Side Lodge 11 and in the mid-1880s served two terms on the city's select council. From 1890 to 1892 he was assistant president of the Iron and Steel Workers, before then assuming its presidency. He resigned from office in 1898 and accepted an appointment as U.S. collector of customs for Pittsburgh, retaining that post until 1915. Garland was a Republican congressman from Pennsylvania from 1915 until his death.

GARRETSON, Austin Bruce (1856–1931), was born in Winterset, Iowa, and in 1884 joined Order of Railway Conductors of America 53 of Denison, Tex. He served the order as grand senior conductor (1887–88, 1891–99), assistant grand chief conductor (1888–89, 1899–1906), grand chief conductor (1906–7), and president (1907–19). From 1913 through 1915 he served on the U.S. Commission on Industrial Relations.

GERMER, Adolph F. (1881–1966), was born in Germany, immigrated to the United States in 1888, and began working as a miner in Illinois at the age of eleven. He served as vice-president (1907) and secretary-treasurer (1908–12) of the Belleville subdistrict of United Mine Workers of America District 12 (Illinois) and then as an organizer for the international union (1913–14). Germer was national secretary (1916–19) and national organizer of the Socialist Party of America, and in 1919 he was convicted under the Espionage Act for obstructing the draft during World War I. He was sentenced to twenty years in prison, but in 1921 the U.S. Supreme Court overturned his conviction. Germer later worked in the California oil fields as an organizer for the Oil Field, Gas Well, and Refinery Workers' Union (1923–25), edited the Rockford (Ill.) *Labor News* (1931–35?), and was active in the Committee for Industrial Organization and the CIO (1935–55).

GOLDEN, John (1863–1921), was born in Lancashire, England, where he worked in the cotton mills and was a member of the Mule Spinners' Union. Blacklisted for union activities, he immigrated to Fall River, Mass., in 1884, where he was employed as a spinner and served as treasurer (1898–1904) of the Fall River Mule Spinners' Association. Golden was president (1904–21) of the United Textile Workers of America and editor (1915–21) of the union's official journal, moving to Brooklyn to oversee its production. He was also a member of the National Civic Federation executive committee from 1913 to 1921.

GOMPERS, Sadie Julian (1883–1918), the youngest child of SG and Sophia Julian Gompers, was born in New York City. After the family's move to Washington, D.C., she studied voice and then for a time sang in vaudeville and on the concert stage. She died in the World War I influenza epidemic.

GOMPERS, Solomon (1827–1919), SG's father, was a cigarmaker who was born in Amsterdam and immigrated to England with his family in 1845. He became a member of the cigarmakers' union there in 1848. In 1863 he immigrated to the United States with his wife, Sarah, and their six children.

GOMPERS, Sophia Julian (1850–1920), SG's first wife, was born in London and immigrated to the United States about 1855. She was living with her father and stepmother in Brooklyn and working as a tobacco stripper in a cigar factory when she married SG in 1867. Between 1868 and 1885 she and SG had at least nine children, six of whom lived past infancy: Samuel, Rose, Henry, Abraham, Alexander, and Sadie.

GOSLING, Harry (1861–1930), was born in London and apprenticed as a waterman at the age of fourteen. He joined the Amalgamated Society of Watermen and Lightermen during the 1889 dock strike and in 1890 became president of its Lambeth branch and a member of the union's executive council. He subsequently served as secretary of the Watermen (1893–1921), president of the National Transport Workers' Federation (1911–21), and president of the Transport and General Workers' Union (1921–24, 1924–30). Gosling was a member of the Parliamentary Committee of the TUC (from 1921, the General Council) from 1908 to 1910 and again from 1911 to 1924, serving as its chairman in 1915 and 1916. Gosling was also active in politics, serving as an alderman (1898–1904), as a member of the London County Council (1904–18, 1919–22, 1922–25), as a Labour member of Parliament (1923–30), and as minister of transport and paymaster-general (1924) in the first Labour government.

GREEN, William (1870–1952), was born in Coshocton, Ohio. He left school after the eighth grade and, at the age of fourteen, became a water boy for track layers on the Wheeling Railroad. At sixteen he joined his father in the coal mines. In 1888 he joined the local chapter of the National Progressive Union of Miners and Mine Laborers, which later became local 379 of the United Mine Workers of America. Green held various offices in his local—secretary, business agent, vice-president, and president—and served as president of subdistrict 6 of United Mine Workers' District 6 (Ohio; 1900–1906), as president of District 6 (1906–10), and as statistician (1911–13) and secretary-treasurer (1913–24) of the international union. In 1910 and again in 1912 he was elected to the Ohio senate. In 1914 Green became a member of the AFL Executive Council and, after SG's death in December 1924, became AFL president, an office he held until his death.

GRIMSHAW, Frank (1879–1953), was born in Quincy, Ill., and learned the stovemounting trade in Ironton, Ohio. Moving frequently in his early years, he lived variously in Ironton, Allegheny, Pa., Kokomo, Ind., and Rock Island, Ill., before settling in Piqua, Ohio, where he served as corresponding, recording, and financial secretary of Stove Mounters' and Steel Range Workers' International Union of North America 23. Grimshaw served as vice-president (1910), president (1910–13), and secretary-treasurer (1913–32) of the Stove Mounters' International Union of North America, as the international renamed itself in 1910. In 1916 he moved to Detroit, joining Stove Mounters' local 1, and from 1934 he was employed by the Kalamazoo (Mich.) Stove and Range Co. and was a member of Stove Mounters' local 74 of Kalamazoo. He retired in 1950.

GUARD, Rosa Lee (1863?–1937), was born near Charlottesville, Va., and began working as a schoolteacher at the age of fifteen. She moved to Washington, D.C., around 1897 and the next year began working as a typist at AFL headquarters, where she became chief clerk and SG's private secretary. After SG's death, she served as chief clerk to his successor, William Green.

HAMILTON, M. Grant (1864–1920), was born in Michigan and moved to Denver in the 1880s, where he joined International Typographical Union 49 and worked as a linotype operator. He later served as an AFL salaried organizer (1903–12, 1914–15, 1918–19) and as a member of the AFL Legislative Committee (1908, 1912–13, 1915–18). In 1919 Hamilton was director general of the Working Conditions Service of the U.S. Department of Labor.

HART, John F. (1871–1940), was born in New York state and by 1896 was working as a retail butcher in Utica, where he joined AFL Butchers' Union 6598. He was a founder of the Amalgamated Meat Cutters and Butcher Workmen of North America in 1897 and served the union as vice-president (1897–1904) and president (1910–21). After leaving office, Hart operated a grocery in Yorkville, near Utica.

HARTWIG, Otto Robert (1887–1972), was born in Manistee, Mich., and as a young man worked on farms, in sawmills, and in a meat-packing firm before becoming an apprentice as a carriage and wagon painter. In 1906 he moved to Portland, Oreg., where he joined Brotherhood of Painters, Decorators, and Paperhangers of America 10. From 1916 until 1925 Hartwig served as president of the Oregon State Federation of Labor. He later served as a consultant for the West Coast Lumbermen's Association (1928–32), on the Oregon State Industrial Accident Commission and Unemployment Compensation Commission (1932–35), as public relations director for the Oregon State Unemployment Compensation Commission (1936), and as Social Security advisor and general safety supervisor for the Crown Zellerbach Corp., a paper manufacturing firm.

HAYES, Frank (1882–1948), was born in What Cheer, Iowa, and after moving with his family to Illinois began working in the mines part time at the age of thirteen and full time after completing high school. In 1904 he was elected secretary-treasurer of the Belleville sub-district of United Mine Workers of America District 12 (Illinois) and in 1908 was appointed secretary-treasurer of District 12. Hayes served as vice-president (1910–17) and president (1917–20) of the United Mine Workers and in 1912 ran unsuccessfully for governor of Illinois as a candidate of the Socialist Party of America. During World War I he served as a member of the National War Labor Board. In 1920 he resigned his office due to ill health and moved to Denver, where he started a mining company. Hayes was a special representative for the United Mine Workers in Colorado from 1920 until his death and in 1937–38 served as Democratic lieutenant-governor of the state.

HAYES, Max Sebastian (1866–1945), was born near Havana, Ohio, and apprenticed as a printer at the age of thirteen. Moving to Cleveland in 1883, he joined International Typographical Union 53 in 1884 and served as an organizer for the international union for the next fifteen years. A founder of the *Cleveland Citizen* in 1891, Hayes worked as the paper's associate editor (1892–94) and editor (1894–1939). He was active in the Cleveland labor movement as corresponding secretary (1896–97) and recording secretary (1898–1901) of the Cleveland Central Labor Union, recording secretary (1902–3) of the United Trades and Labor Council, and recording secretary (1910) of the Cleveland Federation of Labor. Politically, Hayes worked in the People's party campaign in 1896, was active in the Socialist Labor party from 1896 to 1899, and was a founder of the Socialist Party of America in 1901.

In 1919 he chaired the executive committee of the National Labor party (from 1920, the Farmer-Labor party), and in 1920 he was the party's vice-presidential candidate. Hayes was a charter member of the Cleveland Metropolitan Housing Authority in 1933, and from 1933 to 1935 he served on the Ohio State Adjustment Board of the National Recovery Administration.

HAYWOOD, William Dudley (1869–1928), was born in Salt Lake City and at the age of fifteen began working at various mines in Utah and Nevada. He moved to Silver City, Idaho, in 1894, where, in 1896, he was a founder of Western Federation of Miners 66. Within a year he became the union's financial secretary and in 1900 its president. He was elected a member of the Western Federation of Miners' executive board in 1900 and its secretary-treasurer in 1901, moving with his family to Denver in 1901 when the federation relocated its headquarters. He also joined the Socialist Party of America in 1901. In 1905 he chaired the founding convention of the IWW. In 1906 Haywood was kidnapped by Colorado and Idaho authorities and extradited to Idaho where he was jailed on charges of conspiracy in the murder of former Idaho governor Frank Steunenberg; he was acquitted the next year. While in prison, he ran unsuccessfully for governor of Colorado on the Socialist ticket. Disagreements with Western Federation of Miners' president Charles Moyer led to his dismissal as the federation's secretary-treasurer in 1908. Haywood subsequently traveled as a Socialist party lecturer, served on the party's national executive committee, and edited the *International Socialist Review*. He played a major role in the Lawrence, Mass., textile strike of 1912, and he became IWW secretary-treasurer in 1914. In 1917 he was one of the members of the IWW indicted for conspiracy to interfere with the war effort. He was convicted in 1918 and sentenced to twenty years in prison. Released on bail pending appeal, Haywood fled to the Soviet Union in 1921. He died in Moscow.

HENDERSON, Arthur (1863–1935), was born in Glasgow, moved with his family to Newcastle-upon-Tyne, and apprenticed there as an iron molder when he was twelve. In 1883 he joined the Friendly Society of Iron Founders (from 1920, the National Union of Foundry Workers), soon becoming secretary of his local and, in 1892, a district delegate. He served as the union's general organizer from 1902 until 1911 and as its honorary president from 1913 until his death. Henderson also occupied many political offices, both local and national, beginning in the early 1890s. Between 1893 and 1903 he served successively on the

Newcastle City Council, the Durham County Council, the Darlington Town Council, and as mayor of Darlington. He served as a Labour member of Parliament, with brief interruptions, from 1903 until his death, and he was general secretary of the Labour party from 1912 to 1934. In addition, he served under Herbert Asquith as president of the Board of Education (1915–16) and paymaster-general (1916) and under David Lloyd George as a member of the War Cabinet (1916–17), resigning because of the government's opposition to his intended participation in the international socialist conference scheduled to meet in Stockholm in August 1917. He later served as home secretary (1924) and foreign secretary (1929–31). In 1934 he was awarded the Nobel Peace Prize for his work as president of the League of Nations disarmament conference in Geneva.

HILLMAN, Sidney (1887–1946), was born in Zagare, Lithuania. Twice arrested and imprisoned for his revolutionary activities, he went to England in 1906 and came to the United States in 1907, settling in Chicago. He became an apprentice cutter in 1909, joined United Garment Workers of America 39, and emerged as a leader of the Chicago garment workers' strike against Hart, Schaffner, and Marx in 1910–11. In early 1914 he became chief clerk of the New York cloakmakers' joint board of the International Ladies' Garment Workers' Union, but he resigned the post later that year to become president of the newly formed Amalgamated Clothing Workers of America, an office he held until his death. Hillman participated in founding the Committee for Industrial Organization in 1935, chaired the Textile Workers' Organizing Committee and the Department Store Workers' Organizing Committee, and served as a vice-president of the CIO (1938–40) and chair of its Political Action Committee (1943–46).

He was a founder of the Amalgamated Trust and Savings Bank of Chicago in 1922, serving as its director, and the Amalgamated Bank of New York in 1923, serving as chairman of the board. During the 1930s he served on the labor advisory board of the National Recovery Administration, the National Industrial Recovery Board, and the Council for Industrial Progress. In 1936 he was a founder and treasurer of Labor's Non-Partisan League, which supported President Franklin Roosevelt's reelection effort. He later served as a member of the National Defense Advisory Commission, associate director of the Office of Production Management, and head of the labor division of the War Production Board.

HILLQUIT, Morris (1869–1933), was born in Riga, Latvia, and immigrated to the United States with his family in 1886, settling in New

York City. He joined the Socialist Labor party and was a member of the faction that broke with Daniel DeLeon's leadership in 1899. Two years later he participated in the formation of the Socialist Party of America. Hillquit emerged as a leading figure in the Socialist party and served as a member of its national executive committee (1907–12, 1916–19, 1922–33) and as party chairman (1929–33).

In 1888 Hillquit helped found the United Hebrew Trades and was its first corresponding secretary. He graduated from the law school of the University of the City of New York (now New York University) in 1893 and subsequently developed a successful law practice that included serving for many years as counsel to the International Ladies' Garment Workers' Union (1914–33). He was also a director, trustee, and lecturer at the Rand School and the author of a number of works on socialism. Hillquit twice ran unsuccessfully on the Socialist party ticket for mayor of New York City (1917, 1932) and was five times a candidate for the U.S. House of Representatives (1906, 1908, 1916, 1918, 1920).

HOLDER, Arthur E. (1860–1937), was born in Wales and apprenticed as a machinist in England, where he joined the Amalgamated Society of Engineers in 1875. After immigrating to the United States, he settled in Sioux City, Iowa, where he joined KOL Local Assembly 212 in 1883 and International Association of Machinists 178 in 1894. Employed in the railroad shops and as an organizer, Holder moved to Des Moines in 1900 after he was appointed deputy commissioner of the Iowa Bureau of Labor Statistics, serving from 1900 to 1903. He was elected president of the Iowa State Federation of Labor in 1901 and served until 1903. In 1904 Holder moved to Washington, D.C., where he was associate editor of the *Machinists' Monthly Journal* until 1906 and served on the AFL Legislative Committee from 1906 to 1917. He also served as an AFL salaried organizer (1902–3, 1907–9, 1912). From 1917 to 1921 Holder was labor representative on the Federal Board for Vocational Education, and from 1921 to 1923 he was chief of the legislative division of the People's Legislative Service. After working for a time for the U.S. Department of Labor, he retired to Florida about 1931.

HOLLAND, James P. (1865–1941), was born in New Jersey and grew up in New York City. He was the longtime business agent of local 56 (Eccentric Firemen) of the International Brotherhood of Stationary Firemen (from 1917, International Brotherhood of Stationary Firemen and Oilers). Holland also served as vice-president (1907–15) and president (1915–26) of the New York State Federation of Labor (to

1910, the Workingmen's Federation of the State of New York), and he was a member of the New York City Board of Standards and Appeals (1918–25, 1926–34).

HUTCHESON, William Levi (1874–1953), was born near Saginaw, Mich., and became a shipyard carpenter's apprentice at age fourteen. He subsequently worked as a dairy farmer, a farm laborer, a well digger, and a miner before finding employment as a carpenter in Midland, Mich., where he helped organize and served as president of United Brotherhood of Carpenters and Joiners of America 1164. Soon fired for his union activities, Hutcheson returned to Saginaw, becoming a member of Carpenters' local 334 and serving as its business agent for several years. He was vice-president (1913–15) and president (1915–52) of the Carpenters and a member of the War Labor Conference Board (1918) and the National War Labor Board (1918–19). Hutcheson became an AFL vice-president in 1935 but resigned the following year; reelected vice-president in 1939, he held that position from 1940 until 1953.

HYNES, John Joseph (1872–1938), was born in St. John's, Newfoundland, and immigrated to the United States in 1887. He joined Boston local 17 of the Amalgamated Sheet Metal Workers' International Alliance (from 1924, the Sheet Metal Workers' International Association) and was president of the Boston Central Labor Union in 1906 and 1907. He served as general organizer for the Sheet Metal Workers from 1909 to 1913 and as the international's president from 1913 until his death. Hynes also served as a vice-president of the AFL Metal Trades Department (1913–38), the AFL Building Trades Department (1918–33, 1936–38), and the AFL Railway Employes' Department.

IGLESIAS Pantín, Santiago (1872–1939), was born in La Coruña, Spain, where he attended local schools and in 1884 apprenticed as a cabinetmaker. After working briefly in Cuba he returned to Spain in 1886. In 1888 he moved to Havana, where he took part in the independence movement led by José Martí, served as secretary of the Círculo de Trabajadores (Workmen's Circle) from 1888 to 1895, and edited the newspaper *La Alarma* in 1895. He fled to Puerto Rico in 1896 following the suppression of the Cuban labor movement and Gen. Valeriano Weyler's order for his arrest. In Puerto Rico he was a founder and editor of several labor journals: *Ensayo Obrero* (1897–98), *El Porvenir Social* (1898–1900), *Unión Obrera* (1902–6), and *Justicia* (1914–25). In 1899 he helped organize the Federación Libre de los Trabajadores de Puerto Rico (Free Federation of the Workers of Puerto Rico), serving as its president from 1900 to 1933. He was also a founder in 1899 of the Partido Obrero Socialista de Puerto Rico (Socialist Labor Party of Puerto Rico), reorganized in 1915 as the Partido Socialista de Puerto Rico (Socialist Party of Puerto Rico). Iglesias moved to Brooklyn in 1900 and joined United Brotherhood of Carpenters and Joiners of America 309. He returned to Puerto Rico the next year as AFL salaried organizer for Puerto Rico and Cuba, a post he held until 1933. He also served as a Partido Socialista member of the Puerto Rican senate (1917–33), secretary of the Pan-American Federation of Labor (1925–33), and Coalitionist resident commissioner from Puerto Rico in the U.S. House of Representatives (1933–39).

JAMES, Newton A. (1874–1933), was born in Sharpsburg, Md., and moved to the Maryland suburbs of Washington, D.C., as a young man. He joined local 63 (Washington, D.C.) of the International Brotherhood of Stationary Firemen (from 1917, the International Brotherhood of Stationary Firemen and Oilers, and from 1919, the International Brotherhood of Firemen and Oilers), serving for many years as its secretary and business agent and, for a time, as a vice-president of the international union (1907–19, 1930–33). James served as financial secretary (1912?–13, 1925–33), secretary (1917–19, 1923), and president (1914–15, 1916, 1921) of the Washington, D.C., Central Labor Union and was secretary (1917–21) and a vice-president (1922–33) of the Maryland State and District of Columbia Federation of Labor.

JEWELL, Bert Mark (1881–1968), was born in Brock, Nebr., and attended school in Omaha and Ocala, Fla. He worked at a variety of jobs on farms and in sawmills, phosphate mines, and machine shops before becoming an apprentice boilermaker in 1900 in High Springs, Fla. In 1905 he joined the Brotherhood of Boiler Makers and Iron Ship Builders of America (from 1906, the International Brotherhood of Boiler Makers, Iron Ship Builders, and Helpers of America), and by 1910 had moved to Jacksonville, Fla., and joined Boilermakers' lodge 222 (from 1912, lodge 20). Jewell served as the Boilermakers' general chair on the Seaboard Air Line Railroad from 1912 to 1916 and as an organizer for the union from 1916 to 1918. He was president of the Jacksonville Central Trades and Labor Council in 1914. Appointed acting president of the AFL Railway Employes' Department in 1918, Jewell became president in his own right in 1922, serving until 1946. From 1948 to 1952 he was a labor adviser to the U.S. Economic Cooperation Administration, which administered the Marshall Plan, and in 1955 he moved to Kansas City, Kans., to become an adviser to the Boilermakers. He held that post until his death.

JOHNSTON, William Hugh (1874–1937), was born in Nova Scotia and immigrated to the United States in 1885. He settled in Rhode Island, where he apprenticed at a locomotive works, joined the KOL, and, in 1895, helped organize International Association of Machinists 379 in Pawtucket. He later moved to Providence, where he served as president (1901) and business agent (1906–8) of Machinists' local 147. He was also president of Machinists' District 19 (New England; 1905) and president and general organizer of Machinists' District 44 (Navy Yards and Arsenals; 1909–11). Moving to Washington, D.C., around 1910, he joined Machinists' local 174. Johnston was president of the international union (1912–26) and a member of the National War Labor Board (1918–19), and in 1922 he helped organize the Conference for Progressive Political Action. He resigned his union office following a stroke but later served as vice-president of the Mount Vernon Savings Bank and then returned to work at Machinists' headquarters in Washington, D.C.

JONES, Jerome (1855–1940), was born in Nashville, where he worked as a reporter, printer, and editor for several newspapers, including the *Nashville Herald,* the *Nashville Sun,* and the *Journal of Labor.* He joined the International Typographical Union in 1876 and later served as president of the Nashville Federation of Trades and, from the early 1890s, as an AFL organizer. In 1898 he established the *Journal of Labor* in Atlanta, serving as its editor until 1940. He was active in Typographical local 48 in Atlanta and helped organize the Georgia Federation of Labor in 1899, serving two terms (1904–5, 1911–12) as its president. He was also a founder of the Southern Labor Congress in 1912 and its president until its demise in 1919.

JOYCE, John Joseph (1876–1937?), was born in Jamestown, N.Y., and as a young man worked as a freight handler, grain scooper, and timekeeper. Moving to Buffalo, he joined International Longshoremen's Association 109 (Grain Scoopers) of that city and served for a time as its president. Joyce was a vice-president of the Longshoremen (from 1901 to 1908, the International Longshoremen, Marine, and Transport Workers' Association) from 1901 to 1906 and the union's secretary-treasurer from late 1906 until his death.

JOYCE, Martin T. (1876–1931), was born in Massachusetts and left school at an early age to train as a tailor. He soon left that trade to take up electrical work, and on completing his apprenticeship in 1902 joined International Brotherhood of Electrical Workers 103 of Boston, remaining a member of that local until his death. Joyce served briefly as president of the Boston Central Labor Union (1905?) and as secretary-treasurer (1911–31) and legislative agent (1925–31) of the Massachusetts State Federation of Labor.

KELLEY, Florence (1859–1932), was a prominent reformer in the areas of tenement-house manufacturing conditions and child labor and the translator of a number of works by socialist authors, among them *The Condition of the Working Class in England in 1844* by Friedrich Engels. In 1884 Kelley married Lazare Wischnewetzky, himself also a student and a fellow socialist. In 1891, after separating from Wischnewetzky, she reassumed her maiden name and moved to Chicago, residing at Hull-House until 1899 and serving as chief state inspector of factories for Illinois from 1893 to 1897. Moving to New York City in 1899 she became secretary of the National Consumers' League, a position she held until her death. She also served on the boards of directors of the New York State and the National Child Labor Committees, was a founder and board member of the National Association for the Advancement of Colored People, and was vice-president of the National American Woman Suffrage Association.

KONENKAMP, Sylvester J. (1875–1953), was raised in Pittsburgh and began working for the Pennsylvania Railroad in 1892. He joined the Order of Railroad Telegraphers in 1895 and was active in Railroad Telegraphers' local 52 of Pittsburgh until at least 1902, serving as president and secretary. He helped organize the general board of adjustment for the Pennsylvania Railroad and served as its assistant general chair from 1898 to 1900. He also helped organize Brotherhood of Commercial Telegraphers' local 3 of Pittsburgh, which in 1903 became local 6 of the Commercial Telegraphers' Union of America. Konenkamp served as a member of the Commercial Telegraphers' general executive board (1906–8) and as president (1908–19) and acting secretary-treasurer (1916–19) of the international union. He moved to Chicago, where the union had its headquarters, after he was elected president, and he worked there as an attorney after leaving office.

KREYLING, David J. (1859–1938), a Missouri native, apprenticed as a cigarmaker at the age of twelve. He was a charter member of Cigar Makers' International Union of America 44 of St. Louis, serving as its president in 1897, and a founder of the St. Louis Central Trades and Labor Union in 1887, serving as its president (1895–1900) and secretary-organizer (1901–33). He also helped organize the Missouri State Federation of Labor in 1891 and was its first president, serving from 1891 to 1892.

LANE, Dennis (1881–1942), was born in Chicago and after a few years of school began working in the stockyards, where he joined Amalgamated Meat Cutters and Butcher Workmen of North America 87 (Cattle Butchers). Discharged and blacklisted for his participation in the 1904 stockyards strike, Lane worked for a time in other occupations before becoming an organizer for the Meat Cutters. He subsequently served as vice-president (1914–17) and secretary-treasurer (1917–42) of the international union.

LARGER, Bernard A. (1861?–1928), a Cincinnati clothing cutter, was a member of United Garment Workers of America 100 of Cincinnati. He served as president (1897–98, 1900–1904) and secretary (1904–28) of the international union.

LEE, William Granville (1859–1929), was born in La Prairie, Ill. In 1879 he became a brakeman on the Atchison, Topeka, and Santa Fe Railroad and in 1880 was promoted to conductor. He subsequently worked on the Wabash Railroad, the Missouri Pacific, and, from 1891 to 1895, the Union Pacific. He joined Brotherhood of Railroad Trainmen lodge 18 of Sedalia, Mo., in 1890, and in 1891 he helped organize lodge 385 of Kansas City, Mo., which he served as lodge master and financial secretary. Lee served the Brotherhood of Railroad Trainmen as first vice grand master (1895–1905), assistant grand master (1905–9), grand master (1909), president (1909–28), and secretary-treasurer (1928–29). During World War I he was a member of the Committee on Labor of the Advisory Commission of the Council of National Defense.

LEGIEN, Carl (1861–1920), was born in Marienburg, Prussia, and raised at an orphanage in nearby Thorn. He apprenticed to a woodcarver at the age of fourteen. After three years of compulsory military service and two years as a traveling journeyman, Legien settled in Hamburg and joined the local union of woodcarvers in 1886. He was elected president of the Vereinigung der Drechsler Deutschlands (Union of German Woodcarvers) at its founding in 1887. In 1890 he stepped down from this office to become secretary of the newly founded Generalkommission der Gewerkschaften Deutschlands (General Commission of German Trade Unions). He led this organization (from 1919, the Allgemeiner Deutscher Gewerkschaftsbund [General

German Federation of Trade Unions]) until his death and edited its official journal, the *Correspondenzblatt,* from 1891 to 1900. A member of the Sozialdemokratische Partei Deutschlands (Social Democratic Party of Germany), Legien served as a socialist deputy in the Reichstag from 1893 to 1898 and from 1903 until his death. He was instrumental in integrating the concerns of the German trade union movement into the political program of the Sozialdemokratische Partei. Legien helped inaugurate the meetings of the International Secretariat of the National Centers of Trade Unions in 1901 and served as secretary of this organization (from 1913, the International Federation of Trade Unions) from 1903 to 1919.

LENNON, John Brown (1850–1923), was born in Wisconsin, raised in Hannibal, Mo., and in 1869 moved to Denver, where he helped organize a local tailors' union and the Denver Trades Assembly. He later moved to New York City and then to Bloomington, Ill. He served the Journeymen Tailors' National Union of the United States (from 1889, the Journeymen Tailors' Union of America) as president (1884–85), member of the executive board (1885–87), and secretary (1887–1910). He was treasurer of the AFL from 1891 to 1917, served on the U.S. Commission on Industrial Relations (1913–15), and was a commissioner of conciliation for the U.S. Department of Labor from 1918 through at least 1920.

LORD, James (b. 1879), was born in England, immigrated to the United States in 1890, and became a member of United Mine Workers of America 1213 of Farmington, Ill. He served as vice-president (1912–14) of United Mine Workers District 12 (Illinois), president of the AFL Mining Department (1914–22), treasurer of the Pan-American Federation of Labor (1918–24), and, briefly, as an AFL salaried organizer in California (1922). During World War I he was a member of the Committee on Labor of the Advisory Commission of the Council of National Defense.

McCARTHY, Frank H. (1864?–1932), was born in England, immigrated as a child to the United States, and lived in Bangor, Maine, until 1876 when he moved to Boston. He joined Cigar Makers' International Union of America 97 of Boston in 1883 and was its president in 1890. McCarthy served as president of the Boston Central Labor Union (1891–92), as president of the Massachusetts State Federation of Labor (1900?–1902), and as an AFL salaried organizer from 1903 until his death.

McCLORY, Joseph E. (1877–1951), was born in New York and later moved with his family to Cleveland, where in 1898 he joined local 17 of the International Association of Bridge and Structural Iron Workers. McClory was elected to the executive board of the Structural Iron Workers in 1911 and served the international union (from 1915, the International Association of Bridge, Structural, and Ornamental Iron Workers and Pile Drivers, and from 1917, the International Association of Bridge, Structural, and Ornamental Iron Workers) as acting secretary-treasurer (1912–13), vice-president (1913–14), acting president (1914), and president (1914–18). Returning to Cleveland, he resumed his occupation as a structural iron worker and then served for a number of years as deputy county treasurer of Cuyahoga County, Ohio.

MAHON, William D. (1861–1949), was born in Athens, Ohio, and worked as a coal miner in the Hocking Valley district. In the late 1880s he moved to Columbus, Ohio, where he worked as a mule car driver and helped to organize street railway workers in the early 1890s. In 1893 he was elected president of the Amalgamated Association of Street Railway Employes of America and shortly thereafter moved to Detroit. He served as president of the union (from 1903, the Amalgamated Association of Street and Electric Railway Employes of America) until retiring in 1946. Mahon was presiding judge of the Michigan State Court of Mediation and Arbitration (1898–1900), a member of the executive committee of the National Civic Federation (1903 to at least 1923), and an AFL vice-president (1917–23, 1936–49).

MARSH, Ernest P. (1876?–1963?), was born in Ohio. By 1900 he had moved to Skagit County, Wash., and was working as a shingle packer, and around 1905 he moved to Everett, Wash., where he continued working in his trade and edited the Everett *Labor Journal* from around 1910 to around 1914. Marsh served as financial secretary of International Shingle Weavers' Union of America 2 of Everett (1909–10, 1912–13), as a vice-president of the international union (1916–18), and as president of the Washington State Federation of Labor (1913–18). He was a member of the President's Mediation Commission (1917–18) and later worked for the Conciliation Service of the U.S. Department of Labor, retiring in 1949.

MAURER, James Hudson (1864–1944), was born in Reading, Pa., and at an early age worked variously as a newsboy, hat maker, and machinist. He joined KOL Washington Assembly 72 of Reading in 1880 and served as an officer of that local assembly, as a KOL organizer, as master workman of KOL Iron Workers' Assembly 7975, and as a KOL district master workman. During the 1890s he found employment as a steamfitter, newspaper publisher, and cigarmaker, and by 1901 he was working as a plumber and was a member of United Association of Journeymen Plumbers, Gas Fitters, Steam Fitters and Steam Fitters' Helpers of the United States and Canada 42 of Reading. He served as president of the Pennsylvania State Federation of Labor from 1912 until 1928.

Maurer joined the Socialist Labor party in the late 1890s and, after 1902, was a member of the Socialist Party of America (SPA), serving on the party's state and national executive committees. He ran unsuccessfully as the SPA candidate for governor of Pennsylvania in 1906 and then served as a Socialist member of the Pennsylvania House of Representatives (1911–13, 1915–19). He ran unsuccessfully on the SPA ticket for vice-president of the United States in 1928 and 1932, for governor of Pennsylvania in 1930, and for the United States Senate in 1934. In 1936 Maurer left the Socialist party and joined the newly organized Social Democratic Federation.

MITCHELL, John (1870–1919), was born in Braidwood, Ill. He became a miner in 1882 and worked in the Illinois coalfields except for two brief sojourns in the mines of Colorado, New Mexico, and Wyoming. He also read law for a year during the 1880s. In 1885 he joined KOL National Trade Assembly 135. A member of the Spring Valley, Ill., local of the United Mine Workers of America in the early 1890s, he was elected secretary-treasurer of the northern Illinois subdistrict of United Mine Workers' District 12 (Illinois) in 1895, became the lobbyist for District 12 in 1896, and was elected a member of the union's Illinois state executive board and appointed a national organizer in 1897. Mitchell was elected vice-president of the United Mine Workers in 1898, became acting president later that year, and served as the union's president until 1908. He was also an AFL vice-president (1899–1913). A founder of the National Civic Federation in 1900, he served as a member of its executive committee (1901, 1903–10), Industrial Department (1901–2), and executive council (1904–10). He was later a member of the New York State Workmen's Compensation Commission (1914–15) and chairman of the New York State Industrial Commission (1915–19).

MOONEY, Thomas Joseph (1882–1942), was born in Chicago and lived in Washington, Ind., until the age of ten, when his father died; his mother then moved the family to Holyoke, Mass. Mooney went to work at the age of fourteen and soon apprenticed as a foundryman.

He moved to East Cambridge, Mass., and around 1902 joined the Core Makers' International Union of America; from 1903 he was a member of the Iron Molders' Union of North America. In 1908 Mooney moved to California, living first in Stockton and then in San Francisco. He became a socialist, participated in the 1908 presidential campaign of Eugene Debs, attended the 1910 International Socialist Congress in Copenhagen, and briefly joined the IWW. In 1911 he was a founder of the *Revolt,* a weekly socialist newspaper in San Francisco. Mooney was arrested in 1913 for illegal possession of explosives. He was tried three times, the first two trials ending in hung juries and the third resulting in an acquittal. He was arrested again after a bomb exploded during a San Francisco Preparedness Day parade on July 22, 1916, killing ten and injuring forty. He was convicted of first-degree murder in 1917—on what was later shown to have been perjured testimony by a key prosecution witness—and sentenced to death. After widespread protests and the personal intervention of President Woodrow Wilson, his sentence was commuted in 1918 to life imprisonment. He was pardoned by the governor of California in 1938.

MORRISON, Frank (1859–1949), was born in Frankton, Ont. In 1865 his family moved to Walkerton, Ont., where he became a printer. Beginning about 1883, he worked at his trade in Madison, Wis. In 1886 he moved to Chicago, where he joined International Typographical Union 16. From 1893 to 1894 he studied law at Lake Forest University, becoming a member of the Illinois bar in 1895. The following year he was elected secretary of the AFL, serving in that post from 1897 to 1935 and as AFL secretary-treasurer from 1936 until his retirement in 1939. During World War I Morrison was a member of the Committee on Labor of the Advisory Commission of the Council of National Defense.

MOYER, Charles H. (1866–1929), was born in Iowa and moved to Montana in 1882. In the 1890s he worked as a miner in the Black Hills, living in Deadwood, S.Dak., and serving as president of Western Federation of Miners 2 of Deadwood from 1894 to 1896. He was a member of the Western Federation of Miners' executive board from 1899 to 1902, was appointed general agent and organizer in 1901, and served the union (from 1916, the International Union of Mine, Mill, and Smelter Workers) as president from 1902 to 1926. Moyer was a founder of the IWW in 1905 and served briefly as a member of its executive board. In 1906 he was kidnapped by Colorado and Idaho authorities and extradited to Idaho, where he was jailed on charges of conspiracy in the murder of former Idaho governor Frank Steunenberg. After his codefendants William Haywood and George Pettibone were tried and acquitted in 1907 and 1908, charges against him were dropped. Moyer lived in Denver from around the turn of the century until at least 1926 and spent his final years in Pomona, Calif.

NELSON, Oscar Fred (1884–1943), was born and lived his entire life in Chicago. He began working as a newsboy when he was nine, left school at thirteen to work full-time in a department store, and became a post office clerk at eighteen, joining AFL Post Office Clerks' Union 8703, which in 1906 became local 1 of the National Federation of Post Office Clerks. He served as president of the local from 1907 to 1910, as president of the Post Office Clerks from 1910 to 1913, as editor of the *Union Postal Clerk,* the union's official journal, from 1913 to 1917, and as vice-president of the Chicago Federation of Labor from 1910 to 1935. Nelson was chief factory inspector for the state of Illinois from 1913 to 1917 and a commissioner of conciliation for the U.S. Department of Labor from 1917 to 1922. In 1927 and 1928 he served as interim president of the Building Service Employees' International Union. Admitted to the Illinois bar in 1922, he served as a member of the Chicago City Council from 1923 to 1935 and as a superior court judge for Cook County from 1935 until his death.

NESTOR, Agnes (1880–1948), was born in Grand Rapids, Mich., and in 1897 moved to Chicago, where she worked in a glove factory. She joined a local glove workers' union in 1901 and was a founder of International Glove Workers' Union of America 18 in 1902, serving as its president from 1902 until 1906. She served the international union as vice-president (1903–6, 1915–38), secretary-treasurer (1906–13), president (1913–15), and director of research and education (1939–48). During World War I Nestor served on the Committee on Women's Defense Work of the Council of National Defense and on the subcommittee on Women in Industry of the Committee on Labor of the Advisory Commission of the Council of National Defense. She was also a member (1907–48) of the National Women's Trade Union League and president (1913–48) of its Chicago branch.

O'CONNELL, James (1858–1936), was born in Minersville, Pa., learned his trade as a machinist's apprentice, and began working as a railroad machinist. He served as a lobbyist for the KOL in Harrisburg, Pa., in 1889 and 1891. Joining National (from 1891, International) Association of Machinists 113 of Oil City, Pa., around 1890, he became a member of the Machinists' executive board in 1891 and later served the international union as grand master machinist (1893–99) and president (1899–1911). He moved to Chicago in 1896 and to Washington, D.C., in 1900. O'Connell served as an AFL vice-president (1896–1918) and president of the AFL Metal Trades Department (1911–34). He was also a member of the National Civic Federation executive committee (1901, 1903–10) and Industrial Department (1901–2), the U.S. Commission on Industrial Relations (1913–15), and, during World War I, the Committee on Labor of the Advisory Commission of the Council of National Defense.

O'CONNOR, Thomas Ventry (1870–1935), was born in Toronto and moved with his family to Buffalo as a young child. He began working as a ferry boy at the age of eleven, later became a tugboat fireman, and by his early twenties was employed as a marine engineer. O'Connor served as secretary of International Longshoremen's Association 379 (the Buffalo branch of the Licensed Tugmen's Protective Association of the Great Lakes) and as president of the Tugmen's Association (1906–8), and he was a vice-president (1907–8) and the president (1909–21) of the Longshoremen (from 1901 to 1908, the International Longshoremen, Marine, and Transport Workers' Association). He left union office to serve as vice-chairman (1921–24) and chairman (1924–33) of the U.S. Shipping Board.

OGDEN, John William (1863?–1930), served as secretary of the Heywood (England) Weavers' Association (1891–1930) and as president of the Northern Counties' Amalgamated Weavers' Association (1911–30). He was a member of the Parliamentary Committee of the TUC (from 1921, the General Council; 1911–30), serving as its chair in 1917–18.

OLANDER, Victor A. (1873–1949), was born in Chicago. After leaving school, he worked for a time in a factory and then, at the age of fourteen, became a sailor on the Great Lakes. He served as business agent (1901–3), assistant secretary (1903–9), and secretary (1909–20) of the Lake Seamen's Union (from 1919, the Sailors' Union of the Great Lakes) and as vice-president (1902–25), secretary-treasurer (1925–36), and member of the legislative committee of the International Seamen's Union of America. Olander was also active in the Chicago Federation of Labor (FOL) and served as secretary-treasurer of the Illinois State FOL from 1914 until his death. During World War I he was a member of the National War Labor Board (1918–19) and the Illinois State Council of Defense, and he later served on the National Recovery Administration district board for Illinois and Wisconsin, the Illinois Department of Labor Unemployment Compensation Advisory

Board, and the board of directors of WCFL, the radio station of the Chicago FOL. He was a lifelong resident of Chicago.

OUDEGEEST, Jan (1870–1951), was born in Utrecht, Netherlands. A railroad worker, he was a founder in 1898 and the first president of the Nederlandsche vereeniging van spoor- en tramwegpersoneel (Netherlands Association of Railway and Tramway Employees); he continued as an officer of that organization until 1942. He was elected secretary of the Nederlandsch verbond van vakvereenigingen (Netherlands League of Trade Unions) in 1905 and served as its president from 1908 to 1918. During World War I Oudegeest was head of the auxiliary office of the International Federation of Trade Unions in Amsterdam, and from 1919 to 1927 he was secretary of the organization. Also active in local and national politics, he served as a member of the lower (1918–22) and upper (1928–36) chambers of the Dutch parliament and from 1927 to 1934 was chairman of the Sociaal-democratische arbeiderspartij (Social Democratic Workers' party).

PERHAM, Henry Burdon (1856–1949), was born in England, immigrated to Canada in 1871, and became a telegrapher and ticket clerk in Ontario in 1872. Moving to the United States in 1876, he was blacklisted for his participation in the railroad strike of 1877 and became a prospector. In 1889 he took a telegrapher's job with the Denver and Rio Grande Railroad in Gunnison, Colo. He served the Order of Railroad Telegraphers of North America as chairman of the Denver and Rio Grande system (1891–97), secretary and treasurer (1897–1901), and president (1901–19), moving to the union's headquarters in Peoria, Ill., in 1897 and to St. Louis in 1901. He was also an AFL vice-president (1909–18).

PERKINS, George William (1856–1934), was born in Massachusetts and began his career in the Cigar Makers' International Union of America by joining Albany, N.Y., local 68 in 1880. He served as a vice-president of the Cigar Makers from 1885 to 1891 and as acting president for six months in 1888 and 1889. In 1891 he was elected president, an office he held for the next thirty-five years. He became the president of the AFL Union Label Trades Department in 1928, serving until his death.

POWDERLY, Terence Vincent (1849–1924), was born in Carbondale, Pa., apprenticed as a machinist, and moved to Scranton, where he joined the International Machinists and Blacksmiths of North America in 1871, becoming president of his local and an organizer in Pennsylvania. After being dismissed and blacklisted for his labor activities, Powderly joined the KOL in Philadelphia in 1876 and shortly afterward founded a local assembly of machinists and was elected its master workman. In 1877 he helped organize KOL District Assembly 5 (number changed to 16 in 1878) and was elected corresponding secretary. He was elected mayor of Scranton on the Greenback-Labor ticket in 1878 and served three consecutive two-year terms. He played an important role in calling the first General Assembly of the KOL in 1878, where he was chosen grand worthy foreman, the KOL's second highest office. The September 1879 General Assembly elected him grand master workman, and he continued to hold the Order's leading position (title changed to general master workman in 1883) until 1893. Active in the secret Irish nationalist society *Clan na Gael*, Powderly was elected to the Central Council of the American Land League in 1880 and was its vice-president in 1881. He became an ardent advocate of land reform and temperance and, as master workman, favored the organization of workers into mixed locals rather than craft unions, recommended that they avoid strikes, encouraged producers' cooperatives, and espoused political reform.

In 1894 Powderly was admitted to the Pennsylvania bar, and in 1897 President William McKinley, for whom he had campaigned, appointed him U.S. commissioner general of immigration. President Theodore Roosevelt removed him from this position in 1902 but in 1906 appointed him special representative of the Department of Commerce and Labor to study European immigration problems. Powderly was chief of the Division of Information in the Bureau of Immigration and Naturalization from 1907 until his death.

RICKERT, Thomas Alfred (1876–1941), was born in Chicago and attended business college before becoming a garment cutter and joining United Garment Workers of America 21 of Chicago at the age of nineteen. He served as president (1904–41) and acting secretary-treasurer (1934–41) of the international union and was an AFL vice-president (1918–41). During World War I he served on the National War Labor Board (1918–19).

RYAN, Frank M. (1855?–1927), began working as a bridgeman in St. Louis in 1874. By the late 1890s he had moved to Chicago, where he became an active member of International Association of Bridge and Structural Iron Workers 1. He served as president of the Structural Iron Workers from 1905 until 1914. Convicted in 1912 in connection with the dynamite conspiracy case brought against members of the

Structural Iron Workers, he was imprisoned in the federal penitentiary at Leavenworth, Kans., until 1918. Ryan worked as an organizer for the union in 1919 and 1920 and retired as an ironworker in 1924.

SCHARRENBERG, Paul (1877–1969), was born in Hamburg, Germany. After immigrating to the United States, he moved in 1898 to San Francisco, where he joined the Sailors' Union of the Pacific, a regional branch of the International Seamen's Union of America. He served as business manager (1902–13) and editor (1913–21, 1922–37) of the *Coast Seamen's Journal* (from 1918, the *Seamen's Journal*) and as a member of the Seamen's executive board. Scharrenberg was also secretary-treasurer of the California State Federation of Labor (1909–36), secretary of the California Commission of Immigration and Housing (1913–22), and secretary of the California Joint Immigration Commission (1921–36). Expelled from the Sailors' Union of the Pacific in 1935 in a political dispute, he moved to Washington, D.C., and became the legislative representative of the Seamen (1936–37) and, later, a lobbyist for the AFL (1937–43). He subsequently served as director of the California Department of Industrial Relations (1943–55) and as a member of the U.S. Advisory Committee on Public Health (1947–53).

SCHLESINGER, Benjamin (1876–1932), was born in Lithuania, where he received a rabbinical education. In 1891 he immigrated to the United States and went to work as a machine operator in Chicago's cloak and suit industry. He served as treasurer of the short-lived International Cloak Makers' Union of America in 1892 and remained active in the Chicago Cloak Makers' Union until it disbanded in 1894. He was recording secretary of the reorganized Chicago Cloak Makers' Union from 1895 to 1898 and helped organize the International Ladies' Garment Workers' Union in 1900. After serving as manager of the Cloak Makers' Joint Board in Chicago (1902–3), he was elected president of the Ladies' Garment Workers in 1903 and moved to New York City, where the union's headquarters were located. Failing reelection in 1904, he served as general organizer for the union (1904–5), manager of the Cloak Makers' Joint Board in New York, and manager of the *Jewish Daily Forward* (1907–12). He became president of the Ladies' Garment Workers again in 1914, serving until 1923, when he resigned to manage the Chicago office of the *Jewish Daily Forward*. In 1928 he was elected vice-president of the international union, and he assumed its presidency once again upon Morris Sigman's resignation, serving from 1928 until his death.

SCHLOSSBERG, Joseph (1875–1971), was born in Russia and immigrated to the United States in 1888. He settled in New York City, where he joined the Cloakmakers' and Operators' Union, participated in the 1890 cloakmakers' strike, and after 1900 served as editor of several New York City Yiddish-language labor publications. He also joined the Socialist Labor party, remaining a member until 1917. A member of United Garment Workers of America 156, Schlossberg supported an unauthorized strike of New York City tailors in 1913 and then served as secretary-treasurer of the secessionist United Brotherhood of Tailors. In October 1914 a dissenting faction of the Garment Workers elected him secretary of their newly-formed union, which was reorganized in December of that year as the Amalgamated Clothing Workers of America. He served the Clothing Workers as secretary (1914–15, 1915–20), vice-president (1915), secretary-treasurer (1920–40), and editor of the *Advance,* the union's official journal (1917–25).

SEDDON, James Andrew (1868–1939), was born in Prescot, Lancashire, went to work as a grocer's assistant at the age of twelve, and became a commercial traveler when he was twenty-eight. He served as an organizer for the National Amalgamated Union of Shop Assistants, Warehousemen, and Clerks, became a member of the union's executive committee in 1898, and served as its president from 1902 until 1919. He was a member of the Parliamentary Committee of the TUC (1908–15) and served as its chair from 1913 to 1915. Seddon was a founder of the British Workers' National League in 1916 and later a member of its offshoot, the National Democratic party. He served as a member of Parliament from 1906 to 1910 (Labour) and again from 1918 to 1922 (Coalition National Democratic and Labour).

SHORT, William Mackie (1887–1947), was born in Dailly, Scotland, immigrated to the United States in 1905, and subsequently worked as a miner in Washington state and British Columbia. Short served as secretary of United Mine Workers of America District 10 (Washington; 1914–18), vice-president (1915–18) and president (1918–27) of the Washington State Federation of Labor, and editor of the *Washington State Labor News* (1924–28). He left union office to go into banking, serving as vice-president (1927–30), president (1931), and liquidator (1933) of the Brotherhood Bank and Trust Co. (from 1929, the North Coast Bank and Trust Co.). In 1932 he entered the laundry business, serving as manager of the Mutual Laundry Co., administrator of industrial agreements for the Seattle Associated Laundries, and then as administrator of the Laundries and Dry Cleaners Association.

SLATER, George Henry (1876–1940), was born in Brooklyn, moved to Kansas with his family when a child, and around 1902 moved to Galveston, where he worked as a linotype operator. Slater served several terms as president of International Typographical Union 28 of Galveston (1903–7) and was secretary-treasurer (1914–19), president (1919–24), and executive secretary and legislative representative (1924–34) of the Texas State Federation of Labor. After leaving office, he lived in Austin, where he was active in Typographical local 138. He died at the Home for Union Printers in Colorado Springs, Colo.

SPENCER, William J. (1867–1933), was born in Hamilton, Ont., where he apprenticed as a plumber. He immigrated to New York state about 1894 and joined United Association of Journeymen Plumbers, Gas Fitters, Steam Fitters, and Steam Fitters' Helpers of the United States and Canada 36 of Buffalo. Spencer served as secretary-treasurer (1897–1900) and general organizer (1900–1904) of the Plumbers, was a vice-president of the AFL (1904–5), secretary-treasurer of the Structural Building Trades Alliance (1903–8), and secretary-treasurer of the AFL Building Trades Department (1908–24, 1927–33). He lived in Dayton, Ohio, from about 1902 until 1912, when he moved to Washington, D.C., where he became a member of Plumbers' local 5.

STONE, Warren Sanford (1860–1925), was born in Ainsworth, Iowa, and became a locomotive fireman on the Chicago, Rock Island, and Pacific Railroad in 1879. He was promoted to engineer in 1884 and subsequently joined Brotherhood of Locomotive Engineers' lodge 181 of Eldon, Iowa, which he served as first assistant engineer (1896–97) and grand chief engineer (1897–1903). Stone served as grand chief engineer of the Locomotive Engineers from 1903 to 1924 and as president of the union from 1924 until his death. During World War I he was a member of the Committee on Labor of the Advisory Commission of the Council of National Defense.

SULLIVAN, James William (1848–1938), was born in Carlisle, Pa., began working as a printer at the age of fourteen, and moved to New York City in 1882, where he worked for the *New York Times* and the *New York World* and joined International Typographical Union 6. A strong supporter of land reform, he edited the *Standard* with Henry George from 1887 to 1889 and was managing editor of the *Twentieth Century* from 1889 to 1892. He was also a leading advocate of the use of the initiative and referendum during these years, traveling to Switzerland in 1888 to gather information for his *Direct Legislation by the Citizenship through the Initiative and Referendum* (New York, 1892) and lecturing on the subject for the AFL in the 1890s. While in New York City Sullivan participated with SG in the Social Reform Club and the People's Institute of the New York Society for Ethical Culture, and he later worked for a time as an assistant editor of the *American Federationist*. He was assistant editor (1903–4) and editor (1904–6) of the *Weekly Bulletin of the Clothing Trades,* the official journal of the United Garment Workers of America, and he served as a member of the National Civic Federation commissions on public ownership (1906–7), social insurance in Great Britain (1914), and foreign inquiry (1919). An opponent of trade union involvement in socialist political activities, he published *Socialism as an Incubus on the American Labor Movement* (New York, 1909) and a report critical of English socialism (in Commission on Foreign Inquiry, National Civic Federation, *The Labor Situation in Great Britain and France* [New York, 1919]). During World War I Sullivan worked as SG's assistant on the Committee on Labor of the Advisory Commission of the Council of National Defense, and he was subsequently head of the labor and consumer division of the U.S. Food Administration.

SULLIVAN, Jere L. (1863–1928), was born in Willimansett, Mass., worked as a waiter in New England, Chicago, and St. Louis, and founded St. Louis KOL Local Assembly 9124 (Waiters), which later became local 20 of the Hotel and Restaurant Employees' National Alliance (from 1898, the Hotel and Restaurant Employees' International Alliance and Bartenders' International League of America). He was active in Hotel and Restaurant Employees' local 6 of Salt Lake City in the 1890s, returned briefly to St. Louis in 1899, and then moved to Cincinnati, where he joined local 161. Sullivan served as vice-president (1899) and secretary-treasurer (1899–1928) of the Hotel and Restaurant Employees and edited the union's official journal, *Mixer and Server,* from 1900 until his death.

THOMAS, James Henry (1874–1949), was born in Newport, Monmouthshire, and left school to take a job with the Great Western Railway when he was thirteen. He was promoted to fireman in 1894 and later to engineman, and by 1898 he was active in the Amalgamated Society of Railway Servants, serving on its executive committee and then as its president (1905–6), organizing secretary (1906–10), and assistant general secretary (1910–13). After the Railway Servants merged with two other unions to form the National Union of Railwaymen in 1913, Thomas became its assistant secretary (1913–16), secretary (1917–31), and, from 1919, its parliamentary secretary. He led the successful national railway strike of 1919 but opposed the 1921 miners' strike and the 1926 general strike. He served as a member (1916–24, 1925–29) and as president (1919–20) of the Parliamentary Committee of the TUC (from 1921, the General Council) and as president of the International Federation of Trade Unions (1920–24). He served as a Labour member of Parliament from 1910 to 1936, becoming a member of the Privy Council in 1917 and later serving as colonial secretary (1924, 1935–36), lord privy seal, with special responsibility for unemployment (1929–30), and dominion secretary (1930–35). When the Labour party split in 1931, he joined with Ramsay MacDonald to form the national coalition government and was forced to resign from leadership of the Railwaymen. A scandal involving the leak of confidential budget information drove him from public life in 1936.

Thomas, Percy (1869–1941), was born in Leavenworth, Kans., and moved with his family to Oregon as a child. After working as a telegrapher in Portland, Oreg., British Columbia, San Francisco, and Chicago, he moved to New York City in the 1890s and began working for the Hearst newspaper chain. When commercial telegraphers in various cities began to organize a national union around the turn of the century, Thomas was a leader in these efforts, serving first as president of the short-lived Order of Commercial Telegraphers (1902–3) and then as associate president (1903) and executive board member (1903–5, 1908–9) of its successor, the Commercial Telegraphers' Union of America. Thomas also served as deputy international president or organizer (1907, 1918–19), president (1917–19, 1921, 1923) and member of the executive board (1922–23) of the international's New York District Council 16, and president of the Commercial Telegraphers' New York City local. He retired as a telegrapher in 1940.

Tillett, Benjamin (1860–1943), was born in Bristol, England, and started working at the age of six, taking a variety of jobs over the next few years—in a brickyard and in a circus, in the Royal Navy and in the merchant marine, as a shoemaker, as a cooper, and eventually as a dock laborer. In 1887 he was a founder of the Tea Operatives' and General Labourers' Association (reorganized in 1889 as the Dock, Wharf, Riverside, and General Labourers' Union of Great Britain and Ireland). Tillett served as its secretary until 1922. He was a member of the Parliamentary Committee of the TUC (from 1921, the General Council) from 1892 to 1895 and from 1921 to 1931. In 1893 he was a founder of the Independent Labour party and served on its executive council, and in 1900 he helped establish the Labour Representation Committee, the predecessor of the Labour party. In 1910 Tillett helped organize the National Transport Workers' Federation, and in

1921 he took part in forming the Transport and General Workers' Union, taking the post of international and political secretary in the new organization and serving until 1931. Tillett also served as a Labour member of Parliament from 1917 to 1924 and again from 1929 to 1931.

Tobin, Daniel Joseph (1875?–1955), was born in Ireland and immigrated to the United States about 1889, settling in East Cambridge, Mass., in 1890. He worked in a sheet metal factory and then as a motorman for a Boston street railway company, joining a local assembly of the KOL. By the end of the decade he was working as a teamster and had joined Boston local 25 of the Team Drivers' International Union, later serving as its business agent. Tobin was elected president of the international union (from 1903, the International Brotherhood of Teamsters; and from 1910, the International Brotherhood of Teamsters, Chauffeurs, Stablemen, and Helpers of America) in 1907 and moved to Indianapolis; he served in that office until 1952. He was also a member of the National Civic Federation executive committee (1911–14), AFL treasurer (1918–28), and an AFL vice-president (1935–55).

Valentine, Joseph F. (1857–1930), was born in Baltimore, where he apprenticed as an iron molder. After moving to San Francisco, he joined Iron Molders' Union of North America 164 and served as the local's president from 1880 to 1890. He was elected vice-president of the Molders in 1890 and moved to Cincinnati. He held that office until 1903 and then served as president of the union (from 1907, the International Molders' Union of North America) until he retired in 1924. He was also a member of the National Civic Federation executive committee (1904 to at least 1923), a vice-president of the AFL (1906–24), and a vice-president of the AFL Metal Trades Department (1908–24). In 1927 he returned to San Francisco.

Voll, John A. (1867–1924), was born in Zanesville, Ohio, began working in a cotton mill at the age of twelve, then went to work in a glass factory and joined American Flint Glass Workers' Union 95 of Zanesville when he was nineteen. He served on the executive board of the Flint Glass Workers in 1898–99, representing prescription bottle blowers, but when this group withdrew from the Flint Glass Workers in 1901 and joined the Glass Bottle Blowers' Association of the United States and Canada, Voll changed his union affiliation as well and became a member of Glass Bottle Blowers' local 20 of Zanesville. He served as a member of the executive board (1904–6) and vice-president

(1906–17) of the Glass Bottle Blowers and was the union's president from 1917 until his death. Voll also served as president (1909–18) of the Ohio State Federation of Labor. He moved to Philadelphia, the location of the Glass Bottle Blowers' union headquarters, in 1917.

WALKER, John Hunter (1872–1955), was born in Scotland, immigrated to the United States in 1882, and began working in the mines in Coal City, Ill. He returned briefly to Scotland and then settled permanently in the United States in the 1890s. Walker served the United Mine Workers of America as an organizer for West Virginia, president of the Danville, Ill., subdistrict of District 12 (Illinois), and then as executive board member (1905–6) and president (1906–9, 1910–13, 1931–33) of District 12. He was president of the Illinois State Federation of Labor (1913–19, 1920–30), and in 1915 helped organize the Illinois State Cooperative Society, serving as its first president (1915–21). In 1906 Walker ran unsuccessfully on the Socialist Party of America ticket for a seat in the U.S. House of Representatives. He was expelled from the party in 1916. In 1917 he served on the President's Mediation Commission. In 1919 he joined the National Labor party (from 1920, the Farmer-Labor party) and was its unsuccessful candidate for governor of Illinois in 1920. In 1930 he and other opponents of United Mine Workers' president John L. Lewis launched the Reorganized United Mine Workers of America in Springfield, Ill., and he served as secretary-treasurer of this short-lived union. Around 1952 he moved to Denver.

WELCH, Maurice R. "Mike" (1862–1929), was born in Xenia, Ohio, and grew up on a farm in Osceola, Iowa. He began working as a brakeman at the age of nineteen and later became a switchman and then a yardmaster. In 1888 Welch joined Omaha Lodge 11 of the Switchmen's Mutual Aid Association, and by 1890 he was master of Omaha Lodge 166. He joined the Switchmen's Union of North America in 1895 and served on its board of directors from 1895 to 1901. Appointed secretary-treasurer of the Switchmen in 1901, he moved to union headquarters in Buffalo, N.Y., and retained that post until his death.

WHARTON, Arthur Orlando (1873–1944), was born near Topeka, Kans., and apprenticed as a machinist with the Atchison, Topeka, and Santa Fe Railroad at the age of thirteen. By 1900 he was a railroad shop foreman in Osawatomie, Kans., and by 1903 he had moved to St. Louis. Wharton served as business agent of International Association of Machinists District 5 (Missouri Pacific and St. Louis, Iron Mountain, and Southern Railroad) from 1903 to 1914 and as secretary-treasurer of the Machinists' Southwestern Consolidated Railway District from 1908 to 1912. He was president of the AFL Railroad (from 1915, Railway) Employes' Department from 1912 to 1922, although from 1918 department vice-president B. M. Jewell served as acting president of the organization. During World War I Wharton was a member of the Committee on Labor of the Advisory Commission of the Council of National Defense; from 1918 to 1920 he served on the U.S. Railroad Administration Board of Railroad Wages and Working Conditions; and from 1920 to 1926 he was a member of the U.S. Railroad Labor Board. Wharton served as president of the Machinists from 1926 to 1939 and was an AFL vice-president from 1928 to 1940. He spent his last years in Tucson, Ariz.

WHITE, John Phillip (1870–1934), was born in Illinois and later moved with his family to Iowa, where he entered the mines at age fourteen. He served as secretary-treasurer (1899–1904) and president (1904–7, 1909–10) of United Mine Workers of America District 13 (Iowa) and as vice-president (1908) and president (1911–17) of the international union. White was adviser to the U.S. Fuel Administration from 1917 to 1919. He died in Des Moines, Iowa.

WILLIAMS, John (b. 1865), a native of Wales, immigrated to the United States in 1891 and settled Pennsylvania. He served as assistant secretary (1897–98), secretary-treasurer (1898–1911), and president (1911–19) of the Amalgamated Association of Iron, Steel, and Tin Workers and later took a position with the Pacific Coast Steel Co.

WILSON, James Adair (1876–1945), was born in Erie, Pa., where he joined a local of the Pattern Makers' League of North America in 1898. He served as president of the Pattern Makers (1902–34), moving to New York City and then, in 1906, to Cincinnati. Wilson also served as an AFL vice-president (1924–34) and, later, as a labor counselor for the International Labor Organization in Geneva.

WILSON, Joseph Havelock (1858–1929), was born in Sunderland, England, and briefly apprenticed as a printer before running away to sea at the age of thirteen. In 1883 he joined the North of England Sailors' and Seagoing Firemen's Friendly Society and served briefly as its president (1885–87) before founding the National Amalgamated Sailors' and Firemen's Union of Great Britain and Ireland in 1887. He served that union as secretary (1887–93) and president (1893–94). When it was dissolved he organized the National Sailors' and Firemen's Union of Great Britain and Ireland (from 1926, the National Union of Seamen), which he also served as president (1894–1929). In 1896 he helped organize the International Transport Workers' Federation. Wilson served as a member of Parliament (Liberal/Labour, 1892–1900, 1906–10; Coalition Liberal, 1918–22) and as a member (1889–98, 1918–19) and president (1892–93) of the Parliamentary Committee of the TUC.

WILSON, William Bauchop (1862–1934), was born in Blantyre, Scotland, and immigrated to Arnot, Pa., in 1870. The son of a coal miner, he began working in the mines at the age of nine, became a member of a local miners' union, and was later elected its secretary. Blacklisted in 1880, he worked briefly in sawmills and lumber yards in the West and then as a fireman on the Illinois Central Railroad before returning to Pennsylvania. He settled in Blossburg, where he worked in the 1880s and 1890s as a miner and check weighman in the Tioga County mines and, for a time, as a typesetter for the *Blossburg Advertiser.* Wilson was master workman of District 3 of KOL National Trade Assembly 135 from 1888 to 1894 and headed the Independent Order of the KOL, organized by the United Mine Workers of America, from 1894 to 1897. In 1890 he was a founder of the United Mine Workers, serving on its executive board and, during the 1890s, as president of District 2 (Central Pennsylvania). He was secretary-treasurer of the United Mine Workers from 1900 to 1908. Wilson was elected to Congress as a Democrat from Pennsylvania in 1906, serving from 1907 to 1913 and chairing the House Committee on Labor between 1911 and 1913. He was the first U.S. secretary of labor, serving from 1913 to 1921, and a member of the Council of National Defense.

WOLL, Matthew (1880–1956), was born in Luxembourg and immigrated to the United States in 1891. He grew up in Chicago, where he apprenticed as a photoengraver in 1895, and around 1900 he joined International Photo-Engravers' Union of North America 5 of that city. Woll served as president of the Photo-Engravers (1906–29), as an alternate for Victor Olander on the National War Labor Board (1918–19), and as a vice-president of the AFL (1919–55) and AFL-CIO (1955–56). He was also a founder and president (1929–56) of the Union Labor Life Insurance Co.

WRIGHT, Chester Maynard (1883–1964), was born in Milwaukee, worked for the *Milwaukee Journal,* and was later editor of the *New York Call* (1914–16) and the Newspaper Enterprise Association of Cleveland (1917). Wright broke with the Socialist Party of America over its opposition to the entry of the United States into World War I, and during the war he served as director of the news department of the American Alliance for Labor and Democracy. He was a member of the first American labor mission to Europe in 1918 and then worked as a reporter for the *New York Tribune*'s European bureau (1918–19), as English-language secretary of the Pan-American Federation of Labor (1919–27), as director of the AFL information and publicity service (1920 to at least 1925), and as assistant editor of the *American Federationist* (1922 to at least 1925). Wright was subsequently the editor of the International Labor News Service, and around 1933 he founded Chester M. Wright and Associates, a Washington, D.C., news service and research firm that published *Chester Wright's Labor Letter.* After Wright retired in 1948, his colleague John Herling took charge of the publication, which was renamed *John Herling's Labor Letter.*

YOUNG, Charles O. (1858–1944), was born in Carthage, Mo., and moved to Seattle in 1883, where he worked as an operating engineer, joined the KOL for a time, became active in the anti-Chinese movement, and helped organize the Western Central Labor Union in 1888. By 1894 he was living in Olympia, Wash., where he was engineer in charge of the water works, and by the latter part of the decade he had moved to Tacoma, where he joined International Union of Steam Engineers 2. In 1898 Young helped organize the Washington State Labor Congress, predecessor of the Washington State Federation of Labor, and in 1899 he was an organizer of the Tacoma Central Labor Council. In 1904 he became a salaried organizer for the AFL, and he served in that capacity until his retirement around 1933.

ORGANIZATIONS

The Journeymen Barbers' National Union, founded in 1887 by unions formerly affiliated with the KOL, affiliated with the AFL in 1888 as the Journeymen BARBERS' International Union of America.

The International Brotherhood of Blacksmiths organized in 1889 and affiliated with the AFL in 1897. In 1903 it absorbed the AFL's federal labor unions of blacksmiths' helpers and changed its name to the International Brotherhood of BLACKSMITHS and Helpers. In 1919 it amalgamated with the Brotherhood of Drop Forgers, Die Sinkers, and Trimming Die Makers to become the International Brotherhood of Blacksmiths, Drop Forgers, and Helpers.

The National Boiler Makers' and Helpers' Protective and Benevolent Union organized in 1881 and in 1884 changed its name to the International Brotherhood of Boiler Makers' and Iron Ship Builders' Protective and Benevolent Union of the United States and Canada. In 1887 it affiliated with the AFL as the International Brotherhood of Boiler Makers. It withdrew in 1893 and merged with the National Brotherhood of Boiler Makers to form the Brotherhood of Boiler Makers and Iron Ship Builders of America, which affiliated with the AFL in 1896. In 1906 the union adopted the name International Brotherhood of BOILER Makers, Iron Ship Builders, and Helpers of America.

The Boot and Shoe Workers' International Union of America was organized in 1889 by seceding locals of KOL National Trade Assembly 216 (shoemakers); it affiliated that year with the AFL. In 1895 the Boot and Shoe Workers merged with another AFL affiliate, the Lasters' Protective Union of America, and with the remnant of National Trade Assembly 216 to form the BOOT and Shoe Workers' Union.

The Bricklayers' and Masons' International Union of America was organized in 1865 and changed its name to the BRICKLAYERS', Masons', and Plasterers' International Union of America in 1910. It affiliated with the AFL in 1916.

The International Association of Bridge and Structural Iron Workers (from 1915, the International Association of Bridge, Structural, and Ornamental Iron Workers and Pile Drivers; and from 1917, the International Association of BRIDGE, Structural, and Ornamental Iron Workers) was organized in 1896 and affiliated with the AFL in 1901. It soon became involved in jurisdictional conflicts with several metal trades unions and was suspended from the AFL in 1902 for nonpayment of dues. After the conflict was resolved in 1903, it rejoined the Federation. It was briefly suspended again in 1917 during a conflict with the United Brotherhood of Carpenters and Joiners of America.

The Brotherhood of Carpenters and Joiners of America was organized in 1881 and chartered by the AFL in 1887. In 1888 the Brotherhood and the United Order of American Carpenters and Joiners merged, forming the United Brotherhood of CARPENTERS and Joiners of America.

The Cigar Makers' National Union of America was organized in 1864 and changed its name to the CIGAR Makers' International Union of America in 1867. The union received an AFL charter in 1887.

The Amalgamated CLOTHING Workers of America was organized in New York City in 1914 by a seceding faction of the United Garment Workers of America.

The National Brotherhood of Electrical Workers of America was organized in 1891 and affiliated with the AFL the same year. In 1899 it became the International Brotherhood of ELECTRICAL Workers.

The Tailors' National Protective Union joined with members of KOL National Trade Assembly 231 (garment cutters) in 1891 to form the United GARMENT Workers of America. The new union affiliated with the AFL the same year.

The Independent Druggist Ware Glass Blowers' League, founded in 1867, divided in 1884 into two organizations, which affiliated with the KOL in 1886 as district assemblies 149 and 143. The two merged as KOL National Trade Assembly 143 in 1889, which withdrew from the KOL in 1891 to form the United Green Glass Workers' Association of the United States and Canada. The union changed its name to the GLASS Bottle Blowers' Association of the United States and Canada in 1895 and affiliated with the AFL in 1899.

The International GLOVE Workers' Union of America was organized in 1902 and chartered that year by the AFL.

The Granite Cutters' International Union of the United States and the British Provinces of America was formed in 1877 and in 1880 changed its name to the Granite Cutters' National Union of the United States of America. It joined the AFL in 1888, left the Federation in 1890, and then rejoined it in 1895. In 1905 it adopted the name GRANITE Cutters' International Association of America.

The International Hod Carriers' and Building Laborers' Union of America was organized and affiliated with the AFL in 1903. It became the International Hod Carriers' and Common Laborers' Union of America in September 1912 and the International HOD Carriers', Building and Common Laborers' Union of America in December of that year.

The Waiters' and Bartenders' National Union was organized and affiliated with the AFL in 1891. The following year it changed its name to the Hotel and Restaurant Employees' National Alliance and, in 1898, to the HOTEL and Restaurant Employees' International Alliance and Bartenders' International League of America.

The Amalgamated Association of Iron and Steel Workers of the United States was organized in 1876 and in 1887 was chartered by the AFL. In 1897 it changed its name to the Amalgamated Association of IRON, Steel, and Tin Workers.

The International LADIES' Garment Workers' Union was organized and affiliated with the AFL in 1900.

The National Association of Saddle and Harness Makers of America organized in 1887 and affiliated with the AFL in 1889. It merged with other leather workers' unions in 1895 as the United Brotherhood of Harness and Saddle Makers of America. Chartered by the AFL early in 1896, the union changed its name to the United Brotherhood of Leather Workers on Horse Goods later that year. In 1917 it merged with the Travelers' Goods and Leather Novelty Workers' International Union of America and the Amalgamated Leather Workers of America to form the United LEATHER Workers' International Union.

The National Association of LETTER Carriers of the United States of America was organized in 1889 and affiliated with the AFL in 1917.

The National Rural LETTER Carriers' Association was organized in 1903. It did not affiliate with the AFL.

Locomotive engineers organized the Brotherhood of the Footboard in 1863. The organization was renamed the Brotherhood of LOCOMOTIVE Engineers in 1864.

The Brotherhood of Locomotive Firemen was organized in 1873. In 1906 it adopted the name Brotherhood of LOCOMOTIVE Firemen and Enginemen.

The Lumber Handlers of the Great Lakes was founded in 1892 and received its AFL charter in 1893 as the National Longshoremen's Association of the United States. In 1895 it was renamed the International Longshoremen's Association. It became the International Longshoremen, Marine, and Transport Workers' Association in 1901 but changed its name back to the International LONGSHOREMEN'S Association in 1908.

The Order of United Machinists and Mechanical Engineers of America was organized in 1888 and the following year changed its name to the National Association of Machinists. It changed its name again, in 1891, to the International Association of MACHINISTS, affiliating with the AFL in 1895.

The Amalgamated MEAT Cutters and Butcher Workmen of North America was organized and chartered by the AFL in 1897.

The Western Federation of Miners, a regional, industrial union that claimed jurisdiction over mine, mill, and smelter workers in the hard rock mining industry, was founded in 1893 and affiliated with the AFL in July 1896. It paid no dues to the AFL after December 1896, however, and in 1898 it disaffiliated; it subsequently helped organize the Western Labor Union (renamed the American Labor Union in 1902). In 1905 it participated in the formation of the IWW, but it withdrew three years later and reaffiliated with the AFL in 1911. In 1916 it changed its name to the International Union of MINE, Mill, and Smelter Workers.

The United MINE Workers of America was established in 1890 with the merger of the National Progressive Union of Miners and Mine Laborers and KOL National Trade Assembly 135 (miners). The new union affiliated with the AFL the same year.

The Brotherhood of Painters and Decorators of America was organized in 1887, affiliating with the AFL the same year. The union withdrew from the Federation in 1891 but reaffiliated the following year. In 1894 it split between western and eastern factions headquartered, respectively, in Lafayette, Ind., and Baltimore. The eastern faction adopted the name Brotherhood of PAINTERS, Decorators, and Paperhangers of America in 1899, and the two factions merged under that name in 1900.

In 1887 members of nine KOL local assemblies organized the Pattern Makers' National League of North America. It received an AFL charter in 1894 and in 1898 changed its name to the PATTERN Makers' League of North America.

The International PHOTO-ENGRAVERS' Union of North America was organized in 1900 by seceding locals of the International Typographical Union, which recognized its jurisdiction by a referendum vote in 1903. The AFL chartered the union in 1904.

The International Printing Pressmen's Union of North America was founded in 1889 and affiliated with the AFL in 1895. In 1897 it changed its name to the International Printing PRESSMEN's and Assistants' Union of North America.

The National Steel and Copper Plate Printers' Union of the United States of America was organized in 1892 and affiliated with the AFL in 1898. The union changed its name to the International Steel and Copper Plate PRINTERS' Union of North America in 1901 and to the International Plate Printers' and Die Stampers' Union of North America in 1920.

In 1902 pulp, sulphite, and paper mill workers directly affiliated with the AFL joined the International Brotherhood of Paper Makers, and in 1903 that union changed its name to the International Brotherhood of Paper Makers, Pulp, Sulphite, and Paper Mill Workers. The pulp, sulphite, and paper mill locals withdrew in 1906, however, to form the International Brotherhood of PULP, Sulphite, and Paper Mill Workers, which was chartered by the AFL in 1909. The Paper Makers then reassumed their former name.

The Brotherhood of Railroad Brakemen of the Western Hemisphere was organized in 1883. In 1886 it changed its name to the Brotherhood of Railroad Brakemen and in 1890 to the Brotherhood of RAILROAD Trainmen.

The Order of Railway Clerks of America was organized in 1899 and affiliated with the AFL in 1900; it withdrew from the Federation in 1901. The organization adopted the name Brotherhood of RAILWAY Clerks in 1904 and reaffiliated with the AFL in 1908. It adopted the name Brotherhood of Railway and Steamship Clerks, Freight Handlers, Express and Station Employes in 1919.

The Conductors' Union was organized in 1868, changed its name to the Conductors' Brotherhood in 1869 and was renamed the Order of RAILWAY Conductors of America in 1878.

The National Seamen's Union of America was organized in 1892 as a federation of several regional sailors' unions including the Sailors' Union of the Pacific, the Lake Seamen's Union, the Gulf Coast Seamen's and Firemen's Union, and the Atlantic Coast Seamen's Union. The following year it affiliated with the AFL and in 1895 changed its name to the International SEAMEN's Union of America.

The Tin, Sheet Iron, and Cornice Workers' International Association was organized in 1888 and affiliated with the AFL the following year. Its charter was recalled in 1896. The union reorganized in 1897 as the Amalgamated Sheet Metal Workers' International Association, which was chartered by the AFL in 1899. In 1903 it merged with the Sheet Metal Workers' National Alliance, a secessionist group that had broken away from the union in 1902, to form the Amalgamated SHEET Metal Workers' International Alliance. In 1907 the international amalgamated with the Coppersmiths' International Union and, in 1924, absorbed the chandelier, brass, and metal workers, adopting the name Sheet Metal Workers' International Association.

The International SHINGLE Weavers' Union of America was organized and affiliated with the AFL in 1903. In 1913 the union changed its name to the International Union of Shingle Weavers, Sawmill Workers, and Woodsmen, and in 1914 to the International Union of Timberworkers. The union reorganized under its original name in 1916, amalgamated with the International Union of Timber Workers in 1918, and disbanded in 1923.

The International Stove Mounters' Union was organized in 1892 and received an AFL charter in 1894. It was subsequently renamed Stove Mounters' and Steel Range Workers' International Union of North America (1900–1901, 1904–10), Stove Mounters', Steel Range Workers', and Pattern Fitters' and Filers' International Union of North America (1901–2), and STOVE Mounters' International Union of North America (1902–4 and again after 1910).

The SWITCHMEN's Union of North America was organized in 1894 and affiliated with the AFL in 1906.

The Journeymen Tailors' National Union of the United States was organized in 1883 and chartered by the AFL in 1887. It changed its name in 1889 to the Journeymen Tailors' Union of America and in January 1914 to the Tailors' Industrial Union. It merged that year with the Amalgamated Clothing Workers of America but in 1915 seceded from the Clothing Workers and reassumed the name Journeymen TAILORS' Union of America.

In 1898 several team drivers' locals combined to form the Team Drivers' International Union, which received an AFL charter in 1899. Seceding Chicago locals organized the Teamsters' National Union in 1901, and in 1903 the two unions merged to form the International

Brotherhood of Teamsters. In 1910 it changed its name to the International Brotherhood of TEAMSTERS, Chauffeurs, Stablemen, and Helpers of America.

In 1902 the Brotherhood of Commercial Telegraphers amalgamated with independent locals in New York City to form the Order of Commercial Telegraphers, which was then chartered by the AFL. In 1903 the union amalgamated with the International Union of Commercial Telegraphers and changed its name to the Commercial TELEGRAPHERS' Union of America.

Sawmill and logging camp workers in the Pacific Northwest formed the International Union of TIMBER Workers in January 1917; the union received an AFL charter in August of that year. In April 1918 the Timber Workers amalgamated with the International Shingle Weavers' Union of America, which disbanded in 1923.

The National Typographical Union was organized in 1852 by a group of locals that had held national conventions in 1850 and 1851 under the name Journeymen Printers of the United States. In 1869 it adopted the name International TYPOGRAPHICAL Union. The AFL chartered the union in 1888.

The American Wire Weavers' Protective and Benevolent Association was organized in 1882 and subsequently changed its name to the American WIRE Weavers' Protective Association. The union received an AFL charter in 1900.

INDEX

Names of persons or organizations for whom there are glossary entries are followed by an asterisk.

An italicized page number indicates the location of a substantive annotation in the notes following a document. While this index is not cumulative, it includes references to substantive annotations or glossary entries in earlier volumes that are relevant to this one but that are not repeated here; these appear first in the index entry. For example, reference to the annotation of Jacob S. Allen in volume 8 appears in this index as *8:185n;* and the glossary entry for Joseph Barondess in volume 3 appears in this index as *3:**.

621